A HISTORY OF MODERN GERMANY SINCE 1815

A HISTORY OF
MODERN GERMANY
SINCE 1815

Frank B. Tipton

University of California Press
Berkeley   Los Angeles

University of California Press
Berkeley and Los Angeles, California

Published by arrangement with Continuum

Cataloging-in-Publication Data is on file with the Library of Congress

ISBN 0–520–24050–2 cloth
       0–520–24049–9 paperback

Manufactured in Great Britain

10 9 8 7 6 5 4 3 2 1

The paper used in this publication meets the minimum requirements of ANSI/NISO
Z39 .48–1992 (R 1997) (*Permanence of Paper*).

TABLE OF CONTENTS

PLATES

FIGURES

MAPS

TABLES

PREFACE

This book presents an account of the development of Germany in the modern era. It offers an integrated approach of the transformations of the economy, social structure, culture, and politics, but it does not offer a single interpretation of these changes. For reasons that are outlined in the introduction and detailed in subsequent chapters, each succeeding generation of Germans perceived their world differently from those who had gone before, and those perceptions shaped the framework within which economic, social, cultural, and political change occurred. Each generation feared, hoped, planned for, or attempted to control the future, but they could only build on the past. As they did so, each generation shared a set of reference points, a style, an approach, and those commonalities remained even as they disputed the course of economic, social, cultural, and political change. Shifts from one generation to the next might be sudden or not, but they were perceived as ruptures, chasms separating the lives of the "present" generation from "past" generations. The chapters in turn attempt to come to terms with each generation's characteristic style and to focus on the issues that they believed were the most pressing.

Within each generation's framework, there were problems they shared with their predecessors. The rapidity, but also the instability, of economic development left its mark. Agriculture declined, cities spread over the countryside, and a new industrial working class appeared. The social consequences of economic change, though they varied, had in common their ability to excite concerned comment. The gender structure, the role of women, the question of what women should be, of whether there was a "German" woman and if so what she should be, pervaded public discourse. Each generation also worried about what the next generation would become; youth was defined, redefined, and analyzed with almost the same intensity as woman.

That so much of the discourse was public reflected the alterations of the public sphere itself. Again, this was not a linear development, though as with the economy or with the position of women and youth there were underlying trends, especially the emergence of new and progressively broader groups demanding that their voices be heard. Literature and art interacted with and formed part of the changing terms of these debates, part of what Hans Belting has called the "troublesome relationship" of Germans with their art. The terms changed as did the styles, but art in each generation was public, social, and "political" in its implications. Similarly, political structures reflected and interacted with changes in these other spheres. The presentation is organized so that each of these stories can be traced separately across chapters as well as seen together within generational frameworks in each chapter.

German history matters, not only for itself, but also for what Germany means and has meant to the rest of the world. German thinkers, writers, and artists have exercised influence across the entire range of intellectual disciplines. Germany also stands as an exemplar of the problems thrown up by modernization, industrialization, and nationalism. Germans' debates over what these developments meant, and how they reflected and refracted the nation's identity—indeed, the very question of whether there was a German identity and if so what it might be—established the frameworks for similar debates elsewhere in Europe, in the Americas, in Africa, and in Asia. Herder's emphasis on language established one of the defining characteristics of the modern national state, and Hegel's emphasis on law and government officials defined the modern national bureaucracy. Germany's attempts to cope with the various social "questions" also exercised profound influence in distant places. Friedrich List's plans for a railroad network and tariffs were absorbed by the leaders of Meiji Japan in the 1880s, and Bismarck's model for social security funding was taken up by the British in the 1940s.

As one of the main combatants in the First World War, and as the originator of the Second World War and the attendant human disasters, Germany has shaped much of the past century's history. The contrasts and the possible connections between the light and the dark sides of modern history are another of the compelling aspects of the German story. The Holocaust, which many regard as the defining event of modern history, emerged from German history, and much of the urgency that informs study of German history originates in attempts to come to terms with this monstrous event. German history did not end with the Holocaust, but Germans themselves in each generation since have felt the need to deal with questions of guilt, responsibility, and victimhood, and these debates in turn have left their own important marks on Germany's ongoing social and cultural life.

Inevitably the treatment is selective. At the beginning of each chapter I discuss a work or works that appear to me to introduce and represent the concerns of each generation. Within chapters I have opted for examples, of works of art and literature, of problems, and of developments. The selection and weighting reflect my judgments of the balance of contemporary concerns, but also the amount of attention that subsequent scholars have devoted to each. These are contentious choices, and those with particular interests in any of the areas touched on may disagree with the selection, emphasis, and conclusions. However, these are the works and the issues that have particularly excited the interest of my students, and they are the ones that have seemed to open up understanding of each period. As such I hope they prove stimulating and useful to others interested in the history of Germany and in the history of the modern world.

Janet Joyce and Valerie Hall of the Continuum International Publishing Group have supported the project with enthusiasm and with patience, and I am deeply appreciative. Cartographer Peter Johnson, MIMSIA, has my thanks for the preparation of the maps. I have been fortunate in obtaining permission to include images of a number of the paintings and buildings discussed in the text. Norbert Ludwig of the Bildarchiv Preussischer Kulturbesitz in Berlin and Alysa Nahmias of Dia Center for the Arts in New York were particularly helpful in locating and providing images for these illustrations. The manuscript has benefited from careful readings by James Retallack and John Milfull, and John Milfull deserves special mention for his efforts on behalf of German and European studies in Australia, efforts that have provided invaluable opportunities to exchange views with the broadest possible range of international scholars. The book owes much to these exchanges; the errors and shortcomings that remain, remain mine.

This is Elise's book.

FBT

January 2002

CHAPTER 1

INTRODUCTION: FROM GENERATION TO GENERATION

In 1993, visitors to the Venice Biennale confronted a work by Hans Haacke entitled *Germania*. The marble floor of a large room had been jackhammered into fragments, and the fragments left piled randomly on top of one another. At the far side of the room was a blank wall with a gently curved section in the middle, receding slightly from the viewer. On the curved section were inscribed in precise capitals the letters GERMANIA. Visitors had to walk gingerly because the shattered pieces of flooring did not provide a secure footing. As they moved about, microphones picked up the sounds of the shifting pieces, and speakers set above the wall sent the amplified noises reverberating through the room. One critic described the effect of the random echoes as "mournful."[1]

Art and politics have intersected across the generations of modern Germany's history. Haacke was born in 1936, three years after Hitler came to power. He was nine when the war ended, in his teens when the economic miracle began, and thirty-two in 1968, the year of the student revolts against the West German establishment. In the 1970s, he produced posters contrasting the luxurious goods of contemporary consumer society in the affluent industrialized countries with the impoverished conditions of the workers who produced them in the underdeveloped world. In the 1990s he turned his attention back to Germany. For Haacke, for other Germans, and for students of German history, Germania is the embodiment of Germany. Usually a female figure, she has taken many forms, and her forms have reflected the concerns of each succeeding generation. Four years after reunification, Haacke saw Germany as *bodenlos*, without foundations, a broken land, a land of rubble, a land without a floor to stand on securely. We might read the work as saying that Germany's foundations have been destroyed, that they are being rebuilt, that new foundations are under construction, or possibly that Germany has no foundation. In any case, the empty space of Germania/Germany is filled only with the mournful

1

noise created by the viewers themselves, as they unsteadily pass through.

The "German question"

What is special about Germany? Haacke's ironic and deliberately ambiguous work focuses our attention. Unlike the history or national existence of other European states, Germany's very being has been posed as a question. And one of the most recalcitrant aspects of the "German question" is the deceptively simple question of what "Germany" *is*. For much of our period, "Germany" did not exist. Many historians of Germany have considered the history of the region of central Europe that roughly corresponds to the area of the pre-1914 German Empire—the Bismarckian empire—but this approach presupposes simple answers to some very complex questions. Why was there no unified German state until late in the nineteenth century? How did Germany become an industrial power? What did this mean for German women and for German men? What responsibility does Germany bear for two world wars? For the barbarism of the Third Reich? In attempting to answer such questions, many observers focused on Germany's difference from other nations, on the *Sonderweg*, or "special path," of German development. At some point, they argued, Germany diverged from the normal course of modern history, with tragic results. Germany was either a land without foundation or a land that had destroyed its foundations.

Who are the "Germans"? The answer is as difficult as the definition of Germany itself. The present German government attempts to solve the problem by granting citizenship to anyone of "German blood," and by placing severe restrictions on citizenship for those not of German blood. The legal definition of citizenship, as we will see, is racial and based on a law passed shortly before the First World War. Membership in the German community is taken to mean the inheritance of language, that is, descent from German-speaking people. But this is really no solution. Over the centuries language has been no guide, for many of the subjects of the Hohenzollern ruler spoke Polish, and the subjects of the Hapsburg realms spoke over a dozen different languages. In the late eighteenth century, the habitual language of many of the upper classes was French. And many of the "Germans" by "blood" scattered across Eastern Europe and the former territories of the Soviet Union today do not speak German, but rather are descended from people who may have spoken a sort of German centuries ago. Could anyone be a German who has passed through Germany, leaving a mournful echo?

What and where is "Germany"? In the eighteenth century, "Germany" meant the "Holy Roman Empire of the German Nation." It included nearly two thousand separate entitles, among which were the several dozen separate territories ruled by the Hohenzollern prince, who in turn had several different titles. He was subject to the emperor in the western part of his domains, and subject to the King of Poland in the east. The "King" of Prussia until the early nineteenth century was "King *in* Prussia," that is, he was a king in only part of his domains. The empire also included many of the territories of the Hapsburg monarch, who like the Prussian king bore many different titles in addition to ruling as emperor or empress. There was also a "third Germany" of medium-sized and small states, outside of the Hohenzollern and Hapsburg realms, ranging from Imperial Free Knights who might rule over a single landed estate, Church territories, and free cities of varying size, to substantial powers such as Saxony and Bavaria.

The wars of the French Revolution and Napoleon resulted in the end of the old empire and the creation of a new "German Confederation" of thirty-nine separate states. The Vienna settlement resulted in a substantial extension of Hohenzollern territory in the west, and the period from 1815 to 1866 was marked by the conflict between Hohenzollern Prussia and Hapsburg Austria for domination of this new version of Germany. The smaller states played Prussia and Austria off against one another as best they could, and all the surviving states concentrated on organizing and integrating territories they had gained during the wars. The question of whether there was or should be a single "Germany" was one of the most contentious political issues over this entire half century. The broken pieces of Haacke's *Germania* recall the dilemma of which pieces of Germany should be united, and how.

Bismarck, of course, insisted that the empire he created in 1871 was "Germany," but this Germany contained substantial non-German minorities and sizeable irredenta. No one ever convinced the Polish speakers in eastern Germany that they were German, and many in the provinces of Alsace and Lorraine remained stubbornly French. Additionally, many of the Germans who were included in the new empire—in Hanover, Hesse, or Bavaria, for instance—had no desire to belong to Bismarck's creation. And, of course, a very large number of Germans living in Austria and the other Hapsburg realms were not included in this version of Germany.

Nor was being "German" merely a matter of one's native tongue, even within the new empire. Women found their claims to citizenship challenged and undermined by political, legal, and economic codes. Catholics and Jews found their loyalty to the nation questioned, as did workers, who were accused by Emperor Wilhelm II of being "fellows without a fatherland." Many have argued that this failure to define the national community was one of the forces propelling Germany into the First World War.

The Bismarckian empire died in 1918, and the problems engendered by that defeat led to the greater defeat of 1945. Among those problems was the definition of what was Germany and who was a German. In the Polish Corridor, in Silesia, and in Austria, there were violent conflicts over whether or not these territories were to form part of Germany or not. Austria, the remnant of the western portion of the Hapsburg Empire, voted to join Germany in 1919, but was forbidden to do so by the victorious Allies despite their professed adherence to the principle of national self-determination. In 1937, a now very reluctant Austria was forcibly annexed by a new Nazi Germany as part of an attempt to create a "Greater German Empire."

Weimar Germany also proved unable to create a definition of the national community that could comfortably include women, workers, or religious minorities. The national community envisaged by the Nazi leadership, though supposedly including all Germans, in fact excluded many persons who considered themselves to be German—in particular the German Jews, defined in Nazi racial theory as something less than human. The Holocaust—the attempt by the Nazi regime to exterminate the Jewish people—because it seems so monstrous and so incomprehensible, is the event that has led to the impassioned debate over the special path of German history. Haacke's broken floor here could stand for the victims of Nazism, and the echoes of the feet of visitors in the present for the voices of those who cannot speak for themselves.

The Nazi version of Germany collapsed in 1945 into heaps of broken stone and concrete that were cleared by "rubble-women" (*Trümmerfrauen*), and Haacke's work evokes those memories as well. From 1945 to 1989 there were two Germanies and an Austria, as well as substantial German minorities in other countries. Then suddenly "Germany" was "reunited." But this new version of Germany did not include the Germans of Austria or other countries, and it was far from including all the territories that had been included in previous versions of Germany—the western third of Poland now consisted of territories that had been ruled by the Hohenzollerns since the mid-eighteenth century. Again, a more optimistic reading of *Germania* might see the rubble as the prelude to the construction of more lasting foundations, but a more ominous interpretation could view these as pieces of some new version of a greater Germany waiting to be forced together once again.

The broader significance of the "German question": modernization, industrialization, and nationalism

The problem of defining the Germans, and the problem of defining Germany, reflects the fact that the most important questions of modern history have been directly affected by what has happened in this region of central Europe. German history has had an obvious impact on the shaping of the modern world. The rise of Prussia and the decline of Austria reflected competition among national groups and the rise of new national states. The instability resulting from the creation of the Bismarckian empire was one of the contributing causes of the outbreak of the First World War, and the outcome of the First World War in turn paved the way for the outbreak of the Second World War. In the aftermath of the Second World War, the "German question" played a central role in the competition between the United States and the Soviet Union, and in the emergence of the European Union.

On a deeper level, however, the world historical impact of German history can also be read as an exemplification of the main social problems of the past two centuries, problems that continue to affect us today. These can be grouped under three broad headings: modernization, industrialization, and nationalism. Cutting across all three headings are the linked questions of gender, class, and ethnic relations, and the creation of personal identity in a modern and in a postmodern world. In all of these areas and across these linking axes, Germany has been seen as a paradoxical combination of success and failure. Sometimes Germany has been portrayed as a link between "Western" and "Eastern" European patterns of development, and sometimes as a curious amalgam of "backward" and "modern," but in any case German history has been read as going along a separate and distinctive path, a *Sonderweg*.

There are many aspects of Germany that can be seen as forming a middle way between Western European "democratic" traditions and Eastern European "autocratic" traditions. Germany can be seen as somewhere in the middle of a scale of relative modernization, and also in the middle of a scale of modern nationalisms. Germany also has been seen as an important example of the use of nationalism and state power as a means to *achieve* modernization and industrialization, for instance in the work of many economic historians such as W. O. Henderson.

Historians' concern with modernization, sometimes portrayed as "Westernization" or more narrowly as "Americanization," emerged from the sociological conceptions of Talcott Parsons. Drawing on Parsons, in the 1960s sociologists, political scientists, and historians argued that societies moved toward a standard pattern that included industrialization and urbanization, greater political participation, and a tendency to evaluate persons on the basis of individual merit rather than birth. The process of modernization, these scholars held, created greater class mobility and eliminated bars based upon race, religion, or ethnicity. From the perspective of gender relations, this included an expectation that sex segregation and discrimination in all its forms would decline.[2]

When social scientists and historians looked at Germany, however, the country was frequently regarded as having achieved only incomplete modernization, as combining some aspects of modernity with persistent habits inherited from a pre-modern past. In a comparative framework, they argued, this might simply reflect the dangers and tensions inherent in the modernization process, but because of the centrality of Germany in modern history, Germany's failure to modernize completely took on truly tragic overtones. The works of the émigré historian Hans Rosenberg argued along these lines. Produced during his exile in the United States, they influenced a generation of British and American historians in the 1950s, and then a new generation of West German historians in the 1960s.[3] Political scientists reached broadly similar conclusions and remained pessimistic about the chances for true democratization in West Germany.[4] From the 1970s, specialists in women's history also noted the persistence of gender-linked attitudes in German society and politics.[5]

The "German question," intellectual history, and the history of history

Concern for the German question also reflects the position of Germany at the center of European intellectual history. Discussion by German thinkers has deeply influenced the course of development of the entire range of intellectual disciplines. Their very sophisticated discussion underlies the multiplicity of analyses of what it is to be German and what this means. Germans can draw on a tradition of philosophical analysis from Immanuel Kant in the late eighteenth century, through G. W. F. Hegel and Friedrich Nietzsche in the nineteenth century, to Karl Heiddiger and Edmund Husserl in the twentieth century. In the nineteenth century, German scholars pioneered social scientific disciplines such as philology, archaeology, and jurisprudence. Karl Marx and the generations of Socialist scholars following his lead drew on this tradition. So, too, did the founding father of sociology, Max Weber, from whom we have terms such as "charisma" and our concept of the way in which modern bureaucracies operate. In the interwar years, the "Frankfurt School" attempted to combine the insights of Marx and Weber with those of Sigmund Freud, a Jew from Vienna who considered himself German. Exiled by the Nazis, members of the school such as Theodor Adorno and Herbert Marcuse exerted a powerful influence on American social scientists, including Talcott Parsons, and younger adherents such as Jürgen Habermas have played a central role in the discussion of social theory over the past thirty years.[6]

Historians of Germany can look back on an inheritance of six or seven generations of scholarship; German scholars indeed created the historical profession as it exists today. For a half century from the 1830s to his death in 1886, Leopold von Ranke trained young historians in the critical analysis of historical sources in his "seminar" at the University of Berlin. Ranke aimed to reconstruct history "as it really happened" without injecting the spirit of the present into former times. Equally influential have been the ideas of Wilhelm Dilthey, who advocated an empathetic but disciplined "understanding" of the past. Both drew on the German philosophical tradition in seeking patterns and explanations in history, not mere recitations of factual information, and these remain the defining concerns of modern professional historians.[7]

The intellectual and historical concerns of German thinkers were not isolated. They reflected on and engaged in the continuing struggles over the definition of Germany and the German question, and in particular the definition of the German national community. During the Wars of Liberation against the French, the philosopher Johann Gottlieb Fichte called on Germans to surrender themselves to "the devouring flame of a higher patriotism." During the ensuing period of "restoration," there were repeated calls for the creation of a new national state, and the repression of those demands was one of the factors in the revolutionary upheavals of 1848.

Bismarck's success in overcoming both external and internal opponents converted many doubters, in particular the historian Heinrich von Treitschke, who wielded immense influence in propagating the notion that Bismarck's version of Germany was the only answer to the German question. Treitschke reinterpreted the German past to show the Bismarckian empire as the inevitable result of all previous historical development. He and his contemporaries viewed Germany as distinctive and superior, lying between the chronic instability of Western European democracy and the repressive backwardness of Eastern European autocracy.[8]

The shock of defeat in 1918 called the complacent certainties of the pre-1914 generation into question. This led to new interpretations of the German past. Eckart Kehr analyzed the role of key interest groups in determining the policies of imperial Germany, but his was not a popular message, and his works gained influence only after 1945.[9] Scholarship polarized, with Marxists arguing that the war had resulted from the development of the capitalist system, and right-wing thinkers such as Oswald Spengler insisting that Western culture itself had entered its period of decline. Most Germans were incensed that the "war guilt" clause of the Treaty of Versailles made *them* responsible for the war and by extension implied that there was something "wrong" with "Germany." That anger helped Hitler and the Nazis to power.

The aftermath of 1945 led to another reevaluation of the German past. In 1946, Friedrich Meinecke, Germany's greatest historian after Ranke, published *The German Catastrophe*.[10] This book established a trend of seeking a decisive point at which German history had taken the wrong turn, and identifying the groups or individuals responsible for the subsequent tragedy. Meinecke saw this point in the failure of the reformers he had considered in his earlier work to complete their task in the 1820s. Others such as Lewis Namier and A. J. P. Taylor saw the defeat of the 1848 revolution as the point where German history had failed to turn, where Germany had gone wrong.[11] Marxists also concentrated on 1848. They blamed a weak and cowardly middle class for failing to complete its task, to carry through a revolution against the feudal aristocracy. The resulting peculiar combination of rapid industrial growth and continued aristocratic privilege defined the

Sonderweg.[12] Other scholars took a more short-term view and blamed the leaders who had taken Germany into the First World War, or the leaders who had failed to defend Weimar democracy against the Nazis.[13]

Scholars such as Hans Kohn and Leonard Krieger exhaustively re-examined German national consciousness in the light of the war and the Holocaust.[14] They sought to explain what had gone wrong with "German" nationalism, to the extent that the German nation could have been led down the path of Nazism, and they looked back toward the beginning of the nineteenth century, if not before. Leah Greenfeld has also argued that the early nineteenth century is the place to look. Greenfeld concludes that the German national identity was locked in place during the Napoleonic wars. Violent, racist, and anti-Semitic, the German identity did not by itself cause the Holocaust, but, without it, Greenfeld says the Holocaust is inconceivable.[15]

Opinion had reversed itself. Rather than Treitschke's stable synthesis of Western democracy and Eastern autocracy, Germany was now seen as an unhealthy and explosive combination of dangerous and essentially incompatible elements. Within Germany this view was not popular. A storm of controversy greeted the publication of Fritz Fischer's study of German war aims in the First World War, which argued that German leaders had caused the war in order to preserve the conservative aristocratic establishment.[16] However, the younger generation of scholars, influenced by Rosenberg and by American social science and especially Parson's structural-functional sociology, argued that Fischer's fundamental point was correct, that Germany had deviated from the normal course of modernization. Ralf Dahrendorf's *Society and Democracy in Germany* suggested that inherited social structures would make it difficult for Germans ever to achieve a modern democratic political system, and Hans-Ulrich Wehler's history of imperial Germany identified internal contradictions that he believed marked the special path of Germany's modernization and led to the First World War.[17]

More recently many historians have become wary of believing we know what the "normal" course of history ought to be. Specialized studies have shown that many of the things that seem to be special about Germany have parallels in other nations' histories. As we will see in the following chapters, the idea that "Germany was not alone" recurs repeatedly. David Blackbourn and Geoff Eley have emphasized the many positive and stable aspects of pre-1914 German society. Germany looks quite modern in many respects. Especially interesting is their emphasis on the power and influence of the German middle classes, whom many other authors had dismissed as weak or cowardly. They also question the historical basis of the modernization model, in particular its over-simplified view of *British* history, something to which they as British historians have been particularly sensitive.[18]

In addition, two further problems presented themselves. First was the very easy and unproblematic integration of first West Germany and then reunified Germany into the developing structures of the European Union. This did not fit with the essentially tragic terms of the analyses of the German question developed after the Second World War. Second was the rise of postmodernist, post-colonial, and feminist analytical points of view, which called the entire intellectual framework of mod-ernization theory into question. If modernization had only benefited a small group of males, and if it had been achieved at the direct expense of women and subaltern groups, how could this be presented as "pro-gress"? Even more broadly, if economic development was leading toward ecological disaster, as argued for instance by some members of the West German Greens, then how could it represent progress? It no longer seemed so certain that all societies would or should follow a single path of development, and this lack of certainty seemed to indicate a need to rethink the German question once again.

The "German question" and social history

How can we approach the German question and the related problem of Germany's distinctiveness? In their examinations of the German past, many historians have focused on individual statesmen, political institu-tions, or intellectual and cultural traditions. These indeed represent important aspects of the German past, but in addition we need to exam-ine that past through the lens of social history. Social history demands that historians pay attention to the lives of the many as well as the few, to the multiple histories rather than to overarching "grand narratives." Social history demands that we study the poor, the oppressed, and their issues and organizations as well as those of elites. It asks that we exam-ine "private" life as well as events in the "public" sphere, and indeed asks that we question the very basis on which private and public have been defined. This approach insists that in order to do justice to cultural and political issues, the historian must begin from an understanding of the social cleavages in Germany, from an analysis of power relations, not only in the political sphere but also in the broader context of economic, social, and family structures.[19]

The concern with the modernization of German society had the important consequence that scholars began to think in terms of social structures. Social historians are therefore concerned to locate and study social groupings in a society, and the power relations within and among those groups. This has led to studies of the class divisions in Germany and the development of workers' movements and then of workers' culture, of the nature of social and economic elites and the bases of their power, and of the relationship between the state and those groups. Moving beyond class analyses, other historians have explored the regrouping of previously cohesive communities into separate "milieus," of German Catholics, of German Jews, of the Protestant middle classes, and of the aristocracy. They have built on a long tradition of German scholarship, from the first systematic observers of social structure such as Wilhelm Heinrich Riehl in the 1850s through Ferdinand Tönnies in the 1880s, whose distinction between *Gemeinschaft* (community) and *Gesellschaft* (society) remains influential today.

These were gendered processes. Gender theories of social interaction begin with the assumption that whatever men and women do in their daily lives, their choices are constrained by roles that are socially constructed around the division between the sexes. In Joan W. Scott's words, "gender is a constitutive element of social relationships based on perceived differences between the sexes, and gender is a primary way of signifying relationships of power."[20] Women's historians have studied the socio-economic and ideological placing of women, and their political choices as well as their political constraints. What it meant or should mean to be a German woman was a question as hotly contested as any other aspect of the German question.[21] As women came to be coded as consumers, debates over how consumption could or should be regulated linked to these other areas of contention as well.[22]

Changes in social structures and in the relative power of social groups over the past two centuries can often be traced to the process of industrialization. Industrialization is related to, but not the same as, modernization. Indeed, in the case of Germany a rapid and successful industrialization on the one hand is often contrasted with a halting and incomplete modernization on the other. Still, it is clear that industrial growth, the application of modern science to technological processes, the creation of new machinery, and the emergence of new large-scale enterprises would be impossible in a fully traditional society. Germany repeated many of the patterns of early industrial development, but then took the lead in the later movement from steam to electricity, in the direct application of scientific knowledge to industrial processes, and in the creation of new forms of industrial organization. From this perspective German industrialization exemplified German modernity, and the Germans again reflected on the meaning of what was happening. The Conservative Robert Liefmann produced a theory of economic organization centered on German cartels, and the Marxist Rudolf Hilferding developed a theory of finance capital based on the German experience.

At the same time, Germany also experienced the problems associated with industrial growth, the decline of agriculture as the main source of employment, urbanization, the creation of an industrial working class, substantial changes in the position of women, and severe strains placed on the natural environment. The responses of German individuals, groups, and governments to these problems reflected both the very difficult nature of the problems themselves and the intertwining of the problems of industrialization with those of modernization. It is also the case that the response by the German government, beginning with Bismarck, to the "social question" that arose from rapid industrialization, was a modern response. Germany created some of the earliest welfare systems in the world, with health, accident, and aged insurance for workers established in the 1880s.

Again, those responses indicate the importance of social history, for people responded as members of class, gender, ethnic, and religious groups. At the same time, the very problems themselves were often perceived and discussed in social terms. Urbanization, for example, could be linked to the "Catholic question" as part of the debate over the alleged economic backwardness of Catholics, to the "workers' question" regarding poverty and the working class, to the "woman question" focusing on female paid employment, childcare, and morality, to the "youth question" and the danger that undisciplined young people posed, or to the "Jewish question" whereby Jews and cities became a metaphor for the threatening changes of modern life.

Nationalism and questions of ethnicity and race have played a central role in the German question as well, both because of their obvious importance in defining Germany and the Germans, but also because they were related to the problems of modernization and industrialization. A nation today is commonly defined as a contiguous, unified territory inhabited by a people of common culture speaking the same language. It is less commonly realized that this definition itself is largely the product of disputes over the German identity that emerged out of the Napoleonic wars. As seen above, the history of Nazism and the Holocaust led many to see something "wrong" with the German national identity. However, there have been many other cases of state building and of nationalism since. Germany may have differed from Western Europeans in the nineteenth century owing to the lack of a unitary state before 1871, but, more than a half century after the Second World War, it is perhaps clearer that Germany was not uniquely pathological, but shared many of the problems inherent in the creation of a national state.[23]

Although nationalism has usually been examined within the frameworks of intellectual or political history, social historians have brought new approaches to bear. Visions from the mid-nineteenth century of what the German national state might be have been linked to the rise of middle-class groups in German society, and the importance of women in emphasizing the ideals of the national community has been noted. Similarly, the transformation of nationalism at the end of the century into an expansionist and racist doctrine has been linked to interests of particular socio-economic groups, ranging from the aristocratic elite to men of the lower middle class. The changing fortunes of social groups reflected changes in the economy, and this raises the question of how the German economy developed.

The economic context of the "German question"

Economic development results from the growth of population, the increasing skills of the labor force, a rising supply of capital, and especially improvements in the available technology. Germany has shared the major identifying characteristics of modern economic growth with all the other advanced industrial economies. Large increases in population, total income, and income per capita were accompanied by a decline in the share of agriculture in the economy, an initial rise in manufacturing industry, and a later increase in the share of services. In the background, modes of production and distribution altered beyond recognition. Further, sometime in the late nineteenth century, Germany moved from being a "follower" country, an importer of technologies that had been developed in other countries, to being a world economic leader and an exporter of new technologies.

Was Germany "special"? Is economic development to blame for the German tragedy? Volker Berghahn speaks for a large number of historians when he links modern economic growth to "the extraordinarily violent course of Germany's development . . . There would appear to be little doubt that this record of violence was connected with the experience of very rapid industrialisation."[24] However, although the rates of growth and transformation that have characterized German economic and social development have indeed been high, they have not been exceptional among industrializing nations. Hartmut Kaelble and Angus Maddison note that Europe's overseas competitors, the United States, Canada, Australia, and Japan, recorded substantially higher rates of growth and within Europe several countries grew more rapidly than Germany. Nor did German society change especially rapidly. The decline of agriculture, the rate of urbanization, and the decline in the birth rate were no more rapid in Germany than in numerous other countries. If Germany's political problems have economic and social foundations, they cannot lie simply in relatively high *rates* of growth and change.[25]

The generations living in the nineteenth and early twentieth centuries did not know what we know today about long-term economic growth, but they did know that economic development did not proceed evenly. Despite the continuity of the underlying trends, modern economies do not grow at simple constant rates. Modern economies have experienced three main types of cyclical behavior: trade or inventory cycles, investment cycles, and long cycles. Through most of the nineteenth and early twentieth centuries, spending in trade and retail inventories followed a three to five-year cycle, as merchants attempted to keep abreast of consumer demand. In addition, investment in transportation and heavy industry fluctuated over a seven to eleven-year cycle, reflecting the mobilization of large amounts of capital and tens of thousands of workers. Finally, long cycles of some fifty years reflected the introduction of major clusters of technological innovations. The overall condition of the economy at any point depended on the interaction of these three cycles. In addition, the developing German economy also became part of a developing world economic system. Successive revolutions in transportation, communications, capital flows, and migration spread the impulses of change from one center to another, linking them in previously undreamt ways.

The long cycles have been of particular interest to German historians, and they remain particularly contentious. In the 1920s, the Russian economist Nikolai Kondratiev argued that "long waves" in production and prices extended back into the early nineteenth century, and were connected to major shifts in investment. During the long downswing, Kondratiev contended, prices decline and agriculture suffers a severe depression, but large numbers of technological discoveries are made. At the beginning of the long upswing, the new discoveries are applied, and growth accelerates.[26] Kondratiev's methods and conclusions have attracted much criticism,[27] but the notion that there are underlying long cycles in economic development has continued to find adherents. Joshua Goldstein has linked the peaks of long economic cycles with periodic outbursts of warfare, and the subsequent depressions with destruction and exhaustion in the wars' aftermath.[28] Angus Maddison has argued that rather than recurrent cycles, the world economy has passed through distinct "phases" of development since the 1820s, marked by substantial variations in rates of growth of output, and even larger variations in the rates of growth of foreign trade.[29]

The German statistics do show long cycles. The upswings of 1850–73, 1895–1914, and 1950–73 stand out clearly, as do the intervening down-swings, the "great depression" of 1873–95, the interwar decades, and the years of "stagflation" and slow growth in the 1970s and 1980s. We can also see the roles of the changing leading sectors—the railway in the upswing of 1850–73, electricity, chemicals, and urban construction in 1896–1914, and machinery, automobiles, and housing during the 1950s and 1960s. Marked by the costs of reunification and global competition, the 1990s and 2000s have been ambiguous. Whether the application of new information technologies across national and world markets will create the conditions for another long upswing remains for the future to reveal.

The experience of the generations that lived through these periods therefore was not of a gradually unfolding process of growth and pro-gress, but of instability and fluctuation. These experiences marked each generation in distinctive ways. In an upswing, growth meant opportun-ity and optimism. In a downswing, recurrent crises brought insecurity and disaster. For workers depression meant unemployment and hunger for their families, while for wealthy farmers, merchants, and industrial-ists an economic downturn could bring bankruptcy and disgrace. Even in an upswing not everyone benefited. The economy might be in an upward cycle, but changing technologies meant that entire industries and the regions that depended on them might suddenly be laid waste by competition from new firms, new products, or new districts. Most contemporaries found the revolutionary changes in their world confusing, disorienting, and possibly more destructive than creative. As Marx remarked, "all that is solid melts into air."

The social and cultural context of the "German question"

The series of dramatic social transformations that accompanied Germany's modern economic development presented another set of challenges. Old divisions widened, and new fissures opened to divide groups against each other. In each generation, writers and artists drew their themes from these changes, or projected the changes of their own times back onto earlier generations. The possession of culture, of *Bildung*, a disciplined familiarity with literature and the plastic arts, became a mark of high status. Because literature and art dealt with contemporary issues, culture also implied familiarity with and involvement in the issues of the day. The themes changed, but the social and political importance of literature and art remained a constant thread linking across generations.[30]

The social landscape of the first half of the nineteenth century was predominantly agricultural, but split into two very distinct regions. In the east, aristocratic Junker landlords employed landless laborers to till the fields of their large grain-producing estates. Towns were scattered thinly, and opportunities for work outside of agriculture were few. In the west and south, farm families worked on their own lands and often produced manufactured goods between the harvest and planting seasons. A dense network of towns fostered an active exchange of products and services, but most manufacturing was still carried on in farmers' homes or artisans' workshops.

Over the middle decades of the nineteenth century, the shift from agriculture to industry meant not only the decline of agriculture as the self-evident employer of a majority of the population, but also a change in the typical location and structure of industry. The gap between east and west widened, as industry concentrated in the west. Machines replaced handicraft methods, factories replaced homes and workshops, and a new gap opened between large-scale industry and the remaining artisan groups. Family firms in all sectors declined in favor of larger, more impersonal organizations. Another new gap opened, this time between the owners of industrial capital and the new working class.

This affected both men's and women's roles. In the early modern era, the family was the central unit of economic production, and the ideal wife or daughter worked both in the home and outside to help support the family. As a member of a recognized household, a woman's employment placed her in the public sphere. This was not equality. Wages were determined by who the worker was, not by what the worker did. The social hierarchy determined that women should be paid less than men, but the conventional standards assumed that women workers could and should perform skilled tasks as active members of their household unit. Wives produced, sold, negotiated, managed, and, if successful, shared in their family's reputation.

By the late eighteenth century this standard was changing. The ideal wife was now separated from market production, occupied with purely domestic functions. Daughters ideally stayed at home, learning these domestic duties before marriage. The home itself ceased to be considered a place where the family created products for sale. Productive labor, it was thought, occurred "outside" the home, and only men were supposed to venture outside. Therefore wage labor came to be thought to rest solely on the efforts of the husband. Thus the ideal of womanhood exchanged the traits of industriousness, strength, commercial know-how, and public assertiveness for the qualities of dependence, domesticity, modesty, and delicacy.[31]

During the nineteenth century, the terms of the struggle between labor and management changed. In order to lower the cost of production, entrepreneurs introduced machines or other functional changes in some operations that men performed, and they often redefined the jobs as women's work. Male trade workers confronted the new exploitation of factory work with a demand that their wage be sufficient to support their families. This frequently placed men and women in competition with each other, and imposed an impossible goal for those families whose husbands could not earn enough by themselves to support the family. Their wives and children were forced to work, as were single women and their children, but they did so in violation of the social norm of domesticity, as marginalized and denigrated persons.[32]

As people worked less and less in agriculture, so they also came to live less and less in the countryside. Over two-thirds of the German population lived in places of fewer than 2000 inhabitants in 1852. By the 1980s, more than six of every ten persons in both East and West Germany lived in cities of more than 10,000 inhabitants, and many of these cities ran together in extensive agglomerations. Urban growth was seen as a "problem" in many different contexts, and the rise of cities was seen as having opened another unhealthy gap in German society. Writers and artists responded, and in each generation produced some of the most insightful views of the process. In addition, however, the increasing numbers of people concentrated in cities greatly expanded the markets for popular art forms. The easily read melodramatic and sentimental novels, the cabaret entertainment of the late nineteenth century, the stage reviews and films of the 1920s, and the changing fashions of fiction, film, music, sport, and fashion since the Second World War all developed in a kind of symbiosis with critiques of culture, premonitions of its decline, and calls for action in its defense.[33]

As seen above, the rapid growth of population was one of the important background factors conditioning German economic development. However, the rates of increase slowed in the twentieth century. Germany lay in the middle of the "demographic transition" which moved across Europe from northwest to southeast during the nineteenth and twentieth centuries. European birth rates and death rates fell, and by the 1980s the population of Western Europe was not reproducing itself. In Germany the fall in the aggregate birth rate set in during the 1880s and accelerated shortly after 1900. Over the next generation, the tendency to have fewer and fewer children began among affluent urban professional families, gradually spread to industrial workers, smaller towns, and eventually reached the agricultural countryside. The "population problem" seemed to many observers to lie at the heart of the "German question," whether Germans would be inundated by Slavic hordes, as prophesied by Conservatives in the 1890s, or forced to give up their jobs to migrants, the fear of Conservatives in the 1990s.

These changes also framed the position of each generation of young people. Youth, the period of life between totally dependent childhood and independent adulthood, is both a biological and a symbolic structure. Its dimensions and definition at any point in time reflect both existing social relations and previous historical development.[34] They are not constant—for example the spread of compulsory schooling removed children from their parents' homes and placed them under the control of state-appointed teachers, and as the structure of the educational system changed so too did the definition of the young generation, the "youth" who were to be educated. Concern for youth remained, and often reflected other anxieties as well. What young German people did, and even more important what they should do, were issues as contentious as the definition of the German woman.

Industrialization, urbanization, women, wayward youth, and the declining birth rate therefore intersected with inherited structures of German families, and a broad range of commentators debated those changes. The history of families and households forms one of the crucial points of intersection of economic and social history, and not surprisingly it has proved a highly contentious area. From the mid-nineteenth century until the 1920s, upper and middle-class observers expressed horror at the "immorality" of the expanding urban working class. Workers in turn resented and resisted attempts to regulate their private lives and to impose "respectable" patterns on them. The regulation of family life and female behavior played a central role in Nazi ideology and policy. Following the Second World War, the new governments of both West and East Germany attempted to impose new definitions of the family on their citizens, and debate since the 1960s has repeatedly flared over the gaps between "alternative" lifestyles on the one hand and "traditional" family patterns on the other.

The political context of the "German question"

Over the past century and a half, economic, social, and political changes seem to have moved along distinctly separate paths. Germany is not unique in this regard. In all nations the fundamental aspects of economic development and social transformation have resulted from factors over which politicians had little or no control. The basic trends of modern economic growth, and the fluctuations in the growth process, proceeded with very little reference to the needs or desires of political leaders. The underlying trends of social transformation also moved according to their own, sometimes very different, timetables. Contrary to what a large number of patriotic historians wished to believe, the state did not cause economic development to occur, and contrary to what a large number of concerned social commentators hoped would happen, the state could not reverse the direction of social transformation.

In the German case the decline of agriculture is a good example. The imperial, Weimar, Nazi, and West German governments all attempted to protect and preserve their farmers with tariffs and subsidies, and all failed to arrest the decline of the agricultural sector. In addition, attempts to restructure the sector achieved only the most limited success. Programs of peasant settlement under the Imperial, Weimar, and Nazi regimes affected only a few thousand individuals. The program of amalgamation of holdings in West Germany and even the collectivization of agriculture in East Germany did little to alter the distribution of holdings in the west or to improve productivity in the east. Within the process of modern economic growth, the position of agriculture changes, slowly but ineluctably, but attempts to alter the direction or rate of change seem in retrospect to have been largely futile.

Major social transformations such as urbanization and the decline in the birth rate proved equally intractable. In the late nineteenth and early twentieth centuries, it seemed obvious that the growth of cities and smaller families went hand in hand, and that both had resulted from rapid industrialization. In the 1890s, a full-scale academic debate erupted over the threatening consequences of urbanization and declining birth rates, and a generation later the Nazi regime attempted with its characteristic systematic brutality to reverse the process. Without success—urbanization and the decline in birth rates continued. Moreover, it now seems that the link between industrialization and urban growth is not so obvious. In the Third World immense urban centers have emerged over the past generation with little or no industrial development. Similarly, as noted above, the decline in German birth rates is only one example of the common pattern of demographic transition, a pattern linked in complex ways to modernization, family structure, and gender relations, but not simply "caused" by industrialization and also not easily altered by government policies.

However, there have been important points where the paths of economic development, social transformation, and political change have crossed. Over the decades, a broad tendency for the public sphere to expand, and for the number of participants in political life to grow, reflected the underlying trends of economic and social development. Cyclical swings in the economy, both in their timing and their severity, have sometimes been closely linked to political decisions. Moreover, the association has been a two-way relationship. Policies adopted by governments have affected cyclical fluctuations, and conversely cyclical up and downswings have influenced both large and small political changes. Similarly, political change and social transformation have intersected at important points. This is particularly true where family and household structures have been placed under pressure by economic change. The relationships have not been constant, because political, social, and economic structures have undergone profound changes. It is the nature of those changes that make up the substance of historical debate.

Politics does matter, and so do flesh-and-blood politicians. Although economic development and social transformation may have formed the conditions under which political leaders could act, they did not determine those leaders' actions. Most obviously, the outbreak of revolution in 1848, 1918, and 1989, or of war in 1862, 1866, 1871, 1914, and 1939, resulted from specific decisions taken by specific individuals. So, too, with many other events we will be looking at, from the adoption of the Prussian constitution in 1849 to the reunification of 1990—and including the series of decisions leading to the Holocaust. We will see as well, however, that these decisions did not always have the consequences that the leaders who made them had hoped. The effects of decisions taken by a few powerful men depend ultimately on decisions taken by many other less powerful women and men. Hegel called this the "cunning of reason." We might also say it is the outcome of social history.

From generation to generation: ruptures and shared experience

Economic change, social development, and political decisions together made up the framework within which ordinary women and men lived their lives, formed their families, and reared their children. At certain points, however, the economy, society, and political structures interacted in ways that shifted the framework and created something new. The effect was to fracture their experience, disrupt their lives, and alter their way of perceiving the world. Those emerging from such a rupture would look back and see their history differently from the previous generation. They also would see their present differently, and their altered perception affected economic development, social structures, and political action. Commonly it was the emergence of a new cultural style that marked the new generation most clearly. Distinctive modes of literary and artistic expression emerged that shared and expressed the generation's common economic, social, and political concerns.

Generations in this sense were not simply biological. Most were shorter than a human lifetime, and some much shorter. Shared experiences lead to shared modes of perception, and the sense of shared experience and understandings, rather than age or birth date, sets one generation off from another. The political sociologist Karl Mannheim, looking at the "front-fighter generation" in the 1920s, noted that this does not mean that all members of a generation agree with one another, or that all adopt an identical attitude toward social processes or history. Members of any generation may and frequently do disagree violently. However, the shared experience does mean that their beliefs and attitudes will have been shaped in distinctive ways.[35] One could live through more than one generation. Some, like the historian Treitschke, moved seamlessly from one mode of expression and one set of allegiances in the 1860s to another mode and different beliefs in the 1870s with no conscious sense of discontinuity. Others, such as the Conservative Gerlach brothers, could not make the transition and remained marginalized in the new and alien world that Bismarck's diplomacy was creating. "Die at the right time," advised Nietzsche.

No generation could see the future, but each generation looked backward as it set itself off from what had gone before and attempted to make sense of its own unique experience. This has two implications. First, a view of German history as moving inevitably along a "special path" toward an ultimate tragic goal is inappropriate. The works noted above that searched for a decisive turning point and sought to blame particular individuals or particular groups for Germany's "failure" have been superseded. As we will see, many Germans of the Nazi generation knew the Holocaust was happening, but no previous generation knew that it would happen. On the other hand, the second point is that in looking backward every generation picked, chose, and rearranged elements of previous experience, of history. This could come suddenly as a gestalt shift, as in the case of Treitschke's conversion to support of Bismarck. Or it might come gradually, as the spread of anti-Semitism from disreputable fringe groups in the 1880s and 1890s, to more respectable figures after 1900, through the First World War and into the 1920s, to official government policy in the 1930s.

The chapters that follow are defined by the ruptures that opened and closed generations, and they are focused on the experience of each generation as lived, thought, and felt by contemporaries. The sources of economic development and changes in economic structures make up the economic context. Social groups and their interaction make up the social context. Interwoven with social patterns are the cultural products, particularly literature and art, that helped each generation define itself for itself. Political organization and action, both parliamentary and extra-parliamentary, make up the political context. Politics includes foreign policy as well, and this in turn frequently interacts with the development of the international economy. Ruptures could arise from any of the broad fields of action. In the event, again politics does matter, and a majority of the defining ruptures did in fact result from the actions of political leaders.

Each chapter opens with a work that expresses the sense of contemporary belongingness. The selection and interpretation depend on our reading of the text today, and the same point applies to our analysis of economics, society, and politics. The forces driving economic development often framed a generation's understanding of itself, but our analysis of economic growth exists in a tension between the ways contemporaries understood their economy, and our understanding of the way we now believe their economy functioned. Similarly with the social and cultural contexts. Contemporaries struggled to make sense of social change based on their selective appropriation of their own past and, their imperfect knowledge of their own present. Our view is conditioned by what we now know of their past, their present, and, most importantly, their unknown future. Writers and artists also responded to their past, present, and frequently to a hoped-for future. Critical, involved, and individually creative, they often provided insights into social reality that escaped the view of contemporary social theorists or policy-makers. Finally, as argued above politics depended on economic, social, and cultural developments, but did not simply reflect them. Several of the generations indeed are defined precisely by the divergence between the desires of political elites and the thrust of development, and our interpretation of their politics reflects our understanding of the unknown future consequences of their actions.

Notes

1. Hans Haacke, *Germania*, 1993. Marble floor tiles, dimensions unknown. Installed at the Venice Biennale. Reproduced in *Twentieth Century Art* (New York and London: Phaidon). See Bussmann and Matzner 1993.
2. Parsons 1951; Parsons and Smelser 1956.
3. Rosenberg 1943; 1958; 1967.
4. Dahrendorf 1967.
5. Roseman 1995; Abrams and Harvey 1996.
6. Jay 1973; Held 1980.

7. Rickman 1988; Iggers and Powell 1990; see Fulbrook 2000.
8. Dorpalen 1957.
9. Kehr 1970.
10. Meinecke 1946.
11. Namier 1946; Taylor 1946.
12. Engels 1851–52; Kuczinski 1961ff., Vols. 3 and 4.
13. Eyck 1956–57; Fischer 1961.
14. Krieger 1957; Kohn 1960.
15. Greenfeld 1992.
16. Moses 1975.
17. Dahrendorf 1967; Wehler 1973.
18. Blackbourn and Eley 1984; see Hamerow 1983.
19. See Geyer and Jarausch 1989; Breuilly 2001.
20. Scott 1988, p. 42.
21. Roseman 1995; Abrams and Harvey 1996.
22. Confino and Koshar 2001.
23. Tipton 1998b, Chs. 5, 8.
24. Berghahn 1987, p. 267.
25. Kaelble 1983; Maddison 1995.
26. Kondratiev 1928.
27. Spree 1980; Solomou 1987; 1998.
28. Goldstein 1988; see Tylecote 1993.
29. Maddison 1982; 1987; 1989; 1995.
30. Belting 1998.
31. Rose 1992, p. 10; Abrams and Harvey 1996.
32. Secombe 1986.
33. Bowie 1998.
34. Mitterauer 1986.
35. Mannheim 1928.

CHAPTER 2

THE ROMANTIC AGE,
1815–40

Returning from a trip to Italy in the late 1820s, Carl Blechen sketched the finishing stages of the construction of the new Teufelsbrücke (the "Devil's Bridge") at the base of a gorge in the St Gotthard Pass. The resulting painting shows towering dark peaks above, and the powerful rushing waters of the river below. The workers beside the road are portrayed resting, exhausted from their labors. Their struggles have drained them of energy. But they have triumphed nonetheless; the final stone on the primary arch has been inserted, and the completion of the bridge is now assured. Highlighted by a brilliant shaft of sunlight, the road and the new bridge will make the heights increasingly accessible. If the mountains and river represent a vision of wild, untamed nature, nevertheless civilization has established a tenuous foothold of control.[1]

More than most, the Romantic era is known through its painting. Blechen became Professor of the Landscape Class in the Berlin Academy and one of the great landscape artists of his time. His work combines realistic detail with a free rearrangement of scenic structures. In the resulting compositions trees and rocks sometimes appear to take on a life of their own. Blechen's technique has been described as "poetic," and the Romantic generation often expressed their feelings in poetry. The tension between control and wildness, between civilization and nature, lies at the center of the Romantic view. Images of the innocent girl, the peasant, and the peaceful town contrasted with visions of violent, primeval natural forces and a yearning for a timeless, undefinable infinite. Eduard Mörike said he yearned, but that he was "not really sure what for."[2] If Blechen could envision a peaceful end to the struggle with nature, Caspar David Friedrich saw nature as something not only untamed but untameable. Even here, however, as in his famous scene of a solitary man looking down from a rocky promontory onto an expanse of swirling storm clouds, the man is dressed as would suit a member of the leisured upper middle classes, his hiking stick the only concession to the arduous climb.[3]

25

Appropriately, the German sphere in the Romantic era consisted of a multiplicity of communities, ranging from major powers to tiny principalities, from proud trading cities to humble farming villages. Although proud of their history, their culture, and their economic achievements, members of these communities felt themselves living under threat, economically, socially, and politically. France, the defeated foreign invader, was a threat. Revolution, the suppressed yearning for a new society, was a threat. Secularization, the loss of traditional unreflective religious faith, was a threat. "The literature of this time always resonates with the sense of religious loss."[4] For contemporaries, the tensions within the

Plate 2.1   Carl Blechen, *Bau der Teufelsbrücke* (*Construction of the "Devil's Bridge"*), *c.* 1830. Oil on linen, 77.6 × 104.5 cm. Neue Pinakothek, Munich. The Romantic view of nature. Exhausted workers rest amidst overpowering mountain scenery, but they have succeeded in completing the primary arch of the new bridge that will allow travelers easier and safer passage. The details are rendered realistically, but Blechen has rearranged the cliffs and the lighting to illuminate the approach to the bridge and the arch itself. Loan of the Federal Republic of Germany to the Bayerische Staatsgemäldesammlungen. Photo: courtesy of the Bayerische Staatsgemäldesammlungen, Munich.

Romantic vision defined approaches to economic, social, and political life.

The structures that the Romantic generation took for granted in retrospect can appear fluid, subject to processes which contemporaries perceived only dimly. Similarly, the problems and threats they perceived have often been taken as precursors of future developments. For subsequent scholars debate has often centered on the origins of German economic development, the emergence of new social classes, cultural change, religious divisions, and the growth of a "national" consciousness. As seen in Chapter 1, these overarching stories have frequently been combined in the single notion of Germany's "special path."

However, the German women and men of the Romantic generation lived in their own complex present, and they looked more to the past than to the future. Looking at their world through their eyes, we can simplify our picture of the economy by focusing on two Germanies defined by the agricultural landscape in east and west. We can refine our view of social structures if we look at three Germanies marked by patterns of industry and trade in urban communities, protoindustrial districts, and centers of attempts by central governments to stimulate economic development. Politically, we can see that the 39 Germanies, the states of the German Confederation, all tenaciously defended their autonomy. For contemporaries, Germany was more variegated still, being at once their local surroundings, their regional connections, and the broader German sphere. All were changing, and few would have seen the changes as likely to bring good.

The economic context: inherited traditions of economic development

Economic landscapes

In the early nineteenth century there was no "German" economy. Yet the Germanies were not underdeveloped or backward. German women and men produced a broad range of products that they could sell profitably both in local markets and outside their home regions. Sophisticated credit arrangements facilitated trade. But the Germanies were not a single economic unit. Most of the interregional trade from which Germans profited was with regions outside Germany. Even on high-quality roads, wagons and horses were expensive, and therefore goods flowed by water wherever possible. This meant wind-driven sailing ships along the

Plate 2.2   Caspar David Friedrich, *The Wayfarer above the Sea of Fog, c.* 1818. Oil on canvas, 74.8 × 94.8 cm. Kunsthalle, Hamburg. The civilized man confronts nature. We cannot see his expression, although we presume him to be impressed with the immensity of the untamed elements. Nevertheless, he stands at his leisure, comfortably surveying the panorama before him. Photo: AKG London.

coasts, and barges pulled by men and women (again, horses were often too expensive), north along the Vistula, Oder, Elbe, and Weser, west along the Rhine, and east along the Danube.

Contemporaries saw two German economies, lying on either side of a line running from Denmark to the eastern border of Saxony. East of that line large agricultural estates produced grains for export to the industrial regions of Western Europe in the Netherlands, Belgium, and Great Britain. In the west and south small farmers produced a broad range of products for regional markets, and scattered industrial centers sent their textile, metal, or wooden wares to consumers who might be located in the Middle East, East Asia, or North and South America.

On both sides of the east–west divide there were three distinct sources of economic change, all with long histories that in some cases extended as far back as the late Middle Ages. Along with the two German economies, we can speak of three separate models of development: first, development centered in urban communities, the places that Mack

Map 1 The German Confederation in 1815, showing Prussian acquisitions

Walker has called "German home towns"; second, protoindustrialization, the term coined by Franklin Mendels to describe the production of
handicraft goods for export markets; and, finally, state-sponsored development undertaken by the central governments of various states, in
particular the efforts of Prussian government officials emphasized for
instance by W. O. Henderson.[5]

It was tempting for contemporaries to envisage these different kinds
of development as stages leading from a lower to a higher form of
economic organization. The "older historical economists" offered
numerous stage theories of development. Karl Knies argued that financial organization moved from commodity exchange, to the use of

money, and finally to the development of credit. Karl Bucher asserted that, as economic development proceeded, the size and scale of economic relationships would increase, from local economies, to regional economies, and finally to national economies. They were wrong, and in retrospect we can see that their stage theories of development in fact reflected their desire for a politically unified Germany. In fact, none of the inherited types of development was a mere "stage," and none was "higher" or more "advanced" than the others. East and west, protoindustrialization, community-centered, and state-sponsored development were all sophisticated economic systems, but they remained separate. In addition, each possessed its own corresponding gender and social order, and, as a result, the individuals and groups involved in each sort of development had very different political desires.

East vs. west

If we look first to the east, it seems evident today that the interlocking structures of the agricultural, industrial, and commercial sectors severely restricted the region's potential for development. In the early nineteenth century, however, the dynamic, export-oriented agriculture that dominated the eastern economy was one of the most advanced sectors among the German economies. The local landlords were fully capitalist in their outlook, but over the previous centuries they had proved themselves more than willing to use non-economic means—force and guile—to achieve their economic ends.

The eastern landlords were the Junker aristocracy. Throughout Eastern Europe, landlords were attempting to reduce the peasantry to serfdom, meaning that formerly free peasant families would be deprived of much of their land, that they would be tied to the land and forbidden to move, and that men and women would be forced to work on the landlord's land. This progressive degradation of the peasantry, the so-called "second serfdom," extended from Prussia and Poland in the seventeenth century to Russia in the eighteenth century, and was still proceeding in southeastern Europe in the nineteenth century. It was a response to economic development and population growth in Western Europe. In these developing "peripheries," the landlords used the labor of their serfs to grow grain, which they sold to Dutch and English merchants for resale in the expanding urban areas of the industrial "core," the Low Countries and Britain.[6]

Until the late eighteenth century, the techniques used by the East German Junker landlords remained backward, with large open fields on which grain crops were grown for two years, but which were left fallow in the third year to replenish the nutrients required by the grains. Exploiting the peasants still further could raise output, but there were limits to such measures. The more progressive landlords began to search for ways to improve productivity. These were the years during which English landlords were moving from field rotation to crop rotation systems, with grain crops alternated with root crops such as potatoes and beets to aerate the soil and legumes such as clover to replenish nutrients. Karl Kraus, a professor at the University of Königsberg, had studied at Göttingen, at the time a center of British ideas because of the dynastic connection between Great Britain and Hanover. He became one of the early enthusiasts for Adam Smith's ideas of free trade in Germany, and he became one of the chief advocates of enclosure and crop rotation.

The new system was potentially extremely profitable because crops could be grown every year, but it required large amounts of capital for fences and drains, and it also required a reorganization of the fields. Lack of capital, and the problem of how to separate the landlords' land from the peasants' land while still using the peasants' labor, prevented many landlords from enclosing their fields and adopting crop rotation.

Prussia's defeat by Napoleon in 1806 brought to power a group of government officials dedicated to restoring Prussian power, and reform of the agricultural system was one item among many on their agenda. Influenced by the ideas of both the French Enlightenment and Adam Smith, they had concluded that free workers were more efficient than unfree serfs, but also that large estates were more efficient than small farms. Their aim, therefore, was the "regulation" of the peasantry, not "emancipation." The resulting edict in October 1807 was vague, although it both protected existing peasant holdings and permitted peasants to leave the land if they wished. A further edict in 1811 provided that those peasants with hereditary tenure would retain their land, but those without hereditary tenure would surrender one-third to one-half of the land they had previously farmed for themselves, and all peasants owed compensation for the labor services they had previously provided to the landlords. And in 1816, with Napoleon safely defeated, the government further restricted grants of land to peasants to those with enough land to support a pair of oxen. Small peasants and all those with tenure of less than two generations' duration lost their land.

Over fifty further laws were passed in Prussia between 1816 and 1850. The net result was the direct transfer of approximately one million hectares of land from the peasants to the landlords. Those peasants who retained their land owed heavy compensation payments to the landlords. In addition, the landlords benefited from access to the *Landschaften*, rural credit banks originally established in the eighteenth century, but now extended and strengthened. The *Landschaften* sold bonds and lent the money to landlords. The mortgages on the landlords' estates made the bonds an attractive and secure investment, and interest rates were generally low. These sources of capital allowed the landlords to enclose and drain their fields and purchase the new agricultural machinery. The majority of the peasants became agricultural laborers, eking out their wages with earnings from small plots of land allotted to them by their employers.

The position of industry in the east reflected the dominance of large-scale agriculture. Except for the coal mines and iron foundries in Silesia, large industry was absent. There was some production for export markets, such as the extensive linen-weaving industry in Silesia, but in general relatively small numbers of artisans produced goods for local markets. The commercial sector was similarly underdeveloped. The landlords marketed their grains using credit supplied by commercial firms in Königsberg, Danzig, or Hamburg, or in Amsterdam, Antwerp, London, or Newcastle. Towns in the east were relatively far apart, and they lacked the long tradition of independence characteristic of the west.

The contrast with the west and south was striking. In agriculture, industry, and commerce the west appears relatively wealthy, with what we now see as good prospects for long-term development. Agricultural techniques were often relatively advanced, and specialization could reach striking levels. One village in Württemberg produced snails for sale in Bavaria, and others concentrated on cherry juice and dried fruit for overseas markets.[7] The land was worked by peasants who either owned their land or paid a quitrent to local nobles, similar to France before the Revolution. In Bavaria, for instance, though only a small fraction of peasants owned the land they worked, the reforms of 1809 had specified and frozen the services that they owed to the landlords, and had guaranteed the heritability of tenure. However, western German peasants generally did not possess the capital for intensive development in the style of the Netherlands or England. The Bavarian reforms, for example, had made no attempt to redistribute or consolidate holdings, and the government had made no attempt to provide capital to the peasant farmers.

Protoindustrialization and economic development

Industry in the west and south, as in the east, was still overwhelmingly artisan manufacture. Families worked raw materials into finished goods using handicraft methods. Here, however, there was an old tradition of producing high-quality goods for export to other regions. This kind of trade had been increasing since the mid-eighteenth century. As noted above, the consumers of western German manufactured goods often lay in the expanding urban centers of Western Europe, the Americas, or Asia. Manufacturing districts further east, in Saxony or Bavaria, found their markets in the Ottoman Empire, in Bursa, Damascus, or Aleppo.

Protoindustrialization is the term proposed by Franklin Mendels to link several distinct social patterns together into a coherent picture. First, there was the history of the family. As seen below, independent peasant families were cyclical, which meant that the eldest son often delayed marriage until his father retired, and in the urban communities only master artisans with full citizenship rights could marry. In both country and town, younger sons and possibly younger daughters could be left out. This "European" marriage pattern meant that many who would marry could not, or were forced to wait.

However, the opportunity of interregional trade in manufactured goods could lead urban guilds to recruit workers in the countryside. These new employment opportunities would be particularly welcome in poor agricultural areas, especially hilly districts such as areas of Silesia, Saxony, and the Rhineland. Manufacturing employment, combined with a small agricultural holding, could provide a young couple with the opportunity to marry and found a family. Because peak earnings in such peasant/artisan employment were reached at an early age, there was no reason to delay marriage. And, because children could help from an early age, there was no reason to avoid having as many as possible. Therefore population would rise, because earlier and more frequent marriages meant there would be many more children in these rural protoindustrial areas.

The urban entrepreneurs who employed rural peasant artisans often discovered that, above a certain wage level, the supply of labor declined.

Individuals and families aimed for a certain total income, and once they achieved that income, they were content. An increase in the wage rate means that they worked fewer hours or days, because they did not need to work more to achieve their goals. Employers who wished to increase output still further had to move into new country areas to find underemployed poor peasants willing to take up artisan manufacturing. Protoindustrial development was therefore potentially dynamic. As long as demand continued to increase, merchant guilds or individual entrepreneurs continued to seek out poor peasants, who in turn used their new industrial earnings to found families and raise children.[8]

Protoindustrial development provided many families with their livelihoods in good times, but it was inherently risky. A disruption in trade or a poor harvest meant desperate hardship because the farms of protoindustrial families were now very small relative to the needs of the expanded population in these districts. In previous centuries, bursts of protoindustrial development had led to expansion and population growth, but the subsequent decline, caused perhaps by war, by competition from other regions, by harvest failure, or by something as banal as a change in fashion in distant markets, could leave a region to stagnate, with a population too large for its resources, trapped in a kind of economic involution.[9]

However, though precarious, protoindustrial development was real. Across many districts of Germany, increasing population and increasing income from protoindustrial development expanded the potential market. Further, experience in manufacturing production was creating a large pool of skilled labor. Fashion frowned on linen, but smiled on cotton textiles. In England, mechanized spinning of cotton thread lay at the heart of the industrial revolution. The markets for linen cloth and for cotton thread which had been spun by hand in Saxony and the Rhineland declined, but the demand for cotton textiles woven by Saxon and Rhenish weavers increased.[10]

Urban communities and economic development

Commerce in the west and south was centered in the towns. Merchants were organized in guilds, and these guild organizations were restrictive and jealously monopolistic. However, like the landlords in the east, the merchants in the west had extensive contacts with distant regions.

Increases or changes in demand in those distant markets represented opportunities for profit, and western merchants were quick to respond. Artisan manufacture in the towns could be increased and the goods transported by road or water. When the local artisan guilds could not supply sufficient goods to fill the demand, the merchant guild might look outside the town for additional labor power, leading to bursts of protoindustrial development.

In the first half of the nineteenth century, Germany was comparatively highly urbanized. Something like one-quarter of the people of all the German states and Austria lived in towns with populations of 2000 or more. In the west and south, the "individualized land" of the "German home towns,"[11] the proportion was substantially higher. In Württemberg in 1821, for instance, there was one town every German mile (or every seven kilometers), and they contained half of the total population.

The economic organization of the towns followed a standard pattern. The recognized trades were organized into guilds. The guilds were ranked in status and political importance, usually with the guild of merchants who controlled the town's major export trade at the top. Non-citizens allowed to reside in the town, known as "permitted people" or "protected people," normally worked as wage laborers for guild members in the export industries. Peasants in the surrounding countryside were forbidden to carry on guild trades; the town supplied them with manufactured goods, and they in turn were forced to sell their produce in the town's market.

This system remained largely intact through the middle decades of the century. In theory the towns within the expanded territorial states had lost their independence, as had the formerly free cities such as Cologne, annexed by Prussia in 1815. Further, in Prussia the edict proclaiming "occupational freedom" passed as one of the reform measures in 1807 had eliminated the legal power of the guilds over entry into craft trades and ended their role in urban government. In Bavaria, the 1809 reforms placed the guilds under the supervision of the central government and specifically forbade the heritability of mastership. But the members of the urban communities held tenaciously to their traditions, achieving by ostracism and scorn, and occasionally by violence, the desired end of choosing their own members and controlling the local economy. It is important to recognize, therefore, that although they were conservative, their desires were not simply reactionary. The traditional sort of protoindustrial development described above, and much of the new industrial development described in Chapter 3, resulted from the energetic efforts of members of these urban communities.

Central governments and economic development

To analyze the economic role of central government in the economy means to analyze the role of war. This is so not only because of the direct consequences of actual wars, but also because states continually worried about and prepared for war, and this in large part determined their attitude toward economic development. Prussia's successive acquisitions of Silesia, large parts of Poland, and the Rhineland and Westphalia made it a European power. In 1840, Silesia was still the most important industrial area in Prussia, and in subsequent decades the rise of heavy industry in the west supported Prussia's bid for hegemony in Germany.

In addition, the German states inherited the tradition of the "administrative welfare state."[12] In the eighteenth century, political theorists in Central Europe such as Karl Lamprecht argued that the state could and should promote the happiness of its subjects through detailed regulations administered by an efficient royal bureaucracy. Frederick the Great had agreed: "A well-conducted government must be a system as well connected as if it were a system of philosophy." He introduced functionally specialized ministries, with defined areas of authority and their own chain of command from the center to the provincial and local levels. In addition to the army and the royal domains, the administration of Silesia came under a separate department. Another ministry was established to oversee reconstruction following the Seven Years War, including river reclamation projects and the establishment of the *Landschaften* credit banks. The Seehandlung, a combination central bank and overseas trading corporation modelled on the Dutch and British East India Companies, was established in 1763.

On the positive side, rulers saw themselves as the fathers of their countries, and they assumed they knew what was best for their childlike subjects. There was no "private" sphere where government could not intrude.[13] Governments worried about waste. Elaborate sumptuary codes specified the quality of material women of different classes could use in their dresses and the amounts to be spent on weddings and funerals. Governments also worried about production. They attempted to introduce new technologies, and they subsidized industries that they hoped would earn export revenue.

On the negative side, governments interpreted any initiative from outside government as a hostile threat to their authority. Frederick opposed the introduction of English-style machinery in the cotton industry because it might cause unemployment, refused to improve the roads in his western possessions because they might make enemy invasion easier, and slowed the changes in eastern agriculture because they might reduce the numbers of potential soldiers.

Both the positive and the negative aspects of this tradition persisted after 1815. Most German states adopted the new forms of centralized administration and functionally specialized ministries during the Napoleonic period, but recruitment, promotion patterns, and the resulting attitudes toward their subject populations remained very much in the style of earlier generations. The old sumptuary codes disappeared, but in their place were equally elaborate regulations intended to mold behavior to create useful citizens.[14]

The Prussian government's efforts have been the most studied, and the results show the continuing balance of positive and negative. Peter Beuth established a Technical Institute in Berlin in 1821, which supported study trips to Britain (where officials sometimes stole plans for machinery), trained students in the new techniques, and made grants to promising industrialists. Under Christian Rother in the 1820s and 1830s, the Seehandlung constructed in a number of improved highways. The Seehandlung also invested directly in modern industrial enterprises such as the power weaving plant erected in 1842. These were intended to make profits, but in addition were to serve as training centers and models, and therefore they were often located in country areas.

On the other hand, grants made to favored industrialists were sometimes wasted, mining officials opposed new technologies in the Rhineland, and the new highways were toll roads intended to raise revenue. Armies were large and expensive both in Prussia and in the other German states, and all governments were short of money. Memories of bankruptcy during the Napoleonic wars reinforced the reluctance to spend. Railways, a potential solution to the age-old problem of land transport, were particularly expensive. Rother and a succession of finance ministers opposed the construction of railways, because of their expense and because they might compete with the toll roads and reduce revenue.[15]

In 1834, Prussia succeeded in establishing the Zollverein, the customs union that unified most of the German states behind a common external tariff. Later historians often cited the long diplomatic struggle pursued by Friedrich Maassen and Friedrich Motz as evidence of Prussian concern for the economy, as a beginning date for German economic development, and as a step toward political unification.[16] However, the Zollverein excluded Austria, the largest German state and potentially the largest market, because all government officials pursued economic development not for its own sake, but as a means to increasing the power of their state. Motz had written a memo in 1817 in which he argued that Prussia should extend its power in north Germany to secure its position against Austria. Nearly two decades later, the generous terms offered by Prussia for entry into the Zollverein (Prussia bore all the costs of administration, but distributed the revenue on the basis of member states' populations, not according to the value of their trade) were clearly a bribe intended to woo the smaller states away from Austria. The role of the state in economic development was real enough, but it was secondary, and as individual entrepreneurs began to emerge from the old communities involved in the process of growth, this would lead to conflict.

Trends and cycles

The underlying trends of modern economic growth made up a constant background condition in Germany from the early nineteenth century onward, but the patterns are only obvious in retrospect, after several generations of observation and research. Contemporaries were well aware of trade cycles. The export of agricultural and industrial products depended on the state of distant markets, and a decline in foreign demand could spell disaster for individuals, families, and regions. This sort of risk was not new, but it was increasing. The fall of Napoleon ended the so-called "Continental system" which in theory had pro-hibited areas under French control from trading with Britain. Now, a depression that dogged German manufacturers through the 1820s was blamed on competition from a rapidly industrializing Britain. Textile producers in particular suffered as Britain's cheap machine-spun cotton thread appeared in their markets.

However, in the Romantic era economic cycles were not yet determined by activity in the industrial sector. In the preindustrial age, everyone watched the weather anxiously, for the weather determined the harvest. Because of the difficulty of transporting bulky products among regions, a bad harvest drastically raised the price of food. Three-quarters of the population worked in agriculture. With food prices high, the mass of the population suddenly could not afford anything beyond subsistence, and this reduction in their purchasing power led to a depression in the small industrial sector as well. Something like this had happened in 1816–17, when grain prices shot up from 50 to 200 per cent.

Paradoxically, though, the harvest might be "too good" as well. Food has in economists' terms a "low elasticity of demand"—one can only eat so much. A bumper harvest therefore could lead to a decline in food prices to the point where the total income of the agricultural population actually declined. This could result in reduced demand and a depression in the industrial sector. In many of the German states the early 1820s was such a period, a "crisis of agricultural overproduction."[17] Structural change, the pressure of industrialization emanating from Britain, and cyclical change, the fluctuations in the harvest, interacted. Not surprisingly, the experience of those who lived through these decades was often traumatic, confusing, and disorienting.

The social and cultural context: Romanticism as leitmotiv

Parallel to the complexities of economic life were equally complex social structures. However, in one respect the conceptual framework that contemporaries shared was extremely simple. Persons were not individuals, but members of families and of the communities into which they had been born. Despite the disparities among the social and gender orders in the agricultural regions, in protoindustrial districts, and in the towns, the assertion that every person had a particular fixed place in the social fabric gave the pattern of warp and weft a comforting stability. Conversely, any hint that the pattern was being disturbed was that much more threatening.

Germans could also draw on an interwoven fabric of cultural traditions. The Romantic era had its roots in both the *Sturm und Drang* ("storm and stress") and Enlightenment movements of the late eighteenth century. Growing publics enjoyed the ongoing developments in art, literature, history, and philosophy. School systems expanded. Yet another series of reforms had laid down the outlines of a two-track system. In theory, the primary school (*Volksschule*) would impart literacy to all boys and girls and vocational training to the boys, while the *Gymnasium* would train the most able of the boys for entrance into the universities, where they would acquire the broad humanistic culture (*Bildung*) appropriate to an enlightened elite. In fact, the primary schools were poorly funded, the *Gymnasium* was available only to the wealthy, and universities served primarily as certification for would-be clergymen, state officials, and doctors. Over 30 per cent of university students majored in theology, another 30 per cent in law, and 15 per cent in medicine. The number of theology students peaked in 1831 at six thousand.[18] Nevertheless, growing literacy meant larger numbers of readers, and the university system trained and fostered an educated class with a significant set of shared experiences. There was therefore a solid institutional basis for the cultural unity of the socially and politically diverse German communities.

The aristocracy

Aristocracy ruled. Revolution had come and gone, and nobles had managed to bend reform in ways that suited their interests. Symbolized in their exclusive hunting rights, the nobility were the envy of those born into lesser circles. Even Goethe, himself from the wealthy urban elite, had his hero Wilhelm Meister say, "universal and personal cultivation is beyond the reach of anyone except a nobleman." Only an aristocrat could be truly cultivated, because only an aristocrat was truly free, with rights denied to common citizens. The special status of the nobility was embedded in the legal systems of all the 39 German states. Some 80 families of the old imperial nobility, the so-called Standesherren, though they had lost their position as virtually autonomous sovereigns, remained a special group with rights guaranteed by the articles of the German Confederation.

As seen above, the East Prussian Junker nobility did very well indeed out of the government's agricultural reforms. The proposal for a uniform land tax was abandoned, and aristocratic landholdings remained virtually tax exempt. In addition, the nobles successfully resisted government attempts to reduce their power at the local level, and the rural county councilor, the *Landrat*, typically continued to be a member of the local nobility. In the west and south landlords' rights had been protected even under French administration. In Baden aristocrats controlled nearly a quarter of the land, and many of them retained police and judicial rights, as well as the power to appoint church pastors and schoolteachers. In Württemberg their old rights remained largely intact, and in Bavaria they forced revisions in the constitution that protected their interests. Although the incomes they derived from the services and quitrents owed by peasant farmers were fixed, they remained substantial. Even those who had lost their land during the Napoleonic period remained powerful. Their wealth might have been reduced, but they retained their circle of connections, and these could be exploited to find places for themselves and their sons, and suitable marriages for their daughters.[19]

A distinctive feature of the Romantic era was the extent to which nobles depended on expanded and strengthened states to support their position in society. Government service provided many of the sorts of places which aristocrats found congenial. For them a university degree was not essential. Official positions at the three dozen royal and princely courts were reserved for them, and the diplomatic corps of all the German states remained an aristocratic preserve. Around three-fifths of Prussian army officers continued to come from noble families, and the proportion was higher elsewhere. Senior posts in government administration went almost exclusively to nobles. At the middle levels, the proportion of nobles varied depending on the extent of reforms during the Napoleonic period. Very high in Saxony, Anhalt, and Mecklenburg, the share of nobles was much lower in the south. In Prussia the share of the aristocracy in middle-level bureaucratic posts rose from a quarter to a third from the 1820s to the 1840s.

Aristocratic families jockeyed for princely favor and maneuvered to secure advantageous alliances. Aristocratic women led secluded lives, privately tutored, accomplished in literature and music, and possibly active in the management of the family's estates, but never seen in public without an escort. Marriages could only take place within the small circle of the well-born, and therefore typically were arranged by the parents. Even the experiences of exceptional and talented women show the strength of these conventions. Annette von Droste-Hülshoff could write in "Am Turme" (On the Tower) of a woman standing on an open tower in a storm, hair blown by the wind, crying out for freedom and power, but these are denied her by her place as a woman, and the poem concludes with her wish to be a man rather than the polite, well-mannered child that others treat her as. Otto von Bismarck's mother was widely held to have exercised far too much influence in dictating changes in the family residence and her children's education.

Agricultural families in east and west

In the east, the emancipation of 1807 and subsequent legislation had left some 70 per cent of the population without access to any land that was theirs by right. Gender relations reflected the landlords' desire for as large and flexible a labor force as possible. Previously, serfs had required their lord's permission to marry and to inherit their family holding. Although landlords in the nineteenth century no longer held this power legally, in fact they controlled their workers' ability to marry because, in most districts, laboring families could only support themselves if they had the additional income from one of the small plots provided by the landlord. The men worked most of their days on the landlord's land. Women worked on the small family plot, and in addition they were mobilized in gangs to work on the landlord's land during the peak planting and harvest seasons. Further, because local markets in the east were relatively undeveloped, in addition to work on their family holding and on the landlord's land, women had to produce most domestic items for their families, making cheese, baking bread, sewing clothing.

In the west and south, the small farmers' effective ownership of their land and their integration into market networks was accompanied by a standard sex division of labor. Men worked in the family's fields, look-ing after a range of crops, which might be grains, fruit, tobacco, or wine grapes, and managing the horses, sheep, or dairy cattle. Women worked in and around the house. They tended the vegetable garden and man-aged the chickens and pigs. In dairy districts women milked the cattle and transformed the milk into butter and cheese. Markets in the towns provided the outlet for both men's and women's produce. Peasant men and women each exchanged their products for domestic items such as clothing, but also for processed foods such as bread, which peasants were not permitted to make because of the monopoly enjoyed by the bakers' guild in the town.

The affluent peasant family was often "cyclical."[20] The father and mother worked until the father decided to retire. The eldest son then took over the farm, and possibly married at the same time. The retired parents remained in the household, though often in a separate dwelling. In more purely agricultural districts there were apt to be unmarried siblings and male and female laborers present in the household as well. Where alternative sources of income were available, household patterns could be more complex still. Jürgen Schlumbohm's study of a community in Osnabrück reveals a steadily rising population, a small number of families dominating landholdings passed from father to eldest son, and increasing numbers of landless laborers. Many of these took up weaving to supplement their earnings. In this protoindustrial area almost every person in the parish married. In hard times, however, poor families grouped together to save on rent, heating, and childcare. These two distinct household patterns, one large and multiple and the other small and nuclear, interacted with and supported one another.[21]

In agricultural and protoindustrial communities men remained in control. It was the men who could choose to marry. Heads of agricultural families were presumed to be male. In protoindustrial districts men were defined as possessing the skills which potential employers valued. Women's skills were perceived as subordinate to and of lesser value than men's skills. For example, "weavers" were presumed to be men, and their wives and children were assumed to be ancillary workers, preparing raw materials and assisting in the production process.

Further, men were mobile. Husbands of protoindustrial families left their homes in search of seasonal work in agriculture, an ebb and flow of labor that became more widespread and regular as the century progressed. In addition, when times were hard, men left their districts in search of any work they could find. Women were left holding the baby. First, there was the risk of pregnancy before marriage. It was common for marriages to be contracted after the woman became pregnant. In the towns family pressure ensured that the marriage would take place. However, not to be married meant that a pregnant girl would be ostracized, and abandonment was much more likely in the poor rural areas, where there was no family holding.

After marriage, the protoindustrial woman worked in artisan manufacture with her husband. In addition, she often worked the small farm alone. In contrast to the larger purely agricultural peasant households, she often had responsibility for most or all of the agricultural work in the protoindustrial family, both "barnyard" and "field" work (though there was probably no separate barn, and the field would be small). She was left behind when her husband left in search of work, whether on a regular seasonal basis or out of desperation. At these times she bore a triple burden of household and children, the artisan manufacture, and the farm.

Urban communities

The urban communities exercised the strictest control over their members. Guild members had to be full citizens of the town. The position of master in a guild was passed from father to son. Only "honorable" persons could be accepted, which typically meant that all four grandparents had to be proven to be of legitimate birth. Boys served an apprenticeship in their home community, spent time as journeymen (the "wandering years") working in positions arranged with friendly guilds in other towns, and then returned to their home community to apply for mastership. The guild granted the new master permission to build a house, to open his shop, and to marry, and took care to ensure that his wife was "honorable" as well. Citizenship, employment, property ownership, and the family were tied intimately together, and the guilds defended their position vigorously against any interference.

In most urban communities the families enjoying full citizenship rights ranged from 20 to as high as 80 per cent of the total population, with an average of 35–40 per cent. In the larger towns, a small group of families constituted a recognized elite, which ruled in cooperation with representatives of the guild trades. In the remaining three Hanse cities of Hamburg, Bremen, and Lübeck, and in Frankfurt, these formal constitutional structures remained. In cities and towns absorbed by enlarged territorial states, the newly appointed representatives of the central government attempted to undermine the inherited positions of the elite families and guilds. The government's monopolies of taxation and administration in theory eliminated the role of the elite families, and the principle of freedom of occupation in theory allowed even "dishonorable" persons to practice trades. In fact, however, in most of the home towns, elite families remained prominent and influential, and persons who did not enjoy the support of their fellow tradesmen found it extremely difficult to practice their craft.

The gender order reflected these structures. Within urban guild families, provided that she were honorable and married, a woman was typically much better off than a woman in the countryside. The general standard of living was higher in the towns than among the peasantry. A better diet, especially for women, increased their resistance to disease and infection. Medical care was also likely to be better because midwives practicing in towns were more likely to be full time and therefore more experienced. From the early decades of the century, the upper classes in the towns began to use doctors regularly.

Nevertheless, though they were valued as wives, women were not recognized as guild members as they had been in the sixteenth century. Guilds that had previously had female members rewrote their statutes in the late seventeenth and early eighteenth centuries, first to restrict and then finally to exclude women from membership. Martha Howell argues that this decline in the status of urban women was connected with the rise of long-distance trade. Women could not travel or associate freely with strangers, and therefore, as export industries developed, women were confined to crafts and trades which remained "local," or alternatively they were restricted to producing goods which were then traded by others, either the male members of their guild or the male members of a merchants' guild.[22]

By the late eighteenth century, this strictly gendered mode of production had become traditional. Women in the urban communities were confined to invisible roles in the guild trades. Preparation, production, finishing, sales, bookkeeping, management—all, if performed by a woman, were perceived as taking place under the direction of her husband. Though her labor might be crucial, it was unrecognized. Any products she made and sold on her own account would by definition have to be items not produced by one of the guilds, and therefore of little value. Indeed, the fact that she found it necessary to engage in such activity would reflect badly on herself and her husband. Previously, the guild household had been the central unit of production in the urban community. Now, however, as guild regulations came under attack from central governments, the household as such began to lose its formal connection to production, and came to be perceived as a unit of consumption. In consequence, women's work came to be seen as marginal, not essential to the maintenance of the household.

Culture

Following Heinrich Heine, later scholars often labeled the period from 1790 to 1830 the "age of Goethe." In fact, the death of Johann Wolfgang von Goethe in 1832 was itself a literary event of the first magnitude. Every author, in whatever genre, felt the loss and could not help but see themselves as reacting to Goethe in some way, as a model, yet at the same time inimitable, or as something to be overcome. However, artistic and cultural life were complex, and becoming more so. And Goethe himself was isolated, sometimes by fashion and sometimes by choice. He has even been interpreted more recently as an outsider to the age that bore his name.[23] In any event, he seems too protean a figure to give his name to a single age: from early Romantic with *The Sorrows of Young Werther* (1774), which remained the model of frustrated love and suicide through the nineteenth century, to a withdrawn classicism and hostility toward Romantic literature, to periods of intensive scientific study, to a complex and ironic celebration of the world of the urban communities in *Wilhelm Meisters Lehrjahre* (1795–96) and *Wilhelm Meisters Wanderjahre* (1821–29), and to *Faust*, a work which accompanied Goethe throughout his career, in the *Fragment* (1790), Part 1 (1808), and Part 2 (1829–31).

Goethe's Wilhelm Meister experiences his apprenticeship and his journeyman years as a series of allegories on the ways in which modern, commercial society, and its splintered, specialized social roles, undermines the natural wholeness of the world. The conflict is represented in the *Lehrjahre* by Mignon, an androgynous girl in trousers who embodies poetry, and in the *Wanderjahre* by a "secular piety" which might result in a global social mentality and a renunciation of goal-oriented labor. *Faust* moves from a domestic tragedy, the recurrent late eighteenth-century fantasy of the superior man seducing and abandoning a naïve young girl who then murders her child, to the redemptive second part in which Faust engages in all the creative impulses of modernity, is condemned for their destructive impact, but is then saved by a collection of higher spirits, including a transformed Gretchen, the girl he seduces in Part 1. The breadth of these works continues to astonish, and their resonances with the modern condition continue to the present. The experiments in form (the *Wanderjahre* is a connected series of novellas but includes journals, diaries, and letters as well) have provided inspiration for generations of writers, and employment for generations of critics and scholars.

But most readers did not study Goethe's works. Writing had become a profession, and it had become a very competitive one, one indeed which was unlikely to support an independent existence. Most of the writers recognized as serious authors had other means of support. Goethe came from a wealthy urban family, but he trained as a lawyer, worked as a bureaucratic administrator for over a decade, and enjoyed princely patronage. His overpowering eminence did not mean that he earned enough from his writing to support himself. Others were less fortunate, and therefore proportionately more dependent on the tastes of the reading public, and on the estimation of the publishers who risked their money attempting to appeal to public taste.

The reading public was expanding steadily, continuing a development that had begun in the late eighteenth century. Two and a half times as many books were published in Prussia in 1840 as in 1820. In the 1830s, Bavaria had 100 bookshops, and Prussia 300, with 60 concentrated in Berlin. Books remained an expensive luxury, and therefore they were shared through reading clubs and circulating libraries, whose clientele could extend into the countryside. Many of the new readers were women. Partly because of their expense, books from circulating libraries were the main source of reading for women, and for others who wished to read but whose income was limited. In addition, readers now typically read a book only once, in contrast to the religious devotional literature of previous generations, but also in contrast to the demand for repeated and attentive reading imposed by the complex structure of works such as *Wilhelm Meisters Wanderjahre*.

As a result, success for a writer came to depend on the conquest and subsequent defense of market share. An author first had to demonstrate originality, but having done so was likely to repeat the pattern of the first success, and very likely settle into a formula. Publishers sought originality, but at the same time they generally regarded experiments in theme or form as too risky. The results were a proliferation of novels and novellas intended to appeal to the popular audience who read for entertainment, particularly women, and a growing gap between this popular literature and serious writing.

Mimile. Eine Erzählung (*Mimile. A Tale*) was published in 1815 by Carl G. S. Heun under the name H. Clauren. Wilhelm, a Prussian officer and bearer of the Iron Cross, travels to Switzerland after the first War of Liberation seeking peace. In the gorgeous mountain scenery he meets the innocent Mimile (a diminutive of Wilhelmine, the feminine form of Wilhelm), and falls in love. A stern but kindly father insists that they wait a year before they marry, but then Napoleon escapes from Elba, and Wilhelm must return to war. Reports that he has been killed at Waterloo cause Mimile to sicken. The narrator, held in ignorance, at first believes them both to have died, but they survive, marry, and live happily ever after. Clauren appealed to the male audience with stirring battle scenes, and to the female audience with knowledgeable descriptions of Mimile's provincial fashions. In addition, the naïvely coquettish Mimile, with her heaving breasts and shapely thighs, is a constant temptation to the honorable Wilhelm, but he resists, and the text therefore also succeeds as both mildly pornographic and morally uplifting. *Mimile* sold 9000 copies in three years, and Clauren produced 25 further volumes reworking the same themes over the years until 1851. Many appeared in his own journal *Vergißmeinnicht* (*Forget-me-not*), named after the flower which Mimile gives Wilhelm the first time they part.[24]

Clauren was attacked in the 1820s as a typical example of the tendency to neglect not only serious literature but also serious politics, a reflection of the alleged resignation and timidity of Germans in the face of Metternich's reactionary system. The term Biedermeier which is often applied to the period dates from 1855, when two satiric poets began publishing *Gedichte des schwäbischen Schulmeisters Gottlieb Biedermaier und seines Freundes Horatius Treuherz* (*Poems by the Swabian Schoolmaster Amadeus Solidcitizen and His Friend Horace Trueheart*). These parodies, including a hymn to the potato, became associated with the alleged values of the previous decades. For the generation of aggressive and expansive realists examined in Chapter 4, the Biedermeier generation seemed lacking in imagination and quite possibly cowardly. They had retreated into a cosy, limited sphere of home and family, and had renounced danger and ambition in favor of the accepted and secure course of action.

In contrast, literary historians now argue that much of the writing of this period, precisely because of its idyllic depictions of both natural and created environments, has a defensive and fearful quality, and that the insistence on harmony in fact acts as a barrier for chaotic and demonic forces lying beneath the tranquil surface of society.[25] Further, as seen above, the citizens of the urban communities did not retreat into their local sphere, but rather saw themselves as defending that sphere against the aggressive intrusions of central governments. Economic and social structures were contested fields, and the contest was both political and deeply serious.

The political context: Romanticism in politics

To later German nationalists, it was self-evident that Germany should have been united. For historians at the end of the nineteenth century working in the idealist tradition, the contrast between cultural unity and political division appeared a weakness, something to be overcome. Friedrich Meinecke, writing in the first decade of the twentieth century, believed that nineteenth-century Germans had to abandon "cosmopolitanism" in order to realize the ideal of the national state.[26] From the perspective of the generations following the Second World War, both Conservative historians and those leaning more to the left, looking at the origins and development of German nationalism, have also seen the multiplicity of German states as an anomaly, another possible beginning of Germany's "special path." The later story of German unification is often seen as prefigured in the inconsistencies and weaknesses of the German Confederation.[27]

However, contemporaries could not look forward, either to the triumphant unification of the German states by Bismarck, or to the subsequent disasters of the twentieth century. Rather, they looked backward, to the upheavals of the French Revolution and Napoleonic hegemony. The chaotic and demonic forces that political leaders believed lay below the surface were the threat of a resurgent France and the equally frightening possibility of domestic revolution. They therefore attempted to build structures that would contain these forces. These structures derived from earlier models of politics and diplomacy, but they also had to allow for the changes that had occurred.

Political patterns

Looking at the political realm through contemporary eyes, we need to remember that politics was personal. With the exception of the independent cities, these were monarchical states, and the advisor who had the ruler's ear was the one who would influence policy. Thus any statesman had to pursue "geopolitical" policies, based on the objective situation of his state as he saw it, but at the same time he was forced to play the game of "high politics," the competition with rival officials for the ruler's favor.[28] Some Prussian officials might be impatient with their king's hesitancy and deference toward Austria, and Austria's leading minister Clemens von Metternich might despise his emperor, but they nevertheless needed simultaneously to balance their conception of their state's situation with the need to guess the ruler's disposition, while preventing others from gaining influence.

"In the beginning was Napoleon," in Thomas Nipperdey's phrase. The rulers who had suffered under Napoleon lived on through the 1820s and 1830s. Memories of the Prussian disaster at Jena and the Austrian disaster at Wagram haunted King Frederick William III of Prussia and Emperor Francis I of Austria. But not all rulers had suffered under Napoleon, and those who had profited also had to be accommodated. The great powers were constrained by the desires of small and medium states. International power did not depend simply on territorial size or industrial development. Rather, states were judged much more precisely by their populations. "Souls" were counted as potential taxpayers and, more importantly, as potential soldiers. In that world, there were more powerful and less powerful states, but all states represented some degree of power.[29]

Therefore when the victors met in Vienna in 1814 to establish a system that would ensure stability, the lesser powers did influence the outcome. Austria encouraged Prussia to take possession of much of the area along the Rhine that the French had annexed during the wars, as well as the Duchy of Berg and the Kingdom of Westphalia. Metternich intended to commit Prussia to preventing the resurgence of France. However, at the same time the medium and small states that had joined the final coalition against Napoleon had their gains confirmed. Only a few of the smallest states such as Saxe-Weimar and Brunswick were genuine restorations (Hesse-Homburg was also restored in 1817). The others, especially Baden, Württemberg, Bavaria, and Hesse, absorbed large tracts of formerly ecclesiastical lands as well as many of their smaller secular neighbors.[30]

For the historians living in united Germany in the late nineteenth and early twentieth centuries, it was self-evident that the process of state-building in Prussia, the integration of the new western provinces into the existing Prussian state, was the most important story of the first half of the century, because this had led to the creation of the German national state. For contemporaries, however, the problems that confronted officials in all states were similar. Prussia was one among many states, and possibly not the most successful. Government officials struggled with shortages of trained personnel, the stubborn opposition of the recalcitrant leaders of formerly independent urban communities, the claims of

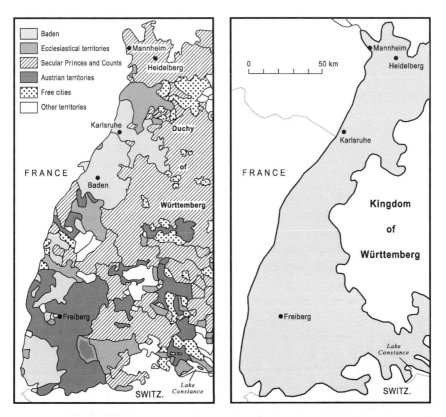

Map 2 State-building in the early nineteenth century: southern Baden and western Württemberg in 1789 and in 1815

displaced aristocrats, unrest in towns and countryside when food prices rose, and demands for a host of expensive improvements in public health, transportation, education, and poor relief. Above all, they attempted to impose uniformity, to extract taxes, and to maintain order across their very diverse possessions.[31]

The German Confederation that emerged reflected the monarchical, personal essence of politics and the determination of each state to exercise its power to the fullest extent. Predictably it took the form of an alliance to defend the independence of the member states. The Federal Diet (*Bundestag*) that met at Frankfurt was a congress of ambassadors, and met in plenary session only sixteen times in its history. Constitutional amendments required unanimous agreement, and a declaration of war required a two-thirds majority. Ongoing business was conducted by a Select Committee (*Engerer Rat*), in which each of the eleven largest states had one vote while the remainder were grouped to share six votes. Having only one vote each, Austria and Prussia were forced to court the medium states to secure passage of measures they favored. When a federal army was established in 1821, the member states retained the right of command over their contingents. Bavaria and Württemberg blocked the establishment of a federal court. No member state wanted the Confederation to have the power to levy taxes, and as seen above the negotiations for the customs union took place directly between Prussia and other states.

The importance of personality and the desire for stability are both evident in the so-called Carlsbad Decrees and subsequent federal legislation. The murder in 1819 of the popular playwright August von Kotzebue by a radical student named Karl Sand gave Metternich an opportunity both to strengthen Austria's position and to repress potential dissent. Meeting with Frederick Wilhelm, Metternich persuaded him that collective measures were necessary. A subsequent meeting with other rulers at Carlsbad resulted in a list of measures that then passed the Confederation Diet unanimously. Universities were subjected to close supervision, censorship was tightened and coordinated, and an office was established to investigate the "revolutionary agitation discovered in several states." Further laws empowered the Confederation to intervene in a member state to preserve public order, especially if the local government had been "rendered unable to seek help," and forbade any member state from introducing a constitution that might "limit or hinder them in the fulfillment of their duties to the Confederation." Metternich appealed to the fears of the rulers that a deep conspiracy threatened their position, but he also undermined the remaining officials in Prussia who favored further reforms to local government and the army, reforms which they intended to strengthen Prussia and which would therefore have run counter to Austria's interests.

The "Metternich system" remained in place until 1848. However, the man who gave the name "restoration" to the period was Carl Ludwig von Haller. From Bern, and like Goethe a member of the urban elite, he published a six-volume work over the years from 1816 to 1822, entitled *Die Restauration der Staatswissenschaften* (*The Restoration of the Sciences of State*), a work he hoped would provide a foundation for a view of the world that would combat and defeat the social contract theory of government, which he believed lay at the bottom of the revolutionary movement.

Instead of human desires and human reason, Haller saw the origins of the natural order in God. Further, rather than all men being equal, Haller argued that the social order which derives from God is fundamentally unequal. This, he said, is an empirical fact, easily observable by all. It was equally obvious to Haller that age-old customs and habits of obedience, reverence, and piety held society together. The weak depended on the strong, children depended on their fathers, and, more generally, subjects depended on their prince. The state therefore was a kind of extended family, and the ruler's God-given authority could not be limited by contract or constitution: "One God, one king, one father." Finally, the aspect of his thought that both ensured his popularity and placed him firmly in the Romantic era was his insistence that small independent states best exemplified this natural order.

The rulers who read Haller probably did not study Georg Welhelm Friedrich Hegel's *Phänomenologie des Geistes* (either *Phenomenology of the Spirit* or *Phenomenology of Mind*). Completed in 1806 just before the Battle of Jena, it remains one of the most discussed classics of Western philosophy. Hegel's vision of absolute spirit unfolding itself in the world led him to examine all aspects of spirit, including the sources of knowledge and reason, the relation between private emotion and the public realm, the organization of the family, community, and state, the origins and content of religious faith, and the forms of artistic expression. Philosophers and social scientists have drawn inspiration from various aspects of this imposing project. The exact way in which spirit overcomes itself and moves to new levels of self-awareness remained contentious (the famous triad of thesis, antithesis, and synthesis was a later simplification), but one of Hegel's lasting legacies was his emphasis on the importance of human history and human agency in realizing the progress of spirit in the world. At particular points in history, spirit might be embodied in individuals, groups, or states. Seeing Napoleon at Jena, Hegel reportedly said he had just seen the world spirit on horseback.

The work of Hegel's that rulers and their servants did read was *Natural Law and the Science of State in Outline. Elements of the Philosophy of Right*, published in 1821. The son of a minor government official, Hegel became a university professor. His appointment at Jena was cut off by the war, but he moved to Heidelberg in 1816 and to Berlin in 1818, where he remained until his death in a cholera epidemic in 1831. The *Philosophy of Right* was "a textbook for the lectures which I deliver in the course of my professional duties." Hegel moves systematically from general principles of right, including property and morality, to the "ethical life" of family, civil society, and corporation, to the state, including Crown, executive, and the legislature which represents the corporate organizations of civil society, and culminates with international law and world history. What he taught his students, most of whom were destined to become state officials, was that their role was central, that they were the "universal class," "the class in which the consciousness of right and the developed intelligence of the mass of the people is found."[32] Mediating between the Crown and the corporations of civil society, they embodied the rational constitution of the state. Only within such a state could the individual be truly free. As such, therefore, the state and its officials represented the highest development of spirit.

Popular protest

Charged by Hegel with the "oversight and care" of society, government officials were particularly perturbed by popular protest, which seemed to threaten the carefully balanced order which they aimed to preserve. We need to remember that not all popular protest was popular. Later nationalist historians interpreted certain privileged examples of protest as precursors or exemplifications of the awakening of the German "national spirit." Three such moments were the uprising against Napoleon in 1813, the gathering of university students at the Wartburg in 1817, and the "national festival" held at Hambach in 1832. However, the campaign against Napoleon had been a war of monarchical rulers, not a popular uprising. There was no popular resistance to the French, as there was in Spain, and volunteer regiments played only a minor role in the final military campaigns. The students at the Wartburg numbered 468. Between twenty and thirty thousand persons came together at Hambach, but again of a list of 187 residents of the Palatinate who attended, 57 were students, another 29 academically trained professionals, and only 11 were farmers or farm workers.

The students at the Wartburg were meeting at the place where Luther had translated the Bible into German while taking refuge during the Reformation three centuries earlier, and on the anniversary of the

"Battle of the Peoples" (*Völkerschlacht*), the allied victory over Napoleon at Leipzig in 1813. They belonged to the *Burschenschaften*, university organizations that had emerged as part of the backlash against Napoleon, and the mode was typically Romantic. Symbols of reaction, including the writings of authors deemed insufficiently patriotic and a corporal's cane, were thrown into a massive bonfire. However, so was a copy of the Napoleonic Code. They yearned, but they were not really sure what for. They opposed the conservative reaction, and they opposed French domination. They sought reform and purification, but they also rejected universalistic Enlightenment values and celebrated inherited "historical" traditions seen as typical of the German *Volk* (the red, black, and gold colors they believed to be from the distant German past in fact were those of one of the volunteer regiments). For some this became a celebration of German "blood," an explicit religious and ethnic chauvinism directed against Catholics and Jews.[33]

The aims of those at Hambach were similarly diffuse. A wave of disorders had followed the French revolution of 1830, and new constitutional regimes had emerged in Hesse-Kassel, Hanover, and Saxony. Two years later, however, the participants still agreed on little beyond the red, black, and gold colors of their flags, and demands for "unity and freedom," "necessary" reform, and a broad education of "public opinion." Karl Heinrich Brüggemann, a university student and member of the underground *Burschenschaften*, threatened an uprising against governments that violated their citizen's rights, but he also conceded that the time had not yet come for confrontation. The only concrete outcome of the meeting was to rename the recently formed *Pressverein* (Newspaper Association) to *Reformverein* (Reform Association). James Sheehan concludes, "the men at Hambach wanted to found newspapers not build barricades."[34]

For rulers and officials, however, such agitation seemed threatening. Karl August, the Duke of Saxe-Weimar who had permitted the Wartburg meeting, was severely criticized. Sand belonged to one of the most radical *Burschenschaften*, and his murder of Kotzebue provided the pretext that Metternich needed to suppress the organizations. Similarly, after the Hambach meeting, Metternich pressured the Diet to pass a series of laws that reinforced the existing restrictions on political activity and tightened the censorship. Austria, Prussia, and Russia signed an agreement to oppose revolutionary change, and threatened any reformist government with outside intervention. The governments of Hesse and

Saxony severely restricted the powers of their new assemblies. The King of Bavaria placed the Palatinate under martial law, and the King of Württemberg forbade any mention of Landtag elections in the press. Hambach participants were harassed and occasionally imprisoned.

There were other sorts of protest, more genuinely popular, but not always recognized as political, by either contemporaries or subsequent historians. Increasing but fluctuating levels of collective violence marked the early decades of the century. These outbursts were only weakly correlated with food prices, and even in years where both prices and violence increased, violence did not concentrate in the areas where prices were highest. Rather, rising food prices appear to have led to increases in individual criminality. Arrests for petty theft were closely correlated with the price of rye and jumped sharply when prices rose, whereas more "political" individual offences such as "insubordination" or "defamation" actually rose in years when food prices declined.[35]

There were upsurges of collective violence in periods of general Europe-wide political unrest and revolution, in 1819–20 and 1830–31. However, the typical protest scenario was a large group in a city, town, or hamlet confronting those who they saw as violating traditional obligations of mutuality. The growth of a large sector of landless and land-poor householders who claimed access to communal privileges in traditional farming communities transformed the community itself into a contested political space. Competition for increasingly scarce resources turned members of the community against each other.[36] In the towns, the objects of collective hostility were grain dealers or bakers who were removing foodstuffs for sale elsewhere, or raising the prices they charged members of the local community. There was also mass trespassing and machine-breaking, again directed at those seen to be violating traditional norms. These actions, says Richard Tilly, were "directed above all against the pressures of commercialization in a rapidly changing, but only slowly growing, economy."[37]

Local officials of course regarded collective protest with horror, but there was little they could do to forestall popular activity, because the limited budgets of all states meant that there were very few police available even in large cities, and none at all in most small towns. Officials confronted by unruly crowds were forced to call for military intervention by regional garrisons, and since army commanders treated these as military operations, the usual result was to worsen the violence. In April 1821, the *Landrat* in Eupen, in the Rhineland close to the Belgian border, reported that a crowd of several hundred local workers had destroyed a quantity of wool-shearing machinery. He requested military support from Aachen "since no armed police are stationed here." The next day he repeated his request in stronger terms. But another day later he changed direction and pleaded that the troops not be sent. He was worried that, because the troops would be quartered and provisioned locally, they were likely to incite the citizens of Eupen.[38]

Notes

1. Carl Blechen, *Bau der Teufelsbrücke*, *c.* 1830. Oil on linen, 77.6 × 104.5 cm. Neue Pinakothek, Munich. Catalog of displayed works, 1982. See Emmrich 1989.
2. Eduard Mörike, "Im Frühling" (In the Springtime).
3. Caspar David Friedrich, *The Wayfarer above the Sea of Fog*, *c.* 1818. Oil on canvas, 94.8 × 74.8 cm. Kunsthalle, Hamburg. View at Mark Harden's texas.net Museum of Art, <lonestar.texas.net/~mharden/artchive/ftptoc/friedrich_ext. html>. Also TCM's Caspar David Friedrich Gallery, <www.geocities.com/ Area51/2229/Friedrich.html>.
4. Saul 1997, p. 203.
5. Henderson 1963; Walker 1971; Mendels 1972.
6. See Wallerstein 1974.
7. Sabean 1990, p. 50.
8. Kriedte *et al*. 1977.
9. See Ogilvie 1996.
10. See Quataert 1995.
11. Walker 1971.
12. Dorwart 1971; Raeff 1983.
13. Hull 1996, p. 95.
14. Raeff 1983, pp. 84–5; Hull 1996, p. 408; Lindenfeld 1997.
15. See Brose 1993.
16. See Henderson 1959.
17. Borchardt 1973; 1991.
18. Ringer 1979; McClelland 1980.
19. Gollwitzer 1957.
20. Berkner 1972.
21. Schlumbohm 1994.
22. Howell 1988.
23. Boyle 1991.
24. Saul 1997, p. 265.
25. Finney 1997, pp. 292–3.
26. Meinecke 1907.
27. Nipperdey 1993a; Wehler 1995.
28. Simms 1997.
29. Hundt 1996.

30. Krahe 1963; 1983.
31. Green 2001.
32. Paragraph 297.
33. Heither *et al.* 1997.
34. Sheehan 1989, p. 612.
35. Blasius 1976, p. 35.
36. Friedburg 1997.
37. Tilly 1975, pp. 191–2.
38. Tilly 1975, p. 219.

CHAPTER 3

A REVOLUTIONARY
GENERATION: THE 1840s AND
THE REVOLUTIONS OF 1848

Two paintings by Philipp Veit frame the revolutionary generation. Both portray Germania, the allegorical female personification of Germany. In 1836, Veit portrayed her in the setting sun, seated under a great oak, the sacred tree of the German tribes and, since the late eighteenth century, a symbol of German freedom and unity. She wears a regal robe, and she has the Golden Bull in her lap and a shield emblazoned with the imperial eagle in her right hand, but the sword of the empire is sheathed, and she gazes in contemplation at the imperial crown, which lies on the ground. On the base of the empty throne behind her are inscribed the arms of the seven electors to whom the Golden Bull gave the right to choose the Emperor of the Holy Roman Empire of the German Nation, which had been dissolved in 1806. The Germania Veit painted in 1848 stands erect in the morning sun, gazing now straight ahead, her sword unsheathed, and raising a banner with the national colors black, red, and gold. There is no crown, no imperial eagle, and no reference to the electoral princes, but a pair of open handcuffs lies on the ground.[1]

In 1843, Heinrich Heine wrote that he could not sleep, "thinking of Germany in the night."[2] At some point, around 1840 the malaise, uncertainty, and foreboding of the Romantic era transmuted into a sense of crisis, and the indefinite yearning crystallized into definite political demands. There seemed an acute threat to the economy in a series of depressions and harvest failures. There seemed an acute threat to social order in uncontrolled population growth, "pauperism," and the "proletariat." There seemed an acute threat to political order in the continued fragmentation of Germany into small states (*Kleinstaaterei*) and in the danger of foreign domination. The target of informed debate was almost always the inadequacies of government policy, and the discussion increasingly turned toward changing the structure of "Germany" so that a new "German" government could address the new range of problems that appeared to be emerging.

Debate revolved around the question of power—but this now meant economic power, which in turn meant industrial power. Therefore debate turned, whether explicitly or implicitly, on the question of how industrial power could be increased. Most looked to the state. Even those who opposed the existing political order, such as Friedrich List and David Hansemann, hoped for action from a central government that would foster modern industrial development. But these proposals raised the issue of the governance of Germany, and any action by a "German" government would cut across the existing cleavages of German society and threaten existing interests.

There was a transformation evident in the decade of the 1840s which affected all Germans, and out of which we can see a new kind of economy emerging. Industrial technologies were revolutionizing the ways in which things could be made, and the railroad was revolutionizing the ways in which people and things could be moved. The intersection of the railway with the new industrial technologies provided opportunities for some individuals and groups, but it also threatened the interests of others. Many suffered acutely. As a result, economic problems, and what could or should be done about them, became social and political problems as well.

The combination of economic, social, and political crises detonated in the explosion of 1848. For a moment Germany was united under a new progressive leadership, and then again it was not, and the old forces returned. As seen in Chapter 4, however, they were not the same, and therefore the 1848 revolutions continue to be a focus of historical debates. Among contemporaries, Karl Marx identified 1848 as the point where the capitalist class turned its back on the working class. After the Second World War, A. J. P. Taylor called it "a turning point where German history failed to turn." For Hans-Ulrich Wehler it is one of several points where Germany did turn, heading off on its "special path" different from the one taken by Western European nations.[3]

The economic context

Population growth

Contemporaries believed their economy to be in a state of crisis. Excessive population growth seemed to be leading to widespread "pauperism," and the growth of a "proletariat," rootless people with no fixed place in the social order. They did not have systematic or comparative figures, but their impressions were correct. We now know that increasing population was one of the background factors to economic, social, and political development throughout Europe. The statistics are poor for the period before 1800, and in the German states they improved only slightly before 1860, but the available estimates show the beginnings of a sustained increase some time in the middle of the eighteenth century. Within the borders of the later Bismarckian empire, population rose from 16 to 18 million in 1750, to some 24 million in 1800. From 26 million in 1820 it rose to 29 million in 1830, 32 million in 1840, and 35 million in 1850. The German states were not unique. Populations rose throughout Europe and in East Asia as well. That is, there is no simple explanation. Rather, a range of factors affecting both death rates and birth rates can be cited as contributing to the increase.

Birth rates did not rise, but they remained high, an average of 39 per 1000 through the 1820s, and then fluctuating around an average of 37 per 1000 until the mid-1890s. As seen in Chapter 2, protoindustrialization had given many young couples the opportunity to marry and found a family. In addition, and possibly more importantly, the end to marriage restrictions on the rural population in purely agricultural areas had also increased the marriage rate. Formerly, peasants required their lord's permission or had to wait to inherit a farm, but increasingly they now worked as wage laborers on large estates in the east or commercial farms in the south and west. By the 1840s, this landless "underclass" made up half the population in most areas, and in some it reached 80 per cent.

Improved agricultural techniques increased the supply of food. More persons could be supported at the same level, and any improvement in average diet made the entire population more resistant to disease. Again, the statistics are poor and incomplete, but average output per farm worker appears to have risen steadily. By 1850, each farm worker was producing perhaps 65 per cent more than she or he would have produced in 1800.[4] In contrast to what contemporaries might have guessed, the rate of improvement did not slow in the late 1830s and 1840s. The introduction of crop rotation systems described in Chapter 2 was complete, but a continual stream of improvements in crop and seed selection, planting, harvesting, and aspects of animal husbandry was available to farmers keen to raise output. Several hundred agricultural improvement societies provided opportunities for discussion, and, from 1837 onward, representatives of local societies met annually. Thousands of books and articles described experimental results and prescribed methods of improvement.

These efforts were directed toward marketable crops. The new methods usually required capital investment, and therefore the improvements were seen primarily on large estates and substantial farms. The benefits in terms of improved diet and increased income were enjoyed by the affluent. Small farmers and landless laborers did not profit. Rather, rising numbers of rural workers became dependent on the potato. Easily grown and widely known as it became a common component of rotation systems, the potato could make a substantial contribution to the diet of families with access to only a small garden plot. The output of potatoes may have risen five times from 1816 to 1840. Conversely, the failure of the potato crop in 1846 caused widespread distress for the poor who relied on this extra source of calories.

The incidence of infectious disease may also have declined. For over a century, observational and experimental science had been influencing medical theory, particularly in establishing correlations of outbreaks of disease with environmental factors. These writers frequently concluded that filth which created strong odors led to "bad air" and caused disease. The "miasma" theory was wrong but plausible in the era before the microscope. However, all of their preferred measures to reduce odors had the unintended effect of reducing insect populations, and it was flies, mosquitoes, lice, and cockroaches that were the vectors for the pathogens causing disease.[5]

To eliminate the suspect strong odors, medical experts recommended draining swamps, cleaning wells, circulating water in cisterns, moving refuse away from houses and burying it, ventilating houses, and cleaning the air in houses in cases of disease, for instance with sulphur fumigation. New and stronger central governments took up these ideas and pursued them actively. Swamp drainage fitted with broader economic plans, and cleaning wells and cisterns and ordering subjects to bury garbage and clean their houses fitted with generally interventionist tendencies. By the early nineteenth century, states had also become adept at quarantining areas of infectious disease. In addition, the notion that strong odors were to be avoided was adopted by the affluent as part of the definition of their private sphere. Homes and the body were to be kept clean, in contrast to the eighteenth century, when the wealthy typically masked unpleasant odors with perfumes.

On the other hand, disease did not disappear. The threats of influenza, cholera, and typhus continued, for instance the cholera outbreak in which Hegel died in 1831, and the typhus epidemics of the 1840s. Infant mortality, the deaths of children who were born alive but died before their first birthday, remained high, just under 300 per 1000 from the late eighteenth century until the 1880s. Therefore the impact of these improvements in public and private hygiene must have been small, though it may have been cumulative.

Trends and cycles: the railroad and early industrialization

The decade of the 1840s appears in Germany as a kind of hinge connecting the old world of agricultural fluctuations and crises with the new world of industrial cycles. As outlined in Chapter 1, in this new world the overall condition of the economy at any point depended on the interaction of three sorts of cycle: the three- to five-year cycle in trade and retail inventories, the seven- to eleven-year cycle in investment in transportation and heavy industry, and the fifty-year "long" cycles reflecting the introduction of major clusters of technological innovations. The railroad was obviously the new major innovation, and it was the obvious means to fulfill the economic potential of the Zollverein. For instance, although the water-borne traffic on the Rhine doubled from 1836 to 1840, there was no increase in the number of freight wagons traveling the road between Nürnberg and Leipzig. The Zollverein would not be an economic unit, any more than the traditional German economies had been, until it was tied together by a modern transportation system.

Contemporaries saw the importance of railroads, but railroads were expensive. The line from Dresden to Leipzig, for instance, required iron for its rails alone equal to four years' output of the entire Saxon iron industry. In addition, much of the rails, rolling stock, and related machinery was being imported from Belgium and Britain. If the German states were to supply their own, then new mines and factories of unprecedented scale would be required. How could this be done? In the 1830s and 1840s, commercial and industrial leaders complained of a "capital shortage," and they said it was especially difficult to obtain finance for new transportation and industrial projects. However, their difficulties did not reflect German poverty or a lack of savings. Rather, the would-be entrepreneurs emerging from the urban communities of western and southern Germany were hampered by the structure of the banking system. Many banks were still small family firms or partnerships whose financial activities had grown as a sideline to their commercial interests. In addition, for individual investors government bonds and quasi-government securities, such as the bonds issued by the Landschaften in eastern Prussia, offered safe returns. Bankers reinforced this conservative prejudice. The Rothschild bank, for instance, consisted of five family firms in Frankfurt, London, Paris, Vienna, and Milan, headed by the sons of the founder. They had grown rich by underwriting loans raised by the Prussian government early in the century, and government business remained their preference. Their resources, though large, were still limited by their personal fortunes, and they were notoriously reluctant to finance large and possibly risky industrial projects.

Contemporaries also saw a connection between economic development and public policy. Would-be railroad promoters and industrialists demanded support from the government. A native of Württemberg, Friedrich List envisaged the radiating spokes of a national railroad system emanating from Berlin and called for a system of protective tariffs to shelter infant German industries from British competition in his *National System of Political Economy*, which caused a sensation when it appeared in 1841. The immense expense of railroads led private entrepreneurs such as Rhinelander David Hansemann to call for government construction. His pamphlet published in 1837 ended each paragraph with the capitalized conclusion, "THEREFORE THE STATE SHOULD BUILD THE RAILROADS."

However, the Prussian government at first opposed railroads. Government officials said it was impossible to contemplate railroad construction from current tax revenues. They worried about potential sources of political opposition. Legally, any loan raised by the government would require the approval of a representative assembly, under the terms of a promise made in 1815. The army was not yet certain that the railroad would be an asset in wartime. And, finally, there was some outright opposition. Successive finance ministers opposed railroads because of the expense and the threat to the government's budget. Christian Rother feared that competition from railroads would reduce revenues from the Seehandlung turnpikes.[6]

Even more important, perhaps, the Prussian government seemed generally hostile to uncontrolled industrial development. When the first concessions for private railroads were hesitantly granted, they were hedged about with restrictions. At first, the telegraph was forbidden because of the danger of subversive groups sending political messages over the wires. Freight rates were strictly controlled, to prevent traffic being diverted from the government's own carrier service. Officials also placed severe restrictions on the introduction of new technologies in mining and smelting, delaying the first deep-mining shaft north of the Ruhr for a decade, and forbidding the smelting of the blackband combination of coal and iron ore for many years. Bureaucrats regarded private banks with particular suspicion. The Darmstädter Bank (1846), as its name implied, was founded outside Prussian territory to evade the government's restrictions.

A very restrictive monetary policy further reduced the funds available. Business leaders complained that the government's refusal to increase the supply of banknotes restricted credit and hampered their activities.[7] They also complained that the government's suspicion of limited liability corporations hampered development, and in particular that the railroads and new larger mines and blast-furnaces in the Ruhr were too large for individual investors and too risky for partnerships with unlimited liability. If the government would not build the railroads, then the huge expense made it imperative that limited liability corporations undertake the task, in order to mobilize the necessary capital with minimum risk to individual investors. This was also true of the new industries needed to supply the railroads. Limited liability corporations spread the risk of investment among large numbers of individuals, and this makes large-scale investments in new technologies easier, but only 67 such corporations gained approval in Prussia between 1826 and 1850. Contemporaries noted that, in states where government policy was more supportive, capital seemed in less short supply and industry developed rapidly, for instance in the Kingdom of Saxony.[8]

Nevertheless, the system began to take shape, linking the key areas of production and consumption with their suppliers and markets. In Saxony, Leipzig and Dresden were connected in 1839, Leipzig and Magdeburg in 1840, and Dresden with Silesia (coal), Prague (and markets in

Austria), Bavaria, and Thuringia in the 1840s. The Rhenish commercial and industrial centers tied themselves together: Frankfurt with Mainz and Mannheim with Heidelberg in 1840, Düsseldorf with Elberfeld and Cologne with Aachen in 1841. List's vision proved accurate as Berlin's radial network began to form: connections with Anhalt in 1841 and Stettin (grain) in 1843 were followed by links with Breslau (coal), Magdeburg (foodstuffs, and onward connection to Leipzig), and Hamburg (the largest port), all opened in 1846.

Investment in railroads, and the induced investment in heavy industry, led to two cyclical crises in 1842 and 1847. These have the marks of investment cycles—an inflationary upswing, a sudden reduction in investment, and a crisis and contraction. However, the Prussian government precipitated the crisis of 1842 by suddenly declaring that railroad bonds would no longer be acceptable as security in transactions by trustees. In the background was the competition of the new railroads with agriculture for capital. Sales of Landschaften bonds had stagnated since the approval of the first railroads in the mid-1830s, and the government hoped to redress the balance. The ensuing depression, however, fed into the growing crisis among the rural population.

Rapid population growth and generally poor harvests had increased prices for food, reducing markets for manufactured products and leading to depression in consumer goods industries. For the landless and peasant and protoindustrial families in the east, particularly in Silesia, this was a classic subsistence crisis. But now, in addition, the pressure of competition from the new factories pressed on certain artisan manufacturers. Then, a disastrous potato blight and failure of the potato crop in 1846 combined with very poor grain harvests. The results were not as severe as in Ireland, but food prices did treble and quadruple in some districts. Harvests improved and food prices declined in 1847, but then the downturn in railroad investment threw tens of thousands of construction laborers out of work, and the effects spilled over into the rest of the industrial sector.

The social context

Culture: literature and politics

In December 1835, the Diet of the German Federation passed a resolution calling on its member states to "bring the penal and police statutes of their respective countries and the regulations regarding the abuse of the press in the strictest sense to bear against the authors, publishers, printers and disseminators of the writings of the literary school known as Young Germany." In fact, the authors targeted by the authorities and grouped together since—prose authors such as Karl Gutzkow and Georg Büchner, poets such as Georg Herwegh and Ferdinand Freilegrath, and the towering talents Ludwig Börne and Heinrich Heine—were extremely diverse in style, mode, and subject matter. Although often identified as outsiders, they did not come from a single social background, and, although denounced, banned by the censors, and pursued by the police, they did not share a common political program.[9]

What Young Germany and the succeeding "Pre-March" (*Vormärz*, that is, before the 1848 revolutions) authors shared was a concern with current events and their opposition to the existing system. Büchner's *Der hessische Landbote* (*The Hessian Courier*, 1834) denounced Germany's 34 tyrants, the princes whose wealthy idleness contrasted so starkly with the harsh impoverished lives of the peasantry, and called for "peace to the hut—war to the palaces." Gutzkow's novel *Wally, die Zweiflerin* (*Wally, the Sceptic*, 1835) portrays a young woman tormented by her dissatisfaction with her female role and her religious doubts. On the day of her wedding to a man she is to marry in accord with convention, she briefly reveals herself naked to the man she truly loves. Several characters commit suicide. Wally herself, stunned by reading a text which presents religion as no more than the response of human despair to the purposelessness of life, stabs herself in the heart. Herwegh's poem "Aufruf" ("Appeal") laments that the national colors represent only the black of death, the gold of the sunset, and the red of a bleeding heart, while Freilegrath's "Schwarz-Rot-Gold" associates them with gunpowder, blood, and the flame of battle.

Börne and Heine were both born into Jewish families, in Frankfurt and Düsseldorf respectively, and both lived much of their lives in exile. Börne is famous among literary historians for his denunciation of Goethe: "Heaven gave you a tongue of fire, but have you ever defended justice? You had a good sword, but you were always only your own guardian." His reply to those who attacked him as a Jew mixes his sense of estrangement and commitment to a future Germany:

Yes, because I was born without a fatherland my desire for a fatherland is more passionate than yours, and because my birthplace was not bigger than the *Judengasse* and everything behind the locked gates was a foreign country to me, therefore for me now the fatherland is more than the city, more than a territory, more than a province. For me only the very great fatherland, as far as its language extends, is enough.[10]

Heine, as well as a brilliant essayist, is one of Germany's greatest lyric poets, and his work continues to excite not only admiration but substantive debate. He met Marx in 1843 and he is frequently portrayed as becoming more radical through the 1840s. He was bitingly ironic in "Germany, A Winter's Fairy Tale," published in 1844, portraying Germans as sleeping and dreaming in their feather-beds, where their souls could "feel themselves free of their earthly chains," the reality of political repression. However, he never identified consistently with any political tendency. He denounced authors who sold out to the market or to the existing system, but he also remained unfailingly hostile to politically committed poets such as Herwegh. "The boldest, the most unbridled singers of liberty turn out to be, on closer inspection, nothing but narrow-minded philistines," he wrote in 1843. But he refused the offer of French citizenship, for "my marriage with my dear Frau Germania, the blond, bearskin savage, had never been happy, but it never came to an actual breach . . . I have not lost the birth of my German nature, not a single bell of my German cap."[11]

Culture had become politicized. The crisis of 1840 led to an outpouring of patriotic poetry, including Max Schneckenburger's "Watch on the Rhine" and August Heinrich Hoffmann von Fallersleben's "Song of the Germans," which, when set to Haydn's Emperor Hymn, became "Deutschland, Deutschland, Über Alles." Prose and poetry explored and publicized the plight of the poor. Bettine von Arnim wrote of the shocking conditions of the "poor colony" in Hamburg in *Dies Buch gehört dem König* (*This Book Belongs to the King*, 1843). Ernst Willkomm detailed the long hours, low pay, and poor health of children working in the polluted atmosphere of a textile factory in his novel *Weiße Sklaven* (*White Slaves*, 1845). In his poem "Arbeite" ("Work!"), Georg Weerth showed how the desperate need for income forced families in effect to exploit themselves. Heine's famous "The Silesian Weavers" weave "A curse for the God to whom we prayed . . . A curse for the king, the king of the rich . . . A curse for the false fatherland," and Louise Aston's "Lied einer schlesischen Weberin" ("Song of a Silesian Weaver") tells of a poor young woman who yields in despair to the sexual demands of her employer in order to save her sister and invalid mother.

The public sphere: Bürger, Bürgertum, Bildungsbürger, bürgerliche Gesellschaft

In the modern world, we regard ourselves unproblematically as citizens of national states, entitled as members of the national community to participate openly in its public life. Government is, or should be, our servant, and government policy is, or should be, formulated in response to public debate and discussion. In the early nineteenth century this was not so. Monarchical states did not recognize citizens, only subjects. Philosophers such as Hegel might see the state as a rational, abstract expression of spirit, but rulers often regarded the state simply as their property. State officials viewed themselves as the active "universal class" authorized and entitled to act in the best interests of all the other classes in society. There was no public sphere, no recognized right to public discussion and debate, and even the laws that governed and punished subjects were sometimes secret.

A contemporary cartoon portrays "The Thinkers' Club," a discussion group of intellectuals. Eight well-dressed men are seated around a long table, and they alternately gesticulate and ponder the topic of the evening: "For how much longer will thinking be permitted?" Speech is already forbidden, and to ensure their compliance, each of the men wears an elaborate muzzle that holds a large gag over his mouth. A supply of muzzles hangs on the wall, ready for any new members who might join the discussion.[12] The target of the cartoon is the censorship of political discussion in the German states, and in addition the cartoonist is poking fun at the ineffectual intellectuals of the "land of poets and thinkers."

But debate and discussion were not crushed. The cartoon itself demonstrates the wide extent of public discourse, as does the outpouring of critical poems, essays, and novels, even those that only exploited poverty and oppression as a titillating backdrop for popularized melodrama. However, the emerging German public sphere had distinctive features. The German *Bürger* translates into English as "citizen," but also as "bourgeois." Whereas in German *bürgerliche Gesellschaft* can mean either "civil society" or "bourgeois society," these are very distinctly different in English. Historically, this points to the origins of German civil society in the *Bürgertum*, which can be translated as "the bourgeoisie," as "the middle classes," or as "burghers," a class that in Germany was rooted in the urban communities. The development of the public sphere in the German realm reflects the dual base of the German bourgeoisie in its shared culture and in these separate and fiercely independent towns.

The English "citizen" and the French *citoyen* both derive from words for "city," as does bourgeois, common to both languages. However, the German *Bürger* retains its connection to *Burg* (town or city), and a *Bürger* is still commonly also understood to be a "townsman." In the early nineteenth century, the connection of *Bürger* to *Burg* was closer still. The only "citizens," in the modern sense of full and free participants in public life, were the honorable men who were full members of the urban communities, the "home towns" described in Chapter 2. Long before political rights and civil freedoms were acquired in France, the citizens of the urban communities of western and southern Germany and Switzerland were already in possession of such rights. They remembered that tradition and resisted the encroachments on their rights by central state officials.

In addition, there was another component of the German citizenry or *Bürgertum*, those men with university educations (the term *Bildungsbürger* or "educated citizens" dates from the 1920s). The ideal of education (*Bildung*) equated it with broad humanistic culture and stressed self-cultivation and spontaneity, along with a disciplined engagement with the recognized great works of philosophy, science, and literature. In fact, rather than this ideal, university education was the passport to a profession, meaning the clergy, medicine, or law. Clergymen depended on the state (or sometimes the nobility) to provide them with their livings. The great majority of lawyers found employment as state officials, and so did many medical practitioners. Therefore state and *Bürgertum* interpenetrated, and the growth of civil society often involved conflict within governments as well as between governments and their subjects. The German realm differed here from England, where professional groups were more self-regulating, and also from Eastern Europe, where the intelligentsia was not so closely connected to the state and where merchants often belonged to a different nationality than the intelligentsia.[13]

Discussion of the public sphere revolves largely around the conception developed by Jürgen Habermas in a book published in 1962 and first translated into English in 1989. In his formulation, participation in the public sphere depends on the willingness of individuals from diverse backgrounds to put aside their particular identities and engage in strictly rational discussion and debate—"private people coming together in public." On philosophical grounds, Habermas argued that within such a public sphere individuals reasoning in universal terms could in principle reach agreement. A common conception of the public good could be identified and then acted upon. Historically, Habermas identified the public sphere with the rise of the middle class in the late eighteenth and early nineteenth centuries. It was discussion among public-spirited members of the European bourgeoisie that both provided the model and forced the actual emergence of this new sphere of debate.[14] Habermas has been criticized, but it is true that, through the middle decades of the nineteenth century, the voices in the recognized public sphere were indeed individual elite persons, almost all male. The low average levels of education (see Chapter 14, Table 14.5) conceal the fact that a few were very highly educated and most had no formal schooling at all. The histories of public discussion in the nineteenth century are therefore histories of individuals and their ideas. The debates between industrial entrepreneurs and government officials in Prussia in the 1840s, or the conflicts among contending advocates of plans for German unification and between them and their opponents in the 1850s and 1860s, were all confined to small groups of privileged persons.

As seen below, the public sphere was gendered and coded as male, and as such required a gendered private sphere coded as female. Further, as social historians have argued, the emerging public sphere was not a purely middle-class realm. The protests of peasants, artisans, and workers were at least as important in defining this new area of contestation as the discourse of privileged members of the elite. Disputes over traditional contractual rights and taxation in the countryside, demands for greater accountability from aloof, unresponsive patricians in the towns, protests over state attempts to regulate religious observances, and demands for redress for economic hardship defined a communal and popular public sphere transmitted through the medium of protest. Well publicized and discussed since the eighteenth century, these disturbances helped frame the contours of bourgeois political consciousness as well. Acculturation in the political realm was reciprocal, flowing from the bottom up as well as from the top down.[15]

To take a regional example, the previously independent communities absorbed by Baden continued to oppose the central state. However, the central government's legislation restructured access to and benefits from political participation in municipalities. Leaders of local urban communities joined increasing numbers of political clubs; in their clubs they articulated political positions, and through their clubs they developed contacts across the state. By the 1840s, a statewide, municipally rooted liberal politics had emerged, with extensive interaction among municipalities at the state level. The demands raised show that this was not simply a negative, localized, and conservative reaction to meddling, tax-collecting central state officials, but a reorientation of local power structures around broader demands for participation in the formulation of government policies. Through the 1840s, this emerging bourgeois liberalism became more radical. Further, although reflecting local middle-class interests, the agitation activated a broader social basis of support arising partly from religious controversies and even more from the economic depression. Agitation from the poor and dispossessed, and from those favoring a broader democracy, interacted with the demands of the urban elite. The growth of local power, organized across the state, undermined central authority so that it collapsed when tested in 1848.[16]

Another regional example is the "Rhenish liberalism" of Prussia's western provinces. The spokesmen were frequently merchant bankers turning to industrial and railroad developments. Numbers of them had relocated from their original home towns to larger cities, notably Cologne. Many were Protestant, and some like the Oppenheim brothers were Jewish. Again, they frequently met in clubs for discussion of public issues. The target of their hostility was the Prussian bureaucracy. Through the 1820s and 1830s, they resisted attempts to undermine their distinctive legal system inherited from the period of French rule, as well as government attempts to control the school system and local government. They also complained that their taxes were heavier than the rest of the kingdom, notably the Junker-dominated east. In the 1840s, their complaints focused more on economic issues, and their proposed solutions extended beyond Prussia to a new reformed German state. They wanted state support, but in their own interests, particularly for the extension of the railway system in which many of them were investing. As in Baden, their complaints intersected with the hardships of the urban and rural poor, and they felt themselves to represent the desires of their regional community as a whole.[17]

But this new public sphere was not necessarily tolerant or democratic. Cologne's leaders attempted to maintain their old exclusion of Jews until the late 1830s.[18] There were democrats among the rising generation, but they were a minority, and most of their contemporaries regarded them as dangerous French-inspired radicals. Rhenish liberals saw themselves as a "middle way" between aristocratic reaction and Jacobin revolution, and their preferred form of government was a constitutional monarchy. Hansemann believed popular sovereignty to be a "pernicious theory" and called for rule by those with education and property, "the real power of the nation." The full citizens of urban communities were typically a minority of the total population, and their demands for participation in public life typically did not extend to all men. And, finally, the poor and dispossessed tended to blame their distress on religious minorities or conspiring merchants, and demanded their restriction or exclusion.

The private sphere: gender and the construction of public life

The obverse of the creation of a public sphere must be the creation of a private sphere. Absolutist states believed themselves responsible for every aspect of their subjects' lives. The theorists of civil society defined a realm of home and family into which the state did not have the right to intrude. As they did so they also created two new images, one of man and the other of woman. The public realm was the sphere of men, the heads of monogamous families and owners of property. This was also the realm of work, of careers, and of production. The private realm was the sphere of women, wives, and mothers raising children. This was the realm of caring, nurturing, and of consumption.

In order for their definition of public and private to have validity, the theorists of civil society required that men and women be essentially different. The rulers of absolutist states had seen their subjects as essentially different, but they divided them by orders, into nobles, clergy, townsmen, craftsmen, and peasants. The theorists of civil society also saw the social system divided into essentially different elements, but for them the crucial divisions lay between men and women and, as seen below, between those who owned property and those who did not.

These ideas came together gradually in the last decades of the eighteenth century. Hegel synthesized them as the building blocks of society as he described it in 1821 in his *Philosophy of Right*:

> The difference in the physical characteristics of the two sexes has a rational basis and consequently acquires an intellectual and ethical significance . . . Thus one sex is mind in its self-diremption into explicit personal self-

subsistence ... The other sex is mind maintaining itself in unity ... In relation to externality, the former is powerful and active, the latter passive and subjective ... It follows that man has his actual substantive life in the state, in learning, and so forth, as well as in labour and struggle with the external world ... Woman, on the other hand, has her substantive destiny in the family ...[19]

The two sexes must come together in marriage, for "marriage, and especially monogamy, is one of the absolute principles on which the ethical life of a community depends."[20] But the family must be supported:

The family, as person, has its real external existence in property ... [but] It is not merely property which a family possesses; as a universal and enduring person, it requires possessions specifically determined as permanent and secure, i.e. it requires capital.[21]

But, finally, the family is a part of society. However, where the absolutist state had claimed the right to govern relations between all of its subjects, male and female, married or not, and also had claimed the right to prescribe how each subject should earn a living and spend an income, in Hegel's view the family and its property were located in a separate sphere:

The family as a legal entity in relation to others must be represented by the husband as its head. Further, it is his prerogative to go out and work for its living, to attend to its needs, and to control and administer its capital.[22]

Hegel's vision is a dream, a dream with two aspects. The first is a fantasy of male domination and female subservience. A man, said Hegel, struggles not only with the external world, but also "with himself." In fact "it is only out of this diremption that he fights his way to self-subsistent unity with himself." However, "in the family he has a tranquil intuition of this unity, and there he lives a subjective ethical life on the plane of feeling." This is so because a woman's destiny is to become a wife, and "to be imbued with family piety is her ethical frame of mind."[23]

The second aspect of the dream was the extension of this model throughout society. As seen in Chapter 2, when Hegel wrote, there were very few such families in any of the German states. Gender orders differed, but virtually all women of all classes contributed actively to the family's income. Indeed, perhaps the only families in which the husband worked outside the home as the family's sole support would have been the families of government officials, and even among these, officials who did not come from aristocratic or patrician backgrounds would not have possessed the capital which Hegel saw as essential to the family's existence.

However, over the next generation the new ideal of the separation of manly work from womanly home spread, through the writings of Hegel and other influential thinkers, through the example of aristocratic households which confined their women, and through the deepening separation of male and female roles among guild artisans in the towns. As the wealthy urban elites looked more and more beyond the walls of their home towns to make their fortunes, they extended the sphere of public discussion as well, but they left their wives at home.

The homes over which the wives of the emerging *Bürgertum* presided were above all orderly and clean. An extremely popular genre of paintings and prints portrayed domestic interiors with plain light walls, contrasting dark timber trim around doors and windows, solid timber furniture with minimal decoration, and multiple paintings and prints hung for display. Windows were large to let light into nurseries where mothers supervised children at play with state-of-the-art toys, into parlors where families (or possibly only a young couple) shared music around the obligatory piano, into studies where fathers read their books, and into nooks in other rooms where daughters read theirs. Walled gardens continued the theme of the home as a place of refuge. The plantings might be romantically unkempt, but the external world lay very firmly beyond the locked gate.

How did women feel about this? Another look at the increasing emphasis on the differences between the sexes in public discourse, and another glance at the idealized domestic interior, suggests that the *Bürgertum* wanted its private sphere confined not only against the threat of external disorder, but also against the threat of female emancipation. Not all women could speak. The wives and daughters of farmers and many sorts of artisans continued as before to support the family enterprise. Many other young women supported their families by seeking work outside the home, as farm workers, domestic servants, or workers in textile factories.

Most girls received basic primary education along with most boys, in most German states. Even for girls from more affluent families, entry into the secondary schools that led to university was impossible, as was entry into the universities themselves. Symptomatically, in all German states secondary schools for girls were supervised by the same officials that oversaw elementary education. A few private secondary schools for girls were established, such as those that catered to the urban patriciate in the Hanseatic cities. Public high schools for girls were founded by city governments, but their numbers remained small. There were 22 in 1820, 34 were founded between 1820 and 1840, and a further 47 opened between 1840 and 1860. Most charged substantial fees for the "luxury" of female education.[24]

Difficult as it was, large numbers of women did obtain secondary education, and large numbers of them put their thoughts into published works. For some, writing was delayed. Bettine von Arnim began writing only after her husband died in 1831. Fanny Lewald's father kept her at home for twenty years after she finished school, and she did not publish until after leaving home in the early 1840s. This became less common, and during the 1840s many female authors emerged into the public sphere. Louise Aston was an outspoken advocate of women's rights, and she was banned from Berlin for expressing thoughts that threatened domestic order and stability. Louise Otto-Peters, in her novel *Kathinka* (1844) and in her essay "The Participation of the Female World in the Life of the State" (1847), argued that girls' education should concentrate on history, science, and physical education, rather than the "crippling" female subjects of sewing, music, and foreign languages.

Many German women authors admired George Sand. Among them, Countess Ida Hahn-Hahn was often referred to as the "German George Sand." An impoverished aristocrat with little formal education, she entered an arranged marriage that ended in a divorce after three years of violence. An open ongoing scandal ensued, as she then lived and traveled extensively with a man who was not her husband. The wide success of her novels made her possibly the leading female German novelist of the first half of the nineteenth century. Many female authors compared loveless marriages to prostitution, and, not surprisingly, the picture of marriage in Hahn-Hahn's *Aus der Gesellschaft* (*From Society*, 1838) and her most famous work *Gräfin Faustine* (*Countess Faustine*, 1840) is negative. In the first, a female character refutes all the conventional reasons for a woman to marry, including social position, protection, domestic happiness, and children. In the second, a loveless marriage and separation frames reflections on the treatment of women "as slaves whom men have bought." *Der Rechte* (*The Right One*, 1839) suggested that girls should be sent to university and boys to sewing school, so the boys could learn what oppression really was while the girls discovered what they were truly capable of. *Zwei Frauen* (*Two Women*, 1845) attacked the notion that women should not think or have wills of their own, and also assaulted the central pillar of the definition of the private sphere, the idea that a woman acquired her place in society only through her husband, regardless of her own talents and accomplishments.

The social crisis: peasants, paupers, and proletariat

For the large majority of ordinary Germans, protoindustrial development and commercial agriculture brought real rewards, but also risks. For protoindustrial families, a decline in demand for their artisan products or a poor harvest meant hardship because the agricultural resources of protoindustrial districts were small compared to the needs of their expanded populations. For wealthy landlords and substantial peasant farmers, increasing commercialization meant contracting loans, and again a decline in demand or a failure in the harvest could bring ruin. For agricultural workers, finally, depression meant unemployment and hunger.

The structural accompaniment of commercialization had been an increasingly wide gap between rich and poor in the countryside. Instability brought insecurity. Large numbers of both aristocratic estates and peasant farms changed hands, and the numbers appeared to be increasing. By the 1850s, some 40 per cent of the former designated "knightly estates" in Prussia were owned by non-nobles. Very large numbers of unemployed protoindustrial artisans and farm laborers moved from one district to another seeking work, and again their numbers appeared to be increasing. The Saxon government worried that only a fifth of "peasant" households could support themselves from their holdings. Emigration rose to unprecedented numbers, from an average of 25,000 per year in the mid-1830s, to 38,000 in 1845, 63,000 in 1846, and 80,000 in 1847.

Contemporaries also perceived a crisis among the artisans. This is difficult to measure. The numbers of masters rose, but this might not reflect prosperity, for, as a contemporary economist wrote, "a master who works without helpers is actually no more than a special kind of wage earner."[25] On the other hand, the number of apprentices and journeymen also rose compared to masters, but this might also be problematical, for it meant that the aspirations of journeymen were being frustrated. This may indicate that the economy was growing too slowly to support new masterships, that existing masters were restricting new entrants into the trade, or that the nature of the trade itself was changing. The best change is no change, as any honorable guildsman could have said.

But there was change, though it affected different trades to different degrees. Mechanized factory competition pressed as yet on only a few trades. For rural craftsmen who served a clientele of farmers, the old saying that "if the peasant has money, all the world has money" held true. Blacksmiths, wheelwrights, leather workers, and a number of the construction trades all benefited when large farmers needed repairs or new equipment. Conversely, when agriculture declined, so did their fortunes. In the towns, the old guild organizations weakened under the continual pressure from government officials. In a number of trades, particularly shoemaking, clothing, and baking, where little capital was required, this made it possible for journeymen to set up as independent masters more easily than before, and for "dishonorable" or "foreign" persons to practice the craft. In others, such as furniture making, many masters became in effect contract workers for merchants who marketed the product while transferring as much of the risk as they could on the dependent artisans. In others still, such as the woodworking, metal, and especially the textile trades, protoindustrial patterns of rural outworkers contracting to urban merchants continued.[26]

In the 1840s, fashion turned from linen to lighter and cheaper cottons, and the hundreds of thousands of families in Silesia whose livelihood depended on the sale of their linen cloth began to go hungry. This was the traditional protoindustrial pattern of expansion followed by crisis and decline, and the outbursts of violence, such as the "weavers' revolt" of 1844, were the traditional response of desperate people. The Silesian weavers had been relatively prosperous independent artisans. The drop in demand for their products meant they became more dependent on the merchants who supplied their raw materials and marketed their output. The merchants, themselves under extreme competitive pressure, used their power to lower the price they paid the weavers. The weavers were also competing, against one another, but they remained bound by their sense of community and saw the merchants as the villains. They demanded higher pay, and they demanded additional payment in compensation for their suffering. Protests and violence increased, but authorities found it difficult to make arrests. In early June a crowd attacked the home of one of the merchants. The next day a crowd assembled to collect payments extorted from another merchant. Troops called in by the local officials arrived. Either frightened or provoked by the crowd, they opened fire, killing eleven and wounding many others.

The threat posed by overpopulation could only be reduced by a genuine industrial revolution that would break through the ceiling. Saxon and Rhenish cotton manufacturers built on the foundations of expertise developed over the previous two generations and successfully laid the basis for the beginnings of industrial development in both regions. However, there were two additional patterns that accompanied this transformation. First, the capital requirements of the new technologies meant that only a relatively small number of entrepreneurs would become the owners of the new factories, and these typically were wealthy merchants, not master craftsmen. A cleft opened which cut across the old solidarity of the citizens of the home towns. Second, the new class of factory owners sought the least expensive form of labor, and this frequently proved to be young women, not the married men who had been regarded as the heads of artisan families. Therefore the industrial transformation revolutionized not only the technology of production, but also the social and gender orders of the industrial districts.[27]

The political context

The "German question"

Hopes were raised by the accession of Frederick William IV as King of Prussia in 1840, but they were disappointed. Frederick William pardoned some political prisoners, settled disputes with the Catholic Church in the Rhineland, and appointed old veterans of the heroic reform era of 1807 to new official posts. However, he also believed in his divine right to rule. He rejected suggestions that he fulfill his father's promise of a constitution by insisting that a "piece of paper" could never come between himself and his subjects. The censorship remained, and Karl Marx, among others, was driven into exile. Heine was again on target in portraying the king as a "a foolish mixture of the extremes of our times," neither good nor bad, neither stupid nor bright, and likely to reverse direction from one day to the next.

Frederick William was indeed a complex figure who adopted and possibly believed in his medieval rhetoric, but who also thought that rhetoric and ceremony would help create a common identity uniting the government with its subjects. He shocked Metternich in 1842 by telling him that his inauguration of the Cologne cathedral was part of an attempt to create a "Prussian tradition" for a country that had no real historical basis. He was also a keen supporter of railroad development, and he was well acquainted and on friendly terms with commercial leaders in the Rhineland such as August von der Heydt.[28]

The Prussian government seemed without a clear vision, but its failures were related to a chronic shortage of funds. Plans for railroads, for new industries, and for programs to alleviate the social crisis all required money. However, the attempts to improve the government's financial position without constitutional reform failed. In 1842, the government convened a grouping of committees representing the provincial assemblies (*Vereinigte Ständische Ausschüsse*). In 1847, all the assemblies were convened together (*Vereinigte Landtage*). The main item on the government's agenda in both cases was approval for loans that would finance railroad construction. In both cases the representatives demanded a series of reforms in return, including Jewish emancipation, the right to approve the government's budget, to meet regularly, and to participate in drafting new legislation. In both cases the assemblies ended in deadlock.

All Liberals opposed the clumsy structures of the German Federation, and Prussian Liberals were also increasingly humiliated by their country's subordinate position. The German Federation was still dominated by Austria and by Metternich, and Metternich's obsessive concern with any hint of resistance had not changed since 1819. He warned Frederick William before the *Vereinigte Landtage* meeting that "Your Majesty will bring together eight separate representative bodies and they will return home as a national parliament." For many, the combination of Austrian intransigence and the *Kleinstaaterei* of the German Federation seemed not only reactionary and out of date, but also positively dangerous in a hostile world. The crisis that blew up in 1840 when some French leaders suggested that France should reclaim its "natural" border at the Rhine raised a palpable threat of foreign domination. The flood of patriotic poems showed the depth of concern, but it also illuminated the weakness of the German system.

Governments and the social crisis

As seen in Chapter 2 and above, the Prussian state was actively involved in the economy, both positively and negatively. The government's efforts in creating the Zollverein, in road-building, model factories, and in the mining industry all contributed to growth, but a persistently deflationary monetary policy, opposition to the railroad, and hostility to joint stock corporations all acted as a drag. The government also made attempts to deal with social dislocation. The response of civil servants to social problems was an authoritarian one that sought to maximize control of the unruly masses while beginning to solve their problems. A new poor law was introduced in 1842. The first protective labor legislation aimed to regulate the conditions of work in the new factories.

However, divisions and conflicts show that the bureaucracy was not monolithic but rather was split between different political factions. Although officials may have sought "the common bond of a Prussian *juste milieu*,"[29] the social crisis accentuated deep divisions within the ranks of government officials. In part this reflected changes in the body of officials. In his famous definition of bureaucracy, Max Weber emphasized permanence of tenure and fixed salaries as bureaucracy's defining characteristics, but the crucial innovation was the introduction of formal examinations.[30] Since the eighteenth century, German states had employed examinations to test the legal knowledge of candidates for official posts, and many had followed Prussia's example in adding a period of unpaid "practical" work. During the 1840s, Prussia added first a second and then a third examination. This was aimed at reducing the pool of candidates, because the chronic shortage of funds meant that the number of positions could not expand. Nevertheless, the universities continued to produce hopeful candidates, and the number of those who failed, or who had passed their exams but languished waiting for an appointment, increased. This was a Europe-wide phenomenon, and these educated but underemployed men constituted a potentially dangerous pool of discontent.[31]

The new examinations were also intended to serve as a filter to ensure that only those with proper social background and political opinions could be accepted; "the exclusion of outsiders."[32] Although they made entry more difficult, they in fact failed to control opinion. Many officials, either precisely because they had passed the examinations and therefore regarded themselves as members of Hegel's universal class, or because noble status or independent wealth gave them security, ignored criticism from their departmental superiors and advocated quite substantial reforms. Judges, for instance, became biting critics of the pretensions of army officers, of the arbitrary actions of the administrative bureaucracy, and of nobles clinging to their feudal and seigneurial rights. They advocated wholesale legal reform modeled on the French Napoleonic Code, administered by an independent judiciary, free from political pressure— that is, themselves. On the other hand, most of those brought before the court for judgment were from the increasingly impoverished lower classes. The judges' liberalism was in no way democratic. Stricter repression, rather than the expansion of political representation, was their preferred way to deal with this dangerously rootless proletariat.[33]

A rising revolutionary wave?

Governments appeared incapable. As in Silesia in 1844, the absence of adequate police forces meant that any protest was apt to trigger intervention by military forces, which almost always resulted in loss of life, and in addition resulted in public scandal when the news spread along the telegraph and through the newspapers. Riots in Leipzig in 1845 and Cologne in 1846 linked religious dissent with protest against unpopular government figures, the Saxon Crown Prince and local Prussian officials respectively. A peasant uprising in Galicia was brutally repressed in 1846, as was the Berlin "potato revolution" of 1847.

Bread riots spread across Germany in 1847. Southern state governments acted fairly effectively, buying grain and distributing it according to need. The Prussian government dithered. Officials at first refused to suspend exports, but then changed direction and began buying grain from dealers, which drove prices up and interfered with the efforts of municipal governments and private charities. The bread riots peaked in the summer and then receded. The harvest in 1847 was better than the previous season, and food prices declined. However, as noted above, the business cycle turned down in 1847.

In the aftermath of hunger came the Silesian "hunger typhus" of 1847. Prussian government officials attempted to cover up the disaster, but then the protests of a Liberal doctor publicized not only the actual suffering of the people in the district, but also the government's incompetence. In December, there were demonstrations across Prussia when city councils were given the right to hold public sessions. Liberals crowded the council chambers and circulated petitions that contained the now familiar list of reform proposals.

Unrest across Europe also distracted governments. A series of uprisings against Austrian rule erupted in northern Italy in 1847. Late in the year, a civil war broke out in Switzerland. In January 1848, revolutionary disturbances began in Palermo. And, in France, an escalating series of demonstrations shook the foundations of the eighteen-year reign of Louis Phillipe.

The revolutions of 1848

Taking a metaphor from one of Heine's poems, in 1844 Marx had concluded his introduction to the *Critique of Hegel's Philosophy of Right* by saying that "when all the inner conditions ripen, the day of German resurrection will be proclaimed by the crowing of the Gallic cock." As it had been in 1831, so it was again in 1848. News of the Paris riots in February, the fall of the French monarchy, and the establishment of the new republic swept across the German states. Incidents of collective violence escalated. The press reported 197 incidents where military force was deployed against rioters in 1848 and 1849, compared with around 50 in 1830 and 1831 and a total of 323 over the entire period from 1816 to 1847.[34]

Riots could be crushed by military intervention, as they had been over the past three decades. However, now huge public meetings were held, too large and too numerous for repression. The crowds demanded the withdrawal of the military, the establishment of civilian militias, new ministries headed by recognized Liberal leaders, an end to remaining feudal privileges, and the creation of a national parliament. In the south and west the changes in government were relatively peaceful. The riots in Berlin and Vienna that toppled the governments were more violent, with some 300 dead in Berlin and 50 in Vienna. By March, although only the King of Bavaria actually lost his throne in favor of his brother, new Liberal ministries had been established in all states, led by opponents of the previous administrations, for instance the moderate Liberal bureaucrat Johann Baptist Bekk in Baden, and Ludolf Camphausen, a prominent businessman and Liberal from the Rhineland, who became the new chief minister of Prussia.

The speed and ease with which the revolutions succeeded reflected the new higher level of politicization of public life, but also the indecisiveness of the governments. None of the regular armies was destroyed. Although violence was widespread, the revolutionary movements that demanded fundamental changes in government were generally confined to the capital cities. From this perspective the revolution continued the previous political conflicts between the municipalities and the central government.[35] However, the revolutionaries were themselves divided. Socially, groups previously excluded from public life demanded a voice, particularly Jews and women, but their efforts excited hostility. Economically, peasants wanted secure title to their land, and artisans wanted an end to "dishonorable" competition, but industrial and commercial entrepreneurs wanted freedom to introduce new technologies without regard for local restrictions. Politically, a few on the left looked forward to a more complete social revolution and a republic, while more on the right saw themselves cooperating with the princes in new constitutional monarchies.

Women played an active part in the demonstrations that brought down the Conservative governments. Louise Aston returned to Berlin and fought on the barricades. She wrote poems celebrating the uprising and as memorials for its defeat. Her novel *Revolution and Counterrevolution* (1849) may be the first and only novel of the revolutions, and, as it happens, it is from the hand of a female revolutionary. Humania, the women's organization founded by Kathinka Zitz-Halein in Mainz, had 1700 members. Louise Otto-Peters' *Frauen-Zeitung* (*Women's Newspaper*) defended the rights of poor women in particular, arguing that only a guarantee of the right to work could save them from the private prostitution of a loveless marriage on the one hand, or descending to public prostitution on the other. However, although some Liberals supported women's right to participate in public life, many more remained opposed to the idea of women stepping outside the domestic sphere.

Similarly for Jews, who in many states and localities had been excluded from public life, the revolution opened up a new opportunity for political activity. As could be expected from their educational and occupational background (enjoined to literacy by tradition, often confined to the Jewish quarter or *Judengasse* in those cities where they were permitted, and usually forbidden to own agricultural land), they often played a disproportionate role in the revolutions and in the new governments. But their new visibility often stimulated anti-Semitic outbursts.

Those on the political left and the urban artisans and journeymen tended to become more radical in their demands. Rioters destroyed machines and pillaged food stores. Confronted by calls for a republic and violent attacks on property, the new Liberal governments defended themselves. In Baden, the Bekk government put down a series of disturbances. This led the radicals Gustav von Struve and Friedrich Hecker to declare a republic in southern Baden. They attempted to put together an army, but their poorly equipped units, made up of journeymen, peasants, and students, were defeated by a force of 30,000 Confederation troops.

Looming in the background was the definition of Germany. Although both Berlin and Vienna were ruled by new Liberal regimes, neither government could rest secure. The weakness and vacillation of the rulers had contributed to the success of the revolutions, but also meant that they might yield to their own instincts and the advice of their reactionary advisers. And any new German government would have to decide whether Austria was to be included in the new state, and, if so, how much of the remainder of the empire should also join.

In the meantime, elections were held for the state parliaments and for the national parliament in Frankfurt. In accord with the accepted definition of the public sphere, members of the national parliament were elected by all "independent" adult males. The results were a cross-section of the German *Bürgertum*. The absent classes were artisans and peasants, only seven together. Of around 800 representatives who served, about 100 were lawyers, 50 were clergymen, and 50 were from other professions. There were about 100 businessmen and landowners. The dominant group by far were state officials, over 400, a result that demonstrated both the high visibility and prestige of officials and the interpenetration of *Bürgertum* and state apparatus.

The Frankfurt parliament worked rapidly and efficiently. A new Provisional Executive was established with a Hapsburg archduke as its nominal head. Rules of procedure were drafted. Nearly 20,000 petitions were read and referred to the appropriate committees. Party groupings formed. The Constitutional Committee presented its recommendations on citizenship and basic rights in less than six weeks. Its decisions reflected the previous decade's debates. The draft abolished the aristocracy as a separate class, guaranteed national citizenship to all Germans, and established the basic rights of free speech, free assembly, and freedom of religion.

On the other hand, the new Provisional Executive remained weak in several respects. No major power granted diplomatic recognition to the new government. The Economic Committee split between protectionists and free traders, and the Provisional Executive therefore remained without a clear economic policy. Unable and unwilling to confront the existing state governments directly, the Provisional Executive did not impose and collect taxes. Combined with its inability to decide on economic policy, this meant that no social policy could be pursued, and economic hardship continued to cause unrest. Even more serious, when it required military power, to confront Polish nationalists over Posen or the Danes over Schleswig-Holstein, or for its own protection, the Provisional Executive remained dependent on the princes. In the dispute with Denmark and in the suppression of uprisings in southwest Germany and in Frankfurt itself, it was the armies of Prussia and the other states that acted.

The public mood began to shift. For some, this reflected satisfaction with the gains they had made. For others, the new mood reflected their fears. Several states announced an end to feudal rights and dues. Landed peasants, now secure in their ownership, ceased to be revolutionary and became supporters of the existing system against the demands of the propertyless rural underclass. Conservatives drew on these new sentiments as they recruited peasants into patriotic organizations such as the Association for King and Fatherland in Prussia. These bodies had already enrolled 20,000 members by mid-1848, and their numbers continued to grow.

Several state governments also substantially increased the supplies of paper money and made credit more readily available. This not only met the immediate needs of firms suffering from the depression but also addressed one of the long-standing complaints of the commercial and industrial classes.[36] As seen above, wealthy entrepreneurs had never favored democracy. Now, particularly in the crucial cities, merchants, industrialists, master artisans, and shopkeepers worried more about the danger of unrest, and they supported energetic action to maintain public order. New and more Conservative governments replaced the Liberal ministries in several states.

Although the Austrian Empire had seemed to be on the verge of dissolution in mid-1848, by the end of the year both the national revolutions in the provinces and the Liberal revolution in the capital had been defeated. Hungarians, Czechs, and Italians had all rebelled. The radical uprising in Vienna had led to the withdrawal of the court to Innsbruck. However, the army had already suppressed the Polish uprising in Galicia in April. The Czech revolution was defeated in June, and northern Italy was reconquered in July. The Hungarians held out longer, but were defeated with assistance from Russia. In the meantime, Vienna had succumbed to a major assault in which more than 2000 lost their lives. A new Conservative government was installed under Prince Felix zu Schwarzenberg.

The Prussian army had also been active, suppressing a revolt of Polish nationalists in Posen in May. In June the army repressed a radical rising in Berlin. Pressured by his Conservative advisors, the king replaced Liberal ministers with more Conservative figures. A notoriously Conservative general was named as military commander of the Berlin district and another as chief minister. Then, on November 2, Count Friedrich Wilhelm Brandenburg, a prominent Conservative, was named chief minister. Several days later 13,000 troops entered the city, martial law was declared, and the commanding general ordered the Prussian parliament to disband. A new constitution was imposed on December 2; following the elections the new chamber was dissolved, shortly after meeting for the first time in February 1849.

Despite the Conservative victories in Austria and Prussia, the Frankfurt parliament continued its work on a constitution for Germany. On October 27, the representatives voted for the "greater German" definition of Germany, which included Austria but none of the non-German dominions. A month later Schwarzenberg rejected the plan and insisted that the Austrian Empire would continue its independent existence. The majority of representatives then moved to a "lesser German" vision, excluding Austria, and eventually decided to offer the crown of Germany to Frederick William of Prussia. He had previously stated he would only agree if he had the approval of the other German princes, and privately referred to the crown as a "dog collar," but he had managed to be equivocal enough in public that there was some hope he might accept the offer. But he did not, and the new constitution, although accepted by a majority of the states, was rejected by the most important, Austria, Prussia, Bavaria, Hanover, and Saxony.

In May 1849, the Frankfurt parliament called on the German states, elected bodies, and the German people to recognize the constitution and bring it into effect. Already, in April, a majority of the Saxon Landtag had voted to compel their government to accept the German constitution, but King Frederick Augustus II defied them and closed the assembly. Angry crowds gathered, and the barricades went up again when soldiers fired on a crowd of demonstrators. The court fled, and a new revolutionary government was established. Unrest spread, notably in Prussia, in Silesia and in the Rhineland, as well as in the south and west. The King of Württemberg also fled, and new revolutionary governments came into being in the Palatinate and in Baden.

However, without military force, the Frankfurt parliament could not enforce its will. Further, although a few army units supported the revolution, the Conservatives commanded overwhelmingly superior forces. The Saxon army remained loyal to the king, and Prussian reinforcements added decisive force. The soldiers recaptured Dresden in early May. Prussian units were also made available to repress the uprisings in other states. The fighting continued in some areas until late July, but the end came with the defeat of a Badenese revolutionary army in June and the surrender of the last insurgents at Rastatt.

Reprisals followed defeat. Hundreds of those who surrendered at Rastatt were executed outright. The Prussian soldiers acquired a particularly ugly reputation for their treatment of suspected revolutionaries in Catholic districts. Thousands more were tried by military courts martial and shot or imprisoned. Additional thousands were prosecuted by civilian courts, sometimes under writs extending back to the very beginning of the revolution and even before. Censorship returned. Otto-Peters' *Frauen-Zeitung* protested the treatment of political prisoners, and was banned in 1852.

Notes

1. Philipp Veit, *Die Einführung der Künste in Deutschland durch das Christentum* (*The Introduction of the Arts into Germany by Christianity*), 1834–36; *Germania*, March 1848. See Gall 1993; Herminghouse and Miller 1997.
2. "Nachtgedanken" (Night Thoughts). See Berman 1997, p. 68.
3. Engels 1851–52; Taylor 1946; Wehler 1995, Vol. 3, pp. 196–7.
4. Helling 1965.
5. Riley 1986.
6. Brophy 1998.
7. Borchardt 1961; Tilly 1966a; Kocka 1978, p. 536.
8. Tipton 1976; Kiesewetter 1988.
9. Finney 1997, pp. 272–91.
10. Quoted in Pinson 1954, pp. 67–8. An early edition of Börne's works was published in Milwaukee in the 1850s by émigrés in the aftermath of the revolutions.

11. Robertson 1988; Liedtke 2000.
12. Blackbourn 1997.
13. Sperber 1997a, p. 276.
14. Habermas 1962; Chambers 1996.
15. See Würgler 1995.
16. Nolte 1994; Green 2001.
17. See Diefendorf 1980.
18. See Magnus 1997.
19. Paragraphs 165, 166.
20. Paragraph 167.
21. Paragraphs 169, 170.
22. Paragraph 171.
23. Paragraph 166.
24. Albisetti 1988.
25. Bruno Hildebrand, quoted in Sheehan 1989, p. 493.
26. Hamerow 1958, Ch. 2.
27. See Quataert 1995.
28. Barclay 1995.
29. Beck 1995, p. 207.
30. Wunder 1993.
31. Gillis 1971; Wunder 1986.
32. Wunder 1986, p. 40.
33. Hodenberg 1996.
34. Tilly 1975.
35. Nolte 1994.
36. Tilly 1990, p. 35.

CHAPTER 4

THE AGE OF REALISM,
1850–71

For contemporaries, the failure of the 1848 revolutions marked a clear break. Defeated Liberals and democrats who had wanted a united and reformed Germany despaired. The victorious Conservative forces rejoiced. However, the rupture of revolution did not lead back to the past, but rather ushered in a new age of realism. Taking its name from a widely read treatise on the "politics of realism" (*Realpolitik*) published by Ludwig August von Rochau in 1853,[1] and for later generations exemplified in Bismarck's diplomacy of the 1860s, the new style was as pervasive in its day as Romanticism had been before.

The new realism revealed itself perhaps most clearly in its treatment of the most "unrealistic" themes. Adolph von Menzel's prints and paintings illustrating the life of Frederick the Great, though entirely imaginary, include detail based on painstaking research into places and costumes of the previous century, sometimes copied from photographs. Unusual and innovative when he produced them in the 1840s, Menzel's compositions place the viewer in the scene with a view that might have been dictated by chance, as if standing beside the artist.[2] Lorenz Clasen's 1860 painting of *Germania on Watch at the Rhine* places the viewer directly next to Germania on a bluff overlooking the river. Crowned with oak leaves, her sword drawn, she rests her hand on her shield and gazes intently ahead, westward toward France. However, in this case the realism of the execution undermines the intended message. This is not the tall, detached goddess portrayed by previous artists, but a quite ordinary young woman dressed up for the part in elaborate robes that do not in fact fit her very well. The painting is obviously a studio pose with the background added later, and the model could not pose with her sword aloft and therefore has been allowed to rest the point on the studio floor.[3]

The distinction with Romantic art lies not in the rendering of detail or the rearrangement of elements in the composition, but in the attempt to create a picture that might plausibly represent what the viewer would

Plate 4.1 Adolf von Menzel, *Frederick II Cheered by Children in Potsdam*, illustration for Kugler's *History of Frederick the Great*, 1840–42. The viewer looks up from the perspective of one of the children running beside the horse of Frederick the Great, the king from 1740 to 1786 and the architect of Prussian greatness. No distant hero, the old man is regarded with ironic affection by servants and subjects. Photo: Bildarchiv Preussischer Kulturbesitz, Berlin.

have seen, if standing where the artist stood. Realism is a shared experience. Reality, rather than depending on a personal vision, is apprehensible to all. Reality stands outside the observer, but is subject to control. In visual art this reflects the viewer's omnipotent gaze, which can range anywhere in the painting and focus on any detail because all have been rendered with equal accuracy and completeness. The skill of the artist is measurable; representations of external reality can be ranked according to their accuracy, and, again, the degree of accuracy is evident to any observer.

This is also the classic vision of physical science. In science the ana-log of the viewer's gaze is the mathematized theoretical description that paves the way to technological control of nature. This was the period in which observational science began to be matched by develop-ments in theoretical science, especially in electricity and chemistry. The first aniline dyes developed in the 1850s were "discovered" by researchers who had a very precise idea of what they were searching for and how to find it. They found immediate application in silk dyeing and caused a fundamental shift in ladies' fashion. Building on generations of university-centered research, the German states led the way. These dec-ades saw the foundation of the Badische Aniline- und Soda Fabrik (BASF), Bayer, and Hoechst. Similarly, Werner von Siemens' discovery and development of the electric dynamo in 1866 opened the way for the application of electric power to dispersed industrial production, urban lighting, and railroads.

Subsequent historians focused on politics and diplomacy, on Otto von Bismarck, and the foundation of the empire in 1870–71. For the next generation this was the event that punctuated their lives, and many experienced the creation of the new state as a new personal beginning as well. The empire and its accomplishments were a source of pride, something to be celebrated. Germany's rise to world economic power confirmed this self-congratulatory world-view. Following the Nazi dicta-torship and the disasters of the Second World War, historians searching for the origins of Germany's "special path" questioned the process of the creation of the Bismarckian empire, the fit between economic and political development, and above all the policies of Bismarck.

But the men and women of the generation of realism had not experi-enced unification. Their focus was on their rapidly changing present, on the economy, on society, and on politics. Optimism derived from their increasing control over nature extended to a belief that they could control political life as well. Bismarck's sudden emergence, and his abil-ity to impose himself on events, could not be foreseen. In the event, the traumatic impact of his actions brought one generation to an end and opened another.

Plate 4.2   Lorenz Clasen, *Germania on Watch at the Rhine*, 1860. Oil on linen, 220 × 159 cm. Kaiser Wilhelm Museum, Krefeld. The viewer stands beside the goddess, the embodiment of German national aspirations, who is, however, far from divine. The robes are too large for the model, and her sword too heavy. She supports herself on the sword point and balances with the shield. The fore-ground stones and background vista of distant walled towns have been added to continue the perspective, which is the one the viewers would have seen if they had been standing on the bluff. Photo: AKG London.

The economic context: the upswing of the 1850s and 1860s

Trends: the railroad and industrial development

The 1850s and 1860s were very good decades for the economies of the German states. There was still no "national" economy, but if we combine the available figures for the separate states of the Zollverein, then certainly on average the German economies were growing, and growing rapidly. While population increased from 35.3 million in 1850 to 40.8 million in 1870, total output rose so that output per person increased by nearly 50 per cent. In Chapter 3, we saw that the 1840s were a kind of hinge between the agricultural past and the industrial future. Now, in the 1850s and 1860s, industrial investment began to dominate the business cycle. Output per worker rose, especially in the industrial sector.[4] The upswing from 1850 to 1873 was marred by only three years of declining output, in 1858, 1861, and 1870. In all three years total output declined only slightly, and it is significant that the declines in total output resulted primarily from declines in agricultural production. That is, problems in agriculture could still affect the entire economy, but not sufficiently to cause a major depression. The expansion of industrial output, and therefore the development of the entire economy, had escaped its dependence on the annual harvest.

Today we expect yearly increases in productivity to result from a stream of new technologies, but in the 1850s and 1860s this kind of change was new and revolutionary. Contemporaries marveled at the new machines displayed at shows modeled on the 1851 Crystal Palace exhibition in London. Newspapers reported on international exhibitions and drummed up support for regional shows. The Karlsruhe exhibition in 1861 drew 100,000 visitors, equivalent to 10 per cent of Baden's adult population.

Some of the improvement in the economy's efficiency resulted from the rapid development of transportation, both the extension of the canal system and the expansion of the railroad network. Canals had a long history. Water transport was (and still is) the cheapest means of moving large bulky cargoes. During the middle decades of the nineteenth century techniques of construction improved dramatically. New canals were built, and older canals were expanded to accommodate larger vessels. Traditionally, barges had been dragged along the canals by men and women harnessed to ropes, because horses were usually too expensive. Now, steam power was introduced, sometimes using engines on the bank to pull barges by cables attached to the vessels or to moving chains on the bottom of the canal, and sometimes to power the new larger canal boats themselves.[5]

But it was the railroads which captured the imagination of the century. "A new chapter in world history begins," wrote Heinrich Heine after observing the opening of a railroad line in 1843. "With each new iron steed that travels the rails, a piece of feudalism falls into the abyss of an irrecoverable past," said historian Johannes Scherr in 1858.[6] The railroads themselves were an unprecedented investment undertaking. Investment in railroads rose at nearly 8 per cent per year, and fluctuations in railroad investment dominated the industrial business cycle from the 1840s to the 1880s. The length of railroad lines in operation rose from fewer than 6000 kilometers in 1850 to nearly 20,000 in 1870. Many thousands of laborers worked to construct the new lines—their numbers were not reported consistently, and they fluctuated sharply, but on average possibly 300,000 men might have been building railroads somewhere in the German realm in any year between 1850 and 1900.

Even more important than the impressive increase in total length of track, however, was the creation of linkages among all the producing and consuming regions in the German states. By the late 1860s, within the Prussian-dominated Zollverein, the outlines of the future German Empire can be clearly seen in the framework of the major railroad lines. There was no plan for this development. Propagandists such as Frederick List had campaigned for a "national" railroad system, but, as seen in Chapter 3, the Prussian government had been less than enthusiastic about the early railroads. Nevertheless, the whole was in fact greater than the sum of the parts, and out of the many individual decisions to build particular lines emerged a single economy whose parts were connected by increasing flows of goods and people.[7]

The new transportation network created "backward linkages" by providing markets for a broad range of industries. Construction required stone, bricks, cement, and timber. Steamboats, barges, rails, locomotives, and rolling stock required iron, steel, and machinery. These in turn required coal.[8] There were crucial "forward linkages" as well. The decreasing cost of transportation reduced the prices that manufacturers and farmers charged their customers. Railways and canals increased the speed and reliability of the delivery of raw materials and finished products. This meant that firms did not have to maintain such large stocks on hand, which permitted a substantial reduction in the amount of capital required for inventories. In turn, the capital released could be made available for other investments. Production therefore expanded and concentrated in those districts where costs were lowest; producers in high-cost areas were forced to move, or fail. The benefits of growth therefore spread very unevenly even among advanced industrial regions.[9] (See Table 4.1.)

The importance of the railroads extended beyond the economic sphere. Socially, the increased movement of persons laid the foundations for accelerating urbanization. Politically, as seen below, the Prussian government and its former Liberal opponents of 1848 came to terms through an agreement to spend increases in government revenue on the railroad system. The Prussian victories in the Danish, Austrian, and French wars owed much to efficient use of the railroad system. Frederick the Great's soldiers had to walk the length of Silesia after digging up the border markers in 1740; in 1866, Helmuth von Moltke's soldiers could

Table 4.1 Indicators of industrial development in Germany, 1820–70

	Railroad lines (kilo- meters)	Iron output (000 tons)	Iron per capita (kilo- grams)	Coal output (million tons)	Coal per capita (kilo- grams)	Steam engines (total)	Steam engines (horse- power)
1820	0	96[1]	3.5[1]	1.2	46		
1830	0	122	4.2	1.7	58		
1840	469	173	5.3	3.2	98		
1850	5856	212	6.0	5.2	147	1416[2]	26,354[2]
1860	11,088	545	14.5	12.3	327	10,113[3]	184,649[3]
1870	19,000	1391	34.1	26.4	647		947,000[4]

Notes:
1. 1823.
2. 1846, Zollverein members.
3. 1861, Zollverein members.
4. 1875, German Empire.

Source: Adapted from Richard H. Tilly, "Banken und Industrialisierung in Deutschland, 1815–70," in *Kapital, Staat und sozialer Protest in der deutschen Industrialisierung* (Göttingen: Vandenhoeck & Ruprecht, 1980), Table 1, with additional figures calculated from data in Walther G. Hoffmann, *Das Wachstum der deutschen Wirtschaft seit der Mitte des 19. Jahrhunderts* (Berlin: Springer, 1965).

catch the morning train from Berlin to Dresden and complete the conquest of Saxony in the afternoon.

In the 1850s and 1860s, finding capital for investment seemed less of a problem than before. Government policy changed significantly, especially in Prussia. In 1848, the revolutionary government had established a separate Ministry of Commerce and Industry. Although the revolution went down in defeat, the new ministry remained, and so did the minister, August von der Heydt. Heydt had been a merchant banker in the Rhineland and a Liberal critic of the government in the 1840s. Appointed to the ministry in December 1848, he survived in office until 1862, and served briefly as Minister–President, but then resigned during the constitutional crisis. He then returned in 1866–67 to help finance the war with Austria. His influence can be seen across a range of policies. In the 1850s and 1860s, the amount of currency in circulation increased much more rapidly than previously, at over 12.5 per cent per year. More limited liability corporations were approved, 201 between 1851 and 1867. The government constructed new railroad lines and purchased others. The old mining laws were reformed. Taxes on the mining industry were lowered, state supervision ended, and the privileges of the miners' guilds eliminated. By 1860, the emerging mining corporations were free to invest when and where they wanted, while wages were set by market forces and the workers' power to resist change had been effectively eliminated.

Most dramatically, the government became less restrictive in its attitude toward the formation of banks organized as limited liability corporations. The emergence of these new banking corporations, which took the French Crédit Mobilier as their model, revolutionized the financial system and became one of the characteristic features of German economic life. The new banks actively sought opportunities to supply capital to industrial enterprises. In some cases they invested their own capital in new or expanding industrial firms. More commonly, they provided capital to new firms and then marketed the firm's shares. The proceeds from the sale of shares repaid their initial investment, and ongoing connections with the firms providing further opportunities for profit.

Cycles: the international economy

Germans were not alone in their good fortune. Exports from the Zollverein rose at 4.9 per cent per year during the 1850s and 1860s.[10] This reflected the buoyant conditions of the world economy. Steamships and railroads moved goods and people, and the telegraph provided information more rapidly than ever before. The outlines of the American, Russian, and Indian railroad systems emerged in the 1860s; in 1869, the first transatlantic telegraph cable was laid and the Suez Canal was opened. Some new markets were opened by force. Following the Opium War in 1839–40, Britain forced China to open several ports to trade, the American navy arrived in Japan in 1854 to demand trading rights, the British imposed a commercial treaty on Thailand in 1855, and the British, French, and Russians forced China to grant further concessions to foreign merchants in 1860. Among themselves the governments of the industrial countries pursued a more civilized approach. Exporters benefited from the extension of an international network of liberal trade treaties during the 1860s. The Cobden–Chevalier Treaty signed by France and Britain in 1860 provided not only for substantial reductions in tariffs, but also for extension of the benefits to other countries through "most favored nation" agreements. Over strong Austrian objections, the Prussian government signed a similar treaty with France on behalf of the Zollverein in 1862. The Zollverein signed further treaties with Belgium in 1863, and with Britain in 1865. Austria signed a treaty with Britain in 1865, and with France in 1866. Others in the emerging system included the newly unified Italy, which signed with Britain and France in 1863, and the Netherlands, Switzerland, Sweden, Spain, and Portugal.

But developing economies now had to share the risks of rapid growth as well, as seen in the world financial crisis in 1857. International credit had been stretched by the demands of rapidly expanding trade between Europe and the United States on the one hand, and Europe and Asia on the other. Europeans imported more goods (silk, tea, cotton, rice) from Asia than they exported, and this negative trade balance had to be covered with silver. In 1856–57, silk imports had been especially high. In addition, the Indian Mutiny and the Arrow War launched by Britain and France to gain diplomatic recognition and further access to markets in China led to an abnormally large flow of silver from Europe to Asia.

Suddenly, an exceptionally large grain harvest in the western United States caused a fall in prices. Farmers who could not meet payments on their outstanding loans attempted to borrow additional money from their local bankers, who in turn could not pay their own creditors. The failure of a major bank in Ohio in August led to runs on banks in Pennsylvania and Virginia in September. Further failures led to runs on banks in New York in October, and eighteen failed. By October, firms in Glasgow and Liverpool which had sent goods to the United States on credit now could not be paid; they and their bankers failed, and their collapse in turn bankrupted several large firms in London.

Commercial firms and manufacturers in Hamburg, who either dealt directly with the United States or used British firms as intermediaries, now came under pressure. During November and early December 150 firms failed. Other failures followed in port cities such as Bremen, Stettin, and Danzig, and inland centers such as Berlin, Cologne, Stuttgart, Magdeburg, and Leipzig. The governments of the German states coped in different ways. The Senate of Hamburg placed insolvent firms under administrators and, having been turned down by Prussia, borrowed 750,000 pounds sterling in silver from Austria, which was shipped by special train and used by the Senate to meet the obligations of the firms most likely to be able to repay the advances in the future. The Prussian government suspended the legal limits on interest rates for three months and authorized the Bank of Prussia to make emergency loans to merchants secured by their stocks of goods. The Zollverein's foreign trade declined by 10 per cent from 1857 to 1859, but output did not collapse and even this severe crisis did not deflect the momentum of the upswing.[11]

With a slightly paradoxical reciprocity, the German states became more closely integrated into the international economy at the very time they were becoming more firmly linked to one another. As detailed in Chapter 2, until the 1840s the German states were still more oriented outward, to the rest of the world, than to other German states. These relationships reflected the availability of transportation, particularly the seacoasts, rivers, and early canals. The railroad and new canals added transport routes connecting west and east, and this led to the emergence of a functionally integrated "national" economy. In theory, the distribution of natural resources would determine the location of production, the most efficient producers of raw materials and agricultural products would exchange them for manufactured goods, and all would benefit. In practice, as seen in Chapters 5 and 6, this caused great hardship and bitterness.

The social context: realism as leitmotiv

Culture: the realistic novel

The realistic novel dealt with the problems of this world, and its prot-agonists were preeminently from the most realistic class, the *Bürgertum*. The central characters of novels of the first half of the century tended to be aristocrats. Now popular fiction placed active, energetic members of the *Bürgertum* in the central roles, and a passive, weak aristocracy receded into the background. Authors and their audiences focused on the problems posed by money, position, and conflicting loyalties, and these reflected their present concerns even when transposed into the past.

One of the most popular novels of the second half of the nineteenth century was Gustav Freytag's *Soll und Haben* (*Debit and Credit*, 1855). The hero Anton Wohlfahrt's surname translates as "welfare" and sym-bolizes his story. Most novelists previously included Jews only as minor characters and portrayed them as speaking a kind of pidgin German, but Freytag makes Anton's training and experiences in the world of business run parallel to those of a Jewish childhood acquaintance, Veitel Itzig. Anton begins as an apprentice in a merchant firm, and Veitel is the apprentice of Ehrental, an unscrupulous moneylender. Anton's dedication, willingness to work, honesty, and his reluctance to take full advantage even of a rival's misfortune intersect and contrast with the ruthlessness and sharp dealing of Veitel and Ehrental. Anton ends in the director's office of a respected firm. He wins the love of Sabine, herself a talented businessperson who has bravely defended the firm's interests. Business is a family affair, and a wife is expected to "throw the last taler of their own fortune into the firm's assets" should it be necessary "to rescue the honor of her husband."

The novel celebrates the details of business from the title onward. "When I set a bag of coffee on the scales, I tie an invisible thread between the planter's daughter in Brazil who picked the beans and the young peasant boy who drinks them for breakfast," enthuses Anton. Freytag brushes against the question of nationalism in the case of the Polish revolt against Russian rule, but this was a sensitive subject for a contemporary novel in the mid-1850s "after the confusions of the past years," and his characters concentrate more on making money than on politics. Exemplifying the accelerating geographical mobility and the pull of the cities, Anton and Veitel both move to Breslau, as does the family of the Freiherr von Rothsattel, in the hope their daughter will enjoy wider cultural contacts and acquire more polished manners. The virtues of the urban merchant class contrast in particular with the fecklessness of the aristocracy. Anton "only rarely" accompanies his aristocratic colleague Fink when he goes riding or shooting on Sundays, and the Rothsattels ruin themselves by speculation and overspending.

Although clearly anti-Semitic in its stereotyping, the novel draws a favorable portrait of Ehrental's scholarly son Bernhard: "I studied at university, and since it is not easy for a young man of my religion to obtain a government position and since I can live with my family, I occupy myself with these books." Bernhard's interest in exotic Asian languages codes him as weak, but Freytag admits Jews into the privileged world of business as full participants. Veitel and Ehrental are sharp, but not criminal. A late confrontation between Anton and Veitel describes both of them as speaking in the experienced, sophisticated tones of seasoned businessmen, exchanging technical legal and financial arguments as they dispute.

Julius von Wickede's *Der lange Isaack* (*Tall Isaack*, 1863) was again set in the popular historical milieu of the wars against Napoleon. Wickede's work centers on the admirable Jewish peddler Isaack and his daughters Rebekka and her elder sister Sara. Some of the compliments paid to them are demeaning, for instance when the narrator describes Rebekka's house as "unusually clean for Jews," but Isaack establishes his character by spying on the French and providing crucial information to the German armies. Sara has disappeared, carried off by the French. We later meet her as the mistress of a French garrison commander; as such, she helps a German noblewoman and later secures her father's freedom. Disqualified from a happy ending by her active sexuality, she renounces her sinful life, and ends the novel in Strasbourg supervising a home for orphaned girls. Wickede thus banishes his marginal females to the traditional borderland of Alsace-Lorraine, in limbo between Germany and France.

Rebekka has been taught by her maternal grandfather, "a learned rabbi," who has instilled in her a deep love for the classics of German literature. With "true Christian [*sic*] charity," she offers to nurse a wounded Prussian officer back to health. The officer is rich, a nobleman, patriotic, and a university graduate. It is too good to last, especially as they meet early in a three-volume work. Rebekka reads Goethe, Schiller, and Kloptsock aloud to the nobleman. To her dismay, however, she discovers that he has no interest in the classics. As he recovers, he orders books "more to his taste" from the lending library, but they "were either so trivial or so risqué that [she] scornfully threw them aside after reading only a few pages." He in fact has no interest in any "higher intellectual calling," and for Rebekka this is incomprehensible, "for although she was also a Jew, she was at the same time a true and genuine German."

Rather than the aristocrat who is patriotic but has turned his back on Germany's cultural heritage, Rebekka finds true love with his friend, a non-noble theologian, who shares her love and reverence for the classics of German literature. Again, it is too good to last, for now religion bars the way. The theologian, about to rejoin the army, finally offers to marry her when he returns if she will convert to Christianity. Rebekka refuses. "God's will ordained that I was born a Jew ... If I had been born a Christian, I would have certainly become a true adherent of your religion." The theologian is mortally wounded in the victorious "battle of the nations" at Leipzig. Rebekka rushes to the hospital, where he dies in her arms. Her nerves collapse, and she in turn sickens and dies, at home in the arms of her father Isaack. The narrator concludes, "The souls of the two lovers were now in that better, eternal beyond, where no religious difference could ever separate them."

Written at the beginning of the constitutional crisis in Prussia, *Der lange Isaack* is a better guide to its own time than to the Napoleonic era. The narrator declares that Germany should be unified under a Prussian king and regrets the failure of the Congress of Vienna to unite Schleswig-Holstein with Germany. For Wickede, the German identity is patriotic and cultured, but it is not aristocratic. As in *Soll und Haben*, the aristocracy is portrayed as wasteful, unintelligent, unreliable, and occasionally opportunistic. However, in addition, *Der lange Isaack* sees identity as religious, and religious identities had hardened. Many Jews of the previous generation had converted (Heine for instance), but Rebekka's good character is exemplified precisely in her refusal to convert and marry the man she loves. In contrast, the German noblewoman befriended by Sara reveals her weakness by marrying a French aristocrat and converting to Catholicism, the religion of the enemy. Her punishment is indirect and symbolic—her mother chokes to death on an excessively large serving of Strasbourg liver pâté.[12]

Social thought in the age of realism

Changing patterns in science, art, and literature paralleled alterations in social thought and political theory. Nature had become something to be defined, analyzed, and manipulated, and this seemed to apply to human societies as well. Historical economists such as Karl Bucher and Bruno Hildebrand developed stage theories of economic development that reflected the increasing integration of regional economies. Demands for a more just social order intersected with calls for more modern and universalistic legal structures. This could mean "occupational freedom" and an end to guild privileges, as seen above in the case of the coal miners, but it could also mean Jewish "emancipation" and the elimination of restrictions on residence, marriage, and occupation that Jews had suffered.[13]

On the left, these were the years when Karl Marx developed his synthesis of German Hegelian philosophy, English classical economics, and French Utopian Socialism. *The Communist Manifesto* appeared in 1848, and the first volume of *Capital* in 1867. Through the 1850s and 1860s, Marx and his collaborator Friedrich Engels produced biting commentaries on contemporary events in which they elaborated their vision. For Marx, the competition among capitalists continually drove down profits. This would lead to continual technical progress, but also to the ruin of small producers who could not afford to invest in the new machines. Society would divide into two classes, the capitalist employers and the proletariat, the working class who owned nothing but their labor. Artisans and rural workers would be forced into the "reserve army" of the proletariat, and competition among workers would hold wages at a bare subsistence level. Cycles of boom and depression would eliminate all but the largest firms. "The big capitals beat the small." However, at some point the remaining monopoly capitalists would attempt to reduce wages below subsistence in order to maintain their profits, the proletariat would seize power, and "the expropriators will be expropriated." Having served its function of raising the possibilities of human existence to a new higher level, capitalism would disappear. In the following generations, Marxism became the official ideology of the organized workers' movement, and the debate over the appropriate policy for the movement has continued to the present.

Though it may seem paradoxical, Conservatism also developed a systematic program of philosophical analysis and a corresponding agenda for social change. Social structure and tradition could no longer be assumed as simply given, but required systematic articulation and defense. History seemed to provide the key. The legal scholar Lorenz von Stein drew general principles from the historical development of German law. Wilhelm Heinrich Riehl's multi-volume "natural history" was explicitly intended as the "foundation of a German social policy."[14] Ernst Ludwig von Gerlach and his elder brother Leopold espoused an anti-revolutionary political theology, opposed to the revolutionary "godlessness" of their times. Ernst argued that for a Christian, compromise with revolution was impossible, because modern revolutions rejected the primacy of divine law. The revolutions of 1830 shocked him and other Conservatives, because they showed that 1789 had not been an aberration. He wrote in 1848, "we are facing years full of revolution."

The Gerlachs defended an idea of Germany's "historical" liberties and "corporative freedom" against all forms of "absolutism." The question was how these inherited liberties could be defended. The brothers belonged to the so-called "camarilla" of Conservative advisors surrounding Frederick Wilhelm IV. But they and the camarilla often found their attempts to influence policy frustrated. As seen below, they unsuccessfully opposed the introduction of the constitution, failed in their attempt to promote a greater role for the corporatist Stände in state policy, and also failed to reduce the power of both the elected Landtag and the appointed bureaucracy. Ernst enjoyed greater influence as a journalist and as a member of parliament. In 1848, he collaborated in the foundation of the Kreuzzeitung, and he and Julius Stahl were leaders of the so-called "Kreuzzeitung party" in the Landtag after 1849. Entry into parliament reflected his conviction that Conservatives had to avail themselves of the techniques of their enemies. He therefore helped to move Conservatives to adapt to the new conditions and opportunities of a constitutional system.

A new "German" woman? Domesticity and social reform

As seen in Chapter 3, women played an important active role in the 1848 revolutions. Not all women fought on the barricades, however. Other activist women sought a new definition of authority and citizenship based on a principle of social harmony, and they aimed to begin at the beginning, with the children. The kindergarten movement became the focus of these efforts and expanded rapidly during the revolutions.

Kindergartens sought to provide the framework for a less authoritarian, "motherly" teaching style in contrast to the existing Church-sponsored day care centers supervised by "fatherly" males, and to infuse familial love into public life. Kindergartens brought women and children out of the home into a public institution. More broadly, the movement broke down the barriers between the public and private spheres.

In 1850, Carl and Johanna Kästner Froebel founded the Hamburg Academy for the Female Sex. The Hamburg Academy was the first institute for higher education for females in the German realm. In addition to its academic curriculum, it offered training for kindergarten teachers, with the explicit intent of developing specifically female and "motherly" powers as a basis for social reform and renewal.

Even among the revolutionaries not everyone was pleased with the sudden entry of women into the public realm, and, following the Conservative victory, activist women were persecuted. The victorious Conservative governments viewed the kindergarten movement as a manifestation of dangerous political radicalism. The Froebel Academy was forced to close in 1851 as "part of a conspiracy to convert the youth of the nation to atheism." Many kindergartens were shut as well, some by force.

The public realm was again closed to women. In 1848, Meyer's *Conversations-Lexicon* paraphrased Hegel in its definition of the "disposition of the sexes." The article linked the physiological differences between the sexes with corresponding mental dispositions and therefore with different social roles:

> The male is in preference individual; the female, universal . . . In accordance with the more universal character of women, sensibility predominates—the female is a more feeling creature; in the man because of his greater individuality, reaction predominates—he is a more thinking creature . . . Next the different destinies of the sexes in the external world must be looked at . . . Reproduction is only possible through the cooperation of both; however, the female has unmistakably the largest part to play in this operation—while the woman in the main lays the foundation for the ties which bind the family, the man is the link with the external world; he is the bond between family and family, [and] it is he who is the basis of the state.

The Conservative legal scholar Lorenz von Stein devoted an entire book to *Woman, Her Education and Purpose in Life* (1851), which repeated Hegel's fantasy of the man returning exhausted from his labors in the increasingly hostile modern world, to be greeted and refreshed by his loving wife in a peaceful home. In 1854, Wilhelm Heinrich Riehl wrote a "sociology of the family" in which he argued

> The state [der Staat] is masculine gender, and the social groups (the peasantry [das Bauerntum] and the bourgeoisie [das Bürgertum]) are generis neutrius: what about women? They should remain in the family [die Familie], which, after all, reflects its predominantly feminine character already in the gender of the noun.[15]

The realistic generation added the authority of historical development to these philosophical principles. The persecuted Liberal historian Georg Gervinus also wrote in 1853 that "the woman of today, like the Greek citizen of ancient times, is removed from the common bustle of life . . . [she] does not suffer the degradation of lowly occupations, the turmoil and heartlessness of work" and therefore has become "the basis of the poetic side of society in modern times." According to Ersch and Gruber's *General Encyclopedia of the Sciences and Arts*, which appeared in 1856, the original, true character of woman could only appear over time, and woman's "moral history" demonstrated that her true destiny could only be realized when the family had correctly been recognized as a "worthy" and "high" institution. This they said had only been achieved in Germany at the end of the eighteenth century. Woman was now defined by the family, and the family in turn was defined by woman's role. It was therefore the laws of nature, morality, and history together which established the boundaries of the female role. Now, to step outside those boundaries would be "going against nature" and against the whole flow of human history.[16]

If there were to be an acceptable public role for women, then it would have to reflect these new views of female nature, the family, and history. When Frederick Wilhelm's mental and physical condition deteriorated in the late 1850s, his brother Wilhelm became regent. One action of the resulting "new era" in politics, discussed below, was the lifting of the ban on kindergartens in Prussia. Louise Otto-Peters founded the Allgemeiner Deutscher Frauenverein (General German Women's League) in 1865. In her writing before and during the 1848 revolutions, Otto-Peters had called for equal treatment of boys and girls in education, but she also insisted that their education should be nationalistic in orientation. The fundamental purpose of education, she said, was to instill a sense of Germanness into all pupils, both boys and girls. Otto-Peters

advocated female suffrage, but others did not see a necessity for women
to vote. The Lette Verein, named after its philanthropist founder Adolf
Lette, was established in 1866. Lette broadened the notion of motherhood as a personal virtue. He and other leaders of women's organizations envisaged an active role for reform-minded women in a broad
range of social contexts, but these women were conceived as "mothers"
of society. It was their distinctive and essentially feminine qualities that
would make that society a better place to live, an enlarged home.[17]

Religious divisions and the problem of separate "milieus"

The generation of realism celebrated man's increasing control over
nature, but remained deeply religious. Religion experienced what some
historians have termed a revival. As part of the reaction to the revolutions, Conservative thinkers such as the Gerlachs wished for a return to
religious values, and governments supported organized religion as a
Conservative force. However, these were manifestations of a broader
trend. As seen above, realistic novelists frequently defined both personal
and national identities in religious terms. The very popular and strongly
feminist author Ida Hahn-Hahn converted to Catholicism in 1850. She
had been disillusioned with the revolutions of 1848, dismayed by the
materialist orientation of Communism, and on a personal level suffered
grief and loneliness after the death of her companion in 1849. She
opened a convent in 1855, in which she spent the remaining twenty-five
years of her life. She continued to write extensively, but her writings now
became highly religious in nature.

The new, more intense religiosity contributed to the creation of
increasingly separate milieus. Within urban communities, members of
the elite traditionally regarded their role as leaders of their local society
as paramount. In Cologne, for instance, family histories and other
sources reveal what from the perspective of later generations appears a
surprisingly high level of interreligious mixing and cooperation within
Cologne's bourgeoisie. Members of the elite shared a common politics.
They met, socialized, and, most tellingly, they sometimes married with
little regard to differences in religion.[18] This became less common after
the middle of the century. As seen below, in the political realm the
Bürgertum came to conceive itself more in regional and national terms,
but this new self-definition was also religious. At the local level, this
made it less likely that Protestant, Catholic, or Jewish families would

entertain one another, or that their sons and daughters would meet and marry.

Why would religious divisions increase? One explanation sees the answer in the changing social position of religious leaders. According to Oliver Janz, after 1850 Protestant pastors came to constitute a "particular sort" of middle class, a separate occupational caste increasingly differentiated from other groups within the *Bürgertum*. In particular, they became separate from the new class of industrial entrepreneurs. The new clerical subculture can be traced through recruitment and training, career profiles, associational activities, and economic position. This encapsulation resulted partly from a loss of traditional status and functions. Protestant pastors faced new competition from alternative forms of communication such as newspapers, from alternative forms of sociability such as voluntary associations, and also the end to clerical monopolies in areas such as marriage registration and school supervision.

The increasing separateness of Protestant pastors also reflected factors internal to the Church. Resurgent orthodox and pietist theologies that stressed the primacy of a pastor's spiritual and liturgical duties caused a significant "resacralization" of the clerical vocation. They therefore emphasized the difference in social identity between the clergy and laypersons, just at the time when the traditional "representational" functions of the clergy were declining. Sacralization was accompanied by an increasing bureaucratization. New pastors' associations and uniform salary schedules indicate a greater degree of professional identity. However, pastors' salaries dropped well behind the incomes of successful industrial and commercial leaders, and the numbers of university students studying theology declined. Pastors compensated by discovering a new sense of identity and purpose in civil service models and their ties to the state. The rhetoric of "throne and altar" and the aggressive anti-Catholicism that marked the next generations therefore may have reflected not a Protestant triumphalism but the status anxiety of Protestant religious leaders.[19]

Parallel developments marked the Catholic religious community. Catholics had periodically found themselves at odds with Protestant rulers. In 1837–39, Catholics had rioted against government intervention in "Church affairs" in the Rhineland, Westphalia, and Posen, and in 1845 and 1846 there were religious riots in Leipzig and Cologne.[20] Nevertheless, Catholic members of urban elites shared their Protestant compatriots' conception of themselves as a unified ruling class. The rise of ultramontane Catholic piety changed this situation, for it forced a process of differentiation. Catholics had to choose between two social milieus, the ultramontane Catholicism that combined personal religious experience with the authority of the Pope in Rome, and the Protestant-dominated public realm.[21]

As in the Protestant case, there were factors internal to the Church. Confronted first by the revolutions of 1848 and then by the increasingly secular Italian national movement, the Papacy moved in a Conservative direction. In the German states, local priests typically came from lower social levels than Protestant pastors. Less well educated, but committed to defending the interests of their parishioners, they blamed members of other religious groups—Protestant capitalists, Jewish moneylenders—for the difficulties of Catholic farmers. The cooperative banks founded by Friedrich Raiffeisen and his followers were intended to provide credit to small farmers, and the movement was intimately connected with the Catholic religious revival. At the upper levels, the Church hierarchy was concerned primarily with discipline and control, but Catholic leaders were also aware of and reacted to the increasingly intolerant attitudes of Protestant Church leaders. The emerging Catholic milieu was a complex mix of class differences, individual demagogy, and populist politics, held together by an increasingly rigid, ideological religious orthodoxy.

The small Jewish community also experienced the increasing separateness and significance of religious identities. The traditional hostility and legal disabilities that Jews suffered had always pressed some Jews toward conversion, but the small size of the German Jewish community (400,000 in 1850 and 512,000 in 1870, 1.25 per cent of the population) made conversion a threat to its existence. Early in the nineteenth century, converts had tended to be women who married Christian men. In the 1830s and 1840s, converts tended to be men seeking careers.[22] Beginning in 1848, extending through the 1860s and finally completed in the North German Confederation in 1869, legal emancipation opened the possibility of moving to previously forbidden places and practicing previously forbidden occupations without conversion. Higher levels of literacy, particularly of women, and experience in mobility enforced by population restrictions in the separate Jewish quarters of the cities, prepared Jews to take advantage of the opportunities of an expanding economy. Prejudice remained and channeled Jews away from government service and the military. Talented Jews came to be over-represented in banking, commerce, the professions, entertainment, and higher education.[23]

Jews could seize the opportunities of the expanding economy, and they could now do so as Jews. One was not forced to be a Jew, bound by the walls and rituals of the ghetto, but one could now be what David Sorkin has labeled a "voluntary Jew."[24] This could lead in the direction of Reform Judaism, which placed greater emphasis on the eternally valid religious and moral elements of Jewish teaching than on the specific ritual observances of the traditional ghetto community. On the other hand, it could and often did lead in the direction of Orthodox Judaism, which emphasized the importance of precisely those rituals often rejected by Reform Jews. With intellectual support from scholars such as the historian Zacharias Frankel, in the new legal context conservatives were now free to establish their own congregations if they wished. Rival Reform and Orthodox synagogues were present in most large cities by the last third of the century. And, even among the most assimilated Jews, actual conversion to Christianity and marriage to non-Jews remained rare. Though they might have discarded traditional dress and observance, "German citizens of the Jewish faith" were conscious and proud of their distinctiveness.

Proposals for Jewish emancipation could become the flashpoint for outbursts of hostility, but this was no longer simply traditional anti-Semitism. James Harris questions the usual dichotomies of "religious" vs. "modern" and "traditional" vs. "racial" forms of anti-Semitism. He argues that, in Bavaria, anti-Semitic attitudes were projected in a "modern" way in the aftermath of the 1848 Revolution, and therefore sees modern anti-Semitism as emerging earlier than most scholars. However, in this case, racism was not a key factor. The "not-so-simple country folk" held a "complex conceptualization of Jews" which combined their hostility toward the parliamentary government introduced in 1848 with a centuries-old anti-Semitism. They typically expressed their hostility through petitions, and Harris analyzes over 500 such petitions, and argues that, despite their opposition to parliamentary democracy and to modernity, farmers were willing and able to use democratic and modern means of mobilization and expression to express their wish not to be obliged to have Jews in their midst.

Most opponents of emancipation argued that, because of Jewish "talent" for business, simple Bavarian peasants were unable to compete and faced economic ruin. On the other hand, in most communities of Bavaria there were no Jews at all, and those supporting emancipation "ridiculed the fear that over four million Bavarian peasants felt toward fewer than 60,000 Jews," and pressed the point home by continuing that if they could not compete, "that said little for the intelligence of the Christians." Bavarian officials were attempting to introduce a progressive program using traditional authoritarian means, and the farmers resisted it using modern democratic forms of expression. An "antirevolutionary conservative state championed Jewish equality with Christians," and in this case the state bureaucrats were opposed by a majority expressing their will democratically.[25]

The political context: the politics of reaction and the politics of unification

Reaction and realism

The defeat of the revolutions brought repression: waves of arrests, the flight of thousands of activists, dismissal of liberal ministers, renewed censorship. Expanded police forces and improved communications enabled governments to pursue opposition leaders and contain popular demonstrations. However, although reactionaries hoped for a complete suppression of all forms of liberalism, they were disappointed. Constitutional government remained after the revolutions in most states. Encouraged by his Conservative courtiers, in 1851 Frederick William IV returned to his monarchical project and ordered that the district and provincial estates (*Stände*) be reestablished. He would have preferred to withdraw the new constitution, but his successive Minister-Presidents Friedrich von Brandenburg, Josef Maria von Radowitz, and Otto von Manteuffel all insisted that it be retained. In their view, the defeat of the revolutions meant that a new struggle with Austria would begin. Repression would create internal opposition and weaken Prussia in this more important conflict. A constitution need not interfere with bureaucratic administration, but it would win internal support and therefore strengthen Prussia.

"We can absolutely rule with this constitution," said Manteuffel. The document was a grant from the king, reaffirmed his right to rule, gave him an absolute veto over legislation, and allowed him to issue emergency decrees should he see fit. Separate articles placed the army outside parliamentary control. The king's rights to appoint his officers and to exercise supreme command were guaranteed, and soldiers swore allegiance to the king, not to the constitution. A new upper house (the *Herrenhaus*) dominated by hereditary peers and royal appointees added a further bulwark to royal authority. The king's senior ministers of course expected to exercise these powers on behalf of their monarch, and they expected their subordinates to obey. The lower levels of the bureaucracy were placed under stricter discipline. Serving officials guilty of "inappropriate expression of oppositional private opinions" were punished. New restrictions on probationary appointees ensured that only those with correct opinions would move on to permanent positions.

The electoral system supported Conservative interests as well, for it reflected the interests of property owners. Elections to the lower house of the Landtag were indirect. Voters cast their ballots publicly for electors who in turn selected the representatives. Though all adult males could vote, voters in each district were ranked and divided into three classes depending on the amount of taxes they paid. Those in the wealthy first class, who paid one-third of the taxes, elected one-third of the electors. Those in the middle elected another third of the electors, and the mass of voters in the third class elected only the final third of electors. For Prussia as a whole, the 153,000 voters in the first class (4.7 per cent of the total) and the 409,000 in the second class (12.6 per cent) could easily expect to outvote the remaining 2.69 million (82.7 per cent) third-class voters. In Berlin, with 430,000 inhabitants, there were 2350 voters in the first, 7232 in the second, and 67,375 in the third class.[26] Local officials were instructed to do all in their power to ensure that only representatives friendly to the government were returned. Many of them stood themselves. Over 60 per cent of Landtag members elected in 1855 were government officials.

On the other hand, the electoral system led many Liberals to look forward to a future in which they too could rule with this constitution. The lower house possessed the important right to approve the government budget. The indirect voting system resembled the systems widely used in local elections in Prussia's western provinces. Indeed, Prussia's constitution looked quite like the plans for a constitutional monarchy advocated by Rhenish Liberals before 1848. As the economy accelerated, commercial and industrial interests would inevitably increase their electoral power. Through most of the decade these potentially liberal tendencies remained repressed.

Frederick William's declining physical and mental condition led to a drift in Prussian policy in the mid-1850s. His replacement by his brother Wilhelm as regent in 1858 opened what contemporaries hoped would be a "new era" in which the system's potential Liberal tendencies would emerge. In the 1858 elections, the government did not pressure voters or harass the opposition. Participation rates shot up, and Liberals won a resounding victory, trebling their numbers from 60 to over 200, while Conservatives declined from over 200 to fewer than 60. The new era seemed to extend to other German states as well. Liberals scored electoral victories in Saxony and Bavaria, and the Grand Duke of Baden launched a series of reforms in alliance with parliamentary Liberals.

The issue of dominance within the German Confederation also hung in the air through the 1850s. Under Radowitz, Prussia had begun a series of diplomatic moves that could have resulted in the creation of a "small Germany" under Prussian leadership and excluding Austria. Austria retaliated with mobilization and a threat of war, and Prussia retreated. The Confederation was reestablished under Austrian leadership as before. In turn, when Austrian leaders suggested a customs union that would combine all the Hapsburg possessions with the Zollverein, Prussia responded first by bringing Hanover and Oldenburg into the Zollverein on very generous terms, and then pressuring the other members to agree to a twelve-year renewal of the Zollverein treaties in 1853. Austria and Prussia signed a commercial treaty in the same year, but the renewal of the Zollverein treaties effectively excluded Austria from the increasingly integrated economy growing up within the Zollverein's tariff walls.

In 1851, the young Otto von Bismarck, aged 36 and without previous diplomatic experience, was appointed as Prussian representative to the German Diet in Frankfurt. Prince Wilhelm, among others, was shocked. Known only as a violent reactionary in 1848, Bismarck owed his good fortune to his connections among Frederick William's circle of conservative courtiers. From his new position he immediately began to attempt to influence policy. Although critical of Radowitz, as he was of all his superiors, he wrote continually to potential supporters of the inevitability of conflict with Austria. He insulted the Austrian ambassador by lighting a cigar at a session of the Bundestag, a privilege reserved for the president of the assembly, who was always the Austrian representative. More seriously, he confronted the Austrians at every opportunity and severely hampered the proceedings of the Confederation. When Wilhelm became regent, Bismarck immediately produced a long memorandum advocating an anti-Austrian policy and promoting himself as the man to implement it. Wilhelm, however, desired better relations with Austria, and Bismarck was removed from Frankfurt and sent as ambassador to Russia, into "cold storage on the Neva," as he put it.

Liberalism and realism: taxes, transportation, and organization

In the Landtag, the Prussian government and its Liberal opponents gradually moved toward an accommodation, concretely embodied in a reorganization and redirection of government finances. Industrial and commercial interests had complained both that the government was insufficiently active in support of modern industry, and that they paid a disproportionate share of taxes. Now, as seen in Table 4.2, taxes rose substantially, but the proportion paid by the industrial provinces declined. The share of tax revenue distributed by the Ministry of Commerce and Industry under Heydt increased substantially. Government spending was redirected, largely toward railroad construction. After a decline through the 1830s and 1840s, the Prussian government debt nearly doubled from 1848 to 1865, and over half of the increase was spent on railroads.[27]

Outside the state parliaments, new relations were emerging among local identities, state patriotisms, and German nationalism. The public sphere extended, but it also deepened. Wealthy members of the urban elites developed interests beyond their home towns, but at the same time a dense network of public, semi-public, and private organizations connected broad constituencies within localities. Further, the common problems they faced led them to develop their relations with like-minded groups across their states, and across their states' boundaries. These processes can be seen in cities as diverse as Dortmund, Munich, and Frankfurt, and at the state level in Saxony.[28]

Men interested in the liberal agendas of economic and political reform and the creation of a new unified political system came together in a number of public organizations. The German National Association and the Congress of German Economists were both established in 1859, the German Chamber of Commerce in 1861, and the German Diet of Deputies in 1862. The German National Association (*Nationalverein*), the largest, had 25,000 members at its peak. It was not a mass organization, although its numbers compare impressively with the half-million

Table 4.2 Central government spending in Prussia, 1815–66

	1821	1838	1847	1849	1853	1856	1866
Spending, current prices (million taler)	82	86	93	94	103	127	158
Spending, 1913 prices (million taler)	78	69	79	62	102	133	147
Spending per capita, 1913 prices (taler)	7.0	4.7	4.9	3.8	6.0	7.7	7.5
Distribution of spending (per cent)							
Military	27	31	28	29		27	29
Debt	13	13	8	8		11	11
Commercial[1]	16	16	19	27		30	31
Administrative	44	40	44	36		32	29
Government debt (million taler)							
Funded, total	207	164	138			228	269
(of which, for railroads)						(83)	(105)
Paper money and note issue	11	18	32			31	79
Distribution of revenue (per cent)							
Non-tax	34	34	34	35		44	51
Tax	65	66	66	65		56	49
Distribution of land tax (per cent)							
Agrarian provinces[2]	25	25					39
Industrial provinces[3]	75	75					61

Notes:

1. Mines, forest, Crown lands, railroads, postal services, and expenditures by the Ministries of Commerce and Industry to 1848, and by the Ministry of Commerce, Industry, and Public Works thereafter.

2. Pomerania, Posen, Brandenburg, Prussia.

3. Rhineland, Westphalia, Saxony, Silesia.

Source: Adapted from Richard H. Tilly, "The political economy of public finance and the industrialization of Prussia, 1815–1866," *Journal of Economic History* 26 (1966): 484–97.

electors in the first two electoral classes in Prussia. Its members were the elite of the *Bürgertum*, merchants, industrialists, academics, lawyers, Protestant clergymen, state officials, and journalists.

The leaders of these cross-state organizations made up an interlocking group of some 80 men dedicated to the cause of German unification. A majority of them were Prussian, but they came from all the German states except Austria. Four-fifths of them were Protestant. A quarter were lawyers, another quarter journalists and writers, a fifth merchants or industrialists. About half depended on their political activities for most of their income. That is, rather than representing any particular class, they were increasingly professional politicians. This group developed and advocated programs that they hoped would promote German unity. Through their organizational work and pragmatic political activity, this "functional elite" worked toward a radical transformation of the German Confederation from a loose grouping of states into a single national state. Their definition of a national state remained a federal structure, but their vision of the future included a strong centralized executive power.

The question remained as to the means to achieve the end. Rochau had written in 1853 that "the practical question has only to do with the simple fact that it is power alone that can rule." These were practical, realistic men, and they were quite willing to consider military conquest. Some of them, and some of the members of their organizations, had careers that extended back to 1848. The Frankfurt parliament had used force against perceived enemies, both external in Schleswig-Holstein and internal in Frankfurt itself. Unification might take the form of a European war, but these men saw war as a road to national unity. War, they felt, if carried out by an army of the people, was an acceptable and obvious means to achieve the desired end of a national revolution. Andreas Biefang, in his study of this group, concludes that, if they had succeeded in their strategy, "the founding of the German empire would have been no less bloody."[29]

And what of Prussia, the obvious key to any "small German" program? The leaders of the national reform organizations saw economic and political unification as tandem processes. Prussia, as the leader of the Zollverein and center of much of the new industrial development, came to seem more and more progressive in the economic sphere, especially compared to Austria. Politically, however, the reactionary Prussian regime seemed out of step with the modern realistic world. Even economic policies that might appear progressive were pursued in an arbitrary and authoritarian manner, often over the opposition of private business interests.[30]

As Minister for Trade and Commerce, Heydt pressed at every opportunity for extension of the government's railroad system. He used his extensive powers of supervision over private railroads ruthlessly, and he was accused of forcing railroads into unprofitable operations such as night trains, in order to bankrupt them so they could be more easily acquired by the government. Private investors were outraged at his exploitation of the legal provisions that allowed him to impose taxes on railroads that could be used to purchase their shares, in effect forcing the railroad companies to pay for their own nationalization. They also opposed his attempts to purge the postal and the railroad departments to eliminate former revolutionary leaders or any employee suspected of "democratic" sentiments.[31] Heydt, however, insisted that, because of their importance, railroads must be run by "reliable persons." He also insisted that the main function of the railroads was to maintain the "authority of the state." "Short-sighted" private economic considerations were unimportant, and even the government's income played a subordinate role in his vision.[32]

The Zollverein gave Prussia another lever of power. The smaller states had become financially dependent on the tariff revenues collected and distributed by Prussia.[33] Industrialists complained that the tariffs were too low; there were free-trade advocates within the Prussian government, but low tariffs were also intended to make any attempt to join by Austria, which had high tariffs, as difficult as possible. Prussia had treated commercial treaties as war by other means for a long time, extending back to the original Zollverein negotiations. In 1861–62, Prussia accepted a French proposal for a most favored nation clause in the proposed commercial treaty, knowing that this would make it impossible to renew the Austro-Prussian commercial treaty of 1853, which had granted special preferences to Austrian goods. The subsequent Austrian protest was rejected by Prussian Foreign Minister Albrecht von Bernstorff: "I must, with the utmost decision, claim for the Zollverein the full right to act in this respect as they themselves think proper." Austria then proposed a new version of the earlier plan for an Austrian–Prussian customs union that would have absorbed the existing Zollverein. The Prussians rejected the proposal because, they said, such a customs union would violate the terms of the new Franco-Prussian treaty.[34]

The Prussian constitutional crisis

Wilhelm declared his intention to rule according to the constitution, but he was also intensely conservative, and he was a professional soldier.[35] He had commanded the Prussian forces that invaded Baden in 1849. When he became regent, he turned his attention to the needs of the army: expansion, new equipment, and improved training. In 1859, he approved proposals for army reform prepared by Albrecht von Roon and named him war minister. This was not surprising, particularly since the army had not grown as rapidly as Prussia's population and remained organizationally much as it had been half a century earlier.

But the program presented to the Landtag by Roon shocked the majority of Liberal deputies. Along with an increase in the number of line regiments and a rise in the period of active service from two years to three, the reforms envisaged a substantial reduction in the militia. Roon made no secret of his contempt for civilians, his intention to use the extended period of service to instill Conservative habits of mind into recruits, and his belief that the militia was militarily ineffective and very possibly subversive. Nourished in part by a diet of novels set in the Napoleonic wars, Liberals cherished an exaggerated vision of the role played by the militia in "national liberation." They feared the effects of extended military indoctrination, they objected to the proposed increase in expenditure, and, most of all, they suspected the government's motives. The army had after all been used primarily to repress domestic political opposition for as long as anyone could remember.

The Landtag refused to pass the budget embodying the reforms, but agreed to a provisional budget on condition that the government not proceed until a regular budget was passed. Wilhelm and Roon reneged on their promise and began the formation of the new regiments, and they refused any compromise on the length of service or on the position of the militia. Wilhelm became king on his brother's death in January 1861, but a new and more determined opposition group had formed in the Landtag. In the December elections, the German Progressive Party (*Deutsche Fortschrittspartei*) won a decisive victory. The new Landtag rejected the budget presented by a new Conservative ministry, and the government dissolved the assembly and called new elections. Held in May, they resulted in an even larger opposition majority. The

Landtag again rejected the budget and was again dissolved. Prince Hohenlohe-Ingelfingen became Minister-President, but failed to find a compromise. Heydt's brief turn as head of the government in 1862 ended in another crushing electoral defeat.[36]

Wilhelm heard contradictory advice. Some advocated confrontation, possibly hoping to provoke violence. Others suggested compromise proposals. Wilhelm seriously considered abdicating in favor of his son Frederick, a man of reputedly Liberal sympathies. However, Roon persuaded him to make a final attempt to appoint a new minister forceful enough to defy the Liberal majority in the Landtag and salvage the army reform. His suggestion for the post of Minister-President was Bismarck, and Wilhelm agreed.

Bismarck[37] was no more successful than his predecessors. At his first appearance before the Landtag's budget committee he said,

> The position of Prussia in Germany will be determined not by its liberalism but by its power. Bavaria, Württemberg, and Baden may indulge themselves in liberalism but no one will assign to them the role of Prussia; Prussia must concentrate its strength and hold it for the favorable moment ... Not through speeches and majority decisions will the great questions of the day be decided—that was the great mistake of 1848 and 1849—but through iron and blood.

The members of the committee were not impressed. They rejected the compromise he put to them. Invoking the king's right to rule by decree in an emergency, Bismarck announced his intention to continue even without a majority. When compromise becomes impossible, he said, "conflicts become a question of power. Whoever holds the power then proceeds according to his own will, for the life of the state cannot remain still even for a second."

Bismarck was able to counter an Austrian proposal to reform the German Confederation, but only by mobilizing the smaller states who feared any change in the status quo. His anti-Austrian policy disturbed Conservatives, and he became the personification of evil for the Liberals when he launched a campaign of censorship and intimidation against them. So long as he retained his king's confidence, Bismarck was invulnerable, but the portents were not promising. The government dissolved the Landtag yet again, but the elections in October 1863 brought another impressive victory for the Liberals. Municipal governments, local meetings, and the spearhead national organizations all condemned

Bismarck and the government. Progressive parties formed in other states in support of the Prussian Liberals, a flood tide of public opinion that appeared irresistible.

Realism in action: war and unification

Bismarck found his salvation in three short, successful wars, each waged against overconfident and isolated opponents. In late 1863, German federal troops occupied Holstein. The Confederation acted in support of the claims of a German prince to Schleswig and Holstein, with broad support from German Liberals. Then, in January 1864, Austria and Prussia together invaded Schleswig. They acted without the support of the other states of the German Confederation, and public opinion was strongly opposed. Austrian leaders hoped to use the joint action to achieve an ongoing relationship with Prussia that would guarantee the Conservative status quo, but Bismarck was considering the possibilities both of annexing the duchies to Prussia and of moving against Austria. Crucially, Britain failed to support Denmark as Danish leaders expected, and they were forced to surrender.

By the spring of 1865, Bismarck had convinced Wilhelm that Prussia should indeed annex Schleswig and Holstein. In addition, he had lured Austria into a complex arrangement under which Austria administered Holstein while Prussia controlled Schleswig. This made the Austrian occupation forces continually vulnerable to Prussian harassment. Further, Austria was friendless among the great powers. During the Crimean War in 1856, when Britain and France had attacked Russia in the Black Sea, Austria had mobilized its army along its eastern border, but had not actually declared war. Austrian mobilization made it impossible for Russia to move an army south to cut the British–French supply lines, and helped ensure Russia's defeat. Russian leaders regarded this as a reprehensible betrayal after the assistance Russia had given Austria in 1849, while, for their part, Britain and France considered that Austria had not done enough to aid them. Then, in 1858, Austria declared war on Piedmont, thereby triggering a secret alliance between Piedmontese leader Camilio Cavour and the French Emperor Napoleon III. Austria lost a province, and, by 1861, Cavour had nearly completed the unification of Italy under Piedmontese leadership. Bismarck ensured Austria's isolation with a three-month promise of support from Italy and series of complex negotiations with Napoleon that seemed to

Map 3   The unification of Germany, 1864–71

promise France some sort of territorial gains without making any definite commitment.

An exchange of threatening notes with Austria over popular agitation in Holstein gave Bismarck the opportunity to tell Wilhelm that there were only three choices he could make: a new Liberal ministry, abrogation of the constitution, or war. A subsequent meeting of the king's advisors supported his decision that the time had come for a final confrontation with Austria. However, public opinion was hostile to Bismarck's policy. In Prussia and elsewhere in the German states, both Conservatives and Liberals opposed the drift toward a "German civil war." In the final confrontation, all the major German states sided with Austria. On June 14, 1866, in the Diet at Frankfurt, Austria moved for a federal execution against Prussia for violating "federal" territory in Holstein, seconded by Bavaria, Saxony, and Hanover. Prussia declared the federal constitution to have been violated, and the Confederation at an end, and the two sides were at war.

The Austrians believed that they possessed superior forces, particularly in cavalry and artillery, and that their infantry would prevail by attacking with fixed bayonets. Foreign observers agreed and rated Prussia's army several notches lower than Austria's. However, the Prussian infantry was now armed with a new breech-loading "needle gun," a rifle with a rate of fire five or six times greater than the Austrian muzzleloaders, and which could be fired and reloaded from a prone position. To take advantage of the new weapon, new, more flexible small unit tactics had also been developed. Tactically, this meant that the Prussians were able to hold ground against Austrian assaults even though outnumbered.

Prussia defeated the other German states with relative ease, and then moved against Austria. The Prussian Chief of Staff, Helmuth von Moltke, made the strategically risky decision to divide his forces and send two separate armies by railroad into Bohemia. The Austrians also moved north by rail. The railroad allowed for the deployment of larger numbers of troops than had ever fought before (a total of 280,000 Prussians and 270,000 Austrians), but, once they left the rail lines, the very size of the armies made effective control difficult. Moltke lost contact with his commanders. The battle that actually occurred was not the one he had planned. In the morning of July 3, 1866, one of his commanders attacked an Austrian force he had encountered between Sadowa and Königgrätz. This proved to be the main Austrian army. The Austrian commanders were divided and did not take advantage of their superior numbers. Instead, the second Prussian force arrived on the Austrian flank, seized the high ground, and held it against Austrian counterattacks. The Austrians suffered heavy casualties and were forced to withdraw under cover of their superior artillery.[38]

In the evening of July 3, one of Wilhelm's aides remarked to Bismarck, "you are now a great man. But if the Crown Prince had arrived too late, you would be the greatest scoundrel in the world." Austria appealed to Napoleon III, and he announced that he would mediate an end to the war. Bismarck accepted, because he feared actual French intervention and possibly Russian involvement as well. He then worked himself close to nervous exhaustion to restrain Wilhelm, now furious and determined to punish and humiliate the Austrians. The peace settlement signed in August 1866 left Austria intact, but it dissolved the German Confederation. Prussia annexed Schleswig and Holstein, Hanover, Hesse-Cassel, Frankfurt, and Nassau. The states north of the Main River joined with Prussia in a new North German Confederation.

In Prussia, the Danish war had already shifted public sympathy toward the government. In another election held coincidentally the same day as the battle at Königgrätz, but before the outcome was known, the Liberal opposition suffered serious losses, and Conservative deputies increased from 38 to 142. News of the victory at Königgrätz resulted in an upsurge of patriotic feeling and created a crisis for the Liberals. Hermann Baumgarten declared Liberalism bankrupt:

> Almost all the elements of our political system have been shown erroneous by the facts themselves . . . Having found out that, in a monarchical state, the aristocracy constitutes an indispensable part, and having seen that these much abused Junkers know how to fight and die for the fatherland . . . we will restrict our bourgeois fantasies a little . . . the citizen is born to work but not to be a statesman.[39]

Heinrich von Treitschke went overnight from scornful opposition to Bismarck ("fancy pants" or *Schönhosen*, a play on Bismarck's family name of Schönhausen) to supporting "the imperial crown of the Hohenzollerns . . . the oldest and noblest in the world." Rudolf Ihering had said he would "prefer to cut off my hand rather than to use it in such a disgusting operation as Prussian policy is now launching against Austria," but months later, after the Prussian victory, he said, "I bow before the genius of Bismarck . . . one of the greatest men of the century."[40] Many others underwent similar conversions.[41]

Bismarck stunned Conservatives as well, first by his ruthless disregard of the rights of legitimate sovereigns in the annexations and reorganization of northern Germany, and second by offering a compromise to the Liberals. In a bill presented to the Landtag, the government admitted that it had collected taxes illegally since 1862 and requested in return that the Landtag retrospectively approve the government's actions. The indemnity bill passed overwhelmingly, opposed only by a few Progressives and Catholics. A new National Liberal Party formed in the new Reichstag in 1867, enthusiastically devoted to Bismarck and dedicated to supporting Prussia unconditionally in foreign affairs, but looking forward explicitly to the day when the four southern states would be united with the north. The *Nationalverein* dissolved itself in October 1867.

Bismarck's final victory also owed much to chance. In 1870, the Sigmaringen branch of the Hohenzollern family was offered the crown of Spain. Bismarck urged them to accept. He was certainly looking for a foreign policy success, and he may have feared that if they refused the offer might go to one of the ruling families of the southern German states. French leaders, intent on scoring a victory against Prussia, opposed the offer. French pressure on Spain led the Spanish government to suggest to the Sigmaringens that they could withdraw, which they did. This stunning diplomatic success left Bismarck wondering whether he should resign. However, the French overplayed their hand, and on July 13, 1870, the French ambassador met Wilhelm, who was on vacation at Bad Ems, and requested that he confirm the withdrawal, which he did, and that he agree that the candidature never be renewed, which he refused to do. Bismarck edited the telegram reporting this incident for public release, but he had already decided to go to war. Napoleon III, his government in a crisis state, could not back down, and France declared war first, on July 19, 1870.

In contrast to 1866, public opinion enthusiastically endorsed the war. Prussia was immediately supported by Baden, Württemberg, and Bavaria. Altogether the German states mobilized 1.8 million men and moved 462,000 to the French border in less than three weeks. France was isolated as Austria had been. The continued occupation of Rome alienated Italy, Britain was suspicious of French attempts to acquire railroad lines in Belgium and Luxemburg, in Austria Liberals and the Hungarian government opposed any new war, and Bismarck put Russia off with vague promises of support for changes in the treaty that had ended the Crimean War. Disastrously, French mobilization was slow, and they could field only half as many men initially as the Germans. The combined German forces pushed through the Lorraine gap. In a series of battles they suffered heavier casualties than the French, but they used their superior numbers to penetrate between Paris and the two main French armies. They pushed one back to Metz, and, when the other moved to assist, they attacked on its flank and pinned it against the Belgian border at Sedan. Napoleon III and 100,000 French troops surrendered; a republic was declared in Paris.

There was more fighting, at Metz and around Paris, but Bismarck now insisted on control. He obtained orders from Wilhelm that forced the army commanders to defer to his political direction. This enabled him to restrain Moltke, in particular, who had been carried away by his hatred for the French and planned a series of humiliations that would have made peace more difficult. The peace that Bismarck imposed was severe enough. Alsace and Lorraine were annexed, a large indemnity imposed, and northern France was to be occupied until the indemnity was paid. As the war with France wound down, Bismarck began negotiations with the southern German states to join in a new German empire. Again despite objections, in particular from Crown Prince Frederick, Bismarck agreed to a federal structure within which the non-Prussian states retained substantial rights.

Finally, on January 18, 1871, in the Hall of Mirrors in the palace at Versailles, the German Empire was proclaimed. Wilhelm had wanted to become "Wilhelm, by the grace of God, King of Prussia, chosen Emperor of Germany." Bismarck, however, insisted on "by the grace of God, German Emperor, King of Prussia." This was the form used in the treaties with the southern states and in the revisions to the constitution of the North German Confederation. These were sufficiently delicate that Bismarck did not want to have to open the negotiations again. Wilhelm agreed that the imperial title must come first, but he wept at the thought that he must "take leave of the old Prussia." He continued to insist on "Emperor of Germany" (Kaiser Deutschlands) rather than "German Emperor" (Deutscher Kaiser) because he wanted it clear that his authority over all of Germany was absolute. Bismarck refused. In the event, the Grand Duke of Baden, as the highest-ranking prince present, simply cried, "Long live his imperial and royal majesty, Kaiser Wilhelm!" Wilhelm descended to accept congratulations, but passed by Bismarck without a word or a handshake.

Bismarck

Bismarck has inspired a great number of biographers.[42] Contemporaries and subsequent historians have all recognized the rupture of the foundation of the empire. Bismarck's role was central. Bismarck himself insisted that his policies had "solved" the German "problem," and he also insisted that his solution was the only one. However, no subsequent diplomatic historian has argued that these wars were in any sense inevitable; indeed, Bismarck's masterful exploitation of a narrow window of opportunity to begin each of his wars, and his careful concern over the limitation of war aims to attainable and sustainable goals, are typically seen as the very essence of his art, even by his detractors.[43] But the ultimate meaning of Bismarck's success remains in dispute, as does his own character. Some see him as a reactionary Junker, some as a forward-looking statesman, some as brutal and ruthless, some as reflective and moderate. And some see his vision of Germany and of Europe as firmly grounded, while others view his creation as essentially flawed and unstable.

The subsequent debates over Bismarck and the meaning of his achievement, however, relate largely to what came after 1871, that is, to subsequent generations. Looked at from the standpoint of contemporaries, at the moment of his greatest triumph, Bismarck seems not so terribly complex. He had been guided by an unswerving loyalty to the royal house of Hohenzollern, imbued with the values of the Prussian ruling establishment, and committed to maintaining and extending the power of the Prussian state. In addition, he was intensely ambitious personally, and he was well aware that he served at the pleasure of his monarch. As previous generations of statesmen, therefore, Bismarck had to pursue "geopolitical" policies, based on the objective situation of his state as he saw it, but at the same time he was forced to play the game of "high politics," the competition with rival officials for the ruler's favor.

Bismarck's great advantages were his tactical flexibility and a remarkable sense of timing. Once given his chance to wield power, he played high politics to perfection, always able to convince Wilhelm that his vision of Prussian interests was the true one, and that his proposed policy was the only way to guarantee those interests. He succeeded in keeping his real and potential enemies divided and off balance. His geopolitical assessment of Prussia's position included reliance on the army (also Wilhelm's primary interest) and the sense that Prussia's position could only be improved at the expense of Austria. He had no plan for German unity, but the demands for unification of the German states were one of the forces he had to consider, and he addressed the issue in stages as opportunities arose. Unity, if it came, would be in Prussia's best interests, and it would be achieved on his terms, no matter whether he was opposed by Liberals in the Prussian Landtag, by Conservative Prussians, by Austria, by the other states of the Confederation, or by the other powers.

Realpolitik was therefore both realism and ideology. Bismarck cultivated the myth that he had merely been realistic, had merely recognized the objective facts and responded to them, or, as he put it, that he had merely seized the hem of the divine cloak and been carried on to the goal of unification. In part this was true, but Bismarck had also shaped events, notably in engineering the outbreak of war with Austria and with France. He claimed that his vision was simply a reporting of objective reality, and that his policies and their success had been inevitable. He therefore appealed to the sensibilities of the generation of realism. But of course it suited his interests, those of his master Wilhelm, and those of the Prussian conservative establishment, to have all those "Germans" who happened to be included in the new empire believe that its foundation was inevitable, and that there had been no alternatives.

Possibly we can obtain a more balanced view of Bismarck if we look at one of his opponents, not among the defeated and coopted Liberals, but among the alienated Conservatives. On the face of it, they should have been delighted by the victory of the Junker over the upstart revolutionaries of 1848. But they were not, and the reasons for their disaffection point to the contradictions contained in Bismarck's solution to the German problem. In an ironic way the contradictions themselves are testimony to Bismarck's genius. Ernst Ludwig von Gerlach was deeply shocked by the war with Austria. Bismarck and the Gerlachs traveled in the same circles, and he had revealed the anti-Austrian direction of his thinking in a letter to Leopold in 1853. They opposed him then, vehemently. Thirteen years later, in 1866 on the eve of war, Ernst wrote that the dualism of Austria and Prussia was "the vital foundation, the real basis for a German constitution." Whatever the deficiencies in the Confederation, "they would not lead me to devastate my family or my fatherland." His opposition to Bismarck continued after 1866, based on his rejection of a politics of "amoral state interest." Finally, he concluded that a renewal of traditional Prussian Conservatism was impossible. Despite his Protestant faith, he decided in despair that the Catholic Center Party offered the only basis for effective opposition to Bismarck's policies.[44]

Notes

1. Rochau 1853.
2. Adolph von Menzel, illustrations for Kugler's *History of Frederick the Great*, 1840–42. See Keisch and Riemann-Reyher 1996.

3. Lorenz Clasen, *Germania auf der Wacht am Rhein* (*Germania on Watch at the Rhine*), 1860. Oil on linen, 220 × 159 cm. Kaiser Wilhelm Museum, Krefeld. See Gall 1993.
4. Hoffmann 1965, pp. 257, 338–43, 390–5, 454–5.
5. Kunz 1994.
6. Blackbourn 1997, p. 280; Brophy 1998, p. 22.
7. Tipton 1994.
8. Fremdling 1975; 1977.
9. Herrigal 2000.
10. Hoffmann 1965, pp. 530–2.
11. Henderson 1975, pp. 119–22.
12. Peterson 1997.
13. See Beck 1995; Lindenfeld 1997.
14. Riehl 1854.
15. 12th edn. 1904, p. 13.
16. Hausen 1981.
17. Prelinger 1987; Allen 1991.
18. Mergel 1994.
19. Janz 1994.
20. Sheehan 1989, pp. 642–3.
21. Mergel 1994.
22. Lowenstein 1994.
23. Lowenstein 1980.
24. Sorkin 1987.
25. Harris 1994.
26. Wehler 1995, Vol. 3, p. 201.
27. Tilly 1966b.
28. Roth 1996; Schambach 1996; Zerback 1997; Retallack 1998, pp. 405–6.
29. Biefang 1994, p. 435.
30. See Breuilly 1996.
31. Brophy 1998, Chs. 3, 4, 6.
32. Bergengrün 1908, pp. 144–6; Brophy 1998, pp. 54–7.
33. Hahn 1982.
34. Henderson 1975, p. 153.
35. See Craig 1955.
36. Brophy 1998, pp. 141, 152.
37. See Pflanze 1990, Vol. 1.
38. Craig 1964; Wawro 1996.
39. Baumgarten 1866.
40. Simon 1968.
41. Faber 1966; see Breuilly 1996.
42. See Pflanze 1990.
43. Engelberg 1990; Hildebrand 1995.
44. Kraus 1994.

CHAPTER 5

AN ANXIOUS GENERATION, 1871–90

From realism to neoclassicism

Adolf von Menzel displayed imperial Germany's public image in *Supper at the Ball*, painted in 1878.[1] A relaxed moment in a gala evening shows a large and very crowded room with groups of guests eating their meal, mingling, and conversing. Banks of candles in candelabras, some held by statues and others in overhead chandeliers, dispense a brilliant but somewhat uneven light. In a pocket of shadow on the left, an officer stands bent over his plate, his uniform hat pressed between his knees, while a man next to him essays cutting his meat while balancing his champagne glass on his plate. Near the center, an abandoned plate lies on the seat of a chair, champagne glass and knife and fork laid across it. To the right, a group of ladies sit, eating, talking, and, in one case, flirting with a seated officer. Another officer bends over one of them, serving her a plate and a full glass. The scene recedes beyond a pair of pillars into a spacious hall, past massive paintings framed in gold and reflecting light back over this relaxed and happy gathering.

But, despite its informal mood and attention to detail, this is not a realistic painting. The canvas is divided into four equal sections by the vertical lines marking the edges of the pillars, and a line formed by the heads of the guests cuts the picture in half horizontally. The guests in the foreground are carefully arranged in balanced groups in each of the four sections in the bottom half of the canvas. In contrast to Menzel's portrayal of Frederick the Great drawn in the 1840s, the view here is impossible. The viewer hangs in mid-air, eyes on a level with the line of heads in the middle of the canvas.

The unusually low "horizon" line means the entire upper half of the painting is devoted to the walls and ceiling. Heavily decorated with gilded carvings, coats of arms supported by angels, and a gigantic human figure emerging from the top of one of the pillars under a cross-beam, the architectural edifice towers over the human guests. They are unconcerned and most are smiling, totally at ease in the extraordinary luxury of their surroundings. For this is a gathering of the elite, either military or uniformed government officials. Of the full figures in the fore and mid-ground, men in uniform outnumber those in civilian dinner suits, thirty to six. There are no servants pictured.

This is a man's world. Despite the occasion, there are only fifteen women, all in virtually identical off-the-shoulder white evening gowns with full skirts that sweep the floor. Eight are sitting. All of the seven not sitting are accompanied by men, and all except one have their arm through their escort's arm. The only one who does not is in the act of making a deep curtsy to an elderly uniformed man in the middle, just behind the chair with the abandoned plate and glass. Five of the seven women appear to be from ten to twenty years younger than the men who are guiding them. These males are all in uniform; in fact, none of the men in civilian clothes has the good fortune to be placed anywhere close to one of the women.

Menzel exhibited *Supper at the Ball* in Paris in 1878. Degas admired it and later painted a copy from memory, thus assuring the painting, and Menzel, a place in the canonical history of modern art.[2] Formally, the contrast of shadow and light, and the bare backs and shoulders of the women in their informal poses, recalls Degas' ballerinas rehearsing or waiting offstage for their cue. But if we contrast Menzel's ball with Renoir's *Ball at the Moulin de la Galette* (1876), where bourgeoisie and working class mingle to dance at a Parisian beer garden, where the "horizon" of heads lies close to the top of the painting and therefore places the emphasis on the people, where the central figures are two women chatting easily with three young men, and where none of the men is in uniform, it is clear that Menzel is contributing to an iconography of gender, class, and power. Entire slabs of German society—civilians, workers—are erased, and women become dependent creatures waiting to be fed or led about by older powerful men. Official culture placed everyone who mattered in uniform, and then placed them carefully in an overpowering edifice that became their accepted and uncontested home.

Appropriately, *Supper at the Ball* found its home in the National Gallery in Berlin. Now known as the Old National Gallery, it was designed by August Stüler and opened in 1876. It is in the form of a Greek temple, with eight Corinthian columns across the front portico, and a flat triangular pediment above them. The curtain walls down the

Plate 5.1 Adolf von Menzel, *Supper at the Ball (Das Ballsouper)*, 1878. Oil on linen, 71 × 90 cm. Old National Gallery, Berlin. The viewer hangs impossibly, several meters in the air, and the painting has been structured into four nearly equal rectangles in the lower half. Each of the four paintings within the painting has its own focus and tells its own story. The surroundings, the predominance of men in uniform, and the submissive and dependent position of their younger female partners create an iconography of the power and gender relations of imperial Germany. Staatliche Museen zu Berlin—Preussischer Kulturbesitz Nationalgalerie. Photo: SMB-PK, Bildarchiv Preussischer Kulturbesitz, Berlin.

side are decorated with half-round columns to complete the effect. However, Stüler placed his classically proportioned temple on top of a plain stone base, nearly as high as the columns, and added a double stairway in front, surrounding a gate and leading up to a platform with a rearing equestrian statue. Possibly intended as a means of raising the temple to give the appearance of elevation in analogy with the Acropolis, the effect is to spoil the proportions, and the result is top-heavy and clumsy. Over the colonnade is an inscription, "Der Deutschen Kunst MDCCCLXXI," that is, "To German Art 1871." A Greek temple on an artificial pedestal dedicated to German art, not in the year of its construction but dating German art from the foundation of the empire.

The neoclassical style in official painting and architecture suggested a timeless stability, but this was obviously false and artificial. Serious problems remained, and new ones emerged. The economy did not function as smoothly as before, particularly for agriculture. Industrial development led to the growth of cities and the emergence of a new industrial labor force. Stability proved elusive, in both domestic politics and foreign relations. Historians continue to debate the rate of economic development, the processes of social change, and the role of Bismarck as domestic politician and as international statesman. Looking backward, contemporaries knew how divided they had been, and how much the creation of the empire had owed to chance. Looking at their own time, contemporaries knew how unstable the new nation and the new national culture remained.

It therefore became all the more important to insist that the divisions and instability did not exist, and that the empire was not an accident, but rather that it was the result of deep and irresistible forces. As seen below, the process of the creation of a new national identity in Germany resembled other cases in Europe and Asia. It involved selective memory, forgetting, and repression, and therefore was marked by bad faith and anxiety. Bismarck presided over the empire of his own making, but continually worried about potential enemies and rivals. The aristocracy once again enjoyed the privilege of position, but continually worried about the upstart middle class. The middle class grew wealthy beyond its dreams, but continually worried about the dangerous working class. Protestants of all social classes celebrated "German" culture, but continually worried about Catholics. Small farmers, artisans, and workers uprooted by change looked for someone or something to blame, and

Plate 5.2   August Stüler, National Gallery, Berlin, 1876. Seen here in a photograph taken around 1915, the National Gallery was designed by August Stüler and carried out from 1866 to 1876, during the Wars of Unification, by J. H. Straack. The inscription "To German Art 1871" is visible over the entrance. The mounted statue of Frederick William IV, by A. Calandrelli, was added in 1886, and the lightning rod some time before 1905. Photo: Bildarchiv Preussischer Kulturbesitz, Berlin.

their discontent focused sometimes on the state, sometimes on the capitalist system, and sometimes on the Jew.

Even Germania suffered from the ambiguities of the new national state. As seen in previous chapters, the eternal symbol of Germany was in fact a historical creation who had already undergone several metamorphoses. She now reemerged as a warrior exhorting her children, as in Ferdinand Freilegrath's poem "Hurrah Germania" written in the enthusiasm of 1870, with its repeated "To the Rhine! To the Rhine! To the Rhine! . . . Hurrah Germania!" In pictorial and sculptural representations after the war she acquired an imperial crown in addition to her armor, sword, flowing drapery, and oak leaves. The new Reichstag building designed by Paul Wallot in 1882 had two crowned Germanias, a sculpture by Reinhold Bega over the main portal showing her astride a horse, and an immense stained glass window. Possibly the best-known Germania of all, the Niederwalddenkmal above Rüdesheim on the Rhine, was erected in 1883. Here she holds the crown aloft in her right hand. In all these representations she has regained her goddess-like quality, with aloof, classical features.

Bega's portrayal of Germania on horseback referred to Bismarck's statement made in 1867 that he would "put Germany, so to speak, in the saddle! She will know how to ride!" The Niederwald monument was intended as a commemoration of Bismarck's victory of 1870–71. But Bismarck disliked the Reichstag versions, and he refused to attend the dedication of the Niederwald monument. Bismarck said the Germania cult was an unacceptable "idolization of the idea of the nation." He also objected specifically to the representation of the nation by a female figure, and further to the idea that any woman might bear arms. He insisted that "a woman (*weibliches Wesen*) with a sword in this aggressive posture is unnatural. Every officer will feel the same way as I do about this." As with so much else about the empire, this was slightly disingenuous. Like the men in Menzel's painting, Bismarck had begun to wear a general's uniform after the foundation of the empire, and he continued to do so until his death, but he himself had never held a military commission. Johannes Schilling, the designer of the Niederwald monument, said that Germania "is showing the crown to the German people, not to the defeated enemy . . . The war is over. Germania watches over the German fatherland." However, although her sword indeed rests point down on the ground, it is draped in laurel as a symbol of her victory, and the debate over whether she looks benignly down on Germany or aggressively toward France has continued to the present.[3]

The economic context: the Great Depression

Bismarck's political and diplomatic triumphs were not matched in the economic sphere. The foundation of the empire was followed not by prosperity, but by the "*Gründerzeit*," the "foundation era," a speculative boom followed by a catastrophic collapse and a depression that bore the name "Great Depression" until the even greater disasters of the 1930s. The interpretation of these events continues to color our understanding not only of the development of the German economy, but of German society and political life as well.

In victory Bismarck imposed a huge indemnity of 5 billion gold francs on the defeated French. He had consulted Gerson Bleichröder, his personal banker and financial advisor, regarding the amount. Bleichröder considered 5 billion too high, but Bismarck persisted because he intended the indemnity to cripple France and prevent military recovery.[4] The indemnity was to be paid over five years, but the thrifty and patriotic French dug into their legendary socks and rushed to purchase the bonds issued by their new government, and the entire amount had been paid by May 1873, a full two years ahead of schedule. The payments were made for the French government by Rothschilds to Bleichröder and Adolf Hansemann, son of the revolutionary leader of 1848 and now head of the Diskontogesellschaft, who acted for the German government. What happened after the money arrived in Berlin became the subject of parliamentary accusations, royal commissions, denunciations in the press, and extended legal actions, and it has remained a topic of debate among historians.

First, the German government spent or gave away most of the money almost as soon as it was received. Both federal and state governments retired their war loans and other bond issues, and this massive repurchasing of government debt may have absorbed 60 per cent of the total.[5] The rest was used for a large number of construction projects including the Reichstag building and expanded army bases, grants to Prussian provincial governments, pensions for war widows, orphans, and invalids, and generous gifts to the successful politicians and generals. Virtually the entire amount of the indemnity therefore passed almost immediately into circulation.

The government also introduced a new gold-backed currency, the mark, but without immediately retiring the old silver-based currency. The new gold mark coins appeared alongside the old gulden and taler, and the government continued to mint additional silver coins, though with metallic content less than their face value.[6] This further increase in the money supply entered an economy already in the final phase of a cyclical upswing and was therefore highly inflationary. Iron output, for instance, increased 61 per cent from 1870 to 1873, but the price jumped 90 per cent.[7] Berlin, where the new gold coins first appeared, became the most expensive city in the world. There were an estimated 10,000 homeless persons in Berlin in 1871, in the midst of a frantic construction boom. Prostitution increased drastically, and the number of rape cases reported in Berlin doubled between 1872 and 1878.

Second, rising prices, the easy availability of capital, and the new, more lenient law of incorporation led to a large number of "foundations" (hence *Gründerzeit*). Nearly 1000 corporations were formed in Prussia alone from mid-1870 to mid-1873. Many of those who had owned the government bonds that had been retired with the indemnity now turned to other forms of investment. The registered capital of incorporated enterprises doubled, and the Berlin stock market rose 50 per cent. Many of the new firms were reorganizations of older companies, but many were genuinely new. Some of the new companies were perfectly sound, but some were less sound, and some were not sound at all. As prices rose and the stock market boomed, investment began to give way to speculation.

Third, the speculative atmosphere provided opportunities for the unscrupulous. Some of the combinations and acquisitions were in the gray area where public and private interests intersect. In 1872, Hansemann and Bleichröder both exploited their connections to secure large loans from the government that they used to gain control of railroads, banks, insurance companies, and also breweries, traditionally the cash cows used to fund takeovers. Some had crossed the line. In February 1873, the Liberal deputy Eduard Lasker delivered a three-hour speech in the Prussian Landtag, during which he denounced the activities of certain railroad companies that had paid certain high officials to exercise their influence with the Prussian Ministry of Commerce. The investigations of the ensuing royal commission resulted in the resignations of Hermann Wagener, one of Bismarck's senior advisors, and Count Itzenplitz, the Minister of Commerce.

Finally, there were the cases where the excessive hope and culpability of promoters on one side met the greed and gullibility of investors on the other. Railroad promoters in particular offered discounted shares in their companies to pay their suppliers and prayed that a continued rise in the stock market would carry their inflated capitalizations and satisfy their creditors. This was the technique employed by Bethel Henry Strousberg, "the railroad king," "the miracle doctor," who was also denounced by Lasker. Strousberg began his career in 1862 as the agent for British investors in the construction of a railroad from Tilsit to Insterburg in East Prussia. By the end of the decade he controlled a business empire that included railroads in Germany, Hungary, Romania, and Russia, as well as ironworks, machinery plants, and real estate. He stimulated interest in his railroad companies by planting favorable articles in local newspapers along the proposed routes. The money from the sale of shares went to finance construction and engineering companies that he also controlled, and the subcontractors who supplied these firms were paid with further shares in the railways. The resulting distortions in the surviving statistics continue to bedevil historians today.

The crash seems almost inevitable in retrospect. In Vienna, a city full of visitors to an international industrial exhibition heard of a wave of selling on the stock market on May 8, 1873, followed over the next week by 300 bankruptcies and the suicides of ruined investors. The government declared a moratorium on all financial transactions and ceased to exchange gold and silver for the paper money of the Bank of Austria. The collapse of credit in Austria placed pressure on German firms, particularly the overextended railroad companies and their bankers. Finally, on October 28, the failure of one Berlin bank led 27 others to suspend payments, and credit dissolved as firm after firm attempted desperately to demand payment while holding off their own creditors. The stock market collapsed, dragging more firms and individual investors into the vortex. Strousberg became only one among many when he went bankrupt. He spent time in a Moscow prison for debt, a meeting of his creditors in Berlin in 1876 learned that most of their money was lost, and he died impoverished in Berlin in 1884. As a personification of the boom and collapse, and as a Jew, he became a convenient symbol and scapegoat.[8]

The statistics we have seem to show that the financial collapse of 1873 did not lead to a decline in output of anything like the same magnitude. However, over the entire period from 1873 to 1895, the rate of growth of total output slowed. This Great Depression was the downswing that inspired Kondratiev's original theory of long cycles discussed in Chapter 1. Some of the previous sources of growth slackened. Investment in railroads grew more slowly, reflecting the maturing of this key leading sector. Industrial investment continued to rise, but the rate of increase in output per industrial worker dropped, as the easier gains of the preceding period had now been largely exploited. In addition, cyclical declines were more numerous and more sustained than in the upswing.[9]

Industrial entrepreneurs once again complained that credit was scarce. The new Reichsbank founded in 1875 used its monopoly of note issue very restrictively. The total of currency and bank deposits rose at less than half the rate of the preceding upswing. In part, this reflected international conditions. Germany had adopted a gold standard currency just as production from the mines of California and Australia began to slow. Under the "rules of the game," countries adhering to the gold standard could only increase their money supply as their gold reserves rose, either from mining or from trade. Germany has no gold mines, and the international economy slowed. The rate of growth of German exports dropped to 3.2 per cent per year over the downswing.[10]

If the foundation of the empire was followed by the onset of a long economic downswing, then Bismarck cannot receive much credit for German economic growth. But many historians see many more ominous connections. In a widely influential article and subsequent book, Hans Rosenberg argued that the 1873 crash and the ensuing Great Depression led to the rise of "neo-mercantilism," "collective protectionism," interest group organization, the rise of mass parties, chauvinistic nationalism, increased militarism, and "modern anti-Semitism and pre-fascist currents."[11] In other words, this is the point at which Germany diverged onto its tragic special path. Though they might rejoice to be part of the new empire, the emergence of the functionally integrated "national" economy meant individuals and families in many regions suffered from the direction of economic development. Their demands for redress and their search for scapegoats made them receptive to the arguments of anti-Semites, and also to the manipulative nationalistic rhetoric of Bismarck and his successors. The desperate attempts of the German Empire's political leaders to maintain the position of the old Junker aristocracy led ultimately to the First World War, the failure of the Weimar Republic, and the rise of Nazism.

Among subsequent historians, Hans-Ulrich Wehler, Heinrich August Winkler, and Jürgen Kocka have argued along these lines. Wehler, for instance, sees a distinctive pattern in Germany's growth and development toward an industrial state. A continued tradition of bureaucratic initiative and the ongoing role of the agrarian elite, on the one hand, were met by the "private crypto-planning" of new large industrial firms on the other. The interaction and interpenetration of these groups resulted in an extension of state intervention in the economy and the development of "corporativist" representation of influential groups.[12] Others such as Thomas Nipperdey, who are more cautious about drawing lines of causation from the economy to society and politics, still see an important shift in attitudes emerging from the depression.[13]

But if the development of the economy had these effects, we need to know how much the German economy had grown in the generation before the foundation of the empire, and how severely the economy declined following the crash of 1873. The arguments are technical, but important. In fact, economists and economic historians have great difficulty measuring economic growth. Complete and consistent data is not always available. Even with complete figures, it is not enough simply to produce lists of goods produced or services rendered. Output series for each industry or income series for each occupation must be combined. Obviously we use prices or wages to do this, but prices and wages change, and we therefore need to create series in constant prices. The figures and tables (Figures 5.1–5.4 and Table 5.1) below give output and capital stock in "constant 1913 marks," meaning that the prices of

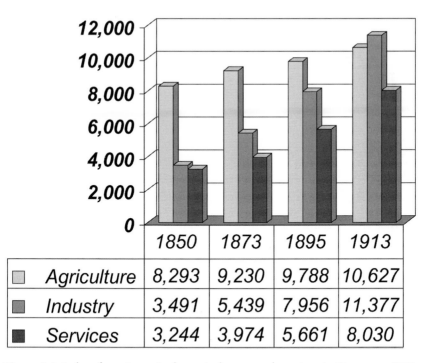

	1850	1873	1895	1913
Agriculture	8,293	9,230	9,788	10,627
Industry	3,491	5,439	7,956	11,377
Services	3,244	3,974	5,661	8,030

Figure 5.1 Labor force in agriculture, industry, and services in Germany, 1850–1913 (thousands)

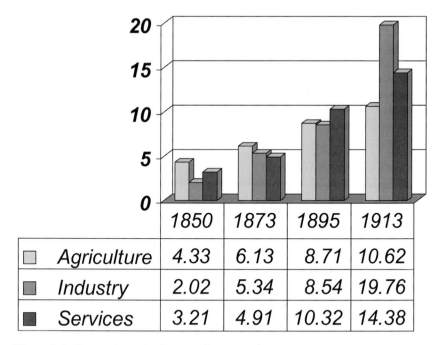

		1850	1873	1895	1913
☐	Agriculture	4.33	6.13	8.71	10.62
◩	Industry	2.02	5.34	8.54	19.76
■	Services	3.21	4.91	10.32	14.38

Figure 5.2 Output in agriculture, industry, and services in Germany, 1850–1913 (five-year averages, net national product in billion 1913 marks)

goods in earlier years have been recalculated in terms of their prices in 1913.

Students of the German economy still rely on the work of Walther G. Hoffmann published in 1965. The data given in the figures and Table 5.1 do show a period of slow growth in the 1870s and 1880s. However, Hoffmann employed a complex series of assumptions and estimates to produce his estimates, and over the years his methods have been criticized repeatedly. Some argue that, if we analyze the cyclical variations in Hoffmann's estimates statistically, the Great Depression simply disappears.[14] Hoffmann's figures may overstate output in the early 1870s, which together would exaggerate the 1873 turning-point and make the Great Depression appear more severe than it was. One intriguing reason for this is his assumption that the face value of the shares in railroad companies actually equaled the amount spent on their construction. As seen above, Strousberg paid his suppliers with discounted shares, and sometimes the discount was as high as 50 per cent. This means that the

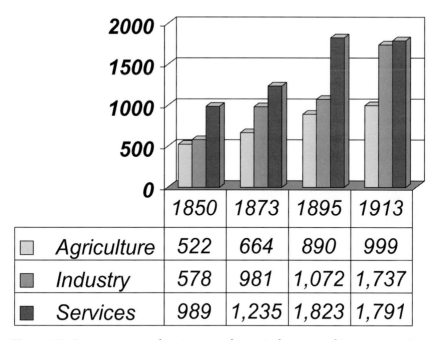

	1850	1873	1895	1913
Agriculture	522	664	890	999
Industry	578	981	1,072	1,737
Services	989	1,235	1,823	1,791

Figure 5.3 Output per worker in agriculture, industry, and services in Germany, 1850–1913 (five-year averages, 1913 marks)

output of the construction industry for the early 1870s is overstated, and therefore that the estimate of total national income is higher than it should be.[15]

Also, though there is disagreement over the timing and severity of the depression, all agree that this was an *industrial* economy; this meant that, though the economy grew more slowly, it did continue to grow. The German population rose 20 per cent from 1870 to 1890. In a pre-industrial economy suffering a long downturn, this would have led to disaster. However, in fact even during this Great Depression total output not only rose, but it rose substantially more rapidly than population, and therefore output per person increased by some 30 per cent.

Some of the increase in German industrial output resulted from the good luck of winning the war. Bismarck had no economic motive for seizing Alsace and Lorraine from France. Initially, the new "Reichsland" appeared more of a liability than an asset. The well-developed textile industry in Alsace immediately became a dangerous competitor for producers in Saxony and the Rhineland, and the iron deposits of Lorraine

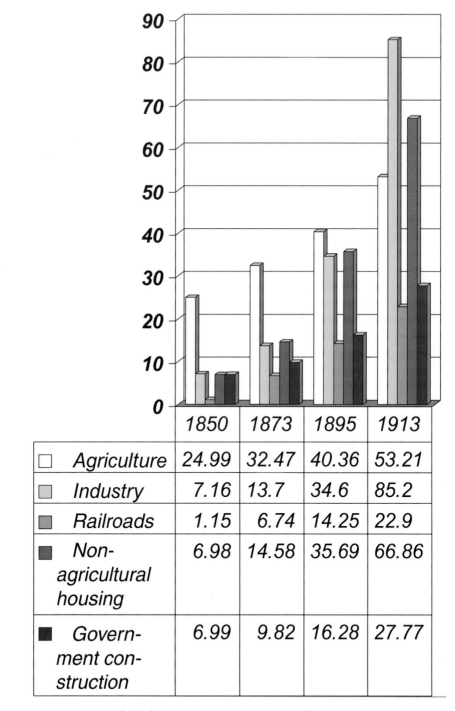

	1850	1873	1895	1913
☐ Agriculture	24.99	32.47	40.36	53.21
▨ Industry	7.16	13.7	34.6	85.2
▨ Railroads	1.15	6.74	14.25	22.9
■ Non-agricultural housing	6.98	14.58	35.69	66.86
■ Government construction	6.99	9.82	16.28	27.77

Figure 5.4 Capital stock in Germany, 1850–1913 (billion 1913 marks)

Table 5.1 Percentage rates of increase in output and output per worker, 1850–1914

	1850–73	1873–95	1895–1914
Output by sector			
Total	2.73	2.39	3.08
Agriculture	1.76	1.61	1.25
Industry	4.98	2.16	5.39
Services	2.15	3.43	2.10
Output per worker			
Total	1.63	1.35	1.48
Agriculture	1.15	1.34	0.73
Industry	2.98	0.40	3.06
Services	1.12	1.79	− 0.11

Source: Calculated from data in Walther G. Hoffmann, Das Wachstum der deutschen Wirtschaft seit der Mitte des 19. Jahrhunderts (Berlin: Springer, 1965). Boundaries of 1913.

were of no value because of their high phosphorus content. However, Alsatian textiles were accommodated, to the ultimate benefit of all. And then, in 1879, two Englishmen discovered that, by changing the type of bricks lining the inside of a Bessemer blast-furnace, phosphoric iron ore could be successfully smelted. German firms rushed to license the Thomas–Gilchrist process, and German iron and steel output doubled in the decade following 1879.

The Great Depression was in large part an agricultural depression. German farmers were not backward. The phosphoric slag produced as a waste by the new iron smelters, with a bit of additional processing, could be turned into a superphosphate fertilizer, or "Thomas-meal" (Thomasmehl). The use of both chemical fertilizers and imported guano and saltpeter rose dramatically. Rather, the crisis of German agriculture arose from changes in the international economy. The railroads that connected regions of Germany also opened up huge new farming areas in Russia, Romania, the United States, Argentina, and Australia. The Junker landlords of Prussia's eastern provinces lost their markets in Western Europe to these new competitors. They demanded protection, and in 1879 the government imposed tariffs on imported grains. As seen below, the shift from free trade to protection was part of a more general transformation of German politics. However, protectionism also reflected the more generally competitive situation in international markets. The era of liberalized trade lasted barely a decade. Austria increased its tariffs in 1878. Russian tariffs on both agricultural and industrial products rose repeatedly from the 1870s to the 1890s. France imposed generally higher tariffs in 1892, and France and Italy waged a tariff war from 1886 to 1898. The United States introduced protective tariffs in 1883 and raised them in 1890. Though the crisis in Germany had its special dimensions, it shared features with a variety of other countries as well.

The social and cultural context

Official neoclassicism

One of the characteristics common to emerging nations is an attempt by a new national elite to impose a common definition of what it means to belong to the "nation." Models are sought in the past and imposed on the present, ranging from public architecture to women's clothing. At the same time that ladies in Germany were being pressed into a standard white off-the-shoulder evening gown by national fashion, ladies in India were being pressed into the sari by Indian nationalists, and ladies in Japan into the kimono by the leaders of the Meiji government. In the public sphere, neoclassicism was an attempt to freeze cultural and social life. It was asserted repeatedly that the Greeks and Romans had discovered the inner harmonies of nature. If nature was an unchanging order, then perhaps the social and political systems were as well. In Japan, neoclassical buildings with Japanese arches demonstrated to the world how successfully the nation's leaders had merged modern Western styles with Japanese tradition. In contrast, in India neoclassicism was the idiom of the foreign British rulers, intended to demonstrate that they would rule forever.[16]

In Germany, neoclassicism was deployed to reinforce the new nation's legitimacy, as in the National Gallery. However, though it had the right "timeless" feel about it, it was not "German." The best-known neoclassical architects were British (Japan sent its bright young men there to study the latest building styles). The trendsetters in ladies' clothing were French. Some insisted that German art and architecture must return to its medieval roots and to a revived Gothic style. Others spoke of the natural and unaffected styles of traditional regional costumes.

Those favoring Gothic motifs and traditional styles argued that they were more purely "German," but for national leaders neo-Gothic or any distinctively regional pattern of dress recalled Germany's lack of unity all too clearly. The search for a new national style therefore remained contentious.

New public buildings aroused controversy, precisely because they reflected the new social and class circumstances that resulted from economic development. The changing situation of the nobility, population movements, the rise of an industrial working class, and the emergence of a workers' culture could all be read in the transformation of urban spaces. The institutional basis of high culture took concrete form in concert halls, museums, parks, and zoos, of political culture in state capitals, town halls, and post offices, and of economic culture in office buildings, banks, department stores, and railroad stations. Behind and between the new avenues of the growing cities, narrow courtyards allowed shafts of light down the sides of multi-story "rent barracks" (*Mietkasernen*) that housed the large floating population of workers. They entertained themselves in bars, beer gardens, in dance halls, or in the parks and department stores where they might rub shoulders with their betters. What to do with masses of people, how to preserve their health and support them in their old age, and how to prevent them from becoming dangerous, all became public issues related to the control of public space.

Old classes and new classes: aristocracy, besitzbürgertum, and proletariat

The aristocracy did not disappear, and indeed occupied a privileged position in the eyes of Bismarck and Wilhelm, but nevertheless this was an anxious age for the nobility. The conflict between Prussia and Austria had cut across family connections and dynastic loyalties that had united aristocrats above regional boundaries. Increasing professionalization of a range of occupations posed problems for the sons of noble families, for their status no longer ensured access to employment. Some areas remained reserved to them, such as the upper levels of the diplomatic services. In German armies, line officers and elite guards' regiments stationed in capital cities also continued as noble preserves, but the increasingly important staff and technical branches, such as engineers and artillery, required formal training in academic subjects.

As the agricultural depression continued, noble families without other sources of income found themselves at a disadvantage. Many of them were wealthy in terms of the value of their land, but found themselves continually short of income. Although exempt from most taxes, on average agricultural land did not pay as well as capital invested in industry. The prestige of holding land meant that there were always eager buyers among the newly rich, but for a landed noble family it was unthinkable to sell and invest the capital in another sector. At the same time, the costs of maintaining the required style of life rose. The house in the capital had to be larger, the rooms had to be filled with new and expensive furnishings, the number of servants had to be greater, entertainment had to be more lavish. Educational expenses for sons and for daughters increased. Sons required formal training, and daughters required "finishing." A noble son might marry the daughter of a wealthy non-noble family, but a noble daughter required a noble husband, and therefore needed a suitable dowry. Stagnating agricultural prices meant that these increasing expenses had somehow to be met out of a constant or declining income.

After the army, government service remained the preferred occupation for a young aristocrat, and at the top levels noble status was still a substantial advantage. The number of administrative officials rose, from around 220,000 in 1875 to around 315,000 in 1895. For many noble families these positions were becoming more important for their existence than their place on the land. However, appointment to state bureaucracies required evidence of academic achievement certified by passing examinations. Although state service was the preserve of the elite, elite status was now defined more by the possession of wealth than by birth. Prussia imposed a formal requirement that the unpaid trainees must prove they could support themselves for a minimum of ten years without contracting debts. As the economy expanded, more ambitious non-aristocratic men appeared with families that could support them. The proportion of higher bureaucrats who were the sons of higher or middle-level bureaucrats increased from 37 per cent in the years 1876–1900 to 44 per cent in the years 1901–18, and the proportion who were the sons of wealthy industrialists rose from 12 to 21 per cent. As a result, the proportion of landowners' sons declined slightly from 29 to 22 per cent.[17]

Among the university-trained *Bildungsbürger*, the professions all defended themselves against outsiders. Boards and associations certified approved practitioners through formal qualifications and examinations. As seen in Chapter 4, Protestant clergymen became an increasingly closed group, and their declining relative status and income made the Church a less attractive option than formerly. Medicine now required not only initial study at university level and certification by government authorities, but also additional years mastering one of an increasing number of areas of specialization. The German professoriate remained one of the most close-knit segments of the *Bildungsbürgertum*. University professors had occupied a privileged position for decades, insulated by the autonomy of institutions and the ever more precise drawing of disciplinary boundaries. Despite a new tendency to recruit from the "German" university system as a whole, the need to prove one was a *Wissenschaftler*, to demonstrate expertise as a specialized researcher in a specific discipline (*Wissenschaft*), reduced the chances of success and made connections even more important. In the natural sciences, one in two professors was related to another professor, the father of one in thirteen was himself a professor, and one in six had married the daughter of a professor. For humanistic disciplines the ties were only slightly looser.[18]

Despite the difficulties of the Great Depression, continuing economic growth created a substantial number of large fortunes. Beside the old *Bürger* of the urban communities and the *Bildungsbürger* with university qualifications, contemporaries noticed a new class, a *Besitzbürgertum* marked by the possession of significant wealth (*Besitz*). As seen in Chapter 3, these families had often begun in urban communities as merchants and manufacturers, but their interests had expanded with their growing wealth beyond their locality. An interest in railroad investment was a common but not the only way for this to occur. Some had political connections, and a few were Jewish. The wealth of Bismarck's banker Gerson Bleichröder was regularly displayed at the dinners and balls he hosted at his Berlin mansion. New wealth attracted the envy of other elite groups, and the satirical gaze of novelists such as Theodor Fontane. The title character of *Frau Jenny Treibel* (1892) is an ambitious social climber who searches for a profitable match for her weak-willed son. She rejects the daughter of a schoolteacher whose culture and character are revealed by his constant citation of the classics. For Jenny Treibel, culture (*Bildung*) is itself a possession, a symbol of wealth, and *Besitz* in turn should itself be sufficient to purchase standing in the right circles.

The obverse of the new wealthy bourgeoisie was a wage-earning working class, a proletariat in Marx's sense. Prussian legislation had reintroduced guilds in 1849, but they were voluntary organizations dominated by masters. In some branches the masters began to become employers, and journeymen gradually recognized that they could never aspire to independent mastership. The Zollverein states adopted the principle of occupational freedom in 1861, but the impact varied from place to place and industry to industry. In Munich, the strength of the guilds and resistance to occupational freedom divided the *Bürgertum* into conflicting groups, though the battle lines shifted as the fortunes of different industries waxed and waned.[19] In Hamburg and other northern coastal cities, the families of the old oligarchy could use their wealth or power to impose their will, and this might override the interests of guildsmen or other groups. In Frankfurt, in contrast, though guilds continued to be strong, the *Bürgertum* remained relatively cohesive. Before the Prussian annexation in 1866, a substantial consensus had to be reached before any major change could be undertaken. This tradition continued, and local industry had to accommodate itself to the guilds. Partly in consequence, commerce, and especially banking, became the most economically innovative sector of the Frankfurt economy, a specialization that remained for the next century.[20]

In the Rhenish-Westphalian industrial district, reform of mining laws and the end to the powers of the miners' guilds encouraged investment in new, deeper mines. Coal was the magnet for iron smelting, metal processing, and machinery industries. In the industrializing city of Dortmund, the population rose from 11,000 in 1850 to 90,000 in 1890. Rapid development brought increasing disparities of wealth within the old *Bürgertum*. Nevertheless, a rather broad segment of the city's old families remained connected both socially and politically. They adopted more voluntarist and associational forms of sociability on the one hand, and supported the introduction of more professional forms of city administration on the other. A network of clubs and associations connected families in this elite with each other and with the new specialized institutions of city government, and they worked actively to promote industrial growth.[21]

The numbers of industrial workers continued to increase. From 1875 to 1895, employment in the "old" industry of textile manufacture remained constant at around 900,000, but this concealed a shift away from linen to cotton and from handloom weaving in rural districts to factory production in towns. Clothing increased from 1.1 to 1.4 million, with the increase again largely in urban areas. In the "new" heavy industrial sector, employment in mining rose from 300,000 to 400,000, and workers in metallurgy and machinery nearly doubled from 750,000 to 1.3 million. As in textiles, the totals concealed a shift from dispersed rural production to concentration in urban districts. In all branches workers labored in larger units than before. The industrial census of 1882 showed 23 per cent of manufacturing workers in firms of 50 or more employees, and this had risen to 34 per cent by the next census in 1895. The share of miners working in giant mines with over 1000 employees rose from 47 to 58 per cent. Symptomatically, the names of new mines changed, from being named after flowers or the locality, to being given the names of members of the owners' families.

The demand for workers in the expanding industrial districts, combined with the continuing problems in agriculture and the decline of industry in rural districts, ensured that many of these workers would be young agricultural laborers, girls in textiles and clothing, and boys in construction, mining, and metals. Individual workers confronted growing firms with owners who insisted on their rights as "*Herr im Hause*" (master of the house). Poor housing, harsh treatment on the job, and the common desire to return home all contributed to a very high turnover of workers. The cities grew, but a large fraction of these new masses of people were transient, present only for the season or a year before moving on. Single workers found little reason to put down roots in the towns. Permanent migrants tended to be married couples with children, and it was those children who became the reason for the exponential growth of the cities' populations.[22]

The new social divisions were reflected in local politics. The *Bürgertum*, whether liberal or conservative, and whether local or outward-looking in orientation, remained united in its belief that only established men of independent means had earned the right to participate in public life. The emerging elite in Dortmund refused to include the lower classes in government. Frankfurt's associational life and the "bourgeois society of equals" were in theory open to all citizens but not to those without voting rights. Wherever the urban elite had the power to determine the right to vote for local elective offices, they restricted the suffrage in ways that ensured that long-term residents and property owners would have the most influence on the outcome. Recent arrivals could not vote, which eliminated the majority of migrant workers. Further restrictions might limit the suffrage to taxpayers above a certain threshold, or limit the impact of a broader suffrage by making elections a two-stage process.[23]

The "worker problem"

Not surprisingly, efforts to integrate the working class into a civil society dominated by the *Bürgertum* failed. Instead, workers began to create their own associational life, frequently centered around the neighborhood bar. In addition, the first labor unions made their appearance, often led by disappointed journeymen. Political parties to represent workers' interests were the logical next step. In 1863, Ferdinand Lassalle, a lawyer and classical scholar, a former friend of Marx, and well known for his radical politics, had formed the German Workers' Association. Lassalle aimed to use the new broader franchise to force the state to subsidize workers' cooperatives that would allow workers to escape dependence on capitalist employers. Bismarck, briefly interested, interviewed Lassalle at one point. Marx, convinced that Lassalle's economics and political strategy were both wrong, but worried about his evident popularity, deputized Wilhelm Liebknecht and August Bebel to establish a rival workers' party. Following Lassalle's death in a duel, the two parties eventually came together. They sealed their union and produced a common program at a meeting at Gotha in 1875. Marx was infuriated by the moderate and reformist tone of the Gotha Program, but his angry critique was not published until 1890, for fear of damaging the morale of the tiny new party. Socialist candidates had won two seats in the first Reichstag election in 1871, and nine in 1874. The newly united German Social Democratic Party (*Sozialdemokratische Partei Deutschlands*, or SPD) received 493,000 votes and won twelve seats in 1877.

The emerging workers' culture and the emerging workers' political movement posed a double threat. Neither Bismarck nor any of his rivals wanted to share power with representatives of the working class. In addition, Germany's elites believed that urban workers were actual or potential criminals, whether through their innately bad character or because of the pernicious influence of the undisciplined urban environment. This was a myth, for criminal behavior was no more likely in the city than in the country.[24] Nevertheless, the idea persisted that urban workers were potential criminals. This had the effect of both problematizing the workers as a group and providing a justification for intervention and regulation.

The "problem" of the working class elicited two responses. The first was repression. Nationally, as seen below, in 1878 Bismarck forced through legislation outlawing the SPD. At the municipal level, local officials harassed workers and attempted to prevent their use of public space, through restrictions on public meetings and through traffic regulations, for instance. They continually interfered in working-class districts to regulate behavior and morals. In a reflection of the older concerns of local communities, they also sometimes restricted the right of workers to marry. While refusing marriage permits to couples they held to be of bad character, they prosecuted unmarried couples for "concubinage." With a criminal conviction for a morals offense, of course, the couple could never prove their good character. Some actually journeyed from northern Germany to England to get married.[25]

The other response was ameliorative. Local, state, and national governments all introduced programs to improve the quality of life for the lower classes. City and town governments could build on an old tradition of poor relief, based on the idea that the community had a responsibility to support its members in time of need. Local authorities developed a broad range of specialized agencies to cope with problems as they were identified. These extended from building regulations, through aspects of public health, to work creation schemes for the unemployed during hard times. National policy developed against this backdrop of local experiences.[26]

Bismarck's motives for taking up the cause of social insurance were mixed. He intended the Anti-Socialist Law to destroy the independent workers' political movement. At the same time, he drew on the tradition of the paternalistic "welfare state," the idea that the king bore a responsibility toward his subjects as a father did toward his children. Lorenz von Stein's concept of a "social monarchy" had influenced some of Bismarck's advisors. Bismarck said he hoped that what he called a program of "state socialism" that extended welfare entitlements to workers would turn those workers into a class of "small pensioners" who would support the government because they had a stake in the existing system.[27]

The sickness insurance law of 1883, the accident insurance law of 1884, and the age and disability insurance law of 1889 have been celebrated as the first "modern" social insurance system. They have served as models for programs in many other countries. At the time, however, their effects were limited, and their structure reflected the constellation of power in Bismarck's empire. The empire was a monarchy, and the government was under no obligation to consult either elected representatives or any of those affected by the new laws. White-collar workers were not included, since their social status was presumed to guarantee that they could and would support themselves. Agricultural workers were excluded. This exempted their employers, and especially the eastern Junker class, from paying contributions, but it also reflected the assumption that in rural communities workers could rely on the charity of local landowners. The system was aimed at the "problem" industrial workers. It rested on compulsory contributions from both workers and employers, but workers' contributions were substantially higher. Payments were low. Employers objected to being forced to contribute, and government officials worried about the financial risks of overly generous payments. Finally, the system was gendered. The old-age pension was only available to men over 70 years old. The system did not recognize young women as permanent workers, and it assumed that elderly women would be supported by their families.[28]

Images of the "German" woman

As seen in Chapter 4, male commentators across the political spectrum insisted that woman's role was to serve as a submissive wife and nurturing mother in a private sphere cut off from public life. Moral, philosophical, and historical arguments had been elaborated and repeated to support this view. Now the authority of the new national state could be invoked as well. Many new national governments have worried about the role of women in the state, and Germany was no exception. Bismarck himself was deeply concerned about the potentially disruptive role of women in public life, as seen in his objections to the idea of portraying Germany as a female Germania, and in his insistence that no female person should even consider bearing arms. In his own home life, his wife Johanna provided him with a near perfect caricature of Hegel's fantasy of a domestic female refuge for the man of public action. Bismarck's overwrought temperament led to episodes of nervous collapse, and these became more frequent and more severe over time. Without fail, Johanna endured his tantrums and arranged for him to be nursed like an infant.

As an aristocrat, Johanna von Bismarck could be expected merely to supervise her numerous servants. Not so far down the social scale, however, the wives of professional men also supervised their servants, but they were expected to set the servants an example through their own energy and diligence. Magazines aimed at middle-class women pre-scribed detailed schedules for cleaning. Floors had to be scrubbed daily, stoves polished after every use, all shelves and cabinets emptied and cleaned once a week, and curtains washed, put through ten separate rinses, starched (with starch made weekly from saved potato peelings), and of course ironed, every three months. The daily cleaning of the bedroom, according to one manual, required the wearing of spotless cotton gloves, an apron, and slippers, lest the room be contaminated as it was cleaned. The process in fact "would have rendered the room almost sterile." The point, as Nancy Reagin emphasizes, lay in the con-tinual comparisons with the less diligent, less thrifty, and, above all, less clean housewives in other countries. Proper household management had served as a class marker since the 1840s, identifying the responsible wives of the *Bürgertum*, but it now became the marker of membership in the new national community.[29]

A further point about housewifely diligence and thrift, economical of money but wasteful of women's time, was that it would leave little or no time or energy for activities outside the home. Male commentators and the editors of women's magazines believed this to be natural and proper. Leaders of women's organizations disagreed, but only in part. Limited feminist activities remained largely within the framework of women's ameliorative groups. Women, they said, should become active in educa-tion and social welfare activities precisely because of their feminine qualities. Female virtues could be drawn on to improve society, not because women were or should be equal to men, but because they were different and distinctively qualified to work in "feminine" areas such as the education of young children, health, and poor relief.[30]

The feminine role, potentially active and reforming yet carefully con-fined, is illustrated in another historical novel set in the Napoleonic period. Louise von François' *Die Letzte Reckenburgerin: Lebensge-chichte einer Deutschen Frau* (*The Last of the Reckenburgers: Life Story of a German Woman*, 1870) was discovered and popularized by Gustav Freytag and was republished in numerous editions. The heroine, Har-dine von Reckenburg, is invited to live at the castle of Reckenburg by her namesake, a divorced and unhappy countess. She might have married the son of the prince who had divorced the countess years before after squandering her fortune, but he seduces Hardine's childhood friend

Dorothee, a lower-class girl who had been taken in by Hardine's family. Dorothee becomes pregnant, has a baby, and eventually is driven insane by her feelings of guilt. Hardine conceals the illegitimate birth, provides for the child's education, and eventually adopts Dorothee's grandchild, thereby threatening her own reputation.

Following the death of the countess, Hardine takes control of the castle and its estates. She educates herself as necessary, and her reforms transform the district into a rural Utopia. A benign autocrat, she refers to herself as "fritzian" in reference to Frederick the Great's rebuilding of Prussia after the Seven Years War. She does not marry. In part, this is a further aspect of her self-renunciation, but she also lacks Dorothee's beauty and feminine charm, and her competence identifies her as too strong a character to become a submissive wife. However, Hardine is not a public character. The novel concentrates on the personal and the domestic. The wars happen almost completely offstage. When the armies do arrive, as Hardine says, "during my 'fritzian' activities I remained a sympathetic observer of public life, whose catastrophes coincided with those of my own new life." The armies move on after several pages, leaving her with only "a sort of connection with the patriots." Hardine is active outside her home, but only in that part of the public sphere that could be conceived as an enlarged domestic arena. The political decisions that will frame and shape the dimensions of that arena are taken elsewhere, by men.[31]

In a society undergoing rapid industrialization, an ongoing crisis in the agricultural sector, and periodic severe depressions, it was unlikely that what women actually did would or could remain constant. We therefore need to look at women's situation in a changing society. Women were not confined to the home as dictated by the official gender ideology. Women worked, in increasing numbers. Working women were forced into a limited number of areas, but female employment was not less strenuous or stressful than men's work. Agriculture remained the largest employer of women, officially 3.9 million in 1882 and 4.1 million in 1895, but in fact many more because the official censuses did not consider "family assistants" to be genuinely "employed." As before in the east, agricultural women were wage laborers mobilized at planting and harvest times. In the west and south, women were more likely to be family members working throughout the year, planting, harvesting, and processing products for sale in local markets. Dairy products were a female preserve, as were a variety of vegetables and fruits. Milk, butter, cheese, and "garden" plants were crucial sources of income for farm households.

In districts of artisan industrial production, wives worked not only in the farm enterprise but also in textile and lace-making, or producing parts for wooden clocks and other objects. In a number of sectors, rural producers were being undermined by competition from mechanized factories. When their husbands, sons, and daughters migrated to find work, wives could be left to tend the farm as well as struggling to produce handicraft goods. A contemporary study of Prussian Saxony, a classic region of mixed protoindustrial and agricultural production, showed that much larger numbers of women went insane than men. More recent work indicates that the general intensification of work in these districts undermined women's health. Even after we allow for the risks of pregnancy, married women between the ages of 20 and 45 were more likely to die than their husbands.[32]

The branches of manufacturing open to women were textiles and clothing. In regions of mechanized textile production such as the Kingdom of Saxony, the Rhineland, or Alsace, girls from surrounding districts moved to work in small or medium-sized factories in small and medium-sized towns. They were temporary, often leaving after less than a year, moving on to another urban place or returning to their home district. Workers in the clothing industry were largely female. As seen above, the recorded numbers rose, though women working at home in the cities tended to be underreported. Many of these were married, and they sewed through the night to add to their family's income.

The largest category of female employment, and indeed one of the largest categories of employment of any kind, with nearly 1.5 million workers, was domestic servants. Particularly in the growing cities, service in a middle- or upper-class household was the most likely source of employment for a girl from the countryside. Again, like her male counterpart employed in transportation, construction, or industry, she was temporary, moving from job to job, and back and forth between the city and her home district. As with female agricultural workers, because she was thought to belong to someone else's household, she also was not considered "employed" by the census office.

The political context: creating a national community

There have been many new national states since 1870. Each is unique, but there are common patterns. A national community does not exist; rather it must be created. Elements of the past must be combined into a version of the nation's history that will establish an acceptable pedigree for the new state. Heroes must be discovered and celebrated. Events, persons, and memories that do not fit the new story must be suppressed. In the German case, history was rewritten. Heinrich von Treitschke forgot his previous opposition to Bismarck, and his five volumes (1879–94) retold the German story as the saga of a rising tide of nationalism leading to inevitable triumph in 1871. Some unlikely heroes were discovered. Friedrich List, considered a dangerous radical during the Restoration period, ironically became a prophet of the Bismarckian state, and as such became influential in Meiji Japan as well.[33]

New national states feel themselves under threat. Villains, those who do not fit the new orthodoxy, must be uncovered and pursued. Catholics were accused of threatening German culture, and Socialists were accused of threatening German society. Both were seen as agents of foreign conspiracies. Influential Heidelberg law professor Johann Caspar Bluntschli argued in "Two Enemies of our State and our Culture" (1872) that, despite their differences, ultramontanism and Communism shared many characteristics. Communists and Catholic clergy might despise each other's beliefs, but they both aimed to destroy the authority of the state. Both, he said, were international movements. Both relied on the lower classes for support. Both appealed to the passions and channeled the raw violence of the masses against the state and society. Bluntschli argued that the present age differed from the age of the Enlightenment because of the spread of democratic rights to the masses. He warned that, as a result, the state must arm and prepare itself now for the inevitable war against both ultramontanes and Communists.

Along with a new written history, new national states embody themselves in monuments that commemorate heroes and events in that history. Contemporaries spoke of a "monument mania." In Paris, the rage for monuments finally led the municipal council to ban statues commemorating anyone who had not been dead for at least ten years. In Germany, well over a thousand major monuments were erected between 1871 and 1914. However, these monuments demonstrate another common aspect of national identity, its contested nature. As seen above, the Niederwald Germania was and remains controversial. This was typical. Not only the form but also the final meaning of many of these monuments aroused intense public discussion and debate. Symbols could be used and abused. They could be exploited, revered, and scorned in turn, on the same artistic and political grounds as any other intervention in the public sphere.

The earliest national-political monuments of the 1870s, such as the Berlin Triumphal Column (the *Siegessäule*), can be seen as depictions of a nation antagonistic to large segments of its own population. The products of the second wave of construction from the late 1880s were less aggressive and more diverse. Both the Niederwald Germania and the Munich Peace Column (the *Friedenssäule*) embodied a conception of the nation that included Catholics and recognized the smaller states. The empire continued to be represented by symbols of the monarchy and the military, not the constitution and the people. But it was not the court, the aristocracy, or the army that erected Bismarck towers and Germanias. It was the middle classes, the affluent *Bürgertum*, that sponsored the contests for their design, organized the fund-raising drives to pay for them, and attended the dedications and the anniversary ceremonies that were their purpose. The organization and the funding were local initiatives, and therefore, although they celebrated the nation, the monuments celebrated local patriotisms as well. Bismarck's refusal to attend the dedication of the Niederwald Germania reflected this tension between the national and the local, a tension that Bismarck's empire never resolved.[34]

Constitution-making

A national constitution can be a written (in the British case, unwritten) set of formal rules that govern the relations among participants in the process of government. At the same time, a national constitution can refer to the entire range of social, institutional, and legal relationships that contribute to the operation of the political system. It is in this broader sense that historians have examined the "constitution" of imperial Germany in the search for the origins of Germany's special path and of the German tragedy. To understand how Germans came to terms with this new structure, we need to examine not only formal constitutional documents, but also legislation, party and interest group structures, and the creation and operation of the institutions of governance.

Looking at the constitutional structure of the North German Confederation and the empire, two facts stand out. The first is that these were federal entities, intended to preserve the identities and privileges of the member states. Bismarck drafted the constitution of the North German Confederation, and he worked frantically to secure its passage. He referred to the Confederation as a "Provisorium," a stepping stone on the way to unification with the south German states, but it was an important one, intended at the time to last as long as was necessary. The compromises embedded in the document assured all the 25 German rulers that their interests would be maintained. Virtually all of the provisions of the Confederation's constitution were carried over into the imperial constitution.

The states remained the focus of identity, and they retained important powers. Regarding citizenship and the all-important question of who is a German, Article 3 announced that "for the whole of Germany one common nationality exists," but then defined this in terms of citizenship in each of the separate states. "Every person (subject, state citizen) belonging to any of the federated states is to be treated in every other of the federated states as a born native." That is, the rights of citizenship were to be enjoyed equally by anyone resident in any particular German state who had been born in another German state, but those rights were not guaranteed by a common national definition of civil liberties. A Polish speaker born in West Prussia was a Prussian and therefore a German, but a German speaker born in Austrian Bohemia was not. However, a Pole born in Prussia who moved to Saxony would be treated as a born Saxon, not as a German. State and local voting rights varied from state to state, and so too did the important powers and procedures of the police. Family law, education, and health were all state responsibilities. Only the member states had the right to levy direct taxes, and the southern states obtained exemptions from the new national excise tax system as part of their price for joining the federation. Bavaria and Württemberg both retained separate military establishments and their own postal and telegraph systems. The states also insisted on keeping control of their own railroad networks.

The second obvious fact is the overwhelming influence of Bismarck on the design of these structures, and the way in which they were intended to preserve and protect his personal position and that of his master, the

King of Prussia.[35] Wilhelm might have wept at the thought of losing "the old Prussia," but he need not have worried. Not only was Prussia preserved along with all of the other states incorporated into the new empire, but its preeminence was ensured as well. The King of Prussia was the German Emperor, or, more precisely, "the Presidency of the Federation belongs to the King of Prussia who bears the name of the German Emperor." As such, Wilhelm determined foreign policy, and he commanded all the armies of the German states. In addition, Article 63 stated that "the Emperor determines the peacetime strength, the structure, and the distribution of the army," although this was subject to the restriction contained in Article 60 that the size of the army must be determined by law. The upper legislative house, the Bundesrat (Federal Council), was an assembly of state representatives. It had the power to initiate constitutional revisions, but Prussia possessed 17 of the 58 votes, enough to veto any measure opposed by the Prussian government.

Parallel to the King of Prussia who was also the German Emperor, Bismarck as Minister-President of Prussia also became Chancellor of Germany. There was no legal provision for this, but Bismarck's constitutional drafts clearly were tailored to his own personal fit. He improved on the Prussian situation by making the heads of federal ministries directly subordinate to the Chancellor. This guaranteed that the occasional resistance he had encountered from his Prussian ministerial colleagues would not be repeated at the national level. He continued to serve as foreign minister, of course. The Bundesrat had an advisory committee on foreign affairs, but Bismarck consulted it only once in the next twenty years.

Along with the Emperor, the Chancellor, and the Bundesrat, there was the legislative assembly, the Bundestag of the North German Confederation and the Reichstag of the empire. In contrast to Prussia's three-class suffrage and indirect election, Bismarck insisted in both cases that the representatives should be directly elected by universal male suffrage. Looking backward to the constitutional conflict, Bismarck believed that his enemies had benefited from the plutocratic voting system, and that the masses of people would support him if given the chance. In 1866 he had written,

> At the moment of decision the masses will stand on the side of kingship, regardless of whether the latter happens to follow a liberal or a conservative tendency ... the artificial system of indirect and class elections is much more dangerous than that of direct and general suffrage, because it prevents

contact between the highest authority and the healthy elements that constitute the core and the mass of the people. In a country with monarchical
traditions and loyal sentiments the general suffrage, by eliminating the influences of the liberal bourgeois [*Bürgerlich*] classes, will also lead to monarchical elections.

He continued to believe this to be true, so in both cases the vote went
to all male citizens aged 25 and above. They elected their representatives
directly, in single-member constituencies, with a run-off between the top
two candidates if there was no clear majority in the first ballot. In a
further contrast to the Prussian system of public voting, national
elections were held by secret ballot.

The government possessed powerful instruments to influence elections. As seen below, campaign activity could be restricted by law. Prussia had confiscated the personal fortune of the royal family of Hanover
in 1866, and this money remained under the control of Bismarck and his
successors. The "Guelf fund" supported newspapers and individual
journalists favorable to the government. For foreign readers their stories
might hint at Germany's intentions, and for domestic consumption they
denounced the government's proclaimed enemies and supported its policies. In addition, state press laws remained in effect, and the national
press law of 1874 lacked guarantees that protected the confidentiality of
sources. Writers and editors of newspapers that offended the government could expect lawsuits, prosecutions, fines, and possibly jail
sentences.

On the other hand, the imperial government never intervened as
heavily as the Prussian government had in the 1850s and 1860s. The
government did not control all newspapers, and many opposed the government. As the cases of the Catholic Center Party and the Socialist
Party demonstrate, despite legal restrictions voters could vote for the
government's enemies, and their chosen representatives could sit in the
Reichstag. The secret votes of individuals remained secret, and the secret
votes were counted honestly.

Was this an effective constitutional structure? The range of measures
introduced by the new government certainly makes an impressive list. In
the financial sphere there were the new currency, adherence to the gold
standard, and the Reichsbank. There were also the Audit Office (1871),
the Statistical Office (1872), the Railroad Office (1873), the National
Debt Administration (1874), the Health Department and the Post Office
(1876), and the Patent Office (1877). Legal scholars worked on a more

standardized system of laws, capped institutionally by the establishment of the Imperial Justice Department and Supreme Court in 1877, and the Imperial Court of Appeal in 1879. In addition, the empire inherited and extended a wide range of official and semi-official institutions that linked public officials and private interests on a consultative basis. Regional Chambers of Commerce and Agricultural Associations had existed since the first half of the century. A national German Agricultural Council was established in 1872.[36] The Prussian State Railroad Council established in 1883 advised on freight rate structures.[37]

However, Germany's subsequent history has led many to emphasize the weaknesses and shortcomings of Bismarck's constitution. Bismarck was no democrat, and the "fig leaf" of manhood suffrage and constitutional provisions could not conceal the empire's fundamentally authoritarian nature. The constitution, like the Prussian constitution of 1849, was a gift from the rulers to the people. When it became obvious that the masses would not automatically vote for his preferred candidates, Bismarck was perfectly willing to consider a coup d'état to change the constitution. The army remained a state within the state. There was no imperial war minister. The Prussian army continued to swear allegiance to the King of Prussia. The Prussian Minister of War exercised internal control over all the armed forces of the empire, and it was he who spoke on military matters in the Reichstag. The new state also remained committed to maintaining the position of the eastern Junker aristocracy, and social divisions led to political divisions. Shifting alliances with the parties conflicted with simultaneous attempts to freeze political life by removing the government budget from Reichstag control. Policy was often hamstrung by conflict within the Reichstag, between the Reichstag and the government, or between Prussia and the other member states. All these contradictions had consequences extending into the next generation, the First World War, and Weimar.

Nevertheless, contemporaries who grew up under this constitution and who considered its structure and its place in German history found much to celebrate. As an example we can take Friedrich Meinecke, one of Germany's greatest and most influential historians, who subjected the history of the German constitution to a searching analysis in *Weltbürgertum und Nationalstaat* (*Cosmopolitanism and National State*), published in 1907. Meinecke considered the tensions between universal and national principles, between state patriotisms and nationalism, between particularism and centralism, between Prussia and the other

German states, and between Prussia and Germany. Within Meinecke's idealistic philosophical framework, Bismarck was not only an active agent in his own right, but also the embodiment of the idea of Germany as it had developed to that point in time. Meinecke saw Bismarck's achievement not as a compromise, but as a dynamic synthesis, to which "all the living forces of the nation have made their contribution."[38] Bismarck's solution to the German problem linked the alternatives of Prussian and German constitutions and of federalist and unitary demands. It was "not an artificial work of strict symmetry." Although it was "apparently formless and complicated," it was a "viable thing," and as such it was a living structure capable of further development.

Bismarck's genius, said Meinecke, was to overcome two essential objections to the unification of Prussia with Germany. The first was the worry that a Prussian parliament would oppress a German parliament. This concern was based on a "parliamentary prejudice" which assumed that a parliamentary majority would in fact have power over the budget, and therefore that in any case of serious disagreement the government would come to a halt. Meinecke believed this opinion was based on an incorrect reading of south German experience. He argued that "moderate constitutionalism" did not necessarily imply parliamentary control, but he admitted that it was the wars of 1866 and 1870 that had restored faith in this "discredited moderate constitutionalism" and broken the parliamentary prejudice.[39]

The second objection was a "unitary" prejudice, which Meinecke traced from pre-1848 liberals to Heinrich von Treitschke. This held that a federal state had to have absolute power, with only limited powers remaining for the member states. Mistrust of Prussia was one reason for the "unitary" emphasis on the powers of the central government, but in addition there were particularist motives. Bismarck's solution was the creation of the Bundesrat to provide protection for the small states while allowing the head of the most powerful state to possess executive power. Treitschke was disappointed because, having swung his allegiance to Bismarck and Prussia, he would have preferred a strong central government, in effect, an expanded Prussia. But, said Meinecke, Bismarck's structure embodied a "moderate federalism" that did not permit individual princes to exercise veto power, and therefore avoided the weaknesses of the pre-1848 Bundestag. Meinecke saw this as parallel to the "moderate constitutionalism" of the Reichstag.[40] For thoughtful contemporaries, therefore, it was not the empire's authoritarianism and rigidity but its moderation and capacity for adaptation that seemed its most important features.

The National Liberal era and the Kulturkampf

The National Liberal parties in Prussia and in the new empire emerged out of splits and regroupings of Bismarck's former Liberal opponents who had been won over by his military successes. They dominated the early elections. In the Prussian Landtag, the National Liberals won 99 seats in 1867, 123 in 1870, and 174 in 1873, while the Conservatives dropped from 125 to 114 and then to 30. In the first Reichstag elections in 1871, the National Liberals won 125 seats, and this rose to 155 in 1874, compared to the Conservatives' 57 and 22. The Conservatives increased to 40 seats in 1877, but the National Liberals won 128 seats and remained the largest party by a substantial margin.

With Germany united and the borders of the empire fixed, many of these men enthusiastically welcomed the opportunity to shape and consolidate the empire not only politically, but also socially, culturally, and morally. They cooperated with the government in passing the range of legislation outlined above that created the institutions of governance for society and the economy. In addition, the "Catholic question" was high on the Liberal agenda. The Catholic problem had become especially pressing because of the annexation of Alsace and Lorraine, not only French but overwhelmingly Catholic. Catholics made up just over 36 per cent of the population of the new empire, dangerously high in the eyes of many Liberals.

As seen in Chapter 4, religious identities had become more unyielding. A tendency of many Liberals to identify the German national identity as a specifically Protestant identity ran counter to a widespread popular Catholic revival.[41] The Vatican Council's declaration of papal infallibility in 1870 appeared to Liberals not only an intellectual aberration in an age of rationalism, but also a direct assault on the state. Catholicism, said the Liberals, was inconsistent with the modern institutions of their new national state, and therefore the power of the state must be used against Catholicism. The *National Zeitung* of February 25, 1872, declared,

> The German will not tolerate a spirit that comes from Rome either among his people or in any of his churches. He does not want clerical rule and *Volksverdummung* ["making the people stupid"]. He wants, rather,

enlightenment, honest conscience, and work. Attaining a new level of moral freedom never before achieved, a morality arising from the people that is shared by Germany's churches and confessions, that is the task for this founding period of the new Reich.

For Liberals the victory over France remained inconclusive. A second campaign was required, this time waged inside the empire against the Catholic Church and its allies to complete the social, cultural, and moral unification of Germany, to secure the future of the nation, and to guarantee the blessings of enlightenment and modernity. Both stages of unification, Liberals believed, required efforts not short of war. The use of force against the inner enemy was as justified as the force that had been used against the outer enemy. Liberals described the confrontation with Catholicism in military metaphors of bombs, swords, and lances. Bismarck was portrayed as a literal knight in shining armor: "Now, Chancellor, show us that you are a knight without fear and reproach. Now, Chancellor, swing your mighty sword. Strike, strike! Plunge your blade with gallant courage!"[42]

The result was the *Kulturkampf*, a "cultural battle" or "clash of civilizations" embodied in a series of measures intended to undermine the political influence of the Catholic clergy. In 1871, Bismarck dissolved the Catholic section of the Prussian Ministry of Ecclesiastical and Educational Affairs. In 1872, the Prussian Landtag enacted legislation abolishing supervision of schools by clerics. Those who had served as school inspectors no longer did so because of their religious status, but were now appointed and removed at the discretion of the government. In principle, the new law applied to all, but, in practice, the government used it only to eliminate Catholic school inspectors. The "Pulpit Paragraph" passed by Reichstag in December 1871 made the discussion of matters of state by clerics "in a manner endangering public peace" a criminal offence. In 1872, Germany broke off diplomatic relations with the Vatican, and the Jesuit order was banned from Germany. In 1873, Adalbert Falk, the minister for religious affairs, introduced the four "May Laws" that imposed regulations on the training and certification of priests intended to undermine the influence of the Papacy, eliminated the disciplinary power of the Church hierarchy over priests, and protected lay persons from the effects of excommunication. Further laws tightened the regulation of the Church by state authorities and provided a range of penalties for violations.

Catholics opposed the new laws. When police authorities moved against the Jesuits in Essen, Catholics rioted and two battalions of troops were required to restore order. Opposition was repressed, but at a high cost. The impact of the *Kulturkampf* was not to consolidate and unify the German nation, but to deepen the divisions and increase the polarization of the population. Catholics now actively resented the state that hounded their religious leaders and attacked their beliefs. Socially, they responded by the creation of a separate milieu supported by an extensive network of Catholic organizations, from singing societies to labor unions. Politically, the majority of Catholics no longer considered Liberalism a political option. Those who had previously voted Liberal turned to the Catholic Center Party (*Zentrum*). Mass mobilization of Catholic voters by the Center was made far easier by their status as members of a pariah community.

The Center increased its representation in the Prussian Landtag from 58 seats in 1870 to 97 in 1879, and in the Reichstag from 63 seats in 1871 to 91 in 1874. In both Prussia and the empire this block of 90 to 100 Center representatives remained constant. Districts with Catholic majorities elected Catholic representatives in election after election. From Bismarck onward, the leaders of the Prussian and German governments therefore had to contend with a hostile party commanding about a fifth of the total seats, a party whose support could only be purchased by repeal of bits and pieces of the anti-Catholic laws. Nor were they grateful. The repeal of each item of legislation was seen by Center leaders and their followers as a humiliating reminder that they remained outcasts in their own country.[43]

All Jewish deputies in the Reichstag opposed the anti-Jesuit bill by either voting against it or abstaining. Although as Liberals they shared many of the anti-Catholic sentiments of their Protestant colleagues, in this particular instance they recognized the threat of the explicit definition of religious differences as the basis for discriminatory legislation.[44] Jews obtained full citizenship in all the member states of the North German Confederation in 1869, and this applied in the states of the empire after 1871, but they remained a small and vulnerable minority. Of the half-million Jews in the empire, most were poor, but some were rich and prominent, and they could easily become a target of hostility.

The anti-Semitism that Rosenberg identified with the Great Depression clearly antedated 1873, but in hard times people looked for someone to blame. Jews such as Strousberg were widely blamed for the frauds of the *Gründerzeit* and the crash of 1873. A journalist named Otto Glagau published a series of articles in the popular magazine *Gartenlaube* (*Garden Arbor*) in 1874 that contrasted the diligence and honesty of the German with the underhanded cunning of the Jew and blamed Jews for the depression. They appeared as a book, reprinted in numerous editions.

A specifically political anti-Semitism was more clearly linked to the depression and to structural change. Artisans and farmers sought an explanation for their difficulties. Organizations representing their interests, and politicians interested in their votes, offered the Jew as a scapegoat. The first explicitly anti-Semitic candidate was elected to the Reichstag in 1887. There were five candidates in 1890, and sixteen in 1893. They remained outside the pale of respectable political activity. Theodor Böckel, who campaigned successfully as an anti-Semite in Hesse, was considered uncouth for his excessively "American" campaign tactics. The number of anti-Semitic deputies declined in the late 1890s, but a few diehard voters remained in virtually every Reichstag district, especially in those that contained small towns. And, as we will see, the anti-Semites did have a lasting impact. The "traditional" Conservative parties and parts of the Catholic Center adopted anti-Semitic slogans, and anti-Semitic attitudes were subsumed within the radical nationalist groups that grew in influence after 1900.[45]

Liberals were happy to follow Bismarck's lead in foreign policy and to cooperate in the creation of the new nation's governing institutions. Bismarck, however, had no intention of relying on any party. Not surprisingly, the old battle lines were drawn again in conflict over the army budget. In the constituent assembly of the North German Confederation, in 1867, Bismarck attempted to establish the principle that the army and its funding should be automatically linked to the size of the population. The Liberals refused, and the deadlock threatened the entire framework of treaties. Bismarck compromised on a budget that set the size of the army at 1 per cent of the population and provided for definite funding until 1871. In 1871, the new Reichstag agreed to extend the 1867 agreement for another three years.

Army leaders still dreamed of independence from parliamentary control. In 1874, with the Emperor's support, they introduced a bill establishing a base size of the army in peacetime and providing that the government could increase the base whenever it wished. A solid majority of the Reichstag of course opposed the proposal, and Wilhelm referred

to them in a speech as "internal enemies" who dared defy "the leadership of the imperial warlord." Bismarck claimed not to have been consulted, and he was probably not enthusiastic about a law that would
have placed the army not only outside parliamentary control, but also
outside his control as Chancellor. He used the opportunity to threaten
leading Reichstag deputies with a dissolution, and then offered a compromise. The size of the army was set at the figure the military chiefs
desired, but the budget was to be fixed for only a seven-year period, after
which it would again be subject to review and approval. Seven years is a
long time, as Wilhelm said, "almost half a century when one thinks of
the years from 1863 to 1870!" Not long enough for the army leaders,
however, who resented interference from anyone, including Bismarck.[46]

The "second founding" of the empire: the Anti-Socialist Law, the bureaucracy, and tariff protection

In 1878, there were two attempts to assassinate Wilhelm. A week after
the first attempt, Bismarck presented a draft law to the Reichstag banning the Socialist Party. The law was vague and in effect threatened any
party that opposed the government. The Liberals led a majority that
rejected the proposal. However, the second attempt shortly after the vote
left the Emperor severely wounded. The two would-be assassins were
unconnected, and neither was connected with the Socialists. Bismarck,
however, dissolved the Reichstag and launched a campaign directed not
only against the Socialist threat, but also against the Liberals, whom he
accused of defending the Socialists. A wave of hysteria washed over the
nation. Treitschke called on employers to dismiss workers suspected of
Socialist inclinations. Courts sentenced dozens of people to long prison
terms for chance remarks. The Socialist Party retained nine of its twelve
seats, but the National Liberals and their allies, the Progressives, suffered severe losses, dropping from 128 to 99 and from 35 to 26. The two
Conservative parties rose from 78 to 116 seats.

Bismarck's Anti-Socialist Law passed the new Reichstag. It banned
any organization that supported "activities designed to subvert the existing political and social order in ways that threaten the public order and
particularly the harmony of the social classes." It detailed activities that
might bring heavy fines and prison sentences, including providing a
meeting place, attending a meeting, collecting funds, and distributing
socialist literature. Party offices, Socialist newspapers, and labor unions

were closed down, and individuals were expelled from Berlin and other cities. However, the law was not permanent, but subject to review and renewal by the Reichstag every three years. And, crucially, the law did not prohibit voters from electing Socialist deputies to the Reichstag. Candidates could still stand for election, and once elected they were protected by parliamentary immunity as long as the Reichstag was in session.

As with the *Kulturkampf*, the Anti-Socialist Law failed.[47] Rather than destroying the Socialist Party and uniting the nation, the law created another separate milieu, supported by an array of circumspect and clandestine socialist organizations. As with the Catholics, Socialist workers experienced the feeling of being outcast, and, as with Catholics, this had the effect of reinforcing their support for the party. The "heroic" period of illegal activities spawned legends, for instance of Julius Motteler, the "red postmaster" who organized the regular distribution of some 10,000 copies of the party's weekly newspaper from his base in Switzerland. Among his tricks were "Socialist funerals," with shipments sent over the border in coffins. The government responded with its own tricks including a network of undercover agents and bribes for information. Possibly 1500 people were imprisoned and thousands driven into exile.

The first wave of repression reduced the Socialist vote to 312,000 in 1881, but the party still gained 12 seats by winning several run-off elections. Thereafter, the party's vote increased in every election. The Socialists won 550,000 votes and 24 seats in 1884. In 1887, the party won 763,000 votes but secured only eleven seats. Bismarck had manipulated a foreign policy crisis to dissolve the Reichstag, and the two Conservative parties and the National Liberal Party united in a "*Kartell*" to pass a renewal of the seven-year military budget. This was the only time Bismarck was able to obtain a friendly majority in the Reichstag.

In 1890, the Socialist Party won 35 seats, and, most shocking of all, its 1.4 million votes were more than any other party. The two Conservative parties declined from 121 seats in 1887 to 93, and the National Liberals from 99 to 42. The Catholic Center's vote declined slightly from 1.5 to 1.3 million, but its seats rose from 98 to 106. The left-liberal Progressive Party, as much an enemy in Bismarck's eyes as the Catholics or the Socialists, rose from 1.1 to 1.3 million votes and from 32 to 76 seats. In contrast to the government's failure in the Reichstag, in the Prussian Landtag the two Conservative parties' representation stabilized in the 1880s at around 200 seats, supported by from 70 to 80 seats held by the

National Liberals. No Socialists were elected until 1908. Bismarck had been wrong. The safest support for the Conservative regime was the plutocratic indirect voting system.

There were other aspects of Bismarck's turn away from the National Liberals, and it is this combination of measures that has led some historians to see a genuine break, a "second founding" of the empire.[48] Along with the Anti-Socialist Law, there were changes in senior personnel, stricter control over junior officials, and the introduction of protective tariffs. The two Conservative parties became Bismarck's preferred supporters in the Reichstag. The National Liberals might be included, as in 1887, but groups to the left among the Liberals were excluded. The campaign against the Catholics ended. Although the anti-Catholic legislation remained in force, when Leo XIII became Pope in 1878 the government took the first steps to reestablish relations with the Vatican.

At the highest level, Bismarck had no desire to foster autonomous ministries or independent ministers. For example, he had relied on the support of Liberal free-trader Rudolf von Delbrück during the constitutional conflict and the Wars of Unification. Delbrück then served as Vice-Chancellor and head of the new Imperial Chancellor's Office, with a broad brief extending over economic, financial, social, and legal policy. However, from 1873 Bismarck progressively reduced the scope of the office because he feared Delbrück's power. In 1876, Delbrück fell, since he would not have supported the turn to protective tariffs. His replacement, Karl Hofmann, "proved himself a pliant official, who executed Bismarck's will."[49]

At lower levels, the demands for conformity by officials became overtly political. Catholic bureaucrats suffered in the 1870s, and, following the decision to introduce protective tariffs, Bismarck placed any official favoring free trade on the same level as one who had failed his examination.[50] There was no "purge" in the sense of large numbers of dismissals, but the pressure increased and the range of permissible opinion narrowed.[51] Prussian Interior Minister Robert von Puttkamer issued a regulation requiring officials to vote for government-approved candidates, and Bismarck defended him, insisting that "activity of officials in the interest of the regime is a requirement of the monarchical state."[52] In 1883, Puttkamer demanded "absolute, unthinking subordination of officials to the will of the all-powerful minister" who had been placed over them by the king. The behavior of officials was continually monitored, and any unsuitable conduct could lead to disciplinary proceedings. In 1899, an official was dismissed for renting a house to a woman thought to be a Socialist "agitator."[53]

As seen above, agriculture suffered worst in the Great Depression, but it was also a period of slower growth and lower profits for industry. Groups of farmers and industrialists in many countries agitated for tariff protection, and Germany was no exception. A petition of 204 Reichstag members calling for protection for agriculture and industry gave Bismarck a public occasion to announce his conversion to the idea of tariff protection. As with his family life, for Bismarck the personal intersected with the political. He belonged to the Junker class and he saw nothing wrong in manipulating policy to ensure the profitability of his own estates. In addition, the revenue from the tariffs would finally free the government from the Reichstag's control over the budget. Not only did he propose tariffs on agricultural goods and iron products, but he also asked for new excise taxes on salt, as well as on tobacco, coffee, and other luxury goods. Once again he failed. He gained the tariffs and the taxes, but he did not escape the Reichstag. The National Liberals proposed an annual review of the new excise taxes, and Bismarck refused. Instead, he compromised with the Catholic Center and accepted their proposal that all revenue above a certain fixed amount would go not to the imperial government but to the states. Peter Christian Witt, and, more recently, John Hobson have emphasized the ongoing financial weakness of the imperial government that resulted.[54]

Bismarck's foreign policy

Bismarck's foreign policy has been praised as a coherent system that preserved Europe's stability, and it has been denounced as an incoherent structure whose contradictions destabilized Europe and resulted in the tragedy of the First World War. Klaus Hildebrand and other diplomatic historians have analyzed the inherent difficulties of Germany's position. As a major power in the center of Europe, Germany was torn between the need for circumspect defensiveness and the desire to break out of the confinement imposed by its position.[55] Konrad Canis adds that both the goals and the means employed by Bismarck and his successors in Germany did not differ markedly from those of the other powers in the late nineteenth and early twentieth centuries.[56] In contrast, social historians such as Eckart Kehr and Hans-Ulrich Wehler have emphasized the connections between domestic politics and foreign policy. The empire's complex constitutional structure and the continuing influence of the landowning Junker class in Prussia contrasted with the thrust of industrial development and urban growth. Germany's authoritarian leaders would always be tempted to use or to create a foreign policy crisis to improve their domestic political position.[57]

One way to approach Bismarck's policy is to view the war against France as a problem rather than as a culmination. As seen in Chapter 4, Bismarck actively sought the war. Defeated, France was then humiliated by the proclamation of the new empire at Versailles. As seen above, Bismarck demanded a huge indemnity and the annexation of Alsace and Lorraine. He intended the indemnity to cripple France, and he justified the annexation of the two provinces on the grounds that leniency would bring no reward. France would never forgive the defeat, and Germany would therefore require the strongest border obtainable. Bismarck rode a wave of public enthusiasm for the annexation, but, as also seen above, in the aftermath of unification the formation of an accepted national identity for the new Germany proved extraordinarily difficult. The problematic heritage of domestic myths of military success and foreign diplomatic vulnerability meant that the Bismarckian system was premised on Germany's position as a "saturated" power with no further ambitions, but also on the assumption of eternal hostility toward France. Therefore Bismarck sought both increased military power and a series of alliances and alignments that would isolate France and secure Germany's position.

Bismarck had a further problem. In the Balkans, as the Ottoman Empire declined, Austria and Russia both sought increased influence and territorial gains. Should they go to war, Germany could be drawn in. Worse, France might fish in these troubled waters and find in either Austria or Russia a powerful ally against Germany. Therefore Austria and Russia had to be convinced both that maintaining the status quo was in their interest and that Germany was a more valuable ally than France. Bismarck's first attempt to solve this problem was the Three Emperors' League of 1873 that linked Germany to both Austria and Russia. These gains evaporated in 1875 when Bismarck attempted to threaten France and found himself isolated. However, the Russians declared war on the Ottoman Empire in 1876, their successes threatened Austrian and British interests, and by 1878 Bismarck found himself hosting a congress in Berlin that brokered a settlement of the conflicting claims in the Balkans. Russian leaders were unhappy, and the tension with Russia led Bismarck to negotiate the Dual Alliance with Austria in 1879 that provided for unconditional support if either party were to be attacked by Russia, and for neutrality if either were to be attacked by some other power. A five-year agreement, it was renewed regularly and lasted until 1918.

The Three Emperors' League was revived in 1881 and renewed for another three years in 1884. Russian leaders wanted a treaty with Germany, but Bismarck insisted on including Austria. The agreement provided for neutrality in case of war with a fourth power and provided for consultation and cooperation in case any of the three should go to war against the Ottoman Empire. Conflict between Russia and Austria in the Balkans continued, however, and the three-power approach failed again. In 1887, Russia refused to renew the treaty. Instead, Bismarck and Russian leaders negotiated a treaty known to diplomatic historians as the Reinsurance Treaty. Germany and Russia agreed to neutrality if either were attacked by another power, and Germany recognized extensive Russian rights in the Balkans.

In the meantime, Bismarck had formed another grouping, the Triple Alliance of Italy, Austria, and Germany. The Italians received the promise of support if attacked by France, and Austria and Germany of support in case of attack by France or by a coalition of other powers. Signed in 1882 for five years, the treaty was renewed in 1887 and remained in force until 1915. Because of conflicting claims in North Africa, Italy wanted allies against France, but had to give up claims to Austrian territory and suffered from the later tariff war with France.

Finally, Bismarck sponsored two Mediterranean Agreements, both signed in 1887. The first included Britain, Italy, Austria, and Spain, and provided for the maintenance of the status quo. The second included Britain, Italy, and Austria, and provided specifically that the Ottoman Empire would not give up its position in the Balkans or the eastern Mediterranean. Should it do so, the three powers would agree to occupy those territories. Germany was not a party, and therefore could disclaim responsibility, but Bismarck was involved in encouraging the negotiations leading to the agreements.

This network of international treaties that Bismarck bequeathed to his successors was complex, but comprehensible. The Dual Alliance with Austria and the Reinsurance Treaty with Russia were defensive treaties, each aimed at the other ally. They were intended to restrain both from aggressive expansion, but they were also intended to reassure each that they were secure from attack by the other. The Triple Alliance brought Italy into the system but also held Italian leaders back from aggression against Austria. The Mediterranean Agreements involved Britain in assisting to guarantee the status quo, and they also made it impossible for Russia to expand its interests in the Balkans by exploiting the Reinsurance Treaty. Together the treaties would have isolated France, and they would have made any change to the existing balance impossible without German approval.

However, the logic of Bismarck's system is only apparent in retrospect, after decades of specialist research. Bismarck never explained his aims to his superior the Emperor, to his subordinates in the Foreign Office, or to his collaborators in the foreign ministries of the other powers. His apparent support of Russia's Balkan ambitions completely confused senior officials in the foreign ministry such as Friedrich von Holstein, for instance, although the Russians realized bitterly that they could never obtain what Bismarck appeared to have promised. Further, beginning with the Dual Alliance, Bismarck's treaties were secret. Other powers knew or suspected that they existed, but did not know their terms. Therefore those other powers would attempt to negotiate agreements to protect themselves. This has led some specialists to argue that the breakdown of Bismarck's balanced system into rival camps was virtually inevitable.

The complexity of the system also meant that it was not consistent. Particularly in the case of the ongoing conflict between Russia and Austria in the Balkans, the treaties might involve Germany in irreconcilable contradictions. In addition, Bismarck insisted that Germany was a saturated and a European power, but he also acquired colonies and became involved in Africa, the Pacific, and the Far East. There were calls for colonial expansion, notably a book published in 1879 by Friedrich Fabri, *Bedarf Deutschland Kolonien?* (*Does Germany Need Colonies?*), and a Colonial Society had been established in 1882, but Bismarck had resisted these pressures. Then suddenly in 1884, Germany established protectorates over Togo and Cameroon in West Africa, Southwest Africa, East Africa, and New Guinea and other islands in the Pacific. These acquisitions almost all cut across British interests. At that particular point in 1884, Bismarck wished to improve relations with the government of Jules Ferry in France. Anti-British moves helped this project, but such momentary gains over Britain were not consistent with his long-term policy. Bismarck initially hoped that colonies would be self-financing supports for German trade. When he discovered this was not true, he decided not to look for further acquisitions, but he was then attacked by colonial enthusiasts.

Bismarck constantly threatened and bullied the other powers. In 1875, the "War in Sight" crisis resulted from a story in a newspaper known to be one of his mouthpieces that asked "Is War in Sight?" and suggested Germany was preparing a preemptive strike against France. In 1887, Bismarck assured the world that Germany was not contemplating a preventive war against France, but the same newspaper carried a story, "The Razor's Edge," that argued France's military build-up made just such a war likely. Bismarck sent his son Herbert to London in 1884 to threaten German opposition to British policy in Egypt if the British did not agree to German claims to Southwest Africa and Fiji. Almost immediately after the Reinsurance Treaty was signed, Bismarck alienated Russia by prohibiting the use of Russian securities as collateral for loans or as approved investments for trustees. Bismarck intended this to make it more difficult for Russia to arm itself and to force the Russians to recognize the necessity of Germany's goodwill. But the result was to force the Russian government to other capital markets, especially Paris. This laid the foundation for an alliance between France and Russia, precisely the development that Bismarck's entire system was intended to prevent.[58]

Bismarck regularly used foreign policy as a means of attacking his domestic enemies. Diplomatic crises were useful weapons in the new electoral politics. In 1884, the acquisition of colonies was intended in part to help in the Reichstag elections. In 1887, Reichstag leaders actually offered to approve the proposed increases in the army, but asked in return for a shorter term before the next review. Bismarck refused. Instead, he dissolved the Reichstag, the election was waged in a crisis atmosphere, and collaboration between Conservatives and National Liberals gave him his majority. Bismarck also still had to play the old game of high politics, and here, too, the string of foreign policy crises was useful. He kept other officials ignorant of his intentions in part because anyone with too much knowledge might become a rival. He could still bully Emperor Wilhelm with threats of resignation, but, looking to the future, he feared the hostility of the Crown Prince and his English wife. Herbert von Bismarck later said that "we had to count on a long period of government by the Crown Prince during which English influence would dominate. In order to avoid this, we had to inaugurate the policy of colonialism, which is popular and can bring on a conflict with England at any moment."

There are also possible deeper links between foreign policy and domestic politics. Eckart Kehr reversed one of Bismarck's favorite phrases and argued that German statecraft did not reflect the primacy of foreign policy, but rather the primacy of domestic politics.[59] Since Kehr wrote, many commentators have pointed out the obvious contradiction between a system of alliances intended to produce stability, and a foreign economic policy of tariff protection, discrimination, and colonial acquisition. Tariffs reflected the interests of Junker landlords and heavy industrialists. Similarly, the causes of imperialism can be seen in the desire of German commercial and industrial interests for sources of raw materials and protected markets. Recurrent crises made the demands for increased military spending plausible and reinforced the position of the army and the officer class. Protectionism and imperialism were also linked to the problem of the working class. Workers might be grateful for the jobs and the improved living standards that resulted from tariffs and colonies. In addition, the waves of patriotism whipped up by crises and heated election campaigns might obscure the divisions in German society and the failure of the government to create a single accepted national identity.[60]

The year of the three Emperors and Bismarck's fall

Emperor Wilhelm died in March 1888, aged nearly 91, and his son Friedrich III succeeded him. A reputed Liberal who had publicly opposed Bismarck's violation of the constitution in the 1860s, married to Victoria, a strong-willed daughter of Queen Victoria known for her preference for English customs and institutions, he was also suffering from a belatedly diagnosed cancer of the throat. Terminally ill when crowned, he died in June, and was succeeded in turn by his son Wilhelm II.

The 99 days of Friedrich's rule are another of the possible turning points in German history. Bismarck feared and hated Friedrich and his wife. His spiteful campaign against the royal couple reveals his character at its worst. Knowing the new Emperor was dying, he blocked proposed appointments to the imperial household and protested against decorations the Emperor wished to bestow on old friends. He created an international incident in thwarting the marriage of Friedrich's daughter to Alexander of Battenberg, whom the Russians had forced from the throne of Bulgaria. Queen Victoria favored the marriage, and Bismarck's claim that this would alienate Russia and reduce Germany to a British satellite set off a vicious campaign in the Conservative press directed against the new Empress and her daughter.

Because any enemy of Bismarck may be regarded as a friend of constitutional government, Friedrich remains an intriguing figure. What would have happened had his father died sooner or if he himself had lived longer? Debate has revolved around attempts to determine the degree of Friedrich's liberalism. A "Liberal" Friedrich might have changed the course of history, but a "Conservative" Friedrich presumably would not. The evidence of his private correspondence indicates that Friedrich believed that the constitution "was a binding agreement between the monarch and the people that had to be upheld at all costs."[61] However, as we have seen, the constitutions of Prussia and Germany placed power securely in the hands of the monarch, and Friedrich believed they bound the people as well as himself. It also appears that Friedrich was neither a deep nor a consistent thinker, nor was he a skillful politician. His views shifted according to circumstances, and his opinions reflected those of other stronger personalities around him. Whatever power he had lay in what he might do when he became emperor, but that power disappeared with his illness.

Wilhelm, just 30, could be expected to rule for a long time. Those hoping for influence, including Bismarck, had flattered him and encouraged him to believe himself capable of ruling. As will be seen in Chapter 6, Wilhelm was subject to fits of enthusiasm. In 1889 and 1890, he convinced himself that, if he could secure legislation limiting working hours and improving working conditions, he could win the working classes away from Socialism. He would earn their gratitude and their loyalty, solve the social problem, and become a "king of the poor." In May 1889, he received a delegation of striking Ruhr coal miners, and after hearing their complaints burst into a meeting of the Prussian state ministers and excitedly insisted that the government intervene to force the mine owners to meet the workers' demands.

Bismarck believed Wilhelm's schemes were naïvely unrealistic and that his enthusiasm for social reform was a passing whim. He may have been correct, but he failed for once to play the game of high politics. Rather than supporting the Emperor, he proceeded with his own plan to make the Anti-Socialist Law permanent. He refused to compromise, his unsteady coalition of Conservatives and National Liberals broke apart, and the law was defeated. He declared in a Crown Council meeting in January 1890 that the government should take the opportunity to push for a confrontation. The elections in February brought triumph for Bismarck's enemies and crushing defeat for his supporters. The votes of the Socialist Party, Catholic Center Party, and Progressives together could block any legislation. Bismarck now proposed to introduce both the Anti-Socialist Law and a new army bill that the Reichstag could never be expected to pass. The war ministry sent instructions to the regional commanders instructing them that the use of force might be necessary to suppress popular uprisings.

Those close to Bismarck were convinced he intended a confrontation with the Reichstag followed by a military coup d'état and a revision of the constitution that would reduce the power of the elected assembly. Some of Wilhelm's friends, such as Philip Eulenburg, also talked of a coup, and Wilhelm himself was deeply alarmed by the gains made by the Socialists. But there were also those who suggested to the Emperor that Bismarck had lost touch with reality, and there were others happy to suggest further that Wilhelm's own plans for social reform provided a much preferable way out of the crisis. Army leaders not only failed to support Bismarck; they encouraged the Emperor to replace him.

A clumsy attempt to prevent other ministers from gaining access to the Emperor, an attempt to have the French government destroy Wilhelm's plans for an international labor conference, and, finally, an unauthorized discussion with Center leader Ludwig Windthorst seeking some sort of accommodation with the intractable Reichstag all gave Wilhelm ample excuses to demand Bismarck's resignation. The break came in March 1890. Bismarck delayed long enough to write an account, published after his death, which placed the blame for his fall on a disagreement over foreign policy. He accused Wilhelm of misunderstanding the issues involved in Russian relations and of a general tendency to make decisions without sufficient knowledge or consideration. He also arranged for the removal of some 12,000 bottles of wine from the basement of the foreign ministry building, and for the sale of large blocks of his shares in German companies, speculating that the news of his departure would send the German stock exchange down.

Notes

1. Adolf von Menzel, *Supper at the Ball*, 1878. Oil on linen, 71 × 90 cm. Old National Gallery, Berlin. Reproduced and discussed in Brettell 1999, p. 159. See Keisch and Riemann-Reyher 1996.
2. Brettell 1999, pp. 158–60.
3. Gall 1993, pp. 26–9; Mazon 2000.
4. Stern 1977, pp. 150–5, 320–7.
5. Nipperdey 1993b, p. 283.
6. Craig 1978, p. 80; Nipperdey 1993b, p. 281.
7. Nipperdey 1993b, pp. 283–4.
8. Henderson 1975, pp. 168–70.
9. Hoffmann 1965, pp. 257, 390–5, 454–5, 530–2.
10. Bopp 1954; Hoffmann 1965, pp. 530–2; Holtfrerich 1988.
11. Rosenberg 1943; 1967, pp. 88–117.
12. Wehler 1995, Vol. 3, pp. 448–86, 662–80, especially p. 666.
13. Nipperdey 1993b, pp. 284–5.
14. Spree 1978; 1980; Solomou 1987; 1998.
15. Hoffmann 1965, pp. 259–61.
16. Chatterjee 1986; Tipton 1998b, Chs. 5, 8.
17. Wunder 1986.
18. Baumgarten 1997.
19. Zerback 1997.
20. Roth 1996; Palmowski 1999.
21. See Crew 1979; Schambach 1996.
22. Jackson 1981; Hochstadt 1999, pp. 107, 156–65.
23. Roth 1996; Schambach 1996.
24. Johnson 1995.
25. Bajohr 1982.
26. Steinmetz 1993.
27. Wehler 1995, Vol. 3, pp. 907–15.
28. Conrad 1994.
29. Reagin 2001a.
30. Allen 1991.
31. Finney 1997, pp. 320–1; Peterson 1997.
32. Imhof 1981.
33. Sugiyama 1994.
34. Applegate 1990.
35. See Pflanze 1990.
36. Aldenhoff 1996, pp. 39–40.
37. Prussia, Ministerium der öffentlichen Arbeiten, *Der preussische Landeseisenbahnrat in den ersten 25 Jahren seiner Tätigkeit, 1883–1908* (Berlin, 1908).
38. Meinecke 1907, p. 436.
39. Meinecke 1907, pp. 418–20.
40. Meinecke 1907, pp. 420–8.
41. Sperber 1984.

42. *Berliner Wispen* 1872, cited in Gross 1997.
43. Sperber 1984; Smith 1995; Hübinger 1996.
44. Gross 1997.
45. Levy 1975; Volkov 1978; Pulzer 1988.
46. See Craig 1955.
47. Lidtke 1996.
48. Barkin 1987.
49. Nipperdey 1993c, p. 113; Wehler 1995, Vol. 3, pp. 642, 860.
50. Wehler 1995, Vol. 3, p. 862.
51. Röhl 1977; Anderson and Barkin 1982; Ritter 1983; Nipperdey 1993c, p. 134.
52. Wehler 1995, Vol. 3, p. 863.
53. Wunder 1986, pp. 89–90; Wehler 1995, Vol. 3, p. 1031.
54. Witt 1970; Hobson 1997.
55. Hildebrand 1995.
56. Canis 1997.
57. Wehler 1973.
58. Nipperdey 1993c, pp. 464–5; Wehler 1995, Vol. 3, pp. 975–7.
59. Kehr 1970.
60. Wehler 1995, Vol. 3, pp. 977–90.
61. Kollander 1995, p. 195.

CHAPTER 6

NEOCLASSICAL FAÇADE AND MODERNIST REVOLT, 1890–1914

Max Klinger was one of the most successful artists in Germany at the turn of the twentieth century, and his paintings, graphic works, and sculpture continue to invite discussion. He caused a scandal in 1893 with a painting that showed Christ completely naked, but became a member of the Academy of Arts the following year, and in 1897 became a professor at Leipzig. In 1897, he painted *Christ on Olympus*, a monumental work that portrays Christ and four female attendants confronting the assembled Greek gods and goddesses. The four women are carrying the cross, and they are wearing what appear to be Roman togas. Christ's robe is an elaborate cloth-of-gold drapery. The Greek deities are naked, except for Bacchus who wears a sarong tied around his waist in addition to his grape-leaf crown. One female figure, identified as Psyche, is at Christ's feet, her raised hands clasped imploringly. Amor (Cupid) cringes away. Christ confronts Zeus, his hand extended, and Zeus recoils in his marble throne, obviously nonplussed. A separate panel below the main painting shows struggling naked figures, possibly the souls of pagans who had not heard the message of Christianity suffering in purgatory.[1]

Klinger also produced a memorial sculpture commemorating Beethoven in 1902. Portrayed in white marble, the composer sits, naked but with his lower body draped, on an elaborate throne. He is leaning forward, staring ahead. The face is the classic portrayal, but otherwise the figure would be unrecognizable, for his body is that of an extremely muscular young athlete. The throne sits atop a square block of dark granite. An eagle hunches before him at a corner of the block, its wings and beak extended, and it is at this eagle that Beethoven is gazing so intently.[2]

In 1905, Adolf Hoelzel painted *Composition in Red*, an asymmetric but balanced arrangement of rounded planes of flat color connected by irregular darker lines. Hoelzel belonged to the Neu-Dachau group of artists who were exploring the artistic possibilities of the landscape of the Dachauer Moor. International in outlook, influenced by the Scottish Glasgow School, and self-consciously post-Impressionist, they employed simplified forms intended to evoke the lyric moods of the wild open spaces in harmonious "tone poems." The painting was almost certainly inspired by a portion of that landscape, but there is no central focus, and no recognizable object is portrayed.[3] Wassily Kandinsky's *Mountain* (1909) retains ciphers of the peak and human figures, but the colors are arbitrary. The overlapping planes of his *With a Black Arc* (1912) avoid any reference to a physical object and consciously distribute the varying weights of size and color to avoid creating an architectonic center.[4]

For contemporaries, a long period of economic expansion and Germany's rising position as a world power were justifiable sources of pride, and the continuing influence of neoclassicism demonstrated this relationship. The prosperity of Wilhelmine Germany created a climate favorable to determinedly edifying works showing historical events, state occasions, and classical allegories. The composition and posing of *Christ on Olympus* and the *Beethoven Memorial* reflect an assertion of enduring truths and continuous heritages. Western, Christian values would triumph over barbarism. Beethoven, the German hero, could be recreated as a classical figure, giving form to chaos through the sheer power of his intellect. At the same time, the wealthy could amuse themselves with the pleasantly thrilling shock of naked flesh—the healthy young figures in Klinger's lower panel are contorted in ways that suggest passion as much as pain. Although anyone from the respectable classes could view the originals, it was illegal to make inexpensive postcard reproductions of the nudes on display in public museums.

Behind the façade of official neoclassicism, however, the unresolved conflicts within German society continued, and perhaps deepened. The message of *Composition in Red* was not clear at all. Even the references to the landscape that had inspired the work were known only to a small group of fellow artists, gallery owners, and sophisticated patrons. *Mountain* and *With a Black Arc* were deliberately obscure. Kandinsky said in 1910, "Mystery speaking through mysteries. Isn't that meaning? Isn't that the conscious or unconscious purpose of the compulsive urge to create?"[5] To admire works such as these, to purchase them, to hang them in a public space, were actions that placed one squarely in opposition to official culture. Visions of the world presented in music, in the

Plate 6.1   Max Klinger, *Christ on Olympus*, 1897. Museum der Bildenden
Künste, Leipzig. Oil on canvas, 550 × 970 cm. Detail, showing Christ, Psyche,
Amor, and Bacchus. A good example of the sort of neoclassical painting that
modernist artists opposed. The uplifting moral is clear and unambiguous.
There is, however, a large amount of naked flesh on display, and although
Christ is a stern judge, Bacchus, realistically flushed with his product, appears
somewhat oblivious to the message. In the background a demon reaches for
another victim, preparing to drag her to the torments of the underworld seen in
the panel beneath the main painting. Photo: AKG London.

novel, and in painting all became fields of contention in their own right,
and, in addition, they symbolized broader conflicts in social and
political life.

Things became confused. *Meyers Conversational Dictionary*, the
bible of the middle classes, said in 1897, "Germania is a conjoining of
the warrior virgin with the German mother who symbolizes the all-
embracing fatherland."[6] By the early years of the twentieth century,
contemporaries realized that their unified view of the world had begun
to fracture. Some attributed the loss of certainty to external threats, and
some accused internal enemies. As seen below and in Chapter 7,
Emperor Wilhelm II and many others feared that Germany, the West,
and civilization itself were under siege from dark forces both without
and within.

Plate 6.2   Wassily Kandinsky, *Mountain*, 1909. Oil on linen, 109.5 × 109.7 cm. Lenbachhaus, Munich. A good example of the sort of work that Klinger's patrons regarded as incomprehensible rubbish. Today Kandinsky's painting is seen as an early example of the move toward pure abstraction, and the artist has a prominent place in the canonical history of modern art. Photo: AKG London. Copyright © Wassily Kandinsky, 1909/ADAGP. Licensed by Viscopy, Sydney, 2002.

What to do? Those who felt threatened by change established organizations and pressure groups to push their case. The General Association for the German Language was founded in 1885 and had over 30,000 members in 1910. Devoted to the "healing of the degeneration and crippling" of the national language, in 1887 the association named as its first Honorary Member Heinrich Stephan, who as Postmaster General had Germanized 760 words used by the postal service, including replacing *Telephon* with *Fernsprecher*.[7] For some of those distressed by social and political conflict, science provided answers and means to shape and control the future. Some argued that Germany's future lay in a program to improve the racial stock. Others argued that the future lay in improved education. Still others sought in various ways to improve the quality of life, of city dwellers, or of working-class families, or of children. But all these proposals involved interfering with individuals and groups, and therefore they proved highly contentious. Theodor Fontane and other novelists resented the Language Association's attempts to restrict their freedom of expression, and workers opposed attempts to control their leisure-time activities.

Partly because of these fascinating cross-currents, Wilhelmine Germany is one of the most intensively studied periods in world history.[8] Basic but difficult questions, such as how economic and social development interact, or what exactly constitutes "modern" culture, have brought into question not only the facts and their interpretation, but also the methods by which the facts should be interpreted.[9] There are high stakes for German historians as well; we want to know whether internal economic, social, and political contradictions led Germany into the First World War, and to what extent the later disasters of Nazism can be traced to the years before 1914. Historians from all specialist fields have debated the severity of the strains within German society. The economic and social contexts, and the conflicts in the cultural sphere, are the subjects of this chapter. The overlapping and equally contentious political context is considered in Chapter 7.

The economic context: the upswing 1896–1914

Trends: the golden age

The long cycle turned up again in the 1890s, and Germany enjoyed very rapid growth from 1895 to 1913 (see Chapter 5, Figure 5.2 and Table 5.1). The upswing was marred by only a single year of declining output. In 1901, Germany's national product dropped 2 per cent, but the loss had nearly been made good by the end of 1902. In every other year Germany produced more than the year before. The upward thrust of the aggregate figures reflected the boom in industry. In the 1890s, the new leading sectors were the industries of the "second industrial revolution," chemistry, engineering, and electricity. The production of chemicals increased 6.6 per cent per year, the output of the metallurgical and machinery industries 8.3 per cent each, and electrical power output rose nearly 18 per cent per year.

The growth in total output was small consolation to agriculture, which grew on average even more slowly than during the Great Depression, and declined in several years. As seen below and in Chapter 7, the problems of agriculture had important political implications. When the 1895 census results showed that agriculture had declined to less than half of the labor force, the news inflamed academic and public debate. However, not all farmers suffered equally, and some did not suffer at all. Agriculture still employed more than one-third of the German labor force in 1914, and, as seen in Figure 6.1, the numbers of farms of under two hectares rose substantially. In the west and south, even very small farms could become specialist producers of fruits, vegetables, or dairy products, and ship their products by rail to consumers in the expanding cities. In the northwest, larger farms predominated, as the number of middle-sized farms declined. The successful farm families raised primarily livestock, and they frequently were net purchasers of grain as feed. Rising meat prices and falling grain prices meant that they had often benefited during the Great Depression, and they continued to benefit during the upswing.

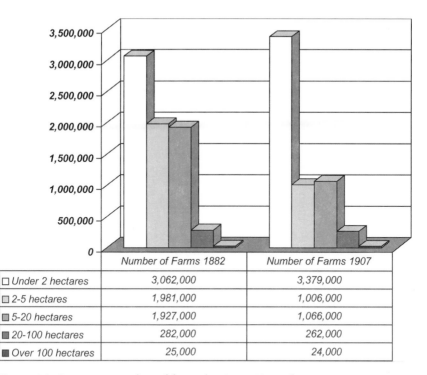

	Number of Farms 1882	Number of Farms 1907
☐ Under 2 hectares	3,062,000	3,379,000
☐ 2-5 hectares	1,981,000	1,006,000
▨ 5-20 hectares	1,927,000	1,066,000
▪ 20-100 hectares	282,000	262,000
▪ Over 100 hectares	25,000	24,000

Figure 6.1 Germany: number of farms by size, 1882 and 1907

In the east the story was mixed. Foreign competition hurt the large estates through the 1890s. Then, at the end of the decade prices began to rise. Exports of grains from Australia, Canada, and the United States did not increase as they had over the previous thirty years. In the United States, especially, rapid population growth and rising incomes increased domestic demand and absorbed potential exports. In the meantime, many owners of large estates had diversified their production to include potatoes, sugar beets, and animals as well as the traditional grains. Many invested in new machinery and improved drainage, and many became heavy users of chemical fertilizers. Diversification and rationalization of production also meant greater control over labor costs. Innovative landowners replaced long-term contract workers and dependent smallholders with flexible part-time workers whenever they could. To the distress of nationalists committed to "Germanization" of the east, these were often Polish migrants.

The international economy boomed. German exports rose 5.9 per cent per year, exports of chemical products 8.9 per cent per year, and exports of machinery 13.9 per cent per year. Angus Maddison designates the years from 1870 to 1913 as "Phase II" of modern capitalist development, a happy period of rising incomes, especially in Britain and the United States. These two countries provided crucial markets for world producers. Britain was either the first or second-most important trading partner of every other country in the world, and the United States grew to be only slightly less significant. From 1895 to 1914, the British national product, measured in constant prices, increased at a rate of 5.45 per cent yearly, and United States national product at 3.53 per cent. British imports, measured in current prices, increased from 417 million pounds to 769 million, and United States imports from 752 million dollars to 1.85 billion.[10]

These gains were achieved despite generally higher tariffs and a series of tariff wars, such as the one between France and Italy in the 1880s and 1890s. The pressure of declining agrarian interests lay behind tariff policies, for instance the campaign for the 1892 Méline Tariff in France. In Germany's case, a series of trade treaties sponsored by Bismarck's successor Leo von Caprivi in 1892–94 lowered tariffs, but this created hysterical opposition in the landowner class, and they regained higher duties on agricultural products when the treaties expired in 1902.

Incomes and productivity

The figures for output and exports are in constant prices, and they reveal our later generation's interest in the underlying processes of economic development. What concerned contemporaries was how much they could expect to earn and how long it took to earn it. Here the news was good. An average worker in the industrial sector brought home 768 marks in the year 1895, but earned 1210 marks in 1913. In addition, average working hours declined from 64 hours per week in 1890–95 to 57 hours per week in 1910–14. But the news was not all good. Rising prices ate into incomes. Working hours declined in industries where the firms tended to be small, and therefore where labor unions were most effective, such as printing and metalworking. In mining and the heavy iron and steel industries, employers resisted and hours did not decline. Workers in agriculture earned substantially less than industrial workers, 444 marks per year in 1895 and 682 in 1913. The hours worked by agricultural laborers did not decline. As in heavy industry, both large landowners and small farmers resisted labor unions. On small farms, in particular, the hours worked by women rose, because, as tens of thousands of young women and men moved to jobs in the cities and in industry, female family members had to take over the work of hired hands.

The rising wages enjoyed by German workers reflected large increases in productivity. This meant new technologies. Individual inventors such as Werner von Siemens, who developed the electric dynamo in the 1860s, established firms that, if successful, grew to be very large. Siemens' great rival was Emil Rathenau, who formed the Allegemeine Elektricitäts-Gesellschaft (General Electric Company, or AEG), in 1883. BASF, Bayer, Hoechst, and several smaller firms such as AG für Anilin-Fabrikation (AGFA) dominated the chemical industry. These firms achieved their advantage as "first movers" by building plants large enough to yield economies of scale. They then moved to exploit what Alfred Chandler called "economies of scope" by diversifying into related areas of production, expanding geographically, and crucially by continually investing in technical improvements and developing new products.[11]

By 1900, the leading firms had all become multi-divisional organizations under the control of a new generation of professional managers. Siemens and the AEG are interesting in this respect, because the Siemens family resisted the professionalization of its management and lost ground to the AEG.[12] For example, to appeal to the expanding market for new consumer products, the AEG hired Peter Behrens, principal of the Düsseldorf School of Applied Art and founding member of the *Deutsche Werkbund*, as architect and advisor on design for new consumer products. Under his leadership, AEG's designs for small electrical appliances and advertisements drew both on the commitment of the *Werkbund* to traditional craft motifs, and on modernist artistic influences. His design for the Berlin Turbine Factory building (1908–09) is a landmark in modern architecture, but the faceted gable roof intentionally recreates the lines of a rural barn.[13]

The new technologies were embodied in new machinery, and the machinery required by the second industrial revolution was expensive. Measured in constant prices, the amount of installed capital per worker in the industrial sector rose some 60 per cent between 1895 and 1907. More concretely, the horsepower of the machinery installed in German mines and factories rose from 947,000 in 1875 to 3.3 million in 1895, but it then more than doubled again to 8.0 million in 1907.

Two generations of heavy investment in education at all levels had provided Germany with the human capital needed to seize the opportunities presented by the second industrial revolution. Developments in pure science made the new technologies possible. They also made it imperative that those working in the new fields had formal scientific training and the support of research and experimental facilities. The day of the insightful amateur and the isolated gentleman researcher were over. Alongside the older universities appeared new "technical universities" (*Technische Hochschulen* or TH). Following a dramatic intervention by Emperor Wilhelm in 1899, they received the right to grant doctorates in engineering. There were eleven by 1914, and they produced a generation of applied chemists and engineers. By 1900, Germany was producing half again as many discoveries in the key scientific areas as Britain and France combined.[14]

Contemporaries noticed the rise of large firms. In mining, predictably, nearly 60 per cent of workers in 1907 were in firms of over 1000 employees. In manufacturing, however, not all firms were large. As seen in Figure 6.2, the greatest increase in employment came among medium-sized firms. Even tiny establishments with five workers or fewer declined only slightly, and if we consider firms of ten workers and fewer as a group, there was a substantial increase.

The desperate complaints about the decline of small establishments therefore need to be qualified. Many artisans became shopkeepers,

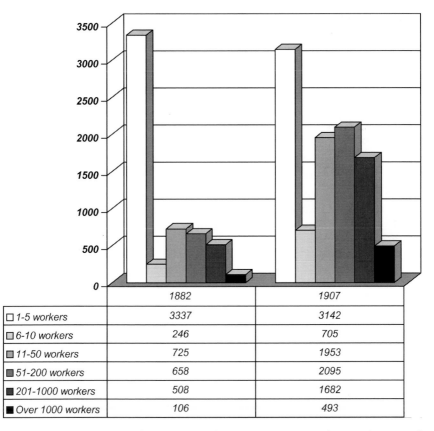

	1882	1907
☐ 1-5 workers	3337	3142
☐ 6-10 workers	246	705
▨ 11-50 workers	725	1953
■ 51-200 workers	658	2095
■ 201-1000 workers	508	1682
■ Over 1000 workers	106	493

Figure 6.2 Germany: workers in manufacturing in 1882 and 1907, by size of firm (thousands)

selling and repairing goods they might previously have made. German employers in small and medium manufacturing firms achieved large increases in productivity by using skilled workers to operate their new machines. They did not adopt the new American approach of subdividing tasks and replacing skilled workers with unskilled and semi-skilled workers. The old artisan networks continued to supply skills to industry. In 1895, over half of the 799,000 apprentices were being trained in firms with fewer than six employees. Guild associations pressed for the extension of continuation schools with artisan masters as instructors. After 1900, employers were required to release male workers under 18 to attend classes for six hours a week, and there were over 500,000 students in the continuation schools.[15]

The complaints of guild masters and skilled workers—and numerous strikes—often aimed at female workers. In trades such as metallurgy and machinery, the requirements for formal training excluded young women. Women were confined to industries where formal training requirements were lower, especially textiles and clothing. Here they worked in factories and operated advanced machinery, but they earned less than men. They also worked full careers, frequently returning to the same jobs after childbirth. The alleged impermanence of women workers and the claimed skill differentials between jobs were excuses to pay women less than men.[16] Women also found employment as proprietors of small shops, in theory independent but in fact acting as branches of larger firms. Again they earned less money and suffered the hostility of male shopkeepers and organizations of male sales clerks.[17]

Money and banking

The massive investment in new technologies and urban construction required funding. Money for expansion was more readily available during the upswing. As seen in Chapter 5, during the Great Depression the Reichsbank limited credit to protect its gold reserves.[18] It had considerable freedom within its statutory guidelines, however, and after 1890 the supply of money increased more rapidly.[19] In addition to currency creation, the Reichsbank could extend credit through its discount policy. In particular, it discounted the bills of the major banks freely. In doing so, despite the clear favoritism shown to large banks and industrial firms, Reichsbank officials claimed that they were merely responding to the demands of the economy. Eventually the rise in the supply of money and credit began to exceed increases in output and productivity, and prices rose sharply. For consumers, rents, food prices, and fees charged for personal services remained more or less constant from the 1880s to 1905, but they then began to increase, and all were on average one-third higher in 1913. For investors machinery prices rose less rapidly, about a quarter from 1905 to 1913, but land prices rose by a third on average, and in the cities speculation drove prices up even further.

Supported by the Reichsbank, the four "D-banks" (Diskonto-Gesellschaft, Darmstädter, Deutsche, and Dresdener) and a handful of others dominated the German financial scene. These large "universal" banks basked in their reputation as the force behind German industrial development. Many observers since have agreed with this view. They argue that the government's discount policy enabled the large banks to hold more risky portfolios than would otherwise have been possible. Therefore they could both "lend to the hilt" and support new ventures directly with their own capital.[20] It has also been argued that the size of the great banks and their multiple functions allowed them to tailor credit and services to the stage of development of each of their client firms, leading to gains in efficiency. The German universal banking model has been recommended as an improvement on the United States financial system.[21]

The banks actively sought opportunities to supply capital to new or expanding industrial enterprises. In some cases they invested their own capital. More commonly, they lent money and then marketed shares in the client firm. They earned further profits by providing regular financial services to "their" firms. These credits often took the form of large current account balances that the banks continuously rolled over, in effect converting short-term debt into long-term financing. Mobilizing the short-term savings of their depositors for long-term investment by industrial firms was an inherently risky strategy, and the banks attempted to insure themselves against unpleasant surprises by insisting on representation on the boards of directors of the client firms. This gave them access to information and, if necessary, control over the firms' investment decisions. In 1914, loans to industry made up three-quarters of the banks' balances. In return, the banks held 20 per cent of all corporate board seats, and the Deutsche Bank alone was represented on the boards of 186 other corporations.

However, the great banks and the government policy that favored them have been criticized. Universal banking may not work as well as claimed. As defenders of their depositors' interests, banks were motivated to exercise caution, and therefore their representatives may have opposed innovative new investments. Alternatively, representation on the boards of "their" firms improved the banks' information, but it also provided the opportunity and motivation for the banks to conceal any difficulties those firms had when they sold their shares to the public.[22] Empirical evidence suggests the system misallocated credit. The banks favored with privileged access to government credit in turn had their own preferred clients, the large firms in heavy industry. They provided very little credit to consumer goods industries, and virtually none to small and medium-sized firms. The resulting segmentation and distortion of the capital market probably reduced the overall rate of growth.[23]

Cartels

Banks also sponsored and profited from the creation of cartels, possibly the most distinctive feature of German economic life before 1914. Cartels are associations of firms established to fix prices, restrict output, divide markets, and share profits among themselves. In the United States, any agreement "in restraint of trade" could be prosecuted under the Sherman Antitrust Act of 1890. Big business had a rather unsavory reputation, and many American politicians made careers as "trust-busters." In Germany, a court decision in 1897 held cartel agreements to be legally enforceable contracts.[24] Bankers and business leaders enjoyed high prestige, and Germany became "the land of cartels." The Cartel Inquiry of 1905 listed 385 cartel agreements, including 92 in heavy industry, but the total was generally believed to be much higher.

The origins and impact of the cartels remain in dispute. The first cartels emerged in the depressed 1870s, and therefore appeared to be "children of hardship." However, they spread steadily from the 1890s onward, and therefore seem more a feature of "organized capitalism," an attempt to guarantee a safe return on the large investments required by the new technologies.[25] The banks pressed Siemens and the AEG together to restrain their intense competition, for example. But the banks were themselves competitors, and not all proposed schemes went smoothly. When Hugo Stinnes attempted to obtain finance for a merger in the coal and iron industry in 1910, his wife wrote, "Hugo tries to get the D-Banks under one roof with regard to the fusion of the Union and Deutsch-Luxemburg, so far without success . . . No one is willing to allow the other a little bit more."[26]

Contemporary economists such as Robert Liefmann celebrated cartels as a new and higher stage of industrial development.[27] On the left, Lenin used data on Germany as key evidence in his theory of *Imperialism: The Highest Stage of Capitalism* (1915). Some of the successful groups, such as the Rhenish-Westphalian Coal Syndicate, were notorious for their predatory behavior. Their high and discriminatory prices hampered industrial development in other regions. On the other hand, the member firms paid relatively high wages and had a good record of introducing new techniques. Many other cartels were not successful, either because they did not control a large enough share of their industry or because they could not police members' behavior effectively, and therefore had limited impact.[28]

How distinctive was Germany? Contemporary British observers worried about German competition, and they blamed British banks. In contrast to Britain, the size and policies of the German great banks seemed to have given Germany a decisive edge. More recent work suggests that Britain did not do so badly, and that British banks played a positive role. Measures of concentration indicate that the banking sector in Britain was at least as concentrated as Germany.[29] In the United States, despite antitrust legislation, these decades saw the rise of merged industry-wide holding companies, often sponsored by bankers such as J. P. Morgan. Measures of industrial concentration do not show great differences between the United States and Germany.

The differences identified by Chandler are more cultural than structural: "competitive managerial capitalism" in the United States, "personal capitalism" in Britain, and "cooperative managerial capitalism" in Germany.[30] Nevertheless, we can say Germany possessed a system that worked very well in the buoyant conditions of the golden age, but that might work much less well in more difficult times. The banks, large firms, and cartels all aimed primarily to monopolize existing markets and to protect existing investment, not to innovate or discover new markets. Like all monopolies, when demand dropped they would reduce output and increase their prices, which would worsen the effect of a depression. During the golden age this possibility seemed remote.

The social context: the problem of the city

Urbanization and internal migration

The expanding industrial sector was concentrated in cities. The rural textile industries, which had supported family income for previous generations, declined. Nationally, employment in textiles rose, but the number of textile workers recorded in rural areas dropped by 20 per cent. Combined with increasing seasonal fluctuations in agricultural work, the decline of rural industry meant that additional hundreds of thousands of young women and men would have to move between city and country or between city and city in search of sufficient work to maintain themselves through the year.[31]

Urban growth followed two patterns. First, existing state capitals and commercial centers grew with their radial railroad networks. Cheap transportation drew industry, which drew workers, who required services, and this growth propelled the need for further improvements in transportation. Berlin was the prime example with 2.1 million inhabitants in 1910, but Hamburg, Leipzig, Munich, Frankfurt, and Stuttgart all expanded along these lines. Second, new industrial centers located close to the coal mines in the west grew explosively from villages into cities. Essen, for instance, had a population of 9000 in 1850, 52,000 in 1871, and 295,000 in 1910, and Duisburg and Dortmund grew at similar rates. Both types of cities now began to add suburban districts, whose growth could also be explosive. In 1910, two of Germany's largest cities were the Berlin suburbs of Charlottenburg with 306,000 residents and Rixdorf (Neukölln) with 237,000.

Most of the huge numbers of people arriving in the cities were temporary residents, but they still required housing. The total invested in non-agricultural housing doubled between 1895 and 1913. The cities also required infrastructure. Local and state governments rushed desperately to provide roads, railroads, and streetcar systems, harbor facilities, water, sewerage, and first gas and then electricity for their urban populations. Total investment in government construction nearly doubled from 1895 to 1913.

Figure 6.3 shows the changing distribution of Germany's population among towns and cities of different sizes. The rise of the largest cities is obvious. Regions where cities did not grow, or grew slowly, lost population. Figure 6.4 shows the out-migration from the major regions of Germany. Over one and a half million persons left the east between 1880 and 1910, and over half a million left the central region. Most of the migrants from the central region moved to Berlin. Those who left the east went first to Berlin, but also increasingly to the industrial cities of the west.

These figures concerned contemporaries. As seen below, social commentators worried about the fates of those who moved to the cities, and they worried as well about the villagers, town dwellers, and farmers. The most important figures were the losses of population in the agricultural eastern provinces of Prussia, home of the aristocratic Junker landowners and now the only reliable electoral base for the Conservative parties in both the Prussian Landtag and the national Reichstag.[32] Nevertheless, in 1910 Germany was still largely a country of villages and small towns, and, as seen above, it was also still largely a country of farmers. These large numbers of people exercised an important

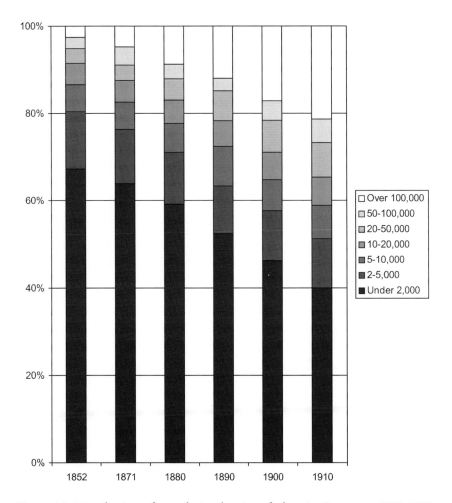

Figure 6.3 Distribution of population by size of place in Germany, 1852–1910 (percentage)

influence in the cultural debates described below, and they played a crucial role in Germany's political system, as we will see in Chapter 7.

Urban culture and German culture

The battles over modern art were fought against this backdrop of rapid change. The city as the center of modern industry became the place

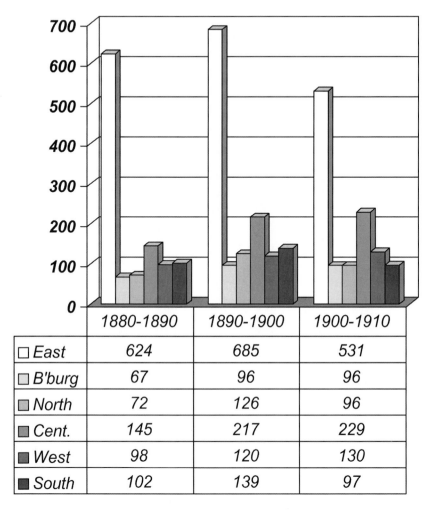

	1880-1890	1890-1900	1900-1910
☐ East	624	685	531
☐ B'burg	67	96	96
☐ North	72	126	96
◼ Cent.	145	217	229
◼ West	98	120	130
◼ South	102	139	97

Figure 6.4 Loss of population through internal migration from regions of Germany, 1880–1910 (thousands)

where the dangers of social dislocation seemed most acute. Urbanization and education also transformed popular culture from inherited local celebrations to professional entertainment. What ordinary people chose to do in their free time became another area of social and cultural contention. The city became a contested space where the forces of order battled to contain the forces of change. Police activity and censorship were pervasive, and applied to all public activity and performances.

They covered not only the obvious areas of political activity and subversion, but extended to the private sphere as well. Audiences were to be protected from seeing or hearing not only criticism of the empire's leaders and institutions, but also any advocacy of sexual liberty or exposure to the scandals of "respectable" society. Spontaneity, the threat of opposition, or the inclination to disobedience—these were the enemies, to be extirpated if possible, and the city was where they were found.

In Berlin, the *Verein Freie Bühne* (Independent Stage Association) was established by a group of modernist actors and playwrights in 1889, with the legal form of an "association" in the hope of avoiding the censors. The association managed to present Ibsen's controversial *Ghosts* without incident. However, during a graphic birth scene at the premier of Gerhart Hauptmann's *Sunrise* (*Sonnenaufgang*, 1889), fights broke out in the audience. The play was banned. Hauptmann's *The Weavers* was also banned when it premiered in 1892, on the grounds that "it was an open appeal to rioting." This time the Liberal press protested. The theater company was prosecuted, but the court found in their favor, holding that the play posed no dangerous threat because the high ticket prices "precluded the attendance of an appreciable number of workers at the performances."

Class prejudice obviously played a role in official attitudes, and the continued rise of the Socialist Party and the labor unions presented an ominous threat to the empire's existing institutions. Therefore what workers did in the urban space appeared especially threatening. If high ticket prices would keep them from seeing an unsettling play, there was no obvious way they could be kept from jostling against their betters in public places. Sales clerks in department stores were instructed when waiting on customers of high social standing to adopt a neutral form of address if they were within the hearing of a "simpler person," in order that the identity of the upper-class client would not be compromised.

After-hours activities required surveillance. Cabaret is a general term that covers the employment of entertainers in bars to sing, tell jokes and monologs, dance, or present theatrical sketches. Workers had more money and more time, and much of both was spent in bars. To attract customers, the owners increasingly employed entertainers. Police in all cities subjected such performers to strict censorship. In Munich, which had a liberal reputation, all material had to be presented in written form for approval fourteen days before its intended performance. Plain-clothes police then periodically attended to check that only approved material was in fact presented. Well-known singer Weiss Ferdl told an unapproved joke in 1910, and the police officer in the audience confiscated his book of jokes, possibly to use as evidence.[33]

Confrontations played on the cities' streets between representatives of state authority and crowds, large and small, organized and spontaneous. We have extensive sources for large incidents. Major strikes, the mass demonstrations in favor of suffrage reform in Prussia, and riots such as the "Moabit disturbances" of 1910 in Berlin are extensively documented. The working-class neighborhood of Moabit erupted when police escorting strike-breakers were provoked by onlookers and attacked them. Bottles and other objects rained down from the windows of apartment buildings, and 30,000 people flooded into the streets. The everyday "guerrilla warfare" between the police and groups of young working-class males is more difficult to reconstruct. Reports of confrontations with unorganized crowds vary depending on the perspective of the reporter. An incident might be the seizure of socialist propaganda, the arrest of strikers threatening property, or police bullying some kids on the street, depending on whether you read the Conservative, Liberal, or Socialist newspaper. There is, however, no doubt about the hostility provoked by the heavy-handed intrusion of the police into working-class neighborhoods.[34] Conversely, there seems little doubt that the respectable middle classes, traditionally distrustful of intrusions by the military and police into the private sphere, came to view the police as enforcers of law and order, as a bulwark between an educated, propertied citizenry and the predatory, undisciplined urban masses.[35]

The city also became a point of crystallization for social protest such as the consumers' movement, and a focal point for concern over old social problems such as prostitution and newly discovered areas of concern such as children and youth. Consumer movements emerged in response to increasing food prices in the early twentieth century.[36] Campaigns against licensed prostitution reduced the number of public brothels in Munich from 32 in 1889 to none in 1910, and the number of licensed prostitutes in Hamburg from 1050 in 1876 to 780 in 1910.[37] The *Verwahrlosung* (waywardness) of urban children and the moral state of young urban workers concerned many groups. Child welfare was an area of particularly intense conflict because it touched on the boundaries between parental rights and the protection of children and therefore between the private and the public spheres. Charities, city governments, courts, state bureaucracies, churches, women's associations, and middle-class reform societies competed to impose their preferred definitions and solutions on this new problem area.[38]

The built environment of the city might be adjusted, some thought, to alleviate the damaging effects of urban life. Architects and urban planners looked with horror on the cramped and unsanitary "rent barracks" that had resulted from rapid and uncontrolled growth. Physicians applied advances in bacteriology to the "illness of housing." Their efforts opened spaces and certainly improved health standards. Often they were ambivalent about the city itself, and they looked for guidance in Germany's past. In smaller cities, newly reconstructed city centers and government offices often incorporated medieval design elements. In Berlin, as noted above, the roof of Behrens' Turbine Factory repeated the lines of a barn. The building formed part of a large complex that Behrens laid out in the pattern of a farmyard. Behrens wanted to recover the sense of common purpose that he believed agricultural communities possessed. Despite extending over hundreds of meters, the buildings' traditional shapes and layout were supposed to evoke a nostalgic response in the workers and recreate that lost sense of community.[39]

The city also became the public arena for women in Wilhelmine Germany. The women's movement expanded and extended beyond the national umbrella organization, the *Bund Deutscher Frauenvereine* (BDF). These diverse organizations, despite overlapping memberships, were often divided by disputes over principles, strategy, and tactics. Moderates such as Helene Lange, leader of the women teachers' association, believed women and men possessed innately different natures, and therefore should perform different roles in society. The role of women in public life was to serve as "social mothers." Moderates advocated specific reforms and non-confrontational tactics, such as the petition campaign for the admission of women into universities launched in 1887. Radicals such as Minna Cauer and Hedwig Kettler asserted that the so-called "nature" of women was the artificial creation of social conventions. They presented more extreme demands and pressed for public campaigns for female suffrage and against the sexual double standard. Kettler particularly advocated equal access to all professions. In

1899, radicals founded a separate league of "progressive" women's associations. Despite disagreements, the two groupings shared common goals, for instance the admission of women to the medical profession. Moderates based their demand for women doctors on the need to protect feminine modesty by ensuring that women were treated by women, while radicals emphasized the issues of equal rights and employment opportunities.

Women also moved into the public realm out of religious conviction. In 1895, Elisabeth Gnauck-Kühne became the first woman ever to deliver a public address to a civic organization in Germany when she spoke before the Protestant Social Congress (*Evangelisch-sozialer Kongress*). The Congress had been formed in 1890 to combat both "the danger posed by the growth of Social Democracy and its growing estrangement from the Church" and "the rival example of Catholic social action." What Gnauck-Kühne told the Congress was that middle-class women could and should work to improve the economic, intellectual, and moral lives of women workers. However, she added,

> in order to be suited for participation in the economic improvement of women workers, the cultivated middle-class woman must put aside her esthetic sensitivities and get involved in real life and in basic economic questions. Love and goodwill are not enough; knowledge and judgment are needed too.

Gnauck-Kühne went on to found both the German Protestant Women's League (*Deutsche-Evangelische Frauenbund*) in 1899, and, following her conversion to Catholicism in 1900, she also founded the Catholic German Women's League (*Katholischer Deutscher Frauenbund*) in 1903.[40]

The link with the city lay in the fact that the entire social service sector depended on the women's movement. In Hanover, as Nancy Reagin has shown, by the first decade of the twentieth century women's associations operated the bulk of all public and private programs that served poor women and children in the city. Women served as almoners and police assistants, and they operated homes for homeless women and unwed mothers, temperance restaurants, and infant care clinics. The disputes over child welfare and prostitution also gave women greater visibility and influence. After the turn of the century, women worked not only as charitable volunteers, but also as legal guardians, professional social workers, and infant health experts. During the 1890s,

Cauer played a major role in creating an organization of women involved in social work in Berlin.

Moderate, radical, Protestant, and Catholic women's movements all remained middle class and respectable. Socialist women's organizations refused to join the BDF in 1894. Women active in urban social work (*Fürsorge* or "care for") used the language of gender (sexual restraint, responsible mothering, housekeeping) as they "put aside esthetic sensitivities" and used their "knowledge and judgment" to help poor women. They did much good, and many of the services they supported were widely popular. Nevertheless, the supposedly non-political activities of middle-class women activists also functioned as class control mechanisms. These women escaped the confines of their own homes and created purposeful lives for themselves, but they did so by invading the homes and lives of poorer women. Middle-class women gained autonomy and exercised agency, but partly through imposing their circumscribed definition of women's roles and their model of the family on poorer women. The regulation of prostitution, for instance, could take the form of criminalizing unmarried working-class couples.[41]

Finally, there were those who attempted to escape the city altogether by "wandering," hiking, and camping in the open countryside. A number of youth groups organized the *Wanderbund* in 1896 and the *Wandervogel* (wandering or migratory birds) in 1900. The "youth movement" reached a peak at a mass meeting held near Kassel in 1913. Members declared themselves against "mechanical" modern life and proclaimed that they opposed "bourgeois" (*Bürgerlich*) society, both because of its "atomistic" individualism and because of its repressive social conventions. Others hoped to preserve or restore the landscape to its pristine preindustrial state. An association for the "protection of the native land" (*Bund Heimatschutz*) was formed in 1904 to sensitize the public to environmental issues.

The youth movement and the *Bund Heimatschutz* recruited their membership primarily from the affluent middle classes. As the children of privileged families, *Wandervogel* members rejected their parents' values while enjoying the benefits of their wealth. A third of the members of the *Bund Heimatschutz* were from the commercial and manufacturing sectors, and therefore participated in the economy that was undermining the "natural" environment. These inconsistencies have remained typical of both adolescent rebellion and environmental activism in the modern world. Other features were more specific to the German condition. *Wandervogel* leaders preached the need for a return to natural organic forms of society and for a new strong leadership. The member societies excluded Jews. Although it may have been intended as a ploy to gain wider acceptance for its goals, the *Bund Heimatschutz* adopted a strongly nationalist stance and pictured the natural unspoiled values of the countryside as the vital source of Germany's military strength.[42]

The cultural context: neoclassicism and the struggle against modernism

Germany possessed an enviably dynamic economy. It was an equally dynamic society, and it also possessed an enviably varied and vibrant cultural life. Neoclassicism remained the official leitmotiv. Officials, beginning on high with the Emperor and ranging down to plain-clothes police officers listening for risqué jokes in smoky cabarets, intervened continually in cultural life to defend an image of unchanging order. In the social realm the Civil Code completed in 1900 can be read as a neoclassical text. It encapsulated the official picture of gendered social harmony, and it looked backward. Fathers ruled over children, and husbands over wives. "The husband takes the decisions in all matters of married life . . . The father's predominance is founded upon the nature of things." Fathers were the legal guardians of children until they reached maturity, or, in the case of girls, until they married. Husbands controlled all property. Wives could not take employment outside the home without their husbands' permission. However, should the husband require the wife to work in a family business, he could compel her to do so. Although a wife's earnings from outside the home were now her own, any profits from the family business belonged to the husband. The public realm was male. Women of course still could not vote, and, until the 1908 Association Law, they were forbidden to join any political organization.

Neoclassicism, the censors, and the law confronted the reality of a divided and changing society. The cultural hegemony of the aristocracy and the bourgeois middle classes came under attack from modern "avant-gardes," from intellectuals on the proletarian left, from leaders of women's movements, and from a new right wing of extreme national-ists and "cultural pessimists." At the level of "high" culture, the pro-fessionalization of the social sciences, the humanities, and the arts accompanied the debates over the structure of "modern" society and over the direction of "modern" art and literature.

Music

Music was the least contentious of the arts. German composers dominated the body of works that musical scholars were beginning to define as the "classical" canon, and German orchestras and conductors dominated the international performance of these works. Across Germany, state and urban governments competed to provide the halls and to train and retain performers. The connection with government and the substantial expense of performance excluded works that did not command an affluent audience. Even self-consciously modern composers worked in an accessible idiom. The "pictures" presented by the music, even though innovative in arrangement and tonal structures, typically remained conventionally sentimental. Music could sweep the listener away, but only within the confines of acceptable and preferably elevated emotional responses.

This did not prevent controversy. Richard Wagner aimed not merely to write operas, but to produce a "total artistic work" (*Gesamtkunstwerk*) that would unite the audience into a collective whole. The works remain as passionate celebrations of honor, glory, heroism, and undying love. They are obviously aristocratic, and they are racist. Wagner intended them to contrast explicitly with the vulgar materialistic world of the middle classes, and he and his wife Cosima believed true culture derived from roots in a pure Aryan racial stock. Nevertheless, his music was too modern for Wilhelm, and the Emperor publicly dismissed him as "nothing more than a conductor—a quite common conductor." Richard Strauss conducted operas at the Royal Opera in Berlin for nearly twenty years, but was forced to premiere his own works in Dresden because they were too risqué for the capital. *Salomé* caused a scandal and was banned because of its sexual themes.

The origins of Gustav Mahler's second symphony, the "Resurrection" (1888–94), show the structure of the music profession, the limits of debate, and the interaction of composer and audience. Mahler's mentor, the conductor Hans von Bülow, championed Wagner, Liszt, Brahms, and other composers of the "music of the future," and he left Berlin in 1892 after a public confrontation with the Emperor.[43] However, he was appalled when Mahler played one of the themes of his proposed symphony. As Mahler wrote, he "became quite hysterical with horror, declaring that, compared with my piece [Wagner's] *Tristan* was a Haydn symphony!" Bülow's disapproval slowed Mahler's work, but when he died, at his funeral Mahler experienced a flash of insight as he listened to Klopstock's chorale "Thou Shalt Rise Again." As he later wrote, "it struck me like lightning and everything stood clearly before my soul. It was the flash that all creative artists wait for! . . . What I then experienced I had to express in sound."

The results still have the power to move. Nevertheless, Mahler's notes make plain the essential banality of the conception. In the first movement:

> We stand by the coffin of a person well-loved. His whole life, his struggles, his passions and his accomplishments on earth once more for the last time pass before us . . . a voice of awe-inspiring solemnity chills our heart . . . "Why did you live? Why did you suffer? Is it all nothing but a huge, frightful joke?"

The second movement brings "a memory, a ray of sunlight, pure and cloudless, out of the departed's life," but in the third this "blissful dream" dissolves again into the agony of a lost identity and the fear that life is meaningless. The fourth movement introduces "the moving voice of naive faith," scored for mezzo-soprano, but in the thunderous finale, "the earth trembles; the Last Trumpet sounds; the graves burst open; all the creatures struggle out of the ground, moaning and trembling . . . All have the same fear; all cry and tremble alike because, in the eyes of God, there are no just men."

This is not the end, however. Mahler's notes continue,

> What happens now is far from expected: the gentle sound of a chorus of saints and heavenly hosts is heard . . . "Rise again, yes, rise again thou wilt" . . . Lo and behold: there is no judgment, no sinners, no just men, no great and no small . . . A feeling of overwhelming love fills us with blissful knowledge and illuminates our existence.

In other words, after a moment of sentimental sorrow, trepidation, and fear, the elite members of the audience can return to their normal lives, reassured that God smiles on all men equally, and that all men will arise and dwell happily in the hereafter. The symphony draws on and reaffirms Germany's gendered identity, and it is specifically men to whom the music speaks. It is the funeral of a male friend that sets the stage, it is male accomplishments and the public male identity that are called into question, and in the final movement we learn that no man will be judged. Male audiences loved it. At considerable risk, Mahler financed the premiere himself, but as his sister reported,

> The triumph increased with every movement. Such rapture is witnessed only once in a lifetime. I saw grown men weeping and young men falling on each other's necks . . . And when the chorus entered, a shuddering sigh of relief broke from every breast. It was indescribable![44]

Literature

With literature we enter a more clearly contested realm, and one where the lines of gender were drawn more explicitly. A professional association for the study of German literature had been formed in 1861, and these were the decades when the history of literature emerged as a separate field, when scholars sought the essence of German literature, and when the canon of great German literary works was established. The experts jostling for position in the new field typically established their reputations through the publication of multi-volume works intended for a broad readership in the middle classes. This was a popular genre, and many of them ran through several editions over decades.

Literary histories were didactic in intent. They offered plot summaries and analysis for readers without time to read the original works themselves, and they delivered authoritative judgments as to which works were worthy for readers unsure of their own competence. Historians of literature explicitly intended to create an accepted and acceptable tradition for their young state. Their "national" emphasis and their desire to define what it meant to be "German" were clearly flagged in their titles, for instance Rudolf Gottschall's *German National Literature of the Nineteenth Century* (*Die deutsche Nationalliteratur des neunzehnten Jahrhunderts*), whose sixth edition appeared in four volumes in 1891.

Only certain elements of the writing actually produced by German language authors were acceptable. Most of the popular novels summarized in previous chapters were not considered serious enough. Heine's ability forced his inclusion, but his reputation suffered because of his radical politics and his Jewishness. Opinions could range from outright rejection to a regretful conclusion that he was somehow not truly German.[45] In contrast to the generation of realism, by the 1890s it was also necessary to identify true literature as aristocratic. Julian Schmitt, a political liberal, nevertheless wrote that German poets had failed "to liberate our nation from the dull confines of middle-class [*Bürgerlich*] atrophy, to imbue it with self-confidence, to awaken its dormant powers, and to introduce it as an equal into the ranks of European nations." He hoped that his five volumes would demonstrate that "the nation does not lack the necessary strength and ability for this task."

As part of this project, literature was defined as a masculine endeavor. Literature, insisted the professional historians of literature, belonged to the esteemed public realm, which excluded women by definition. Schmitt went out of his way in his final volume to insist that "in matters of politics, women are on the outside and it cannot be any other way." Literary historians repeatedly denied that women could write. They were incapable of writing historical novels, for instance, because they "are only able to see in history chance materials for memoir-like chit-chat." Writing that was valued was identified as masculine, and writing that was not valued was identified as feminine. Gottschall praised the "manly verse" of the Young German movement that had "attempted to influence the nation." He contrasted their writing with the feminine "flower verse" (*Blumistik*—a word he invented), the "sweet and pretty, shallow literature of the day."

Literary historians coopted the prestige of both history and science for literature. Heaping scorn on the writers who preceded the Young German movement, Gottschall returned to the Napoleonic wars. He insisted that "a race of men who had gone through the wars of liberation could only turn away from this trivia with contempt." In turn, praising the Young German authors, he concluded that "these men brought about . . . the new realistic literature of the present, which promises such an auspicious renewal of the age-old relationship of science and poetry." This of course further disqualified women, for, as all literary historians argued at great length, women were incapable of scientific thought.

Women were only admitted to universities as observers in the 1890s, so there were few women among the students who heard the lectures, and of course none among the professors who defined the field. But women read, and they also wrote. In fact, they wrote quite a lot, and it seemed that the amount they wrote was increasing. Literary historians all discussed the large numbers of women who seemed to be writing. Gervinus had worried about an "epidemic" of women writers in the 1850s. In 1892, Gottschall was deeply concerned by the "mob" of female would-be poets who "swarmed about the gates of the German temple of the muses."

The anxiety over past women authors could be alleviated by simply omitting them from the histories. The works of many nineteenth-century women are only now being rediscovered and appreciated. In addition, those women authors too prominent to ignore could either be interpreted in ways that fitted them into the accepted mold, or denigrated for their personal shortcomings. Annette von Droste-Hülshoff was praised for her "harsh masculine style," and for her supposed opposition to women's emancipation and "the mere play of emotions." The open scandal of Ida Hahn-Hahn's divorce and her subsequent life with a man who was not her husband reverberated through the decades. In 1916, Otto von Leixner referred to a "demonic streak" (*dämonischer Zug*) in her nature that marked her writing.

The rising numbers of women writers in the present posed a problem, and literary historians solved it for themselves by insisting that what women did write was not writing, but something else. Gottschall attempted to categorize "female singers" (*Sängerinnen*) into those who were unmarried and those who were married. The former "write pure moonlight lyrics," while the latter "are more solid in their thoughts and feelings." Other phrases used included "literary ladies" (*literarische Damen*), "women who write" (*dichtende Frauen*), or "ladies of the pen" (*Frauen der Feder*). All these circumlocutions were to avoid calling them simply *Dichter/-innen*, for *Dichter* had become the accepted term for authors of serious literature (*Dichtung*). Women's writing, rather than *Dichtung*, was "female scribbling" (*weibliche Schriftstelerei* or *weibliche Dichterei*, both phrases with strong negative connotations).

Literary historians noted reluctantly that the "woman's novel" was becoming increasingly popular. And, since women seemed to be writing so many novels, and since women seemed to be reading them in preference to the canonical great works by male German authors, the novel was downgraded as a literary form. Women, it was argued, could produce novels precisely because prose narrative did not require the discipline that other forms demanded. This was given a nationalist twist as well. Gottschall insisted that "a catalog of German novels now has a great deal of resemblance to an English one, in which the 'eternal feminine' predominates. Of course, only a few of these women writers have any significant intellectual profile."[46]

Five women who did write with success were Gabriele Reuter, Helene Böhlau, Lou Andreas-Salomé, Franziska von Reventlow, and Else Lasker-Schüler. Reuter's *From a Good Family* (*Aus guter Familie*, 1895) details the increasing desperation of a talented young woman smothered by her respectable parents, who cannot see any other role for her than to become the wife of a rich husband. Böhlau's *Half-animal!* (*Halbtier!*, 1900) showed the degradation of women to the status of domestic animals that lay beneath the conventional reverence that men showed for them. Andreas-Salomé, friend of the philosopher Friedrich Nietzsche, the poet Rainer Maria Rilke, and Sigmund Freud, published controversial works on female psychology and sexuality. In her fiction she returned to themes of direct emancipation considered by women novelists earlier in the century. In *Fenitschka* (1886), a young man meets and learns from a Russian woman university graduate who considers genuine love incompatible with marriage. In *A Debauch* (*Eine Ausschweifung*, 1898), the woman narrator comes to realize that the conventional love of a woman for a man is in fact masochistic, and that she would prefer to renounce love rather than suffer the damage to her sense of self. Von Reventlow took a different approach, believing that the woman's movement would destroy femininity. Her semi-autobiographical *Ellen Olestjerne* (1903) portrays a strong female character who escapes her repressive family, learns from Ibsen's plays to value her individuality, and experiences the sexual and artistic freedom of the bohemian world in Munich. She finds happiness and self-confidence as a mother, but it is as an unmarried one. In her poetry, Lasker-Schüler addresses gender much less directly. She is more concerned with the creation of a private world of feeling in which colors play a distinctive role as emotional markers, "golden" for sexual release, for instance. Her writing also includes *The River Wupper* (*Die Wupper*, 1909), a drama of class conflict utilizing the dialect of her native Rhineland. As she became more conscious of her dual identity as both German and Jewish, she chose themes that celebrated the "wild" traditions of ancient Judaism, as in her *Hebrew Ballads* (*Hebräische Balladen*, 1913).

Among male novelists, Theodor Fontane, "the gentle critic,"[47] subtle, ironic, and usually indirect in his treatment of controversial themes, concerned himself with the pressures of convention on individuals. As women occupied the most confined social spaces, his novels often focused on their problems. These could be seen in the desperate if unreflective search of Jenny Treibel for social respectability, noted in

Chapter 5. More frequently, they surfaced in the sexual longings of women trapped in unhappy marriages to older men. In *The Adulteress* (*L'Adultura*, 1880), Melanie van der Straaten is twenty-five years younger than her husband, who regards her as a possession to be proud of rather than a person to be cherished. In his great *Effi Briest* (1894–95), the title character is seventeen when she marries the thirty-eight-year-old Baron Innstetten. Melanie manages to separate from her husband and goes to Italy to have her lover's child. Effi does not love the man who seduces her, but, six years after the affair, her husband discovers her infidelity and kills the former lover in a duel. Convention triumphs, for both women are alienated from their former friends and from their children. But Fontane's view of the absurdity of convention is clear, particularly in the emptiness of Innstetten's life following his separation from Effi.

The struggle against convention also marked modernist plays with themes of sexuality and social justice. Frank Wedekind's *Spring Awakening* (*Frühlings Erwachen*, 1891), subtitled "A Children's Tragedy," remains a confronting piece over a century after it was written. Fourteen-year-old Wendla, shielded from all sexual knowledge by her mother, is seduced by the schoolboy Melchior, becomes pregnant, and dies from an attempted abortion, although the cause of her death is concealed as a case of anemia. Another boy, Moritz, commits suicide after failing a school exam. Melchior is sent to a reformatory, but escapes. The themes of sexuality are explicit. Wendla and Melchior make love in a hayloft during a thunderstorm, the two boys share a homosexual love, and another girl, Ilse, reports graphically on her promiscuous life in the nearby city. There are fairy-tale motifs that recall Romantic literature from early in the century, but there are also several characters representing authority figures (schoolmaster, prison officer, pastor) who appear as abstract modernist puppet-like caricatures, and there is a mysterious Masked Man who guides Moritz into a future in which his will to survive will compensate for the undermining of all his conventional beliefs.

Gerhart Hauptmann's plays considered the consequences of class oppression more directly. *The Weavers* (*Die Weber*, 1892), a historically based portrayal of the 1844 uprising of the Silesian weavers, deemphasizes individual characters to concentrate on the actions of the entire class of impoverished workers. An exception is a pious old weaver who does not join the rebellion but dies from a stray bullet after praying for the rebels' safety. The play's episodic structure and the repetitious sound of the spindles emphasize the theme of collective consciousness. *Hannele's Ascension to Heaven* (*Hanneles Himmelfahrt*, 1894) centers around a young girl living in the slums who is beaten by her drunken father, taken to a poorhouse, and experiences a series of visions before dying of her injuries. *And Pippa Dances!* (*Und Pippa Tanzt!*, 1906) stresses the tension between the delicate but inert products of a glass factory and the living energy of the human characters, whether a brutish glassblower or the dancing girl. *The Rats* (*Die Ratten*, 1911) portrays life in one of the "rent barracks" of Berlin, where the people pick over refuse, nibble, and scrape at everything as if they have become rats, leading to murder and suicide. Emperor Wilhelm twice intervened to prevent Hauptmann from receiving the Schiller Prize, but Hauptmann's international reputation continued to grow, and he received the Nobel Prize for Literature in 1912.

The visual arts

The kinds of art preferred by the elite, and particularly by the Emperor himself, were certainly no secret. Wilhelm was proud of his artistic abilities and confident of his artistic judgment. His standard was simple:

> When faced with the magnificent remnants of classical antiquity we are overwhelmed with the same emotion: here too an eternal law dominates; the law of beauty and harmony, the law of aesthetics . . . we are proud when a particularly fine achievement is praised with the words: "That is virtually as good as the art done 1900 years ago."[48]

An interesting and ironic example of the influence of neoclassical models is the sculptor Adolf von Hildebrand. Like the Emperor, he was impressed and influenced by ancient classical art. His own style was austere and formal, as seen in the Wittelsbach Fountain in Munich (1890–95). However, his influence and his reputation rest on his book *The Problem of Form* (*Das Problem der Form*, 1893). In the book, Hildebrand argued that sculpture was the search for timeless universal forms conceived by the intellect, rather than the imitation of superficial details perceived by the eye. This meant that for the working sculptor overall form was to be preferred to minute detail. Translated into English, the book became very influential in international circles. Here lies the irony, for Hildebrand's ideas anticipated the approach, but not the character, of twentieth-century sculpture. The ideal forms as he conceived them were timeless universals derived from the models of Greek antiquity. However, his emphasis on the artist's insight into the essence of form became the justification for the authority of the idiosyncratic vision of an individual artist, as seen later for instance in the abbreviated and simplified forms of Henry Moore, which both Hildebrand and Wilhelm would have rejected out of hand.

Wilhelm took every opportunity to denounce modernism in the arts, wherever found. In 1898, he vetoed a medal that was to have been awarded to Käthe Kollwitz for her cycle of prints illustrating the 1844 uprising of the Silesian weavers. Conversely, artists favored by the Emperor and his circle were lavishly rewarded. His favorite sculptor was Reinhold Begas, and one of his favorite projects was the 700-meter long Siegesallee (Victory Avenue), a broad carriageway laid through the Tiergarten and lined with 32 massive marble statues of Hohenzollern rulers from Alfred the Bear in the twelfth century to Emperor Wilhelm I. At the opening ceremony, Wilhelm declared that the art of Berlin was "of a quality rarely seen even during the Renaissance," and that Begas was superior to Michelangelo.[49]

In painting, Anton von Werner "ruled at the Kaiser's side."[50] He specialized in monumental paintings commemorating state occasions. His portrayal of the Berlin Congress of 1878 shows an elderly but massively solid Bismarck greeting an equally elderly but less substantial Shuvalow, the Russian ambassador. Bismarck's exaggerated size makes him the focus. Most of the other participants are arrayed behind a long table. The similarity to Michelangelo's *The Last Supper* is obvious, as is the attempt to portray the "character" of each of the nations of Europe through the expression of its representative. Adolf von Menzel was another of the Emperor's favorites. When he died in 1905, Wilhelm walked behind the coffin and provided a military guard of honor dressed in eighteenth-century uniforms in honor of Menzel's works detailing the life of Frederick the Great.

But not everyone shared Wilhelm's limited vision of art and what it could be. Berliners referred to the Siegesallee as the *"Puppenallee"* (a *Puppe* can be a doll, a puppet, or a tailor's dummy), and to the overdecorated monument to Wilhelm I as "Wilhelm in the Lion's Den." In 1889, a group of young artists led by Max Liebermann participated in the Paris International Exhibition. Because it commemorated the centenary of the French Revolution, with its anti-monarchical implications, it was ignored by the official custodians of culture in Germany. In Berlin, Liebermann and other progressive artists formed the Alliance of Eleven (*Vereinigung der Elf*). Also in 1889, the Norwegian painter Edvard Munch had been invited to exhibit in Berlin by the Society of Fine Artists (*Verein Bildender Künstler*). Munch's work includes *The Scream* (1893), which has become an icon of modern art. He had already begun to hang his paintings when Werner proposed that the exhibition be closed and carried the motion in a meeting of the society by 120 to 105.

Hugo von Tschudi, the director of the National Gallery in Berlin, exhibited a group of modern paintings in 1896, some of which had been donated by liberal collectors known to oppose the ruling neoclassical style. Conservatives saw the showing of "foreign" acquisitions as a "desecration of the German temple of art." Tschudi was eventually forced to resign in 1908. In 1911, the board of the Bremen Museum purchased a Van Gogh landscape. A landscape specialist named Carl Vinnen collected 118 artists' signatures in protest. Vinnen argued that Van Gogh "ignored the three dimensions of reality—line, color, and atmosphere," but he also asserted that, through such purchases, "millions of marks meant for German art are lost every year."[51]

French art dominated the invention and propagation of new artistic movements and avant-garde groups. Modernist German artists typically found themselves followers of the new trends working in a hostile official environment. They were not completely without allies, and they benefited from Germany's diverse regional culture. In 1892, the Munich Succession formed the Society against the Association of Artists (*Gegenverein zur Künstlergenossenschaft*), dedicated to spreading knowledge of Impressionism and to promoting international exchanges. In 1893, a Dresden Succession was founded, with a continuing emphasis on encouraging the Arts and Crafts movement. In 1897, the Vienna Succession emerged under Gustav Klimt and declared itself open to all new tendencies in art. The Grand Duke of Saxe Weimar appointed the Belgian designer and architect Henry van de Velde as professor in the new Grand Ducal School of Arts and Crafts in 1904, and his commission to design the school's new premises became the nucleus of the later Weimar Bauhaus.

The idea of a Berlin Succession, independent of official pressure, was discussed over several years following the cancellation of the Munch exhibition. The break came in 1898 when a painting by Walter Leistikow was refused by an official exhibition. He suggested an enlargement of the Eleven, and the Berlin Succession was formed, with Liebermann as president. In 1902, they mounted an exhibition of Munch's work, and, in 1903, another including works by Cézanne, Van Gogh, and, Gauguin as well as Munch.[52]

The combative art critic Julius Meier-Graefe publicized and propagandized in favor of modern trends in art. He was also influenced by the English Arts and Crafts movement, particularly its effort to combat the standardizing effects of mass production by defending and developing individual craftsmanship. His journal *Pan*, founded in Berlin in 1895, was joined by *Jugend* and *Simplizissimus* in Munich in 1896, and by *Ver sacrum* in Vienna in 1897. These became the organs of the *Jugendstil* (Youth Style) in interior decoration as well as modern architectural trends. His curved desk was designed by Van de Velde and stood under Ferdinand Hodler's Symbolist painting *Day*.[53]

Meier-Graefe's book on Manet and his circle introduced younger artists such as August Macke to Impressionism. His *History of the Development of Modern Art* (1904), when translated, influenced the development of the international canon of modern art, with its argument that the movement from Impressionism to non-representational art denoted a continuous and progressive development. Meier-Graefe has been given credit by art historians for "goading" German artists into the formation of the first "authentic" avant-garde in Germany, the Expressionist movement.[54] *Die Brücke* (The Bridge) was founded in Dresden in 1905, with Ernst Kirchner as possibly its most prominent member. *Der Blaue Reiter* (The Blue Rider) was founded in Munich in 1911. Its members included Franz Marc, Gabriel Münter, and the Russian Wassily Kandinsky who had lived in Munich since 1896.

Not content to defend modern art, Meier-Graefe went over to the attack in 1905 with a denunciation of Arnold Böcklin, whose very popular dreamy imaginary landscapes and genre pictures were reproduced in thousands for display in the living rooms of the middle classes. Böcklin, said Meier-Graefe, "unites in one person all the sins committed by Germans against the logic of art," with his contextual pathos, theatricality, and the obvious subtext of chauvinistic nationalism. The resulting battle demonstrated how thoroughly art and politics had become entangled. Meier-Graefe welcomed the new "international language" of art that "transcends the natural diversity of place and race." He was attacked by

Henry Thode, professor of art history at Heidelberg, and coincidentally the son-in-law of Cosima Wagner. Thode insisted that art could never be independent of its "national character," but was "something thoroughly natural" like language.[55]

Urban culture and modern culture

As a contested space, the city also became the symbolic focus of economic, social, and moral concerns. When Thode wrote that the foreign influence of French modern art "is being forced upon Germany from Berlin," he allied himself with a broad range of commentators deeply concerned about the pernicious effects of large cities on the national body.[56] The industrial census of 1895 added fuel to the debate, because it showed that agriculture employed less than half the labor force. In 1897, the economist Karl Oldenburg published a small book entitled *Germany as an Industrial State* (*Deutschland als Industriestaat*). He asked whether Germany had ceased to be an "agricultural state" (*Agrarstaat*) and, more importantly, whether anything should be done to halt Germany's movement toward becoming an "industrial state" (*Industriestaat*). The book was a runaway success and inspired a number of imitators.[57]

Oldenburg touched on several sensitive nerves, but in particular he worried about life in the city. Whereas people in rural society possessed a willingness to sacrifice and a sense of duty, and had large families, the inhabitants of the city were marked by egotism and ambition, and had small families. The bright lights along the avenues, the nightlife, and the luxury shops with their displays of goods all worked to create an unhealthy envy and desire for material goods. Workers in the city therefore prevented children in order to be able to spend their incomes on frivolous luxuries. The evil consequences of the modern, individualistic, capitalistic, and urban way of life could be clearly seen, said Oldenburg, in the degenerate French with their low birth rate, and in the immoral Jew.[58]

Although Oldenburg emphasized the susceptibility of workers to the seductions of the city, the subtext implied that the luxuries themselves, because they were equally available in the city to all who could afford them, threatened to dislocate the social order. Others extended this theme. Women, it was asserted, confronted with the enticing goods in city shops, could resist neither the desire to purchase nor the temptation to steal. Consumption needed to be restrained and "disciplined" or the primary values of hard work and sacrifice would be undermined.[59]

Germany's rapid growth and the concomitant changes in the structure of the economy posed serious problems for traditional classes and values. We do not have to adopt the romantic nostalgia of contemporaries to sympathize with small communities that suffered as their industries declined and their young people moved to strange new places. Migration was often labeled and discussed as *Landflucht*, the "flight from the land." What would happen to the areas depopulated by the masses fleeing to the cities? Might they be lost to foreigners? For concerned Germans a danger lay in the higher birth rates of the Slavs to the east. "Thank God," said Oldenburg, "that until now our farmlands could supply enough men to fill most industrial places without resorting to Poles."

Modern sociology grew out of observations of rapid social change. In 1893, Max Weber analyzed the condition of agricultural laborers in Germany's eastern regions, looking for the reasons for the flight from the land. His study was part of a broader report sponsored by the *Verein für Sozialpolitik* (Association for Social Policy). The *Verein* included many of Germany's leading social scientists among its members. Their political opinions differed, but their shared commitment to systematic analysis of social problems and to social reform earned them the common nickname "socialists of the chair" (*Kathedersozialisten*) in reference to the fact that most were university academics. Their reports remain one of the best sources for study of Wilhelmine Germany.[60]

Weber concluded that workers were being driven out of eastern agriculture and into the industrial cities, not by the effects of the agrarian reforms of the early nineteenth century, or by the falling grain prices of the late nineteenth century, but by capitalism itself. Capitalism, the opportunity for profit combined with the need to compete in the market, had caused a change in the attitude of rural employers. As he put it, "the old economic order asks: 'how can I give, on this piece of land, work and sustenance to the greatest number.'" Under the modern capitalist order, however, landlords sought only the highest profits. They would use the cheapest labor and the latest technology, and they would ignore their old paternalistic obligations to their less fortunate neighbors.[61]

Weber's notion of the corrosive effects of rational calculation and market relations on traditional societies remains influential today. Others shared his regrets. Ferdinand Tönnies, another of the founders of modern sociology, examined the structures and values of traditional rural societies. He contrasted them with the corresponding structures and values of modern urban societies. In a traditional "community" (*Gemeinschaft*), individuals were born into a dense web of relationships, and the small scale of institutions meant that individuals experienced each other as whole persons. In modern "society" (*Gesellschaft*), this network of relationships was lost, and in the cities each individual was only concerned with others insofar as they could be useful. For Tönnies the tragedy of modernity lay in the transition from *Gemeinschaft* to *Gesellschaft*, the traumatic dislocation caused by the shift from small, face-to-face community life to existence in large, impersonal social structures.[62]

The concern and pessimism that marked the work of economists and sociologists also affected philosophers. Friedrich Nietzsche attacked the complacency of official culture. His critique extended to virtually all aspects of the modern world that conventional opinion viewed as sources of pride. The ideal of personal equality, he insisted, was a sham, for men are not equal, loving, or free by nature. The national state was "only an increment in the general insecurity and menace." It forced men to conform but then unleashed their worst instincts in the service of despots. He was especially critical of Bismarck, who had caused "the extirpation of the German spirit on behalf of the German Empire," but he also damned Socialism as a road to despotism and Liberalism as a sham. Education had become indoctrination, divided between irrelevant academic specialists and popular journalism, the "pseudo-education" of the herd of slaves.

Christianity had provided the core of Western civilization, but in one of his most famous aphorisms Nietzsche said, "God is dead." We have killed him, but we have not yet noticed. That is, science had undermined supernatural sanctions as a basis for values, but the habit of obedience to external authority remained. Religion had therefore become simply empty piety, intrinsically hypocritical. Culture itself was dissolving, but there was no reason to expect that "progress" would improve the human condition. Nietzsche opposed the claims of science to present a universal truth, and argued that human beings required myth. "Without myth every culture loses its healthy, natural, creative vigor."

Nietzsche desired the restoration of heroic and potentially tragic values. He looked for the sudden, unpredictable emergence of a Super-man, someone "beyond good and evil." Capable of joyfully affirming the life-process, the Superman would create his own values and live by moral standards infinitely more demanding than those of the existing conventional morality. But the innate superiority of the Superman would also mean that he would not be bound by existing norms. "What does not kill me, strengthens me." Nietzsche was a friend of the Wagners and his ideas connected at several points with their aristocratic prejudices. He celebrated the role of the artist, "for only as an esthetic phenomenon is existence in the world justified."

Nietzsche wrote in the 1870s and 1880s. His mental breakdown in the late 1880s coincided with the beginning of his public impact. His sister edited his works in ways that identified the Superman as a racially superior being, emphasized the need for a leader who would command obedience from the masses, and appeared highly nationalistic in calling for a return to primitive Germanic values. She released these works in carefully controlled packages to maximize their impact and her income from the publishing rights. In this form his ideas were popularized and deployed to reinforce the arguments of many others. After the First World War, these others included Adolf Hitler and his followers in the Nazi Party. Following the Second World War, Nietzsche was held to "bear the historic responsibility for helping to create the intellectual climate" that had given rise to Nazism.[63] As with so much else in the debate over possible turning points in German history, this judgment has been disputed. Because his work reached the public in distorted form, Nietzsche's defenders have attempted to exonerate him from the authoritarian and irrational implications of his thought. Professional philosophers have systematized and developed his insights, and his ideas have played an important role in post-Second World War thought, especially through their influence on Michael Foucault.[64]

Nietzsche's mode of argument was aphoristic and unsystematic. In *Thus Spake Zarathustra*, we hear "Why? Thou askest why? I am not of those who may be asked after the Why." Nietzsche's rhetoric was often unclear, although it was always evocative. For instance, claiming in *Twilight of the Gods* (1889) that the Greeks had discovered the principle of ever-renewed life and energy in the cult of Dionysus, he exclaimed,

> Eternal life, the eternal return of life; the future promised and affirmed in the past; the triumphant Yes to life, beyond death and change; *true* life as the collective survival through procreation, through the mysteries of sexuality . . . All this is meant by the word Dionysus.

The people influenced by Nietzsche were extraordinarily diverse. They included emancipated female authors such as his friend Lou Andreas-Salomé and modernist playwright Frank Wedekind, whose characters discovered a will to power in themselves. Young Expressionist painters found in his celebration of individual artistic insight a justification for their own personal visions. The architect and industrial designer Peter Behrens designed buildings in a "Zarathustra style" that he believed expressed a "will to form" embodied in their shape. His employer Walther Rathenau, head of the AEG after his father Emil's retirement, drew on Nietzsche and wrote in his *Criticism of the Times* (*Zur Kritik der Zeit*) that "understanding will never be able to tell us what to hope for . . . what to offer up sacrifices for."

Nietzsche also provided arguments for a large group of conservative authors known as "cultural pessimists," who denounced modern culture and particularly the culture of the city. Paul de Lagarde called for the elimination of all "Semitic" and "Roman" elements from German culture, and for a return to the pure Germanic culture of the distant past. Arthur Moeller van den Bruck wrote several volumes of portraits of German heroes (*Die Deutschen*, 1904–10), and attacked contemporary cultural relativism because it undermined the "Prussian style" of simplicity, honor, and personal courage (*Der preussische Stil*, 1914).

Julius Langbehn's *Rembrandt as Educator* (*Rembrandt als Erzieher*, 1890) was reprinted 39 times in two years. It attained immense popularity as one of the books presented to teenage boys at birthdays or graduations, and achieved cult status among *Wandervogel* members. Langbehn identified and celebrated Rembrandt as a "pure" German and a model for modern young Germans to emulate, a "free" man who gave expression to his inner, simple, instinctual feelings through his art. Knowledge creates pygmies. "The professor is the German national disease; the present German education is a kind of massacre of the innocents." Faith, however, brings forth heroes. For Langbehn the "faith-hero" Luther was "the greatest German hero of all; in him Germany first recognized itself." Langbehn adopted Nietzsche's elitism, but also identified the peasantry as the basis of the German race, and insisted that pure German values were found in traditional local societies. Intellectuals were the enemy, and they were found in the city. "In the end it may happen that the peasant will kill the professor; that what is innate in the nature of the German will predominate over what is artificial and conquer it . . . The provinces should be mobilized and ordered to march against the capital."[65]

The fringes of scientific thought and cultural criticism overlapped. Once more Germany was not alone. Writers in many countries concerned about a decline in culture also worried about the dangers of racial degeneracy. Charles Darwin's ideas were popularized in Germany by zoologist Ernst Haeckel. Haeckel believed both that acquired characteristics could be passed on to children and that the process of competitive natural selection would ensure the survival of the best. A Liberal who opposed clericalism and aristocratic privilege, he also favored the elimination of "weak and sickly" babies and opposed universal education because it was an "artificial" attempt to improve the status of inferior races. Many scientists accepted Italian criminologist Cesare Lombroso's theory that some men were "natural criminals" and analogously that some women were "natural whores."[66] This notion intersected with the idea that a bad environment could damage not only individuals but also future generations, and together they became widely influential. Hauptmann's play *Sunrise* revolves around a case of inherited alcoholism, and the characters in *The Rats* are destroyed by their urban environment. As in France, Britain, the United States, and Japan, Darwin's ideas were applied to human society, and his phrases "struggle for survival" and "survival of the fittest" were transformed into nationalist slogans. Social Darwinism referred loosely to national groups as "races" and saw nations pitted against each other in competition for the world's resources.[67]

The Wagners and their circle introduced the ideas of the Frenchman Arthur de Gobineau into Germany. Gobineau had published his four-volume *Essay on the Inequality of the Human Races* in 1853–55. He interpreted all of human history as a struggle between races, and he emphasized the dangers of racial degeneracy in the competition among human groups. In 1881, shortly before his death, he visited the Wagners at Bayreuth. They published a series of articles and excerpts from his works. In 1898, his *Essay* appeared in a complete German translation (the first volume appeared in English in 1856 and again in 1915). He was best known and most widely read as the author of *The Renaissance*. This book, which portrayed the conflict between the creative hero and the mob in a time of decadence, was another favorite gift for teenage boys. The future Emperor Wilhelm received his copy from his English mother, who was an admirer of Gobineau. He said later that it had made a deep impression that he had retained throughout his life. Wilhelm almost certainly derived his idea of the Yellow Peril from Gobineau as well, probably through his close friend Philipp von Eulenburg, a personal friend of Gobineau and co-founder of the Gobineau Association in 1894–95.[68]

If national groups were races, and if they competed against each other, then it made sense to attempt to improve the national race whenever possible. Darwin's cousin Francis Galton proposed that a science of eugenics could detect both the desirable and the undesirable members of the nation. Legislation, intervention, and social controls or negative eugenics could reduce the opportunities for undesirables to reproduce and multiply, while measures of positive eugenics could encourage reproduction of superior types. In Germany, the academic journal *Archiv für Rassen* began publication in 1903, and the German Society for Racial Hygiene (*Deutsche Gesellschaft für Rassenhygiene*) was founded in 1905.

The rhetoric of race found legal expression in 1913. The government introduced a new citizenship law that was accepted by the Reichstag, although only reluctantly. As seen above, Conservatives worried about foreign immigrants, and they also worried about Germans who emigrated elsewhere. The government wanted to make it easier for "Germans" outside the empire to gain citizenship, and it wanted to prevent undesirable aliens, especially Poles and Jews, from becoming citizens. The new law built on the existing principle that descent conferred citizenship, but imposed a racial definition by defining a "community of descent" that made it extremely difficult for anyone who did not possess "German blood" to become a German citizen.[69]

Notes

1. Max Klinger, *Christ on Olympus*, 1897. Oil on canvas, 550 × 970 cm. Museum der Bildenden Künste, Leipzig. Reproduced in Dube 1972, p. 8.
2. Max Klinger, *Beethoven Memorial*, 1902. 300 × 100 cm, approximately. Marble, granite, bronze. Leipzig, Gewandhaus. View at <www.kunst-und-kultur.de>, index Klinger.
3. Adolf Hoelzel (1853–1934), *Composition in Red*, 1905. 68 × 85 cm. Günther Wagner collection, Hanover. Reproduced in Dube 1972, p. 11.
4. Wassily Kandinsky, *Mountain*, 1909. Oil on linen, 109.5 × 109.7 cm. Lenbachhaus, Munich. Wassily Kandinsky, *With a Black Arc*, 1912. 188 × 196 cm. Nina Kandinsky collection, Paris. Reproduced in Dube 1972, pp. 113, 126.

5. Ibid.
6. *Meyers Konversationslexikon* (Leipzig, 1897), p. 402.
7. Polenz 1978, pp. 159–61.
8. Retallack 1995; Chickering 1996; Eley 1996.
9. Wehler 1996; Eley 1998.
10. Maddison 1995.
11. Chandler 1990.
12. Kocka 1969; Feldenkirchen 1994.
13. Frampton 1980, pp. 110–13.
14. Nipperdey, 1993b, pp. 602–18.
15. Kocka 1978; Herrigal 2000.
16. Canning 1992; 1996.
17. Adams 1988.
18. See Bordo and Kydland 1995.
19. Hoffmann 1965, pp. 814–15.
20. Tilly 1986; 1989; 1991.
21. Calomiris 1995.
22. Fohlin 1999.
23. Neuberger and Stokes 1974; see Fremdling and Tilly 1976; and Neuberger and Stokes 1976, listed with Neuberger and Stokes 1974.
24. Blaich 1973.
25. Winkler 1974; Eley 1986.
26. Fohlin 1999.
27. Liefmann 1910.
28. Wehler 1995, Vol. 3, pp. 632–7.
29. Collins 1991.
30. Chandler 1990.
31. Hochstadt 1999, pp. 201–11.
32. Tipton 1976.
33. Sackett 1982.
34. Lindenberger 1995.
35. Spencer 1992.
36. Nonn 1996.
37. Wehler 1995, Vol. 3, p. 520.
38. Linton 1991; Dickinson 1996.
39. Frampton 1980, p. 112. See Ladd 1990; Zimmermann 1991.
40. Hübinger 1996, pp. 175–6.
41. Mitchell and Koven 1990; Reagin 1995; Dickinson 1996.
42. Laqueur 1962; Rollins 1997.
43. Richie 1998, pp. 222–3.
44. Alan Bunin, program notes for Gustav Mahler, Symphony No. 2 in C minor, "Resurrection" (1888–94), Honolulu Symphony Orchestra, 1999–2000.
45. See Robertson 1988; Liedtke 2000.
46. Herminghouse 1997; see Hohendahl 1989; Roper 1991.
47. Remak 1964.
48. Speech of December 18, 1901. Richie 1998, pp. 923–4.

49. Richie 1998, pp. 231–2, and pictures following p. 196.
50. Dube 1972, p. 7.
51. Belting 1998, pp. 64–8.
52. Paret 1980.
53. Frampton 1980, p. 97, illustration p. 78.
54. Brettell 1999, pp. 30–2.
55. Belting 1998, p. 66.
56. Lees 1975.
57. Barkin 1970.
58. Karl Oldenburg, *Deutschland als Industriestaat* (1897).
59. Breckman 1991.
60. See Lindenfeld 1997.
61. Weber 1893, p. 367.
62. Tönnies 1887.
63. Pinson 1954, p. 270.
64. Aschheim 1992.
65. *Rembrandt als Erzieher* (Leipzig, 1891), pp. 138, 193. See Stern 1961; Mosse 1964.
66. G. Ferraro, *Das Weib als Verbrecherin und Prostituierte* (Hamburg, 1894).
67. Weindling 1989; Hawkins 1997.
68. Blue 1999, pp. 127–8.
69. Brubaker 1992, pp. 114–37.

CHAPTER 7

POLITICS, GOVERNANCE, AND DIPLOMACY BETWEEN NEOCLASSICISM AND MODERNISM

In 1895, Emperor Wilhelm II commissioned an engraving based on a pencil sketch of his own. The picture portrays the nations of Europe as mythical armored figures, gathered on a bluff overlooking a broad valley with towns and church towers receding into the distance. They are all female. Germania stands at the front, and at the rear Britannia is clearly holding back from the others. A luminous cross floats in the air above. Before them, on the edge of the precipice, a vibrantly male Archangel Michael, breastplate outlining his muscular torso, sword in hand, gestures toward the horizon, urging them to action. For there, in the distance, astride a black dragon, sits a Buddha, a huge looming figure framed in fiery smoking clouds. An inscription in French reads, "Nations Européenes! Défendez vos biens sacrés!" (Nations of Europe! Defend your sacred possessions!). Wilhelm sent the original of the finished engraving to his cousin Tsar Nicholas II of Russia, and wrote (they corresponded in English) that it "shows the powers of Europe represented by their respective Genii called together by the Arch-Angel Michael,—sent from Heaven,—to *unite* in resisting the inroad of Buddhism, heathenism and barbarism for the Defence of the Cross. Stress is laid on the *united* resistance of *all* European powers which is just as necessary also against our common internal foes, anarchism, republicanism, nihilism."[1]

Politics, but also the constitutional structures of governance, were caught between the orderly pillars of neoclassicism on the one hand, and the disorderly waves of modernism on the other. For defenders of the status quo, the world appeared increasingly threatening, both externally and internally. Internally, the battles over art, culture, and economic change outlined in Chapter 6 reflected deep social divisions. Political life split along the resulting fault-lines. Some of the fractures were vertical, separating religious and ethnic groupings. Others were horizontal, separating rich and poor, and the small ruling elites from those less fortunate in their choice of parents. Externally, conflicts between and among groups inside and outside of elected assemblies, between the elected representatives and their unelected masters, and among those masters themselves, made it very difficult for Germany to present a single face to the outside world. The lines of causation and the allocation of blame remain subjects of dispute, but the net effect was to place Germany in a vulnerable and dangerous position.

The political context: separate milieus

The public sphere

National communities depend on the existence of a public sphere, but one of a particular type. Nations claim that all citizens can and must participate in the public sphere, and the actions of national states vastly increased the number of persons capable of participation. However, the claim to rationality is undermined by the propagation of myths about the nation through the schools, and the claim to universalism by the exclusion of non-citizens by definition, and by the unwillingness of elites to allow the majority of citizens to exercise their theoretical rights. In Germany, the number of voices in the public sphere increased. As educational levels rose and the media expanded, previously suppressed groups made themselves heard. Catholics defended themselves from attack, workers demanded the right to collective agitation, farmers demanded protection, the gendered public realm came under attack from feminists, and the radical right wing attacked the ruling elites.

Jürgen Habermas argued that the "bourgeois" public sphere declined during the later nineteenth century. In Habermas' terms, the claims of these new movements represented the special pleading of particular interests. Neither the leaders of new movements nor their supporters entered the public realm as "abstract" individuals, and therefore could not logically represent themselves as "the" public.[2] Critics have questioned his privileging of the role of the bourgeoisie and the normative value he places on the specific bourgeois public.[3] Historically, however, the significant fact was the access of previously excluded or unheard groups to the means to be heard, noticed, and discussed, and Germany shared in this development with the other national communities of the late nineteenth and early twentieth centuries.[4]

Among contemporaries, historian Friedrich Meinecke, cited as an admirer of Bismarck's constitution in Chapter 5, was also forthright in enumerating the problems he believed that imperial Germany had not mastered. He regretted the rise of the Catholic Center Party and the Socialist Party, and he lamented the breakdown of Liberalism. In Prussia, he said, the three-class suffrage produced Liberal majorities until 1879, but since then had become "the suffrage of the possessing classes" and particularly the landowners. Nationally, the imperial universal suffrage had led "under the double pressure of economic-social and confessional forces" to a division of the rest of Germany along class and religious lines. The result in his view was the absence of any effective political force that was neither "Conservative-Prussian" nor "confessional."[5]

Voting patterns have been intensively analyzed, charted against economic and occupational variables, and linked to aspects of community life.[6] The results have confirmed Meinecke's contemporary insight and shown the expansion of the public sphere. Germans participated actively in the political system. The men entitled to vote generally did so. By the 1890s, participation rates in national Reichstag elections had risen above 80 per cent. In addition, as Meinecke and other contemporaries sensed, Germans lived in a divided society. Karl Rohe has argued that German voters split into three "camps" (*Lager*), the national, the Catholic, and the Socialist.[7] Others have preferred Rainer Lepsius' notion of socio-political "milieus" as a framework linking political behavior to social networks.[8] The men who voted can be seen as members of families that belonged to separate social and moral "communities of sentiment" defined by historical tradition, religion, and economic development. Although the edges of the groupings overlapped, in their daily lives individuals interacted primarily with other members of their own milieu. When the male members of these families cast their votes, they both responded to and reaffirmed their membership in these particular social groupings. Members of other milieus, and those who voted for the parties of other camps, were portrayed in stereotypes and regarded with suspicion and hostility.

National minorities, Jews, and anti-Semitism

In an age of aggressive nationalism, and in an age of scientific racism, minority groups confronted increased prejudice, and prejudice took political form. In the Romanov Empire, "Russification" created the Finnish national movement of resistance, and, in the Hapsburg Empire, "Magyarization" worsened the national divisions within Hungary. In Germany, national minorities came in conflict with "Germanization" policies in Schleswig, in Alsace and Lorraine, and in East Prussia and Posen. By 1900, Danes in Schleswig, the French in Alsace and Lorraine, and the Poles in the east were more likely to identify themselves in terms of their "own" nation and in opposition to the "German" national identity than in the 1870s. Teachers in these districts regularly punished schoolchildren for speaking their family language. The government made attempts to settle German peasants in the east, and in 1910 expropriated a number of Polish landowners in order that their estates could be turned into small farms for Germans.[9] In response, the minorities organized, and the men voted. In 1906, over 40,000 Polish schoolchildren went on strike to protest the language policy. Even in the Prussian Landtag, Poles elected between 13 and 17 deputies from the 1890s onward. Votes for Polish candidates in Reichstag elections increased from 200,000 in the 1870s to over 450,000 in 1907, and the number of Polish deputies rose from 14 to 20. The votes for Alsace-Lorraine candidates peaked at 234,000 in 1887, declined to 101,000 in 1903, but then rose again to 162,000 in 1912. A Danish member was elected in every Reichstag election. And in Hanover the separatist Guelph Party remained a force and paralleled Alsace-Lorraine with a peak of 113,000 votes in 1887, a decline to 78,000 in 1907, but a rise to 85,000 in 1912. Together, the disaffected separatists polled 546,000 votes in 1874, 461,000 in 1893, and 705,000 in 1912, and their 33 deputies opposed the government whenever it suited them.

Jews suffered as well. Germany was not France, and there was nothing to match the conflict over the Dreyfus affair. Germany was not Austria, and German citizens of the Jewish faith could live where they chose and practice any occupation for which they were qualified. Germany was not Russia, and there were no pogroms. Jews moved from Russia and the Austrian Empire to Germany to find a better life and relief from discrimination, not the other way around. However, after 1880, state and national governments imposed measures restricting immigration of

Eastern European Jews. These laws and a low birth rate ensured that their numbers remained small, 512,000 or 1.3 per cent of the population in 1871 and 615,000 or 1 per cent in 1910.

Previous restrictions on residence meant that most German Jews were urban. The earlier history of discrimination had also pushed them in the direction of commerce, manufacturing, and the professions. Jewish women were among the first to demand entry to universities in the late 1890s. Solidly middle class, German Jews were nonetheless diverse. As noted in Chapter 4, there were substantial differences among the more religious in belief and observance. Like their Protestant and Catholic counterparts, the leaders of both Orthodox and Reform congregations struggled to maintain attendance and public observance. Among the less religious or those who had rejected religion altogether, beliefs and attitudes could cover the entire palate from conservative to radical and from traditional to avant-garde. In public, these solid members of the middle classes might be indistinguishable from their Christian neighbors. In private, however, Marion Kaplan argues that Jewish women insisted on keeping dietary laws and maintained a distinctive religious atmosphere in their homes even as some rituals fell into disuse.[10]

There were communities in which Jews were quite well integrated. In Königsberg, a center of agricultural trade with Eastern Europe, Jews made up between 3 and 4 per cent of the population. They concentrated in trade and the professions, and they lived and worked comfortably with the non-Jewish middle and lower-middle classes of the city. Their occupational structure corresponded more closely with that of the non-Jewish middle class than in many other cities. This made them less conspicuous and allowed even the social inclusion of Eastern European Jews, as long as they were regarded as economically useful. Corresponding to the commercial spirit of the Königsberg middle class was an "old-fashioned liberalism," which clung to the ideals of the emancipation era.[11]

Nevertheless, there remained areas from which Jews were excluded, notably the higher ranks of the civil service and the army. Not a single Jew gained a regular commission in the Prussian army between 1878 and 1910. Even in generally supportive environments, such as Königsberg, there were circles dominated by bureaucrats and army officers that refused to receive Jews. In addition, Jews faced anti-Semitic groups that lumped all Jews together and blamed them for society's ills. A number of anti-Semitic political parties contended for voters. As seen in Chapter 5, they had won 16 Reichstag seats in 1893. They dropped to 100,000 votes and 3 seats in 1912, but, in the meantime, other, more respectable parties adopted anti-Semitic rhetoric and policies, such as the Conservative Party's Tivoli Program of 1892. Conservative parties might exist in tension with anti-Semites, as in Saxony and Baden, or collaborate with them, as the National Liberals did in Hesse and Thuringia, or wink at local expressions of prejudice, as Catholic Center Party leaders did.[12] As noted in Chapter 6, the *Wandervogel* excluded Jews, and many student organizations did so as well. Jews became a symbol. Conservatives found it easy to dismiss anything they disliked in the modern world as foreign, Jewish, or both.

All Jews coped with prejudice, but they did so in different ways. At one extreme were those who advocated a complete assimilation and disappearance into the broader society. Some Jewish leaders actively encouraged intermarriage. In Prussia, the number of Jewish marriages remained constant at around 2500 per year, but there were 248 mixed marriages in 1885, 297 in 1895, and 493 in 1903. At another extreme, other leaders advocated a new and more forceful insistence on a separate Jewish identity. Zionism, the attempt to create a Jewish national homeland in Palestine, was discussed intensively in Germany, a German Zionist Association (*Zionistische Vereinigung für Deutschland*) was founded in 1897, and many German Jews supported the movement.

Most found themselves somewhere between the extremes. Most German Jews married Jews. German Jews were not among the main theorists of Zionism, who were Russian and Austrian, and German Jews did not themselves migrate to Palestine. They typically considered it more appropriate for the less advanced Jews of Eastern Europe. Many German Jews believed that excessive immigration of poor Eastern European Jews into Germany was undesirable because it could place German Jews in a bad light with German Gentiles. Jewish female university students joined protests against "foreign" students auditing courses at the University of Berlin in 1900 as part of their campaign to gain full rights of matriculation at Prussian universities—the foreigners were Russian, but they were all women and almost all were Jewish.[13]

Acculturation might mean assimilation but this did not necessarily mean denial of Jewishness, and it did not mean passively tolerating the attacks of anti-Semites or relying on the assistance of well-meaning Gentiles. In 1893, alarmed at a series of violent anti-Semitic outbursts, Jews organized the *Centralverein deutscher Staatsbürger Jüdischen*

Glaubens, an organization that explicitly defined its members not as "German Jews," but as "German citizens of the Jewish faith." The Central Association decided to pursue anti-Semites through the courts. Grounds for prosecution were narrow, and early failures led to discouragement. However, repeated attempts gradually overcame the prejudice and reluctance of public prosecutors, and, by 1902, the Central Association's legal department was handling an average of 100 cases each year. In addition, the Central Association itself changed. The opening paragraph of its constitution had called upon every member to cultivate a sense of German identity, but, by 1900, its leaders had become committed to an aggressive internal mission to reinforce Jewish identity. The Central Association continued to see this Jewish identity as German, however, and this led to conflict with Zionists, who emphasized the unity of all Jews regardless of citizenship.[14]

Individuals exemplified these cross-currents. Max Liebermann was unusual among the modernist painters in being Jewish. However, in addition to being a Jew, he was a Berliner, a Prussian, and a German, "all at the same time, and with no obvious strain."[15] The writer Else Lasker-Schüler moved away from assimilationism toward a sense of a dual German-Jewish identity. Walther Rathenau, head of the AEG electrical conglomerate, also published extensively on contemporary intellectual and social problems. An admirer of Nietzsche, as noted in Chapter 6, he saw himself as a prophet of despair along with the other cultural pessimists, but he also looked forward to a future in which technically trained elites would guide modern economic and social development. He criticized the continued influence of the "feudal" aristocracy on the government system. He was scathing in his criticism of members of the middle classes who had capitulated to the aristocracy. However, he also criticized Jews for failing to assimilate. By remaining an alien and uncultured Asian stock, he argued, they had themselves caused the prejudice they suffered. He remained a Jew, because he saw conversion as an opportunistic means of escaping prejudice, but he refused to join the Central Association because of its defense of Orthodox rituals.

Catholics and the center

The role of anti-Semitism in German history has been of central importance to historians. However, this was not the religious issue that divided contemporaries in the nineteenth and early twentieth centuries.

Friedrich Meinecke does not mention Jews once in his study of the German national state. Rather, for Meinecke and for most Germans, the crucial religious divide lay between Protestants and Catholics. Meinecke saw Catholicism historically as a part of the "cosmopolitanism" that had to be discarded if the German idea was to realize itself, and he was particularly suspicious of political Catholicism. In 1848, Catholics in the Rhineland favored both a new German central government and the greatest possible degree of provincial autonomy, in both cases in order to reduce the influence of the Prussian central government. This meant in Meinecke's view that they opposed the forces he regarded as crucial in the creation of the German national state. Since then, the "failure" (*scheitern*) of the *Kulturkampf*, had led, he believed, to the emergence of the Catholic Center Party as a dangerous "state within the state," pursuing a narrow "confessional" politics to the detriment of the German nation.[16]

More recent research has confirmed the hostility with which Protestant and Catholic Germans regarded each other. Rohe concludes bluntly that "religious division was *the* deciding reality of life, of thought, of self-perception, and of politics in Germany."[17] As seen in Chapter 5, for many Protestants the *Kulturkampf* and a war on Catholics had been the necessary next step in national unification. Although the government made peace with the Vatican and began to dismantle the anti-Catholic legislation in the 1880s, Protestant attacks on Catholicism continued. The Protestant League (*Evangelische Bund*) was founded in 1886 ostensibly to promote the Protestant faith but actually to propagandize against Catholicism and the Catholic Center Party. The Protestant League had 100,000 members in 1897 and 500,000 in 1914. Its leaders came largely from the professional upper-middle classes. Luther and Bismarck were their heroes. They typically supported the National Liberal Party, and they adhered to a liberal "free Christianity" that they believed to be less dogmatic than either Catholicism or devout Protestantism. Their mass publications regularly denounced the Catholic clergy and the Catholic Center Party as "creatures of Rome" who mobilized voters as "electoral cattle" (*Stimmvieh*) and threatened the German Empire from within.

The number of Catholics recorded in the censuses rose from 14.9 to 23.8 million from 1871 to 1910, but their share of the German population remained constant at just over 36 per cent. They concentrated in the south and west, and in the Polish districts in the east. Within Prussia, they were a majority in the western provinces of Westphalia and the Rhineland, and the eastern provinces of West Prussia, Posen, and Silesia. In the south, they made up 60 per cent of the population of Baden and 70 per cent of Bavaria, but only 30 per cent of Württemberg. Through central and northern Germany they were often a very small minority, under 5 per cent in Saxony in 1910, for instance. Catholics developed a dense network of organizations that reinforced religious identity. The People's League for Catholic Germany was founded in 1890 and claimed 800,000 members in 1914. There were substantial regional variations, but, at the local level, the local priest often led Catholic organizations, with women as the key active members. Their aim was as much control as defense, and they attempted to restrict contacts with non-Catholics. Fewer than 10 per cent of all marriages celebrated in the German Empire were between Catholics and Protestants. Although there were spectacular exceptions such as Elisabeth Gnauck-Kühne, very few persons changed their religious affiliation.

Compared to their Protestant neighbors, in the areas where Catholics were numerous they were more likely to live in villages than in larger towns. They were more likely to be farmers, and among farmers they were more likely to be small farmers. If employed in industry they were more likely to be ordinary workers and less likely to be managers or owners of firms. Primary schooling was universal, but Catholics were less likely than Protestants to move on to secondary school, the *Abitur*, and university. Therefore they were also underrepresented in the professions. They were also underrepresented in the army officer corps and in the upper bureaucracy, particularly in Prussia.

Protestant propagandists cited these figures as evidence of the cultural backwardness of Catholics. They blamed the Church, the priesthood, and the Center Party for keeping Catholics in ignorance. Max Weber was subtler, but he shared the concern for religious differences and their consequences. He wrote his most famous and influential book on the link between capitalism and the Protestant religion. In *The Protestant Ethic and the Spirit of Capitalism* (1904), Weber argued that certain characteristic features of Protestant belief, particularly the notion of a religious "calling," fit especially well with certain fundamental aspects of capitalism. He began with the statistics showing low secondary school attendance by Catholics in Baden in 1895, 42 per cent, compared to their 61.3 per cent of the total population. Baden's Catholics were also poorer. They possessed only 589 marks of taxable capital per person, compared to 954 marks per person for Protestants. Without correcting, for instance for family occupational background or place of residence, Weber then projected these differences backward. Protestant morality and the capitalist spirit, said Weber, had reinforced one another from the sixteenth century to the present, and therefore Protestantism could be seen as one of the primary causes of modern economic and social development.

The Protestant Ethic is also the work in which Weber developed his notions of ideal types and ideal-typical analysis, and so, in addition to generating an immense literature on the role of religion in economic life, it has been extremely important for the development of the social sciences in general. However, as with his study of rural migration, it is rooted in its time. Like Nietzsche, Weber worried that the loss of religious belief had robbed life of meaning, leaving man imprisoned in an "iron cage" of empty rationality. Like Meinecke, he worried about the deep divisions in German society, and it was the divide between Protestant and Catholic that worried him most. Weber noted in his footnotes that Jews in Baden possessed over 4000 marks of capital per person and that they made up 10 per cent of secondary school students despite being only 1.5 per cent of the population, but rather than seeing these figures as a problem for Protestants, he concentrated on the evidence of Catholic backwardness. His scattered references indeed portrayed Jews as quite similar to Protestants.[18]

Like Jewish leaders, prominent Catholics adopted a dignified and principled public stance in opposition to prejudice. Catholic intellectuals and the leaders of the Catholic Center Party generally refrained from direct anti-Protestant attacks. Reform-oriented Catholic leaders such as Georg von Hertling, a professor of philosophy in addition to his role in the party, and editor Julius Bachem combined calls for an end to discrimination with appeals to Catholics to improve themselves and to abandon their life as an isolated subculture. The People's Association for Catholic Germany, in addition to defending Catholicism in general, sought to educate and uplift the Catholic working class. Its propaganda was directed against Socialism rather than Protestantism.[19] The Catholics who did engage in "disturbing the confessional peace" were usually rural or small town clergy.[20] They were pursued by government authorities under Article 166 of the Uniform Criminal Code of 1876, which outlawed blasphemy and the defamation of the institutions and practices of any incorporated religious body. A Catholic priest who said during a sermon that all evil came from Protestants was indicted for insulting the Evangelical Church and convicted—this case particularly incensed lawyers working for the Jewish Central Association because the courts consistently refused to convict those who made similar statements about Jews.[21]

The Catholic Center Party's vote in Reichstag elections rose from 1.3 million in 1890 to 2.2 million in 1907. The number of deputies depended on the results of run-off elections, but fluctuated around 100, although, in 1912, the Center's vote dropped to 2.0 million and its seats to 91. In the Prussian Landtag, the Center was even more consistent, with 95 seats in 1893, 100 in 1898, 97 in 1903, and 104 in 1908. As the largest single party in the Reichstag from 1878 to 1907, the Center Party was a force that the government had to negotiate with. The price for its support was legislation in areas that concerned Catholics, for example the repeal in 1904 of Paragraph 2 of the anti-Jesuit law, which had forbidden even individual members of the Society of Jesus from entering Germany.[22]

However, the Center Party relied on voters in rural districts and small towns, and these districts were often static or declining in population. Although Catholics took their religious identification with them when they moved to the cities, they usually did not constitute the absolute majority necessary to secure a Reichstag seat. In addition, the reinforcing structures of authority and sociability became weaker and class divisions stronger in urban environments, and working-class Catholics might be lost to the Socialist Party. In the eastern provinces of Prussia the role of religion cut across the question of national identification. Poles were overwhelmingly Catholic, and the national Center Party supported Catholic Poles, but this clashed with the feelings and resentments of both local Catholic Germans and nationalistic Poles.

These considerations led Center Party leaders to consider ways of reforming the party and broadening its appeal beyond the bounds of religion. This brought them into conflict with both bigoted rural priests and conservatives in the Church hierarchy. Many lay women and men had also come to return the hostility of Protestants. The Catholic German Women's League refused to affiliate with the national BDL, and the Catholic labor unions remained separate from the Socialist "free" union movement. In addition, a broader appeal was necessarily a democratic appeal, and this cut against the interests of Catholic aristocrats, landowners, and employers. The result of these conflicting forces was vacillation. Hertling celebrated the transformation of the Center into a "party of national cooperation" in 1907, but there were many Catholics and many Center Party leaders who did not support the reformers.[23] In Cologne, the Catholic clergy's one-sided attempts to enclose working-class Catholics and isolate them from contamination by Marxist socialism broke down, and the Socialist Party won Cologne in the 1912 Reichstag elections.[24]

Socialists, labor unions, and workers' culture

Meinecke ranked the problem of socialism—the political expression of "economic-social" forces—along with Catholicism as one of the fundamental problems confronting the German nation. As we have seen, the masses flowing into the cities were overwhelmingly young workers, fluid and impermanent. Frequently harassed by local officials, often poorly housed and without social support networks, they could expect sympathetic assistance from the Socialist men and women's organizations in working-class neighborhoods. The Socialist Party therefore was well placed to mobilize young men who might not otherwise have voted. As seen in Chapter 5, the great Socialist victory of 1890 ended Bismarck's career. Votes cast for the party increased in every subsequent election, from 1.4 million in 1890 to 1.8 million in 1893, 2.1 million in 1898, 3.0 million in 1903, 3.3 million in 1907, and 4.2 million in 1912. Socialist deputies rose from 35 in 1890 to 44 in 1893, 56 in 1898, and 81 in 1903. In the election of 1907, the government campaigned against the Center Party and the Socialists as unpatriotic opponents of Germany's colonial activities, orchestrated alliances in the run-off elections among the other parties, and reduced Socialist deputies to 43. In 1912, however, poor harvests and the rising price of food allowed the Socialists to campaign effectively against the government's tariff and taxation policies, the other parties failed to cooperate, and the Socialists rolled to victory with 110 seats.

A large and well-organized labor union movement supported the Socialist Party. The Socialist "free" unions (*Freie Gewerkschaften*) were grouped under a General Commission founded in 1890 and led by Karl Legien. Under Legien's leadership the Socialist unions restructured themselves during the 1890s. By 1900, most were centralized national bodies that carefully weighed the chances of success before declaring a strike. They preferred to strike against isolated and vulnerable employers, a tactic they referred to as *Einzelabschlachtung* or "butchering them one at a time." Best of all was not to strike at all, but to negotiate collective bargaining agreements for higher wages and improved working conditions. By 1905, a substantial fraction of workers in medium-sized industrial plants were employed under these "industrial peace treaties."[25] Many union leaders also sat as Reichstag representatives.

The bureaucratic structures of the Socialist Party and the labor unions attracted the attention of Robert Michels, a student of Max Weber. Too radical for a German university appointment, he migrated to Italy. His study of the German workers' movement, *Political Parties* (1915), focused on the role of salaried party employees and the party's Reichstag representatives. Their specialized knowledge of internal administrative procedures gave them control over the party's machinery and power over its members. Despite the formally democratic procedures of the party and the unions, they became an entrenched elite. Michels generalized this development into an "iron law of oligarchy" that he predicted would affect all large organizations in the modern world, and his theory has continued to influence political scientists and sociologists.[26]

As seen in Chapter 6, what workers did in their leisure time was of great concern to the ruling establishment. The Socialist Party and the labor unions also disapproved of disorder. Their leaders insisted on the respectability and dignity of the working class, and if workers were not respectable and dignified they regarded it as their duty to encourage them to become so. They campaigned against excessive consumption of alcohol, and they organized expeditions into the countryside. Workers' libraries attempted to steer their readers away from popular novels and toward the German classics, and worker's choirs included works of the canonical great composers. Party and unions consistently rejected any claims that their members had instigated disturbances. They claimed that street violence resulted either from police provocation, or else it was the actions of an unorganized and undisciplined sub-proletariat. The unions and party did not support the Moabit strikers in 1910, for instance.[27]

Party and union leaders regarded the workers as a single class in the Marxian sense, with their conditions of life and therefore their consciousness determined by the fact that they were proletarians in a capitalist system. They envisaged the worker as an employee working for a wage in a large industrial plant. Other forms of labor were "pre-capitalist" or "transitional" and they and their corresponding modes of thought would disappear as the economy developed. This ignored the fact that most workers were young, single, and temporary, that most of them did not work in industry or in large plants, and that the majority would return to their home districts after holding a variety of jobs in a variety of places. It also ignored divisions among workers. For most of those active in the labor movement, a worker was a worker, not a Catholic or a Pole. He was not an artisan, and he certainly was not a woman. Some historians, such as Klaus Tenfelde, have found evidence that workers overcame an artisanal consciousness and came to see themselves as members of a single working class. Others, such as Stephen Hickey, emphasize the divisions among workers resulting from inter- and intraregional migration, religious divisions, and ethnic differences. August Bebel's *Women and Socialism* (1883) argued strongly in favor of women's rights, and Klara Zetkin edited the Socialist women's newspaper *Die Gleichheit* (*Equality*) from 1891 until 1917. Nevertheless, Kathleen Canning's study is one of many that demonstrate the ways in which gendered social conceptions marginalized women in the labor movement.[28]

There remained the problem of what to do. The Socialist Party was committed to the overthrow of capitalism. Following the end of the Anti-Socialist Law in 1890, the party held a congress in Erfurt and approved a new program that looked forward to a revolution that would expropriate capitalists and create a new Socialist commonwealth. But the continued upward trend of the Socialist vote opened a new possibility of changing the existing system by reform from within. Parallel to developments in the Catholic Center Party, some Socialist Party leaders came to believe that they should appeal to groups outside the urban working class. Georg von Vollmar, a party leader in Bavaria, argued that Socialists needed to gain the votes of small farmers to win seats in rural constituencies. The Marxist dogma, that small farmers would disappear as capitalism developed, was not an effective campaign slogan in these districts.

The reformists or "revisionists" were led by Eduard Bernstein. In *Evolutionary Socialism* (1899, translated into English in 1909) he argued that none of Marx's predictions had come true. Crises were not becoming more severe, the number of capitalists was increasing not decreasing, small farmers remained numerous, and wages were rising. Surely the task of Socialism was to use the existing levers of power to gain social reforms.[29] Union leaders, with their emphasis on bread-and-butter issues, generally supported the revisionists.[30] Activists and intellectuals who remembered the heroic days of struggle under the Anti-Socialist Law, and who continued to believe that the Marxian theory of economic development would prove correct in the long run, opposed revisionism. They also reminded the revisionists of the undiminished hostility of the government and the difficulty of genuine reform under the existing constitutions of the empire and especially of Prussia. In addition, a new generation of leaders such as Rosa Luxemburg and Karl Liebknecht called on the party to reestablish its connection with the masses and press toward a genuine revolutionary confrontation with the government. For them the Russian Revolution of 1905 provided a model, and the general strike seemed a viable tactic. Union leaders replied that it was hard enough to organize an ordinary strike, and they agreed that "the general strike, as advocated by anarchists and persons without the slightest experience in the field of economic struggle" was simply "not discussible."[31]

Revisionism was officially rejected first by the German Socialist Party, and then by the international Socialist movement that was dominated by the German party. But within Germany, Socialist Party leaders did not challenge the essentially reformist activities of the labor unions and did not risk a direct confrontation with the government. The reformist and radical wings of the party continued in a kind of stasis. As with the Catholic Center Party, this has seemed to later historians a missed opportunity.[32]

The Conservative milieu: Prussia and the aristocracy

In one sense there could be no Conservative "milieu." Possibly the most important factor in the creation of a separate sphere was the sense of being outcast and under threat from the establishment. Conservatives were not under threat from the establishment because they were the establishment. Aristocratic landowners continued to dominate. Under Wilhelm, the aristocracy retained and possibly enhanced its privileges. Positions in the upper levels of the bureaucracy, in theory open to any, and in theory open only to those who passed the strenuous series of examinations, in fact were reserved for nobles. The Emperor intervened personally in the selection process to secure positions for the sons of well-connected noble families who had been so unfortunate as to fail their examinations.[33] Similarly, the upper levels of the army officer corps were largely closed to non-nobles. Private firms continued to recruit titled members for their boards of directors.

Aristocrats did have their problems. Prestige and influence in high places contrasted with the difficult economic position of landed estates outlined in Chapter 6. Change was possible, but the new techniques were expensive. Regional studies of Pomerania and Prussian Saxony have shown that the most progressive landowners tended to be non-noble. Aristocrats preferred to extend their cultivated area without changing their methods or their output mix. When they contracted debts it was more likely to be to maintain their level of consumption, and when they fell into difficulties they attempted to use their political influence to obtain favors from the government. At the local level, this might be the dredging of a river, the construction of a new road, or the convenient siting of a branch railroad line. At the national level, it meant the demand for tariff protection.[34]

Conservative power rested on the power of Prussia. Meinecke listed the unresolved issue of Prussia's position as one of the most urgent problems facing Germany.[35] Historians since have all agreed, though with a shift in emphasis. Meinecke as a patriotic contemporary saw Prussia as a positive force that required more effective integration to fulfill its role in the ongoing development of the German idea. For those writing after the Second World War, Prussia has been the bulwark of reaction, "the hegemonic power of the empire" in Thomas Nipperdey's phrase, with a "conservative internal structure that supported and secured the conservative power complex monarchy, nobility, military, and bureaucracy—that is what distinguished Prussia from all other federal states."[36]

In Prussia, Conservative power rested on the unequal three-class suffrage described in Chapter 4. The system remained in force until 1918, and district boundaries remained the same despite population changes. In the Reichstag, the two Conservative parties dropped progressively from 121 seats in 1887 to 75 in 1903, rose to 84 in the government victory of 1907, then collapsed to 57 in 1912. In the Prussian Landtag, in contrast, their 193 seats in 1888 rose to 212 in 1908. The Prussian franchise seems to us increasingly anachronistic, out of step with the thrust of national economic development, the accompanying social changes, and the general movement toward mass political participation. The voting procedure seems simply silly. Voting was not only unequal and indirect, it was also public. Voters could spend entire days in unheated halls simply to hear votes being cast. Nevertheless, as Thomas Kühne emphasizes, elections cemented a symbiotic relationship between the legal and constitutional framework and the structures of local society and local politics. The Conservative milieu was not limited to the aristocracy; it included many poor families as well. Kühne believes the Prussian franchise lasted for over sixty years because it accurately reflected the social realities of the relatively closed, hierarchical, and conformist communities of rural Prussia.[37]

Voting was a local festival, and politics revolved around local issues and relationships. Of course the public casting of votes offered government officials, employers, and clergy many possibilities to influence the outcome. The electoral system and the political culture that surrounded it reinforced traditional deferential "communitarian" patterns of politics. However, Conservative candidates had to meet challenges from well-organized opponents, including Poles, Catholics, and Socialists, but also anti-Semites, economic pressure groups such as the Agrarian League, and mass-based patriotic organizations such as the Pan-German League.[38] Over time, the more open contests for the Reichstag had a spillover effect. The inherited assumption, that districts should be represented by local notables as "natural" community leaders, frequently broke down. In some cases, electors and deputies came to be chosen as representatives of specific social groups. Deals could be done and alliances formed. At the local level the milieus may not have been so impermeable as they might appear. Conservatives and Catholics sometimes worked together.

The Prussian suffrage became one of the key issues in German politics, both practically and symbolically. Prussia's role made the Conservative majorities in the Prussian Landtag a practical problem of the first importance. In addition, whereas the Reichstag suffrage became a symbol of modernity and democratic reform, the Prussian suffrage came to symbolize political backwardness and reaction. In 1908, a series of mass demonstrations in favor of reform prompted Wilhelm to promise some sort of "organic evolution." In 1910, the government presented some minor changes to the Landtag. Passed by the lower house, they were rejected by the upper house. Creating new peers to secure a majority for reform, a threat used periodically by the British government against a recalcitrant House of Lords, appeared to risk further dangerous change and was rejected. Within the Landtag the parties could not agree on the structure of a new system, and in

1912–13 reform efforts were blocked by a "Blue–Black" alliance of Conservatives and Catholics.

Elsewhere in the empire, change was possible although the story was mixed. Some of the federal states moved toward the Reichstag model, but some did not. In the Kingdom of Saxony, the franchise was altered in 1896 to an indirect three-class voting system modeled on Prussia's. Although the total electorate was increased, the change eliminated Socialist Party representation from the Saxon Landtag. In embarrassing contrast, in 1903 Socialist candidates won 22 of Saxony's 23 Reichstag seats. In the Landtag, Saxon National Liberals who had supported the change found themselves confronting a Conservative majority that favored agriculture over industry. Younger National Liberal deputies around Gustav Stresemann began to advocate reforms that would include the obviously frustrated masses. Their efforts intersected with large street demonstrations beginning in late 1905, and in 1909 the three-class system was abolished—"a symbiosis," in Simone Lässig's phrase, "of a partially successful modernization 'from below' and a modernization 'from above.'"[39]

The Protestant middle classes and the Liberal parties

The economic and cultural achievements detailed in Chapter 6 were overwhelmingly the products of the middle classes. In Germany's cities, middle-class political parties developed sophisticated political machines that mobilized voters around a range of issues. Jan Palmowski's study of Frankfurt's Liberals shows them playing a productive and innovative role. Their efforts, and their conflicts, shaped the city's development just as much as the increasing influence of the professional bureaucratic municipal administration. The local Democrats, Progressives, and National Liberals contended over issues of education, welfare, and of course taxation. The Democrats, in particular, won votes by allocating municipal resources to the advantage of their voters. Their identification with progressive taxation paid particularly high political dividends.[40]

But these local successes did not translate into national political power. Liberals encountered severe problems as they attempted to assemble coherent constituencies within the very different municipal, state, and national political arenas. The problem was the structure of the federal system, which made it very difficult for Liberals to recreate their success in local elections. From 1890 to 1912, the National Liberals remained confined to around 50 seats in the Reichstag. In the Prussian Landtag they dropped from 86 in 1888 to 65 in 1908, and, as noted above, their alliance with the Conservatives in Saxony ended disastrously. The left Liberals divided and together gained only 36 seats in the 1903 Reichstag elections, although they then recovered under Friedrich Naumann's leadership. In Prussia, the two left Liberal groupings together gained fewer than 40 seats from 1893 to 1908.[41]

Divisions among the middle-class parties reflected divisions within the middle classes.[42] The National Liberals were the party of big business, connected to industrial pressure groups such as the Central Association of German Industrialists that represented heavy industry in the Ruhr and Silesia and the League of Industrialists that spoke for textile and clothing manufacturers in Saxony. Left Liberal parties were often linked with specific industrial or commercial groups in the southern states. Again we find some leaders seeking ways in which their party's constituency could be broadened, such as Gustav Stresemann in Saxony. And again we find that other leaders and many of the parties' supporters opposed these initiatives, peeking fearfully over the fences of their separate milieus at the enemy in the other camps.

Meinecke deplored the decline of Liberalism, and Weber has been described as "a liberal in despair."[43] Changing conditions fueled nostalgia for the old days. Freytag's *Soll und Haben*, with its celebration of honest upright merchants and their hardworking wives, retained its popularity as a birthday or graduation present for teenage boys. Their parents read Thomas Mann's *Buddenbrooks*. Published in 1901, it sold more than 1.3 million copies over the next thirty years. Subtitled the "decline of a family" and modeled on Mann's own family in Lübeck, the novel spans the years from 1835 to 1875. The Buddenbrooks belong to the city's ruling elite, and their grain-exporting business places them in the same milieu as Freytag's merchants. However, from the foundation of the Zollverein to the foundation of the empire, the three generations of Buddenbrooks become progressively less able to cope with the changing structure of the economy. They lose money when an associate firm in Frankfurt goes bankrupt following the Prussian conquest in 1866, and they lose more in an attempt to emulate their aggressive competitors in a speculative purchase of an unharvested crop, destroyed by "a bit of hail." As their business sense declines and their physical vitality decreases, however, their qualities of "spirit" (*Geist*) rise, a linkage that Mann took from Nietzsche. The family ends with the death of the sickly but musically talented Hanno from typhoid. The inevitability of the tragedy, and its symbolic nature, are heightened by Mann's trademark device, the identification of each character with a repeated leitmotiv, a musical technique Mann borrowed from Wagner's operas.

By the beginning of the twentieth century, a new term had begun to be used widely, *Mittelstand* or middle class. And no sooner had the term appeared than its users began to speak of both an "old" and a "new" *Mittelstand*. The old *Mittelstand* included a portion of the old *Bürgertum*, the urban artisans. Some of these continued to produce their traditional goods, some became small factory owners, and others became shopkeepers or providers of services. The father of the Munich entertainer, Karl Valentin, worked for twelve years with a furniture upholsterer beginning in the 1850s, but, when his employer retired, he shifted the business to furniture transport.[44] In addition, the old *Mittelstand* was commonly taken to include small farmers, a group that would never have been included in the old notion of *Bürgertum*. The old *Mittelstand* saw itself under threat. Large industry threatened artisans and small factories because the low prices it charged for finished goods could drive them out of business. Large industry threatened farmers because the high prices it charged for machinery and chemical fertilizers could drive them out of business. Large department stores threatened artisans who had transformed themselves into shopkeepers. Socialists threatened to organize workers to demand higher wages, and their revolutionary rhetoric threatened private property. Catholics and Jews threatened the sense of national identity by being somehow "different."[45]

The new *Mittelstand* were the "black-coated" classes, a group that in the United States or Britain were called white-collar workers, and, in Japan, salarymen. The range was broad and the boundaries indistinct. Salesmen in department stores and bookkeeping clerks in large firms wore the distinctive clothing. But so, too, did their supervisors and the senior managers in those same firms. Doctors and lawyers did as well, but their secure position in the *Bildungsbürgertum* eroded as new groups (surveyors, architects, and others) claimed equal status as "professionals." Public servants had always worn the black coat, when not wearing uniforms. Here, too, status became more problematic, because the public service had expanded and now included very large numbers of railroad workers (237,000 in 1890 and 492,000 in 1913), postal employees (104,000 in 1890 and 272,000 in 1913), and teachers (215,000 in 1890 and 380,000 in 1913).[46] Again those threatened by change or insecure in their new status organized to press their case. The German National Association of Commercial Clerks, for instance, regarded itself as an organization of professionals, not a labor union. It agitated against "unfair" competition from women who worked as salesclerks or managers of small branch shops, adopted a violently nationalist rhetoric, and denounced Socialists and Jews as the source of Germany's problems.

Protestantism divided as well. As seen above, the anti-Catholic Protestant League grew to over 500,000 members, and the *Evangelischersozialer Kongress* came into being in 1890 to combat both Socialist and Catholic activism. The Congress at first included Adolf Stoecker's antiSemitic group, but he was expelled in 1896 and moved toward the new radical right wing. Another group under Friedrich Naumann branched out as the *Nationalsozialer Verein* in 1896. A crushing electoral defeat in 1903 led to a regrouping, and eventually Naumann emerged as the leader of a new united left Liberal party, the Progressive People's Party (*Fortschrittliche Volkspartei*) in 1910, which won 42 seats in 1912.

Interestingly, and in the view of Protestant nationalists ominously, the truly devout Protestant circles associated with the Conservative Party frequently cooperated with the Catholic Center Party.[47] Often from Pietist backgrounds, these Protestants shared with Catholic Conservatives a hostility to modern industry, capitalism, and individualism. Among these groups, the series of small but active organizations led by Stoecker combined elements of patriarchal conservatism and Protestant piety with anti-Semitism. Blaming Jews for all they regarded as wrong with the modern world, they advocated social reform but insisted that the way to improve the lot of the disadvantaged lay in a return to the values that had supported traditional community life.[48]

High politics in the modern world: the power of the monarch

It would have taken exceptionally imaginative, sympathetic, and focused leadership to have bridged these gaps and brought Germany together. Germany did not possess such leadership. At the top the Emperor himself suffered from what today would probably be diagnosed as a histrionic personality disorder. Wilhelm's symptoms fit the standard criteria.[49] He suffered acute discomfort when not the center of attention. He continually ran through rapidly shifting and shallow expressions of emotion. He used his dress and physical appearance to draw attention to himself. He was notorious for his fluent but impressionistic style of speech and for his inability to give reasons for his strongly held but changeable opinions. He was self-dramatizing and theatrical, continually on stage and acting a role, though the role varied from one moment to the next. Cunning courtiers could exploit his suggestibility and the ease with which he adopted the opinions of others. Although not sexually flirtatious, his interactive style was persistently coquettish, designed to charm ladies and win over men, so long as he remained the focus of their attention. He could and would talk and act out stories for hours to entertain a group of women. For men, he had a repertoire of dirty stories and practical jokes. He possessed an overdeveloped and immensely strong right arm and hand, with a series of rings with jewels turned inward to crush an unsuspecting victim. His left arm and hand were withered as a result of an injury at birth, and they rested on his sheathed sword, carefully concealed in a tailored short sleeve and glove. Dogged, obsessive practice made him a good horseman and a good shot, with thousands of dead animals carefully recorded.

His aides knew that Wilhelm quickly studied the area of expertise of anyone he was scheduled to meet in order to impress them with his knowledge. They and his ministers also knew that he was easily bored by any subject requiring sustained mental effort, but that he could return from a yachting cruise bursting with ideas that might disrupt months of planning and negotiation. They also knew that he found domestic politics tedious and foreign policy exciting, that he loved military affairs, that he was positively passionate about the new German navy and overseas expansion, but again that his opinions were labile. When frustrated he was evasive, and when his role-playing did not have the desired effect of keeping unpleasant realities at a distance, he could descend into depression and develop symptoms of acute neuralgia.

However, the key point in any clinical diagnosis is that the disorder must cause present distress or disability, or impose a significant risk of suffering death, pain, disability, or an important loss of freedom. Wilhelm's problems did not cause him distress. Instead, Germany's constitutional system and the power of the monarch meant that the problems of this particular monarch were reflected on the nation. The arrogant junior officers in the army aped his mustaches and his manner. Officials at all levels pretended to arcane knowledge beyond the understanding of ordinary subjects. German diplomats threatened, bullied, and occasionally thumped on tables. And ordinary patriotic Germans took pride in their nation's military strength, deferred to the expertise of officials, and celebrated colonial acquisitions. Though they joked about his excesses and were appalled at his public blunders, even the most critical did not know how badly their country was governed.

As biographical details have accumulated, the picture of Wilhelm has deteriorated. Michael Balfour, in the 1960s, portrayed Wilhelm as a man who "could make rings around most of the people he associated with" but who was hamstrung by the contradictory elements of his combined English and German background. More recent works see him as either a reflection of the weaknesses and contradictions of German society, or simply as a failure as a human being.[50] In a parallel manner, evaluations of his impact on policy, whether for good or evil, have changed. The older picture of his "personal rule" gave way to a chaotic picture of a confused "polycracy" of competing power centers in which he played only a peripheral role.[51] As his reign wore on, he was frequently marginalized in debates that took ever more technical forms.[52] He could and did intervene in whatever area had excited his interest, but he was incapable of developing and supporting a consistent policy program.

It was unlikely that such a man would select strong and independent subordinates. The four Chancellors who followed Bismarck were Leo von Caprivi (1890–94), Chlodwig zu Hohenlohe-Schillingsfürst (1894–1900), Bernhard von Bülow (1900–09), and Theobald von Bethmann-Hollweg (1909–17). Caprivi has the best reputation among historians. A serving army general, he accepted the post of Chancellor only reluctantly and refused to serve concurrently as Prussian Minister-President as Bismarck always had. His period in office is seen as a brief interlude in which Conservatives were "willing to learn."[53] Realizing that Germany depended on exports of manufactured goods, Caprivi negotiated reciprocal trade treaties that lowered German tariffs on agricultural imports, particularly Russian grains. Only some Conservatives were willing to learn, however. Furious agitation by landowners culminated in the formation of the Agrarian League (*Bund der Landwirte*) in 1893. In the east, the League recruited large numbers of members and campaigned effectively against any candidate who did not support agricultural tariffs. Its success has been seen as a stepping stone on the path toward the formation of a radical right wing that mobilized the masses for Conservative ends, and as a precursor of Fascism in using democratic methods to achieve anti-democratic goals.

The Prussian Minister-President undermined Caprivi's position, and eventually both were replaced by Hohenlohe, an elderly nonentity. Bülow, in turn, was a smooth but unprincipled courtier. He renegotiated the trade treaties when they expired to secure increases in grain tariffs to please the landowners. The tariff income was important, because tariffs and excise taxes were the imperial government's primary sources of revenue. Bülow did manage to assemble a coalition of parties including Conservatives, National Liberals, and both the left Liberals and the anti-Semites that gave the government a majority in 1907. The alliance was inherently unstable, and Bethmann-Hollweg came to power following the dissolution of Bülow's bloc.[54] He was pessimistic and vacillating, and, when his worst expectations were exceeded in 1912, he simply attempted to avoid dealing with the Reichstag.[55]

All four Chancellors struggled with the budget. The imperial government could neither tax nor spend as it wished, because the states perceived increases in the government's budget as increases in Prussian power. Excessive federalism led to excessive reliance by the central government on borrowing, and economists cite the German Empire as evidence in favor of a strong central monetary authority in today's European Union.[56] Only the member states had the right to levy direct taxes. Legislation limited the amount of tariff revenue that the imperial government could retain, and the balance went to the member states. Any resulting deficit then required contributions negotiated with the states. Fiscal policy therefore faced severe constraints, which worsened as demands on the budget increased.

In fact, the government generally succeeded in obtaining increases in military spending from the Reichstag. Caprivi dissolved the Reichstag and won approval for a large army bill in 1893. As seen below, the army itself asked for only modest increases in 1899, 1905, and 1910, and Bethmann obtained the largest army bill in history in 1913. In the meantime, Hohenlohe pushed through the first large navy bill in 1898. A supplementary bill and another increase passed in 1900. In 1906, Bülow secured a bill that increased the tonnage of the ships approved in 1900. In 1908, he gained a further large increase in the number of ships and approval of an open-ended commitment to increases in the size of future ships. Bethmann passed another navy bill in 1912.

The government was far less successful in increasing taxes. Building on earlier work by Peter-Christian Witt, John Hobson places Germany in a comparative perspective and concludes that the government was only a "semi-strong" state.[57] In contrast to Britain, the government could not deepen its tax base by extracting resources from the wealthy classes. Taxes and tariffs bore most heavily on those with low incomes. The Socialist Party was most successful in those elections where taxes, tariffs, and military spending were the key issues.[58] However, the government could not rely on the support of the Conservative parties to increase revenue. Tariffs, trade treaties, major construction projects, such as the *Mittellandkanal* intended to connect the Rhine and Elbe rivers, increases in the size of the army, and expansion of the new navy, all became bitterly contested confrontations. In 1912 and 1913, the Socialists voted for the army bills because the money would come from a new tax on inherited land, and they regarded this precedent as more important than opposition to militarism. The Conservatives voted against the new taxes, the first time any major finance bill had been carried over their opposition.

In the years before the First World War, the budget deteriorated into a permanent crisis. Table 7.1 shows the dependence of the government on consumption taxes, tariffs, and income from state property such as the railroads, telegraph, post, and banking services. It also shows the rise in military spending and the large gap between income and expenditures. The share of the military in net expenditures rose from 65 per cent in 1900–05, to 80 per cent in 1910–13. The government overspent its net income by 40 per cent in 1900–05 and by 20 per cent in 1910–13, when the net deficit averaged over 400 million marks per year. The outstanding debt of the imperial government rose from a negligible 16 million marks in 1876 to 4.84 billion marks in 1910.

The Chancellor was required to negotiate with the Reichstag over the budget, and they all did so despite the difficulties. Although the Chancellor was appointed by the Emperor, in fact failure to maintain a viable majority meant dismissal. In addition, although the parties could not introduce legislation, all large parties were represented on the committees that discussed proposed laws before the government formally introduced them. In some cases parties and their representatives developed reputations and acknowledged expertise in particular areas such as education or social welfare. Manfred Rauh put this and other evidence forward to argue that Germany experienced a "silent parliamentarization."[59] This fits with much of the more recent work that sees Germany confronting and coping with the same problems that concerned all other nations at the time. Nevertheless, it remains true that the governing structures of Prussia and the empire did not change. Wilhelm expected the Chancellor not to maintain a working Reichstag majority, but to manage the Reichstag and secure the funds he wanted for the army and navy. As concerned Reichstag leaders knew, there were people close to Wilhelm, such as his friend Philipp von Eulenburg and army Chief of Staff Alfred von Waldersee, who periodically suggested a coup d'état to change the suffrage and reduce the Reichstag's powers. And, in the critical areas of the military and foreign policy, the powers of the Emperor remained intact.

Table 7.1 Imperial government income and expenditure, 1872–1913 (millions of marks)

(Yearly averages)	1872–75	1880–85	1890–95	1900–05	1910–13
Net income	345	491	930	1281	2045
Total indirect taxes	224	335	623	819	1311
(tariff revenue)	(110)	(191)	(360)	(488)	(701)
(excise taxes)	(114)	(144)	(263)	(331)	(610)
Total direct taxes	–	–	–	–	44
Net state property income	43	101	128	275	598
Loans	–	38	193	165	40
Contributions from states	78	17	–14	22	52
Total expenditure	1095[1]	776	1553	2294	3244
State property expenses				502	792
Net expenditure				1792	2452
Military expenditures	418	461	883	1155	1965
Civilian expenditures	41[2]	312[2]	670[2]	637	487
(administration)				(513)	(338)
(social welfare)				(124)	(149)

Notes:
1. Includes indemnity payments from France.
2. Includes State Property Expenses.

Source: Adapted from John M. Hobson, The Wealth of States: A Comparative Sociology of International Economic and Political Change (Cambridge: Cambridge University Press, 1997), Tables 2.5, 2.8, 2.10. Hobson argues that State Property Expenses should be deducted from Total Expenditure, as they went to produce State Property Income.

The Emperor, the military, and foreign policy

Wilhelm the conqueror

In 1890, Germany was the center of the system of alliances that isolated France and effectively blocked any other power from action without German support. In 1907, France was firmly allied with Russia and Britain, and Germany's two remaining allies, Austria and Italy, were weak and unreliable. Seven years later Europe was at war. How did this happen? Critics of Bismarck's foreign policy have argued that his system was excessively complex and inherently unstable. Critics of his domestic policies point to the structural weaknesses and divisions in German society and politics detailed above and in Chapter 5. There remain the roles of the Emperor and of his senior advisors.

Wilhelm saw himself above all else as a soldier, but he never progressed beyond a dangerously amateurish image of himself on horseback in full dress uniform, charging the enemy at the head of a troop of cavalry. His imaginary charges were all victorious; he never led troops in battle, but he sometimes cheated on maneuvers to ensure a successful result. Among themselves his generals laughed at his impulsiveness, contradictory orders, and refusal to take advice. However, they were happy enough to flatter him to his face, and he remained cocooned in his belief that he had inherited his ancestors' talent for military leadership.

Similarly, Wilhelm loved the excitement of foreign policy and believed himself to have a particular gift for it. Any area where he developed an interest became an area in which he would interfere personally, but, as always, his interventions were episodic, erratic, and sometimes simply hysterical. In 1896, he sent a telegram to President Kruger of the Transvaal congratulating him on defeating the Jameson raid and forestalling a pro-British takeover. Badly judged and intemperate in its language, it deeply offended British leaders and led to violent public outbursts of anti-German feeling in Britain. Wilhelm had wanted to send troops, declare a German protectorate over the Transvaal, and fight the British in South Africa in a war that he believed would somehow be localized, not extend to the seas, and not affect European affairs. Foreign Secretary Adolf Marschall von Bieberstein agreed to the telegram only to prevent something worse.

The Chancellors who followed Bismarck found the game of high politics much more difficult to play. Wilhelm spent most of his limited working time with his military advisors. The Chancellor met with the Emperor on most but not all Saturday afternoons. In comparison, Wilhelm had regular weekly appointments with the Prussian war minister, the Chief of the General Staff, and the Chief of the Admiralty, three appointments each week with the head of the military cabinet, and constant contact with the generals and adjutants of his own large Royal Headquarters staff. This meant that army and navy leaders could bypass the Chancellor, and it created a space in which an ambitious general or admiral could press directly for his preferred policies.

Bismarck's system of treaties began to unravel almost immediately. On March 21, 1890, three days after dismissing Bismarck, Wilhelm instructed his new Chancellor Caprivi to begin work on a renewal of the Reinsurance Treaty with Russia. Friedrich von Holstein, Bismarck's senior assistant for fifteen years, insisted that Caprivi delay a decision until he had consulted with officials in the foreign ministry. Holstein, as noted in Chapter 5, did not understand Bismarck's aim of preventing either Austria or Russia from gaining too much in the Balkans and thereby provoking the other to war. He worried more about the inconsistency between the Reinsurance Treaty and the Dual Alliance with Austria. He had become increasingly anti-Russian, believing Russia to be both ungrateful and unreliable. Privately, he believed he would lose his job if Bismarck returned to power and therefore wanted to create a decisive break with Bismarck's policies. The meeting took place on March 23, Holstein and the other officials convinced Caprivi the Russian treaty should be dropped, and he in turn convinced Wilhelm.

Despite Russian pleas, the Reinsurance Treaty was not renewed, but the Triple Alliance with Austria and Italy was renewed ahead of schedule in 1891. Fearing German support for Austria, Russia looked for other allies. Important financial links with France already existed because Bismarck's action banning Russian bonds from the Berlin money market had caused the Russian government to fund its industrial development policy with loans raised in Paris. In 1891, Russia and France signed a convention to consult in the event of a threat to peace, in 1892 they drafted a military convention, in 1893 they exchanged notes ratifying the convention, and the alliance was reaffirmed and strengthened in 1899. France and Russia each agreed to attack Germany if Germany attacked the other, or supported either Italy or Austria in an attack. Further, if any of the three Triple Alliance members mobilized their armies, both France and Russia would mobilize immediately.

Germany needed some other combination to counteract the threat posed by the Franco-Russian alliance. An understanding with Britain, the only major power without an alliance partner, has seemed the obvious solution to diplomatic historians—if not an alliance, at least great care to avoid alienating British leaders and driving them toward France and Russia. Possibilities for cooperation existed. Britain feared Russian expansion on the northern borders of India and in Manchuria and Korea. Britain and France were rivals as well, particularly in Africa, and nearly went to war over the Fashoda crisis in 1898. In 1895, British Foreign Secretary Lord Salisbury suggested a cooperative partition of the Ottoman Empire to Wilhelm, and, in 1898, Prime Minister Arthur Balfour and his Foreign Secretary Joseph Chamberlain discussed a British–German agreement with Wilhelm and Bülow.

Rather than working to gain British support, Germany rejected British advances and launched into a program of overseas imperialism. The German colonial empire eventually included German Southwest Africa, Togoland, the Cameroons, German East Africa, German New Guinea, the Marshall, Caroline, Palau, and Mariana Islands, parts of Samoa, and the concessions in China centered on Jiaozhou (Kiaochow). The colonies turned out to be financial liabilities rather than assets. Pacification campaigns, administrative costs, and subsidized freight services all proved expensive. They did not provide raw materials or markets for industry, and they did not provide an outlet for excess population, or "German" areas of settlement where emigrants could settle and still remain German. The "green twig" often referred to in the early days of overseas expansion did not grow into a mature tree. Rather, spread across the globe, the colonies became potential points of conflict with the other powers and particularly Britain.

Wilhelm ignored the dangers and difficulties of colonialism. He was an imperial enthusiast, desperate to play a role in history and confirm Germany's position as a world power. Other European, American, and Japanese leaders also sought imperial possessions, and all were strongly supported by popular opinion. In Germany, Conservative historian Heinrich von Treitschke's belief that colonies were "a matter of life and death" was shared by thinkers as diverse as sociologist Max Weber and Socialist intellectual Eduard Bernstein. The Colonial Association enjoyed funding from industrial pressure groups and included many prominent academics among its members. The pale green of German possessions took its place on world maps beside the pink of British and the purple of French territories. The colonies seemed to secure Germany the "place in the sun" that patriotic Germans felt it deserved. Wilhelm was possibly never so popular as in 1896 when he brought German relations with Britain to an all-time low with the Kruger telegram.[60]

A corollary of the establishment of an overseas empire was the development of a navy strong enough to protect it, and to pursue the new course of "world policy" (*Weltpolitik*). Wilhelm was also a naval enthusiast who doodled pictures of battleships when bored in meetings with his ministers. Other world leaders shared his enthusiasm. American naval theorist Alfred Thayer Mahan argued in *The Influence of Sea Power upon History, 1660–1783* (1890) that command of the sea decided conflicts between great powers and that the sea could only be dominated by fleets of heavy battleships. The book became an international bestseller. Mahan was celebrated in the United States, revered in Britain, and studied by naval strategists everywhere. German imitators included Ernst von Halle's *Sea Power in German History* (*Die Seemacht in der deutschen Geschichte*, 1907). Wilhelm ordered a copy of Mahon's book placed on every German warship.

The Tirpitz Plan

Alfred von Tirpitz made his career in the navy by strenuously advocating new technologies. Returning from a tour of duty in the Far East, he became navy secretary when his predecessor failed to gain Reichstag approval for the navy budget. He secured passage of a new larger navy bill in 1898, and the subsequent bills of 1900, 1906, 1908, and 1912. A tireless lobbyist and ruthless intriguer, he played the modern game of political public relations as well as the older game of high politics. In sharp contrast to most other ministers, he cultivated and flattered Reichstag deputies, especially members of the Catholic Center Party whose votes were crucial to pass his bills. In the Navy Office a "News Bureau" orchestrated a propaganda campaign for overseas expansion and for the navy. It fed stories to friendly reporters, arranged tours for academic speakers, and cultivated contacts among potential supporters in patriotic organizations. Founded in 1898, the Navy League (*Flottenverein*) had over 300,000 members in 1914.[61]

At the highest level Tirpitz exploited his right of direct access to the Emperor. He appealed to Wilhelm's weakness for arguments couched in technical terms but, at the same time, promised simple solutions to complex problems. The battleships Tirpitz championed embodied cutting-edge technology. Mahan's analysis appeared to demonstrate that the possession of a sufficient number of them would guarantee success in foreign affairs. Tirpitz also argued that the economic and patriotic impact of the fleet would "offer a strong palliative against educated and uneducated Social Democrats."

The first navy law of 1898, increasing the number of German battleships from 7 to 19, was only the beginning. "The construction of a fleet is in general the work of a generation," Tirpitz said. The second law in 1900 provided for a fleet of 38 battleships. The 1906 law increased the size of the planned battleships and enlarged the size of the canal linking the Baltic Sea and the North Sea to accommodate them. The 1908 law moved toward a program of three new ships a year and a shorter 20-year lifespan, or a fleet of 60 ships. Tirpitz was already thinking of a program of four ships a year "in the first instance" and a fleet of possibly 77 ships. The Emperor strongly supported his request for a further large increase in 1912, but Bethmann favored the army's demands instead, and the final navy bill was relatively modest.

The fleet was aimed at Britain. "We must have a fleet equally strong as England's," wrote Tirpitz in August 1914. "This natural and single aim could not, however, be announced during the past two decades." Not only did the ultimate goal have to be concealed from British leaders, Tirpitz also hid the full extent of the planned construction from the Reichstag because of the immense costs. He also concealed his ultimate aims from army leaders because the expense would undermine their own plans and his strategic conception would reduce their role. In the meantime, he insisted that Germany needed a navy only strong enough to pose a "risk" to Britain in order for German policy to be realized.[62]

Would Britain, the world's preeminent colonial and naval power, accept a substantial reduction in its relative position? In the early 1890s, Wilhelm and Holstein persuaded themselves that Britain would be an unreliable ally even if an agreement could be reached. Later Wilhelm and Tirpitz persuaded themselves that the risk of naval conflict with Germany would force Britain to seek Germany's friendship instead. There was a psychological dimension here. His failure to resolve his own and Germany's relations with Britain was the "thread that ran through Kaiser Wilhelm II's entire life."[63] His mother's English origin and her chronic unhappiness in Germany led her to desperate attempts to force him to accept the superiority of England. The accident at birth that had left him with his withered arm was blamed on the English doctor who had devoted too much attention to his mother. In addition, there was Bismarck's implacable hostility to her and to his father.

Tirpitz appears "unbelievably inflexible" in his pursuit of an ever larger fleet of battleships, all based in the North Sea. A convinced social Darwinist who had absorbed much of the common cultural pessimism analyzed in Chapter 6, he sincerely believed in the superiority of German culture over Britain's materialistic individualism. He "came to regard Britain not only as being a real power-political and commercial threat to Germany but also as representing in the most extreme degree an ideological, almost a spiritual, foe."[64] He wrote in his memoirs that his attitude toward Britain had been determined by his family and his profession. The son of a judge and the son-in-law of a doctor, he came from the professional middle classes. His father was a Liberal who combined admiration and jealousy in his ambivalent feelings toward Britain. More generally, the navy enjoyed the support of the middle classes from 1848 onward and provided the road to a successful military career for middle-class boys. The British base at Plymouth served as the main supply base for the small Prussian navy in the 1860s, and in his memoirs Tirpitz recalled being humiliated by the condescending treatment he received from British naval officers.

Tirpitz's calculations were wrong. Britain did not allow Germany to build sufficient ships to become the "risk" his theory required, let alone to approach equality. British financial resources proved far greater than Tirpitz had thought. In contrast to Germany, the British government demanded and received substantial increases in tax revenues from the wealthy classes.[65] His opponent in Britain was Sir John Fisher, whose career shows remarkable parallels with Tirpitz. As Tirpitz was creating the new German battle fleet, Fisher was modernizing and expanding the much larger but older British fleet. By 1902, British leaders perceived Germany as a naval threat, and began a new building program. In 1906, Britain launched the *Dreadnought*, armed with ten 12-inch guns, which made all existing ships instantly obsolete. Worse, Britain matched and exceeded the later increases in German naval construction. Worse still, Britain sought and found allies. A treaty with Japan in 1902 was followed by the two Entente agreements with France in 1904 and Russia in 1907. Cooperation with the French navy freed the British Mediterranean fleet for redeployment to confront the German fleet in the North Sea, destroying the premise of Tirpitz's risk theory.

The Schlieffen Plan

As Tirpitz pressed for a battle fleet aimed against Britain, army leaders had concluded that a two-front war against France and Russia was unavoidable. This posed serious problems. The large size of the Russian army made a quick victory in the east appear unlikely. But in the west, although the French army was not as large, the fortified positions along the border of Alsace and Lorraine also made a quick victory difficult if not impossible. Alfred von Schlieffen, Chief of Staff from 1891 to 1906, agonized over the problem of the two-front war, and he proposed a solution. Russia would be slow to mobilize, he reasoned, and therefore, if Germany could defeat France quickly in the west, German troops could then be moved east to equalize the numbers against the Russians.

Schlieffen considered that to defeat France quickly would require German forces to avoid the fortifications along the border. He decided the only path lay through the Netherlands and Belgium. German troops in Lorraine would retreat, drawing the French across the border, while a great mass of German soldiers would sweep through the Netherlands and Belgium, across northern France to the west of Paris, and then eastward. The entire French army would be surrounded as Hannibal had surrounded the Romans at Cannae in 216 BC. Cut off from the capital and from their sources of supply, presumably the French would then surrender.

The Netherlands and Belgium were neutral countries, and Belgian neutrality and inviolability were guaranteed by treaty. Britain, it was well known, would not tolerate a major power gaining control of the area across the English Channel. Therefore Schlieffen's plan virtually guaranteed that Britain would enter the war against Germany. France had not surrendered after the defeat of the army in 1871, and could have been expected to continue to fight on in any new war, tying down the troops needed to defeat Russia. Army leaders simply dismissed such worries. As in the case of Tirpitz's navy, technical military considerations would somehow overcome political and diplomatic difficulties.

Schlieffen's plan became the dogma of the army planners. His successor, Helmuth von Moltke, was the nephew of the general who led the Prussian armies in the Wars of Unification. He was a cautious man, partly because of his sense of standing in the shadow of his uncle. In addition, he had professional doubts about Schlieffen's plan. Concerned about creating another enemy, he decided not to invade the Netherlands.

This also reduced the range of the wheeling movement the German army would make and shortened the supply lines. He did not want to allow any enemy forces into German territory. Therefore, rather than retreating through Lorraine, he planned to hold the border against French attack. To do so he moved troops from the right to the left wing. These forces would have strengthened the thrust across Belgium and into France, but now they were stationed in a static defense of the German border.[66]

After the First World War, Moltke was blamed for altering Schlieffen's original plan. Specialists continue to dispute exactly what the general staff might have achieved, but the demands imposed on men and animals, the need for perfect coordination over long distances, and the difficulty of dislodging entrenched opponents all suggest that the plan could never have succeeded. As the analogy with Cannae revealed, Schlieffen's plan was a brilliant strategy but designed for an era when armies numbered in the thousands and tens of thousands, not in the hundreds of thousands and millions. Nevertheless, for these contemporaries, the details of planning seem to have provided the basis for a pervasive confidence that they could win the war that they believed would happen, and that they could win it quickly.

There was a more fundamental problem, however. The troops required to execute the plan did not exist. In 1906, Schlieffen's final version of his plan specified a full eight army corps that had not yet been created. As noted above, the bills proposed by the army in 1899, 1905, and 1910 were very modest. Astonishingly, the general staff did not tell the war ministry the details of Schlieffen's plan, and the war ministry continually opposed increases in the size of the army. Help came from an unlikely direction. In 1910, Ernst Bassermann, leader of the National Liberal Party, broke with tradition and attacked army leaders for not introducing general conscription and generally neglecting the army. Bethmann, who hoped to improve relations with Britain and therefore opposed further large navy increases, used the opportunity to force the war ministry to draft a request for nearly 40,000 additional soldiers. Then, in late 1912, Moltke, prodded by senior officers on the general staff such as Erich Ludendorff, demanded another 300,000 men. This was reduced to 120,000 by the war minister, and then approved with the again unlikely support of Tirpitz, who said the navy would not be ready to fight Britain before 1914 at the earliest.

As with the navy there was a psychological dimension. Schlieffen was obsessed with the need for a short war to avoid the collapse of the economy. Modern commerce, with its thousands of interlocking wheels, he said, could not stand still for a moment. In addition, he and his subordinates worried about the danger of social dislocation, and the possibility of a revolution, if a war were prolonged. But his solution, an army large enough to ensure a quick victory, raised an additional and even more fundamental fear among army officers. A large army would have to be drawn from all classes of the population. The new officers might not be aristocrats, and their soldiers might not be peasant boys. This was the basis of the war ministry's opposition to the general staff's demands for increases in manpower.

Army leaders had made desperate efforts over the previous thirty years to insulate the army from undesirable elements. As noted above, there were no Jewish officers in the Prussian army (by comparison there were over 2000 in the Austrian army including a field marshal, and Jews were overrepresented in the Austrian reserve officer corps by a factor of three). The prejudice against middle-class officers was almost as great. There were only 230 higher officers from middle-class families who served from 1871 to 1914, 29 per cent of the total, and of these 131 had been ennobled. One-third of all entering officers from non-noble families were already the sons of officers. The one exception was the Second Section of the general staff, responsible for the critical mobilization and supply functions. Here brains were more important than connections, and none of the serving officers came from noble families. Ludendorff, head of the Deployment Department, typified this small group. His father had been an army officer and he owned a manorial estate, but he was not noble and suffered prejudice as a result. Ferociously energetic and talented, with a broad knowledge of military engineering and technology as well as tactics and military history, he pressed for increases in the size of the army to fulfill the needs of his plans without regard for the economic, social, and political obstacles.

In the ranks the army recruited when possible from rural districts. In 1911, 64 per cent of recruits came from the countryside, 22 per cent from small towns, 7 per cent from middle-sized cities, and only 6 per cent from large cities. Army authorities were especially careful in selecting noncommissioned officers from among the least well educated applicants from Conservative rural backgrounds, because the NCOs had primary responsibility for training the other recruits. The point was to avoid recruiting possible Socialists. "I prefer a monarchist and religious soldier to a Social Democrat," the war minister told the Reichstag in 1904, "even if he is not as good a shot." Since 1896, a standing order had banned soldiers from having any contact with Socialists, and requiring them to report any of their fellows whom they suspected of having such contacts.[67] The enemy was in the cities. In 1907, the general staff prepared a report on "battle in insurgent cities," and, in 1908, the orders dating from 1890 preparing for a coup were reviewed and reconfirmed.[68]

The problem was not Schlieffen's plan, or even the contemplation of urban insurrection—all countries expect military planners to develop options for all contingencies. Germany's problem lay in the fact that there was only one plan, and only one response to social change. Here technical military details intersected with foreign relations, but also with domestic politics. The soldiers assumed Austria was Germany's only ally. Not only did they make this assumption, but they acted on it. Moltke assured Austrian leaders of German support against Russia in 1907. He exceeded his authority in doing so, but his right of direct access to the Emperor meant that he could not be controlled by the Chancellor. Wilhelm in turn believed himself a soldier destined to lead, and sharing the great secret of the plan and being assured that the care in its formulation guaranteed its success led him to accept the assurances that its foreign policy implications were not important. If civilian officials, elected representatives, or the people in the streets should object, the army could be relied on to manage them as well.

The road to war

Germany and Europe

Possibly the most important fact about the First World War is that no one expected it to happen. The chance of war had existed for some time. A series of crises disturbed the decade before 1914. The rigid alliance system and the even more rigid military mobilization plans meant that any of these crises could have led to war. All of Europe's powers were ruled by more or less unrepresentative and irresponsible elites, and all of them used nationalist imagery to deflect internal dissent onto external enemies.[69] External imperialist competition could and did lead to direct conflict. In addition, the threat of internal instability made the leaders of Europe's great powers willing to gamble on a war to fuse their divided societies into unified nations. But until August 1914 they did not do so.

War was possible, but not inevitable. Specialist historians in all the belligerent countries continue to debate the question of how each country made the decision for war.[70]

These considerations applied to Germany as well. Germany pursued a policy of imperial expansion, but so did all the powers. The quest for supremacy, for positions of strength, for exclusive markets, for exclusive spheres of influence, and attempts to divide and undermine the positions of rival powers had characterized European international relations for centuries.[71] From the specific perspective of the late nineteenth and early twentieth centuries, if imperialism and war were the inevitable results of monopoly capitalism, as Lenin argued in 1915, then all capitalist powers were equally guilty. Germany was bound by the alliance system, but no more so than any other power. Germany possessed a rigid military plan, but it was no more rigid than for instance the Russian scheme of mobilization. The divisions that marked German society were severe, but certainly not as serious as the national antagonisms within the Austrian Empire, or the impending civil war in Ireland. Germany's elites were under challenge, but elections were honest and demonstrations usually peaceful. No senior German official had been attacked since the two attempts on Wilhelm I's life in 1878. In Russia, the Tsar was murdered in 1881 and the Prime Minister in 1911, along with numerous other officials. The Queen of Italy and the President of France had also been murdered. The British Prime Minister was attacked and horsewhipped by suffragettes.

Nevertheless, although the war was a European phenomenon, in the view of historians such as Fritz Fischer, Germany appears to bear a particular burden of responsibility.[72] German leaders rejected opportunities to reach an understanding with Britain in the 1890s. The first Moroccan crisis in 1905, pressed by Germany to drive France and Britain apart, in fact pushed them together. Later in the year, a promising opportunity to reestablish relations with Russia foundered because the angry French would not participate. In 1906, Germany was isolated at the Algeciras conference and shut out of Morocco. An opportunity to limit the naval arms race was lost at the Second Hague Peace Conference in 1907, also the year of the Entente agreement between Russia and Britain. Austria did not inform Germany of the planned annexation of Bosnia and Herzegovina in 1908, but Germany felt compelled to give support. The resulting friction between Germany and Britain was worsened by Emperor Wilhelm's intemperate remarks published in *The Daily*

Telegraph. In 1909, a German note to Russia demanding an end to Russian support of Serbia appeared to Russia and Britain as an ultimatum, and a German mission to London to repair and improve relations failed. In 1911, the second Moroccan crisis, set off by German protests at French advances, was worsened by the arrival of the German gunboat *Panther* at Agadir. Isolated again, Germany was forced to consent to a French protectorate in return for slices of territory in the Congo. Encouraged by this, in 1912 Italy annexed Tripoli, and, as with Austria, Germany felt obliged to support an increasingly unreliable ally.

In February 1912, the mission of British War Minister Lord Haldane to Berlin looking for an agreement failed, because navy secretary Alfred von Tirpitz would not consent to limits on the German navy and because Wilhelm insisted on a political alliance as a precondition for negotiations over naval armaments. Wilhelm boasted, "I have shown the English that, when they touch our armaments, they bite on granite." In December, in view of the defeat of Turkey in the First Balkan War and Austrian threats to Serbia, Haldane warned the German ambassador that Britain would intervene if Austria attacked Serbia and that Britain could not tolerate a defeat of France. Wilhelm, in a meeting with Tirpitz, army Chief of Staff Helmuth von Moltke, and other senior naval officials, raged that Germany must declare war on France and Russia at once. Tirpitz said the navy could not be ready for a war with Britain before spring 1914 at the earliest. Moltke, concerned about military reforms in France and Russia, endorsed a preventive war "the sooner, the better."[73] Nothing was decided, but the Chancellor Theobald von Bethmann-Hollweg was not even informed of the meeting for over a week. Moltke remained convinced that the rising power of Russia must lead to war, and in the aftermath Tirpitz agreed to support the record increase in the army passed in 1913.

Since the war historians have pored over this record and debated the intentions and actions of Germany's leaders. Fischer's arguments have been subjected to particular scrutiny.[74] Those such as Klaus Hildebrand, broadly sympathetic to Bismarck, his successors, and the ruling establishment, have emphasized the primacy of foreign policy. They have viewed Germany and its leaders as essentially tragic figures caught between east and west and between the need for cautious conservatism and the need for effective military force to maintain the nation in a hostile world. Mistakes there certainly were, but the dilemmas imposed by Germany's foreign policy position made it extraordinarily difficult for even the most gifted of diplomats to balance the increasing tensions in a way that would ensure peace and stability.[75]

Thomas Nipperdey focuses on Germany's situation from 1907 onward, and he highlights the errors committed by Germany's leaders in dealing with the other powers. He is particularly severe on Chancellor Bernhard von Bülow. The conclusion of the Entente between Britain and Russia he believes marked the final failure of "Bülow's world policy." After that "little remained."

> One could wager on détente, with England and Russia above all, one could wager on testing the opposed alliances, whose solidity was not guaranteed, through crises, or one could wager on achieving some sort of breakthrough through crises. All of these were tried.

The problem, Nipperdey concludes, lay in the external structural factors affecting Germany's foreign policy. Germany was "completely unlikely" to renounce its world policy because that would have contradicted the ambitions of both the ruling establishment and—"not less"—"the nation." But, he continues, this would not have solved Europe's problems in any case. The "European problems" of "the land in the middle" with France, Austria, and Russia would not have been resolved but rather sharpened if Germany had abandoned its new role as a world power. "A limitation to the Continent was no longer a guarantee of security, but a further risk to security."[76]

More critical interpreters have taken their lead in particular from Eckart Kehr's notion that Germany's diplomacy reflected not foreign policy imperatives but rather the "primacy of domestic policy." Kehr emphasized the influence of the Junker landowners and heavy industrialists on the government. In attempting to maintain the position of the Prussian aristocracy and the profits of industry through subsidies and tariffs, the government severely damaged its relations with the other powers. The army remained a sacrosanct state within the state, and the navy imposed further very large demands on the budget. The failure to reform the tax system, combined with increased military spending, led to a financial crisis. The failure to democratize the Prussian franchise, combined with a refusal to treat the majority of deputies in the Reichstag seriously, led to a political crisis. Germany's aristocratic leaders, insecure and therefore aggressive in their domestic and foreign policies, pushed for war as the solution to their unresolved domestic social and political dilemmas.

Hans-Ulrich Wehler concentrates on these internal structural factors. He identifies three phases of armaments policy, an increase in the army from 1890 to 1897, a double tendency of slowing army growth and increases in the navy from 1898 to 1911, and a "hectic" increase in armaments beginning in 1912. He attributes the adoption and the continued adherence to the Schlieffen Plan to the "fantastic nimbus" of prestige enjoyed by the military. This was "not a temporary preponderance of the military planners . . . but a genuine social-historical problem" and one of the "specific qualities" of Germany's "special path." The contrast of the demands of the Schlieffen Plan with the limited size of the army resulted from the army's "domestic political tasks," and especially the need for a politically reliable military to repress the rapidly growing urban working classes. The expansion of the navy in turn was intended to "block off the claims for power of the middle class and proletariat," to "stabilize the traditional power structures," but also to "satisfy influential interests in heavy and shipbuilding industry including their workers." When this attempt at "social imperialism" failed, Germany's leaders "fled forwards" into a preemptive war.

> If the Faustian rule of history applies, that states institutionalize or at least cultivate the arrangements to which they owe their rise to historical greatness, then the greater Prussian empire of 1871, born in war, in early summer 1914 based its policy on a position that had already brought Berlin the longed-for success three times one after the other and now ought to bring it again.[77]

The failure of diplomacy

On June 28, 1914, a young Bosnian named Gavrilo Princip stepped out of the crowd lining a street in Sarejevo to watch the Archduke Franz Ferdinand, heir to the throne of the Austrian Empire, and his wife Sophie pass by. Their open car had taken a wrong turn, stopped, and was attempting to reverse. Princip fired two shots from a pistol and fatally wounded both Franz Ferdinand and Sophie.

Austria's annexation of Bosnia and Herzegovina had caused an international crisis in 1908. Serbia wanted to expand and saw the provinces as likely additions. The provinces were openly rebellious and were under martial law in 1914. Austrian leaders suspected Serbian agents of attempting to destabilize their rule. They were correct. They did not know it, but the Bosnian nationalist organization to which Princip belonged was supported by the head of Serbian military intelligence. What they did know was that nationalist and pro-Serbian agitation in Bosnia threatened their empire's stability by encouraging other national minorities to demand self-government. Therefore Austria wanted to reduce Serbian power. Russian leaders saw any Austrian gains in the Balkans as damaging Russian interests. Russia supported Serbia.

Austria had suffered a series of humiliating defeats at the hands of the Serbs. The Austrian Chief of Staff, Franz Conrad von Hötzendorff, had advocated war against Serbia for years. After the Balkan wars other senior officials also decided to "settle accounts with Serbia" at the next opportunity. Franz Ferdinand had been extremely unpopular in conservative court circles in Vienna, but his murder provided the excuse for the war they wanted. They drafted an ultimatum intended to be so severe that Serbia would reject it. Foreign Minister Leopold Berchtold pressed Emperor Franz Josef to sign the subsequent declaration of war because he feared it was "not impossible that the Triple Entente Powers might yet try to achieve a peaceful solution of the conflict unless a clear situation is created by a declaration of war."[78]

The Austrians requested German support. They were particularly concerned about the possibility that Russia might intervene in support of Serbia. The Austrian representative met with Wilhelm, members of his military entourage, and Chancellor Bethmann. He received assurances that Germany would support Austria. He also received encouragement to move against Serbia as quickly as possible. The promise of support is known as the "blank check" because German leaders made it without reservations or conditions on Austrian actions.[79]

Why did Germany's leaders do this? Bülow, the former Chancellor who still hoped to return to power, said at the time that they had stumbled blindly into war. In his opinion the blank check was the first of a series of stupid mistakes that a more intelligent and better informed leader, such as himself, could have avoided. In contrast, Theodor Wolff, the respected editor of the *Berliner Tageblatt* and after the war one of the founders of the German Democratic Party, believed "the men of 1914," both civilian and military leaders, wanted war and that active encouragement of Austria was part of their plan. Kurt Riezler, the Chancellor's personal assistant, told Wolff that "Bethmann calculated the risk very carefully." Historians ever since have tended to lean toward one or the other of these two contemporary views. Nipperdey and Wehler emphasize the accidents and the mistakes. Fritz Fischer and his students have argued that industrial capitalists and agrarians actively planned the war as a way to maintain themselves in a potentially revolutionary situation.[80] John Röhl believes "the decision was taken not in response to the Sarejevo assassination, but some time before" and possibly as early as 1911 or 1912 in response to Germany's humiliation in the second Morocco crisis.[81]

If we look at these men and ask what concerned each of them most, it is clear that none of them opposed a war to achieve their goals. Wilhelm was a dynastic ruler, prone to emotional outbursts and demands for instant, dramatic activity with himself in a starring role, as in 1912. He had been close to Franz Ferdinand personally and believed the Serbs to be "a gang of criminals" who "should be wiped out, and quickly at that! It is now or never." As for the possible conflict with Russia, Wilhelm's fears of the "yellow peril" had become entwined with dark forebodings of a looming race war between Slavs and Germanic peoples in which the Anglo-Saxon British had allowed themselves to become the creatures of the Slavs. But Wilhelm would have never followed through on his enthusiastic call for drastic action, for war, unless his advisors pressed him past the point of no return.

Bethmann as Chancellor confronted a hopelessly intransigent Reichstag. The government's enemies, the Socialists, Catholic Center Party, and Progressives, together held a near veto over proposed legislation. On the horizon, the Socialist unions had announced plans for a series of major strikes in heavy industry, and employers' organizations planned to retaliate with mass lockouts. From the right, the Pan-German League denounced the government's weakness. Bethmann felt that he needed a major foreign policy victory to strengthen the government internally. Externally, Germany's failed diplomacy had left it isolated and dependent on Austria. The risk of a general European war looked like a fair gamble against both the possibility of a quick Austrian victory over Serbia and the additional possibility of splitting the Entente. If a general war were to occur, a victory would bring annexations that would benefit the economy and quiet internal discontent.[82] Bethmann may have been gambling, but he also believed he had no choice.

Moltke and other army leaders believed the Schlieffen Plan would bring victory, but they also feared Germany was slipping behind France and Russia. Germany's window of opportunity would close, Moltke calculated, by 1917 at the latest. In addition, Moltke himself had promised German support to Austrian military leaders. He now urged his

Austrian counterpart Conrad to move to a full mobilization against Russia. Again there seemed no choice, and in arguing for war army leaders drew on their prestige and unquestioned position as technical experts to overcome the hesitancies of others around the Emperor. In particular, Moltke insisted that there could be no delay in invading Belgium because of the necessity of overcoming resistance from the fortress at Liège as quickly as possible.

Meanwhile, the French President Raymond Poincaré, the Prime Minister René Viviani, and their senior foreign policy advisors were visiting Russia. They proposed an international conference. Forcing Austria to accept mediation by the other powers would have imposed a defeat on the Triple Alliance. This was another case of policy having been decided beforehand, because they adopted this position before the Austrian demands on Serbia were known. Poincaré believed war to be inevitable and he intended to support Russia. He delayed, hoping Germany would declare war, because he wanted to ensure domestic support and because he wanted to be certain that Britain would definitely support France.[83]

The Serbian government refused to agree to the crucial points in the Austrian ultimatum, and ordered their army to mobilize before they replied. Russia offered support to Serbia. Not quite another blank check, because the offer came after the Serbian reply to Austria's demands, but good enough for Serbian leaders to continue on a course they knew would lead to war. Russia's leaders had confidence that the military reforms instituted since their defeat by Japan in 1905 put them in a strong position. Army leaders had been prepared for war against Austria during the First Balkan War in 1912. A majority of the Tsar's senior advisors considered the failure to intervene then, and of course the Austrian annexation of Bosnia and Herzegovina, as major defeats. They believed that another setback would seriously undermine Russia's status as a great power.[84] Another policy decided beforehand, and another gamble that seemed necessary.

The British cabinet was badly split. The majority opposed British intervention. Foreign Secretary Edward Grey believed that Britain must intervene, because friendly relations with Russia were essential to Britain's imperial interests. Grey believed in addition that Britain was obligated to defend Belgium and to support France. But he could not act without a cabinet majority. His opponents pointed out that there were no formal treaty commitments, that Britain was unlikely to gain from a war, and that British commerce would suffer. Britain supported an international conference. Both Germany and Austria rejected the idea. In response to a direct inquiry, France said it would observe Belgian neutrality, but Germany refused to answer on the grounds that this might reveal military plans.[85]

To prevent intervention by the other powers, Austria declared war on Serbia and invaded. Russia began to mobilize its army, but this was only a partial mobilization, and it was directed only against Austria. Russian army leaders attempted to modify their general mobilization plan so that it would not be directed against Germany, but they failed. Redrafting the complex orders for men, supplies, and railroad transportation could not be done in the time that seemed to be available. They attempted to conceal their general mobilization as long as possible.

German intelligence was quite good. There were a number of "commercial travelers" in Russia who reported on evidence of Russian troop movements, and German army leaders revised their recommendations as new information was received. However, when signs were posted in Russian villages along the eastern border of Germany ordering all reservists to their assembly points, it was obvious that Russia had moved to a general mobilization. If this were true, then Germany would have to mobilize as well or be left at a hopeless disadvantage when the Russians attacked. This meant attacking France, through Belgium, because that is what the Schlieffen Plan prescribed.

Germany delivered an ultimatum to Russia to end its mobilization. On July 31, the German ambassador inquired what French leaders intended in case of war between Germany and Russia. On August 1, he returned, but with the additional demand that France surrender the principal fortresses along its eastern frontier as a guarantee of "sincerity." French leaders were still unsure of British support, and replied that "France would be guided by its own interests." French troops were authorized to repulse any attacking forces, but ordered not to pursue them across the border. At 7.00 p.m. Germany declared war on Russia, but at 11.30 p.m. Poincaré told the Russian ambassador that it was still necessary "that mobilization should be taken as far as possible before war was declared," and that "it would be better that we were not obliged to declare it ourselves." The next day, on August 3, Germany declared war on France and the German army invaded Luxemburg and then Belgium. In London, on August 2, Grey still had to threaten to resign in order to secure an agreement that the British navy would aid in defending the French coast against German naval attack, and two ministers opposed to intervention did resign. But, on August 3, the news of the German declaration of war on France and invasion of Belgium led Britain to demand that Germany halt its invasion, and on August 4 Britain declared war on Germany.

Notes

1. Blue 1999, pp. 122–3.
2. Mah 2000.
3. Blaug 1999.
4. Tipton 2002.
5. Meinecke 1907, pp. 444–5.
6. Fairbairn 1997; Sperber 1997b; Anderson 2000.
7. Rohe 1990; 1992, p. 21.
8. Lepsius 1993.
9. Wehler 1995, Vol. 3, pp. 961–5, 1068–71.
10. Kaplan 1991.
11. Schüler-Springorum 1996.
12. Blaschke 1997; Retallack 1999.
13. Albisetti 1988, pp. 245–6.
14. Schorsch 1972; Reinharz 1975.
15. Gay 1978, p. 105.
16. Meinecke 1907, pp. 364–68, 444, 445.
17. Anderson 1991; Rohe 1992, p. 114; Heilbronner 2000.
18. Weber 1904–05.
19. Klein 1996, pp. 49–50; see Hübinger 1996; Lönne 2000, pp. 137–53.
20. Smith 1995, p. 102.
21. Schorsch 1972, p. 124.
22. Smith 1995, p. 127.
23. Cary 1996; Hübinger 1996.
24. Sun 1999.
25. Imle 1905.
26. Michels 1915.
27. Lidtke 1985; Lindenberger 1995.
28. Lidtke 1996; Canning 1992; 1996.
29. Bernstein 1909; Gay 1952.
30. Steger 1997.
31. Paul Barthel, *Handbuch der deutschen Gewerkschaftskongresse* (Dresden, 1916), pp. 130, 133.
32. See Schorske 1955.
33. Wunder 1986.
34. Aldenhoff 1996.
35. Meinecke 1907, p. 426.

36. Nipperdey 1993c, p. 611.
37. Kühne 1994.
38. Chickering 1984; Eley 1991.
39. Lässig 1995, p. 151.
40. Palmowski 1999.
41. Thompson 2000.
42. Blackbourn and Evans 1991.
43. Mommsen 1974, Ch. 5.
44. Richie 1983.
45. Gellately 1974; Blackbourn 1987.
46. Kocka 1981.
47. Smith 1995.
48. Hübinger 1996, pp. 166–7.
49. *Diagnostic and Statistical Manual of Mental Disorders, Fourth Edition* (Washington, D.C.: American Psychiatric Association, 1994), pp. 655–8.
50. Balfour 1972, pp. 83, 142; Röhl 1987; Cecil 1989; 1996; Kohut 1991.
51. Wehler 1995, Vol. 3, pp. 1016–20.
52. Cecil 1996.
53. Nichols 1958; Röhl 1967; Wehler 1995, Vol. 3, pp. 1005–6.
54. Lerman 1990.
55. Jarausch 1973.
56. Hefeker 2001.
57. Witt 1970; Hobson 1997, pp. 62–70.
58. Fairbairn 1996, p. 324.
59. Rauh 1977.
60. See Friedrichsmeyer *et al.* 1998.
61. Steinberg 1965.
62. Steinberg 1965; Kennedy 1984; Sondhaus 1997.
63. Cecil 1996, p. 194.
64. Kennedy 1984, pp. 125, 152.
65. Hobson 1997, Ch. 4.
66. Bucholz 1991.
67. Förster, Stig 1996.
68. Wehler 1995, Vol. 3, p. 1122.
69. Mayer 1981.
70. Wilson 1995b.
71. Canis 1997.
72. Fischer 1961; see Moses 1975.
73. Balfour 1972.
74. See Moses 1975; Berghahn 1993.
75. Hildebrand 1995.
76. Nipperdey 1993c, p. 670.
77. Wehler 1995, Vol. 3, pp. 1118, 1121–2, 1131, 1152.
78. Fellner 1995, p. 16.
79. Williamson 1991.
80. Fischer 1961.

81. Nipperdey 1993c, pp. 696–7; Röhl 1995; Wehler 1995, Vol. 3, p. 1159.
82. Fischer 1961, pp. 98–106. See Chickering 1998, pp. 62–3, 86–7.
83. Keiger 1995.
84. Cornwall 1995; Nelson 1995.
85. Wilson 1995a.

CHAPTER 8

THE FIRST WORLD WAR

Over two million German soldiers died during the First World War. Something like 50 per cent of the traumatized bodies of these dead soldiers could not be identified, because their wounds had obliterated their features, or because they had simply been blown to pieces and the pieces mixed and confused with pieces of both comrade and foe. The formal letters that families received were a fraud, as were the later cemeteries and their neat rows of crosses. The junior officer who wrote the letter often had no idea who the young man was or how he had died, and the graves might or might not contain the remains named on the marker. The letters and the cemeteries were an attempt to preserve the idea that somehow the individual identity of each of these young men could be held in memory, kept intact, and preserved.

The First World War traumatized Germany. The war seemed as if it might galvanize and unify the divided limbs of the German body, but defeat called into question the very essence of the German identity—national, unified, Protestant, and male. The failure of the army led to the collapse of the traditional sources of authority. The royal governments of the states and the imperial government of the nation evaporated. Into the void stepped the undisciplined forces that had been contained by law, by police power, by custom and convention—Socialists, workers, Catholics, and women. Adolf Hitler, recovering in a Pomeranian hospital from a mustard gas attack that had blinded him, wrote that when he heard of the revolution, "again everything went black before my eyes."[1]

The dawning disappointment as the war continued without success and without end, and then the sudden and unexpected collapse, opened the rupture that divided the war generation both from the prewar generation and from the generation that followed. Those who fought in the war felt themselves irrevocably changed, with experiences that could not be shared through normal discourse. Artists struggled to express these feelings, and historians of both the plastic and visual arts and of literature have argued that modes of artistic and literary expression have never been the same since. Our language and our expectations of the meanings of artistic works continue to reflect the experiences of the generation of the First World War.[2]

Two examples are Ludwig Meidner's *Apocalyptic Landscape* and Franz Marc's *Tyrol*. Meidner's painting is figurative, but surreal. A naked male body lies sprawled in a depression in the left foreground, amid a confusion of broken forms. On the horizon, darkness, storm, and fire engulf buildings to the left of a valley and threaten buildings on the right.[3] Marc's work is an abstraction, but equally violent, formed of intersecting diagonals. An explosion just above the center sends confused, jagged shards of contrasting colors flying toward the viewer.[4]

These two works are particularly good examples, firstly because they so clearly seem attempts to come to terms with the wartime experience, and secondly because they were both painted in 1913. Viewing them today, and then being told their actual date, they seem somehow to express an eerie premonition of the war and its destructive force. This is wrong. Rather, we see a connection with the war because we know the outcome. As contemporaries, Meidner (1884–1966) and Marc (1880–1916) were both struggling with inner demons. A friend of Meidner's wrote that "there is probably no other artist whose hand is directed as absolutely . . . to force, to hurl out his inmost being on canvas and paper." For Marc, who died at Verdun, abstraction was an escape:

> I felt the human form to be ugly . . . animals seemed to be more beautiful, purer; but in them too I came to discover so much that was repulsive and ugly that my depiction of them instinctively, on an inner compulsion, became increasingly more schematic, more abstract. Trees, flowers, the earth, everything revealed more ugly and repulsive sides to me every year, until now at last I have become fully conscious of the ugliness of nature, its impurity.[5]

Artists who did attempt to express the inexpressible horrors of the war drew on the approaches developed by the modernist avant-gardes before the war. If the war was a great divide, it also carried with it all the previous conflicts and contradictions of imperial Germany. Otto Dix painted an abstract *War* in 1914 using the same crossing diagonals to break images into exploding fragments that Marc had employed in *Tyrol*. Dix moved back to figurative imagery in the 1920s. The central panel of his *War* triptych painted in 1929–32 employs both the arrangement and the surrealist devices of Meidner's *Apocalyptic Landscape*.

Plate 8.1   Franz Marc, *Tyrol*, 1913–14. Oil on linen, 135.7 × 144.5 cm. Bayer-ische Staatsgemäldesammlungen, Munich. In this painting, which has been seen as a premonition of the war and which was used by later painters to visualize their wartime experience, explosive violence becomes the focus of abstract art—or, rather, abstract art becomes explosively violent.

The male figure on the left is now squatting, wearing a helmet and wrapped in a blanket, staring at a scene of devastation that includes wounded and bleeding limbs protruding from the rubble. Meidner's plume of fiery smoke extending over the left background has become a decayed body hanging from a protruding girder over the squatting soldier.[6]

Dix's 1929–32 *War* (see Plate 10.1) has been controversial. Some read it as an indictment of war and others as an idealization of male violence.[7] As a social document, it seems no accident that it was painted just as the German economy was collapsing into the ruin of the

Plate 8.2 Ludwig Meidner, *Apocalyptic Landscape*, 1913. Oil on linen, 80 × 116 cm. National Gallery, Berlin. Another painting that has been seen as a premonition of the war. The reverse side is also painted, an eerie work entitled *Revolution (Battle on the Barricades)*, which makes it appear that Meidner foresaw the Russian Revolution. Meidner produced several other versions of the *Apocalyptic Landscape*. As with the Marc painting, however, rather than a prediction, Meidner's works became models for other artists coming to terms with the violence of the twentieth century. Staatliche Museen zu Berlin— Preussischer Kulturbesitz Nationalgalerie. Photo: Jörg P. Anders, Bildarchiv Preussischer Kulturbesitz.

depression. As such it embodies both the centrality of the First World War in twentieth-century history, and the questions that remain. Economically, socially, and politically, the war can be seen either as creating new patterns, or as carrying forward tendencies already present. How could this have happened? The debate over the reasons for the war has continued to the present. What was the war's impact? Did the war merely magnify Germany's existing problems, or did it launch Germany in a new direction? Answers to these questions vary, and they remain contentious, for they relate directly to the question of whether German society was essentially stable, or whether indeed Germany was different, pursuing its own tragic special path.

The failure of strategy

The failure of the Schlieffen Plan

As seen in Chapter 7, the outbreak of the war came as a surprise. Once it had begun, however, all of the participants expected to win. In this Germany's leaders did not differ greatly from the leaders of other countries. However, as with the war's origins, their errors stand out above the rest. Their misconceived plans, their faulty execution, and their failure to see the implications of their mistakes created the conditions for the war's traumatic outcome.

At first all seemed to go well for the Germans. German forces moved through Belgium and toward Paris as they had been intended to do. However, they were delayed four days by an unexpectedly effective Belgian resistance around Liège, allowing the British time to land a force to reinforce the French around Mons. The French and British then retreated, but their flank was not turned. As the German armies penetrated deeper into France, men scheduled by the plan to advance over 40 kilometers a day began to tire, and supplying them by horse-drawn wagons became more difficult. Reinforcements had to move even more rapidly, over roads crowded by the supply wagons. Communications among the field commanders and between them and Chief of Staff Helmuth von Moltke's headquarters also became more difficult the further they advanced. Most information and orders traveled by couriers on horseback or motorcycle along those same roads. However, as long as each unit followed the plan exactly, other units could assume they were where they were intended to be, and act accordingly.

A gap opened between the two army groups on the right wing, and Moltke agreed when the commander of the group on the extreme right suggested that he turn his forces east of Paris to keep contact with the group to his left. This meant that Paris would not be cut off and surrounded, and it exposed his right to a counterattack. It also meant that commanders could no longer assume the positions of other units according to the plan, and communications among the armies on the German right broke down severely. Along the Marne river, the British counterattacked into the gap between the two German armies, and the French attacked the extreme right.

Meanwhile, in the east, the Russians had mobilized faster than the Germans thought they could, and they invaded East Prussia. Moltke,

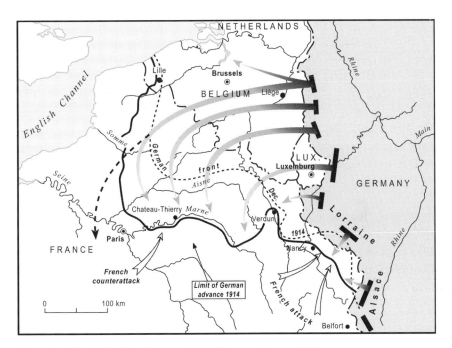

Map 4 The Schlieffen Plan and the Western Front, 1914

possibly overconfident of victory in the west, and determined that no German territory should be lost, ordered two full corps of troops to reboard their trains and head eastward. Before they arrived, the Russians had been defeated at Tannenberg. They were missed in the west, where the German right wing required reinforcements to defeat the French and British counterattack and move to the offensive again.

The French also launched an attack in Lorraine. They were defeated, with heavy losses. Again, Moltke could not bear that German territory fall into enemy hands, and he was tempted by the successful defense against the French attack. He therefore ordered an offensive against Nancy. This was expensive in losing large numbers of men, and again drew on manpower that was needed on the right wing close to Paris.

At this point, the strain of directing two uncoordinated battles caused Moltke to suffer a breakdown. An order was issued by a junior officer to the commanders on the right wing to break off the attack southward and eastward. The Germans withdrew to the Aisne river. They dug in and were then attacked by the British and French, who suffered heavy losses. In a series of flanking moves, the armies now moved west and north, as each tried to extend their lines around the end of the enemy's lines. The result was a "race to the sea" that ended when both armies reached the English Channel at Ypres in Belgium.

The Schlieffen Plan had failed. Strategically, the war was over. The Western Front stabilized, and there was no movement in either direction of more than fifteen kilometers until 1918. Tactically, the defense always had the advantage over the offense. The attacking army could move men and guns up to the front by rail. This gave them local numerical superiority, and commanders in their headquarters in the rear believed that this would bring victory. At the front, the troops had to move forward under concentrated fire from repeating rifles, machine-guns, and artillery. The bolt-action rifles carried by German soldiers were accurate at a range of two kilometers. Each infantry regiment also had a machine-gun company with six guns that could fire 500 rounds per minute over an effective range of four kilometers. Artillery batteries added fire from breech-loading 77-millimeter field guns. Their effective range of 8.4 kilometers meant they could be placed well behind the front line.

Despite their inevitable losses, the attackers might overrun the enemy's front-line trenches. To break the enemy line they would also have to take the support trenches to which the enemy would have retreated. But even if they broke through, they now had to move forward on foot. The enemy, well aware where the attack was concentrated, could move reinforcements up by rail. The rapid arrival of these new troops would turn the local advantage in the enemy's favor, and the attack would stall. In every battle, the attackers lost more men than the defenders, and no attacking soldiers ever achieved the breakthrough that their commanders planned.

Westerners and easterners

The failure in the west was not appreciated because of successes in the east. The elderly Paul von Hindenburg, recalled from retirement, and Eric von Ludendorff, who had been appointed his Chief of Staff, received credit for the German victory at Tannenberg. In reality, the two Russian armies had advanced beyond their effective supply lines, and they had lost contact with each other. The German army facing them had initially retreated, but a plan for luring one of the overextended Russian armies into a position where it could be surrounded had been worked out by staff officers before either Hindenburg or Ludendorff arrived. The victory was sealed through clever deployment of troops by rail to cut off the Russians' possible escape route. The following victory over the second Russian army at the Masurian Lakes seemed to open the possibility of defeating Russia completely, if Germany concentrated its forces in the east.

War minister Erich von Falkenhayn had replaced Moltke as Chief of Staff. He insisted that victory could only be won in the west. He believed that the experience of Napoleon showed that the vast spaces of Russia could not be conquered. Even if Russia were defeated, he reasoned, France and Britain would not give in. Falkenhayn in fact did not believe that Germany could win directly. Rather, he said, "if we do not lose this war, we will have won it." The failure of the Schlieffen Plan meant a different kind of war, a war of attrition in which the victor would be the power with the greatest reserves of men and material. Falkenhayn believed Britain was Germany's most dangerous enemy, and he therefore advocated a submarine blockade to prevent Britain from drawing resources from its overseas empire, combined with a major offensive in the west to demonstrate German invincibility. At the same time, he hoped a limited offensive against Russia would lead to a negotiated peace in the east. In the intrigues that followed, he was supported by members of the Emperor's entourage and by Alfred von Tirpitz, who wanted as large a role for the navy as possible.

Hindenburg and Ludendorff led the opposed party of "easterners" in the army command. They insisted the war could only be won by a "decisive battle" in which the enemy's main forces were crushed in one blow. Russia, as the weaker of the major opponents, should be dealt with first. They envisaged a huge encircling movement deep into Russia that would trap the main Russian army between two gigantic pincers. As the "victors of Tannenberg" they had already acquired legendary status. They got their offensive, although it was not the one they had wanted. A substantial German force was assembled to aid the Austrians in the southern Polish district of Galicia, where they had suffered severe losses to the Russians in 1914. An initial thrust regained the passes through the Carpathian Mountains. Hindenburg and Ludendorff requested more troops, and Falkenhayn agreed to a dual attack in Galicia and to the north from East Prussia. The result was a spectacular breakthrough that drove the Russians back past Warsaw and out of Poland entirely. German armies occupied Lithuania and Latvia as well.

Hindenburg and Ludendorff pressed for a further offensive in the east, but Falkenhayn resisted. He noted, correctly, that the strains on German resources would weaken Germany in the west. Further, the gains in the east had been achieved against a Russian army that was far inferior in equipment, but they had not defeated Russia. He insisted that Russia's huge spaces and immense population posed the same problems as before. In retrospect, we can appreciate that, despite the appearance of movement, strategically the Eastern Front resembled the Western Front. The level plains and sandy soil made defensive entrenchments less strong, and the thinner rail network made it more difficult to move reserves to a threatened sector. However, as in the west, although the attacker could gain local superiority and push the defender back, the attack would stall and stop as the attackers' supply lines lengthened and the defenders brought up reinforcements.

The great test of Falkenhayn's western strategy came in 1916 at Verdun, where he attempted to "bleed France to death." This was an indirect attack on Britain, in that it would devastate Britain's partner and prove German invincibility. Combined with submarine attacks on British shipping, Falkenhayn believed that the realization that Germany's army could not be defeated would force Britain to seek peace. He discounted the danger of the use of submarines bringing neutral countries into the war, because he expected to end the war quickly. Falkenhayn remembered that his own attack in Flanders in October and November 1914 had failed to break through along the coast as planned, and he noted that frontal assaults by the French and British in 1915 had failed to break the German lines. But these battles had also demonstrated that the attacker could gain a local advantage through superiority of numbers. He reasoned that, if Germany could seize a point in the French lines so important in itself that the French would be compelled to attempt to recapture it, then Germany would have the advantage of defense. The French would lose so many men that they would be forced to ask for peace.

Verdun was a good symbolic choice, a system of forts originally designed by the legendary Vauban in the days of Louis XIV, whose fall during the French Revolution had set off the Reign of Terror. The initial German success in capturing Fort Douaumont, in theory the anchor of the entire system, appeared to support Falkenhayn's analysis. A huge outpouring of emotion and calls to retake Douaumont at any cost reverberated across France. Again, however, the defense had bent but not broken, and French reinforcements began to flow to the Verdun sector before the Germans had secured their new position. The campaign swung back and forth, and rather than enjoying the defense, the Germans found themselves attacking as often as they defended. From February to the end of 1916, the battle claimed possibly 750,000 casualties, but nearly as many of these were German as French. The failure of the Verdun offensive weakened Falkenhayn's position and the entry of Romania into the war on the Allied side brought about his fall. He was replaced by Hindenburg and Ludendorff.

Allies and enemies on land and at sea

Germany's poor relations with its allies and the creation of new enemies contributed to the failure of German strategy. The problems began before the war. There had been no communication between German and Austrian military leaders on the possible joint actions that their alliance might force upon them. Moltke, while encouraging Austrian Chief of Staff Franz Conrad von Hötzendorff to full mobilization and promising support, had never shared the secrets of the Schlieffen Plan or its implications. Conversely, Conrad had never informed Moltke of the true state of Austrian preparedness or the details of Austria's operational plans. When the war broke out, Germany ignored Austrian desires from the outset, despite the fact that it was Austrian actions that the war was intended to support. In his telegram to Franz Josef informing him of Germany's mobilization, Emperor Wilhelm said,

> In this hard struggle it is of the greatest importance that Austria directs her chief force against Russia and does not split it up by a simultaneous offensive against Serbia. This is all the more important, as a great part of my army will be tied down by France. In this gigantic struggle on which we are embarking shoulder to shoulder, Serbia plays a quite subordinate role, which demands only the most absolutely necessary defensive measures.[8]

Conrad felt that German planners neglected his needs and wishes. He was correct, but defeats by the Russians in 1914 and again in 1916, and his failure even to defeat Serbia, led German generals to a sense of scornful superiority over their ally. By late 1916, Germany had imposed a unified supreme command on the Austrian armies and added German units along with staff officers to "brace" them. Mutual distrust hampered the effectiveness of these units. The Germans took credit for

successes and blamed failures on the slackness of their Austrian colleagues. More seriously, the old army that had seen itself as a corporate
identity and the support of the Hapsburg dynasty disappeared. The new
"Austrian" junior officers, noncommissioned officers, and enlisted personnel called up to make good the terrible losses were far more likely to
see themselves as members of national groups.

Italy abandoned the Triple Alliance and entered the war on the Allied
side in 1915. France and Britain offered to reward the Italians with
Austrian territory; Germany's counter-offer was limited by the fact that
Austria was its chief ally. Repeated Italian attacks along the Isonzo river
failed to break the Austrian lines, but the new front tied down Austrian
and German divisions needed elsewhere. Turkey and Bulgaria entered
the war on the side of Germany and Austria, but Romania joined the
Allies. In the Far East, Japan declared war on Germany. Serbia was
finally overrun, but a substantial remnant of the Serb army escaped and
retreated into Greece. Similarly, Turkey defended the Dardandelles
against an Allied landing, but required German aid to maintain itself on
several scattered fronts. The British and French attack on the Somme
failed, but cost the German defenders another 500,000 casualties. Strategically, Germany and its allies were on the defensive on all fronts by
the end of 1916.

At sea, the Tirpitz Plan failed even more abjectly than the Schlieffen
Plan. The huge expense of the fleet of battleships had caused immense
political difficulties and created a financial crisis. Although most German taxpayers would have been surprised to hear it, in 1914 the navy did
not have any plans to defend Germany's colonial empire. There were no
naval bases in the Pacific colonies and none planned. Rather, Tirpitz
concentrated his forces in the North Sea to challenge Britain. As seen in
Chapter 7, his calculations proved wrong. Germany could not build a
fleet large enough to defeat Britain, but the naval arms race poisoned
relations between the two countries. Tirpitz bears as much responsibility
for the war as any other leader.

Schlieffen and Tirpitz had pursued their plans in complete isolation
from each other. The army plans made no mention of the navy's role,
and, as noted in Chapter 7, Tirpitz had attempted to conceal his ultimate intentions because he feared the army would object to the expense.
When the war broke out, Tirpitz had sixteen of the new large "dreadnought" battleships, but the British had 25. A single confrontation
would have been suicidal. The British imposed a "distant blockade"

from safe bases in Scotland and the English Channel, so the Germans also had no hope of catching elements of the British navy close to German ports. The two main fleets did meet once, in 1916, off Jutland. The battle revealed design, communications, and gunnery weaknesses in the British fleet, and the Germans sank six British ships while losing only two themselves. But the odds were still too great, and after the battle the German fleet returned to port and, except for a few limited sorties, it remained there for the rest of the war.[9]

The alternative to attacking the British navy on the surface was to attack British shipping from under the water. Britain and Germany had both declared blockades, but, while the British controlled the surface, the German blockade remained an empty gesture. Tirpitz now pressed for the use of submarines, although he had despised them before the war as a distraction from his battle fleet, and he knew there were not enough to be effective. Of the total of 37 submarines Germany possessed in 1914, only an average of six could be placed on patrol in British waters during the first submarine campaign in 1915. They achieved considerable success, but Bethmann argued that the danger of alienating neutral countries, particularly the Netherlands and the United States, was too great. The submarine campaign was called off, but debate continued.

In 1916, Falkenhayn leant his weight to a resumption of the submarine campaign. Bethmann insisted that restrictions be imposed. During the struggle that followed, Tirpitz, who now suffered from Wilhelm's displeasure as the man who had convinced him to build the wrong sort of ships, offered his resignation and Bethmann persuaded the Emperor to accept. The neutral countries objected again, and again the submarine campaign was called off. This, in turn, opened the way for those in the navy who wanted to contest the surface to launch the series of operations that culminated in the Battle of Jutland. And, in turn, the inconclusive result tipped the scales once more in favor of the submarine.

Ironically, after his fall, Falkenhayn led one of the mixed German and Bulgarian forces that defeated Romania and occupied Bucharest in late 1916, a genuine victory in the east. In the meantime, his successors Hindenburg and Ludendorff, previously committed to the Eastern Front, now adopted Falkenhayn's strategic arguments that the Western Front was the crucial theater, and that submarine attacks on British shipping could tip the balance in Germany's favor. They also adopted the navy's wildly optimistic forecasts of British losses and the navy's further assurance that submarines could prevent American troops from arriving soon enough or in sufficient numbers to give significant aid to Britain. Bethmann still resisted, but Hindenburg and Ludendorff gained Wilhelm's support. Germany announced the resumption of unrestricted submarine warfare in February 1917, and the United States declared war on Germany in April.

The German submarines managed to sink their planned quota of Allied shipping for three months, but, as the British navy moved to a more systematic convoy system, the losses dropped. By the end of the year, Britain and the United States were building twice as much new shipping tonnage per month as the Germans were sinking. Tellingly, no United States troop transport ship was lost.

In the meantime, the German army in the west adopted a defensive attitude, while the British and French attacked. The resulting losses demoralized the French and mutiny spread through 45 divisions. In the south, the Austrians counterattacked and gained a substantial victory over the Italians at Caporetto. In the east, the Tsarist government collapsed and was replaced by a provisional government under Alexander Kerensky. Against his better judgment, he agreed to Allied demands for a new offensive in Galicia, but the attack stalled and the Austrian and German counterattacks pushed the Russians back. This new defeat caused the beginning of a complete dissolution of the Russian army.

Ludendorff continued to pursue the chimera of a decisive break-through leading to a definitive final victory. Defending in the west was a prelude to assembling enough men and equipment to achieve that break-through. In March 1918, the "Ludendorff offensive" initially drove the British and French back as much as 70 kilometers along the Somme. Once again the attack stalled as reinforcements arrived. The losses here delayed the second attack, to the north, blunting its effectiveness. Ludendorff persisted with two further attacks that brought German troops back to the Marne. The net result was a strategic loss. The break-through had not come, and the territory gained now required defense along a longer front with several vulnerable "salients" that the enemy could attack from two sides at once. Another 500,000 casualties, the decimation of many of the best units, and the huge losses of material seriously weakened the army that now had to withstand the Allied counterattacks.

German generals did not differ from their opposite numbers among the Allies. The British attacks on the Somme and at Passchendaele and the French "Nivelle offensive" stand as monuments to mindlessness. American John J. Pershing believed in the offensive that would lead to a breakthrough and a "war of movement" as deeply as any European commander, and the Americans lost 35,000 casualties in their first major action at Chateau-Thierry. The difference lay in the disparity of resources. In early 1918, the Allies had three times as many machine-guns per division, 20 per cent more artillery pieces, a third more air-planes, and four times as many trucks. Against 800 Allied tanks the Germans had ten, all captured. Allied troops were better fed—German soldiers sent packages of captured rations home to their families during the Ludendorff offensive. And crucially there were more Allied troops.

The economic context: the problems of mobilization and coordination

The economic impact of the war arose in large part from the fact that no one expected this sort of war. There had been no planning for the war that actually took place. Schlieffen believed a war simply had to be short if the economy were not to collapse. As the years passed, some including Moltke himself had begun to think of the planned campaign against France as the first step in a long war rather than as the way to win a short war.[10] Wilhelm's initial order to the navy to return to its bases aimed to preserve it for the next war, directed against Britain.[11] However, Wilhelm had also promised the departing troops that they would be home from this war "before the leaves fall from the trees," and general staff planners continued to think in terms of a war that would not last longer than eighteen months, and would probably be over within six months.

The soldiers used ammunition at unprecedented rates. In 1914, along the Marne, German soldiers fired more ammunition every day than the whole Prussian army had used in the entire war against France in 1870–71. The British and French fired 1.5 million artillery shells at German lines over a week before the attack that began the Battle of the Somme in 1916, but the Germans replied with 150,000 shells a day over the entire period of the battle.

The war also used soldiers at an unprecedented rate. Germany raised 22 new divisions in 1915, but reduced the number of infantry regiments in each division from four to three, and the number of artillery pieces in each battery from six to four. At the end of 1915 along the Western Front, the German army of 2.3 million men in 118 divisions confronted the Allied army of 3.5 million in 145 divisions. Then came the losses in

1916—350,000 casualties at Verdun, 500,000 at the Somme, and a total on all fronts of 1.5 million. The age of conscription was lowered to eighteen, which added 300,000 to the cohort of young men scheduled for induction in 1917. Enemy losses were greater still through 1916, and the ratios were even better in 1917 because the Germans were on the defensive in the west. But the Allied reserves were also greater, and even the successful defenses claimed further hundreds of thousands of casualties. Then German losses mounted again in 1918. By the war's end 13.3 million men had been mobilized, over 2 million killed, and 4.1 million wounded.

The lack of planning for a long war showed in the complete absence of reserves of food or raw materials. There could not have been adequate reserves, given the institutional and political structure of Germany. No one wanted anyone else to control such stockpiles. Government agencies regarded each other with jealous concern. Agricultural and industrial groups would not permit the government to amass huge amounts of basic commodities outside their control. And of course there was the question of the expense. Not only were government finances in a chronic state of crisis. Even more important, any appropriations for stockpiles would require the approval of the Reichstag, and this would raise the question of Reichstag control over the budget.

No other country was any better prepared than Germany. In Britain, it was "business as usual" because "the boys will be home by Christmas." The preferred models for military planning were taken from the experiences of the Austro-Prussian, Franco-Prussian, or Russo-Japanese wars, all of them short, sharp, strategic confrontations leading to decisive victory. The example of the American Civil War, a long war with several instances of static fronts where the opposing sides dug into trenches, was dismissed as the result of incompetent leadership. The trenches on the Mukden Front in the Russo-Japanese war were also considered unlikely to recur in a European conflict; the success of Japanese frontal assaults, though their high cost was noted, seemed to confirm the general faith in a spirited offense.

In all countries stocks of munitions were exhausted in the first few weeks of combat. By the end of the British and French counterattack on the Marne, Germany was thrown back on day-to-day production to keep the troops supplied. In November, artillery units had only four days' supplies of shells on hand. Here was another problem, because the initial mobilization of reservists caused dislocation in industrial production. All countries eventually discovered and implemented a system of exemptions for male workers in strategic industries. Production was maintained and increased by employing greatly increased numbers of female workers. All countries discovered the need to allocate raw materials on a priority basis to strategic industries. They also all discovered the need to ration food supplies in order to feed the soldiers at the front while ensuring minimal nutrition for the civilian population at home.

Germany moved more rapidly toward centralized control over the economy than other countries. The credit goes not to the army and not to the bureaucracy, but to Walther Rathenau, head of the AEG electrical conglomerate. He worried about how production could be maintained to support to army. On August 8, he "could no longer stand the agony," and he visited the war ministry to inquire what had been done about supplies of raw materials. War Minister Falkenhayn told him that he had issued no orders and that he personally did not believe that an effective policy to guard against shortages of strategic materials could be devised. Rathenau suggested an idea developed by Wichard von Moellendorff, a senior AEG executive, to conduct a survey of available supplies and to establish a central office to control their acquisition and distribution. Falkenhayn accepted the offer the next day. A War Raw Materials Section (*Kriegsrohstoffabteilung*, or KRA) was established in the war ministry. In the initial enthusiasm, even the federal states agreed to grant the new body authority within their boundaries. Rathenau and a group of his executives now set about gaining control over strategic resources.

The KRA began with a staff of five, but it expanded rapidly and by December already occupied 60 rooms. "War raw materials corporations" were organized in the form of joint stock companies. The government played the role of lead investor and the larger firms in each industry put up the bulk of the capital. The corporations were given the power to buy or, if necessary, confiscate all supplies of critical raw materials. Available stocks were then allocated to firms under contract to produce war materials. The first, War Metals Incorporated, was established on September 2, 1914. A combine of 22 of the largest metal processing firms, it established control over supplies of non-ferrous metals such as copper. By mid-1915, when Rathenau handed over his functions to an officer in the war ministry, there were 25 war raw materials corporations that extended over the range of direct military production.

By the end of the war, there were 200, and they covered the entire industrial sector. The large number of industrial cartels and the links between banks and industry eased the process, and in some cases such as coal the KRA simply adopted the framework of the existing cartel.

The KRA also worked out an arrangement with the leaders of the labor unions. The unions had patriotically renounced strikes for the duration of the war. Now officials in the war ministry agreed to consult union representatives in cases of disputes. They encouraged the formation of new unions as well, notably in the state-owned railroad systems, where unions had been forbidden. Industrialists of course objected, but they wanted to hold their skilled workers in order to fulfill their contracts with the government. The shortage of labor meant upward pressure on wages. The KRA used its leverage to force employers to accept the wage rates set in collective bargaining agreements modeled on those the unions had fought for before the war. Now, however, collective bargaining spread into heavy industry, where powerful employer groups had previously resisted negotiating with the unions.

The organization of the war raw materials corporations benefited the large firms that were their chief shareholders. Describing the KRA, Rathenau said, "in its methods it is closely akin to communism and yet it departs essentially from the prophecies and demands resulting from radical theories." He also believed "our methods will leave their impress on future times."[12] He envisioned a new system, a unique "German" or "national socialism" that would replace the market mechanism with intelligent public planning.[13] Others appealed more openly to self-interest. A senior war ministry official defended the high profits and other benefits large firms enjoyed. "Exploiting the national emergency to promote private interests . . . is the logical outcome of capitalism's basic philosophy and a fruitful field for the employment of capitalist expertise."[14]

The 22 members of War Metals Incorporated, for example, were the major contractors supplying non-ferrous metal products to the government, so of course they received the bulk of allocations of raw materials. The AEG itself produced a substantial fraction of Germany's copper wire. The war raw materials corporations bought the raw materials at fixed and usually relatively low prices that they passed on to their members. However, the terms of the military supply contracts set no limits on costs and guaranteed suppliers a 5 per cent profit. Small firms faced increasing difficulties, and the corporations frequently closed them down or forced them to merge. The number of shoe firms declined from 1500 before the war to 400, for example. Since raw materials and labor were allocated to army suppliers first, firms and entire industries supplying civilian needs contracted drastically. Employment in war industries (metals, machinery, chemicals, electrical) rose 44 per cent from 1913 to 1918, but employment in civilian industries (textiles, clothing, food processing, printing) dropped 40 per cent.

Nor did the large firms need to worry about taxes on their extraordinary profits. The imperial constitution prohibited the federal government from levying direct taxes, and the states were no more willing to give up their financial powers during the war than they had been in peacetime. In addition, the head of the Treasury, Karl Helfferich, believed that any taxes on profits would merely discourage enterprise and initiative. The only new federal tax introduced was the 1916 value-added tax on the "excess" profits of war contractors. This was politically popular, but firms found that they could pass the additional "cost" of the tax back to the government in their negotiations with procurement agencies.

Table 8.1 Germany: foreign trade and industrial output, 1913–19 (millions of metric tons, unless otherwise noted)

	1913	1914	1915	1916	1917	1918	1919
Index of exports	100	74	25	29	20	28	na
Index of imports	100	79	55	59	39	39	na
Index of industrial production	100	82	67	64	62	57	38
Hard coal	190	161	147	159	168	158	117*
Brown coal	87.2	83.7	87.9	94.2	95.2	101	93.6*
Pig iron	16.8	12.4	10.2	11.3	11.6	10.7	6.3*
Steel	17.6	13.8	12.3	14.8	15.5	14.1	8.7
Railroad freight traffic	677	529	368	416	na	387*	287*
Electricity (gigawatt hours)	8.00	8.80	9.80	11.0	12.0	13.0	13.5*
Beer (million hectoliters)	69.2	59.4	45.9	36.8	23.8	24.8	29.4*

Note:
* Excluding Alsace and Lorraine.

Sources: B. R. Mitchell, International Historical Statistics: Europe, 1750–1988 (Basingstoke: Macmillan, 1992); Gerd Hardach, The First World War 1914–1918 (Harmondsworth: Penguin, 1987).

Germany relied on imports for one-quarter of its food supplies in 1914, especially eggs, dairy products, fish, and meat. The British blockade cut off a large fraction of this trade, and the war with Russia cut off a major grain supplier. The army initially insisted that its orders take precedence over civilian needs. Prices rose. In November 1914, the Socialist Party demanded price ceilings and controls on food producers, and union leaders warned of possible labor unrest. The government responded by nationalizing the production and distribution of food. Farmers were required to declare any supplies, and wheat and rye were forbidden as animal fodder. A new Imperial Grain Corporation was established to purchase and distribute supplies of grain. By June 1915, bread rationing had spread over the entire country. In October 1915, an Imperial Potato Office extended control over another basic food, and potatoes were also forbidden as animal fodder. In addition, the commanding generals in each army district, who knew that food shortages might create social unrest, imposed their own price ceilings and allocation mechanisms. As George Yaney shows in the important case of Berlin, the resulting system was complex, inconsistent, and inefficient. The central bureaucracies could not deal effectively with the logistics of storage and transportation. When successes were achieved, they were often due to the superior ability of local organizations to respond to unanticipated emergencies, and to communicate and cooperate with each other despite their rivalries and conflicts.[15]

Farmers found that although the government attempted to freeze the prices they received for their output, at the same time the prices of their inputs increased drastically. Chemical fertilizer became very expensive when it could be obtained at all because of the need for nitrates to manufacture explosives, and machinery and spare parts disappeared. There were fewer workers. Several hundred thousand seasonal workers from Russian Poland were no longer available. The conscription of young men hit the rural sector hardest, and further thousands of young women were drawn into industry. Although nearly 1 million prisoners of war were working in German agriculture in 1918, on small farms wives, in particular, were forced to take up the slack. The bans on the use of grains and potatoes as animal fodder meant the farmers would either have to slaughter their animals, as they were ordered to do in 1915 when 9 million pigs were killed, or break the law. Many decided to break the law. Fixed official prices that did not even cover costs meant that farmers would either have to absorb losses, forgo profits, or break the law. Again, many decided to break the law. Farmers diverted supplies to markets or products where prices were high or not yet controlled—a ceiling on the milk price caused a milk shortage as farmers shifted to butter or cheese, for instance. Or, supplies disappeared into a black market where prices might be eight or ten times the official levels. Farmers, consumers, and government officials all came to regard each other with hostility and suspicion.

The government paid for its purchases though inflation. Helfferich said in March 1915 that "the compelling necessity for raising new taxes does not exist for us, in contrast to England . . . We hold fast to the hope of presenting our opponents at the conclusion of peace with the bill for this war that has been forced upon us . . . It is not we who have brought on this war, and it is for our enemies to carry the leaden burden of billions in the future."[16] In the meantime, Helfferich believed all the extraordinary expenses of the war could be met through loans. Nearly 100 billion marks were in fact raised through war loans. Marketed every

Table 8.2 Germany: agriculture, 1913–19 (millions of metric tons, unless otherwise noted)

	1913	1914	1915	1916	1917	1918*	1919*
Imports of all grains	7.56	na	na	na	na	na	na
Output							
Wheat	5.09	4.34	4.24	3.29	2.48	2.53	2.32
Rye	12.2	10.4	9.15	8.93	7.00	6.68	6.10
Barley	3.67	3.13	2.48	2.80	1.87	1.85	1.67
Oats	9.71	9.04	5.99	7.03	3.72	4.38	4.49
Potatoes	54.1	45.6	54.0	25.1	34.9	24.7	21.5
Sugar beet	18.5	16.9	11.0	10.1	9.97	9.88	5.82
Animals, in millions							
Horses	4.56	3.44	3.34	3.30	3.32	3.42	3.47
Cattle	21.0	21.8	20.3	20.9	20.1	17.7	16.3
Pigs	25.7	25.3	17.3	17.0	11.0	10.3	11.5
Poultry	82.1	na	na	65.2	59.0	51.3	na

Note:
*Excluding Alsace and Lorraine.

Source: B. R. Mitchell, *International Historical Statistics: Europe, 1750–1988* (Basingstoke: Macmillan, 1992).

six months, these became important morale and propaganda exercises as well, but they still came nowhere close to covering the costs of the war. For most of its expenditures, the government simply asked the Reichsbank to extend credit to it. The government also created a series of new credit institutions empowered to extend credit to state and local government and to issue their own currencies. (See Table 8.3.)

If the KRA had not been established, Germany could very well have lost the war in 1915. Despite their shortcomings, the systems of industrial and agricultural allocation worked reasonably well through 1916. The troops were supplied and fed. The civilian population was fed. There was very little industrial unrest. But the situation was grim and could only worsen. Tables 8.1 and 8.2 show the declines in industry and agriculture compared to 1913. They also show that output was maintained in heavy industry, but their final message is that Germany was

Table 8.3 Germany: finance, prices, and wages, 1913–19 (billions of marks, unless otherwise noted)

	1913	1914	1915	1916	1917	1918	1919
Central government expenditure	3.5	8.8	25.8	27.8	52.2	44.9	54.9
Of which, military	2.0	7.0*	24.0*	24.8*	42.5*	34.0*	
Government income		2.5	1.8	2.1	8.0	7.4	
Budget deficit		6.3	24.0	25.7	44.2	37.0	
Banknote circulation	2.9	5.9	8.4	11.4	18.2	33.1	50.1
Savings bank deposits	19.7	20.5	20.4	21.4	25.4	31.8	37.0
Wholesale price index		100	133	143	169	205	393
Consumer price index		100	125	164	244	292	401
Index of wages in war industry		100				252	
Index of wages in civilian industry		100				181	

Note:
* Fiscal years, 1914–15, 1915–16, 1916–17, 1917–18, 1918–19.
War industry includes metals, machinery, chemicals, electrical; civilian industry includes textiles, clothing, food processing, printing.

Sources: Calculated from data in B. R. Mitchell, *International Historical Statistics: Europe, 1750–1988* (Basingstoke: Macmillan, 1992); Roger Chickering, *Imperial Germany and the Great War, 1914–1918* (Cambridge: Cambridge University Press, 1998); Gerd Hardach, *The First World War 1914–1918* (Harmondsworth: Penguin, 1987).

unable to increase output significantly. The drop in beer output typified the experience of civilian consumer industries. Germany was cut off from overseas trade by the British blockade, and from most European markets by the land war. Of Germany's five major trading partners, only Austria remained. Britain, France, Russia, and the United States were all enemies. Previous exports such as machinery and chemicals could be diverted to the war effort. Some raw materials such as nitrates and cellulose could be replaced using new synthetic processes. But shortages of food, raw materials, and labor meant that Germany could only hold even with France and Britain through extraordinary efforts, and had no hope of matching the Allied totals after the United States entered the war.

The replacement of Falkenhayn by Hindenburg and Ludendorff in 1916 brought changes in the administration of the economy as well. Hindenburg's immense popularity lent authority to Ludendorff's energy and single-mindedness. Ludendorff regarded war as the foundation of human society, a standard social-Darwinist view that he pursued with exceptional conviction. From a non-noble family, he rejected the aristocracy's claim to leadership. All the resources of the nation must be mobilized for war, and mobilization must ignore social and political convention. The only criterion that mattered was one's contribution to the war effort. This meant that military matters should be in the hands of professional soldiers, not aristocrats. It also meant that government should be guided by soldiers, and indeed that military dictatorship was the normal form of government in the modern age.

Ludendorff's attitudes overlapped with those of industrial leaders. Employers were unhappy with the conditions imposed on them by the war ministry and the KRA. They believed the prices they received were too low, and they especially feared the long-term implications of negotiating with workers' representatives on equal terms. The heavy industrial firms in particular were as stubbornly intransigent as before the war, and they looked forward to a postwar world where the gains of unions could be rolled back and the absolute authority of employers restored. Rather than their previous family rhetoric, with employers as fathers and workers as children requiring guidance, they now adopted military analogies. An employer could not negotiate with his workers any more than could "a colonel in the trenches permit negotiations with his troops."

The government announced the Hindenburg Program for "total mobilization." New plants would be constructed and an additional three million workers concentrated in the armaments industry. Output of ammunition would be doubled and the production of artillery pieces and machine-guns tripled. All "non-essential" industries would be shut down and their capital, labor, and raw materials channeled into war production. A new War Office was organized under Wilhelm Groener, like Ludendorff a non-aristocrat and previously head of the railroad section of the general staff. An Auxiliary Service Law was proposed to the Reichstag. The draft placed all men between the ages of 17 and 60 under military discipline and, in theory, made all liable equally for service wherever the army decided they were needed. The law ignored women, who were leaving their jobs in agriculture, domestic service, and the textile and clothing industries and taking positions in the metal and machinery industries.

The army leadership was forced to compromise on the Auxiliary Service Law. Reichstag deputies and labor leaders also ignored the role of women, but they insisted on sharing power over Germany's "workers." They were willing to agree to restrictions on the rights of male workers to move from job to job, but only if elected representatives shared in the law's administration and if unions received parity with management in wage negotiations. Employers of course opposed parity in negotiations, but they still wanted to hold their workers, and they expected to pass any increased costs on to the government in higher prices. Hindenburg and Ludendorff wanted simple compulsion and militarization of the labor force. However, Groener argued for compromise because he knew that the hardships brought by the war were beginning to undermine domestic morale. The final bill provided for labor representatives on the committees overseeing labor allocation in each military district, created joint management–labor committees to resolve disputes in all firms with over 50 employees, and made collective bargaining agreements legal contracts for the first time.

As shown in Table 8.1, the Hindenburg Program did not result in significant increases in output. The War Office and the Auxiliary Service Law were supposed to simplify and rationalize control over production, but they produced administrative chaos and opened the door to pressure groups representing all organized interests. Inflation began to accelerate. Conflicts erupted between local commanding generals and their administrative committees and the new local branches of Groener's War Office. It proved very difficult to identify "non-essential" firms for closure. Soldiers had to be returned from the front to work in industry,

1.2 million in September 1916 and another 1.9 million in July 1917, and this created another area of conflict. Groener attempted to restrain industrial profits. He also opposed the construction of new plants. He argued that building new factories diverted raw materials and labor from current production, and the new plants then could not be operated because of the shortages. This and his willingness to deal with labor leaders alienated industrialists. The obvious failure of the program created further tension, and he was fired in August 1917.

By 1918, possibly 90 per cent of those firms still operating were producing war materials, but Germany had slipped irretrievably behind the Allies. The Austrian economy was near collapse, and the Austrian army increasingly unreliable. Although Russia was out of the war, a large German occupation force remained in the east. Italy had recovered from the previous defeat and raised new armies, and a large mixed Allied force still threatened in Macedonia. In the west, as seen above, French and British forces were better equipped than German units, and the gap was widening even before the arrival of large numbers of United States troops.

The social and cultural context: the battle front and the home front

Another crucial fact to remember about war is that no one expected it to have serious cultural or social consequences. The battles would be waged outside of Germany. The soldiers would leave their jobs temporarily, and then return. The resources needed to supply the armies would be supplied without serious change or inconvenience to those who remained at home. And, crucially, there would be no alteration in social structures, political institutions, or official culture.

Some did hope for changes, and they saw the war as an opportunity. The war itself fascinated participants in all countries:

> Most radical imaginations, whether of a political or aesthetic bent, were engrossed from the outset. The war offered extremes of emotion and effort ... sights, sounds and images that bore no relation to the staid Edwardian or even the febrile Wilhelminian world. The war thus acted as a veritable exhortation to the revolutionary renewal for which the prewar avant-garde had striven.[17]

Not only radicals were engrossed—a broad range of social reformers with a wide variety of agendas saw a chance to have their preferred programs adopted during this period of national emergency. For them the war might provide the means for implementing needed reforms in moral behavior, by exploiting the enthusiasm of a national emergency or using the convenient presence of the army and its ability to decree change through martial law. In Germany specifically, these kinds of reformers intended change to utilize rather than alter Germany's existing institutions. Then, as the war continued and hardship increased, new kinds of reformers emerged that demanded much more extreme sorts of change. Their demands in turn appeared a deadly threat to Germany's elites.

Culture goes to war

The initial overwhelming enthusiasm for the war was pre-programmed.[18] The desperate insistence on a single national identity in the 1870s had solidified into a school curriculum that celebrated Germany's institutions as a middle way between the undisciplined and decadent democracies of Western Europe and the uncivilized Slavic hordes of Eastern Europe. From top to bottom, high and low culture were saturated with patriotic imagery that celebrated Germanic myth, Luther, Bismarck's unification, Germany's rise to "world power," the old army, the new navy, and the Emperor. For years, twice daily and three times on Sundays, Berliners could watch British ships go down, sunk by German broadsides, in a gigantic indoor pool on the Kurfürstendamm.[19] The more reflective, or those without small children, could study the dozens of works by the cultural pessimists outlined in Chapter 6. As competitors in a crowded market, they offered differentiated and conflicting messages, but they all insisted that German culture was under attack and that desperate measures were required for its defense.

Popular enthusiasm for the army, the navy, and imperialist expansion sometimes ran ahead of official intentions. As seen in Chapter 7, the Navy League was initially supported by the navy itself to drum up support. It grew rapidly into one of Germany's largest organizations. However, its leaders began to turn against the government because the navy was not expanding rapidly enough. The slower pace of construction following the launching of the British *Dreadnought* caused the Navy League leaders to attack Tirpitz himself for his timidity. Officials in the navy office, unwilling to allow civilians to interfere in military policy, forced the radicals out of the Navy League. They then joined the

Pan-German League and, disillusioned with Tirpitz and the failure of "world policy," began to agitate in favor of increasing the size of the army.

During the days following the Sarejevo assassinations, crowds assembled to read the latest news bulletins posted in public places. They were concerned and earnest. Some of the expressions of patriotism were suspect. Theodor Wolff, the editor of the *Berliner Tageblatt*, believed the government had organized the demonstrations in favor of an Austrian attack on Serbia that he had witnessed on July 25 and 26.[20] As the drift toward war gathered momentum, there were a number of anti-war demonstrations. In Berlin, 100,000 people demonstrated against war on July 28 and 29, and they were joined by half a million in other cities.[21]

This changed with the declarations of war, the first movements of troops, and especially the first German victories. An obscure young man photographed in a state of euphoria in the middle of a huge crowd in Munich was typical. "Overpowered by stormy enthusiasm," wrote Adolf Hitler, "I fell down on my knees and thanked heaven from an overflowing heart for granting me the good fortune of being permitted to live at this time."[22] Actress Tilla Durieux said in Berlin,

> Every face looks happy: We've got war! Bands in the cafés and restaurants play "Heil dir im Siegerkranz" and "Die Wacht am Rhein" without stopping, and everybody has to listen to them standing up. One's food gets cold, one's beer gets warm: No matter—we've got war!

Others who we now believe should have known better shared these feelings. Sociologist Max Weber wrote to his colleague Ferdinand Tönnies on October 15, 1914, that "this war with all its ghastliness is nevertheless grand and wonderful. It is worth experiencing." The feelings were genuine enough, and the enthusiasm for the war was repeated in all countries. In Germany, the outpouring of emotion provided possibly even more relief than elsewhere, because, as we have seen, Germany was deeply and intransigently divided into separate milieus. Here perhaps was the great crisis that might overcome those divisions.

Intellectuals continued to wrestle with the problem of cultural decay, but they found reasons to assert the superiority of German culture over others. In *Decline of the West* (1917), Oswald Spengler advanced a theory of culture based on a Darwinian struggle for survival. Man, he said, is a mere "zoological expression" fated to pass away. "We no longer believe in the power of reason over life. We know that life rules reason."

Drawing on a pedigree that he claimed extended back to Goethe, Spengler insisted that, just like an individual person, any culture passes from
birth and growth to decline and death. Germans, however, had reason to
hope, for theirs was still a "young nation" that had been "kept back" by
its rivals, but now would begin to use its vast potential and would soon
rise to greatness.

Writers across a range of fields produced works that expanded on this
theme, and again they include many who should have known better.
Historian Karl Lamprecht predicted the victory of Germany's young
culture over the old and decadent English and French. Economic historian Werner Sombart portrayed Germans as noble self-sacrificing
"heroes" struggling against calculating selfish English "traders." Georg
Simmel, another of the founders of modern sociology, published works
before the war that, like those of Weber and Tönnies, lamented the
impersonal nature of modern culture. He believed the market economy,
in which the use of money comes between needs and the things that
satisfy needs, had led to a split between the human subject and the world
and a loss of direct contact with "life." Now, in *War and Spiritual
Decisions* (1917), Simmel argued that "the 'machine of war' has a completely different, infinitely more living relationship to him who uses it
than the machine in the factory." That is, a soldier in the midst of war
experiences "life" directly, overcoming the abstractions of civilization
and bridging the artificial gap between himself and reality created by
modern culture. Similarly, Thomas Mann's *Reflections of a Non-
political Man* (1918) rehearsed all the clichés of German culture as a
superior middle way and viewed the war positively, as an opportunity
for a "self-recognition" of German culture. From another perspective,
Hans Blüher's *The Role of Eroticism in Male Society* (1917) celebrated
the erotically charged male-bonded group (*Männerbund*). He believed
such male groups to be the source of cultural progress, and he attributed
their creative potential to sublimated homosexual feelings. He believed
the prewar *Wandervogel* to have been a particularly pure example. His
enthusiastic readers, including Mann, saw the *Männerbund* as the
model for the relations among the men at the front.

However, it is difficult to be certain as to the true state of popular
opinion. One of the duties of the generals commanding in military
districts was to enforce censorship. Once war had been declared and
their powers became operative, oppositional voices could not make
themselves heard. No one would have been allowed to organize an anti-

war rally to match those on July 28 and 29, for instance. Police reports, prosecutions, and private diaries show that for most Germans any initial hesitancy was swept away in the euphoria of the first three months of victories. As the deaths mounted, the assurances of the clergy that the sacrifices were sanctified by the nation's need began to sound less reassuring. Käthe Kollwitz lost one son and feared for the other. "My whole life as a mother is behind me. I often have a terrible longing to be back there, to have my children—my boys—one to the right and one to the left."

The government not only attempted to prevent opposition to the war, it also made efforts to stimulate enthusiasm. As noted above, the sales of war bonds became public rituals. Schoolchildren were given free days to canvass their neighborhoods. Public institutions and private firms bought them and sold them to their employees against advances in their wages. The early enthusiastic letters of soldiers at the front were collected and published. Foreign authors disappeared from bookstores. Most foreign films were banned, and Ludendorff personally supported the establishment of Universum-Film AG, or Ufa, in December 1917. He believed modern warfare depended on the mobilization of popular sentiment, and he wanted to exploit the propaganda possibilities of this new visual medium. The government did not always speak with a single voice, however. Tirpitz had been one of the most effective manipulators of public opinion before the war, and he continued to appeal to the public mood. Since his battle fleet had failed, he now advocated submarines. He believed the public would respond to the promise of a wonder weapon, and would demand enough submarines to defeat Britain. The popular enthusiasm for the submarine campaign and the failure to appreciate its consequences reflected his efforts.

Popular culture is a business. There was a wide market for romantic evocations of glorious and victorious struggle. Publishers competed to bring out stories of heroism or celebrations of new technologies. Flying ace Manfred von Richthofen's *Red Fighter Pilot* became a particularly successful best-seller. However, the popular market was fickle and not always subject to direction. The would-be moral reformers who hoped the war would cleanse the nation of foreign artistic styles and cheap frivolous literature (*Schundliteratur* or "smut") were bitterly disappointed. Edifying neoclassical art began to look ridiculously outdated. Popular novels remained cheap and frivolous, even though set in wartime contexts. In addition, the escapist, sensual, and erotic possibilities of cinema proved irresistible. Already in 1918, Ufa's civilian film-makers dismayed their military sponsors by producing films with "loose and fast living" heroes and heroines who appealed particularly to young audiences of apprentices and clerks.[23]

The need to escape into popular art increased as the hardships of the war multiplied. At a higher level, avant-garde artists who hoped for fulfillment in the war were as disappointed as the moral reformers. Some began to oppose the war, though only when out of the country, for instance in Zurich, in their homes, or in private clubs such as Club Dada in Berlin. Born in Zurich, Dada expressed revolt but without any promise of redemption or regeneration. Ironic cynicism deployed through Expressionist motifs, a typical mode of Weimar artists such a George Grosz, emerged out of these circles.

The battle front: the "front-fighter generation"

The Western Front is our image of the war. The trenches with their parapets, traverses, angled approach, and support trenches, the artillery barrages and assaults, and the meaningless slaughter created the overarching unity of destruction that defined the experience of the "front-fighter generation." While ordinary soldiers huddled in their dugouts, officers remained at the rear, planning new offensives. Over and over again, soldiers died by the tens of thousands struggling to seize the blasted and cratered stretches of ground. German soldiers called themselves *Frontschwein* (front pigs), a sardonic label like the French *poilu* (hairy one). Today, nearly a century later, senior figures of all large organizations are regularly accused of not knowing what goes on "at the front" or "in the trenches."

It took time for this image to develop. As with academics and intellectuals, the initial response of young men was enthusiastic support for the war, and again the response had been pre-programmed. The formulation of plans to deal with the "problem" of young workers had occupied official and unofficial groups intensively since 1900. Municipal governments established vocational schools that would take young men off the streets as well as offering them training. The Protestant and Catholic Churches both established youth clubs. The Youth Cultivation Decree and the foundation of the Young German League in 1911 represented an explicit militarization of these "youth salvation" efforts. They emphasized patriotism and respect for and willingness to serve in the army. By 1914, tens of thousands of young workers in urban centers had belonged to and presumably been influenced by the conservative rhetoric of municipal and religious youth clubs and the extreme patriotic rhetoric of the Young German League.[24]

New recruits began their trip to the front in training camps. But, despite the efforts of the authorities, the experience was still a shock, and not everyone fitted in. Artist Ernst Ludwig Kirchner was driven to a near breakdown by a combination of stress and physical ailments. He was furloughed home on medical grounds because by chance he was assigned to a unit commanded by an influential prewar acquaintance. Back in Berlin, he painted two of his greatest pictures. *Artillerymen in the Shower* (1915) shows naked boys crowded together, cringing against the flow of the water from the ceiling. One, possibly Kirchner himself, is kneeling, attempting to stoke the boiler. Weak and vulnerable, feminine except for their penises, they are virtually indistinguishable from each other. A uniformed NCO in riding boots and peaked cap, with a mustache worn in the style of Emperor Wilhelm, barks orders at the right.[25] His famous *Self-Portrait as Soldier* (1915) presents Kirchner in his uniform in the foreground, cigarette dangling from his mouth, staring out of the canvas to the viewer's right. His arms are raised to shoulder height, but his right arm ends in a bloody stump. In the background a naked woman stands in front of a large painting. The woman could be a lover, a prostitute, a model, or the personification of his art. His missing hand is the terrible fear that the war will take the one thing he must have to pursue his life and his art. Soldiers worry about castration; for an artist the worry can easily be figured as loss of a hand.[26]

Together the paintings show the regimentation, vulnerability, and fear of the young men on their way to becoming soldiers. They also point to the gendered perceptions Germans brought to the war experience. The recruits' exposure to the officer's gaze renders them vulnerable, and Kirchner expresses this by portraying their bodies as soft and feminine. In the self-portrait, he shows himself as the artist who has produced both the painting and the painting within the painting, despite his missing hand. In turn, the woman's hands are not visible. Her right hand disappears behind Kirchner's uniform collar, and her left hand is cut off by his remaining left hand. The soldier, wounded and marked by defect, has paradoxically recovered his powers of expression as shown by the paintings. His ability to function in a sexually charged setting is shown

Plate 8.3   Ernst Ludwig Kirchner, *Artillerymen in the Shower* (*Das Soldaten-bad*), 1915. Oil on canvas, 140 × 152 cm. Solomon R. Guggenheim Museum, New York. For the front-fighter generation the terrors of war began in training camps, subjected to the dehumanizing discipline of noncommissioned officers determined to eliminate individuality and produce soldiers who would sacrifice themselves without question. © Dr. Wolfgang and Ingeborg Henze-Ketterer, Wichtrach/Bern. The Solomon R. Guggenheim Museum, New York, by exchange, 1988. Photograph by Robert E. Mates © The Solomon R. Guggenheim Foundation, New York.

by the woman's presence in his studio, and the capability to mutilate her as well.[27]

Of course, one had to get to the front. One newly commissioned lieutenant exclaimed delightedly that "war is like Christmas!" but then died of an accidental gunshot wound on the way to Liège.[28] Once there, even the terror held its own fascination. Hitler said he was never truly alive before the war. Many returned to the front after recovering from

Plate 8.4 Ernst Ludwig Kirchner, *Self-Portrait as a Soldier (Selbstbildnis als Soldat)*, 1915. Oil on canvas, 69 × 61 cm. Allen Memorial Art Museum, Oberlin College, Ohio. The soldiers at the front lived in fear of wounds and death. But some wounds are worse than death, and for an artist such a wound would be the loss of a hand. © Dr. Wolfgang and Ingeborg Henze-Ketterer, Wichtrach/ Bern. The Allen Memorial Art Museum, Oberlin College, Ohio: Charles F. Olney Fund, 1950. Photo: John Seyfried, 1990.

wounds. This was common among soldiers of all countries. It was also common for those who "missed" the war or who could not return to the front to regret it deeply. This was a male community, even more so in the

German army than in others—there were no female drivers or messengers as in the British army, no female doctors as in the Austrian army, and none of the female support staff that served in the Italian army. The only women were the French and Belgian prostitutes in the occupied territories, many of them in bordellos supervised by army medical authorities.

Again, not everyone found the experience a positive one. Religious and class prejudice remained strong. Regiments were usually either Protestant or Catholic, and an isolated member of the "wrong" confession could expect harassment and brutalization. So, too, could Jews, and so could the middle-class enlisted men who found themselves serving among farmers or industrial workers. The continual strain took its toll. Tiredness could overtake one. Boredom and repetitive tasks could literally put one to sleep; it was possible, for instance, to fall into a deep sleep while continuing to pass shells to a field gun. There were those whose nerves snapped. During the Allied bombardment that preceded the attack on the Somme, German soldiers lay in their bunkers, sometimes as much as 10 meters below the surface, and waited through the week for the howitzer shell that would either kill them outright or entomb them. Some cracked, went berserk, and were shot by their comrades.

"Hysteria," regarded by Freud and other contemporary psychologists as the classic female response to stress, applied to the symptoms of stressed soldiers—paralysis, muteness, blindness, debilitating anxiety. Over 600,000 cases were reported. But, because these were men, the disorder needed to be redefined and became either "war neuroses" when sympathetically handled, or "cowardice" if less sympathetically regarded. The doctor who treated Hitler believed his patients to be cowardly slackers. He hypnotized them and then shouted at them that they could overcome their weak and unmanly impulses through an act of will. In theory, the post-hypnotic suggestion would remove the symptoms and enable them to return to the front.

Morale deteriorated as the war went on. In 1914, hundreds of young recruits and reservists died at the "Battle of Langemarck" in the Ypres district, reportedly singing "Deutschland, Deutschland über alles" as they charged the enemy. By 1916, newspapers circulating at the front presented images of a stoic endurance, a kind of matter-of-fact heroism combined with the hope that peace might still come soon. Letters from the front no longer made suitable propaganda, and, indeed, censors became deeply concerned that their cynicism and disillusionment would undermine morale at home. The favored treatment of wealthy and aristocratic officers, including their preferential access to the women in the bordellos, came to seem the result of corruption and connections rather than as part of the natural order.

By 1918, equipment and food had deteriorated severely. Things never got to the point where horse-meat was reserved for officers, as happened in the Austrian army. There were no mass mutinies as in the French army. The German army did not dissolve as did the Russian army, or fracture along national lines as did the Austrian army. Discipline held, despite the addition of large numbers of striking workers sentenced to service at the front. Nevertheless, the final Ludendorff offensive severely strained morale, physical endurance, and material support. On August 8, the day that Ludendorff called "the black day of the German army," the British attack near Amiens cost 20,000 casualties, but also saw 30,000 Germans surrender. Many others surrendered, disappeared during transport or while on leave, or pretended injury or illness. As many as 750,000 to 1 million may have avoided battle during the final months of the war, a "covert military strike," in Wilhelm Deist's phrase.[29] The soldiers knew they could not win, and many wondered who was responsible for the defeat they now feared.

The war produced wounded, crippled, and disfigured veterans. The statistics show 4.1 million wounded, half seriously. At the end of the war, the national insurance office listed 1.35 million "war wounded," and, of those, a half million were judged to be "more than one-third disabled." For them and for their families, possibly even more than for those of the dead, the questions of whether their sacrifice had been worth the cost and of who was responsible hung in the air.

The home front: a divided society at war

The experience of the home front also reflected initial enthusiasm, followed by declining morale as conditions worsened and the war did not end. Some of the measures of deprivation can be read or inferred from the tables above. Money wages rose, nearly doubling in civilian industries and rising two and a half times in war industries. But prices rose faster, and were nearly three times higher at the end of the war than at the outset. Real wages therefore declined. Workers in some civilian manufacturing branches suffered a 50 per cent loss in their purchasing power.

The middle classes also suffered. At the lower levels, sales clerks and bookkeepers' pay rose only from 20 to 70 per cent depending on the size of their firm. Shopkeepers, artisans, and small firms strained to survive, and many did not. Supervisors and senior managers in large firms in the war industries did somewhat better, but neither they nor the independent professionals could recoup the rise in prices. Public servants also lost purchasing power. By 1918, lower-level bureaucrats' salaries were twice their 1914 levels, but they had lost a third of their prewar real incomes. Higher officials had always earned several multiples of their junior colleagues' salaries, but their salaries rose by less than half, and therefore their purchasing power declined drastically.

As their real incomes declined, members of the middle classes found it more and more difficult to maintain their status relative to unionized workers. They felt, they said, as if they were being "proletarianized." They also felt that they lacked political representation. In 1916, the Conservative and anti-Semitic association of male shop assistants called for a reform of the Prussian franchise, which would give their members more political weight in elections. In the case of public officials, this sense of declining status led to a previously unthinkable expansion of labor unions. Erich Remmers, a postal assistant with Liberal political connections, had attempted since 1898 to organize public employees, but the hostility of the government and the reluctance of individual officials limited his success. Responding to the integration of manufacturing workers' unions into the war effort, Remmers established an umbrella organization for associations of government employees in 1916. By 1918, its associated groups, mostly of postal and railroad officials, had 600,000 members. In 1917, central organizations of government officials were established in Bavaria and Baden. Remmers pressed for the creation of a national Union of German Officials (*Deutscher Beamtenbund*, or DBB) dedicated to the "creation of modern, uniform regulations" for public employees. Success came only after the outbreak of the revolution in December 1918. Remmers' twenty-year struggle was capped by his election as the new organization's first president.[30]

As the war went on, the attention of those whose real incomes were declining concentrated on food. Harvests in 1914 and 1915 were good, but 1916 was a poor year and the winter of 1916–17 was exceptionally cold. The agricultural statistics show the decline in food supplies. As noted above, farmers held back as much as they could to sell to friends, acquaintances, or anyone who could pay more. The official figures do not take black market prices into account. They do not show the decline in quality or the consumption of poor quality substitutes. They do not show the complete disappearance of many high-quality foods from the diets of ordinary Germans. Although officially prices may have risen 300 per cent between 1913 and 1918, not very much was available at those prices. Price controls failed. Estimates suggested that as much as one-third of all food was purchased on the black market or obtained through non-market transactions by 1918. The figures also do not account for the time, energy, and anxiety of this search for food. Mothers and grand-parents sought out and purchased from black market suppliers, and those who could, traveled to the countryside to obtain food directly from farmers. (See Table 8.4.)

Malnutrition registered in the statistics. Civilian mortality increased from 16 per 1000 in 1910–13, to 21 per 1000 in 1914–18. Death rates for young children rose, and the causes reflected an increase in nutritional deficiencies. Adults lost weight, and for the elderly this too could be deadly. During the "turnip winter" of 1916–17, food supplies tightened, and the shortage of coal meant delayed food shipments, interrupted electric power, cold apartments, and frozen and burst pipes. At the same time that Thomas Mann was writing *Reflections of a Nonpolitical Man*, his family were collecting and eating the snails in their garden.

In theory, all sacrificed to the war effort equally. But Germany was a class society, and the upper classes sacrificed much less than the poor.

Table 8.4 Wartime rations as a percentage of peacetime consumption

	July 1916– June 1917	July 1917– June 1918	July 1918– December 1918
Meat	31	20	12
Fish	51	—	5
Eggs	18	13	13
Lard	14	11	7
Butter	22	21	28
Cheese	3	4	15
Sugar	49	56–67	80
Flour	53	47	48
Potatoes	71	94	94

Source: Gerd Hardach, *The First World War 1914–1918* (Harmondsworth: Penguin, 1987).

A HISTORY OF MODERN GERMANY

Parallel to the experience at the front, the traditional elite classes did not suffer unduly, and the owners of the firms in war industries did the best of all. The wealthy had privileged access to food and to coal for heating. As at the front, the decline in the standard of living increased the sensitivity of all classes to existing differences. Because they came after a period of rapidly increasing affluence, the gaps between employers and workers, between landlords and tenants, and between rich and poor were not accepted passively.

Germany was also a gendered society. If the battle front was a male community, the home front was in large part a female community. Gertrud Bäumer, leader of the Association of German Women's Organizations, immediately founded a new National Women's Service in 1914 to coordinate women's contribution to the war effort. She published *The War and Woman* (*Der Krieg und die Frau*, 1914) and compared mothers' sacrifices to death on the battlefield. Women were wives and mothers, but they were also workers, an unacknowledged double burden reflected in the absence of women in the disputes over the Auxiliary Service Law. The government at first made no plans for the employment of women. As the war industries expanded and drew in more women, the government and Reichstag party leaders assumed, and union leaders insisted, that women's work in war industries would be temporary, and that after the victory men would return to their jobs and women to the private sphere of home and family. They therefore believed allocation of and control over "workers" meant regulations governing male workers.

The employment of women paralleled the changes in the economy described above. The contradictions between the gendered public realm and the private sphere widened with the strain placed on farm wives due to the labor shortage in agriculture, and even more openly with the dramatic increase in the number of women working in industry. Workers in firms with more than ten employees increased their share of total employment substantially from 1913 to 1918. However, the number of adult men they employed dropped 25 per cent, while the number of boys under 16 rose 10 per cent and the number of women increased by over 50 per cent, to more than 2 million. The total number of women working in industry rose 17 per cent, and by the end of the war over one-third of the industrial labor force was female. In the previously male-dominated metal and machinery industries, the increase was particularly large. Krupp employed almost no women in 1913, but nearly 40 per cent of its workers were women in 1918.

Women became more visible in public. Confined before the war by the principle that respectable women did not appear on the streets without a male escort, women now moved about on their own. They went back and forth between home and work. They stood in lines outside shops, waiting to purchase their food rations or other supplies, "dancing the Polonaise" as it was known. The authorities worried that these unsupervised groups could turn violent.[31] They also worried about single women alone on the streets at night. Men serving at the front, the army assumed, needed the sexual relief provided by the women in the bordellos behind the lines, but unsupervised prostitution posed a threat to public order. The additional fear that these women were the faithless wives of soldiers seeking sexual gratification (*Kriegerfrauen*) undercut the entire symbolic structure of power and dependency upon which the relation between battle front and home front rested. When the war began in 1914, Kirchner was working on *Two Women on the Street* (1914) and *Potsdamer Platz* (1914), which also focuses on two women on the street. In both paintings he changed the color of the dresses to black and added a widow's black veil to one of the women. The burst of quick marriages at the beginning of the war meant that in fact there were soon large numbers of young widows. However, all the women in Kirchner's 1913–15 series of Berlin street scenes are presumed to be prostitutes. His changes in these two pictures may have reflected the common belief that prostitutes had quickly adopted widow's clothing as a disguise or even as an additional morbid thrill for their customers.[32]

Historians looking back from the 1960s and 1970s interpreted the employment figures as a decisive break, a sudden seismic shift in women's working patterns that laid the foundation for women gaining the right to vote in 1919 and for later waves of feminist emancipatory movements. More recently, interpretations have swung toward a view of wartime changes as a continuation of prewar trends. Ute Daniel argues that the number of women working in industry would have increased by nearly the same amount if the war had not happened. The war did cause a shift in the employment of women, but the majority of these women were already employed, in agriculture, domestic service, food processing, and particularly in the textile and clothing industries. Many women simply moved from operating machines in factories in these branches, to operating similar machines in factories making munitions. The hours were long, the work boring, and handling explosives dangerous. An explosion in an ammunition factory in Fürth killed 40

Plate 8.5   Ernst Ludwig Kirchner, *Potsdamer Platz*, 1914. Oil on linen, 200 × 150 cm. New National Gallery, Berlin. On the home front, one of the most threatening changes brought about by the war was the appearance of women on the streets. When Kirchner began this painting in 1913, he intended the women to be prostitutes, as all unescorted women were presumed to be. Changing the colors of their dresses to black and blue and adding a veil transformed them at least nominally into war widows, but the ominous sexual charge of the work remains. © Dr. Wolfgang and Ingeborg Henze-Ketterer, Wichtrach/Bern. Staatliche Museen zu Berlin—Preussischer Kulturbesitz Nationalgalerie. Photo: Jörg P. Anders, Bildarchiv Preussischer Kulturbesitz.

women workers in 1917. Although they were the highest paid among female workers, women in the war industries still earned on average only half what men in the same industries earned. There is also evidence that they themselves expected these jobs to end when the men returned from the war, though they anticipated returning to their previous jobs rather than retreating to their homes.[33]

Germany was also a society divided along religious lines. The gulf between Protestant and Catholic narrowed as the clergy of both Churches supported the war with unrestrained enthusiasm. Churches filled again, which the clergy saw as a gratifying reversal of prewar trends. Protestant leaders had always believed the German national identity to be uniquely Protestant, and they continued until the end to preach a victorious peace including large annexations. German Catholic priests preached no less fervently than Protestant pastors that German soldiers were the agents of God's will. They also managed to persuade themselves that French Catholics deserved punishment for having fallen away from the true faith into the sins of secularism, rationalism, and modernism. Some Catholics even allowed themselves to hope that the war would bring about a healing of the great schism and allow the reconstruction of a single united Christian Church with Germany as its center. This was a fantasy, as they ought to have realized during the massive Protestant celebrations in 1917 of the 400th anniversary of Luther's posting of his Ninety-Five Theses. Protestant suspicions of Catholic patriotism also revived in 1917 when Pope Benedict XV broke his silence and called for a negotiated peace.

If Catholics and Protestants could both appeal to a common German identity, the divisions that contemporaries saw as racial deepened. Externally, all of the prewar rhetoric of race was deployed against Poles, Russians, and Slavs generally. Incapable of higher culture, their hostility toward Germany made them a danger that would have to be controlled into an indefinite future. Internally, the war years saw a substantial increase in the level of anti-Semitism. Jewish leaders responded as patriotically as Protestants and Catholics. Over 10,000 Jewish men volunteered in the first weeks, and a total of 12,000 died fighting. The army agreed to commission Jewish officers, and the commanding generals in army districts suppressed the writings of known anti-Semites. However, as the frustrations and privations mounted, the number of anti-Semitic incidents in the army increased, while at home anti-Semitic publications reappeared. The failure to achieve victory, bureaucratic bungling, deteriorating transportation, declining public services, and above all the food shortages, all were explained by the anti-Semites as the results of the machinations of Jewish profiteers. Walther Rathenau, who had organized the supplies of raw materials that kept Germany's armies functioning during the crisis of 1915, as a Jew became a primary target of these attacks.

Most German Jews responded to anti-Semitism as they had before the war, insisting that they were German citizens of the Jewish faith, a confessional group as were Protestants or Catholics. Zionists disagreed in part, arguing that the connection with other Jews, such as the Polish Jews that came under German administration as the Russian armies retreated, was the most significant aspect of Jewish identity. The internal debate was overshadowed by a broader discussion of whether Jews were a confession and therefore essentially German, or whether they were a separate ethnic, national, or racial group and therefore essentially foreign. The army contributed to the debate, and to the rising tide of anti-Semitism, in an underhanded way. Military authorities announced that they were undertaking a census of Jews in the army. The results showed predictably that Jews were better educated than the average, and that they were serving in relatively large numbers. But the military authorities did not publish the results, and thereby supported the attacks on Jews as slackers who were evading military service.

Both production and the food distribution system began to break down seriously during the winter of 1916–17. Pewter dishes were turned in for their tin, lightning rods for their copper, bicycle tires for their rubber. Damp weather bred fungus, and the potato harvest dropped. During the "turnip winter," the continued failure of the government to ensure supplies turned the state itself into a symbol of the problem. "The population has lost all confidence in promises from the authorities . . . particularly in view of the earlier experiences with promises made in the administration of food," reported the general commanding in the Nürnberg district in September 1917. Crimes against property and for disturbing the public peace increased. Significantly, the number of women convicted of theft climbed sharply, and in 1917 over 1200 women were convicted of threatening violence against police officers or other public officials.

On May Day 1916, a demonstration in Berlin in favor of "Bread, Freedom, Peace!" was broken up by police and the Socialist leader Karl Liebknecht arrested and sentenced to prison. In protest, 55,000 metalworkers struck in Berlin, supported by workers in several other cities. Between January and March 1917, there were a number of strikes in the Ruhr, Berlin, and elsewhere. The strikers demanded higher wages and improved rations. On April 16, there were mass strikes in Leipzig and Berlin, triggered by an announced decrease in the bread ration. Another series of strikes followed in June and July in Silesia and again in the Ruhr. The martial law regime allowed military authorities to suppress protests and strikes by arresting the participants. Women could be sentenced to prison. Men could be court-martialed and conscripted for military service. Repression became less effective, however, as discontent rose. During 1917, an average of 50,000 workers were on strike in every month. In 1918, the average rose to 100,000, and strikers became more likely to voice political demands. In Berlin, in January 1918, 400,000 workers went on strike for peace without annexations, and there were parallel actions in Kiel, Hamburg, Halle, and Magdeburg.

The political context: military leadership and the opposition

The role of Germany's leaders

In his memoirs, the former Chancellor Bernhard von Bülow reported a conversation with Walther Rathenau in autumn 1914. They were standing on Unter den Linden in Berlin. Pointing toward the Brandenburg Gate, Rathenau said,

> Can a monarch of such arresting personality, so charming and human a man, so utterly inadequate as a ruler, as is the Emperor Wilhelm II—with an impossible chancellor like Bethmann and a frivolous chief of staff like Falkenhayn—ever expect a triumphal return through that gate? If he gets it, history will have no meaning.

Rathenau had just begun his work with the KRA. He was devoting his entire energy to the war effort, but he had seen Germany's top leadership at work. His misgivings were well founded. The weaknesses of these men both as individuals and as members of elite groups must be considered in examining both the outbreak and the final outcome of the war.

As seen in Chapter 7, none of the influential individuals or groups opposed war, and all had motives to welcome war, "the sooner the better," as Moltke had said in 1912. Germany's leaders had dreams of annexations. Army leaders thought in military terms. Ludendorff said in February 1918, "if Germany makes peace without a profit it has lost the war."[34] His aims had come to embrace most of Europe from the

Atlantic to the Caucasus. Other generals looked forward to future wars, but they saw them in terms of the campaigns just past. Falkenhayn thought Belgium "must remain at our disposal for the initial assembly of our troops." Lithuania, said Hindenburg, was necessary "for the maneuvering of my left wing in the next war."

The King of Bavaria put in a claim for a "Bavarian Burgundy" including portions of Alsace-Lorraine, Belgium, and the Netherlands with control over the mouth of the Rhine. Both the Bavarian and Württemberg royal families also laid claim to the throne of a restored Poland. The King of Saxony wanted part of Alsace-Lorraine as well as portions of Poland and Lithuania. Industrialists looked back to the preceding generation of imperialist competition. They planned to acquire raw materials, food supplies, and access to overseas markets through the annexation of Belgium, northern France, Russian Poland, and further stretches of territory in the east, as well as overseas colonies. They also remembered their struggles against organized labor before the war. Alfred Hugenberg, a member of the Krupp board of directors, worried about the impact of the war on discipline.

> One will probably have to count on a very increased sense of power on the part of workers and labor unions . . . It would therefore be well advised, in order to avoid internal difficulties, to distract the attention of the people and to give fantasies concerning the extension of German territory room to play.[35]

These men believed a glorious "victorious peace" (*Siegfrieden*) on these terms would secure their positions of privilege. Still, their lack of realism gives one pause. Friedrich Meinecke, one of Germany's most prominent historians, had explained in some detail in his work on the German national idea we have looked at in previous chapters that statesmen during the Napoleonic wars had been deluding themselves by thinking that territories and populations could be transferred from one ruler to another without consideration of the wishes of the people affected.[36] The annexation plans simply ignored the intervening century of rising nationalism. More immediately, they made any negotiated peace impossible. As seen above, a military victory became less likely the longer the war lasted, but, paradoxically, the demands for annexation increased in extent and intensity.

Under Hindenburg and Ludendorff the power of the army's supreme command expanded into what some historians have labeled a "military dictatorship."[37] As seen above, Ludendorff believed that war was the normal condition of modern states and that military dictatorship was in fact their inevitable form of government. The martial law regime, the strength of military tradition, and the undoubted prestige and power of the army leaders certainly give an impression of unified power. Contributors to the Red Cross received the right to drive iron nails into huge wooden statues of Hindenburg. His massive fatherly face stared out of recruiting posters. Once again, however, Germany was not so different from other countries. Recruiting posters featuring Tsar Nicholas, Emperor Franz Josef, General Kitchener, and Uncle Sam appeared in the same format, a single fatherly face telling prospective recruits, "I WANT YOU." Clemenceau in France and Lloyd George in Britain ruled autocratically through small war cabinets. The need to conserve and allocate resources led to central planning, to control, and to a suspension of parliamentary oversight of the executive. A similar process took place in Italy following the disaster of Caporetto. In contrast, the war efforts of Russia and Austria were undermined by their failure to streamline administration and establish effective central control over resources.

As seen above, administration was not efficient. The military districts did not correspond to state or provincial boundaries. The commanders of these districts were responsible as army officers directly to the Emperor, but he was incapable of directing their activities. The new agencies created to guide the economy competed with both military and civilian authorities. Therefore, despite efforts to clarify and simplify the structures, there were several overlapping administrations in each district, and they might cooperate, or they might not. There was also the Reichstag, and, as seen above, Hindenburg and Ludendorff were forced to compromise on the centerpiece of their mobilization plans, the Auxiliary Service Law.

Nevertheless, although not a dictator, in 1917 and 1918 Ludendorff was unquestionably the most powerful man in Germany. Kurt Riezler, Bethmann's personal assistant, believed he typified "those who have risen in the war . . . explosive, bombshell energy, crassest lack of culture . . . really an American type." His power rested on Hindenburg's popularity. Hindenburg symbolized Germany. However, Hindenburg the man was an aging, intensely conservative soldier of limited intelligence who left policy in the hands of his energetic subordinate. They controlled the Emperor by threatening to resign, as Bismarck had controlled his grandfather. Wilhelm virtually disappeared as a leadership figure. His erratic behavior had already substantially impaired his effectiveness before the war. He now spent most of his time traveling among his estates and to command centers behind the front. He was photographed consulting with Hindenburg and Ludendorff, but he had no impact on operational decisions. He remained the object of intrigue because of his constitutional powers, but he declined to "a neglected, ill-informed, and increasingly inconsequential figurehead," significant only in that his consent was required before changes in senior personnel could occur.[38] Wilhelm's weakness gave the army leaders leverage over the Chancellor, constitutionally the Reichstag had no real power, and despite the increasing unrest, public opinion remained under the control of the censors and the police.

Ludendorff regarded proposals for constitutional reform as a disastrous "surrender to the Zeitgeist" that were "bound to lead to perdition." In particular, he insisted, "we cannot live" with a reformed Prussian franchise. He believed victory in the west and a new empire in the east would create a firm foundation for the absolutist state. His plans, however, degenerated into an inchoate megalomania. His offensive in the west lacked a strategic objective. The first attack may be seen as an attempt to strike through toward Paris at the hinge between the British and French forces, but the subsequent attacks made no sense, and the entire offensive has been labeled a "military absurdity."[39] In the east, he envisaged a string of puppet governments. The largest would extend from the Ukraine past the Don Basin to the Caucasus, with a "German Riviera" on the Crimea, and with connections to central Asia that would challenge the British in India. He ignored the shortages and the decline in civilian and military morale detailed above. Anyone who doubted or opposed his vision was silenced or driven from office.

The aura of success that gave Hindenburg and Ludendorff their authority would dissipate if they failed to deliver the victory they promised. But as long as victory seemed possible, no civilian leader could challenge them. Bethmann had gambled on the war, of course wanted victory, and privately favored large annexations. By late 1916, he had come to see the impossibility of complete victory, and he had begun to recognize the need to offer political reform as compensation for the suffering the war had brought.[40] Hindenburg and Ludendorff refused to contemplate anything short of total victory and rejected all suggestions of internal reform. They believed Bethmann had failed them in the struggle over the Auxiliary Service Law. They were infuriated when he opposed their demand to resume unrestricted submarine warfare. And they were determined to have his head when he publicly committed himself to constitutional reform in February 1917, established a Reichstag committee to examine "the structure of the representative body of the nation and its relationship to the government" in March, and in April persuaded Wilhelm to promise the abolition of the Prussian three-class voting system and a reform of the Bundesrat as soon as the war ended. In the meantime, Bethmann's equivocal style had also alienated Reichstag leaders, so he had no support there. Hindenburg and Ludendorff threatened to resign, and Bethmann had to go.

In July 1917, days after Bethmann's fall, the Catholic Center, the Progressives, and the Socialists united to pass a resolution drafted by Matthias Erzberger calling for a "peace of understanding" without "forced acquisitions of territory." Bethmann's replacement was Georg Michaelis, who told the Reichstag that he would accept the peace resolution "as I understand it." Given the constitutional situation and the fact that Michaelis owed his position to the army leaders, this meant that the war would continue. Michaelis in turn was replaced by Georg von Hertling, the 74-year-old veteran Center Party leader. He had been chosen with the consent of Reichstag leaders but was equally unable to counter the influence of the army. Following the French Nivelle offensive, the British losses at Passchendaele, and the Italian defeat at Caporetto, the British Foreign Secretary Lord Lansdowne had publicly called for peace negotiations. The new Russian Bolshevik government then announced they wished to end the war. Hertling saw this as an opportunity. A moderate peace in the east might pave the way for a negotiated settlement in the west as well. Ludendorff, however, insisted that huge losses of territory be imposed on Russia, and he and Hindenburg again threatened to resign if their demands were ignored. The result was the Peace of Brest-Litovsk. Russia surrendered Finland, the Baltic states, Poland, most of what is now Belarus, the Ukraine, and the Caucasus. Forty German divisions, 1.5 million men, remained in the east as an occupying army. In the west any thought of a negotiated peace evaporated.

The return to politics

Thomas Mann wrote in *Reflections of a Nonpolitical Man*, "I hate politics, because it makes men arrogant, doctrinaire, obstinate, and inhuman." In fact, Germans were not nonpolitical, any more than they had been before the war. However, the unexpected outbreak of the war, the lack of preparation for a long war, and the failure to see the social and cultural implications of the war, certainly did influence the politics of the war. At the war's outbreak, the Emperor told the members of the Reichstag "I no longer know any parties, I know only Germans." The parties agreed to suspend political conflict, a "fortress truce" (*Burgfrieden*). The government did not carry out its plans to arrest Socialist Party and labor union leaders. In return, the Socialists voted for the war credits, and, as noted above, the unions pledged not to strike for the duration of the war. The Reichstag agreed to a special act that placed all power in the smaller Bundesrat. It convened at regular intervals to review decrees issued by the Bundesrat and to approve the funding that allowed the war to continue.

In the rush toward war, the parties in the Reichstag had no direct influence. In fact, apart from a few individual enthusiasts, none of the deputies had systematic views on foreign relations, and none of the parties possessed a developed foreign policy. This was another of Bismarck's legacies. Foreign policy was the business of the government, which did not depend on the Reichstag for approval. On the other hand, no one in the Reichstag opposed the war. The members of the Reichstag, from right to left, virtually all shared the general enthusiasm for the war, assumed a quick German victory, and expected that Germany would annex large amounts of territory. In these attitudes they faithfully reflected the opinions of their constituents. Germans thought they had been forced to fight, they expected to win, and they assumed substantial gains. Those gains would guarantee Germany's position in the future.

The limited horizons of German party leaders partly explains their aggressive support for the government and the army's expansionist policies. In 1914, leading Center deputy Matthias Erzberger was only one of many who outlined grandiose plans for annexations. In 1915, Reichstag leaders supported unrestricted submarine warfare. They foresaw victory over Britain and discounted the risk of alienating the United States, knowing nothing of its strategic military potential. National Liberal leader Ernst Bassermann said in July 1915, "German submarines rule the sea."[41] Again in 1917, most ignored the danger when submarine warfare was resumed.

As the war progressed and their constituents became more and more unhappy, the parties in the Reichstag began to insist that their wishes be considered. The debates over the budget became genuine struggles. When the government introduced the Auxiliary Service Law, the parties demanded a share in its administration. This moved into an area previously reserved for the bureaucracy. The Socialists, the Catholic Center, and Liberal parties cooperated to pressure the government. Their refusal to accept the bill forced the government to redraft the legislation to suit the will of the parliamentary majority. On one interpretation this was an important precedent in establishing the power of the nation's representatives over the Crown, the bureaucracy, and the army, another step in the "silent parliamentarization" of the prewar period.[42] As before, however, as long as the constitutional structures of Prussia and the empire did not change such precedents meant little. In addition, a less optimistic view sees the unions joining industrial and agricultural pressure groups as merely another intransigent interest to be satisfied.[43]

Erzberger represents the dilemma of Reichstag deputies committed to an increase in parliamentary power, but still confronting Germany's authoritarian establishment. He opposed submarine warfare because his calculations showed it could not work. The navy angrily rejected his calculations, but did not refute them—it could not because they were correct—but he could not prevent the resumption of the campaign. He also contributed to Bethmann's fall. He hoped that Bülow would be recalled to replace Bethmann, and that together they would be able either to collaborate with or to control Hindenburg and Ludendorff. The merits of this plan were questionable. More important, he was easily outmaneuvered by the army leaders in the contest for the Emperor's approval. Michaelis was their creature, and although his successor Hertling enjoyed Reichstag support, he was equally unable to deflect Ludendorff's intentions. Erzberger's great triumph was the peace resolution, bringing together the government's prewar nightmare coalition of enemies, the Socialists, the Catholic Center, and the Progressives, but again it had no impact on policy.

As the situation on the home front became more desperate, debate in the Reichstag linked with extraparliamentary politics on both the left and the right. The Socialist Party split. The Socialists had voted for the war credits in 1914 on the understanding that this was a defensive war, and that it was directed primarily against a tyrannical Russian autocracy. The *Burgfrieden* seemed like an opportunity to represent workers' interests inside the government at last, and the subsequent sacrifices carried the implicit promise of further reforms to come after victory.

When the strikes began in 1916, Carl Legien, head of the General Commission of the Socialist unions, claimed that the strikers were not union members but undisciplined young workers brought into industry by the war. He and other union leaders also suggested ominously that they were having great difficulty controlling their own members, who were losing confidence in the government. In the debates over the Auxiliary Service Law, the unions offered to restrain workers and prevent strikes, if the government would grant them equal rights in wage negotiations. In February 1918, Legien was one of the authors of a memorandum to the army high command that argued that any new offensives must be undertaken only after the German people had been assured that every effort had been made to make peace and that Belgium would remain independent.

On the left, radical Socialists and the small syndicalist unions pointed to the government's refusal to give up its annexation plans and the opposition of the ruling elites to any reform. Censorship prevented many from reading Lenin's *Imperialism: The Highest Stage of Capitalism* (1915), but as Marxists they had no difficulty in identifying the war as a crisis of capitalism. Hardship had led to increased polarization and rising class conflict. Legien was wrong and perhaps disingenuous about the strikers, for the workers' protests built on prewar activism, and many workers resented the new disciplinary functions that union officials had begun to exercise.[44] Liebknecht's arrest and conviction in 1916 made him a hero on the left. The protests arising out of the hardships of the "turnip winter" were reinforced by the news of the Russian Revolution in March 1917. The Tsarist government, the primary justification for Socialist support of the war, was no more, and in its place was a Socialist provisional government. The majority of the Socialists in the Reichstag voted in March to expel eighteen of their members, who had voted against the latest round of war credits. The mass protests of April demanded immediate peace with no annexations. They were coordinated by workers' councils similar to the soviets emerging in Russia. Independent of the existing unions and frequently led by elected shop stewards, the councils linked up with the expelled radical members of the Socialist Party who became the nucleus of the Independent Socialist Party.

On the right, the government sponsored the new Fatherland Party. An umbrella organization of right-wing groups, it gathered together organizations claiming to represent the interests of farmers, various divisions of the *Mittelstand*, and of industry, patriotic societies such as the Pan-German League, and the Conservative Party led by Count Westarp. The public leaders of the Fatherland Party were Tirpitz and Wolfgang Kapp, later leader of a putsch against the Weimar Republic. The forces behind its formation were the chief of military intelligence and Ludendorff personally. He had encouraged Tirpitz and others to establish a mass party to agitate for a victorious peace, for annexations, against the peace resolution, and against the parties and individuals who supported a negotiated peace. Lavish funding came directly from the government and from industrial pressure groups. Founded in September 1917, by July 1918 it had 2000 chapters and nearly 1 million members, more than the Socialist Party. It combined its extreme annexationist position and calls for the repression of internal dissent with violent racial and anti-Semitic rhetoric. Local leaders were often Protestant pastors, and members included Anton Drexel, the founder of the Nazi Party.

Collapse

The euphoria at the announcement of the Brest-Litovsk peace rivaled the enthusiasm of 1914. Then came the initial successes of the attack in the west. For a moment in March 1918 it seemed that Ludendorff had been right after all, and that a glorious victorious peace still lay within Germany's grasp. In the Reichstag only the Independent Socialist Party voted against the treaty. Paralyzed by dissention, the Majority Socialists abstained, and both the Progressives and the Catholic Center voted in favor. Erzberger insisted that the terms of the treaty were compatible with the peace resolution. The peace resolution renounced "forced acquisitions" and Erzberger could argue that a negotiated settlement for, say, the French iron mines would be compatible with the resolution. The new states envisaged in the Brest-Litovsk treaty were technically independent and therefore also not forced acquisitions.

The apparent victory in the east made the sudden collapse and surrender in the west appear all the more incredible. As noted above, the Germans did not have the men or the material to exploit their initial gains. The Allied offensive began with a French attack on the Marne in July 1918. Despite losing 100,000 casualties (compared to the German 25,000), the French forced the Germans back once again to the Aisne. A British assault near Amiens followed, and again stalled, but the Germans had no reinforcements. Large numbers of surrenders and desertions, and the additional impact of the influenza epidemic during the summer, further weakened German forces. By October, the German army was retreating back through Belgium. In September, an Allied assault into Serbia had caused Bulgaria to sue for peace, as did Turkey. In late October, after a final failed Austrian offensive, the Italians broke through along the Piave, and the Austrian army broke apart into national groups.

Ludendorff's nerves finally cracked, but he refused to take responsibility. On September 29, 1918, he announced without warning to the Emperor and Chancellor that the war was lost and that they must negotiate an immediate armistice. They and everyone else in the country were stunned. Rathenau wrote in an article published on October 7, 1918,

> The premature request for an armistice was a mistake. The enemies should have been made to see that the new spirit of the state and the nation also strengthens the spirit and the will power of the fighters . . . The country is not broken, its means are unexhausted, and its people are unweary . . . A beginning must be made with national defense, the rousing of the people; a Ministry of Defense must be created . . . This Ministry . . . appeals to the people in the language of truth, pure and simple . . . We do not want war, but peace. However, not a peace of submission.[45]

Meinecke wrote to a friend on October 21,

> although my hatred of the enemy, who remind me of beasts of prey, is as hot as ever, so is my anger and resentment at those German power politicians who, by their presumption and their stupidity, have dragged us down into this abyss. Repeatedly in the course of the war, we could have had a peace by agreement, if it had not been that the boundless demands of the Pan-German-militaristic-conservative combine made it impossible. It is fearful and tragic that this combine could be broken only by the overthrow of the entire state.[46]

However, the old elites did not want a "rousing of the people," and they did their best to save the old authoritarian state. Ludendorff, other army leaders, and senior civilian officials believed that an appeal to United States President Woodrow Wilson for an armistice based on his "fourteen points" offered their best chance. They pressured Wilhelm to announce a series of political reforms. Hertling gave way as Chancellor to the liberal Prince Max of Baden, the head of a new responsible ministry resting on the support of a Reichstag majority made up of the Catholic Center, Progressives, and Majority Socialists. The powers of the new federal government included authority over the army and foreign policy. The Prussian franchise was reformed.

Ludendorff recovered from his panic, and actually began to envisage new offensives in 1919. He attempted to deny he had asked for the armistice, and when it became obvious that Wilson and the Allies were not going to be satisfied with cosmetic changes, sent a telegram to army commanders ordering "resistance with every means at our command." The telegram became public because one of the military wireless operators was an Independent Socialist. Prince Max insisted that Ludendorff must go or he and the entire new cabinet would resign. He went, and was replaced by Groener. In turn, on November 9, 1918, Groener and Hindenburg presented the very reluctant Wilhelm with the demand for his abdication.

The armistice went into effect at 11 o'clock on November 11. The war was over.

Notes

1. *Mein Kampf* (1925), p. 204.
2. Fussell 1975; Eksteins 2000.
3. Ludwig Meidner, *Apocalyptic Landscape*, 1913. Oil on linen, 80 × 196 cm. National Gallery, Berlin. Reproduced in Dube 1972, p. 178. Meidner painted several other works with the same title, which show cities being destroyed by explosions in the air above them.
4. Franz Marc, *Tyrol*, 1913–14. Oil on canvas, 135.7 × 144.5 cm. Bayerische Staatsgemäldesammlungen, Munich. Reproduced in Dube 1972, p. 135.
5. Dube 1972, p. 135.
6. Otto Dix, *Der Krieg*, 1914. Kunstmuseum Düsseldorf im Erhenhof. Otto Dix, *War*, 1929–32. Reproduced in Tatar 1995, p. 83.
7. Tatar 1995, pp. 84–5.
8. Fellner 1995, p. 22.
9. Tarrant 1995.
10. Förster, Stig, 1996, p. 473.
11. Balfour 1972, pp. 360–1.
12. Pinson 1954, p. 323.
13. Chickering 1998, p. 40.
14. Chickering 1998, p. 39.
15. Yaney 1994.
16. Williamson 1971, pp. 121, 141.
17. Eksteins 2000.
18. See Verhey 2000.
19. Richie 1998, facing p. 388.
20. Röhl 1995, p. 32.

21. Blackbourn 1997, p. 462.
22. *Mein Kampf* (1925), p. 161.
23. Kreimeier 1996, p. 39.
24. Linton 1991.
25. Ernst Ludwig Kirchner, *Das Soldatenbad* (1915). Oil on canvas, 140.5 × 152 cm. Solomon R. Guggenheim Museum, New York. Reproduced in Grisebach 1999, p. 129.
26. Ernst Ludwig Kirchner, *Selbstbildnis als Soldat* (1915). Oil on canvas, 69 × 61 cm. Allen Memorial Art Museum, Oberlin College, Ohio. Reproduced in Grisebach 1999, p. 128.
27. Tatar 1995, pp. 173–95.
28. Friedrich Meinecke, *Ausgewählter Briefwechsel* (Stuttgart, 1962), p. 326, cited in Craig 1978, p. 339, note 2.
29. Deist 1992.
30. Wunder 1986.
31. Davis 1996.
32. Ernst Ludwig Kirchner, *Two Women on the Street*, 1914. Oil on canvas, 120.5 × 91 cm. Düsseldorf, Kunstsammlung Nordrhein-Westfalen. Ernst Ludwig Kirchner, *Potsdamer Platz*, 1914. Oil on canvas, 200 × 150 cm. Staatliche Museen zu Berlin—Preussischer Kulturbesitz, Nationalgalerie. Reproduced in Grisebach 1999, pp. 109, 111, 115–116.
33. Daniel 1989.
34. Pinson 1954, p. 326.
35. Feldman 1966, p. 136.
36. Meinecke 1907.
37. Kitchen 1976.
38. Cecil 1996, p. 219.
39. Chickering 1998, pp. 179–80.
40. Fischer 1961, pp. 98–106; Jarausch 1973.
41. Opelland 1995, p. 90.
42. Rauh 1977.
43. Feldman 1966.
44. Patton 1998; Thorpe 2000.
45. Cited in Pinson 1954, p. 344.
46. To L. Aschoff, October 21, 1918, *Briefwechsel*, p. 97, cited in Craig 1978, p. 395.

CHAPTER 9

AN EXPRESSIONIST AGE: THE WEIMAR REPUBLIC, 1918–33

The novel *Michael: A German Fate through the Pages of a Diary* was published in 1929. It tells the story of Michael, a young man who returns from the war, and the heroism of the front-line soldier's life to confront peace in his beloved but defeated Germany. Michael defines his generation:

> Our decade is absolutely Expressionistic in its inner structure. This has nothing to do with how fashionable the word is. We people today are all Expressionists. People who want to form the world from inside out. The Expressionist builds himself a new world within himself. His secret and his power is passion. His mental world usually breaks against reality.
>
> The soul of the Impressionist is the microscopic picture of the macrocosm.
>
> The soul of the Expressionist is the new macrocosm.
>
> A world in itself.
>
> Expressionistic sensation is explosive.
>
> It is an autocratic feeling of being oneself.

Michael, whose name marks him as the representative German Everyman, is not much of a character, and *Michael* is not much of a novel. The diary form delivers little in the way of plot structure. The entries report Michael's conversations, first with a girl named Hertha whom he meets at the university, and then with a revolutionary Russian student named Ivan. Michael does little but talk, until he decides to take a job in a mine. "Soldiers, students and workers will build the new Reich. I was a soldier, I am a student, a worker I will be." He hears that Ivan has been killed, the victim of a political assassination. And then Michael dies in an accident in the mine. Hertha learns in a letter from one of the miners that he died with a smile and that he had marked a passage in Nietzsche's *Thus Spake Zarathustra*: "Many die too late and some too early. Strangely still sounds the lesson! Die at the right time."[1]

Michael repays our attention despite its shortcomings, for two reasons. First, its author was Joseph Goebbels. In 1929, he was one of

Hitler's senior aides and responsible for the Nazi Party's election propaganda, but he also had serious literary ambitions. The novel was published by the party's publishing house in Munich. As such, it sheds light on the aims and fantasies of the Nazis before they came to power. Second, *Michael* was typical of the contemporary Weimar scene in identifying Expressionism as its key. Expressionist modes ranged from painting to literature, drama, film, and architecture, and the "autocratic feeling of being oneself" could be seen at work in economic and political life as well.

What is Expressionism? In 1912, the *Sonderbund* exhibition in Cologne announced that Expressionism was

> the most recent movement in painting, which has made its appearance in the wake of atmospheric naturalism and Impressionism, and which seeks to simplify and intensify the forms of expression to achieve new rhythm and colorfulness, to create in decorative or monumental forms.

As seen in Chapter 6, many artists had revolted against official neoclassicism, but usually by adopting one of the new French styles. For a short period there was some hesitation as to whether this new term referred to a group of French Fauves and Cubists. Then, in 1914, Paul Fechter published the first monograph on Expressionism. He referred to a German avant-garde, and defined their work as a specifically German countermovement to Impressionism, parallel to but distinct from Cubism in France and Futurism in Italy.

Some of the artists involved dismissed the label, but they substituted a vision of what they hoped to accomplish. Karl Schmidt-Rottluf said, "I have no program, only the unaccountable longing to grasp what I see and feel, and to find the purest means of expression for it." Franz Marc wrote that,

> It is impossible to explain the latest works of these "wild beasts" as a formal development and reinterpretation of Impressionism. The most beautiful prismatic colors, and the famous Cubism, have both lost their meaning as the goal of these "wild beasts." Their thought has produced another goal: the creation, through their work, of symbols for their age, which belong on the altars of the coming religion of the spirit, and behind which the technical creator disappears from sight.

As noted at the beginning of Chapter 8, Marc felt driven to abstraction by the ugliness of human and animal forms. Others such as Ludwig

Kirchner retained a figurative approach, but not a photographic realism. The smoothly modeled and shaded nudes of neoclassicism disappeared. So, too, did the carefully judged tricks of "realistic" perspective. In Kirchner's case human figures are elongated and bent, and the backgrounds distorted and fragmented. Most of Marc's colleagues did not want to disappear from sight, but most would have accepted identification as "wild beasts." Marc's word was *Wilde*, synonymous with the French Fauves, and the use of flat planes of shockingly garish and contrasting colors that made the Fauves notorious marked much Expressionist painting.

The First World War cut across all such developments. The movement, contrast of color, and distortion offered by Expressionism helped younger artists such as Otto Dix to come to terms with the war in their art. The war's end left a void, however. Dix said that "color and form alone cannot make up for the experience and excitement that are missing. I am deeply concerned to achieve an interpretation of our age in my pictures, for I believe a picture must first and foremost express a meaning, a theme." Many sought meaning, hungered for wholeness, in Peter Gay's phrase,[2] but meaning can be elusive. Dix's triptych portraying *War*, painted at the same time as Goebbels' novel was published, remains controversial, an ambiguous celebration of both the human horror and the gendered heroism of war.

Others took the need for meaning out of the artistic realm and into public life. Art had been highly politicized in Germany before 1914. Now politics became an art form. For many, this meant that the social realm had become an arena where something new could be constructed. Influenced by the new freedom in the arts and by new theories in physics and psychology, artists, writers, social scientists, reformers, and political leaders launched into experimental projects. Where this would lead remained an open question, and the meanings of "Weimar culture" are still debated. As we will see in Chapter 10, some looked left, to the new Soviet Union. Others, shocked by defeat, never reconciled themselves to the republic that replaced the empire. But though they might look right, they too were searching for something new.

The economic context: the search for stability

The failure of the interwar economy

The structural tendencies of development continued through the war. Agriculture continued to decline. Heavy industry continued to expand. Women continued to increase their share of industrial employment. However, the war caused substantial dislocation, and the war's end ushered in a new and very difficult period. The population of Germany was nearly 70 million in 1913 and had been increasing at a rate of 1.4 per cent per year since 1895. Over 2 million died in the war, and under the Treaty of Versailles Germany lost Alsace and Lorraine, North Schleswig, Posen, West Prussia, and part of Silesia. The Saar district with its valuable coal resources was placed under French administration for fifteen years. In 1922, the population was 61.9 million. And from 1922 to 1938 the population increased to only 68.5 million or 0.64 per cent per year. These figures were important economic facts. The shortage of young men, loss of raw materials, and slowly growing markets slowed growth. But the statistics were even more important as social symbols and political issues. The young men were a sacrifice, the lost territories were sacred soil, foreigners hampered German recovery, and the small number of babies was evidence that something had poisoned the national body.

Not only Germany, but the entire world economy seemed to have fallen out of adjustment, and it stubbornly resisted attempts at repair. What had gone wrong and what should be done were contentious issues at the time, and they have remained so. Russian statistician Nikolai Kondratiev published his theory of "long waves" in 1928.[3] Many scholars since have identified the interwar generation years as a long downswing. Angus Maddison's "Phase III" from 1913 to 1950 was "a bleak age, whose potential for growth was frustrated by a series of disasters."[4] The cyclical up and downswings of the major Western economies became increasingly important, as they became more closely integrated into patterns of regional and world trade. British national product measured in constant prices grew at only 1.81 per cent yearly from 1920 to 1938. The United States boomed through the 1920s, but the depression saw a massive contraction of the American economy. British and United States imports declined precipitously. In current prices, British imports were 1.93 billion pounds in 1920, but only 920 million in

1938, while United States imports were 5.37 billion dollars in 1920 and only 2.19 billion in 1938.[5]

Germany suffered with the rest of the world from the slow growth of Britain and the United States. Before the First World War, Britain was by far Germany's most important export market. The United States was Germany's second largest source of imports, behind Russia, but significantly the United States was also the third largest market for German exports, behind Britain and Austria-Hungary. After struggling through the 1920s, the prewar patterns had nearly reestablished themselves in 1929 and 1930, but world trade then collapsed. In addition, the slow growth of Britain and the United States of course hurt other trading nations; as they in turn grew more slowly this also affected German trade and German growth, and, finally, slow German growth hurt those other countries as well.

Policy-oriented explanations focus on the operation of the international gold standard before 1914, the failure of attempts to reestablish the gold standard system in the 1920s, and responses to the downturn of the late 1920s. Although all responsible officials in the interwar years believed that the gold standard had fostered growth before 1914, and that they understood its operation, specialist scholars today do not agree on exactly how the prewar gold standard worked its magic.[6] The "rules of the game" specify that a balance of payments deficit is a signal to raise interest rates, which will depress investment and domestic incomes. This will lower wages and domestic prices, reducing both imports and the price of exports. As exports rise, balance will be restored, with net gains in overall economic efficiency and income. However, the evidence that this in fact happens, or that governments before 1914 actually followed the rules of the game, is ambiguous. Consequently, there is widespread disagreement as to what could or should have been done to promote growth in the 1920s and, most importantly, to avoid the collapse of 1929 and the depression.

It may be that the gold standard was not the reason for the smooth operation of the international economy before 1914. Rather, the unique position of Britain, with its large and open market, its positive balance of payments which permitted massive international lending, and the overwhelming dominance of sterling and of the London money market, both facilitated the growth of international trade and investment and worked to minimize fluctuations and instability. Following the war, Britain grew slowly and suffered a chronic negative balance of payments, and its role as a lender declined. Britain held over 40 per cent of the world's total foreign investment in 1914, but only 29 per cent in 1929. The role of sterling and of London declined relative to other "key" currencies and other centers, and because exchange rates were fixed but not stable, there was far more opportunity for speculation.

In the 1920s, Britain continued to export raw materials and "traditional" manufactured products, such as coal, basic iron products, and cotton textiles. Britain lost markets to Germany and other industrializing countries in Europe, the United States, and to Japan. Britain's problems led significant groups to protectionism. The Federation of British Industry called for safeguarding traditional industries in the home market and expanding those industries through "trade-preference" principles in the colonies and other traditional markets. Bankers abandoned free trade because of tensions in world capital markets. Labor unions demanded tariffs to defend jobs and wages. Against the background of both structural weaknesses in production and increased international competition, Britain rationed international credit and attempted to exploit its bargaining power over markets for primary products and financial services.[7]

Most students agree that, above all, government officials in Europe and the United States failed to cooperate effectively. The responses of political and financial leaders to downturns were both deflationary and protectionist. Most countries including Germany attempted to maintain the gold standard, that is, to hold the value of their currencies constant in terms of gold or gold-backed "key" currencies. This "made economic conditions worse instead of better," but they believed that this unpleasant but strong medicine would restore economic health.[8] In addition, however, governments did not allow their economies to adjust if this meant injuring the interests of politically powerful groups. Restrictions on output imposed by cartels and reductions in wages, it was hoped, would maintain profits while making exports more competitive. Tariffs and quotas were introduced to shut foreign competitors out, and, finally, in the crisis following 1929, the gold standard was abandoned as countries devalued their currencies to make their goods cheaper than their competitors' products.[9]

Reparations and inflation

The hatred that all governments had encouraged during the war left a bitter legacy, symbolized in the question of guilt and embodied in reparations. For the Allies, Germany was guilty, and should pay for the costs of the war. Americans believed German reparations would make it possible for Britain and France to repay the loans the United States had made to them during the war. The British also demanded repayment of the loans they had made to France, Belgium, and Italy. The French believed German reparations should pay for the reconstruction of the northern region where the battles had raged. For Germans, reparations were an illegitimate demand based on a manifestly false premise—the assertion written into the Versailles Treaty (Article 231) that Germany alone had been responsible for the war. In addition, Germans claimed that reparations imposed an intolerable burden on their fragile economy. They were supported by English economist John Maynard Keynes, whose small book *The Economic Consequences of the Peace* (1919) insisted that Germany would be unable to pay the reparations demanded by the Allies. Keynes' arguments, and the awe-inspiring figure of 132 billion gold marks that the Germans were to pay, resonated through the contemporary debate and were still quoted in both German and British textbooks over seventy years later.[10]

As with the outbreak of the war, so with the war's aftermath there is more than enough blame for all to share. Objectively, the United States and Britain could have written off the loans, and France and Belgium could have financed reconstruction through taxes. To do so would have required sacrifices from the property-owning classes, but these were sacrifices they were uniformly unwilling to make. Leaders in all countries had justified the hardships of the war with the assertion that the enemy would pay. Lloyd George promised to "squeeze the German lemon until the pips squeak." But all countries had financed the war through inflation rather than taxation, imposing a disproportionate share of the burden on the lower classes. Now, elite groups hoped that the promise of reparations would help maintain social stability and quiet demands for political change.[11]

Germany could have paid the reparations. A series of conferences had progressively reduced the total from a vague 500–800 billion marks discussed at Versailles. The final total of 132 billion announced on April 27, 1921, was a compromise suggested by Belgian representatives. Privately, the German negotiators were pleased to have reduced the overall figure. Further, the complex mode of payment divided the total into three classes of bonds, and until all charges had been met, the 82 billion marks of so-called "C" bonds could not even be issued. This effectively reduced the nominal total to 50 billion, and since the bonds were issued below the market rate of interest, they could not be sold at par value. This may have reduced the real burden to as little as 25 to 35 billion, and this in turn would be close to what the German negotiators had suggested, though Allied representatives had contemptuously refused their offer.

Politically, to admit these things was impossible. Among themselves, the negotiators agreed that Germany could not pay more than around 3 billion marks per year, which they worked out at 2 billion plus 26 per cent of the value of each year's exports. Capitalizing this income stream at 6 per cent yields a principal sum of 50 billion, so some way had to be found to make the total appear to be higher. No German leader would admit that the real total was low or that Germany could pay, for they opposed reparations in principle, and public opinion in the Allied countries would demand more. Similarly, no Allied leader could confess to having lowered the total, for fear of appearing to have sold out to the Germans.[12]

This is not to say the totals were insignificant, especially in view of the rapidly depreciating German currency. As seen in Chapters 6 and 8, Germany had entered the war on the crest of a credit-fueled inflation, and like all other countries had financed the war through further inflation. Following the war, the government continued the wartime practice of covering its expenses by asking the Reichsbank to extend credit. By May 1921, the mark had dropped to 60 to the dollar. The first payment of 1 billion gold marks (250 million dollars) demanded by the Allies was met by creating marks to purchase dollars on foreign exchange markets, and the mark plunged to 310 to the dollar in November 1921.[13]

The Allied ultimatum and demand for payment led to the resignation of the German government. Josef Wirth of the Catholic Center Party became Chancellor. Walther Rathenau, prewar head of the AEG and the organizer of the wartime War Raw Materials Office, became foreign minister. In his first speech to the Reichstag after his appointment, Rathenau insisted on a policy of "fulfillment" of the reparations demands. His argument to German public opinion was that Germany was unable to pay, but that a sincere attempt to pay would lead the Allies to reduce their demands. His approach to the Allies was to continue negotiations on specific concrete points until some basis for agreement on broader issues of principle could be established.

At first, Rathenau's approach seemed to succeed. He reached an agreement with French representatives that would have allowed Germany to substitute industrial products for monetary payments. However, French industrialists denounced the agreement because they feared German competition. French Conservative parties attacked the government, and the moderate Prime Minister Aristide Briand was replaced by the intransigent and vengeful Raymond Poincaré, who viewed German financial policies as a deliberate attempt to destroy the value of the mark. He wanted the Allies to impose controls on Germany's finances and seize territories to gain revenue directly.

The policy of fulfillment aroused hysterical opposition in Germany, and Rathenau was murdered by right-wing assassins in June 1922. His death weakened the government and Wirth resigned in November. In the absence of any leader who could command a majority in the Reichstag, President Friedrich Ebert intervened and named Wilhelm Cuno, head of the Hamburg-America shipping company, as Chancellor. Ebert hoped Cuno, who belonged to no party, would gain the support of business interests and find a way out of the twin crises of reparations and the deteriorating currency. Cuno formed a "cabinet of experts" who were claimed to be "above" the parties. Without a Reichstag majority, Cuno relied on President Ebert to issue emergency decrees to implement his policies. However, he also failed to secure the support of industrialists such as Hugo Stinnes, who resisted any reparations settlement that might injure their interests.[14]

In December, the French pressed for an occupation of the Ruhr industrial district, using the excuse of German defaults on deliveries of raw materials. Cuno, after consultation with business leaders, offered a payment of 20 billion gold marks. Business leaders, especially Stinnes, refused to agree to higher taxes or to a special levy on their foreign currency holdings. Therefore Cuno proposed to raise the money through an international loan. In addition, Cuno suddenly proposed a peace treaty with all countries along the Rhine, to be guaranteed by the United States. The Allies rejected both offers, and French and Belgian troops moved into the Ruhr in January 1923.

An inept politician and a worse diplomat, Cuno believed until the last minute that the French would back down, and had no plans to meet the occupation. A cabinet meeting chaired by President Ebert decided unanimously that Germany must not yield to military force, and that a campaign of passive resistance should be organized. The government ordered railroad and factory workers not to cooperate with the French, and the French responded by taking over the railroads, bank branches, mines, and factories. They arrested and imprisoned those who resisted. Cutting off the country's main coal reserves damaged industry in other regions as well. The number of families across the country who required government assistance rose rapidly.

Committed to supporting the victims of the passive resistance policy, but unable to increase taxes because of business opposition, Cuno resorted to the inflationary expedient of his predecessors. The annual government deficit rose from 6.1 billion marks in 1922 to 11.7 billion in 1923. The deficits were covered with additional credit granted by the Reichsbank. Prices increased and the government began to print additional money to meet the demand for currency. The decline in the exchange rate accelerated, and further money was created to meet the deficit in the balance of payments.

In mid-1923, the velocity of circulation of the currency began to increase. That is, people became wary of holding money as its value deteriorated, and attempted to dispose of it as quickly as possible. By late 1923, the government had 133 printing firms running 1783 presses twenty-four hours a day to print new Reichsbank notes. Local governments such as the city of Cologne were empowered to issue their own supplementary currencies. Workers were paid in shopping bags full of money twice a day so that they could spend their morning earnings during their lunch break, before the afternoon exchange rate quotations were published. In January 1923, it already took 18,000 marks to buy a United States dollar, by July it took 353,000, in August 4.6 million, in September 98 million, in October over 25 billion, and on November 15, 1923, the final quotation was a meaningless 4.2 trillion. The 4 and the 2 were selected arbitrarily because the exchange rate had been 4.2 marks to the dollar in July 1914, and it was felt that the arithmetic would be easier for the subsequent conversion.[15]

The collapse of the German economy would have made any further reparations payments impossible, and the collapse of the German currency threatened the French franc as well. A solution had to be found, and it was found. Cuno left office and was replaced by Gustav Stresemann, former Saxon Liberal and now head of the German People's Party. Stresemann committed Germany to fulfilling the terms of the reparations agreement. The campaign of passive resistance ended. Taxes were raised, government budgets cut, wages reduced, and working hours increased. The old currency was replaced by a new temporary currency, the rentenmark. Based on a proposal by wartime finance minister Karl Helferich, the change was carried through by Hjalmar Schacht. The number of rentenmarks was to be strictly limited, and the government could no longer call on the Reichsbank to create additional marks to cover its expenses. The rentenmark was supposedly based on a mortgage on all the land and industrial buildings in Germany. This was a convenient myth, but, as with all currencies, the willingness of people to accept the new money ensured its success.

An international committee chaired by American Charles Dawes scaled down the reparations payments to 1 billion marks in 1924–25, with a program of increases to 2.5 billion in 1928–29. A special banking institution in Berlin was created to ensure that the transfer of these funds did not destabilize exchange rates. In return for the program of currency stabilization and austerity, a consortium of lenders arranged for substantial loans to provide Germany with sufficient foreign exchange both to ensure the initial reparations payments and to support the value of the new currency. The "Dawes Plan" seemed at last to have provided the basis for economic stabilization.

Where did the inflation leave the German economy? Counter-intuitively, economic historians such as Carl-Ludwig Holtfrerich have argued that Germany benefited. Both public and private debt disappeared. Governments at all levels emerged debt free and much stronger than their counterparts in other countries. Rationalization and consolidation encouraged by both inflation and the following stabilization strengthened German industry. Increased efficiency and reduced wages made German exports more competitive. Measured in constant prices, exports rose steadily and were nearly 50 per cent higher in 1929 than in 1925. The holdings of German currency by foreign speculators were wiped out, again with gains in stability and productivity.[16]

Those who argue the contrary case, such as Gerald Feldman, emphasize the negative social and political consequences of the inflation. In addition, they question the economic benefits. However one might delight in seeing foreign speculators punished, their effective expropriation meant that Germany paid higher interest rates for international loans during the 1920s. Inflation disrupted normal patterns of economic exchange. Instead of saving and investing, Germans spent and speculated. The sudden stabilization meant unemployment for many. Also as seen below and in Chapter 10, where economics and politics intersect, the policies of Germany's leaders in the crisis of 1929 and 1930 were constrained if not determined by what had happened in 1923 and 1924.[17]

Investment and industrial organization

Investment is the engine of growth, and Germany's slow and spotty growth in the 1920s reflected low investment compared to the preceding upswing. According to Hoffmann's estimates, net investment averaged 15.5 per cent of total national product in 1910–13, but only 11.8 per cent from 1925 to 1928. Total net investment rose above pre-1914 levels in only one year, 1927, and even then it reached only 15.3 per cent of national product. From the peak of 1927 investment declined steadily, becoming negative in 1931 and 1932 before turning upward again.[18]

Why should investment have been low, and why did it decline from 1928 onward? Contemporaries blamed reparations, foreign trade, and first the rise and then the collapse of the New York stock market. None of these suspected causes was at fault, however. Reparations did rise as scheduled under the Dawes Plan, but rising exports actually reduced the deficit in the trade balance. The stock market boom did not reduce American lending to Germany. German capital imports peaked in 1927, whereas total American capital exports continued to rise into early 1928. The New York stock market did not crash until October 1929, nearly two full years after German investment began to drop.

The components of investment shown in Table 9.1 have been intensively scrutinized. Local German government agencies have sometimes been blamed for excessive borrowing and spending on construction projects, but their new investment was a small component of total investment, returned to prewar levels, and did not decline until 1930. Investment in the railroads (consolidated into a single national agency during the war) was lower than prewar levels, but again was relatively small and did not decline until 1931. Housing investment also remained below prewar levels, but declined only slightly in 1929. Investment in agriculture, including rural housing, dropped from a peak in 1927 to zero in 1929. That was about a quarter of the total decline, but because of a substantial increase in animal stocks, agricultural investment actually returned to its 1927 level in 1930.

The culprit is net investment in industry. Investment in the industrial

Table 9.1 Components of net investment in Germany, 1910–13 and 1924–34 (billions of 1913 marks)

	Total	Public con-struc-tion	Rail-roads	Hous-ing	Agri-culture	Indus-try—total	Build-ings	Machin-ery	Inven-tory
1910–13	7.8	0.8	0.6	1.9	1.1	3.3	0.8	2.5	
1924	na	na	na	0.9	na	6.0	0.8	0.5	4.8
1925	5.4	0.5	0.2	0.9	0.6	3.1	0.7	1.2	1.2
1926	3.3	0.7	0.3	1.2	0.2	1.0	0.7	0.9	−0.6
1927	8.1	0.8	0.2	1.4	1.2	4.3	0.9	1.3	2.1
1928	6.9	0.9	0.2	1.4	0.9	3.5	0.8	1.6	1.2
1929	3.4	0.9	0.1	1.3	0	1.3	0.8	0.9	−0.4
1930	2.8	0.6	0.2	0.9	1.2	−0.1	0.7	0.3	−1.1
1931	−1.3	0.3	0.1	0.5	0.7	−2.8	0.4	−0.5	−2.7
1932	−0.7	0.2	>0.1	0.5	0.2	−1.5	0.3	−1.2	−0.7
1933	2.3	0.4	0.1	0.7	0.9	0.1	0.3	−1.0	0.8
1934	3.3	0.6	0.3	0.9	−0.5	1.6	0.4	0.2	0.9

Note:
Public construction includes public buildings and public works (*öffentlicher Tiefbau*). Housing is non-agricultural residential construction. Buildings (*Gebäude*), machinery and equipment (*Anlagen*), and inventory (*Vorräte*) are components of the total for industry. Some yearly totals do not add up due to rounding.

Source: Walther G. Hoffmann, *Das Wachstum der deutschen Wirtschaft seit der Mitte des 19. Jahrhunderts* (Berlin: Springer, 1965), pp. 246, 258.

sector fluctuated wildly, from a peak in 1924 to a low in 1926, another peak in 1927, and then a decline to negative figures in 1930, 1931, and 1932. Further, almost all of the fluctuation in industrial investment was the result of changes in inventory. Industrial firms' investment in new buildings remained quite steady, at about the level of the immediate prewar years until 1931. Net investment in machinery and equipment (new investment, less depreciation) continued to increase through 1928. The 1928 rise was more than canceled by the 900-million-mark decline in inventory investment, however, and the drop of 700 million marks in machinery and equipment investment in 1929 was dwarfed by the further decline of 1.6 billion marks in inventory investment.

The components of industrial investment are usually held to reflect different factors. Buildings result from long-range strategic decisions, and, because firms often build with borrowed money, these decisions are affected by interest rates. New machinery and equipment may also be purchased with borrowed money, but the timing of decisions is more flexible, and reflects judgments as to the likely state of business in a year or eighteen months. Inventory investment shows no connection with interest rates. Rather, it reflects immediate expectations. Firms look at their recent sales and current unfilled orders, try to guess how demand will change over the next month, three months, or six months, and then either place additional orders with their suppliers or else run down their current stocks.

Peter Temin argued that, since exports continued to rise, the drop in inventory investment must have been a response to declining domestic demand. The available statistics and his interpretation of them have been questioned, but other data (foreign and domestic orders for new machinery, for instance) support his conclusions. Most specialists now agree that there was a "crisis before the crisis," that is, a downturn in the domestic German economy that began before the crash in the United States and the collapse of the world economy in 1929–31. Changes in investment in machinery and equipment generally followed the changes in inventory investment with a year's lag. This suggests that disappointing experiences with sales led to reductions in inventory, and that this in turn led to pessimistic expectations of future sales and reduced investment in machinery and equipment, and further reductions in sales and inventories, creating a vicious circle of decline.[19]

Were there features of German industry that would make it particularly sensitive or vulnerable to a decline in demand? As argued in Chapter 6, Germany possessed a system that worked very well in the buoyant conditions of the golden age, but that might work much less well in more difficult times. Banks and industry were concentrated—Germany was the land of the "great banks," of giant industrial firms, and of cartels. Elementary theory tells us that if demand declines, in a competitive market firms will lower their price and produce the maximum amount they can sell at that price. However, a firm with a monopoly position faced with declining demand maximizes its profits by raising its price and reducing its output. Like all monopolies, when demand dropped, Germany's large firms and cartels would reduce output and increase their prices, which would worsen the effect of a depression.

Concentration continued during the 1920s, first during the inflation and then in a series of mergers in the middle years of the decade. From

1921 through 1923, in addition to providing credit to the government, the Reichsbank also discounted private commercial bills. As inflation accelerated, these bills were ultimately repaid in depreciated currency worth only a fraction of the amount originally borrowed. Those who were quick, cunning, and who enjoyed access to the Reichsbank's credit facilities could purchase firms with borrowed money, use the firms' earnings to pay the interest on the loans, and easily repay the loans as prices rose. Under the aggressive leadership of its chairman Kurt Schmitt, Allianz, today the world's largest insurance company, took advantage of the opportunities to acquire more than a dozen other insurance companies. The Flick industrial conglomerate also originated in the inflation. Friedrich Flick, a director of the Charlottenhütte steel firm, began buying the firm's shares in 1915. Wartime profits gave him the leverage to gain access to credit following the war, and he emerged in 1924 in control of a number of heavy industrial firms.

In 1925, the major chemical firms combined as IG Farbenindustrie AG (*Interessen-Gemeinschaft*, or community of interests, in the dye industry). In 1926, Fritz Thyssen, heir to one of the most important steel firms in the Ruhr, merged his company, the Flick firms, and others to form the United Steel Works (Vereinigte Stahlwerke AG or Vestag). The new combine had 250,000 employees and controlled nearly half of Germany's steel output. With a monopoly position in Germany, IG Farben was also able to use its market power to recapture many of Germany's export markets, sometimes competing and sometimes collaborating with foreign firms such as DuPont in the United States and the newly formed Imperial Chemical Industries (ICI) in Britain. Vestag played a leading role in the establishment of both the European and international steel cartels, which aimed to fix international prices for steel products.

Some combinations were pressed by the government. In the case of aircraft, the government planned a national airline system based on regional airlines. Deutscher Aero Lloyd had been formed in 1923 in Berlin, and Junkers Luftverkehr was established in 1924 by the aircraft manufacturer Junkers. They were merged, along with all other German airlines, in 1926 to form Deutsche Luft Hansa AG. The Paris Air Traffic Agreement lifted the restrictions on German air transport imposed by the Versailles Treaty, and Lufthansa became a member of the International Air Traffic Association. Lufthansa was a quasi-public corporation with the national government holding 26 per cent of the firm's shares, and city and provincial governments 19 per cent. The chairman of the board was Emil Georg von Strauss, a director of the Deutsche Bank, and another board member was Konrad Adenauer, the Mayor of Cologne.

Contemporary scholarly observers viewed the combinations very positively. Robert Liefmann's work on cartels appeared in a fifth edition in 1922. Business leaders congratulated themselves and portrayed their activities as "rationalizing" German industry both in the sense of combining small units into larger and more efficient ones, and in the sense of imposing a systematic standard of rationality on existing practices. Their favorite models were Americans: Henry Ford, whose production-line techniques were revolutionizing the automobile industry, and Frederick Taylor, whose detailed time-and-motion studies promised great improvements in labor productivity.

However, the American model did not appeal in its entirety. Rather, as Mary Nolan argues, it provided "a working version of modernity from which Germans could pick and choose different elements as they strove to imagine not an ideal future, but at least an updated and improved one."[20] There was little change in human resource management. Managers of the Siemens electrical equipment plants in Berlin, for instance, made serious attempts to model production on Ford-style assembly lines and to control labor costs by subdividing the work as recommended by Taylor. However, though they attempted to introduce unorganized female workers drawn from the textile industry, they maintained a strict separation of male and female domains of work, and they continued to rely on a high proportion of expensive male "skilled" workers.[21] More generally, German managers continued to think in terms of centralized national organizations, and there was no change in their tendency to look to the state for support.

Consolidation did not lead to full employment or to notable improvements in efficiency. Unemployment rose to over 10 per cent in 1923 and 1924, dropped to 7 per cent in 1925, but then rose to 18 per cent in 1926. It still remained at 8 to 9 per cent in 1927 and 1928, before beginning to rise again. In early 1929, there were some 1 million workers out of jobs, and unemployment reached 13 per cent before the New York stock market crash in October. Productivity is extremely difficult to measure, but a number of studies indicate that productivity did not increase in Weimar Germany as rapidly as before the war.

The interwar combines and cartels caused unemployment by closing small plants, but they did not invest enough either to restore full employment or to improve productivity. As noted above, in the aftermath of the inflation interest rates may have been excessive, and this would have hindered investment. More controversially, Knut Borchardt suggested that the relatively powerful position of labor unions in the Weimar period allowed workers to gain wage increases substantially in excess of productivity growth. This restricted potential investment by raising the share of wages in national income. By reducing investment, the increase in real wages also reduced potential employment. In a kind of vicious circle, low levels of employment reduced the market for goods and services, and this lowered investment still further. Not surprisingly, the "Borchardt thesis" has stimulated extensive debate. In addition, as seen in Chapter 10, Borchardt traced his argument through to examine the effects of high wages on the possibilities open to German leaders in the crisis of 1929–30, and concluded that the structural weaknesses of the economy severely limited their options.[22]

These analyses of course have all come after the collapse, the rise of the Nazis, the war, and the Holocaust. At the time, however, business executives basked in the glory of their role as heroic leaders. Some financial entrepreneurs became household names, and some actively sought public status as legendary figures. The inflation provided them with an opportunity to create new combinations, to paint as it were with an entirely new palate. Alfred Hugenberg and Hugo Stinnes both attempted to transmute their wealth into political power. Stinnes, whose control of the Deutsch-Luxemburg mining and smelting firm had led to acquisitions in electric power generation, shipping, and shipbuilding before the war, expanded his holdings into a vast conglomerate during the inflation. He saw himself as the spokesman for German industry, and attempted to dictate policy to the government. He and the newspapers he controlled violently opposed Wirth and Rathenau's policy of fulfillment of reparations, new taxes or capital levies, the introduction of the new currency, and Stresemann's conciliatory foreign policy. Believing the French to be more reliable than the British or Americans, in 1923 he supported the efforts of Cologne mayor Konrad Adenauer to establish an autonomous government in the Rhineland and Westphalia that would collaborate with France after the campaign of passive resistance was ended. He died in 1924, and much of his empire collapsed under its load of debt in the stabilization.

Hugenberg, a director of the Krupp firm and one of the organizers of the Pan-German League before the war, created the Scherl newspaper syndicate, which eventually expanded to three daily papers in Berlin and fourteen provincial papers. In 1927, he purchased control of the Ufa film company. A member of the German National People's Party (DNVP) and Reichstag member since 1919, he aimed for national leadership. The newspapers and their profits supported his radical nationalist campaign against the republic. When the moderate Conservatives in the DNVP agreed to participate in a coalition government in 1928, he led a revolt that ousted the moderates. He supported the campaign for a plebiscite against the reparations settlement offered by the Young Plan in 1929. He became one of many who thought they could tame Adolf Hitler and use the Nazis for their own purposes. He expected to lead a broad-based coalition of right-wing parties that would include the Nazis; disappointed, he became for a brief period the designated "economic dictator" in Hitler's first cabinet.

The social and cultural context: Expressionism as leitmotiv

Josef Goebbels had a great deal of sympathy for Expressionism. For a while it even seemed that this uniquely German avant-garde might become the recognized official artistic movement of the Nazi Party. As seen in Chapter 11, this did not happen, and the Nazi government condemned Expressionism as "degenerate" art. The ambivalence and hostility are already evident in Goebbels' novel *Michael*. Michael identifies his age as Expressionist, but he also denounces "un-German" artists and intellectuals and exclaims that "this whole foreign rabble will have to be removed!"

As with his definition of Expressionism, Goebbels was recycling contemporary clichés. Expressionist modes spread, to the extent of blurring any meaningful definition, but at the same time their very pervasiveness contributed to an ongoing anxious discussion over what art was, what it should be, and what its purpose was. This, in turn, led not only to conflict over whether there was a "German" art, but also to violent dispute over what it ultimately meant to be "German" at all. Prewar themes of cultural pessimism continued. The second volume of Oswald Spengler's *Decline of the West* appeared in 1922, and Arthur Moeller van den Bruck's *Das Dritte Reich* (translated as *Germany's Third Empire*) in 1923. Both argued that an organically restructured Germany could overcome internal division and external defeat and still fulfill its destiny. For those fearful of change, hostile to experiment, or opposed to the republic, anyone and any group identified with Weimar could be identified as "foreign rabble" and something that "will have to be removed." Carl Schmitt, professor of public law at Bonn, said bluntly that only the state can judge who is a "friend" and who an "enemy." Further, a state is only unified insofar as it is able to eliminate those factions it identifies as "enemies." Finally, echoing both the contemporary right wing and the more distant legacy of Bismarck, he concluded that the ultimate value of a state depends solely on its ability to control internal dissension and external threat.[23]

The dispute over art and German culture was not confined to the right. On the left, the role of art in society and politics was also intensely debated, ranging from the creation of more pleasant physical environments for living to the possibilities of leading a proletarian revolution against the capitalist system. In exile in the 1930s, four of the major protagonists formalized their views in the "Expressionism Debate." Philosopher George Lukács believed progressive art should reflect social reality and serve an educational function. He favored a politically committed and easily understood art, and he criticized Expressionism because it denied and disrupted the connection between individual perceptions and broad social movements. Dramatist Bertolt Brecht replied that the realism favored by Lukács in fact blocks contact with social reality by encouraging an unreflective identification with the characters in the work. His solution was pragmatic. It is not the particular form of art, but the mode of its presentation that enables people to overcome ideological deception and see social relations as they really are. Literary theorist Walther Benjamin and sociologist Theodor Adorno wondered how any critique of culture could be grounded. Benjamin thought modern technologies might, even as they undermined the traditional notion of art works as unique products, provide an opportunity for a new kind of revolutionary culture. Adorno replied that the use of art for directly political purposes would reduce it to the same status as any other tool of "instrumental reason," and mass reproduction would reduce it to the same status as any other commodity. In a later work he concluded by refusing to conclude: "The promise of the work of art to institute truth by imprinting shape into socially transmitted forms is as necessary as it is hypocritical."[24]

The Expressionist style extended to encompass scientific discourse. Reformers across the entire spectrum claimed the authority of science for their preferred programs. Both Taylorist rationalization of industrial

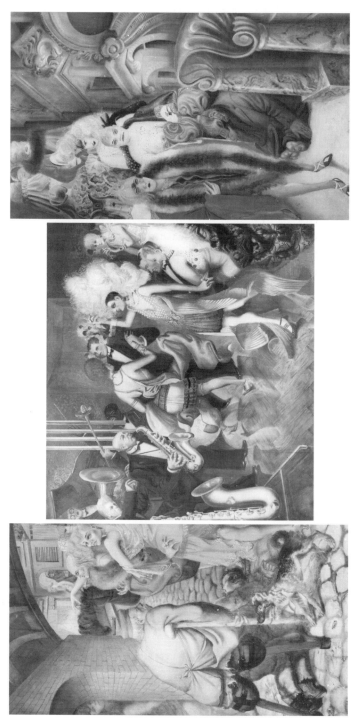

Plate 9.1 Otto Dix, *Metropolis (Grossstadt)*, 1927–28. Triptych, mixed media on wood. Center panel 181 × 210 cm; right and left panels 181 × 1005 cm. Städtische Museum, Stuttgart. Even among those who might have been expected to celebrate its freedom and openness, Weimar elicited ambiguous or negative sentiments. Dix, a radical and a leading exponent of the New Objectivity in painting who was later denounced as "degenerate" by the Nazis, shared the widespread hostility to the garish excesses of the city. In the streets, as legless war veterans beg and die, old and ugly prostitutes preen and parade. Inside an expensive nightclub, young women and men dance feverishly to the new jazz music. Dix codes the music as violent and disorderly through the musicians' postures, and reminds viewers that the music is foreign by adding a black musician in the background. Photo courtesy Otto Dix Stiftung. Copyright © Otto Dix, 1928/Bild-Kunst, licensed by VISCOPY, Sydney 2002.

work and predictions of Marxist proletarian revolution claimed to be based on dispassionate scientific observation. So, too, did the eugenics movement discussed below. Even as they did so, however, a range of scientific thinkers was debating what exactly science was, and whether there was a truly "German" science. They were attempting to discover the secrets of the macrocosm, and like Expressionist artists and writers they sought to step outside the bounds of previous thought. German authors advocated a new holistic grounding for science, whether in a notion of a context or surrounding world (*Umwelt*) whose operation took precedence over the mechanistic interactions of its parts, or the purposive biological striving of a cosmic power to realize itself.

Today they seem cranky, but, in 1920, fully 44 per cent of all scientific publications in the world were written in German, and leading German scientists' views on the ultimate structure of the universe commanded attention. Internationally, the Newtonian view of the world and of the human being, with the machine as a metaphor for nature and for the human mind, was being undermined by Einstein's theory of relativity and Freud's theory of the unconscious. German advocates of holistic approaches to nature participated in this discussion. In Germany, the debates took on an added political dimension, and their visions could lead in opposite political directions. Belief in the *Umwelt* and privileging wholeness could translate into a preference for monarchy and opposition to democracy. The search for a "German" science could be directed against Anglo-Saxon Newtonian physics, but also against the theories of prominent Jewish scientists. Alternatively, others argued that learning how to think not in piecemeal reasoning, but with "gestalt logic" that identified whole patterns at once, prevented demagoguery and supported a truly free society.[25]

The range of expression

Expressionism is less clearly defined in literature than in painting. The dissatisfaction with received modes of representation affected authors as well as artists. Although not an Expressionist writer, Rainer Maria Rilke deviated from standard grammatical forms, treating abstract ideas as if they were concrete objects and coining completely new words and combinations of forms. These techniques already appear in his prewar poetry. His poem-cycle *Duineser Elegien* and the companion piece *Sonette an Orpheus* were published in 1923. They deploy language not to describe reality but to encourage the reader to experience reality from a new perspective. Meanings are hinted at, not prescribed. The results are some of the best poetry ever written in German. However, for the poets usually identified as Expressionist, Rilke's approach seemed still too removed and too consciously esthetic. Instead of examining the feelings of individuals, they tended to present themselves as speaking for humanity as a whole. The best were brilliantly original. Else Lasker-Schüler's work is often compared to Rilke. Ernst Stadler died at Ypres in 1914, and Ernst Trakl committed suicide in 1914, probably as a result of his horrific experiences on the Eastern Front. Less original writers such as Johannes Becher often adopted a stylized approach of presenting grim or shocking contemporary subject matter and displaying it with grotesque metaphors and a strident declamatory style.

In drama, the language of Expressionist poetry was stretched even further, and the claims for representativeness and relevance became more obvious. The dialog of Oskar Kokoschka's *Murder Hope of Womankind* (*Mörder Hoffnung der Frauen*, 1909) consists largely of inarticulate shouts, meaningless without the stage directions, and in *The Burning Bush* (*Der brennende Dornbusch*, 1913) the polarity of man and woman is symbolized by the imagery of moon and sun. Georg Kaiser refined other typical elements, such as the alternation of monologs by the main characters with choruses and staccato exclamations, contrasts between isolated main characters and undifferentiated masses of people, and shifts from one symbolic set to another, as in *Die Bürger von Calais* (1914) and *From Morning to Midnight* (*Von Morgen bis Mitternachts*, 1916). The last years of the war and the revolution—and the end of censorship in 1918—saw a number of plays that attempted to capture the horrors of the war or to advocate the possibility of a new transformed humanity. Ernst Toller's *The Transformation* (*Die Wandlung*, 1919) follows its hero, Friedrich, on his spiritual path from naïve militarist to revolutionary leader. The main female character of *Masses and Man* (*Masse Mensch*, 1922) is named Sonja Irene L. ("wisdom" and "peace"). Drawing on Toller's experiences during the Munich Soviet in 1919, the alternation of her monologs with mass choruses outlines the tragic conflict between her call for love and non-violence and the demands of the revolutionary leader ("The Nameless One") for the "hard deed" and revenge against the state's violence.

Bertolt Brecht's works include over forty plays, poetry, and a large body of critical writing on theater. Of several classics, the musical *The*

Threepenny Opera (*Die Dreigroschenoper*, 1928), a collaboration with composer Kurt Weill and translator and author Elisabeth Hauptmann, is the best known of his works written during the Weimar years. He is in many ways an archetypal Weimar figure, a carefully calculated proletarian image supported by dark leather jacket, dirty white shirt, and cigar. Married, he conducted a series of affairs, and suspicion lingers as to the unacknowledged contribution of his female partners to his works. His appropriation of material from his lover Marielouise Fleisser damaged her career and obscured her revival of the genre of plays centered on rural and small-town life.

Brecht rejected Expressionist drama as too abstract, for containing "proclamations of humanity without human beings." He also criticized the implausible spiritual transformations on which Expressionist drama rested. However, the structure and staging of his own plays drew on Expressionist techniques. Several of his works use choruses to explicate the action. This is part of his famous *Verfremdungseffekt* or "estrangement effect" which was simultaneously to distance the audience from the play's action and to involve them in the play's ideas. In addition, in the version of Marxism that he adopted, ideas embodied in "epic" theater would have the potential to transform society. His own directions to his actors also drew on Expressionist ideas. He instructed them not to attempt to "be" the character, but to play their role in a deliberately exaggerated style in order to highlight the play's philosophical message. Audiences in turn were not to be entranced or to identify with individual characters, but to remain detached, alert, and critical. He said he preferred cigar smokers in the audience, because when one smokes a cigar one must pay attention or the ash will fall, and the need to stay alert kept such an audience awake for the play's message.

Path-breaking as they were, Expressionist dramatists found it difficult to present the spectacular effects they envisaged on stage. Film could overcome some of the limitations. Robert Wiene's *The Cabinet of Dr. Caligari* (1920), with its distorted angular sets and exaggerated performances, defined Expressionist film. Fritz Lang's *Metropolis* (1927) drew on Kaiser's portrayal of the oppressive social structures of modern industry in his play *Gas* (1917). The spectacular sets in this case blew the budget out to an unprecedented 5.3 million marks. Friedrich Murnau's *Nosferatu* (1922), the first vampire film, and Lang's portrayal of a serial killer in *M* (1931) drew on Expressionist techniques in their use of lighting and camera angles to create their oppressive and threatening atmosphere.

Specialists usually group the novelists of the Weimar years into modernist and realist camps. Expressionism is not generally deployed as an interpretive category, but modernist novelists took advantage of Expressionist modes and motifs. The search for individual authenticity, "the autocratic feeling of being oneself," frames Hermann Hesse's *Demian* (1919) which, like Goebbels' *Michael*, is a confessional novel, and *Der Steppenwolf* (1927), in which the hero, Harry Haller, tests himself through a series of fantasy experiences in a Magic Theater. The final experience sees Haller and a retired professor of theology ambushing automobiles and shooting the people riding in them. Haller justifies his actions, partly on the grounds that there are too many people in the world, but also philosophically:

> Yes, what we are doing is probably mad, and probably it is good and necessary all the same. It is not a good thing when a man overstrains his reason and tries to reduce to rational order things that are not susceptible to rational treatment. Then there arise ideals such as those of the Americans and the Bolsheviks. Both are extraordinarily rational, and both lead to frightful oppression and impoverishment of life, because they simplify it so crudely. The likeness of man, once a high ideal, is in the process of becoming a machine-made article. It is for madmen like us, perhaps, to ennoble it again.

Thomas Mann's *The Magic Mountain* (*Der Zauberberg*, 1924) built on his prewar techniques, but extended them into a series of contrasting symbolic structures. Hans Castorp visits a mountain sanatorium, becomes infatuated with a female patient, is himself diagnosed as having tuberculosis, and remains for seven years. During his stay he meets characters who embody conflicting positions: Nietzsche's Apollonian and Dionysian traditions, religious and secular views of the world, and the tension between erotic attraction and conventional morality. The Italian Liberal Settembrini and the Jewish Jesuit Naphta attempt to win his allegiance to their respective political programs. Mann, a fervent supporter of the war, had been shocked by Rathenau's murder and delivered a lecture supporting the republic in 1923. If there is a single central message in *The Magic Mountain* it may be the essentially liberal position that since no individual possesses absolute truth, truth will always need to be approached through argument. But, in the novel the rationality on which liberalism depends confronts very powerful irrational forces. Although Settembrini is the victor in his duel with Naphta, Castorp returns from the hospital only to the carnage of the First World War.

Alexander Döblin practiced medicine in the working-class districts in East Berlin where *Berlin Alexanderplatz* (1929) is set. The structure is fractured and chaotic, reminiscent of Kirchner's streetscapes. An omniscient narrative voice accompanies and comments on the action, moves in and out of the characters' minds, and sometimes announces future events, but the voice itself changes like the voices of the city, a ballad-singer at one point and a boxing commentator at another, for instance. A montage technique juxtaposes elements from the life of the city, such as advertisements, newspaper stories, weather reports, and train timetables, interspersed with the action. The subtitle is "the story of Franz Biberkopf," the central character, and critics are still divided over whether the book has Biberkopf or the city of Berlin as its subject. The narrator invites us to sympathize and identify with Biberkopf. "Step by step, we could have done what he did and experienced what he did." But Biberkopf, though he attempts to remain "decent," is a violent and extremely stupid man who brutalizes and exploits a series of women. He successively murders, rapes, and nearly beats to death the women he relies on for emotional and economic support.

His vicious criminal acquaintance Reinhold first injures Biberkopf and then murders his girlfriend Mieze, blows that drive him insane. Near death, he encounters the figure of Death, who shows him that he is responsible for his own sufferings. The ending is ambiguous and still disputed. On one reading, Mieze, the gold-hearted prostitute, has through her death redeemed Biberkopf by giving him the opportunity to achieve insight and agency, a theme extending back to Goethe's *Faust*. On another, the religious imagery Döblin deploys throughout the novel seems to demand Biberkopf's conversion and redemption through faith. Döblin became a Catholic in 1941, but, according to this line of interpretation, in 1929 could not provide this religious closure to his story.

As with poetry, so with drama and the novel: along with the genuinely innovative there were many works that deployed Expressionist modes as a formula. Gerhart Hauptmann adopted the new style in a play about Montezuma and Cortez and had one of his characters declaim, "Words are confused speech. Screaming is clarity! Screaming is truth!" Goebbels was one of many would-be Expressionist novelists whose characters declaimed or screamed, and whose works shifted abruptly from one setting to another in supposedly symbolic fashion. In addition, many writers continued to produce in a realist idiom, and some went on a counteroffensive against Expressionism. This was the *Neue Sachlichkeit* or "new objectivity." *Neue Sachlichkeit* also referred to the reintroduction of figurative techniques in painting, as in the work of Otto Dix, and as with Dix's paintings the cool, distant view was adopted as a means of approaching traumatic events from the war, revolution, and class conflicts of the republic. Several of these writers adopted pseudonyms. Erich Maria Remarque (Paul Remark) produced a classic anti-war statement in *All Quiet on the Western Front* (*Im Westen nichts neues*, 1929). Erich Reger (Hermann Dannenberger) detailed the struggles between workers and employers in the Ruhr from the revolution in 1918 to the crisis of 1928–29 in *Union of the Firm Hand* (*Union der festen Hand*, 1931). Hans Fallada (Rudolf Ditzen) described a farmers' revolt in Holstein he had witnessed as a reporter in *Farmers, Functionaries, and Fireworks* (*Bauern, Bonzen und Bomben*, 1931) and the consequences of unemployment for a young man and his wife in Berlin in *What Now, Little Man?* (*Kleiner Mann, was nun?*, 1932).

Self-consciously critical artistic innovation invited controversy. *The Threepenny Opera*, with its petty crime, seedy prostitution, and casual violence, was attacked by the right-wing press. The *Kreuzzeitung* denounced it as "literary necrophilia." Despite or because of the scandal, it was hugely successful. An article in the Weimar constitution proclaimed "there will be no censorship," but the continuity of personnel and attitudes from prewar to Weimar meant continued official hostility to avant-garde art, and to left-wing artistic expression. At all levels, officials connived with right-wing and anti-Semitic movements. Authorities reflected the insecurity of conservative elements in attempting to repress what they could not understand. An exhibition staged by surrealist artist Max Ernst was closed in 1920. Police first accused the organizers of fraud, because they were charging admission to see works that obviously had no artistic merit, and then shut the exhibition on the grounds that it was pornographic. Dix, Brecht, and many others also faced charges of pornography. George Grosz's satirical cartoons brought him three court appearances, all of which resulted in judgments against him. Attacks on the army, such as the dummy in uniform with an animal's face at the 1920 Dada Fair, were also regularly prosecuted. In 1925, poet Johannes Becher, who was also a Communist member of the Reichstag, was formally accused of "literary high treason." The case was dropped, then reopened in 1927. The trial was called off as part of an amnesty for left-wing literary figures following the victory of the Socialist Party in the May 1928 Reichstag elections, a temporary respite that demonstrated the depth of cultural divisions and their close relation to politics.[26]

The Bauhaus stood at the vortex created by the intersection of these currents. Established with money from the state and municipal governments in Weimar in 1919, its name was intended to evoke the medieval workshops connected with cathedrals (*Dombauhütte*). The founding director Walter Gropius drew on the prewar Arts and Crafts movement and on Wagner's idea of the total artistic work. Charismatic teacher Johannes Itten derived his conviction that "we must counter-balance our externally orientated scientific research and technological speculation with inner-directed thought and practice" from "the horrible events of World War I and a close study of Spengler's *Decline of the West.*" Lásló Maholy-Nagy replaced Itten as director of the basic course, and added a "constructivist-elementarist" approach derived from contacts in the Soviet Union. The staff included Marcel Breuer, Wassily Kandinsky, Paul Klee, and other well-known names in twentieth-century art and design. The Bauhaus basic course has influenced training in design schools around the world, and the simplified forms of the "Bauhaus style," ranging from furniture and wallpaper to kitchen appliances, has helped define "modern" interior decoration. When the opposition of Conservatives in the Weimar city government forced the school to move to Dessau in 1925, Gropius' design for the new building became another classic. The mayor of Dessau hoped to use the prestige and resources of the school to upgrade the city's image and contribute to his housing program, but right-wing opposition continued and intensified with the onset of the depression. In 1932, the Bauhaus was closed, and an "Aryan" pitched roof added to the already famous horizontal façade.[27]

Protecting the race: population and eugenics

Conflicts over what it might be, or should be, to be German stepped to center stage in the debate over population policies. The losses of the war needed to be made good, the national body healed. The declining birth rate suggested that something was wrong. As seen below, there was widespread concern over women working, and there were periodic scandals over abortion prosecutions. A variety of reform leagues, medical organizations, women's movements, churches and denominational organizations all pressed their particular interpretation of the available statistics and attempted to exploit the public attention generated by concern and scandal to further their own agendas. The eugenics movement benefited from this public concern, and its ideas spread to a far wider audience than before the war. Eugenics could claim a scientific pedigree that held out the promise of transforming mankind and lent itself to various social engineering projects in Germany's health and welfare sectors. As part of an international movement, German eugenicists debated the merits of positive policies to promote the "fitter" elements in society as opposed to negative policies to discourage breeding by the "less fit" (*Minderwertigen*). Also disputed was the question of whether the aim of eugenics was to improve the single human race, or whether there were a number of separate competing races.

Debates over population policy, and debates within the eugenics movement, therefore reflected both Weimar's social and political polarization and the desire to impose a preferred vision on German society. The eugenics movement split between those, generally in Berlin, who rejected excessively racist ideas or the extreme claims of chauvinistic nationalists, and those, generally in Munich, who accepted the arguments of racial (*völkisch*) nationalists that there was a "German" or "Nordic" race. Separate research institutes were founded, in Munich in 1924 and in Berlin in 1927.

It may seem surprising to find Socialist and Communist writers actively involved in eugenics debates. Left-wing intellectuals shared the general faith in science and they were patriotic Germans as well. Socialist writers before the war had framed social policy issues such as improved hygienic conditions at home and in the workplace, advocacy of birth control, and liberalization of abortion restrictions in the language of eugenics. This tendency became more widespread after the foundation of the republic, when Socialist eugenicists attempted to push through healthcare certificates and establish marriage counseling centers. They also attempted to enact eugenics legislation at state and national levels, and these included negative as well as positive measures. It is not always clear why Socialists embraced "negative" eugenics. Michael Schwartz suggests it was easier to sell politically. In addition, however, Socialists attempted to "biologize" (that is, to label as genetically defective) those already marginalized groups in German society that had never enjoyed public support. For Weimar Socialist eugenicists and the skilled workers who formed their constituency, it was the underclass or *Lumpenproletariat* who, along with the mentally handicapped, should be socially engineered out of existence. The money saved could then be used on social programs to improve the quality of life of the majority of genetically healthy citizens.

Attempts to pass eugenics laws were almost completely unsuccessful. During the depression some Socialists suggested the need for a sterilization law. This became caught up in the ongoing controversy between the Catholic Center Party and Socialists over just how to regulate national health. The Center stressed population policy programs and rejected Socialist attempts to introduce eugenically based birth control and abortion legislation as well as sterilization. However, many members of the Catholic clergy also advocated a eugenics-based argument for the defense of the family. It was the Center and not the Socialist Party that drafted a voluntary sterilization law in Prussia in 1932, which was not passed but that later served as a model for the Nazis.[28]

Eugenics issues were viewed as especially relevant to women. Reforms did bring improvements in maternal and child protection. The Weimar period saw efforts to increase knowledge and accessibility of birth control and abortion among poor and working-class women. Legislation in 1926 reduced the punishments for those convicted of abortion. A campaign among doctors favoring decriminalization of abortion in 1930 led to the simultaneous arrest of over 300 physicians in 1931. The subsequent national campaign to defend the doctors and decriminalize abortion also became a "women's" issue. The Communist Party in particular attempted to exploit its advocacy of abortion, but, limited by the rigidity of their ideology, Communists were unable to mobilize the potential political force of a women's politics.

Disputes over population policy intersected with the notion of a "body politic." For the parties this was intensely practical. Female leaders in the Socialist and Communist Parties, under the banner of scientific eugenics, attempted to promote policies that would mobilize women voters. The bourgeois women's organizations were less tied to particular parties, but they opposed policies that promised to deliver votes to the left. Religious women's organizations were also very important, and they refused to make a common front with either bourgeois or left-wing women's organizations. Symbolic issues were also at stake. The national body was disputed, but it was conceptualized as feminine. In the abortion debate, those who opposed abortion defended unborn children as limbs of the national body, a body threatened by social decay which was responsible for the declining birth rate. Those who campaigned to decriminalize abortion did so on the grounds that women's special responsibility for the protection and nurturing of the national body could only be guaranteed if the offspring they produced were of the highest quality. All expressed their concern for the quality of German children rather than mere numbers. All expressed their concern for the family's role, and all demanded that the state intervene to prevent its collapse.

Cornelie Usborne highlights the generally conservative tone of the debate. The specific legal reforms and improvements in social services were substantial. Weimar Germany was relatively progressive compared to other countries of interwar Europe. Pope Pius XI condemned all forms of contraception and declared abortion a mortal sin in 1930, for instance. However, even the support of those advocating specific reforms was qualified. The Socialist and Communist Parties had great difficulties fitting gender into their class perspective. Female party members played a crucial role in pushing the parties toward more progressive policies on all women's issues, but they placed women in the context of other collective interests. Male party leaders, intellectuals, and ordinary members and supporters shared traditional views of motherhood as woman's primary role and of the authority structures within the patriarchal family. Women did not have an independent political voice, so when the support of left-wing parties wavered or disappeared, so did progressive initiatives.[29]

The "new woman" and the "woman question"

On November 12, 1918, the new voting law enfranchised women and men on an equal basis. On August 11, 1919, the new Weimar constitution proclaimed "Men and women have fundamentally the same civil rights and duties" (Article 109), "Marriage is based on equality between the sexes" (Article 119), and "All citizens without distinction are to be admitted to public office" and "All discriminatory provisions against female civil servants are abolished" (Article 128). A "new woman" appeared on the streets and in the newspapers and magazines, with short hair, silk stockings, cigarettes, and an independent income. Forthright and assertive, familiar with sexual technique and birth control, her desires and morals were objects of intense interest and scrutiny. Once more Germany was not alone—the "new woman" bore a striking resemblance to the Japanese "moga" (*modaan garu* or modern girl) and to the American "flapper," and the debates over her existence and significance closely paralleled the anxious discussion in those countries.

Goebbels' novel *Michael* typified the reactions of those for whom the new woman posed a threat. In one of his conversations with Hertha, Michael defines human existence as struggle. "Struggle the moment man sets foot on this earth. Struggle till the moment of leaving it." But it is man who must struggle, for only he can conquer and defend the land. Woman is subordinate. Her duties are to be lovely and to bring children into the world. Hertha interrupts at this point and accuses him of being "reactionary," but Michael is unrepentant. "If being modern means unnatural, utter collapse, putrefaction and deliberate corrosion of all morality, then I am being reactionary." Once again the text deconstructs itself. As with the eugenics movement and disputes over population policies described above, Michael is not describing what women and men actually do, but rather what he believes they should be doing. He is speaking to a "new woman" and the text allows her to interrupt his diatribe, but she is then effaced in a string of epithets.

Michael's vision of man struggling in the world while his wife maintains his home and cares for his children repeats clichés derived from Hegel. The image of struggle as specifically the acts of conquering and defending land derives from the cultural pessimists (the phrasing is sometimes lifted from Nietzsche) and even more directly from the lost war. But Michael, Goebbels, and the Nazis were not alone. Male political leaders across the spectrum from left to right believed that the proper roles for women were as wives and mothers, and that the proper place for women was in the home. Demobilization and reconstruction meant that women lost their jobs.[30] The war ministry insisted in 1917 that women must be "returned to the family" as quickly as possible. In the midst of the revolution, the agreement between the unions and industrial leaders specified that all returning soldiers would have the right to "immediate" reemployment. In virtually every industry in 1919 and 1920, newly empowered male workers and their shopfloor organizations insisted that women workers be the last hired and the first fired. During the 1920s, those who called for rationalization of industry also advocated a rationalization of housework, but it was women homemakers who were to be made more efficient, in order that their children could enjoy the benefits of modern, up-to-date mothering.[31]

The celebrated "new woman" had little resonance in policy, except for her exploitation as an image deployed as evidence of the breakdown of the family. When she did step outside the home, she became a threat, or a victim, or both. The women in *Berlin Alexanderplatz* are under constant threat from male violence, but when they die they disappear from the text. It is the suffering of the men that receives attention and sympathy from the narrator. Bertolt Brecht's first play *Baal* (1918) presents its male hero as an isolated, amoral being who rejects society and dies alone. He associates women with nature, and for Baal sex repeats immersion in the flood. However, the actual women with whom he has sex are discarded, and Baal feels no remorse when they drown themselves. His true love is another man, whom he kills from jealousy. This was a common set of themes from left to right. Brecht deploys the same set of symbols used by extreme right-wing authors, as Klaus Theweleit shows in his study of the writings of members of the *Freikorps* military units. The imagery associates sex and women with water, floods, swamps, and disease, and contrasts with portrayals of men as firm, dry, steadfast, and healthy, and of male bonding as superior to heterosexual relationships.[32]

A series of gruesome sexual serial killings engrossed the popular media, and sexual murder became a repeated theme in art. The murderer in the film *M* preys on young girls who are late returning from school, but, as in *Berlin Alexanderplatz*, it is his suffering that receives the work's sympathy. Dix, Grosz, and other painters produced repeated images of dismembered and disemboweled women lying on disheveled and blood-soaked sheets. Maria Tatar confirms Theweleit's finding that these works gave expression to a deep anxiety arising from the fear that to allow women into the public space would undermine the foundations on which patriarchal society and the male identity rested. News and art reinforced a triple message. Terrible things were happening, usually in the disorderly and depraved cities. But, in addition, the detailed reports and the explicit portrayals were themselves exciting. And finally the underlying message was also clear—respectable women were only safe at home. Artists figured women alone in public, and the victims of their imagined murders, as prostitutes. In *M* we see posters warning girls off the streets.[33]

Who was the "new woman" and what was she doing that could have been so threatening? The census reported that 35 per cent more women were working in 1925 than in 1907, and that many more married women were working. These figures were widely noted and discussed. Observers frequently blamed the rise in female employment for causing the high levels of male unemployment, and cited the figures for married working women as evidence of the breakdown of the family. In fact, as women writers pointed out, male employment had risen as well, and the share of women in the labor force had increased only slightly. In addition, a change in definition led to more complete reporting of women working in family businesses, so a large share of the reported increase in married working women was artificial.

The number of women recorded working in agriculture rose substantially to 5 million in 1925, half of all working women. The extension of the eight-hour day to agricultural day laborers (mostly male), and the increased availability of machinery for planting and harvesting, led small farmers to cut back on hiring and to replace their former day laborers with their wives and daughters when they could. In industry, around 2 million women workers made up about one-third of the total labor force, and, of these, two-thirds were single and under 30 years old. Women were as before confined to certain branches, but some of the newer areas in which they were employed were expanding quite rapidly, such as "light" assembly of electric bulbs, telephones, or radios. Domestic service remained large, though declining slightly. Other services, and particularly white-collar jobs such as sales clerks, expanded rapidly. These other services employed 1.4 million women in 1925, and 90 per cent were single and under 30 years old.

Female sales clerks were most visible in the central areas of cities, they were rapidly increasing in numbers, and they were young and hired for their looks in order to appeal to customers. If there was a "new woman" she was probably a sales clerk. Fantasies about her independent income were precisely that. Wages in the service sector were below subsistence and three-quarters of sales clerks lived with their families. Low wages and discrimination marked other sectors as well. Women were less likely to own a farm in the 1920s than before the war, and they were excluded from management positions in the new dairy cooperatives that cut into a traditionally "women's" area of agricultural production. Women workers in industry earned 30 to 40 per cent less than their male colleagues, and unskilled males typically earned more than skilled females.

There were also more female professionals and female public servants than before the war. Legal and medical associations complained and did what they could to restrict women. The public service suffered a

backlash. Despite the constitutional guarantees, there was a purge of
married women from the public service in 1923–24. There was no debate
over whether they should go, only whether women were entitled to
receive their severance pay when they married and were dismissed.
Although women made up 32 per cent of teachers in Prussia in 1925,
only 30 of the 317 heads of girls' senior schools were women. Hiring was
restricted, and by 1931 teaching was effectively closed to women.

Women's movements coped as best they could, both with the disorienting new opportunities that Weimar appeared to offer, and with the
continued discrimination. Women, even those committed or sympathetic to the activist women's movement, were themselves divided. The
older generation of leaders such as Helene Lange and her life partner
Gertrud Bäumer continued to argue that women were essentially different from men. This meant that only women could properly educate
women, so teaching positions in girls' schools should be reserved for
women. It also meant that women in the public sphere should not aim
for equality with men, but rather to infuse the feminine qualities of
compassion and understanding into the public realm. They continued to
emphasize both the reality and the metaphor of women as mothers, in
the private sphere and in those parts of the public sphere they viewed as
an extension of the family.[34]

Younger feminists adopted Expressionist rhetoric, insisting on their
rights to equality and to seek individual authenticity. This might lead
them to abstain from public activity altogether, and many insisted on
their right to "refuse" to participate in the existing male-dominated
institutions. One young contributor to *Die Frau* argued that at the
moment "the absolute" was no longer clear, and that the worship of
"idols" such as the state, culture, or art, or indeed the women's movement itself, could not be justified. The search of youth for a new absolute, a "wish for a radical critique from a point beyond all existing
possibilities" meant "that dualism was no longer possible, which
imposed different norms on public life than those of the personal relations of person to person." Relations with men might also be different,
defined on a basis of equality within a restructured private sphere rather
than in separate spheres of public life.[35]

Contemporary feminists were particularly concerned, not only that
the younger generation seemed to reject the movement's accepted principles, but also that many young women rejected the movement
altogether. Religious organizations pulled away potential converts, and

so did the Nazi youth and women's organizations. The appeal of conservative and nationalist groups for women has remained a concern of subsequent historians. Nancy Reagin believes many of the leaders of the women's movement were comfortable with authoritarianism and with aggressive anti-Socialism, nationalism, and sexual repressiveness. Their conservative values reflected class differences and led in an authoritarian direction, in which "technically competent" and therefore allegedly non-political elites provided services to groups allegedly unable to care for themselves.[36] This argument is extended by Claudia Koonz to explain women's support for the Nazi movement. Koonz argues that there were clear lines of continuity leading from the prewar women's movement through Weimar and on to the Nazi period. She emphasizes in particular the insistence by leaders of women's organizations that women were essentially different from men, that they therefore had a special role, and should exercise special functions in society.[37]

Other historians such as Ann Taylor Allen believe the accusations of these critical scholars are unfair and anachronistic. Allen sees German feminism as a movement rooted in its own time, and very progressive for its time. Prewar German women could not be expected to aim for equality with men as their primary goal. Rather, they concentrated on the issues that concerned them, children and education. The content and delivery of education, the questions of what children should be taught, how it was to be taught, and who should teach them brought them into conflict with male-dominated educational establishments. The search for less authoritarian models of child-rearing brought them into conflict with the core structure of the model of the family established in the early decades of the nineteenth century. Their alternative vision, a transformation of society into an organic realm of cooperation and harmony based on communal values and free of individual egoism, overcame the gap between public and private and allowed the concept of "social motherhood" to become the basis for an expanding range of public activities. And Allen also notes that the practices of the German women's movement were very similar to those in the United States, so it is particularly unfair to identify German feminists as tragically different, or their activities as part of Germany's "special path."[38]

Wayward youth

Debates over the social problems posed by youth and young workers also built on prewar developments. And, as with the women's movement, the appeal of Nazism to youth has led to intense scrutiny of Weimar's plans to deal with the "problem" of young workers. The many groups that had contended for influence over policy before the war—charities, municipalities, courts, state bureaucracies, churches, women's associations, middle-class reform societies—continued to offer competing visions of what should be done.[39] Edward Dickinson defines "two opposing middle-class cultures" that crystallized around issues of child and family welfare. One was secular, scientific, materialist, statist, and centralist, but also participatory. The other was religious (especially Catholic), patriarchal, and voluntarist, but tended to be authoritarian. Before 1914, a network of vocational schools supported by municipal governments and religious youth clubs of Protestant and Catholic Churches had spread across the country. These years also saw a rapid expansion of correctional education, juvenile courts, and infant health clinics. The terms of debate shifted in a "scientific direction," from repression to prevention and from moral to medical, psychiatric, and eugenicist models of reform. But there was still no centralized, uniform child welfare bureaucracy.

The reorganization of German society during the war and the hardships of the home front not only made the expansion of child welfare a practical necessity, but also effectively transformed relief into a legal right. As a critical aspect of the defense of the national body, child welfare could be seen either as a cornerstone for Weimar democracy or as a lever to restore society to its traditional stability. Weimar child welfare reform was not surprisingly a corporatist compromise. The National Child Welfare Act of 1922 embodied the secular, social-liberal model of reform, but it also created a place for Christian charities within the national youth bureaus established by the new law.[40] In addition, despite the article in the constitution against censorship, many authorities managed to agree that young persons must be protected from the "trash and dirt" that they might read or see in movies, and their concerns culminated in a campaign in 1926 for the "Harmful Publications (Young Persons) Act" intended to filter material that boys and girls might see.[41]

But tensions continued. Progressives favored science and medicine, while conservative reformers continued to advocate force and authority to crush godless youthful rebellion. The child welfare initiatives of the Weimar state also came under attack, not only from those who opposed democracy and refused to recognize the state's legitimacy, but also from eugenicists and racial hygienicists who opposed initiatives that might promote the survival of the "unfit" and "inferior." The welfare bureaucracy also became identified as a center of female power. Government departments would only consider women for senior positions if their presence was "desirable," a principle that virtually excluded them from areas outside of education or welfare. As specialists in girls' education, infant health experts, and professional social workers, women could and did play prominent roles, but as such they and their departments became targets for conservative attack.[42]

Left-wing parties were generally less successful in recruiting youth than groups on the right. Religious youth clubs and the Young German League had been very successful before 1914. When the war broke out, German youth were enthusiastically patriotic, and in the aftermath of the war many were willing to listen to the arguments of extreme nationalists. In contrast, the Socialist youth organizations were far less successful. Socialist youth clubs only emerged later and were not very well organized compared to the religious clubs. The attempts of the prewar Socialist Party and Socialist "free" unions to organize the leisure time and influence the attitudes of young workers reached fewer young persons than their competitors and appear to have had much less impact on attitudes.[43] The same was true of both Socialist and Communist youth organizations in Weimar. They competed with each other, and both hurt themselves in competition with "nationalist" societies by identifying themselves as exclusively working class. It may have been that young German workers, usually raised in religious or conservative milieus, were usually religious and usually patriotic, and that the "top-down" efforts of conservative moral reformers fitted with the "bottom-up" dispositions of their targets. If so, they therefore were inevitably more effective than any Socialist effort was likely to be.

The working class

The working class also remained an object of contention, but the terms altered following the war. First, the changed political system meant that parties claiming to represent the workers could contend directly for power. Second, the extension and multiplication of government activities made a broader range of aspects of individuals' lives into objects of government policy, but it also made those individuals aware of themselves as groups with particular interests. Young-sun Hong emphasizes the increasing conflict generated by the rising number of groups demanding government support. As seen above, in the cases of women and youth, the proposals to deal with publicly perceived "problems" emanated from groups with very different values and agendas. National programs resulted from the push and pull of the interests of political parties, social work professionals, would-be reformers, and representatives of the target groups, who also often disagreed among themselves. The division between Socialists and Communists, both claiming to represent "the" working class, was only one of the most visible of these divisions. These conflicts and the multiplying claims for support placed a heavy burden on the available political and financial resources of the republic, and the resulting frustrations embittered political life.[44]

The conflicts were often fought out at the local level because national legislation reserved extensive areas of action to state and municipal governments. Older traditions of independent urban communities continued even under the new and formally centralized administrative systems. The complexities, and the local focus, can be seen in Wilfried Rudloff's study of Munich, and in the intentional pun in its title (The Welfare City, or *Wohlfahrtsstadt*, rather than the welfare state or *Wohlfahrtsstaat*). Munich differed from other cities in the small relative size of large-scale industry, and in being the center of a Catholic state, but it was typical in the determination of the middle classes to deliver social services in combination with a program of moral improvement. The poor working classes were to be uplifted as well as cared for. At the same time, local elites believed in holding pure welfare, and the costs of all programs, to a bare minimum. Voluntary effort was both cheap and exemplary, but might require supplementation from newly emerging professional groups. A broad array of private and semi-private organizations sometimes filled gaps left by public agencies, and sometimes competed with those same agencies.[45] And again, Germany was not unique, for the same issues and the same messy complexities can be seen in the parallel debates in Britain, France, the United States, and Japan.

Who were the workers? As in previous generations, most were young, and many of them were women, obvious facts that were often ignored in the debate. However, they were less mobile than before the war, a fact that has only come into focus more recently. After increasing for half a century, the rates of migration into German cities stabilized from 1900 to 1912 and then declined. The rates in the 1920s were half those of the two decades before the war. As seen in previous chapters, the high rates of migration into cities were the net results of very much higher rates of total in and outmigration, much of it seasonal. Family groups, the main contributors to the net increase in urban populations, became less likely to move than before. And young men, the major contributors to the huge total flows, became much less likely to move.

Steve Hochstadt argues that this change reflected a fundamental structural shift in employment patterns. The war played a role. One-third of the men born between 1892 and 1895 had died by 1918, and among the war dead, single men and men from rural districts were overrepresented because of the pattern of mobilization and exemptions. The pool of those most likely to migrate was therefore greatly reduced. However, the available figures show that the decline began before the war. Further, although we might be inclined to blame the dislocations of Weimar and the depression for the low rates of the 1920s and 1930s, the rates of total migration have remained at these new low levels since the Second World War as well.

What had happened? Throughout the middle decades of the nineteenth century, millions of young men moved from village to town to city and back again through the year, eking out their living with spring planting, summer brickmaking, construction, possibly the shifting of materials in a factory, and fall harvesting. The use of machinery for planting and harvesting increased, and this accelerated after 1900. As noted above, the number of women recorded working on family farms increased. Families that owned larger farms dispensed with more expensive day laborers when they could, and many families that owned very small farms found that they could produce a living income without the need for the husband to migrate among jobs through the year. "The increase in the agricultural population after 1907," concludes Hochstadt, "represented a move of landowning peasants back to their farms, where they found a greater investment of time and machines could replace migration as a source of income." Meanwhile, in the towns and cities some previous sources of temporary work, such as brickmaking, were mechanized. And a key aspect of the rationalization movement in large-scale industry was the creation of a more permanent labor force, including where necessary married women. Available figures show a large increase in the proportion of industrial workers over 40 and in the proportion of married women among female workers.[46]

The decline in migration may be the underlying cause of the decline in investment in new housing, compared to the prewar period. In the case of Munich and other cities, public debate led to a widely perceived shortage of housing, but measures of housing shortages were confused with plans and proposals for housing improvement. This had both political and cultural aspects. The infamous "rent barracks" of prewar cities were widely held to cause social dislocation, but also to produce a common class consciousness and solidarity among the poor workers who lived in them. Governments at all levels intervened in the housing market during the war to restrict the powers of landlords. As with other social welfare measures, these initiatives were extended and systematized after the war, and culminated in the Tenant Protection Law of 1923, which greatly limited the right of landlords to evict tenants. A wide consensus held that renter protection was a useful mechanism for ensuring social and political stability. But if rents were to be held "low" and the "rights" of renters protected (that is, rents set below market rates and tenants made safe from eviction), governments would have to intervene further. Private interests would construct housing only if it were profitable, and, if rents were fixed by law, this was unlikely. Either government authorities would have to build, or rely on private builders, who demanded profits. The result was often to construct some public or "social" housing and to grant subsidies in both directions, both to renters and to private builders.[47]

The blocks of housing constructed in Berlin by Martin Wagner's GEHAG cooperative, by Frankfurt city planner Ernst May, by Gropius and the Bauhaus staff in Dessau, and elsewhere between 1925 and 1930, defined the look of "modern" multi-unit housing, with flat roofs, undecorated exteriors, common garden spaces, and clean austere interiors. Frequently sponsored and subsidized by Socialist municipal governments, they were intended both to house and to civilize the working class. The flat roofs were not functional, but an announcement of the programmatic style. The apartments replaced the traditional combined kitchen–living area (*Wohnküche*) with the separate "Frankfurt kitchen," intended to shift the focus of the dwelling toward a modest version of the bourgeois salon. In this new living room, the husband and father would hold sway. The wife and mother would prepare food in the kitchen. The children would work on their school assignments in their "workrooms," which became their "sleeping rooms" when the collapsible "Frankfurt bed" was unfolded. Outside the family dwelling were communal meeting halls, and carefully managed building arrangement would maximize both open space and housing density. Heiligenthal's rule, that rows should be spaced no less than twice their block height apart, was extended by Gropius to prove the efficiency of high-rise slabs. The simple exteriors and stripped interiors were intended to reduce costs and make the production of prefabricated elements possible. A dwelling, said Gropius, is a "machine for living," a "technical-industrial organism," and since "most individuals have the same living requirements," all dwellings should be the same in order to avoid a "wasteful and misplaced emphasis on individuality."[48]

Mass culture and popular culture

Today it seems obvious that high incomes and wide participation in popular culture are crucial sources of economic growth, and that modern mass culture works to break down class barriers.[49] This was less obvious to contemporaries between the wars. Popular culture, the things that ordinary people enjoyed in their free time, remained suspect. Conservative government leaders such as Heinrich Brüning believed that excessive consumption was wasteful and fundamentally immoral. On the left, Communists insisted that the role of workers' culture was only to aid in bringing about the revolution, and Socialists believed that workers should rise to participate in Germany's inherited high culture. Manufacturers, as members of the upper classes, believed that consumption was and should be restrained by the existing class structure. As a result, they believed that the domestic market was limited, and their production and marketing decisions were based on that belief. Their beliefs and their actions therefore worked to keep the market limited, slowed growth, and made the economy less resistant to downturns.

The story of the automobile illustrates these points. Before the First World War, automobile ownership in Europe was restricted to the upper classes. Emperor Wilhelm was an auto aficionado, but the Munich police decreed that there could be no more than 25 motor cars allowed in the city. In 1907, there were only 1000 "fuel distribution places" in the entire empire. Just over 16,000 cars were produced in Germany in 1912, and just under 50,000 were in use. In the United States, Henry Ford had introduced his Model T in 1908. In 1912, Ford produced half of the

356,000 cars made in the United States, and there were 902,000 automobiles in use. The divergence continued in the 1920s. In 1929, there were 422,000 automobiles in use in Germany, and in the United States 23.1 million. At five or six persons per car, every single American could have a seat in an automobile at one time, but only 2.1 million of the 65 million Germans.

German auto makers suffered in the postwar depression and inflation. Stabilization brought recovery but not profitability. As in other industries, the response was a series of mergers, such as the formation of Daimler–Benz in 1926. Daimler and Benz were encouraged to join together by the Deutsche Bank, one of Daimler's major shareholders. However, the new models of the combined firm still targeted the upper-middle class. The least expensive Mercedes cost 6000 marks. Daimler–Benz abandoned the lower end of the market to American-controlled firms. All major American firms constructed plants in Germany during the 1920s. The cheapest model of the General Motors-controlled firm Adam Opel was priced at 2500 marks. In 1928, over one-third of all newly registered automobiles in Germany were produced by foreign companies.

Radio provides another example. In the United States, there were 60,000 radios in 1922, 1 million in late 1923, 4.5 million in 1925, 10.2 million in 1929, and 19.3 million in 1933, slightly behind the number of automobiles. In Germany, there were 9000 radio licenses in 1924, 1 million in 1925, 2 million in 1927, 3 million in late 1929, and 4 million in early 1933, or roughly one per family and roughly the same relative number as in the United States. However, in the United States broadcasting was almost exclusively in the hands of purely commercial stations that vied with one another in giving their audience what they wanted— comedies, soap operas, detective serials, and quiz shows in addition to popular music. In Germany, in 1923–24, the postal ministry, which administered the state's monopoly over radio licensing, divided the country into regions and granted one monopoly license per region. Foreigners, political parties, individuals with close political links, and anyone engaged in producing radio sets were prohibited from owning shares in radio program companies. The ministry maintained majority voting rights through preferred shares in all the companies, and it built and operated the broadcasting stations, which the companies rented on an hourly basis. In 1932, the private companies were taken over by the ministry.

The ministry needed revenue, and the rental charged to program companies and the monthly license fees charged to radio listeners were to balance its budget. But there were social motives as well. In the postal ministry's view, "dirty competition" (*Schmutzkonkurrenz*) had brought forth the "trash and dirt" that polluted the newspapers and movies, and these measures were intended to keep the airwaves clean, German, and above politics, all at once. Hans Bredow, the most influential official in radio matters, said that "While foreign nations strive for a wider range, we strive for deepening." Listening to worthwhile cultural offerings should relieve listeners from the "exhausting restlessness" of modern life. Their houses would become "home" (*Heim*) and would provide a shelter to counteract the superficiality and anonymity of modern society. Serious classical music would enable listeners to discover their "soul," and lectures on music and science would round out the radio's educational mission. The leveling tendencies of modern society would also be combated by a strong regional content in each district, and the flow of people from country to city would be slowed by making urban entertainment available to rural districts.

In fact, economic and technical factors shaped and limited the audience. Only expensive sets could receive outside the immediate vicinity of the transmitters, and the two marks a month charged by the ministry for a license were a substantial fraction of a working-class family's disposable income. The audiences were overwhelmingly urban, and only about 20 per cent were working class. The rapid increase in the total number of licenses conceals very large numbers of cancellations, for instance 221,000 new subscribers in Rhineland-Westphalia in 1929, but 156,000 cancellations. Limited survey information shows the lectures were disliked even by upper-class listeners, and across the social spectrum subscribers simply refused to listen to programs that did not interest them. Radio officials persisted, however, and in 1929 rejected proposals to give listeners a choice between "a coffee-house program every evening for listeners who have no taste and a program of high quality for the others." The Socialists regarded the system as the best one imaginable, one that would familiarize workers with Beethoven and Schiller. The Communists feared "ideological contamination" of workers' minds, and the KPD recommended its members use their sets to tune into broadcasts from the Soviet Union instead.[50]

The number and size of movie theaters also increased rapidly. Contemporary estimates held that two million Germans went to the movies every day by the mid-1920s. Many of the viewers were young, and many of them were female. What they were watching therefore worried the various groups interested in the nation's welfare. Many of the most popular films were American, and this (along with the statistics that showed that 70 per cent of novels published were "trash") contributed to the move for the 1926 law to protect young people from "filth and dirt." However, the "Hollywood invasion" and the threat of "Americaniza-tion" were met by a countervailing "boredom with America" (Ameri-kamüdigkeit), which in retrospect appears part of the ebb and flow of popular genres and the continual search for novelty in the commercial world of popular culture.[51]

German film in fact did well against foreign competition. The intro-duction of sound placed greater stress on national content, and reduced the popularity of American films. It also helped that German films were of high quality. In addition to Expressionist films, the *Kammerfilm* or "chamber films" focusing closely on character, the New Sobriety move-ment with its emphasis on hard-edged understated realism, a range of more or less explicitly "proletarian" films inspired in part by the success of Sergei Eisenstein's *Battleship Potempkin* (screened in Berlin in 1925), and *Strassenfilm* or "street films" concentrating on the problems of indi-viduals in urban environments provided a rich variety of experience. *People on Sunday* (*Menschen am Sonntag*, 1930), a variation on the *Strassenfilm* set in a white-collar milieu, followed five young people on an outing to the Wannsee. It featured improvisation by amateur actors and was a collaborative effort by four future Hollywood directors, Robert Siodmak, Edgar G. Ulmer, Billy Wilder, and Fred Zinnemann.

Alfred Hugenberg gained control of Ufa, the largest company, in 1927. He faced the same problems that had bedeviled Ludendorff during the war. Marxists and Jews played key roles. No one could control output entirely. Ufa was a business, and success depended on experimen-tation and on the reception of the films by the audience.[52] With the introduction of sound, Ufa added to its already impressive technical skills and produced an ongoing series of light and lively films, many in multi-language versions for export. *The Blue Angel* (*Der blaue Engel*, 1930) with Marlene Dietrich was both a critical and popular success and remains a classic. More typical was Eric Charell's lavish and hugely popular period piece *Congress Dances* (*Der Kongress tanzt*, 1931). Charell returned to the Napoleonic wars, but this time to the aftermath at the Congress of Vienna, which becomes the background for the story of a poor milliner played by Lilian Harvey who has a bitter-sweet romance with Tsar Alexander I, played by Willi Foertsch. The romantic theme song "It comes only once/ It doesn't return" (*Das kommt nur einmal/ Das kommt nicht wieder*), like the film, provided a respite from the deepening depression, but did not pretend to deeper meanings.

Historians have been at least as interested in Weimar film as contemporary moralists. Siegfried Kracauer wrote a version of the *Sonderweg* thesis applied to Weimar film, arguing that German films repeatedly returned to an obsessive fascination with fate, with the need for authority, and with the dilemmas of individuals trapped between the unpleasant but unavoidable alternatives of tyranny or chaos.[53] Detlev Peukert focused on youth and particularly the young working-class people who caused so much contemporary concern. "The early entry into working life, living conditions of the family, and a sort of realism focused on obtaining the necessities of life" led to "an appetite for gripping stories without complex characters, combined with wishful thinking derived from the real world even if, when seen in detail, the characters strove for goals that were difficult or impossible to obtain."[54] Klaus Kreimeier emphasizes the "anti-democratic" and "authoritarian" qualities of films such as the very popular *Fridericus Rex* (1922). He regrets that the left did not appeal to the "psychic and emotional life" of the nation and allowed "reactionary forces" an uncontested monopoly over the "imagination of the masses."[55]

Popular culture must appeal to the market. Mass culture may be produced by large centralized interests, but it cannot simply be imposed on an unwilling audience. It may not belong to the lower classes in the same way that historical popular cultures did, but it is not only "the culture of the 'other.'" Youth, as noted above, may very well have absorbed conservative values from their schooling and from a range of associations. All Germans had been stunned by the defeat and resented the terms of the Versailles Treaty. All shared the general economic insecurity. It would be surprising to find that popular culture did not reflect these facts. An entire genre of popular novels invented imaginary endings to the war in which Germany emerged victorious.[56] Nevertheless, when asked why they went to movies, the majority of young people said they went to pass the time. Movies were a social event, and an entertainment. They did identify with the characters they watched on the screen, but they knew the world portrayed in film was fictional.[57] As we will see in the next chapter, the problem for Weimar's political leaders was not the fictional world of popular novels and films, but the disjointed and unstable world of reality.

Notes

1. Joseph Goebbels, *Michael: A German Fate through the Pages of a Diary* (*Michael. Ein deutsches Schicksal in Tagebuchblättern*) (Munich, 1929). These and the following quotations are from Richie 1983.
2. Gay 1968.
3. Kondratiev 1928.
4. Maddison 1995, p. 65.
5. Figures from Mitchell 1992; 1993.
6. See Bordo and Kydland 1995.
7. Rooth 1993.
8. Eichengreen and Temin 2000, p. 183.
9. Eichengreen 1992; James 1992.
10. Eberhard Kolb, *The Weimar Republic* (London and New York: Routledge, 1998. German edn., 1984; English trans. 1988), pp. 41–2, 167; William Carr, *A History of Germany, 1815–1990* (4th edn., London: Arnold, 1991), pp. 270–2.
11. Mayer 1967; Maier 1975.
12. Marks 1969.
13. Felix 1971.
14. Maier 1975; Feldman 1977.
15. Feldman 1993.
16. Holtfrerich 1986, export figures from Hoffmann 1965, p. 822.
17. Feldman 1993.
18. Hoffmann 1965.
19. Temin 1971; 1989; Kruedener 1990; Spoerer 1997.
20. Nolan 1994, p. 9.
21. Homburg 1991.
22. Borchardt 1991.
23. Schmitt 1927.
24. Bowie 1998, pp. 147–9.
25. Ash 1995; Harrington 1996.
26. See Willett 1978; McCloskey 1997.
27. Whitford 1984; Neumann 1993.
28. Weindling 1989; Schwartz 1995.
29. Usborne 1992; Grossmann 1995.
30. Rouette 1997.
31. Nolan 1994, Ch. 10; Hagemann 1996.
32. Theweleit, 1977–78.
33. Tatar 1995.
34. See Hong 1997.
35. Stoehr 1985.
36. Mitchell and Koven 1990; Reagin 1995; Dickinson 1996.

37. Koonz 1986.
38. Allen 1991.
39. Peukert 1986.
40. Dickinson 1996; Crew 1998, Ch. 7.
41. Stieg 1990; Petersen 1992.
42. See Hong 1997; Crew 1998, Chs. 2–3.
43. Linton 1991; Dickinson 1996.
44. Hong 1998.
45. Rudloff 1998.
46. Hochstadt 1999, pp. 226–33.
47. Führer 1995; Saldern 1995.
48. Willett 1978, Chs. 11–12; Frampton 1980, Ch. 15.
49. Abrams 1990.
50. Führer 1997.
51. See Saunders 1994.
52. Kreimeier 1996, p. 3.
53. Kracauer 1947.
54. Peukert 1986, p. 185.
55. Kreimeier 1996, pp. 96, 176.
56. Denham 1992.
57. Saldern 1990.

CHAPTER 10

THE POLITICS OF FEELING AND
THE SEARCH FOR STABILITY

In 1918, Max Weber delivered an address entitled "Politics as a Profession" at the University of Munich. Published in 1919, like so many of his works it has been immensely influential. The first crucial fact about professional politicians, said Weber, is that they are paid. Political leaders no longer live "for" politics, but "off" politics. They need their jobs and they need jobs for their followers, and therefore the struggle for patronage increases as the number of parties increases. In addition, professional politicians need to attract votes. Democracy means candidates must "woo" the masses. These two facts Weber believed had led to a fundamental change in political leadership. Previously leaders emerged from the class of qualified and principled "notables." Democracy and professionalization, however, had led to rule by party "machines." Politics, thought Weber, had become corrupted. Competition among party machines leads to an emphasis on the "demagogic effect of the leader's *personality*," on his "will," and particularly on his "speech." Parties with such leaders, Weber believed, would succeed. Parties of the educated middle classes could not compete with mass-based machines, and individual notables could not compete with charismatic demagogues. However, the pursuit of power for its own sake leads to an "intoxication" that replaces the sense of struggle for a cause. This sense of responsibility and commitment is a necessity for good government, but in the competition among political machines, leaders no longer accepted personal moral responsibility for their decisions. Germany, said Weber, faced a "polar night" in public life.[1]

Ten years later, when Josef Goebbels' novel *Michael* turned to politics, it again reflected contemporary Expressionist mannerisms, but also the attitudes of Nazi leaders, both toward the educated elite and toward the masses. Michael becomes a student but is distressed to find the universities full of weak-willed pale faces, the "bespectacled highbrows." It is not here that "the future leaders of the nation" will be found. Michael, named after the German Everyman figure, is himself of

370

solid peasant stock, and he will always retain his connection to the land: "I stand with both feet on the hard soil of the homeland. Around me is the smell of the soil. Peasant blood mounts up slow and healthy within me." But the peasant is not the leader either. Rather, Michael argues that a leader must be a combination of the poet and the politician, someone able to act on the people (*Volk*) as a sculptor acts on a block of stone. Politics is the creative art of the state, just as a painting is the creative art of the painter. "To turn the masses into a *Volk* and form the *Volk* into a state, that has always been the fundamental essence of all true politics."

Michael does meet the man he believes to be the leader:

> That evening I sit in a big hall with a thousand others and see him again, hear him who awakened me.
> Now he stands in the midst of a loyal congregation.
> He seems to have grown in stature.
> There is so much strength in him, and a sea of light gleams from those big blue eyes.
> I sit among those others, and it seems as if he is speaking to me quite personally.
> About the blessing of work! Whatever I only ever felt or guessed at, he puts into words. My confessions and my faith: here they gain shape.
> I feel his strength filling my soul.
> Here is young Germany, and those who work in the blacksmith's shop of the new Reich. Anvil 'til now, but a hammer before long.
> Here is my place.
> Around me are people I never saw and I feel like a child as tears well up in my eyes.[2]

Many young people listened to the arguments of the extreme right wing. In contrast to the Conservative or Liberal Parties, the Nazis effectively portrayed themselves as a party of youthful vigor. Many young people were also willing to listen to the arguments of the Communists. A gap opened up between an older generation of Socialist Party members and voters and a younger generation of workers who appear to have looked either to the right or the left for more extreme solutions than the Socialist Party was able to offer. The rhetoric of right and left overlapped. Poet and Communist Party Reichstag representative Johannes Becher opened his book *Forward, Red Front!* with a hymn to "Struggle" ("Kampf"):

This book is born of struggle.
It is struggle.
It wants more struggle.
Pure works of art are for after the victory.
We however are in the midst of the battle.
O that all artists, writers and
Thinkers might realize this!
Start seeing!
The day of decision is near.
Forward!
Struggle![3]

Nevertheless, youth alone cannot be blamed for the difficulties of establishing and maintaining democracy, nor can the masses of ordinary German women and men, nor even can demagogic leaders. The images of the political leader as artist, life as struggle, the healthy peasant, degenerate intellectuals, and the need to energize the masses were common clichés. Many agreed with Weber that threats of radicals from both right and left reflected the unfortunate consequences of the rise of mass society and the decline of the autonomous individual and the possibility of rationality in public life. Later historians have noted as well that all of the older dimensions of the German question remained after the war, compounded by defeat. But despite their ominous parallels with Weber's analysis, in his novel Goebbels, the Nazi Party functionary, is currying favor with his party's leader, and Becher's rhetoric was directed against other left-wing intellectuals with whom he disagreed as often as against the capitalist system. When their books were written, both the Nazi and Communist Parties were on the fringes of political life, with no prospect of gaining power.

Weber withdrew from active politics and died prematurely in 1920, so those who heard or read his address did not have the opportunity of accepting his invitation to join him in ten years' time and look again at German politics. His analysis appears prescient because of what did happen. But his lament is rooted in its time. His nostalgic picture of the prewar world bore little relation to the reality of politics in Bismarckian or Wilhelminian Germany. Rather, it expresses the deep dissatisfaction felt by the *Bildungsbürgertum*, the affluent and cultured academically trained upper-middle class, when they looked at the emergence of the masses as a political force. Democracy had enemies, but perhaps more importantly it had few friends. In what appeared to be a crisis, it was

Weber's notables who surrendered the republic in the hope of turning, or returning, to something better. Whether that outcome was inevitable and whether Weimar "failed" are questions that continue to motivate research across a range of specializations.[4]

Establishing democracy, 1918–24

Despite Goebbels' call for a leader, Becher's call for revolutionary struggle, and Weber's pessimism about the quality of public life, the new republic survived. As seen in Chapter 9, by 1924 the economy had achieved a new stability. The same could be said in politics, though, as with the economy, stability only came after a series of severe shocks. Putting ourselves into the minds of contemporary women and men, however, we can see that many members of the middle classes worried about the decline in standards represented by the intrusion of the masses into public life. Their fears reflected their prejudices, but the fact that they were afraid was important in its own right. In addition, the deep division between right and left was both a psychological and an objective fact. The Fatherland Party sponsored by the army had more members in 1918 than the Socialist Party, and government officials continued to support right-wing agitation. They had widespread support especially among the property-owning classes and in the countryside. This broad pool of Conservative support might be difficult to organize, but it was a potent force opposing radical social and political change.

On the left, the Socialist Party had split into a Majority Socialist Party (SPD) and an Independent Socialist Party (USPD). Radicals in the USPD in turn formed the nucleus of the Communist Party (KPD). In Russia, the collapse of the Tsarist regime and its successive replacement by a provisional government, a Socialist government, and a Communist government provided a model of revolutionary change propelled by mass action. The workers' councils aligned themselves with the expelled radical members of the Socialist Party in 1917, and they became the main support first of the Independent Socialist Party and then of the Communist Party. The councils, and more importantly their members and supporters, remained outside the control of any organized body, and therefore remained suspect in the eyes of even leaders on the left, in the unions and the Socialist Party, for instance. Those such as Karl Liebknecht and Rosa Luxemburg who called for "all power to the councils" were a tiny minority even among the radicals of the Independent Socialist Party.

Another aspect is the collective emotional roller coaster Germans had all shared. From the bitterness of the protests of 1917, to the rekindled enthusiasm in 1918 when the Brest-Litovsk Treaty and new victories in the west made it seem that victory was within Germany's grasp after all, the nation suddenly descended into the shock of the armistice, collapse, defeat, and the "dictated" Treaty of Versailles. The psychological trauma reflected the government's continuing control over information. The widespread calls for annexations had been combined with a suppression of dissenting opinion. The public was not informed of the weakening military situation. On the other hand, information did not flow the other way either. One of General Wilhelm Groener's complaints as head of the War Office had been that field commanders were not told of the economic difficulties at home. At the level of ordinary women and men, those who experienced the front, almost all men, did not know how those at home, many of them women, suffered. In turn, the civilians at home did not know what those at the front had experienced.

Those to blame refused to take responsibility. Having demanded an armistice, Ludendorff then attempted to deny he had done so. Having been forced to abdicate, Emperor Wilhelm left for a comfortable retirement in the Netherlands. He lived until 1941, incapable of any awareness that his actions might have contributed to Germany's defeat. Hindenburg personified the army's continued refusal to admit its incompetence, and also provided the label that has persisted, when he told a Reichstag inquiry that "the German Army was stabbed in the back." Bureaucrats and officials at all levels, religious and educational authorities, leaders and members of the array of semi-official and voluntary organizations, all continued to believe that Germany's governing institutions were not only good but superior, and therefore that, if Germany had lost the war, then Germany must have been betrayed.

Authority seemed to dissolve. Navy commanders planned a suicidal assault on the British blockading forces to redeem the navy's honor, and confronted a mutiny. The sailors adopted the council form of government, and the rebellion spread in the first days of November 1918 to other navy bases, to Hamburg, to Hanover, to Cologne. Army garrisons proved unreliable. In Munich, Kurt Eisner, leader of the Independent Socialist Party in Bavaria, was released from prison, placed himself at the head of a radical coalition of workers, soldiers, and farmers, and on November 7 seized power and declared a "democratic and social republic." In Berlin, on November 9, Prince Max surrendered power to Friedrich Ebert, head of the Socialist Party. Ebert had lost two sons in the war and would probably have preferred a reformed constitutional monarchy, but allowed himself to be persuaded that a republic must be declared.

To ensure that Germany did not descend into the chaos of a Bolshevik revolution as in Russia, Ebert accepted an offer made by Groener. Groener placed the army at the new Chancellor's disposal, in return for promises to facilitate the orderly return of the troops to Germany, and especially to combat the forces of the radical leftists. Ebert also accepted the additional demand of Groener and his aide Major Kurt von Schleicher that he reject proposals to disband the existing army and replace it with a people's militia with elected officers. Confronted with further disorders in Berlin and Russian Bolshevik activity on the eastern borders, Ebert and his advisors called on the army to maintain order. There were not many regular army units remaining that could be considered reliable. Hindenburg and Groener instead encouraged demobilized officers to recruit "free corps" among their former non-commissioned officers and enlisted men. A minority of returned soldiers found it congenial to slip back into the violent life they had known before, and predictably they tended to be extremely conservative. The government used them to suppress the radical uprisings in Berlin and then in other centers. Among several thousand killed were Liebknecht and Luxemburg.

In Munich, Eisner had attempted to govern through the councils of workers, soldiers, and peasants. In foreign policy he demanded that Germany accept blame for the war as the basis for reconciliation with France. The economic situation deteriorated. His support in Bavaria eroded, and Socialist leaders in Berlin were hostile. His party was defeated by the Socialists in elections, and he was on his way to tender his resignation as Prime Minister when he was murdered. A subsequent attempt to establish a Communist government was defeated by local free corps units and reinforcements from Berlin. The revolution in Bavaria ended as in Berlin with a violent wave of right-wing repression.[5]

The Socialist government had alienated a portion of its natural constituency in the working class by using the army and free corps units to defeat the left, but without winning any support on the right. During the negotiations over the Versailles Treaty and reparations, the government had to contend with repeated threats of military insurrection. A loose anti-republican National Association had formed, including prominent figures such as Ludendorff. Wolfgang Kapp, an East Prussian politician, began to seek support for a coup among party and business leaders, but in early 1920 his associate General Walther Lüttwitz impetuously demanded that Ebert revoke orders to disband the free corps units, call new elections, and appoint a non-party government of experts. When Ebert refused he ordered free corps units to march on Berlin. The regular army took its lead from General Hans von Seeckt, who insisted that soldiers could not fire upon their wartime comrades, and then went on leave. Ebert and his ministers left Berlin for Dresden and then Stuttgart. They called on the working class to defend the republic, and the unions imposed a general strike that paralyzed the transportation and public utilities systems. Kapp and Lüttwitz also discovered that business leaders were surprised and angered by their actions, and that they could not rely on the military garrisons for support. They were unable to establish a coherent administration, and by March the coup had collapsed.

As seen in Chapter 9, the republic now confronted the challenges of reparations and inflation. As seen in Table 10.1, the elections of June 1920 drastically reduced the power of the Socialists, temporarily increased the power of the Independent Socialists, and also increased the power of the middle-class and Conservative parties. The Socialists withdrew from the government, leading to instability and finally the appointment of Cuno's non-party cabinet by Ebert, who had been elected President by the constitutional assembly. The hardship created by the hyperinflation by mid-1923 caused strikes, in Upper Silesia and the northern port cities in June, in the Berlin metal industry in July, and among agricultural laborers across the country in late July and August. Demonstrations in a number of cities turned into riots, and when the printers' union went on strike the capital faced a threatening shortage of paper money.

Gustav Stresemann, head of the People's Party (*Deutsche Volkspartei* or DVP), became Chancellor and, as noted in Chapter 9, succeeded in ending the passive resistance, negotiating a reparations settlement, and implementing a currency reform to end the inflation. However, again there were threatened coups from the right, and again there were attempts to exploit the economic discontent to stage a Communist revolution from the left. Military units raised secretly by the Cuno government to defend the eastern border plotted to march on Berlin, and, in Munich, Adolf Hitler attempted to seize power. Poorly organized, neither of these movements succeeded, but the threat of a right-wing counter-revolution based in Bavaria appeared very real for a time. The expanding Communist Party, encouraged by the Soviet-sponsored international organization (the Comintern), launched threatening actions in Saxony and Thuringia. Here Stresemann intervened using Ebert's emergency powers under Article 48 of the constitution. These successes, however, alienated both right and left. Stresemann's coalition government weakened and he faced opposition from the right within his own party. Finally, the Socialist Party withdrew its support and joined with the Nationalists to bring about his fall in late November 1924, shortly after the restoration of stability in Bavaria.

Ebert was outraged at the behavior of the Socialist Party's leaders. "The reasons why you have toppled the Chancellor will be forgotten in six weeks, but you will feel the effects of your stupidity for the next ten years." The Socialists' decision to leave government and their decision not to support Stresemann have been interpreted as tragic errors that undermined Weimar democracy. In turn, Ebert's detractors insist that his use of the army to restore order damaged Weimar democracy at its moment of birth, and that his use of emergency powers to appoint Cuno and to repress the left set the dangerous precedents that paved the way to its death. As always, this is hindsight. As with the economy, it seemed in 1924 that forceful action by responsible leaders had secured the republic against both external and internal threats, precisely the sort of principled commitment Weber believed unlikely in a democracy.

The old milieus in a new generation

Hardening religious identities in the middle decades of the nineteenth century and the emerging class identities of the later decades formed the basis of separate social-cultural milieus. Catholics, urban workers, Jews, and more loosely rural and urban Protestants divided, and, as seen in Chapter 7, these group identities structured the voting patterns of pre-war Germany. One of imperial Bismarckian and Wilhelmine Germany's great failures was its inability to overcome these divisions, and one of the reasons for that failure was its inability to recognize the divisions as legitimate. Here democratic Weimar Germany, beginning from different premises, possessed the potential for success. However, the heritage of division and the search for new absolutes made that success more difficult to achieve.

German Jews and anti-Semitism

In one crucial respect Weimar Germany did fail. German Jews were forced to cope with a widespread and threatening anti-Semitism. Bizarre beliefs and prejudices moved from the fringes to the main-stream. Goebbels' novel *Michael* was violently anti-Semitic. Jews make Michael physically ill. He believes they have despoiled his people, con-taminated German customs, and ruined the nation's morals. The Jew, Michael says, is the lie personified. Christ is truth nailed to the cross. Christ was their first great enemy, and that is why they killed him. "Christ cannot have been a Jew. I do not have to prove this scientifically, it is so!"[6]

Goebbels was an official in a political party that included anti-Semitism as one of its key beliefs. The Nazis were far from power when Goebbels wrote *Michael*, but they rode a wave of bigotry. Ten years earlier, Artur Dinter's novel *Die Sünde wider das Blut* (*The Sin Against the Blood*, 1919) became a best-seller. Dinter's hero Hermann Kämpfer falls in love with Johanna and marries her. She does every-thing that could be expected of the perfect wife. But she has a dark past that comes to light when she gives birth to Hermann's child. To his horror, the baby is a "genuine" Jewish child with swarthy skin and black curly hair. Johanna confesses that ten years before she had been seduced by a Jewish officer, who abandoned her. The baby she bore then died at birth, but her new baby looks like the first. Hermann is then told that a thoroughbred mare is ruined if she is mated with an inferior stallion, for this corrupts her, and she will be incapable of producing thoroughbred offspring. And, similarly, a single sexual contact with a Jew will ruin the reproductive system of a healthy Aryan woman. Hermann demands the name and regiment of the officer, seeks him out, and challenges him to a duel. When the officer refuses, Hermann shoots him dead on the spot. He returns home to find that Johanna has killed both the baby and herself. The poisoned hypodermic needle is still sticking out of her breast. Dinter hammered home his message: "Now consider the damage that year in, year out is inflicted upon the German race by Jewish youths who every year seduce thousands upon thousands of German maidens!" At his trial, Hermann labels Jews vampires and calls for their extermination.

Possibly even more pernicious was the widespread deployment of less overt stereotypes in literature and film that portrayed Jews as degenerate, sinister, and foreign elements. Thomas Mann's story *Blood of the Wälsungs* (*Wälsungenblut*) centers on the incestuous love between twin brother and sister, denied normal outlets because of the excessively sophisticated and oppressively artificial environment of their Jewish family. Mann had written the story in 1904. He did not publish it then for fear of offending the Jewish family of his fiancée, but he did publish it in 1921. Murnau's *Nosferatu* rests on a text that associates vampires with Jews, foreigners that prey on innocent victims and suck the blood of the national body, and, in the film, a Jew monitors the hero's movements and ensures that he does not miss his carriage to the vampire's castle. Lang's *M* casts Peter Lorre, a foreign Hungarian-born Jewish actor, as the serial killer who preys on young German girls. He exists outside society, driven by some unknowable compulsion, and even murderous criminals see him as an alien being that must be eliminated for normal life to proceed. As seen in Chapter 9, the film has an anti-feminine subtext and turns the killer into a victim, but the Nazis simply lifted segments showing Lorre cringing in fear and included them in documentaries that pretended to present "the eternal Jew" as the cowardly murderer he really was.[7]

As mass entertainment, popular novels and film must appeal to the audience's hopes, fears, and prejudices. Anti-Semites did not have the field to themselves. Dinter's novel deconstructs itself—there were no Jewish officers in the army before the war, and Hermann's "medical friend" is retelling legends from a century before. *The Sin Against the Blood* was parodied by Hans Reimann, who worked a series of puns to produce the title *Arthur the Sinner: The Ink Against the Blood*. Published in 1922, it sold 693,000 copies by the end of the year. The evidence is subject to several interpretations. Obviously there was a widespread market for bizarre anti-Semitic fantasies. On the other hand, there was an equally wide market for a cutting parody that emphasized the ridiculousness of anti-Semitism. Again, this reflects divisions in German society inherited from before 1914, and the two books together illustrate the nearly unbridgeable gap between opposing sides in the debate over the German identity.[8]

The experiences of individual Jews and Jewish families varied from region to region. The German defeat in 1918 hit Königsberg harder than most other German cities. Trade with the east broke down. New borders isolated the city, separating East Prussia from the rest of Germany. Inflation then destroyed the savings of the predominantly middle-class population, including many of those with whom Jews had socialized before the war. The climate within the city deteriorated, and Jews were among the first victims. As noted in Chapter 7, military and bureaucratic circles had never received Jews. The anti-Semitism propagated by radical nationalists since the 1890s now became more common. In contrast to the pre-1918 period, liberal forces were no longer strong enough to keep this hate campaign at bay. With the rise of the Nazi movement, in particular after 1928, Königsberg became the scene of frequent violent attacks and riots against Jews. By then hardly any non-Jew would defend Jewish rights. Here the social exclusion of Königsberg's Jews was a process that began long before 1933.[9]

In contrast, when we look at Hesse, specifically the liberal metropolis of Frankfurt, the university city of Giessen, or a small town such as Geisenheim, local archives, interviews, and memoirs show Jews to be well integrated, but also realistically engaged in the cultivation of their own Jewish identities and in self-defense. Jews were involved with non-Jews at many levels. Ludwig Landmann, the Lord Mayor of Frankfurt from 1924 to 1933, was Jewish. Class was more important than religion in determining sociability, and upper-class Jews and upper-class Gentiles were more likely to socialize with each other than either were to socialize with lower-class co-religionists. Many of these contacts were strained and ambivalent, but many were genuine and unforced.

Zionists and refugees from Eastern Europe were relatively rare in Hesse. This removed a potential source of conflict among Jews as well as a potential focus for increased anti-Semitism, as seen in other communities such as Königsberg where these groups were larger. In Hesse the rise of Nazism resulted from economic desperation, not anti-Semitism. However, few Gentile Germans considered the "Jewish problem" to be a major issue. Tolerance did not translate into active support. Under the Nazi regime, the majority of Gentile Germans accepted legal discrimination against Jews. They might not approve of or show any enthusiasm for direct violence against Jews, but only a few opposed the laws openly, or expressed publicly their disgust for officially sanctioned violence, for instance the Kristallnacht riots.[10]

Among Jews themselves, Michael Brenner argues that there was a "renaissance" of Jewish culture during the Weimar years. As seen in previous chapters, secularism and mobility had eroded traditional Jewish practices and the traditional knowledge that accompanied them. Jews experienced pressure to assimilate. Then the confrontation with racist anti-Semitism had provided an impulse for some to rethink their identifications and their identity. Jews of all social classes and political inclinations considered themselves Germans, and they found republican Weimar a generally congenial environment. Weimar provided new outlets, both for Jews as individuals and for Jews as communities. In addition to contributions of individual Jews across the entire range of Weimar culture, there was a widespread search for identity among German Jews, contributing to the revival of Jewish culture. Large areas of knowledge about Judaism and Jewish history that had been neglected for a generation were revived. The search for community led many to adopt "ethnicity" in place of "faith" as the central bonding element. Jewish community councils increasingly took on such secular tasks as social welfare, education, and culture, and they became politicized as a result.

The expanded transmission of Jewish knowledge often occurred through adult education and promotion of Jewish scholarship. Jewish scholars and publishers found audiences for histories of the Jews, multi-volume Jewish encyclopedias, and translations of Hebrew classics. Franz Rosenzweig was instrumental as the leader of the Jewish *Lehrhaus* movement. The "houses of study" provided opportunities for thousands to study Jewish history and culture. Lectures and discussions appealed across a broad spectrum of Jewish opinion. They succeeded in raising interest among non-practicing Jews as well.

The motives of participants varied, reflecting previous divisions. Zionists studied in a *Lehrhaus* to discover the limits of their integration into German society. Liberals attended the same lectures and discussions because they believed increased knowledge of Jewish culture would further their goal of German-Jewish synthesis. An Eastern European Jewish intellectual community appeared in Germany in the early 1920s, and many German Jews encountered Hebrew and Yiddish culture directly for the first time through these contacts. There were authors who sought to portray "authentic" Jews, often portrayed as Eastern European, in unfavorable contrast to the German Jews who denied their heritage. On the other hand, writers such as Else Lasker-Schüler were widely read by the whole German public, and their particular message was not necessarily singularly Jewish. Specifically Jewish music and painting were often religious, not ethnic. And, despite the resurgence of interest and activity in the Jewish cultural sphere, divisions remained, among classes, among political persuasions, and between recent migrants and the majority.

Simultaneously, some German Jews felt obliged to reconsider their traditional ties to Liberalism. For some this constituted a reshaping of Jewish Liberalism, parallel to developments among other Liberals, and for others it meant a break with the Liberal tradition itself. Most Jews continued to vote for the Liberal parties until their collapse after 1930. Many Jews then cast their votes for the Social Democrats or the Catholic Center as the only parties committed to defense of the republic. The proportional representation system meant that these votes all counted, but German Jews were a small group, unable to influence electoral outcomes except in local elections in municipalities where they were especially numerous. Brenner concludes that the advent of the Nazi regime fundamentally altered the conditions under which Jews lived, a break more like that in the Hessian urban centers than the thickening fog of prejudice and discrimination in Königsberg.[11]

Catholics in the Weimar system

The religious divisions that marked prewar German society had isolated Catholics in a social and cultural ghetto. For the majority of Catholics the war brought a significant change. However, they emerged from their ghetto in two directions at once. Catholics fought to defend imperial Germany in the First World War. In doing so they supported a ruling establishment that still considered them enemies of the state. At the same time, the Catholic Center Party collaborated with the Socialists and left Liberals in disputes with the government during the war, especially the debates over the Auxiliary Service Law, the peace resolution, and the establishment of the republic. Therefore Catholics reflected the divisions of Weimar into those who looked backward and those who looked forward. Some, particularly in rural areas, did not want to leave their enclosed social system. Those Catholics who wished to step outside their old milieu did not necessarily agree on the role of the Church or the aims of specifically Catholic organizations.

The Church hierarchy leaned to the right. Although opposed to extreme right-wing political parties, Catholic clergy were often anti-Semitic, and frequently supported a notion of a "folk community" based on family descent. This continued a prewar tradition of hostility to social divisions based on economic class. It was also a response to the influence of the Socialist Party and even more to the rise of the extreme left, the Communist Party with its connections to the Soviet Union. Catholic lay leaders favored a stronger and more authoritarian form of government, and remained ambivalent or opposed to the republic. But although they were conservative they did not return to the ultramontane position that Church leaders had adopted in response to the *Kultur-kampf*. Most believed that the German Catholic Church and German Catholic society must not be isolated as before the war. Rather, German Catholics must participate in the broader society, and the Church must adapt to social trends.

The Church encouraged an intensification of piety among individual Catholics and Catholic communities. However, rather than supporting the comprehensive range of associations that had marked and set off Catholic society before the war, their focus came more and more to concentrate on life within the Church itself. This meant that class-based Catholic associations no longer enjoyed the automatic support of the hierarchy. This reflected the political prejudices of the Church hierarchy. Siegfried Weichlein's study of the competing social milieus in Hesse shows the decline of Catholic trade unions, workers' societies, youth organizations, and the broader Catholic People's Association, all of which lost the support of the Church because of their relatively left-wing stance and their support for the republic. Their membership dropped drastically in the mid-1920s.[12]

Within the Center Party, leadership remained with the moderate Wilhelm Marx, a committed supporter of the republic, until his retirement in 1928. The new leader Ludwig Monsignor Kaas and the new parliamentary leader Heinrich Brüning were more conservative and much less supportive of the republic. The Center's 60-plus deputies made it an essential coalition partner, and Marx served four times as Chancellor. However, looking forward in comparison to the postwar world, Weimar Catholics had not managed to conceive of themselves as simply "Germans of the Catholic faith," and the Center Party had not yet managed to conceptualize itself as a broad "people's party" that could appeal to all voters regardless of their religion. As seen in Table 10.1, the Center vote fluctuated within a narrow band, and it never challenged for leadership in its own right.[13]

Membership in Catholic organizations began to grow again after 1929. Now opposition to Communists on the left and Nazis on the right stimulated a Catholic response from both clergy and lay persons. Many of the new members were middle-aged, possibly those who had left or failed to join over the previous decade. Local studies show increasing participation in the sacraments. Where Catholic organizations revived, the Center Party's share of the vote also rose, and the Nazis had little success. However, Brüning's appointment as Chancellor began the period of rule by presidential decree, his policies worsened the depression, and the Center Party's votes gave Hitler the power he needed to establish his dictatorship.

The working-class milieu: Socialists, Communists, and workers

The division of the working-class milieu into Socialist and Communist camps has been seen by left-wing and structuralist historians as a key factor in the Weimar tragedy. Some have blamed the Majority Socialists and argued that the Independent Socialists had a much more realistic view of the realities of power at the end of the war. A more radical policy opposed to the continuation of the old structures and the old leaders in the army, in rural areas, in the bureaucracy, and in industry might have placed the republic on firmer foundations.[14] On the other hand, once the republic came into existence, the Socialists were its staunchest supporters, and other historians have blamed the Communist Party for splitting the labor movement and undermining the republic. In this view, after 1924 the increasingly "Stalinized" leaders of the KPD in Berlin dictated policy from above, expelled dissidents as they emerged, and created another isolated social milieu. As competitors for members and voters, the Communists saw the Socialists as their chief enemy. The ultimate source of this disastrous policy lay not in Berlin but Moscow. Communists had either broken from their Social Democratic heritage or had not absorbed it at all, because they were younger, less skilled, and poorer than Socialists. Rather than former Socialists, Communist workers were likely to be lapsed Catholics, and they were apt to be even more radical than their leaders.[15]

Looking at working-class politics from the standpoint of the national leadership, on the one hand, it is clear that Soviet Russia posed a serious challenge to the ideological standing and the practical political position of the Socialist Party. The response was negative. Ebert and other SPD leaders rejected the Bolshevik revolution as chaotic, and the Soviet model as dictatorial. And, of course, the Soviet Union supported their main rival for working-class support, the German Communist Party. However, the Soviet model could not be ignored, either in the revolutionary years or in period of the first five-year plans after 1929, when the Soviet Union appeared to be escaping the ravages of depression. The SPD failed to press for nationalization of industries during the revolution, because of the agreement between union leaders and employers ensuring jobs for returning soldiers and because of the danger of stimulating further disorder and possibly a right-wing counter-revolution. Over the next decade, support for the republic entailed acceptance of the existing capitalist system as well. The ideas of "economic democracy" advanced in the late 1920s pointed toward developments seen later in postwar West Germany, but the SPD could do little for the millions of unemployed in the early 1930s.

On the other hand, the KPD was an explicitly revolutionary party, committed to the immediate overthrow of capitalism in Germany. Its hyper-masculine, militaristic language and symbols, and its willingness to contemplate violence and civil war, clearly differed from the SPD.[16] The KPD in addition was committed to fostering a worldwide uprising of the proletariat. As the country with a Communist regime in place, the Soviet Union assumed leadership of this movement. Although their relationship with Moscow was not constant, German Communist leaders were not independent. Comintern policies reflected the internal politics of the Soviet Union and especially the rise of Stalin to absolute power. Moscow directed German Communists after 1928 to concentrate their attacks on "social Fascists," that is, on the Socialist Party. This widened the split between the working-class parties, and made effective action against the Nazis more difficult for both.

Looking at working-class politics from the perspective of local members, from Chapter 9 we may make two inferences about the working-class milieu. There was an opportunity for community building among the workers arising from the greater stability of urban populations, because of the decline in seasonal migration. Industrial workers as a class were becoming somewhat older, somewhat more settled, and somewhat more likely to be married. The leaders of working-class parties exercised real power, and particularly at the state and municipal level could introduce new programs to help their constituents, for instance, subsidized housing schemes. At the same time, however, the resources needed for such community-building were eroded by the high levels of unemployment and the violent fluctuations in the economy. Workers, male and female, married and single, were insecure and sometimes hungry. Union membership, about 3 million before the war, declined during the war and then exploded to 6.5 million in 1919 and 9.2 million in 1920, but it then declined to less than 5 million in 1924 before rising again slightly in the late 1920s. The old divisions among Socialist free unions, Catholic Christian unions, and the moderate Hirsch-Duncker unions remained, and the free unions split among Socialist, Communist, and anarchist tendencies. And there was further competition, not only among working-class organizations, but also between them and the institutions established by religious and right-wing groups.

Differences that seemed clear on the national plane blur at the local level. In the Saar district, for instance, the leaders of the Communist Party in Berlin were never able to control local branches or individual party members as they wished. The lived world of Communists overlapped with the Social Democratic social-cultural milieu that KPD leaders denounced obsessively. In striving to forge a disciplined "Red Army" that would also enjoy a mass base, party leaders continually ran up against this left-proletarian "niche society." Efforts to eradicate Social Democracy's reformist, passive legacy were foiled by indifference, circumvention, and hostility. District leaders, as well as ordinary members, skipped meetings and ignored directives. Communist trade union officials only reluctantly implemented separatist policies, while Communist workers disdained them. Members and local leaders refused to abandon leisure organizations that included both Communists and Social Democrats. In order to win their weekly match, a Communist soccer team would play a Socialist striker, and vice versa. Or a Catholic, for that matter. Many Communist and Socialist Party members who came from Catholic backgrounds maintained at least nominal ties with the Church.[17]

The commonalities among working-class members of political organizations seem more significant than their differences. At least until 1930, the KPD was neither an unstable movement of the "uprooted" nor one dominated by unskilled workers. Rather than being extremely young, the plurality of its activist members were men of the "front generation" who had been affected by the war's violence. As such they looked much the same as recruits to the Nazi Party in working-class neighborhoods. Radical right-wing organizations, including and especially the Nazi

Party, made substantial inroads into the working class during the Weimar Republic. Contacts with Nazi organizers showed local Communist leaders that they were in direct competition for members and supporters. Appealing to the same classes of voters, in both the working and lower-middle classes, they sometimes did so by deemphasizing the differences between them. Some Communists believed that Nazis were less conservative and more open to argument than their rhetoric suggested. If Nazi supporters had misunderstood their "true" class position, or had been misled by deceitful Nazi propaganda, then a modified and less dogmatic appeal might win them over to the Communist side. Conan Fischer believes local Communists were more flexible than Socialists or Socialist labor union leaders. He presents evidence of a slight broadening of the KPD's social base in the early 1930s.[18]

As with the Catholic Center, the Socialist Party did not succeed in moving significantly beyond its working-class base to appeal to all classes. Its leaders, especially those from the labor unions, have been criticized as uninspiring and unimaginative. Carlo Mierendorff and a few other young representatives attempted to increase the party's emotional appeal and broaden its electoral base, and their failure has been seen as yet another possible missed turning point.[19] Although the largest party in the Reichstag until 1930, the Socialist Party was generally locked out of the coalitions that included the right-wing Liberal or Conservative Parties. It lost support to the KPD from 1928 onward. The KPD, in turn, despite its successes, was excluded from government, and even if the two parties could somehow have come together they would still never have commanded a majority.

The Conservative milieu

Before 1914, Conservatives dominated their rural strongholds through the Prussian three-class voting system, and some of that local power transferred to the Reichstag as well. The middle classes, in contrast, divided along regional and economic lines, and Liberal parties experienced difficulties at both state and federal levels. For those with inherited position or acquired wealth, however, voting strength did not matter because they were protected by the empire's constitutional system. Weimar was different. Men and women now voted, and under the proportional representation system their votes counted equally. Socialists and Communists not only sat in parliament but also might determine policy. Defeat, revolution, and inflation seemed to place not only the nation but also property itself at risk. Peter Lösche and Franz Walter argue that the sense of threat and the felt need for defense now created the necessary preconditions for a single Conservative milieu. "Millions of Conservative citizens campaigned aggressively in associations of soldiers, gymnasts, shooters, and singers." Demonstrations particularly on the anniversary of the foundation of the empire became a Conservative counterweight to the Socialist celebrations on May Day and the Catholic processions marking religious holidays.[20]

There was no shortage of prophets seeking to lead Conservatives into a new promised land. One who continues to interest historians is Ernst Jünger. Born in 1895, he attempted to run away from home and join the French Foreign Legion. His father prevented him, and he finished *Gymnasium* before the outbreak of war in 1914. He enlisted, was promoted to lieutenant, and fought at the Somme, Cambrai, and in the 1918 offensive. He was wounded seven times, and in 1918 was awarded the *Pour le Mérite*, the army's highest decoration. His memoir of his war experiences, *Storm of Steel* (1920), was hugely successful.[21] His success with this and his subsequent books encouraged a flood of war literature in mid-1920s. During the 1920s, Jünger associated with right-wing figures such as cultural pessimist Moeller van den Bruck, constitutional theorist Carl Schmitt, and Nazi leader Otto Strasser.

Like many others, Jünger was influenced by Spengler and looked to Nietzsche as a mentor. And again, like so many of his generation, his writing embodies "the vaunting posture of German Expressionism, with its cultivation of an internal dynamic that is supposed to discharge itself with stunning energy."[22] Or, as he put it himself, "Write with blood and you will find that blood is spirit." References to will, to struggle, and to the superiority of strength over weakness abound. The details of his writing paint a realistic picture of a new kind of war in which technology had transformed the traditional role of the warrior. But also, in Jünger's view, this new kind of war had created a new race of men. In *Battle as Inner Experience* (1922) he wrote:

> This war is not the end, but the chord that heralds new power. It is the anvil on which the world will be hammered into new boundaries and new communities. New forms will be filled with blood, and might will be hammered into them with a hard fist. War is a great school, and the new man will be of our cut.

The new man of course would be a German and a nationalist, but a different kind of German nationalist. Jünger called for a new consciousness. He and like-minded intellectuals formed a loosely grouped movement of "Conservative revolutionaries" that detested the Weimar Republic but also rejected the Conservative traditions of the Wilhelmine era. Antiparliamentary and antimonarchist, they envisioned themselves playing a tutelary role for the masses by synthesizing nationalism with socialism, thereby reproducing in a civilian context the comradeship of the trenches and permanently transforming the German spirit. All insisted that the republic had to be replaced by some radical change in political system.

Jünger had no political program. His work was contradictory, and some Conservative revolutionaries doubted his utility. However, Roger Woods argues that Jünger exemplified the "new nationalism" precisely in his growing vacillation. Jünger had originally believed that the movement could be unified by a common commitment to what he called the "four pillars of nationalism," the national, the social, the military, and the dictatorial, but, by the late 1920s, he was becoming resigned to the fact that consensus among the new Conservatives was elusive. Disenchanted with the programs that he now believed to be unattainable, Jünger embraced the notion of the "single great personality" who could ultimately provide the movement with the leadership and direction it so obviously lacked. Others also converted to this vision of activist politics. The new nationalist state they wanted could not be built on a programmatic foundation. They had originally intended to become the intellectual vanguard of a movement transcending the political divisions of left and right. Increasingly, however, they came to view nationalism as something intangible that could only be experienced, in effect leaving to others the challenge of political mobilization.[23]

At a more abstract level, Conservative theorists such as Carl Schmitt also had deep misgivings about democracy in general and the Weimar system in particular. He was closer to the centers of power than Jünger, and acted as an advisor to Kurt von Schleicher. Schmitt's worries paralleled those of Weber. His critique of Liberalism was grounded in a broader critique of modern thought, which he regarded as having been infiltrated by the technological. Schmitt saw no emancipatory potential here, and like Weber he saw modern politics as machine-like and dehumanized.[24] In addition, however, Schmitt relativized law to power and to the contingencies of a particular situation, and this led him to emphasize the need for power and decision. He argued, in his 1921 book *Dictatorship*, that in an emergency situation where the life of the state was at stake, only a decisive dictatorial leader could overcome internal divisions. Again, we find the pervasive influence of Nietzsche, and the absolutist Expressionist motifs in Schmitt's friend–enemy distinction, noted in Chapter 9. Schmitt discounted the dangers of emergency powers, of the notion that a leader can represent the common good, of law as the servant of the state, and of the state as an abstract good above all others, and his thought slid from Conservatism to Fascism.

The defining characteristic of prewar social-cultural milieus was their close connection to specific political parties. The Weimar party that should have united the various Conservative groups and thinkers was the Nationalists, the German National People's Party (*Deutschnationale Volkspartei* or DNVP). The DNVP at first looked as if it might develop into a broadly based Conservative opposition party. DNVP representatives participated in the negotiations that resulted in the drafting of the new constitutions for both the national government and the state governments. As seen in previous chapters, there was a rich history of Conservative constitutional thought on which they could draw. However, instead of a loyal opposition or a contender for power, the party became an obstructive element stubbornly opposed to the republic on principle and only reluctantly cooperated in government even when offered the opportunity. Why this should have been so has remained another of the tantalizing puzzles of Weimar's history.[25]

The Nationalists faced competition for the votes of property owners from several other parties that could claim to represent the interests of the middle classes. The DNVP itself was almost impossibly heterogeneous, including not only the rural centers of power of the old Conservative parties, but also industrialists, craftsmen, white-collar workers, radical anti-Semites, and also the newly enfranchised women voters. The party looked backward to the empire. But the party's leaders and members also included not only Conservative monarchists, but also the new Conservative revolutionaries who disliked the old monarchy as much as the new republic, and also another group of younger Conservatives who were willing to accept a republic provided it gave predominant power to the executive.

In addition, the DNVP suffered from a gap between its leaders and the rank-and-file members. Notwithstanding its diversity, the membership was always far more radical than the leadership. Leaders had to live with their parliamentary colleagues, and as professional politicians they desired office. The more intellectual among them offered analyses of the new situation based on their understanding of the traditions of Conservative thinking regarding the relationship between state and society. These included the rights of property, the relations between executive and legislature, and limits on the civil rights of potentially dangerous individuals and groups. Many called for a strong leader. Oskar Hergt, for instance, favored an "orderly state" (*Ordnungsstaat*), even a republic, so long as the executive possessed ultimate power. The members, on the other hand, simply hated the republic that had replaced their empire, and their emotional refusal to accept the new situation grew stronger as the years passed. It was among this group that the shock of the Versailles Treaty was felt most severely. Their bitter and irreconcilable opposition forced the parliamentary leaders into obstructionism rather than collaboration with parties that accepted and supported the republic.

The DNVP's leaders in turn failed to educate their followers. The DNVP suffered from an absence of effective leaders. From the earliest period of constitutional drafting to the end of the republic, the party frequently found itself unable to take a clear position because the leaders failed to discover compromises that its disparate wings would find acceptable. It was easier to evade the hard business of hammering out inclusive positions and then selling them to the voters, and instead to denounce the republic, foreigners, Jews, and other unspecified enemies. The apocalyptic rhetoric could cover over the divergent desires and interests of the party's supporters, and gained votes in crisis situations such as 1924, but it left the party vulnerable to takeover by those whose rhetoric was the strongest and whose opposition to the republic was the most implacable. In the end, the well-financed campaign of Alfred Hugenberg gave him the leadership of the party, but in turn he lost out to the even more radical and better organized Nazis.

The structures of Weimar politics

The problem these divisions posed for Weimar democracy is evident from Table 10.1. The Socialists, the largest party until 1932, were generally excluded from office. The Center failed to broaden its appeal beyond Catholics. The Liberals also failed to expand. On the right and left were parties that rejected the republic, the Communists (KPD), the right wing of the Nationalists (DNVP), a collection of rural and

Table 10.1 Weimar elections: popular vote in millions, and numbers of deputies

	Jan. 19, 1919	June 6, 1920	May 4, 1924	Dec. 7, 1924	May 20, 1928	Sept. 14, 1930	July 31, 1932	Nov. 6, 1932	Mar. 5, 1933
Total voters	36.8	35.9	38.4	39.0	41.2	43.0	44.2	44.4	44.7
Votes cast	30.5	28.5	29.7	30.7	31.2	35.2	37.2	35.8	39.7
Deputies	423	459	472	493	491	577	608	584	647
SPD	11.5 (165)	6.1 (102)	6.0 (100)	7.9 (131)	9.2 (153)	8.6 (143)	8.0 (133)	7.2 (121)	7.2 (120)
USPD	2.3 (22)	5.0 (84)							
KPD		0.6 (4)	3.7 (62)	2.7 (45)	3.3 (54)	4.6 (77)	5.3 (89)	6.0 (100)	4.8 (81)
Center	6.0 (91)	3.8 (64)	3.9 (65)	4.1 (69)	3.7 (62)	4.1 (68)	4.6 (75)	4.2 (70)	4.4 (74)
Dem	5.6 (75)	2.3 (39)	1.7 (28)	1.9 (32)	1.5 (25)	1.3 (20)	0.4 (4)	0.3 (2)	0.3 (5)
DVP	1.3 (19)	3.9 (65)	2.7 (45)	3.0 (51)	2.7 (45)	1.6 (30)	0.4 (7)	0.7 (11)	0.4 (2)
WP	0.3 (4)	0.2 (4)	0.7 (10)	1.0 (17)	1.4 (23)	1.4 (23)	0.1 (2)	0.1 (1)	
DNVP	3.1 (44)	4.2 (71)	5.7 (95)	6.2 (103)	4.4 (73)	2.5 (41)	2.2 (37)	3.0 (52)	3.1 (52)
Reg	0.1 (1)	1.5 (26)	1.2 (21)	1.5 (23)	1.1 (19)	1.2 (22)	1.3 (22)	1.2 (21)	1.1 (18)
Other	0.1 (2)	0.3 (0)	1.8 (14)	1.1 (8)	2.7 (17)	3.7 (46)	1.0 (9)	1.3 (10)	0.6 (7)
Nazis			1.9 (32)	0.9 (14)	0.8 (12)	6.4 (107)	13.7 (230)	11.7 (196)	17.3 (288)

Note:

Parties: SPD—Majority Socialist Party; USPD—Independent Socialist Party; KPD—Communist Party; Dem—Democrats; DVP—People's Party; WP—*Wirtschaftspartei* or Economics Party; DNVP—Nationalists; Reg—regional parties, the Bavarian People's Party and the German Hanoverian Party; Other includes the *Deutsches Landvolk* (1.1 million voters and 19 deputies in 1930) and the *Christlich-sozialer Volksdienst* (0.9 million voters and 14 deputies in 1930).

Source: From the figures published by the Reich Statistical Office. The popular vote is given in millions; the number of deputies is given in parentheses.

THE POLITICS OF FEELING 393

anti-Semitic parties, and the Nazis. The results for May 1924 and for 1930 show that, when the economy declined, voters turned to them and away from moderate centrist parties. That is, they blamed the system for their troubles, not the parties in power. In hard times they voted not for a different policy mix within the existing system, but for the destruction of the system itself.

Not only were many alienated from the system or prepared to support parties that promised to replace it; many were also prepared to go into the streets to battle against those with different visions. Expressionist politics here did paint with a new palette compared to the neoclassical empire. Building at first on war veterans and then on core activists supplemented by occasional sympathizers, right and left organized armed groups to attack their enemies and defend themselves. As in the social and cultural spheres, the police and judiciary often leaned toward the right. Police intervention frequently provoked violent responses from left-wing demonstrators. Nevertheless, as Richard Tilly showed in an early quantitative study, the dimensions of the problem had changed substantially. The number of "major" disorders, those that local police needed reinforcements to contain, increased from around seven per year before 1914, to over ten each year from 1919 to 1932. Worse, their size exploded, from an average of around 850 persons, to an average of 17,800. There were many public protests in the prewar years, for instance the mass demonstrations demanding a change in the Prussian franchise, but they only rarely led to violence. Now public demonstrations regularly became violent confrontations between the demonstrators and their opponents.[26]

The constitution, the President, and the parties

The Weimar constitution enjoyed a very positive international reputation. Hugo Preuss, left Liberal and noted professor of law, had been appointed to draft a new constitution. Rigorously democratic, it attempted to resolve the tension between the executive and legislature that had plagued German politics over the previous century. Sovereignty resided in "the people"—a fundamental break with monarchical tradition that Germany's constitutional theorists found deeply troubling.[27] Accordingly, the President was directly elected, for a seven-year term. The first ballot in a presidential election could only be won by an absolute majority. The second ballot, however, would be won by the candidate with the most votes. The President possessed extensive powers under Article 48, a provision influenced by the disorder of the revolution and intended to allow government to continue in the absence of a clear parliamentary majority. As seen in Chapter 9 and above, the first President, the Socialist Ebert, used his powers to appoint the Cuno government in 1922, and Stresemann employed presidential decrees to suppress the Communists in Saxony and Thuringia in 1923.

Ebert died in 1925, making a new election necessary. Seven candidates ran in the initial ballot, and not surprisingly none obtained the necessary majority. The leading contenders polled very nearly the same vote as their respective Reichstag parties had in December 1924. Karl Jarres, Mayor of Duisburg and a joint candidate of the People's Party and the Nationalists, received 10.4 million votes. Otto Braun, the Socialist head of the Prussian state government, received 7.8 million. Wilhelm Marx of the Center received 3.9 million. Well behind were the Communist candidate, Ernst Thälmann, and candidates from the Democrats, the Bavarian People's Party, and the *Völkische Partei* candidate Ludendorff.

For the second ballot, the Socialists, Democrats, and Center agreed to support Marx, former Chancellor and head of the Center Party, and a committed supporter of the republic. He seemed almost certain to succeed if the voters of these three parties followed their leaders' suggestion. Casting about for a candidate with the widest popular appeal, the Conservative parties found him in Hindenburg. Now 78 years old, he had withdrawn from political life, but was persuaded to stand as the candidate of a "*Reich* bloc." The Communists refused to support Marx, and Thälmann ran again. The Bavarian People's Party decided to support Hindenburg, a Protestant from north Germany, over Marx, a Catholic from the Rhineland. The working-class vote and the Catholic vote therefore split. Thälmann received 1.9 million votes, Marx 13.7 million, and Hindenburg with 14.6 million became the republic's new President.

Hindenburg impressed his opponents and disappointed his supporters by unequivocally declaring himself in favor of the principles of popular sovereignty and the democratic and republican essence of the constitution. He did, however, warn the Reichstag that he could fulfill his task more easily "if the parties in this high house will not indulge in petty quarrels about advantages for a party or an economic group, but will compete with each other in serving our hard-pressed people faithfully and effectively." That is, he confused politics with administration, and did not recognize the conflict of interests as legitimate. He also believed himself to have virtually unlimited powers under Article 48, and he believed that he had the right and duty to exercise those powers. In 1926, the Ministry of the Interior developed a draft law guiding the implementation of Article 48. Hindenburg opposed the law as inappropriate and unnecessary. "A strictly formalistic definition of the manner of exercising the President's rights, or even a limitation of those rights, would weaken his authority and gravely endanger the security of the state."

Hindenburg's prejudices influenced the formation of governments from 1926 onward. He wanted the Nationalists to be included if at all possible, and he wanted the Socialists to be excluded if at all possible. This made the achievement of a stable coalition more difficult. In addition, Hindenburg reverted to character in coming under the influence of his close advisors, particularly from the army. Schleicher, now a general and the most politically influential figure in the military after Seeckt's dismissal in 1926 (he had invited a grandson of Wilhelm II to attend military maneuvers), became the most important of those advisors. He suggested that should a right-wing coalition without the Nationalists prove impossible, then the President should "appoint a government in which he had confidence" and not only prepare for a dissolution of the Reichstag "to give the government every opportunity to get a majority," but also prepare "to govern 'against' the Reichstag" if a majority could not be obtained.

The Reichstag with which the President had to deal was elected by a system of proportional representation. The country was divided into 37 electoral districts. Voters cast their ballots for lists of potential representatives ranked by the parties, not for individual local candidates. Each party received one representative in the Reichstag for each set of approximately 60,000 votes. All adult men and women were entitled to vote, but voting was not compulsory. The size of the Reichstag therefore fluctuated depending on the number of voters the parties could mobilize. Socialists especially favored the new system, because they remembered the many times they had been shut out in the elections to the old imperial single-member constituencies by alliances of their enemies.

Proportional representation was highly regarded by political theorists and was also adopted by a number of other European countries in the 1920s. Historians since have identified a number of problems with the system. Apart from each party's "number one," most voters would not recognize most of the names on the lists. This gave great power to the parties' central national organizations and distanced them from local concerns. Because all votes in each district counted, small parties representing narrow interests could hope to win seats. A proliferation of splinter parties could make it impossible for any party to obtain a clear majority and could also make it difficult to form the necessary coalitions after an election.

In the event, although a large number of parties competed, splinter parties ("Other" in Table 10.1) gained few representatives. The more significant problem lay in the intransigence of the larger parties. The system encouraged parties to emphasize their distinctiveness, to present themselves as saviors of the nation, and to denounce their opponents in the most extreme rhetoric possible. They had no motive to merge with other parties or to seek the middle ground in policy programs in order to secure local majorities. The parties of the middle classes, the Democrats, the People's Party (*Deutsche Volkspartei* or DVP), and the Economics Party (*Wirtschaftspartei* or WP) failed either to unite or to expand. To the right, the DNVP would have had very few seats under the old system if it had remained confined to the small rural Protestant communities in the north and east where it had natural majorities, but would almost certainly have campaigned differently if competing in single-member constituencies across the nation. Rather than becoming more moderate in order to win local majorities, the DNVP was further radicalized by the need to compete with extreme right-wing parties.

The "woman question" also had a political dimension. Female suffrage doubled the voting population, and women's voting patterns differed from men's. They voted less often, and they voted more conservatively. A contemporary joke held that wives voted one party to the right of their husbands. The Catholic Center, the Conservative DNVP, and the People's Party gained disproportionate numbers of women's votes, the Socialists and Democrats gained about the same share of the women's as of the men's vote, and the Communists consistently failed to attract as many women as men. There were activist women in the KPD, but the party made little effort to appeal directly to women. What women might want was secondary to what Communist leaders believed the working-class needed. Their open commitment to revolutionary change alienated many, as did their hostility to religion. Their advocacy of equal pay and improved working conditions was offset by demands for equal legal treatment of illegitimate children, abortion, and divorce on demand, all opposed by solid majorities across the political and social spectrum.

The Reich, the states, and the bureaucracy

Two old problems the constitution did not address were the relationship between the central and state governments and the position of Prussia in Germany. Preuss had followed the old Liberal centralizing tradition. His original draft proposed that Prussia be divided and the country reorganized into twelve administrative units subordinate to the central government. This proposal was strongly opposed by the states, especially Baden, Württemberg, and Bavaria. It was also opposed by the Socialists, despite their preference for a strong central government. The SPD had become the dominant party in Prussia and did not want to surrender their position in the largest state and the leverage this gave them in national politics. The separatist ambitions of Rhineland leaders such as Konrad Adenauer and the danger of creating one or more intransigently reactionary states in the east were additional concerns. The states were redesignated as *Länder* but not dissolved, and they retained control over churches, schools, and the police.

Prussia in fact became one of the bulwarks of the Weimar system under a coalition of the SPD and the Center led by Socialist Otto Braun from 1920 to 1932. Then in 1932, the Braun government lost its majority in state elections and was ousted by the Chancellor Franz von Papen on the grounds that they had favored the Communists and failed to maintain public order. Papen appointed himself head of the Prussian government and began a purge of officials loyal to the republic. Papen hoped this decisive action would impress right-wing voters and woo them away from the Nazis, but, as seen in Table 10.1 and below, he was wrong. Hitler became Chancellor and Hermann Goering became Minister of the Interior of Prussia and, as such, head of the Prussian police, which he augmented with Nazi "auxiliaries" and exploited as one of the key means of consolidating Nazi power.

However, as we have seen at several points in Chapter 9 and above, the central Reich government did possess greater powers than under the empire. The Socialists supported Preuss' draft in this regard, because they saw a strong central administration as a check against Conservative tendencies in the states. The principle of the unitary state was adopted over the federalist concept put forward by the Center and the Nationalists. The Reich could dictate principles of legislation and administration to the states over a wide range of areas, including their form of government. The Reich also finally gained control over direct taxation, and, in a neat reversal of the pre-1914 system, reserved only a few indirect taxes to the states.

The new system was administered by the old bureaucracy. In November 1918, Ebert, struggling to retain social control, assured all serving public officials that they would retain their salaries and pension rights, and he also granted them full freedom of association, political opinion, and expressions of opinion. These rights were later incorporated into the Weimar constitution. For many, including both supporters of the republic as well as those who opposed it, the continuity of bureaucratic administration was one of the few assurances of stability in an uncertain world. These included Max Weber, and once again Weber remains important because his analysis of bureaucratic power has become the basis of all subsequent studies of bureaucracy. Based on Hegel's philosophical reflections and the empirical studies by Gustav Schmoller of the Prussian central government and urban administration, Weber located the "status honor" of government officials in their professional training, their lifetime tenure, and their fixed salaries. Weber believed the rise of mass politics threatened the integrity of the bureaucracy. Lawyers, he said, are drawn to politics because they are especially suited to plead cases. Though officials also have legal training, they should engage in "impartial administration," and it is the ethical sense imparted by their special position that guarantees they will do so. Professional politicians almost by definition will attempt to subvert the impartiality of state administration, to the detriment of all.

Weber, though critical of specific aspects of bureaucratic administration and gloomy in his vision of a bureaucratized future, accepted much of the mythical self-image of the Prussian-German bureaucrats in creating his immensely influential model. As seen in previous chapters, recruitment had never been open, and administration had never been impartial. The examinations, unpaid apprenticeships, and purges of politically unreliable officials had created a remarkably homogeneous group, but they were unbendingly conservative and increasingly out of touch with the modern world. Study in a university law faculty was the only avenue of entry, but legal training was becoming less and less adequate as a background to the growing number of technical areas in which the government was involved. These were men who before 1914 would be punished if they were seen carrying their own suitcases on a train platform.[28] Under the thirty years of Wilhelm's erratic rule they had also become accustomed to exercising wide discretion within their ministries. Rather than acting as the agents of responsible political leaders they considered themselves the only ones properly qualified to judge policy and its implementation.

Three directions of development can be seen in the interwar period. First, the extension of the government's range of activities had already made the government an employer on a large scale. The bureaucracy divided, with a small elite at the top and large numbers of workers at the bottom. This led to mobilization on the lines of occupations and interest groups, but the representatives of public employees, though in effect playing the role of labor unions, found their position confused by the claim that they enjoyed a special status. As seen in Chapter 8, Erich Remmers finally succeeded in 1918 in establishing the German Union of Public Officials (DBB). In 1920 the DBB had over 1 million members, but there was a separate 200,000-strong organization of Catholic public officials, an association connected with the Hirsch-Duncker unions, and

Table 10.2 Germany: employment in government services, 1895–1939 (thousands)

	Public administration	Higher officials	Railroads	Post	Education	Military
1895	311		263	129	233	606
1907	416		432	236	299	664
1913	460		492	272	380	864
1925	865		793	356	383	142
1928	1046	754	769	371	406	144
1929	1070		785	377	410	145
1930	1069	707	753	378	415	145
1933	1094	682	661	355	399	147
1939	1535		992	532	450	923

Note:
Higher officials (*Beamte*) are included in the total for public administration, but the underlying sources are different. Railroads and post figures exclude "technical personnel" before 1925.

Sources: Walther G. Hoffmann, *Das Wachstum der deutschen Wirtschaft seit der Mitte des 19. Jahrhunderts* (Berlin: Springer, 1965), pp. 200–6; Bernd Wunder, *Geschichte der Bürokratie in Deutschland* (Frankfurt: Suhrkamp, 1986), p. 131.

another organization of elite "higher officials" with 55,000 members. The DBB split in 1922 when railroad workers went on strike. The central organization declared itself opposed to any strike by public officials, and over 300,000 left to form a Socialist-oriented organization. The DBB regained its preeminent position when the Catholic association joined it, but the separate Socialist union, higher officials' union, and Hirsch-Duncker association remained.

Second, the expansion of government functions intersected with the claim to be omnicompetent, and led the bureaucrats into more extensive attempts to manage economic and social development. These efforts ranged from public housing to the "non-party" or "expert" national governments of Wilhelm Cuno, Heinrich Brüning, and Franz von Papen. Political conflict could stalemate policy. Weimar ministers found their orders subverted by unsympathetic bureaucrats, and the officials in turn bitterly resented the parliamentary government's somewhat hesitant attempts to democratize the bureaucracy. They accused the government of an illegitimate "politicizing" of the state service, and their complaints were supported by hysterical outbursts from the leaders of right-wing parties. Following the Kapp Putsch and again after Rathenau's murder, the Prussian state government pressed some officials into retirement, and the busts of the Emperor were finally removed from official offices. But in 1926, of just over 1000 senior "political officials" in Prussia, the DBB listed only 16 per cent as supporters of the Socialist Party. Nearly half gave no party affiliation, but were presumed to be Conservatives, opposed to the republic.

Finally, the claim to be an elite had negative consequences as well. The upper levels remained bound by the image of themselves as a separate estate (*Stand*), by the distinction between state and civil society, and by their image of themselves as non-political professionals, their status validated by their mastery of their own elaborate rules and procedures. Their hostility toward the republic redoubled with the reductions in public sector employment and cuts of as much as 20 per cent in the salaries of tenured officials, as the Reich and state governments slashed their budgets in the depression. In the view of many historians, the senior civil servants, determined to protect their privileges at any cost, compromised with the Nazis, contributing to their rise to power and giving the Nazi government crucial stability and legitimacy in the early days of its rule. Looking forward to Chapter 11, Table 10.2 shows why civil servants as a group might have supported the Nazi regime during its early years, but they, like so many others, eventually found themselves subject to an arbitrary power, one that unlike theirs knew no rules at all.

The depression and the collapse of Weimar

The elections of 1928 brought substantial gains on the left, both to the Socialists and to the Communists. The Socialists finally returned to government and their leader Hermann Müller became Chancellor and head of a coalition that included the Center, the Bavarian People's Party, the Democrats, and the People's Party. The power behind the new government was Stresemann, who had served as foreign minister since losing the Chancellorship. He had succeeded in negotiations at Locarno in gaining withdrawals of some of the foreign troops that still occupied districts in western Germany, French and British agreement to Germany's entry into the League of Nations, and a guarantee of Germany's western borders that protected Germany from French intervention in case of a confrontation in the east with Poland and Czechoslovakia. He was, however, bitterly attacked by Conservatives for implicitly surrendering Alsace and Lorraine, and some of the promises made by the French at Locarno were slow to be fulfilled. He needed further successes. He aimed to remove the final occupation troops and the restrictions on rearmament. This would eventually make it possible to regain some of the territory lost in the east, but that was not a goal that could be announced publicly. To aid in the negotiations and protect himself from right-wing attacks, he wanted the backing of a broad-based government with impeccable democratic credentials.

The main losers in 1928 were the Nationalists, and their losses paved the way for Hugenberg's rise to leadership. The old leaders had finally agreed to participate in government in 1927. The appointment of Martin Schiele as agriculture minister raised hopes among farmers that the government would address agriculture's ongoing problems. Schiele was a leader of the Reich Rural Federation (*Reichslandbund* or RLB), the largest agrarian association. He had announced plans for the formation of a new movement that would unite agricultural interests. Hugenberg and the DNVP faction within the RLB sabotaged this idea because it would have reduced the power of the party and the large landlords in the organization. In addition, the new DNVP executive forced the withdrawal of Schiele and the other Nationalist ministers from the government. They then eliminated other moderates and those who did not support the right wing of the DNVP from leadership from the RLB.

Under Hugenberg, the Nationalists rejected the idea of parliamentary democracy entirely. This also had negative consequences for the RLB and for farmers after the onset of the depression, because the party continually opposed the government while at the same time agitating for narrow agrarian interests, and therefore lost influence and in effect dragged the RLB down with it. Farmers in many districts turned away from both, toward the Nazis and other parties on the radical right.

The Müller government also faced problems. Hindenburg distrusted Stresemann and was, it seems, simply incapable of understanding the logic of Stresemann's policies. He preferred, he said, foreign ministers who simply "knew how to pound on the table." He also distrusted any government that included the Socialists. Stresemann's party, the People's Party, wanted to be included in the Prussian state government, but the Center opposed this because the People's Party would not support the Prussian concordat with the Papacy. The Socialists split over the construction of new naval cruisers. The right wing of the People's Party supported employers in the iron industry when they locked out workers in the hope of undermining the system of compulsory arbitration in labor disputes. They then in effect rejected Stresemann when they announced that they could not continue to support the Müller coalition unless there were changes to its financial policies. This would have undermined the social programs for which both the Center and the Socialists had been fighting.

In August 1928, Stresemann had persuaded the French to consider the final evacuation of western Germany, and, in February 1929, a commission under American Owen Young began the planned reexamination of reparations foreseen under the Dawes Plan. The resulting Young Plan substantially reduced both the nominal total of reparations and the annual payments, and Stresemann was able to maneuver the French and British into agreeing to the final end of the occupation in return for Germany's agreement to the new terms. This did not satisfy the right, and Hugenberg used the constitutional provisions of initiative and referendum to circulate a petition to reject the Young Plan, abrogate the Versailles Treaty, and try ministers for treason if they should accept any agreement that implied Germany's war guilt. The Reichstag rejected it comprehensively (even DNVP representatives voted against it). In the subsequent poll, Hugenberg allied himself with the paramilitary

Plate 10.1 Otto Dix, *War (Der Krieg)*, 1929–32. The "old" version. Triptych with predella, mixed media on wood. Center panel 204 × 204 cm; right and left panels 204 × 204 cm; predella 60 × 204 cm. Gemäldegalerie Neue Meister, Dresden. Ten years after its end, the First World War continued to haunt Weimar, and Dix's work reflects the ongoing debate over the war and responsibility. Whether Dix intended to celebrate masculine endeavor and heroic comradeship or to denounce war and its brutalizing effects remains a disputed topic. The central panel, with its horrible parody of a crucifixion, recalls the arrangement of the elements in Meidner's *Apocalyptic Landscape*. Dix produced another right panel that shows a soldier holding a dead comrade, leaning against a beam, with suggestions of medieval and Renaissance paintings showing Christ's descent from the Cross, but this early version seems to emphasize the shock and horror experienced by the participants. Photo: courtesy Otto Dix Stiftung. Copyright © Otto Dix, 1933/Bild-Kunst, licensed by VISCOPY, Sydney 2002.

Stahlhelm organization, and with the Nazi Party. Their combined efforts persuaded 5.8 million persons to vote for the so-called "Freedom Law," far short of acceptance but demonstrating the depth of hostility to the republic. The campaign brought Hitler and the Nazis to national prominence for the first time, setting the stage for their success in the 1930 elections.

In the background was the downturn in the economy beginning in 1928. Chapter 9 examined the possible sources of weakness in the domestic economy and links between Germany and the world economy. In early 1929, nearly 1.5 million unemployed workers had applied to the Reich Labor Insurance Office for unemployment benefits. The agency was running a sizeable deficit. Prohibited from creating money through the Reichsbank, the government attempted to cover its obligations with a bond issue, which failed. Employers and Conservatives insisted that unemployment benefits should be drastically reduced and taxes cut to stimulate investment.[29] The unions, and therefore the Socialist Party, refused to accept reductions in the unemployment benefits and argued for increased employer contributions instead. An ailing Stresemann barely held his People's Party colleagues in the government at a meeting on October 2, 1929, but he died the next day. Later in October, the New York stock market crashed, leading to a series of financial crises, drastic declines in agricultural prices, and the virtual collapse in world trade. Hjalmar Schacht, now president of the Reichsbank, first attempted to dictate budget reductions to the government and then resigned, further discrediting the government. The Socialists rejected a final attempt at compromise on unemployment insurance, and Müller resigned at the end of March 1930.

Hindenburg now listened to his military advisors, Groener and especially Schleicher, who had become convinced that only a government "above the parties" would have the necessary determination to confront the deepening crisis. To lead the new government they settled on Brüning, known for his Conservative fiscal views, hostility to Socialism, and support for the army and revisions of the armaments restrictions imposed by the Versailles Treaty. Groener at least honestly thought Brüning to be both extremely knowledgeable and politically gifted. As head of the large Center Party, he had some hope of obtaining the cooperation of the Reichstag. They also believed that, as a committed Catholic, he would not oppose authoritarian measures should these prove necessary.

Brüning said in his memoirs that, when approached by Groener, he suggested a general such as Groener or Schleicher instead, but Groener insisted he wanted to keep the army out of politics. He also claimed that Hindenburg would follow his advice and support Brüning with his powers under Article 48 if necessary. That is, rather than keeping the army out of politics, Groener planned to manipulate policy but without taking responsibility. Hindenburg did in fact promise he would back the new government with his emergency powers, "but naturally only so far as it is consistent with the constitution."

Brüning had a clear economic agenda, which rested on a set of moral and social attitudes. He believed that only a rigorous policy of deflation could overcome the depression. He also believed the depression was a kind of divine judgment for the excesses of the 1920s. He blamed the Socialist Party for encouraging unreasonable expectations among the working classes. In this, and in his hostility to the materialism and hedonism of the modern world, he epitomized the attitudes of the German upper classes and reflected the platitudes recycled by two generations of cultural pessimists. Germany's elites were not unique in this respect. Politicians, senior officials, bankers, and employers across Europe and the United States believed that only strict adherence to the gold standard and reductions especially in wages—the "rules of the game" outlined in Chapter 9—would overcome a depression. Together their efforts worsened the depression.[30]

Brüning's political agenda is less clear, and remains a disputed topic. An earlier controversy over the implications of the shift to a "presidential system" was superseded by the publication of his memoirs in 1970, which suggested that he aimed to recreate an authoritarian system and ultimately to reestablish the monarchy. Memoirs are not always reliable, and after sifting through a range of evidence William Patch concludes that Brüning wanted to preserve parliamentary democracy and the rule of law. He interpreted these in a traditional Prussian sense as embodying the virtues of diligence and self-denial while serving the common good, but Patch believes that Brüning intended to restore parliamentary rule when the economic crisis had passed.[31]

Brüning's budget reduced spending and increased taxes. The Nationalists objected to the rise in taxes on higher incomes, and the Socialists objected that there was no cut in military spending. When the Reichstag rejected the budget, Brüning promulgated it by presidential decree, an action regarded by legal experts as unconstitutional. The Reichstag in turn demanded the decree be abrogated as an attack on popular sovereignty. Brüning withdrew the decree, but then dissolved the Reichstag, put off the new election for as long as he legally could, and then again imposed his budget by decree. Further deflationary measures followed in 1931. The downward spiral continued. By 1932, industrial production had declined to a little over half its 1929 level, and unemployment, officially over 6 million, in fact was probably over 7 million, a fifth of the total labor force.

Brüning was damned as the "hunger Chancellor" because he seemed to be ignoring the misery of the depression and the way in which his policies were making the situation even worse. Economists and historians since have debated the question of whether there were alternatives. As noted in Chapter 9, Knut Borchardt argued that there were not. Germany had been living beyond its means, granting wage payments in excess of productivity improvements, and redistributing income away from productive investment, leading to the slump in the domestic economy. Then, during the depression itself, the limits on the public budget forced the adoption of deflationary policies. Albrecht Ritschl extends this argument. He emphasizes in particular the role of the new requirement imposed by the Young Plan that reparations payments would take precedence over repayment of private loans. In contrast to the situation under the Dawes Plan, this placed the economy and the government under a rigid foreign exchange constraint.[32] In addition, even a government that wanted to introduce an expansionary program would have found its options limited by the legal cap on the credit that the Reichsbank was allowed to give.

The underlying reasons why there were no alternatives to Brüning's policy were not so much economic, financial, or legal, however, but ideological and political. Brüning detested the notion of giving money to those who had not earned it, and he believed as well that Germany could "not afford" a large program of public works to provide jobs for the unemployed. He believed, like leaders in the United States, Britain, France, and elsewhere, that government policies of any kind could have only a limited influence on the economy. Depressions were natural, and ultimately self-correcting if proper policy were maintained. In his New Year's Day message of 1931, he cautioned the nation, "I am anxious to stress the limitations of any policy so that you will not indulge in any illusions." This was a problem for all parties. Even the Nazis in 1932 were torn between the need to "do something" and the perception that any expansionary program would be inflationary. The 1923 hyperinflation was still a recent memory, and in speaking for instance to potential supporters in heavy industry, Hitler was careful to emphasize his financial conservatism.

Brüning also believed that what he himself called his "draconian" measures were necessary to enable Germany "to meet its international obligations." This is a different point from the economic impact of the shortage of foreign exchange. Brüning's aims here were political and diplomatic. By demonstrating its financial conservatism, and indeed precisely by sinking deeper into depression, Germany would show the Allied nations that it could not pay reparations. The cancellation of reparations would be a foreign policy triumph, enough perhaps to win a friendly Reichstag majority and secure the government's position until the economy turned upward once again. Brüning also hoped to reduce or eliminate the restrictions on Germany's armaments, and he began negotiations with Austria to form a customs union. The French and Czechs immediately opposed the Austrian scheme, and the World Court held against it, a defeat so complete that Brüning claimed he had merely inherited the project from the Müller government. Proposals to increase German armaments sat badly beside claims that Germany could not pay reparations, and were rejected. In the aftermath of a further financial crisis in 1931, President Hoover proposed a moratorium on reparations payments, but the French had become suspicious of German motives and delayed until threatened by the Americans. The final end to reparations therefore not only brought no credit to the Brüning, but also came too late to help his government's financial problems.

By 1931, even Brüning was aware that something had to be done, but policy options remained limited. As agricultural minister, Martin Schiele insisted on increased agricultural tariffs. As head of the RLB he was representing his constituency, and other countries were raising their tariffs as well, but tariffs became another difficult point of dispute in foreign policy. A government study commission in 1931 recommended some stimulation. In April 1932, a modest program of 135 million marks was announced. The new spending had no visible effect before Brüning left office. His successor Franz von Papen introduced a tax credit for employers who hired new workers, and added a further 167 million marks for job creation. This may have resulted in some 25,000 new jobs, in the face of 6 million registered unemployed. Papen in turn gave way to Schleicher, who increased spending on direct job creation to 500 million marks. Socialist Party leaders rejected a public works program proposed by trade union leaders in the spring of 1932.[33] Instead, Nazi Gregor Strasser picked up their ideas and demanded a 10-billion-mark program to create 2 million jobs. This, too, was attacked as inflationary, and he reduced his proposal to 3 billion marks. Hitler was worried both about accusations from the right that spending would lead to another inflation and social instability and about claims by the left that he and the right were actually planning another inflation to wipe out the debts of the rich.

Most specialists agree that Brüning's decision to dissolve the Reichstag was a serious error. As seen in Table 10.1, the results of the 1930 election confirmed the disaffection already evident in the Young Plan referendum. On the left, the Communists, and on the right, the Conservative splinter parties increased their vote substantially. And the Nazis scored their stunning success, rising from twelve to 107 seats. Opposed by the Communists, Nazis, and Nationalists, Brüning only survived because the Socialist Party decided for "reasons of state" to "tolerate" his government and not to support the votes of no confidence that would have invalidated his emergency decrees. The campaign was violent, and the violence continued, the Nazi *Sturmabteilung* (SA), the *Stahlhelm*, the Communist Red Front Fighters' Union, the Socialist and labor union Iron Front Against Fascism, and others battling in the streets, and the Nazis seeking out their enemies to bomb, burn, beat, and murder. Organized gangs of thugs moved about by truck. The police, though more numerous and more heavily armed than ever before, could not be everywhere.

Hindenburg's term as President expired in 1932. Brüning's attempt to convince the Nazis to support a move to extend his term without an election failed. With difficulty, he persuaded Hindenburg to stand again. The campaign was disorderly and violent. Hindenburg was humiliated to be opposed by the Nationalists and forced into a second ballot against Hitler, a former corporal, and Thälmann, a Communist. Hindenburg won easily, with 19.4 million votes to Hitler's 13.4 million and 3.7 for Thälmann, but the vote for Hitler showed how far he and his party had come.

Having lost the confidence of the voters, Brüning also lost the confidence of the elites. Hindenburg now actively resented him. State governments feared the rising Nazi movement and blamed the Chancellor for the decline in public order. Business leaders, though not supporting the Nazis, feared that Brüning's dependence on the Socialists would lead him to increase taxes, and they, too, began to wish for a leader who could impose order. Groener continued to support him. Schleicher, however, wanted Brüning to demand an end to the Versailles Treaty's restrictions on Germany's armed forces. Brüning's refusal and his evident failure to rally Conservatives behind his government turned Schleicher against him. When Groener, serving as interior minister, convinced Brüning and Hindenburg that Hitler's SA and SS units should be banned, Schleicher organized a campaign of protest that turned Hindenburg against both. Without the President's support, Brüning had no choice but to resign.

Schleicher persuaded Hindenburg to appoint Franz von Papen, an extremely conservative Center Party leader, as Chancellor. He also influenced the selection of the cabinet and intended to control the government from the background. Papen secured an agreement with the Nazis to "tolerate" his government. The price was the lifting of the ban on the SA, and new elections. Over the next five weeks, nearly 100 persons were killed and 1000 injured in fighting in Prussia. As seen above, this was the decline in public order that Papen then used as the excuse to overthrow the Prussian government. The elections at the end of July 1932 returned 230 Nazi deputies to the Reichstag. Hitler demanded the Chancellorship, and Papen, Schleicher, and Hindenburg refused. Hitler then declared the Nazis would no longer "tolerate" the government, and Papen dissolved the Reichstag to avoid the inevitable vote of no confidence. The election in November cost the Nazis 2 million votes and 34 seats. However, Papen now launched a plan to revise the constitution by presidential decree, which would turn Germany into a corporatist state ruled by the propertied classes. Schleicher persuaded Hindenburg that the scheme was impractical and dangerous, Papen was ousted, and, in early December 1932, Schleicher himself became Chancellor.

Schleicher's two months in office were devoted to preventing Hitler from coming to power, or, failing that, finding some way of including the Nazis in government while still retaining control himself. Schleicher also had a plan, based on ideas drawn from Spengler, Jünger, and others, of a coalition of labor groups, Nazis, and the army that would foster not only a political but also a spiritual revolution. He attempted to forge an alliance with the supposed "left wing" of the Nazi Party led by Gregor Strasser, the second ranking leader behind Hitler himself. Hitler easily outmaneuvered Strasser and emerged with his power within the party greater than before. Schleicher then asked Hindenburg for a decree banning both the Nazi and Communist Parties. Hindenburg refused and began to negotiate with Papen regarding a new government, and Schleicher resigned.

Papen decided the only way to gain the support of the Nazi Party was to give Hitler the Chancellorship, but he believed Hitler could be controlled with himself serving as Vice-Chancellor, Hugenberg as economics minister, *Stahlhelm* leader Franz Seldte as labor minister, and General Werner von Blomberg representing the army as defense minister. Wilhelm Frick as interior minister and Hermann Goering without a portfolio were the only other Nazis in the cabinet. On January 30, 1933, Adolf Hitler became Chancellor of Germany.[34]

The rise of Nazism

How could this have happened? The summary above shows that there were a large number of points where a different or better decision might have deflected Germany onto another path. The reasons why those other paths remained closed varied. Some of the reasons were subtle and structural. There were serious weaknesses in Weimar's economic and social systems. Divisions between the social-cultural milieus remained. There were unresolved problems in the political arrangement. Some of the reasons were obvious and personal. Germany lacked leadership. Although all would-be leaders spoke of the need for a "leader" and many called for struggle and revolution, too many of them were irresponsible, motivated by prejudice, personal ambition, or visions of Utopia. In Weber's terms, they had become intoxicated by power but unwilling to accept the consequences of their decisions.

Nevertheless, the short answer is that Hitler came to power because he was the leader of far and away the largest party in the Reichstag. Who voted for the Nazis? How were they mobilized? Which groups supported the Nazis and why? The Nazis themselves claimed to appeal to all Germans. The party, after all, was a national, socialist, German, workers' party. There was a party program, but Goebbels himself, the master of Nazi propaganda, wished it did not exist. Some historians, such as Ernst Nolte, have attempted to define the movement negatively, in terms of what the Nazis opposed rather than what they favored. Gregor Strasser screamed in 1932 that "National Socialism is the opposite of what exists today!"—an evocative Expressionist turn of phrase, but not much of a guide to Nazi policy or the motives of Nazi voters.

Voting patterns have been repeatedly correlated against economic and social variables.[35] These are "ecological" data, meaning we do not know the behavior of individuals. Problems arise with correlations at the national level. For instance, the Nazi vote increased as unemployment rose, but, looking at smaller districts, the correlation between unemployment and the Nazi vote breaks down. More recently analyses of voting patterns have been supplemented by local and regional studies that include interviews, memoirs, local press reports, and records of local organizations.[36] Much of the attention paid to the social-cultural milieus described above and in previous chapters has been addressed either explicitly or implicitly to the shift toward the Nazis.

The September 1930 elections were the Nazis' great breakthrough, and the July 1932 elections their high point. Compared to 1928, in 1930 the number of voters had risen from 41.2 million to 43.0 million, and the total votes cast increased from 31.2 million to 35.2 million. The number of votes cast for the Nazis rose from 810,000 in 1928 to 6.4 million. Two years later, of 44.2 million voters, 37.2 million cast their votes, and of these 13.7 million voted for the Nazis. Discussion has focused particularly on non-voters, young voters, rural voters, workers, affluent urban voters, and women voters.

The percentage of non-voters rose from 17 per cent in 1919 to 24 per cent in 1928. This is still a far higher rate of voting than, for instance, in recent United States elections, where fewer than half of the electorate cast ballots, but non-voters did provide an opportunity for a party that could mobilize them. Non-voters are hesitant about participating or are more or less alienated from the existing system. Many of them hold authoritarian, intolerant, and anti-intellectual beliefs. The increase in participation in the 1930 and 1932 elections aided the Nazis.

In a classic article, Peter Loewenberg analyzed young voters.[37] Many of them were non-voters; possibly 3.5 million young persons failed to vote in 1928. Young adults were particularly hard hit by the depression, as young workers were often the first to lose their jobs. Recent university graduates looking for employment were unlikely to find jobs, especially as government bureaucracies cut back. University enrollments increased as students delayed the search for a job as long as possible. Forty-two per cent of the members of the Nazi Party in 1931 were between 18 and 30. Born between 1901 and 1913, as children they had suffered the privations of the home front described in Chapter 8. Separated from their fathers during the war, their idealized picture shattered when the fathers returned home, defeated, and the political father of the country, the Emperor, abandoned them. Loewenberg argues that this early shock predisposed them to a "traumatic reliving" of their earlier experience. In the new crisis of the depression, they regressed and sought out a new father figure, finding him in Hitler.

Rural voters in the Protestant north and east made up the core of Nationalist Party support, but they moved to more radical right-wing parties in 1924 and again in 1930. This reservoir of Conservatism could be tapped by a party that promised better times for farmers. In another classic study, Rudolf Heberle noted that, in areas with large numbers of small independent farmers, the Nazi vote was highly correlated with the average level of indebtedness.[38] As seen above, the DNVP under Hugenberg gained control of the largest agrarian pressure group, the RLB, but lost influence by refusing to participate in government. As the economic distress of the countryside intensified, farmers and others, discouraged with their leaders and frustrated with the political process, began to act on their own, with boycotts of agricultural equipment suppliers, refusal to pay taxes, and other similar initiatives. The Nazis stepped into this vacuum, with claims that for the rural population, as for everyone else, things would be "different" and "better" under a Nazi government. They recruited significant numbers of Protestant pastors, schoolteachers, and large farmers, the traditional opinion leaders in rural communities, but they also projected an image of youth, energy, efficiency, and unity, a sharp and effective contrast to the tired and selfish maneuvering of the old leaders.[39]

The Comintern defined Fascism as the final stage of monopoly capitalism, and therefore had no easy way to explain the appeal of Nazism to workers. This has remained a problem for leftist historians and it relates directly to the question of the genuine popularity of Nazism, and therefore the question of working-class support for Nazism has engaged the attention of many specialists.[40] At the local level, as seen above, Nazis and Communists frequently competed for members in the same neighborhoods. There was probably no great flood of workers from the Communists to the Nazis in the early 1930s, but there was a good deal of movement back and forth between the Nazis and both the Communists and the Socialists. In 1928, the Socialists collected many voters who had cast their ballots for the Nazis in 1924, but in 1930, and especially 1932, many of those voters shifted back again. Jürgen Falter estimates that 27 per cent of all workers voted for the Nazis in 1932.[41] Neither the Communists nor the Socialists seem to have understood the appeal of the Nazis' nationalist message. When local Communists encouraged appeals based on common nationalist sentiments, the idea that the nation had been betrayed and therefore that the system had to be changed, this proved a dangerous tactic, because the Nazis were much better placed to succeed in a contest of chauvinistic protest parties.[42]

Affluent urban families provided another important reservoir of voters for the Nazis. The parties of the Protestant middle classes collapsed. The Democrats, People's Party, and Economics Party together dropped from 83 deputies in 1928 to 73 in 1930 and 11 in 1932.[43] The correlation of average income levels with the Nazi vote in urban districts is a strong one. Government officials, shopkeepers, and the sort of artisans who had become small factory owners were people whose economic situation was more precarious in the depression. For these voters, the threat of a Communist uprising seemed serious enough to require strong and even dictatorial measures.[44] As seen in previous chapters, these families had been one of the bulwarks of the empire, consistent supporters of the National Liberals and deeply suspicious of Catholicism and Socialism, so again the vague but resonant nationalist appeal of the Nazis struck home.

Nazi leaders openly opposed female suffrage. Gottfried Feder said, "the insane dogma of equality led as surely to the emancipation of the Jews as to the emancipation of women. The Jew stole the woman from us . . . We must kill the dragon to restore her to her holy position as servant and maid." Hitler himself remarked pragmatically, "I am no friend of female suffrage. If however we must continue with this tomfoolery, then we should draw what advantage we can . . . Women will always vote for law and order and a uniform, you can be sure of that."[45] Women voters did support the Nazis in large numbers, but the pattern differed from men. Not all districts recorded votes by gender, but it appears the Nazis did poorly with women through the 1920s, and then attracted many more in 1930 and especially in July 1932. Many of these women may have been non-voters, many must have previously voted for the parties of the Protestant middle classes, and, in 1930, many of them probably voted for the various smaller parties.

Local studies show the Nazis developed their power bases in quite prosaic ways. Under a system where voting is not compulsory, parties do best not when they attempt to convert supporters of opposing parties, but when they concentrate their efforts on ensuring that all of their own supporters are taken to the polls to vote. Though the party's vote declined from 1924 to 1928, its membership did not. A committed and enthusiastic cadre of activists solicited funds, organized meetings, marched, and demonstrated their solidarity. The activists were crucial in mobilizing voters on election day. Organization played a critical role in the Nazis' ability to gain support. They were better than their competitors among other Conservative and right-wing parties at structuring meetings, providing entertaining speakers, and mobilizing volunteer workers for local community projects. Speakers told their audiences things would be different and better under National Socialism, and they avoided points in the party program that might provoke hostility, such as opposition to capitalism or anti-Semitism.[46]

As noted above, Nazi activists were often young, but they did not belong to any single class. Regional membership lists show that large numbers came from the "lower class" or "working class," and also that the "middle class" was only slightly overrepresented.[47] As the economic crisis deepened, and as initial successes in local and state elections were reinforced by the rising national vote, membership rose, from 100,000 in 1928 to 1.5 million in late 1932. Behind the brown-shirted men increasingly there were formations of women, in blue skirts, brown blouses with white collars, with neckerchiefs and swastika armbands. Women were underrepresented as party members, fewer than 8000 before 1930, and fewer than 50,000 of the 1 million members of 1931. However, corresponding to the ideology of separate spheres, Nazi women's organizations expanded and claimed over 200,000 members. In addition, Nazi district leaders reported that from 50 to 80 per cent of the women who supported them did not belong officially to any Nazi organization.

The party also had an effective publication and propaganda campaign manager in Goebbels, the *Gauleiter* of Greater Berlin. He founded *Der Angriff (Attack)* as a "fighting paper" in 1927. By 1930, it was appearing six days a week and had a circulation over 100,000. The paper is credited with winning segments of the Berlin working class to Nazism and was particularly important in maintaining the party's presence during the period when the SA was prohibited from demonstrating in public. Goebbels worked in a standard pattern. First, he arranged for the SA to attack the party's enemies. The resulting notoriety, celebrated in the pages of *Der Angriff*, gained new recruits for the Nazi cause. The paper also libeled opponents, particularly the Jewish deputy police president Bernhard Weiss, and when the victim sued, again the resulting publicity could be exploited.[48]

Goebbels' propaganda style included the staging of public events, particularly funerals, party rallies, and the use of music. Nazis were able to organize spectacular stunts that had a widespread impact on public opinion and on undecided voters. One stunning example is the opening of a play, a work set again in the Napoleonic period. This particular play, A Hundred Days, had been written by none other than Benito Mussolini, dictator of Italy since 1922 and model for would-be Fascist leaders across Europe, Latin America, and Asia. The Nazi Party sponsored the German premiere on January 30, 1932. It took place in Weimar, the city where the republican constitution had been ratified, and the event was intended as a direct and deliberate provocation of the republican system. The state of Thuringia had been under Nazi rule since 1929, so the production had the support of the local government as well. In a hall draped with swastika flags, Hitler and other leading Nazis entertained Italian diplomats. Elisabeth Förster-Nietzsche, the elderly sister of Friedrich Nietzsche, who had edited the published versions of his works, was also present. Reporters from all major European news-papers were on hand, as were theater directors from Frankfurt, Leipzig, and even London, where productions were planned in the near future.

Of course, the typical Napoleonic novel or drama in Germany did not take Napoleon as the hero. In this case, however, the image of the heroic leader, who only fights when forced to do so, who struggles against incompetent parliamentary leaders, and who only loses the Battle of Waterloo due to mistakes made by others, was one that the audience could appreciate. The scene that brought the audience to its feet, how-ever, was the portrayal of the Prussian general Blücher confronting the defeated French soldiers, the reminder of Germany's victorious past, and the hope for defeated Germany of victories yet to come. Six months later, in the elections of July, the Nazis reached their highest share of the popular vote.[49]

Effective political agitation is expensive. Der Angriff was still losing money in 1932. The cost of the campaigns raises the question of who supported the Nazis financially. Nazi campaigns depended at critical points on donations from wealthy supporters. A Communist poster depicted Hitler giving his characteristic salute, and, from the rear, a large potbellied capitalist laying money onto his upraised hand. The caption was Hitler's own proud boast: "Behind me stand millions!" Many contemporaries and many subsequent historians have accused big business of responsibility for the rise of Nazism. East German Marxist historians saw the depression as the product of a crisis in the capitalist system, and the Nazi seizure of power as the establishment of a regime of state monopoly capitalism (*Staats-monopol-kapitalismus*). Some business groups made contributions to the Nazi Party, and some of Hitler's wealthy benefactors were industrialists, but the "*Stamokap*" argument breaks down in the face of the well-documented divisions among industrial leaders and the general lack of enthusiasm for the Nazis among leaders of big business in particular.[50]

Each region and each locality has it own features, but the rise of Nazis in most areas shared these general characteristics. Benjamin Lapp has traced developments in Saxony, particularly interesting as one of the strong points of the Socialist Party before 1914. In the early years of the Weimar Republic, Saxony boasted the most left-wing government in Germany, but, in the late 1920s, it was one of the first states to fall to the Nazis.[51] The revolution of 1918 and subsequent political emancipation of the working classes shocked and terrified the Saxon middle classes. In contrast to the rest of Germany, the tide of revolution did not recede after 1919 but remained high. A coalition of Social Democrats, Independent Socialists, and Communists remained in power and was able to enact a series of leftist measures. May 1 and November 9 were made state holidays. Free from the restraint imposed in Prussia by political alliance with the Catholic Center, Saxon Social Democrats introduced changes in the school system that greatly reduced clerical influence. Though more symbolic than substantive, such legislation heightened middle-class fears that revolution was just around the corner. Their fears led to strong local support for right-wing paramilitary organizations.

Unstable economic conditions exacerbated political polarization. The small, outdated structure of Saxon industry made it extremely vulnerable to the more difficult economic conditions of the postwar years. Heavily oriented toward textiles, Saxon industry employed large numbers of women, usually poorly organized. For many Saxon firms bankruptcy was a constant threat. Uncompetitiveness combined with and led to high rates of unemployment. Owners facing ruin confronted workers facing hunger.

Confrontation between the left and the right reached a crisis point in

1923. Working-class political demonstrations and economic protests, which often turned violent, frightened the property-owning classes. Right-wing paramilitary maneuvers, especially in neighboring Bavaria, in turn frightened the left. They were met by the formation of left-wing, but government-sponsored, paramilitary formations, the "proletarian hundreds." Saxony seemed on the edge of violent revolution and civil war. As seen above, Chancellor Stresemann, himself a Saxon, invoked the President's emergency powers and repressed the left-wing armed units. Federal intervention restored nominal order, but it did not reduce class conflict. The middle class welcomed the federal troops as saviors, but the working classes saw them as a hostile occupation force.

The "golden twenties" led to an appearance of stability in Saxony, but Lapp argues that class conflict in fact increased. Rationalization struck at small business owners and workers. Unemployment, and, even more important, the instability of employment, remained high. In the political realm, the traditional German party structure disintegrated as the "parties of the middle" divided and lost support. These conditions combined to provide the background for the huge increase in support for the Nazis that followed the downturn from 1928 onward.

Determined to prevent a revival of the radical left-wing "Soviet" Saxony of the early 1920s, the middle-class parties combined in a "*Bürgerblock*." However, differences over economic policy hampered the effectiveness of the alliance. Commercial, industrial, and agricultural elites—the class of notables Weber believed had provided the principled leaders of the past—remembered the crisis of 1923 and regarded the federal government as too accommodating toward the left. As the crisis deepened, they turned against democracy and the republic and began to favor some sort of authoritarian solution. At the same time, the less affluent voters who had supported the traditional middle-class parties deserted them, first for special interest splinter parties, and then for radical right-wing groups that called for the creation of an anti-Marxist national community, a *Volksgemeinschaft*.

Saxon voters did not remain with either the special interest parties or the radical right groups for long, but Lapp argues that they served as important stages in the shift toward eventual support for the Nazi Party. The decisive breakthrough for the Nazis came in the Saxon state elections of 1929. In an ironic reversal of the situation of the early 1920s, bourgeois parties now collaborated with the Nazis. Their search for stability seemed to be over at last.

Notes

1. Weber 1918.
2. Translation from Richie 1983, p. 42.
3. Willett 1978, p. 175.
4. Mommsen 1989; Kershaw 1990; Winkler 1993; Fritzsche 1996.
5. Mitchell 1965.
6. Translation from Richie 1983.
7. Tatar 1995, pp. 57–61, 171–2.
8. Richie 1983, pp. 19–20 and note 22.
9. Schüler-Springorum 1996.
10. Friedman 1998.
11. Brenner 1996.
12. Weichlein 1996; see Müller 1996.
13. Weichlein 1996; Lösche and Walter 2000.
14. Mommsen 1989.
15. Weber 1983.
16. Rosenhaft 1983.
17. Mallmann 1996.
18. Fischer 1991.
19. White 1992; Harsh 1993.
20. Fritzsche 1990; Lösche and Walter 2000, p. 478.
21. Jünger 1920.
22. Nevin 1997.
23. Woods 1996; Nevin 1997.
24. Schmitt 1985; Dyzenhaus 1997; McCormick 1997; see Caldwell 1997.
25. Trippe 1995.
26. Tilly 1975, p. 213.
27. Caldwell 1997.
28. Wunder 1986.
29. See Crew 1998, Chs. 8–9.
30. Eichengreen and Temin 2000.
31. Patch 1998.
32. Ritschl 1998.
33. Harsh 1993, p. 190.
34. See Turner 1996.
35. Childers 1983; Kolb 1988, pp. 187–96; Falter 1991.
36. Fritzsche 1998.
37. Loewenberg 1971.
38. Heberle 1963.
39. Baranowski 1995; Pyta 1996; Merkenich 1998.
40. Fischer, Conan 1996.
41. Kele 1972; Falter 1991.
42. Fischer, Conan 1991; Harsh 1993.
43. Jones 1988.
44. Hamilton 1982.

45. Koonz 1986, pp. 53–4.
46. Pridham 1973; Grill 1983; Lapp 1997.
47. Kater 1983; Mühlberger 1991; Brustein 1996.
48. Lemmons 1994.
49. Richie 1983, p. 55.
50. Turner 1985.
51. Lapp 1997.

CHAPTER 11

A "GERMAN STYLE":
THE NAZI GENERATION

Leni Riefenstahl's film depicting the 1934 Nazi Party Day rally in Nuremberg is entitled *Triumph of the Will* (*Triumph des Willens*, 1935). Technically brilliant, it portrays a Germany magically revivified and unified by a collective act of faith, focused on the figure of Hitler. The Führer descends from the heavens in the latest two-engine airplane. Wagner's music accompanies him through billowing white clouds toward the landing field. Women and children carrying flowers press forward to greet him, straining at the rope along the edge of the field in their eagerness. Intercutting between the approaching airplane and the excited crowd heightens the tension, and continues as Hitler emerges and salutes the crowd. Elevated tracking shots show his progress through the thronged streets of the old city. The tracking shots follow him as he passes across a huge open space, between dozens of orderly squares, each of them containing hundreds of the members of various Nazi organizations, standing at attention as he places a wreath on a tomb symbolizing the dead heroes of the First World War. The next shot, from below, outlines Hitler and other senior officials on a dais backed by huge banners with swastikas, against a now cloudless sky. Later, a series of low-angle shots shows the heads of boys against the sky, shouldering shovels as if they were rifles. They respond in turn to the question "where are you from?" in their regional accents, proud to be part of building this new Germany. Later still, a torchlight parade culminates in a hall, the raised shields of local party branches illuminated by the flickering light. A series of addresses heightens the tension, and finally near pandemonium erupts as Hitler himself speaks.

Hitler and the Nazi movement proposed a "revolution" that would solve all of Germany's problems. A "German style" rooted in the community of German people would define and perfect that same community. Riefenstahl's camera captures the revolution, and the style. But the Nazi regime ended in war and genocide, a word that had to be created to describe their crimes. The awesome destruction of the Second

World War shaped the world in which the human race lived for the next half century. The Holocaust, the systematic attempt to kill every person identified as a Jew, is arguably the defining event of the twentieth century. The search for its origins and meaning has framed the discussion of Germany's "special path" and much of the debate over modern civilization itself.[1]

With the evidence of the Second World War and the Holocaust before us, it seems obvious that there must have been something extraordinary about the Nazi state. As we will see, many Germans participated in the Nazi regime, many participated in its crimes, and many more knew of those crimes. Yet, at the same time, for most ordinary Germans the Nazi government was simply "the government," and Nazi society was simply "society." As we will also see, in later years many of these same women and men distanced themselves from the government and from those they remembered as "Nazis." Nevertheless, even when they disagreed with the "Nazis," they still remembered much that was good and valuable. One of the things they remembered was being "together" with other people, and Riefenstahl's film repeatedly returns to individual faces to illustrate that sense of belonging. Each Nazi organization has its place in the field before the dais, and each member has his or her place with the group, yet each remains an individual to be cherished for his or her specific contribution to the collective effort of creating the new Germany.

"Generation" in the sense we have been using it refers not to a biological cohort but to a group with distinctive shared experiences, perceptions, and modes of expression. In Mannheim's sense, the people alive in Germany between 1933 and 1945 constituted a distinct generation, in that their shared experience shaped their beliefs and attitudes in distinctive ways. Two conversations, twenty years after the war, introduce the experience of the Nazi generation and illustrate the clear ruptures that set this generation off from what had gone before and from what then followed.

A conversation with a housewife in her mid-forties in 1965, in a suburb of a southwestern city:

[Were there many convinced Nazis?]

Oh yes. Many. I could not be a Nazi. I remember I thought myself stupid. The neighbor two doors up, he was a convinced Nazi. But he doesn't talk about it now. But I don't know why, I just could not.

[Were you in the Girls' League?]

Oh yes. We hiked and camped and had such lovely community times together. And of course the Women's Association after. We were together so often and helped each other. There were speakers and helpers. Music and books. Cooking and babies and women's things. Of course my husband was in the Hitler Youth, and then the air force.

[What about Strength Through Joy?]

Oh, we never won any of the cruises, but the workplace had outings, community times together, entertainment, hotels for weekends. We saved for our car, too. There was music, real culture, serious, not like now when everything is nothing but American.

[Were there any Jews in your neighborhood?]

I didn't know any Jews. It was horrible, horrible, what was done.

[But a lot of people didn't like Jews?]

Well, yes. You—you have to remember the Jew had done much that was bad. But it was horrible what was done.

[What about Hitler?]

I remember him speaking. We had a radio. "Everything will be made the same." He was brutal. I hated that.

[But was there anything good?]

Oh, jobs. No one had work, and then there came a man, and suddenly there was work. And the highways. Hitler built the highways.

[And the war?]

I changed jobs. There was a lot of work. I was collecting tickets in the central train station when the Americans bombed us. I ducked inside the booth. There were pieces of people flying. My husband was captured and sent to work in France. He hated the French. But that's all gone now, thank Heaven.

A conversation with a dairy farmer in his early forties in 1965, in a village in the southern highlands:

[Were there many convinced Nazis?]

Oh yes. In the village. Our village was full of them. They don't like to talk much now. But I couldn't be bothered with that stuff.

[Were you in the Hitler Youth?]

Oh yes. We hiked and camped and had times together. Community. We spent a lot of time in the mountains. And the wife of course. Girls' League, Women's Association, Strength Through Joy, all that. And my mother. And my father and the cooperative. He saved for a car.

[And then the army?]

Right. To get away. I didn't like what was happening in the village.

[You mean with the Nazis?]

Right. I couldn't be bothered with that stuff.

[Were there any Jews in your village?]

I didn't know any Jews. Of course it should never have been done, what happened. But there was—well, you have to remember the Jew had done much that was bad.

[What about Hitler?]

I remember him speaking. On the radio. "Everything will be made the same." I couldn't be bothered with that stuff. And the Jews, it should never have been done. But, well, like I said, the Jew had done much that was bad. But he did build the highways. And jobs. No work, and then there came this man, and there were jobs. A lot of people, even here in the village. But I joined the army.

[And the army?]

Real camaraderie. Real fellowship. A community. Together. Faithfulness. That's the thing. German faithfulness. Different from Americans—German faithfulness.

[You were on the Eastern Front.]

Right. It was hard. I remember idiots running around in shorts if the sun came out. Pneumonia. What pulled us through was German faithfulness. Like they say, "My honor is my faithfulness."

[So you were the elite.]

Oh yes. You had to be hard. Volunteer. It was hard. But we pulled through. Faithfulness pulled us through. German faithfulness. But that's all gone now.

Of course not all conversations with Germans who lived through the Nazi years were quite as strikingly similar as this. Experiences varied, and so did responses. But the themes recurred, and so did the phrasing. In 1999, an extremely elderly lady managing a guest house in Berchtesgaden insisted, "you must remember that no one had jobs. Then there came a man. Hitler built the highways, gave people jobs." She also insisted, "you must remember the Jew had done much evil." We will see again in Chapter 13 that very few Germans remembered themselves as having been convinced Nazis. But here we see the penetration of Nazi organizations at all levels of society, and we get a hint of what those organizations meant. The words "community" (*Gemeinschaft*) and "together" (*beisamen*) express part of what the Nazi generation experienced. The experience of German culture for some and the sense of faithfulness and loyalty for others add another dimension.

Hitler for most was a disembodied voice over the radio, but he was clearly a presence, and he received credit for making things the same (*gleichen*), for building the highways (*Autobahn*), and for providing jobs. His arrival, signaled in the phrase "there came a man," marked the beginning. Typically, Jews, in the memories of the Nazi generation, were absent. The Holocaust was universally condemned, but the condemnation has a ritual and perfunctory ring. Not every German would have added the hesitant qualification that "the Jew" might have brought punishment on himself for the evil he had done, but many would. For both the timid suburban housewife and the bluff dairy farmer, who quoted the motto of the SS to support his idea of German "faithfulness" (*Meine Ehre heisst Treue*), the war was hard, but it was a closed book. The era was gone, and something new had replaced it.

The seizure of power

Hitler had insisted as one of the conditions of his appointment as Chancellor that the Reichstag be dissolved and elections held once again. The nation, he argued, must pass judgment on the new government. Hugenberg's fears that this would further strengthen the Nazis and make Hitler harder to control failed to persuade the other ministers. Hermann Goering, a cabinet minister without portfolio, now also served as the Prussian interior minister and therefore as head of the Prussian police. Wilhelm Frick, the national interior minister, granted wide powers to the state interior ministers to maintain public order. A presidential decree allowed suppression of publications or public meetings that abused public institutions or officials. Armed with these powers, Goering ignored Papen, the Vice-Chancellor, who also remained as the emergency commissioner for Prussia and in theory was his superior. Goering forced senior and intermediate police officials into retirement and appointed some 50,000 members of the Nazi *Sturmabteilung* (SA) and *Schutzstaffel* (SS) and the *Stahlhelm* as auxiliary police. Police and auxiliaries were authorized to use their weapons "unconditionally" to suppress left-wing organizations. "Every bullet that now leaves the mouth of a police pistol is my bullet," said Goering. "If you call that murder, then I am the murderer, for I gave the order, and I stand by it."

Goering and Nazi ministers in other states attempted to sabotage Communist and Socialist election efforts by banning their publications, breaking up their meetings, and suppressing all protests. Josef Goebbels masterminded the Nazi campaign, including the use of the government-controlled radio to ensure that Hitler's speeches were broadcast along with commentary that emphasized the enthusiasm of his audiences. On February 27, 1933, the Reichstag building burned down. An unemployed

Dutch worker, Marinus van der Lubbe, was arrested and later tried and executed for the crime. After the war, the Nazis were accused of setting the fire themselves, but this seems not to have been true. The documents published by East German historians were forgeries. However, it is true that Hitler and Goering immediately accused the Communist Party of planning to use the fire as the beginning of a revolutionary uprising, and it may be correct that they had convinced themselves that this was true.[2] Waves of arrests had already begun before Hitler persuaded Hindenburg to sign yet another presidential decree that harked back to the 1820s, as it empowered the Reich government to assume power in any federal state whose own government was unable or unwilling to maintain public order. A range of new crimes, including arson committed against public buildings and treason, but also incitement to riot and resistance to the decree itself, were made subject to the death penalty.

The results of the election of March 5, 1933 (see Chapter 10, Table 10.1), increased the Nazi vote to 17.3 million and their seats to 288, but did not give them a majority. The Communist vote declined, but the Socialists and Center held. Hitler proposed an Enabling Act (*Ermächtigungsgesetz*) that would grant the government emergency powers for four years. Decrees with the force of law could be issued without the President's approval so long as they did not interfere with the rights of the Reichstag, President, or state governments. Governments in other countries also suspended normal parliamentary rules to cope with political division and economic crisis. Similar laws were introduced in the Netherlands, Belgium, and Switzerland, and in Fascist Italy the electoral law had been changed so that the largest party automatically received two-thirds of the seats in the assembly. However, even with the Nationalists, the Nazis did not command the two-thirds vote they needed to enact such constitutional changes. The leader of the Catholic Center, Ludwig Monsignor Kaas, persuaded his colleagues that it would be better to vote for the Enabling Act and hope for moderation on Hitler's part, rather than face the certainty of a further escalation of violence. The Center's votes gave Hitler the powers he sought on March 23.

The "coordination" or *Gleichschaltung* (bringing into line, or shifting to the same gear) of institutions and organizations began immediately. In early April, a law eliminated permanent tenure for civil servants, who now had to satisfy their immediate superiors and who also had to prove themselves to be of pure Aryan descent. Another law imposed the same political and racial requirements on lawyers and forced all remaining practicing attorneys into state-controlled bodies under Hans Frank. The Communist Party had been declared illegal following the Reichstag fire. The Socialist Party was outlawed in June along with the Democrats. Franz Seldte, leader of the *Stahlhelm* and member of the cabinet, joined the Nazi Party and offered the headship of the *Stahlhelm* to Hitler. This undermined Hugenberg, and when he resigned from the cabinet the DNVP was dissolved as well. Hitler outflanked those Center Party leaders who wished to remain independent by signing a concordat with the Vatican, and both the Center and the Bavarian People's Party dissolved themselves in early July. On July 14, 1933, the Nazi Party was declared the only legal party in Germany.

The Reichstag continued to meet, but Nazi leaders heatedly debated the form a new national assembly would take. Some wanted to replace the Reichstag with the NSDAP's own *Reichsparteitag*. Others, linking older traditions with contemporary Fascist theory, argued in favor of a chamber of social and occupational estates (*Ständekammer*). Still others suggested something like Hermann Goering's new remodeled Prussian Council of State. One official argued the Nazi Party itself should become a hierarchical order of progressively narrower elites, topped by a senate of sixty members. Hitler decided to retain the Reichstag. He used it frequently, particularly for foreign policy purposes. He announced the remilitarization of the Rhineland in 1936 in the Reichstag, and asked the Reichstag for approval of the unification with Austria. Domestically, the Reichstag passed the Nuremberg racial laws in 1935, and Hitler regularly requested that the Reichstag reapprove his special powers. The Reichstag last met in 1942, but Hitler planned to use it again following the successful conclusion of the war to help design institutional machinery to ensure an orderly succession to his rule.[3]

In March 1933, Reich officials were appointed as heads of all the state governments, in April they were given the power to issue decrees in their states without consulting the state legislatures, and, in January 1934, the separate state legislatures were dissolved, the sovereign rights of the states passed to the Reich, and the governing officials brought under the supervision of the Reich interior minister. Labor unions first fell victim to a takeover by the SA and SS, and then were absorbed into the expanding Labor Front under Robert Ley. Organizations representing elements of the lower-middle class such as shopkeepers and artisans also disappeared, first into a National Socialist "fighting league" and then into a large umbrella organization of handicraft, trade, and industry. Farmers' associations had dissolved themselves when the DNVP disappeared. They were replaced by new peasant leagues controlled by the Reich Food Estate (*Reichsnährstand*) under Walter Darré, who was named Reich Peasant Leader in January 1934. Over the night of June 30, 1934, the murder of several hundred potential opponents both inside and outside the movement led to the *Gleichschaltung* of the SA as well. Following Hindenburg's death in August 1934, Hitler combined the offices of Chancellor and President and became both Führer and *Reichskanzler*. Later came the Party Day rally in Nuremberg, and one of the functions of Riefenstahl's *Triumph of the Will* was to demonstrate that Germany's divisions, and the divisions within the Nazi movement, had been overcome.

Gleichschaltung did not affect all equally, and some seemed to escape. Hjalmar Schacht remained president of the Reichsbank. "Germany is Hitler, and Hitler is Dr. Schacht," said the wits in Berlin. Although Nazi supporter Fritz Thyssen began to develop plans for the reorganization of heavy industry on corporatist principles, Hitler declared that industrial leaders had proven themselves to be an elite and did not require the process of "renewal" that others did. After Hindenburg's death, army officers swore a personal oath of allegiance to Hitler, but this did not differ significantly from that required of civil servants, or from the oath sworn, for instance, by United States army officers to the President. Army leaders regretted the end of their covert collaboration with the Soviet Union, but they approved Germany's withdrawal from the Geneva disarmament conference and welcomed Hitler's hints that he would begin to expand the armed forces.

The Nazi economy

The experience of the 1930s varied from country to country and region to region. Among the fully industrialized countries, the slump was especially severe in Germany and the United States. The United States, however, had not quite recovered when it slumped again in 1938, while Germany continued to expand. Britain, Italy, and France all suffered less severe initial downturns. They returned to their 1928 levels in 1934, 1935, and 1936 respectively, but like the United States they slowed again in 1937 and 1938. In addition, while Germany achieved virtually full employment by 1938, the other advanced industrial economies still suffered from high levels of unemployment. Capitalist economies also faced the challenge of the Soviet Union. The success of the five-year plans was not merely propaganda. Despite the traumatic dislocation of agricultural collectivization and the purges, the Soviet economy grew rapidly and steadily.[4]

On balance, in Germany by 1936 most of the unemployed were back at work, over the next years the economy boomed, and, compared to other nations, Germany performed exceptionally well. Table 11.1 gives some indication of how this happened. It continues the story of net investment from Chapter 9, Table 9.1. The changes are obvious. Total investment in 1935 was the highest since 1928, and in 1936 investment finally returned to the average levels of 1910–13. Construction boomed. Both new housing and public construction were consistently high from 1935 to 1938. Private companies also invested heavily in new commercial buildings. In addition, in 1937 and 1938 industry made exceptionally heavy investments in new machinery, and there was a massive increase in inventories.

What role did Nazi economic policy play in this record of recovery

Table 11.1 Net investment in Germany, 1933–39 (billions of 1913 marks)

	Total	Public construction	Railroads	Housing	Agriculture	Industry—total	Buildings	Machinery	Inventory
1933	2.3	0.4	0.1	0.7	0.9	0.1	0.3	−1.0	0.8
1934	3.3	0.6	0.3	0.9	−0.5	1.6	0.4	0.2	0.9
1935	5.8	1.5	0.2	1.3	0.1	2.7	0.7	1.0	1.0
1936	7.3	1.8	0.1	1.5	1.6	2.2	0.9	1.4	>0.1
1937	11.2	2.0	0.2	1.4	0.5	7.2	0.8	2.9	3.5
1938	12.0	2.1	0.2	1.2	1.4	7.2	0.7	3.5	3.0
1939	na	na	na	0.9	0.9	2.6	0.5	2.8	−0.7

Note:
Public construction includes public buildings and public works (*öffentlicher Tiefbau*). Housing is non-agricultural residential construction. Buildings (*Gebäude*), machinery and equipment (*Anlagen*), and inventory (*Vorräte*) are components of the total for industry. Some yearly totals do not add due to rounding.

Source: Walther G. Hoffmann, *Das Wachstum der deutschen Wirtschaft seit der Mitte des 19. Jahrhunderts* (Berlin: Springer, 1965), pp. 246, 258.

and expansion? Barry Eichengreen and Peter Temin argue bluntly that
only new leaders could implement the radical changes in policy needed
to overcome the depression.[5] Heinrich Brüning of course disagreed and
claimed that his policies had begun to show results and the economy had
begun to turn up when he lost office, "shot down," he said, "100 meters
from the finish line." Some historians have agreed with Brüning. Harold
James insists that Nazi economic policy was orthodox and conservative,
merely extending the initiatives already taken by the "presidential" cabinets of Brüning, Papen, and Schleicher and the policies of the Reichsbank under Hans Luther. The output of producers' goods and consumer
durables had already begun to rise from their troughs in mid-1932, and
though unemployment continued to increase for another quarter, by
early 1933 investment in inventory and housing had also risen, well
before any possible impact of Nazi policy.

Hitler himself insisted he had no economic theory. Nazi speakers
could be vague. However, as noted in Chapter 10, although Gregor
Strasser claimed that National Socialism was simply the opposite of
everything, he also put forward a sophisticated stimulus package. These
policies resonated with people whose lives had been ruined by the
depression. William Brustein argues the Nazis' successes in attracting
the votes of skilled blue-collar workers, livestock farmers, and
independent artisans can be attributed to their coherent economic programs, a combination of eighteenth and nineteenth-century state intervention and what we would now call Keynesian "pump priming,"
designed specifically to aid farmers and to revive industrial employment. Brustein points out the narrowness and inadequacies of the programs advocated by other political parties. As Hitler himself said, all
the other major parties had had their chance to rule and had left
Germany "a heap of ruins." That is, rather than anti-Semitism, hyper-
nationalism, or irrational anxieties, the motive of many voters for
choosing the Nazis may simply have been the superiority of their
economic program.[6]

Hitler adhered to financial orthodoxy in his public speeches. In 1934,
he claimed both victory in "the battle for work" and that "the German
Mark has remained stable." He had reappointed Hjalmar Schacht as
president of the Reichsbank in March 1933 and named him economics
minister in 1934, decisions welcomed in Conservative international
financial circles. The high levels of taxes introduced by the Brüning
government, which had been extremely unpopular, were retained. Table

11.2 shows that, as the economy recovered, government revenue also increased.

But the Nazis had promised that things would be better under their rule, that there would be jobs, that farmers would receive higher prices, that Germany would be strong again. This required programs to create employment, interference in markets, and increased armaments. One important story told by Table 11.2 is that government spending rose even more rapidly than income, and the Nazi regime ran substantial deficits from the beginning. Schacht nurtured his international reputation for financial conservatism, but he developed a range of expedients that allowed the government to conceal these deficits. This could be done through anticipations of revenue, subsidies paid in the form of credits against future taxes, or credits advanced by the Metallurgical Research Corporation (*Metallurgische Forschungsgesellschaft*), the so-called Mefo bills used in particular to conceal military expenditures. Another important story told by Table 11.2 is the large increase in the importance of the central Reich government compared to the states, and, along with this, the massive increase in military spending.

There were contradictions. When governments run large deficits they absorb available savings, and this makes it more difficult for private firms to obtain capital. Private firms are "crowded out" and private investment is reduced. The Nazi regime directed investment toward its political ends, not where the market would have led. It is difficult to estimate what would have happened in the absence of these distortions, but Albrecht Ritschl believes that Nazi policies deliberately crowded out private demand to ensure high rates of rearmament. When account is taken of these effects, Ritschl believes that the residual, the additional stimulus provided by "active policy," was small in 1934 and 1935. From 1936 onward, the continued increase in government spending may have prevented the slump that hit the United States in 1938, but this came from a trebling of military spending on top of the previous rises.[7] That is, the Nazis purposefully redirected the German economy, but did not stimulate extra growth.

The Nazi government intervened directly in the labor market. Men were sent to work in agriculture, and if they refused they lost their unemployment benefits. Women were encouraged to leave employment through marriage loans and direct measures, such as the 10 per cent ceiling on their share in university enrollments. The Labor Service introduced under Brüning (which Hitler had said at the time had "no value")

Table 11.2 Germany: government income and expenditure, 1928–38 (billions of marks, current prices)

	1928	1932	1933	1934	1935	1936	1937	1938
National product in current prices	89.5	57.6	59.1	66.5	74.4	82.6	93.2	104.5
Reich government expenditure	11.9	8.7	9.9	14.4	16.0	21.1	23.1	30.7
(of which military expenditure)	0.8	0.7	1.3	3.5	5.5	10.3	11.0	17.2
State government expenditure	11.6	8.9	8.9	8.5	7.9	7.7	7.7	7.9
Total government expenditure	23.5	17.6	18.8	22.9	23.9	28.8	30.8	38.6
Total government revenue	20.5	14.8	15.9	17.5	19.1	21.6	25.0	30.0
Total government deficit	3.0	2.7	3.0	5.4	4.9	7.3	5.7	8.6
Deficit as percentage of national product	3.4	4.7	5.1	8.1	6.6	8.8	6.1	8.0
Increase in government debt	3.6	0.6	1.7	2.4	3.9	5.1	4.3	10.9

Source: John Turnbull, "How Conventional Was Nazi Economic Policy?" (Thesis, University of Sydney, 2000), Table 4, Table 7, Appendix 2.

was maintained and expanded, and became compulsory in June 1935. Under Hitler, the Reich government trebled the amount of money for work creation programs, adding 2 billion marks under the first and second "Reinhardt" programs, and a further 2 billion from the railroad, post office, and highway agency to the 1 billion allocated by the Brüning, Papen, and Schleicher governments. The 4 billion marks were close to 3 per cent of the total national income for the two years 1934 and 1935. The end of the labor unions meant that, as the economy approached full employment, upward wage pressure was minimized.

Again, there were contradictions. The Labor Service was inspired by a conservative vision of taking young people out of "dangerous" cities and returning them to the countryside. However, numbers employed in the program actually fell from 1932 to 1935. The main source of employment in the countryside was not agriculture but the new highway system. Fritz Todt, head of the agency responsible for the autobahn project, emphasized the military and economic importance of a modern system of mass transport. Its potential importance as a work creation program was significant but secondary in his view. With Hitler's support, Todt pushed the highways through over the opposition of the railroad, transport, and finance ministries. Building contractors objected to using unemployed workers from the cities, because they would require housing and were less suited to hard physical labor than rural workers. Town and district governments pushed to have their own unemployed hired by autobahn contractors and opposed the resettlement of urban workers in their neighborhoods. On balance, the projects may have taken workers out of the country by drawing them away from rural industry.[8]

Declining prices were bankrupting farmers and therefore destabilizing the banking system. As noted in Chapter 10, the Nazis did well in areas where farmers were particularly heavily indebted. Darré's Reich Food Estate imposed price controls on agricultural goods. The government also froze interest rates. This helped to end the decline in prices and put a ceiling on interest expenses. There were contradictions here as well. As it happened, the introduction of price supports coincided with the low point in world agricultural prices. From 1935, price controls actually had the effect of holding prices down, increasing the disposable incomes of urban consumers.

The government stimulated building and construction. In addition to the highway program, housing schemes of state and local governments that had been cut during the deflation were reinstituted. Tax credits were offered for renovation and for the division of large buildings into smaller units. Ley's Labor Front gained control of housing policy, and, in 1940, Hitler appointed Ley Reich Commissar for Social Housing. Once again there were contradictions. Some of the increase in housing investment was recovery from the bottom of the cycle, so again Nazi policies cannot be given much credit. In addition, policy was caught between a vision of homes appropriate for German families as envisaged in Nazi ideology, and the need to provide as many housing units as cheaply as possible. The emphasis on cutting building costs, as local government budgets were restricted, resulted in the construction of large numbers of poor-quality dwellings.

Under Schacht's direction, Germany began to cut itself off from the international economy. The end to reparations payments removed one of the constraints that had hampered Weimar policy-makers. Germany was known to have a trade deficit and to possess only small international reserves. Germany therefore could hold foreign debt hostage. Foreign countries had to compete for German favor to secure better treatment for debts owed to their citizens. Foreign assets had already been frozen and all foreign currency registered, and a law of August 1931 made payments abroad subject to government approval. Schacht built on this, and his New Plan announced in September 1934 organized trade on bilateral principles. Individual deals for the exchange of specific amounts of goods were negotiated, and payment held in special accounts. By the late 1930s, Southern and Eastern European countries had large positive balances, but were unable to spend the funds on German goods. Desperate for trade and shut out of other markets, these small countries in effect subsidized a portion of Germany's recovery and expansion.[9]

Rapid recovery through 1934 and 1935 led to increased imports and negative trade balances. Some manufacturers who depended on imports suffered, especially those in textiles. Some armaments producers were having difficulty obtaining raw materials. Schacht attempted to cut imports further, especially consumer goods and particularly food fats. This led him into conflict with Ley of the Labor Front and Darré of the Reich Food Estate. Germany again faced a foreign exchange constraint, and could either continue to separate itself from the world economy, or reintegrate itself particularly with Western Europe and the United States. Reintegration would require the end of bilateral agreements, repayment of debts, and devaluation of the mark.

The Nazi government debated the possibility of devaluation after the Tripartite Stabilization Pact signed by Britain, the United States, and France in September 1936. Schacht favored devaluation to improve the balance of payments, but Walter Funk, State Secretary in the Propaganda Ministry, was opposed. Goebbels noted in his diary that "Funk went straight to the Führer. And he intervened." A broad range of public opinion opposed devaluation because it might set off a new inflation. Gestapo reports showed that the fear of inflation was widespread, and they also show that Nazi leaders were very concerned about those popular fears. Hitler believed that inflation had undermined the morale of Germans during the First World War: "The last war was lost because of a limitless lack of understanding for the susceptibilities of the masses of small savers and housewives . . . I have pledged my word. I will not make a new inflation. The people would not understand it."

Germany remained on the gold standard at the old parity, but at the same time the regime continued to detach the German economy from the world economy through direct controls and bilateral agreements. The pretense did not last much longer. Armaments expenditures had already risen substantially. The unilateral decision to remilitarize the Rhineland announced Germany's reemergence as a military power. Through 1936 and 1937, the government was split by the dispute over the Four-Year Plan and the technical question of the best use of iron ore. The centerpiece of Goering's empire, the Reichswerke Hermann Goering, was to be constructed with capital raised from private firms, and Goering had further plans to develop low-grade German iron deposits. The point was to make Germany less dependent on imported iron ore. Schacht opposed Goering, and he was supported by industrialists who opposed the plan on technical grounds and resented the favoritism shown Goering's enterprise.

The conflict over the Reichswerke Hermann Goering is seen by many specialists as the decisive political struggle between big business and the state, and big business lost. In James' view, under Goering's Four-Year Plan Germany became a "state-planned economy." Schacht lost as well. Funk replaced him as economics minister. He remained at the Reichsbank, but continued to oppose rapid rearmament because of the danger of inflation and possible foreign opposition. In 1939, he was ousted from the Reichsbank as well, remaining a minister without portfolio but without influence.

The social and cultural context

If the economy could be subjected to an act of will, then society and culture could also be bent to serve the purposes of the Nazi leadership. If Hitler and others pretended to be following an orthodox economic policy, there was no such pretense with regard to social and cultural policies. The regime proclaimed itself to be revolutionary and committed itself to the creation of a new society and a new German style based on German culture. "In fact," said Hitler, "the power we enjoy cannot be justified, in my eyes, except by the establishment and expansion of a mighty culture."[10]

Nazi culture seems a contradiction in terms. Goering is widely reported to have said, "When I hear the word 'culture' I reach for my pistol." The Nazi cultural program was fundamentally incoherent, based on a notion of reality that was both eternal and unchanging, and also malleable through an act of will. Nevertheless, culture became both leitmotiv and façade as society was restructured. Hans Frank, as head of the General Government in occupied Poland, took the old Polish royal palace as his official residence, created a state theater and symphony orchestra, and fostered the publication of a range of German-language journals, while at the same time overseeing the extermination of the Jews and the Gentile Polish intelligentsia and debating whether to deport the entire remaining Polish population eastward, or perhaps exterminate them as well.

Nazi culture

Conservative intellectuals accepted the new government. With the fall of the Weimar Republic and the Nazi seizure of power, the loose group that Roger Woods and others label Conservative revolutionaries "shifted from seeing themselves as the 'earthquake' which would bring down the Weimar Republic and clear the way for a dictatorial order to seeing themselves in retrospect as the 'seismograph' which merely registered the inevitable upheavals of their time."[11] Some had higher ambitions. Political theorist Carl Schmitt had initially opposed the Nazi Party, but the fragmentation of Weimar political parties led him to view Hitler as the only possible source of authority, and the only one who could maintain a unified state, which, as we have seen, he believed to be the essential framework for a stable system of law. He joined the Nazi Party in 1933, and defended the purge of June 30, 1934. Until 1936, he enjoyed recognition as the leading legal theoretician of the Nazi regime.

Academics across all disciplines aligned themselves with the Nazi regime. They copied the rhetoric of renewal, restoration, and struggle for living space and applied it to their own disciplines. In many cases, they continued conservative agendas reaching back before the First World War, but, in addition, the dismissal of Jews and others the new government considered its enemies opened career paths and possibilities for expansion. Psychiatrists, for example, had become increasingly dependent on the state for funding and therefore had to respond to changes in government policy. In addition, some such as Ernst Rüdin now actively pressed forward eugenics proposals that ended in compulsory sterilization programs and the systematic murder of the mentally ill and the handicapped.[12] Similarly, the nationalistic movement in music studies initiated after the First World War dominated academic musicology departments. Musicologists who discovered new examples of traditional German music enjoyed opportunities for publication and promotion, while Marxists and modernists were excluded. The Nazi regime therefore caused little institutional disturbance. The vast majority of musicologists benefited from Nazi rule and supported the regime enthusiastically. Musicology justified the annexation of the Sudentenland and claims to the South Tyrol by searching out "German" traits in their folk music. The battle against modernism continued as well. In 1938, musicologists mounted an exhibition of "degenerate music" in Düsseldorf.[13]

Philosopher Martin Heiddeger shows the continuity of ideas and the adaptation of academics to the Nazi regime. Heiddeger's most influential work, *Being and Time* (*Sein und Zeit*), was published in 1927. In Heiddeger's view, man is thrown into a world that he has had no hand in creating. Lost, with no firm foundation on which to stand, he must learn to face nothingness and death. In a world itself convulsed by revolutionary upheavals, man must act, but he will never know the outcome or ultimate significance of his actions. In a crucial sense, therefore, the consequences of any act are far less important than the act itself. Heiddeger's concern for questions of being and meaning has interested many subsequent philosophers, including Christian existentialists, for instance. In their context, however, his use of common Expressionist terms and phrases reinforced the prejudices of readers searching for an outlet for their inchoate and frustrated feelings. His emphasis on the need for action regardless of possible consequences provided a seemingly more sophisticated justification for the claims of others such as Ernst Jünger. His deliberately cultivated provincialism and hatred of the city again reinforced antimodernist clichés. For those who rejected the Weimar Republic, it was an easy step from reading Heiddeger to asserting that the revolutionary situation (*Umsturzsituation*) of Germany required violent action, and it was also easy to say that the consequences of action did not matter.

Heiddeger not only accepted the Nazi seizure of power, he welcomed it. Further, he believed that he could play the role of philosophical tutor to the new Nazi generation. In May 1933, he was appointed rector of the

University of Freiburg, and in his inaugural address he defined the role of the university in the new Nazi state. He rejected objective science and called for an end to academic freedom. The essence of the university could only be achieved, he said, when "the leaders themselves are the led—led by the inexorability of that spiritual mandate that forces the destiny of the German people into the mold of its history." Based on blood and soil, the will of the students and the will of the people together must ready themselves for the struggle. "All powers of will and thought, all the forces of the heart and all the capacities of the body, must be unfolded through struggle, elevated in struggle, and preserved as struggle."[14]

For a time it seemed that intellectuals and academics might influence or even control the development of the ideology of the "new" Germany. There were obvious tensions within the Nazi movement. There were significant disagreements among Nazi leaders. However, as with all other elite groups, Germany's *Bildungsbürgertum* discovered that divisions among the Nazis were overshadowed by their ruthless monopoly of power. We can criticize, for instance, the Conservative revolutionaries for failing to provide a viable alternative or a "fundamental philosophical critique of National Socialism."[15] But after January 1933 this was no longer an effective option. Although they might draw on their ideas, Nazi leaders were not going to share power with intellectuals.

Hitler named Joseph Goebbels Reich Minister and head of the new Reich Ministry for Popular Enlightenment and Propaganda in March 1933. This deeply disappointed Alfred Rosenberg, who had founded the Combat League for German Culture in 1927, and led the organization in highly publicized attacks on modern artists and museums that showed their works. Rosenberg's definition of traditional popular (*völkisch*) sources of German art appeared poised to become official policy with the seizure of power. However, there was widespread opposition, even among Nazi student organizations, and Hitler decided to place art policy under Goebbels instead. Goebbels then pressed for the establishment of a Reich Chamber of Culture, and again was victorious, this time over the opposition of both Rosenberg and Hermann Goering, who as interior minister of Prussia believed culture should come under his control. Goebbels became president of the new Reich Chamber in September 1933, and it expanded and subdivided into subordinate chambers that covered all of the artistic and communications professions.

Goebbels, however, could not dictate policy. He would have preferred a broad definition of acceptable styles that in particular would have included Expressionism. He argued that a more inclusive policy would stem the flow of writers and artists who were leaving Germany for more hospitable countries. Expressionism was the only identifiably German movement in modern art. Hitler, however, had strong views, especially about painting: "There are really men who on principle feel meadows to be blue, the heaven green, clouds sulfur-yellow . . . In the name of the German people I have only to prevent these miserable unfortunates, who clearly suffer from defects of vision . . . from presenting them as 'art.'"[16] When Hitler, after some vacillation, declared himself and the National Socialist movement unequivocally opposed to modernism in the arts, Goebbels reversed himself, and ordered the watercolors by Emil Nolde that he had "borrowed" from the National Gallery removed from the hall of his ministry building.

In 1937, nearly 16,000 works of "degenerate art" were confiscated from museums across Germany, and some 700 were exhibited in a show in Munich intended to demonstrate the difference from the works on display in the opening exhibition of the new House of German Art. All major Expressionists were declared "degenerate" and their works featured prominently. This included Nolde, despite his having been a Nazi Party member since 1920; he was forbidden to paint in 1941.[17] Over 2 million saw the exhibition in Munich, and when it moved to Berlin, it attracted over 20,000 visitors per day. The Nazis had tapped the deep vein of hostility to modernism. Most of the viewers who left comments agreed with the captions that presented the works as the products of "diseased minds" and "Jewish Bolsheviks." One wanted each artist tied up beside his work so "every German can spit in his face."[18]

The only acceptable "German style" became either an imitation of medieval and early modern works identified as being "purely" German, or an edifying and inspirational neoclassicism based on allegorical or romantic themes. Hitler echoed Wilhelm II in his preference for the idealized picture of Greek and Roman art, and in his boast that "never was humanity in its eternal appearance and frame of mind nearer to the ancient world than it is today." In return for doing Goebbels' bidding, the subsidiary chambers that governed the artistic professions gained a certain latitude in negotiating accreditation and rates of pay for their members. Painter Alfred Ziegler, president of the chamber of the visual arts and organizer of the exhibition of "degenerate art," had begun his career as an Expressionist and admirer of Franz Marc. He now specialized in studies of female nudes that included detailed renditions of the models' pubic hair. This common element in Nazi painting in theory reflected the more "natural" openness of the new Germany. Hitler lectured guests in his Munich residence on Ziegler's *The Four Elements*, which hung over the fireplace. In contrast, like other enemies of the regime, "confessional, communistic, and art-Bolshevik" artists and their works were denounced to the security services. Suspect artists lost their jobs as teachers, could not exhibit, and suffered harassment by SS thugs, their houses searched and vandalized, their works destroyed, and they themselves beaten, and possibly arrested and beaten again.[19]

The frame for the new German style was to be a new reconstructed Berlin, to be known as Germania. Albert Speer was named Inspector General of Buildings for the Renovation of the Federal Capital in January 1937. The capital would become a city of 8 million. Railroad stations would be shifted and a new system built to make space. The city would be crossed by four thoroughfares each wider than the Champs Élysées in Paris. The proposed center included a meeting hall several times larger than St. Peter's in Rome, so large that clouds could form within it and rain would be a real possibility. Hitler said, "I am too proud to move into former palaces . . . Everywhere they're squatting in some old building. My simple ambition is to present the new German Reich with buildings it need not be ashamed of." His own palace, at the very center, was planned to cover a plot of 22 million square feet.[20]

The regime's emphasis on propaganda implied recognition of the importance of popular culture, and the need to control and manipulate it. But this opened another area for disagreement and conflict among Nazi agencies. Jazz, for instance, was banned from German broadcasting when the Nazis came to power in 1933. Rosenberg and other *völkisch*-inclined Nazis believed that jazz represented "negrification" of culture. Its associations with blues and its improvisation and spontaneity made jazz the quintessential manifestation of decadence and American lack of culture (*Unkultur*). But the ban was not always enforced. What Michael Kater calls "the haphazard totalitarianism of Hitler's regime" in this instance meant that local Nazi leaders could either enforce the ban more effectively than could be done from the center, or neglect to enforce it at all. Some senior officials enjoyed jazz music and continued to listen to it. During the war, the army entertained soldiers with jazz groups and broadcast jazz over its radio network to prevent the troops from listening to British or American broadcasts.[21]

Hitler and Goebbels prized cinema highly because it married ideology, propaganda, and esthetics to a modern technology. Goebbels gained control of Ufa. The film corporation's previous successes had depended on experimentation, carried out despite Hugenberg's conservative agenda, and Marxists and Jews had played key roles. Under Goebbels, the best talents emigrated, production costs rose, and exports collapsed. But popular culture remained a business. Film under the Nazi regime certainly imparted propaganda messages, but still had to entertain to be effective. Goebbels himself cut off the initial wave of films such as *Hitlerjunge Quex* (*Quex of the Hitler Youth*, 1933) that celebrated the seizure of power because "we National Socialists place little value in having the SA march about on stage or screen. They belong in the street." Relatively few of the films produced under Goebbels were overtly propagandistic. Most were comedies, musicals, and domestic melodramas. The war brought more explicit propaganda, including the purported documentary *The Eternal Jew* and the anti-Semitic drama *Jud Süss* (both 1940). Goebbels' last major film project, *Kolberg* (1945), returned to the Napoleonic wars. Intended to inspire its viewers to resist the Allies to the last, it presents a mythical retelling of German resistance to the French and a spectacular resurrection from the ashes of defeat.[22]

The divisions and competition among the Nazi leaders and among their institutional empires could be exploited by astute careerists, but they also could result in individuals and groups being caught in the crossfire of contending power centers. Folklore studies (*Volkskunde*), for instance, attracted the attention of Nazi leaders because of its relevance to the identification of the roots of German culture. Leading folklore scholars had already politicized their discipline before 1933, and with few exceptions they collaborated with the Nazi government after 1933. Many had advocated the establishment of a central Reich institute of folklore studies. The intended purposes of this institute included national regeneration, reversal of rural migration to the cities, authentication of foreign-born Germans as part of the German *Volk*, and verification of German claims to ethnically mixed border areas.

Because of its obvious political uses, the Nazis promoted *Volkskunde*. New professorships, research institutes, and umbrella organizations were funded, and the Reich Institute was finally established in 1942. As the field expanded, younger scholars proved eager to take advantage of these new opportunities. Many of these worked under an office headed again by Rosenberg, who viewed *Volkskunde* as a means of supporting the racial theories he had advanced in his *Myth of the Twentieth Century* (1930). The older generation of folklore specialists were denounced for adhering to outdated methods and beliefs and displaced from leadership. Then, however, Rosenberg's control over folklore studies was challenged by a rival agency, the *Ahnenerbe* (Ancestral Inheritance), sponsored by Heinrich Himmler. The resulting conflicts over the distribution of resources and power were couched in ideological terms, as each side fought to have its position recognized as the correct interpretation of the National Socialist vision. The losers lost funding and sometimes their positions. In the aftermath of the war, the conflict proved convenient for numbers of folklore scholars, who claimed that they had been harassed and suffered professional discrimination under the Third Reich, even though they had in fact suffered only as the result of losing in the struggle between rival Nazi agencies.[23]

Purges in the arts and the universities ran parallel to the "renewal" of the bureaucracy. Under Goebbels' Reich Chamber of Culture, any person involved in professional music, theater, architecture, the visual arts, or journalism required membership in the relevant subsidiary chamber. Those who were Jewish and those defined as "dangerous" or "undesirable" were refused membership and deprived of their livelihood. In the universities, about 1400 out of a total of 11,000 teachers were dismissed. Jews were excluded as they were from the civil service generally, as were any Gentiles suspected of political unreliability. All fields were affected, but the losses were heaviest in economics and social science faculties. Marxists and other students without the proper "national conviction" were forbidden to enter universities in August 1933. The yearly intake of students was restricted to 15,000, including the permitted 10 per cent of women. At first, the intake also allowed 1.5 per cent of Jews. After July 1935, prospective students needed their secondary schools to attest to their national conviction, and they also had to submit proof of their ancestry.

Those who lost their positions as entertainers, artists, writers, or academics faced either prolonged unemployment or exile. Many chose to leave Germany. The exiles included many prominent scientists, especially physicists, including Albert Einstein. Hitler dismissed Einstein's theories as "Jewish physics" and partly as a result Germany did not develop the atomic bomb. Also among the exiles were members of the Frankfurt School, such as Theodor Adorno and Herbert Marcuse, who laid the foundations of postwar social science in the United States. Ludwig Mies van der Rohe and Bauhaus director Walter Gropius moved to the Illinois Institute of Technology in Chicago and Harvard University respectively and became two of the most influential architects of the twentieth century. Some exiles produced notable works, such as Bertolt Brecht's plays *Life of Galileo* (1937–39) and *Mother Courage and Her Children* (1939) and Thomas Mann's novel *Doctor Faustus* (1943–45, published in 1947). Others did not fit in, especially creative artists and writers. Communist poet and Reichstag representative Johannes Becher and Marxist theorist Georg Lukács narrowly escaped death in the purges in the Soviet Union. Some despaired. The long list of suicides includes literary theorist Walther Benjamin, playwrights Kurt Tucholsky and Ernst Toller, and painter Ernst Kirchner.

Women and the family: mothers in the fatherland

Male intellectuals and academics were not the only ones who believed they could impose their vision of a better future on the regime, and they were not the only ones to be disappointed. Leaders of women's organizations also discovered that there were elements of the Nazi ideology that were not negotiable, and that the regime's leaders would not share power with anyone outside their circle.

As we saw in Chapter 10, women had supported the Nazi Party in large numbers. In addition to 50,000 full party members and more than 200,000 members claimed by Nazi women's organizations, over half of the people who cast their vote for the Nazis were women. The local, regional, and national leaders who mobilized these women remained largely independent and outside the formal party hierarchy. They attacked the leaders of the old middle-class women's movement unmercifully, particularly for emphasizing gains for individual women at the expense of changes that would benefit all women as members of the national community. They disagreed with each other as well, but they shared a common vision. The new national community would contain a separate public space in which women would exercise autonomy, a female *Lebensraum* to correspond to the male *Lebensraum*. Many women activists requested guidance in the points of Nazi doctrine and Adolf Hitler's thought, but this was to arm themselves "to answer questions by bitter opponents," or to translate "My Struggle" into "Our Struggle." "The activation of the male world has been achieved," said one, "but the woman's unique potential has not yet been tapped. The Party has not yet appreciated the faithfulness of its women and their emotional fanaticism."[24]

In the tension and excitement of the campaigns before Hitler finally became Chancellor, definitions of the space that women would occupy remained loose. As in other areas, Hitler was willing to let his followers compete among themselves as the movement expanded. Already in 1932, however, the growth of the Party and its ancillary organizations posed serious administrative problems, and as part of a general reorganization, Gregor Strasser, head of the party apparatus, began to bring the women's organizations under central control. A number of prominent women activists received national recognition, but women's organizations were placed under the direction of the male *Gauleiter* in each district. In May 1933, Robert Ley, head of the Labor Front, announced the formation of a women's grouping that would amalgamate more than two hundred existing women's associations. Along with a pledge of allegiance to Nazi ideology, this required them to exclude Jews from leadership positions, submit their financial records and agendas for approval, and appoint only Nazi women to office. Conservative organizations such as the Queen Louisa League agreed at once, but so too did the powerful Federation of German Women's Organizations (BDF), whose executive overruled the advice of its long-time leader Gertrud Bäumer and voted to dissolve itself.

Initially the position of women and the role of women leaders in the Nazi movement appeared secure. The elite Nazi Women's Organization (the *NS Frauenschaft*) increased in membership to 2 million members in 1935. Under its control the remaining organizations were grouped into the German Women's Work (*Deutsches Frauenwerk*), which had 2.7 million members in 1935, and 4 million by 1940. Leaders of the old women's organizations were not harassed and many emerged as the leaders of the growing Nazi organizations. Bäumer initially lost her position as a specialist in youth welfare in the interior ministry, but following protests she was offered another position. Although her name disappeared from the masthead for a few months, she continued to publish her journal *Die Frau* until 1944. She supported the restrictions on women attending universities because she said standards had dropped, and she now defined the women's movement as a non-political

force motivated only by a "longing for outlets for its spiritual powers."
She also revised her curriculum vitae to identify herself as an early
"National Socialist" and lived to insist after the war that she had never
published a word under the Nazi regime that contradicted her
principles.[25]

Interior minister Wilhelm Frick went out of his way to assure women
in the public service that the government had no intention of dismissing
them, but merely that he wanted to ensure that women who did not need
the extra income should give up their jobs. In fact, the Nazis systematically excluded women from public life. The Prussian state service had
already dismissed all married women by early 1934. Eventually, all
senior female officials and virtually all of some 19,000 women holding
regional and local government offices lost their positions. These
included Jews and supporters of left-wing parties, but they were
replaced by men, not by Nazi women. As noted above, women were
limited to 10 per cent of university enrollments. In 1934 came a requirement that all female doctors be unmarried. In 1936, a personal directive
from Hitler excluded female lawyers from positions as judges and advocates and confined them to the middle levels of state legal departments.
Women were excluded from jury duty because they could not "think
logically or reason objectively." In 1937, Hitler personally barred women
from positions in the higher civil service.

Although the number of women teachers declined by 15 per cent,
there were few limitations on "female" occupations. At first, the government's assurances that dismissed female public servants could find
positions in voluntary activities or within appropriate female areas of
administration seemed hollow, since these new bureaucracies did not yet
exist. Over time, however, large numbers of women did make careers in
new Nazi social service structures. Nazi child welfare policies, for
instance, were continuous with aspects of both progressive and conservative reform from earlier periods. Here *Gleichschaltung* meant dis-
placement of some agencies by the Nazi Party apparatus, but not a
decline in the number of positions.[26] In the case of birth control and sex
education, the new Nazi regime brought a more complete break. The
subordination of procreation to "racial and political purification"
changed the meanings of birth control and abortion. Expulsion of
female, Jewish, and Socialist and Communist doctors who had led in the
foundation and extension of birth control and sex education clinics, the
destruction of private organizations dedicated to sex education, and

the *Gleichschaltung* of remaining clinics to serve Nazi purposes created a wholly new situation, although the Nazis emphasized continuities in their propaganda.[27]

A eugenic biological vision lay at the center of the Nazi ideology. The "racially fit" were to be identified and encouraged to bear as many children as possible. The role of women in Hitler's view was to serve the *Volk* by producing these racially pure children. "Your body does not belong to you," said a government pamphlet, "but to your lineage [*Sippe*] and your . . . people [*Volk*]." The government levied a new tax on unmarried persons, and used the proceeds to fund substantial grants to newly married couples, on the conditions that both husband and wife could prove their pure Aryan descent for two generations and that the new wife did not work outside the home. To ensure against wastage, the grants came as coupons that could only be used for the purchase of household goods.

When the war began, Nazi agencies sought out suitably "Aryan" stock wherever it was to be found. Young women with Aryan features were placed in brothels to mate with SS officers in the hope they would become pregnant and bear Aryan children. Some 200,000 Polish children were identified as Aryan and taken to Germany for "Germanization." The Nazis preferred children ten years or younger, because they would not be attached to their "Polish" past. They were graded on a 62-point scale, with an emphasis on physical traits. Arms, legs, and heads were measured. The size of a girl's pelvis and the size of a boy's penis were noted as an index of future reproductive capacity. Given a German name and ordered not to speak Polish, they were then adopted into racially approved German families.

Conversely, the "unfit" and those "unworthy of life" were to be identified, discouraged from reproducing, and ultimately eliminated. In July 1933, the government required nurses and social workers to report all "genetically defective" individuals to health authorities, who were empowered to decide whether they should be sterilized. However, *voluntary* sterilization was made illegal. Over 200 special courts heard the applications that flooded in from social workers, 100,000 in the first year, resulting in over 50,000 sterilizations, with nearly equal numbers of men and women. Official totals were not published after 1936, but estimates place the total number of forced sterilizations between 300,000 and 400,000. As Claudia Koonz notes, other countries, and a number of American state governments, had sterilization laws based on eugenics principles, but only in Germany did the full power of the state focus on the systematic weeding out of groups of persons the regime found undesirable.[28] The 1933 law increased penalties for abortion, but a revision in 1935 permitted eugenically approved abortions before sterilization, and in 1940 local health officials were instructed to consider abortion in cases of rape or undesirable racial combinations. The war brought over five million forced workers into Germany, and female foreign workers who became pregnant, and German women who became pregnant by foreign workers, were regularly forced to have abortions.

As elsewhere in Nazi policy, there were contradictions. Although the family was praised as the "germ cell" of the nation, the state interfered continually in its functioning. The choices of marriage partner and children were constrained by racial and eugenics laws. The authority of the father was undermined by the demand for total loyalty to the Führer and the state. In addition, though husbands were intended to support their wives and children, the marriage law of 1938 made divorce easier for men, who were able to plead "irretrievable breakdown" of their existing marriage and then avoid alimony and support payments by claiming to want to establish a new family.[29] The role of the mother was circumscribed by a host of regulatory agencies that guided her as she nurtured her offspring. High social status was no defense; all mothers were equal in the eyes of the state. Wealthy women found to their shock that their servants were recruited into Labor Front organizations along with all other workers. Antenatal clinics, infant care, nutrition, and household management had all been concerns of government and voluntary organizations before the First World War and during the Weimar years. This form of surveillance now expanded and intensified as the Nazi state identified the production and nurturing of the next generation as one of its highest priorities, but also insisted on guiding mothers and housewives in the most efficient use of scarce resources.[30] Finally, once children reached the appropriate age, they were taken out of the family for large portions of each day, not only in Nazified schools but also in Nazi youth organizations.

Women could play a role, but paradoxically it was outside the family, in the expanding array of institutions and organizations that supplied advice and services, offered courses in home economics, structured leisure time activities, and provided the background labor required for the new calendar of official ceremonies. Careers could be and were made by many, most notably the head of the *Frauenschaft*, Gertrud

Scholtz-Klink. A widow with four children and therefore a self-sacrificing mother, she was conveniently unimpeded by her wifely duties to a husband. Younger than her rivals, and with impeccable Aryan looks, she was an antidote to the joke making the rounds that the new regime wished to produce children "as blonde as Hitler, as slim as Goering, and as athletic as Goebbels," an unkind reference to the clubfoot of the last-named.

Scholtz-Klink had united local Nazi women's organizations in Baden in 1930 and successfully allied them with non-Nazi women's societies. She had no national experience, but she had a powerful male patron, director of national welfare Erich Hilgenfeldt. Scholtz-Klink later denied rumors of a sexual relationship, but Hilgenfeldt only married on the day after Sholtz-Klink's wedding to an SS general in 1939. In 1933, it was Hilgenfeldt, a shrewd infighter capable of "a viciousness rare even among Hitler's deputies," who set out the policy program. He announced the regime's intention to end "racial poisoning" and "to create the type of woman who is needed in our era . . . as the complement of the heroic and fighting man." Scholtz-Klink remained in the background, speaking only vaguely of woman's "spiritual duties."

Hilgenfeldt mounted a smear campaign against Scholtz-Klink's main rival, who had the support of his superior, interior minister Frick. Her supporters responded in kind. They accused Scholtz-Klink of neglecting her children, of an affair with a Nazi functionary, and of a "miscarriage" that might have been an abortion, and they accused Hilgenfeldt of homosexuality. In late 1934, Hilgenfeldt was forced to withdraw his charges, but, in the meantime, with additional support from Rudolf Hess, Scholtz-Klink had become the head of the *Frauenschaft*. As head of the new organization, as she said, "I want my wishes accorded the same respect that would be given to a man . . . I insist on this attitude from my co-workers and I am determined to make it an iron law right down to the smallest local group." However, every single order she issued required Hilgenfeldt's signature before it could be implemented.[31]

Equally ambitious, Leni Riefenstahl, like Scholtz-Klink, benefited from the patronage of powerful men. She had already produced the official film record of the 1933 Nuremberg party rally under a special contract with Hitler. In 1934, for the shooting of *Triumph of the Will* she commanded battalions of camera operators and other technicians, and her demands created "frequent conflicts with the Party organization, which was soon up in arms against her," according to Albert Speer.

She could rely on her supporters, however, including particularly Julius Streicher, the *Gauleiter* in the Nuremberg district. Following the 1934 party rally, he sent her a telegram addressing her in the familiar Du form and recalling their last time together. Her party file also includes a power of attorney, giving Streicher authority to act on her behalf in a dispute with "the Jew Bela Balacs."[32] She went on to a privileged existence in the Nazi world, and to produce another technically outstanding film under special contract to Hitler, this one commemorating the 1936 Olympics (*Olympia*, 1938).

The requirement that women not work outside the home, except in the approved "feminine" social service occupations, corresponded not only to Hitler's personal preferences and to Nazi ideology, but also to the interests of some of the movement's key supporters among the middle classes, shopkeepers and professionals, for instance. For the majority of women, however, the demand for labor resulting from recovery and then rearmament meant that female employment continued its long-term upward trend. Employers could not resist the appeal of women who earned on average from 50 to 70 per cent of male wages. Nazi Party members expressed dismay that in 1936 there were 600,000 more women employed outside the home than there had been when the Nazis came to power.

The outbreak of war and the mobilization of men led inexorably to a further expansion of female employment, but not to the extent that might have been expected. The percentage of women in the German industrial work force rose only from 26.2 in 1940 to 26.5 in 1943. In May 1940, restrictions on the employment of married women were lifted, but official encouragement such as the American government gave women to contribute to the war effort never appeared. Germany utilized a far smaller share of its potential female labor force than either Britain or the Soviet Union. Middle-class women did find more employment in the administrative jobs they had been forced out of previously. In heavy industry, however, the lack of training available to German women over the previous decades reduced the pool of skilled workers. In agriculture and in less skilled occupations the regime decided to exploit foreign workers whenever possible, rather than use German labor. Despite the commitment to "total war," the ideology of sex segregation combined with Hitler's determination to avoid the hardships of the First World War therefore prevented Germany from complete mobilization.[33]

Daily life in Nazi Germany

How did the experience of living under the Nazi regime affect women and men as individuals and workers? More pointedly, did ordinary German women and men support Hitler and Nazism? One important aspect of daily life was the continuing role of the bureaucracy. The face of the state remained largely the same for most Germans. Nazi Party secretary Martin Bormann attempted repeatedly to force official departments to give the party the right to approve appointments and promotions of all public officials. The Civil Servants' Association (DBB) was renamed and absorbed into the Nazi Party in January 1934. However, a stubborn battle waged by Wilhelm Frick, the interior minister, resulted in a compromise public service law in 1937 that limited the role of the party in the personnel policies of the bureaucracy. This apparent victory then evaporated in the war. In 1942, the Reichstag granted Hitler's request that as commander-in-chief he be given the right to insist that every German obey his orders and to punish them should they refuse "without being bound by existing Reich legislation." Nevertheless, in the meantime, although virtually all senior "political" officials had been replaced by Nazis, 90 per cent of the remaining higher civil servants and almost all lower-level officials who were not Jews, women, or leftists remained in their positions.

The new members who flooded into the Nazi Party were labeled cynically by the "old fighters" as the "March victims" (*Märzgefallene*), a reference to those who had died in the 1848 revolution. In fact, as Jürgen Falter has shown, although over 62,000 new members joined in March 1933 and more than 203,000 in April, 1.3 million lodged their applications in May, just before the publicly announced deadline. Compared to those who joined before September 1930, the new members were slightly more likely to be male (95 per cent compared to 93), and they were significantly older (34.4 years compared to 27.9), more likely to be married (62 per cent compared to 45), less likely to be workers (35 per cent compared to 41), and much more likely to be academics (9.2 per cent compared to 4.7) or public officials (12.5 per cent compared to 4.2).[34] Officials, that is, might be party members, but most likely their membership was recent.

Another aspect was the proliferation of Nazi organizations, some of them renamed successors of Weimar associations and some of them new. As noted above, women worked in an expanding range of social service positions. Girls and boys moved seamlessly through the Girls' League and Hitler Youth, into school associations, and on to the various chambers into which most occupations and professions had been organized. The Labor Front's Strength Through Joy (*Kraft durch Freude* or KdF) programs extended into the workplace and provided entertainment, recreation, and vacation facilities. In the context of the depression and recovery, many country restaurants and hotels were taken over by the KdF, and many professional musicians depended on KdF functions for their livelihood.

Life, even within the new structures of Nazi organizations, continued. Middle-class women continued to lead women's organizations and to work as teachers, social workers, and public health nurses. Painters, sculptors, composers, and musicians, if they were male and Aryan, continued to produce and perform.[35] Senior professionals such as doctors and lawyers, if they were male and Aryan, continued to exercise their professions.[36] Social scientists, if they were male and Aryan and if their work could be reformulated in politically acceptable ways, continued to research and publish their results.[37] So, too, in the physical sciences.[38] Even in physics, one could argue that the rigorously empirical approach of the officially approved "German" physics could produce results as readily as the despised "Jewish" theoretical physics. Hitler's personal hostility toward "Jewish" theories slowed work on atomic energy, but did not halt it. Some internationally recognized physicists such as Werner Heisenberg remained in Germany. Heisenberg played a key role in the understanding of nuclear fission and in recognizing that the isotope Uranium 235 could be used as a nuclear explosive. At first, the rapid success of the German armies made new weapons appear unnecessary, and when the war began to go against Germany in 1941–42, it was already too late to develop an atomic bomb in time to influence the war's outcome.[39]

Most importantly for most Germans, there were again jobs. There were no labor unions, but this was not supposed to matter, for "German work" itself would bring joy and overcome previous class divisions. A Law for the Ordering of National Labor of January 1934 specified that there would be no collective bargaining over working conditions. Therefore, although employers' bodies such as the Reich Group Industry continued to exist, they had no role as such. In theory, all, both employers and employees, were "workers," but within each firm conditions would be regulated according to the Nazi leadership principle, with the

employer being the Führer of the plant or office. Every industrial establishment with over ten employees was required to have an elected works
council, but the list of candidates was drawn up by the Nazi Party cell
with the advice of the employer/leader. In general, wages did not rise,
although with recovery and rearmament workers put in increasing
amounts of overtime.

On the surface the Nazi system appears cynically exploitative. Nevertheless, as Tim Mason and others have shown, the system did not work
simply for the benefit of employers. Conditions of employment were
regulated both by the Labor Ministry and by the Labor Front. They
pressured employers to provide a broad range of social welfare programs, including housing, childcare, health, recreation, and entertainment. The Labor Front, as a major owner of leisure and entertainment
facilities, insisted that firms adopt the programs of its KdF subsidiaries.
At the same time, various agencies responsible for military output
attempted to increase productivity, "rationalizing" work practices and
introducing output-linked modes of payment along lines mapped out in
previous decades. The ceaseless infighting of party, government, and
management for control, and the conflicts among competing agencies,
often created a space in which workers, like other ordinary Germans,
could live. The labor courts that heard disputes decided in favor of
workers at least as often as in favor of employers, and individual workers could use connections with local Nazi Party officials to exert further
pressure on employers.[40] For most workers, and for most Germans, these
were "good times" in marked contrast to the "bad times" of the revolution, Weimar, and the depression, and the good times lasted until bombs
began to drop in 1942 or 1943.[41]

Jews in Nazi Germany

It is easy to see the Nazi regime as somehow "normal" in the view of
most ordinary Germans, and therefore to see their lives as "normal" and
ordinary as well. However, in one crucial respect these were not normal
times. The Nazi regime was founded on a hierarchical notion of races.
Among its principles was the belief that one race, the Jews, was
irredeemably evil and so dangerous as to be potentially deadly to the
German race. In consequence, all the power at the disposal of the state,
and all the energies of a mobilized society, must be directed to the
struggle against this pernicious enemy.[42]

The Jewish cultural renaissance of the Weimar years could not continue.[43] Jews were progressively stripped of their civil rights. One of the first acts of the new regime was to expel Jews from public employment. At first there were exceptions, for those of only one-half or one-quarter Jewish ancestry, for those who had been appointed before 1914, for those who were war veterans, and for those married to Aryans, but in 1935 these people too were forced to retire. Some Jews, especially academics and professionals in fields or with qualifications that would be recognized in other countries, emigrated. What looked from the outside like a flood of Jews into the world's universities, however, was only a small minority of German Jews. The possibility of emigration for those Jews who remained was restricted by a series of ever more stringent decrees, and finally prohibited outright in 1941.

The restrictions placed on Jews multiplied through the entire Nazi period. The Nuremberg Laws of 1935 deprived Jews of full citizenship and prohibited sexual relations with Aryans. In turn, Jews were banned from using public transportation, banned from library reading rooms, banned from public parks, banned from the streets bordering on public parks, banned from restaurants, banned from theaters and cinemas. They were confined to their homes after 9 p.m. and required to wear the yellow star to identify themselves as Jews. They were forced to give up their telephones in 1936. In 1938, Goebbels seized the opportunity of the murder of a German consular official in Paris and pressed Hitler to authorize a full-scale attack on Jews by the SA. On the night of November 9–10, synagogues in Berlin and other cities were burned down, and so many shop windows broken that the glass shards littering the streets gave the incident its name, the *Reichskristallnacht* or crystal night. Jews had to meet the costs of the damage themselves, as Allianz and other insurance firms refused payment, and a fine of 1 billion marks was levied on the Jewish community for allegedly having provoked the attack. Further legal restrictions followed, including the seizure of commercial and industrial assets. In addition to the yellow star, which made the bans on public movement enforceable, Jews were forced to add "Sara" or "Israel" whenever they signed their names.

The outbreak of the war brought further restrictions. Some appear as precursors of rationing and the other hardships that the war eventually brought to the whole population; Jews were treated differently, not only in being first, but also in the fact that they were not restricted, but prohibited, from doing or consuming the few things that remained to them by 1939. They were limited to shopping between 3 and 4 p.m. in 1940. In 1941, they were banned from owning a car, banned from receiving home deliveries of milk, banned from smoking, forced to surrender any typewriters they owned, and banned from using public telephones. Early in 1942, they were forbidden to buy flowers or newspapers, and also forbidden to arrange for any teaching of their children either privately or communally. Later in the year they were forbidden to buy eggs, vegetables, meat, or white bread.

In March 1942, Jews were prohibited from keeping pets of any kind. Further, it was made specifically illegal for a Jew to give a pet to anyone else. It was also made specifically illegal for a Jew to kill a pet. Rather, pets were required to be delivered to official centers where they would be killed. This meant walking, carrying for instance a canary in its cage, across an entire city to a distant suburb, because Jews could not own cars or ride on public transport. It also meant walking well around any public parks to avoid infringing the ban on appearing on streets bordering parks.[44]

Equally important, perhaps most important, Jews were stripped of their position as human beings, a "social death" imposed by the government but, crucially, "sustained, with some notable exceptions, by the German population."[45] Beliefs that had been on the fringes of acceptability before the First World War, and which as we have seen became more widespread in the war's aftermath, now became official policy, backed by the full power of the state. In his diary, Victor Klemperer records the voice of a woman. "The most terrible thing for me," she says, "is that people always say: 'But your husband *must* have done something. They don't just kill someone for no reason!'"

In working life, which the Nazis conceived as a male preserve, government policy first pressed Jewish men out of government employment, and then also out of jobs in non-Jewish firms. Under Hans Hinkel, one of Goebbels' assistants, a separate Jewish Cultural Association was established to absorb Jewish musicians and actors dismissed from state-sponsored institutions and forbidden to join the Reich chambers. It had some 50,000 members by 1937. They were prohibited from performing works by "German" composers and authors and confined to intentionally stereotyped "Jewish" works.[46] Professionals of all kinds were banned from practicing, first in any way that might bring them into contact with Aryan clients, and then altogether. Lower-class and middle-class Jewish men found themselves working for each other in a "Jewish" economic sector. Their firms suffered systematic discrimination. Individually, men might suffer violence, imprisonment, and various forms of "legal" persecution. Nevertheless, their work continued to yield them some form of fellowship and compensation.

Jewish women and Jewish children suffered the loss of social identity earlier and more directly. Shopkeepers refused them service. Officials at all levels refused them consideration. Neighbors refused them hospitality and support. In school, the children were attacked by other children. Bullying took place with the support and connivance of their teachers. Two generations of selection and indoctrination, particularly in Prussia, had created a class of Conservative and opportunistic schoolteachers not only willing but positively eager to bend to the latest Conservative breeze blowing from on high.[47] What should a mother do? Many Jewish mothers told their children not to tell their fathers of the harassment, because their fathers already had more than enough to cope with. Fathers who did learn of their children's hardship frequently insisted that their children remain in school, hoping that a "thicker skin" would protect them.

The question of what the family should do hung in the air. Some did nothing, hoping for a better future. Some attempted to fit in with the direction of government policy. Some prominent Jews, such as the Bleichröders, attempted use their influence with government officials to have their status altered. Some considered emigration. Marion Kaplan argues that it was frequently the women in the family who read the signs the earliest. Men tended to wish to stand firm, and because gender roles dictated that such a decision was the husband's to make, the decision was often delayed. Klemperer, an academic, hesitated because he feared losing his pension and because his foreign languages were not good enough. Then the turning point of November 1938 meant that it was often too late. Many men were arrested. Wives now struggled desperately to obtain visas and emigration permits, because without these documents their husbands could not be freed from the concentration camps.

The pressures and discrimination that the law imposed on Jews were widely known. In the particular case of mixed marriages, the fate of the Jewish partner impinged directly on their Gentile relatives as well. Responses varied, from divorce to a courageous refusal to submit. Holding fast to one's Jewish partner could alienate one's own family, but could sometimes save the Jewish partner if the marriage fell into the favorable category of "privileged" mixed marriages. A large proportion of the few Jews who survived were married to Gentile Germans.

The expulsion of Jews from their homes and the assignment of their houses and apartments to trustees, the collection of Jews into *Juden-häuser*, the reduction in the rations allocated to Jews, the restrictions on movement, and the requirement to wear the identifying yellow star, occurred openly. Jews found their neighbors and their business associates unwilling to assist them. Worse, they found that their neighbors often extorted "presents" of money and other valuables in return for small favors, and those same neighbors frequently looted their homes after they were taken away. Businessmen used their contacts with SS officials to profit from the "Aryanization" of Jewish businesses. That is, the theft of Jewish property was not only immoral from the outset, but was also systematically corrupt.

There is no question of the existence of widespread anti-Semitism. Government policy was tolerated and supported by most Gentile Germans. The sufferings of Jewish Germans did not result from ignorance. Nor was it a result of indifference. On the other hand, there was no single "eliminationist" anti-Semitism that demanded the annihilation of all Jews. Hitler and leading Nazis knew less than half of the German people had voted for them. They also knew, because police reports told them, that there was widespread opposition to their anti-Jewish policies. During the war Goebbels responded to Hitler's concerns about opposition to the anti-Jewish measures with an outburst of anti-Semitic propaganda, and the feature films *The Eternal Jew* and *Jud Süss*.[48] Klemperer records many small instances of kindness, such as gifts of illegal food, and his Christian wife and a female friend risked death to preserve the pages of his diary as he was recording the experiences of himself and his fellow Jews. This was state policy, executed with the full trappings of legality. Opposition was illegal and subject to civil and criminal penalties; in November 1941 it was made illegal to show friendship for a Jew by appearing in public with them, for instance. How and by whom state policy was decided remains a matter of intense controversy, as seen in Chapter 12.

Notes

1. Fischer, Klaus P., 1996; Stackelberg 1999; Burleigh 2000; Kershaw 2000b.
2. Tobias 1962; Mommsen 1964.

3. Hubert 1992.
4. See the figures in Maddison 1995, Table C.
5. Eichengreen and Temin 2000.
6. Brustein 1996.
7. Ritschl 2001.
8. Silverman 1998.
9. Berend and Ranki 1974, Ch. 11; Leitz 1996.
10. Trevor-Roper 1988, p. 82.
11. Woods 1996, p. 115.
12. Blasius 1994.
13. Potter 1998.
14. Gay 1968, pp. 83–4; Wolin 1993.
15. Woods 1996, p. 132.
16. Trevor-Roper 1988, p. 371.
17. Barron 1991.
18. Richie 1998, p. 449.
19. Steinweis 1993; Richie 1998, p. 450.
20. Richie 1998, pp. 469–72; Speer 1970, pp. 119–29.
21. Kater 1992, p. 45.
22. Welch 1983; Kreimeier 1996; Rentschler 1996.
23. Lixfeld 1994.
24. Koonz 1986, pp. 119–20.
25. Koonz 1986, pp. 147–48.
26. Dickinson 1996.
27. Grossmann 1995, p. 136.
28. Bock 1986; Koonz 1986, pp. 150–1.
29. See Bock 1994.
30. Reagin 2001b.
31. Stephenson 1981, pp. 114–15; Koonz 1986, pp. 167–71, 182.
32. Koonz 1986, p. 181 and note 10.
33. Stephenson 1975; Rupp 1978.
34. Falter 1998.
35. Kater 1997; 2000.
36. Jarausch 1990.
37. Derks 1999.
38. Beyerchen 1977.
39. Walker 1989.
40. Mason 1972; 1977; Siegel 1985; 1989; Campbell 1989; Frese 1991.
41. Herbert 1986/1987.
42. Friedlander 1997.
43. Brenner 1996.
44. Klemperer 1999; 2000.
45. Kaplan 1998, p. 229.
46. Steinweis 1993, pp. 120–3.
47. Jarausch 1990, pp. 108–9; Lamberti 2001, p. 81.
48. Bankier 1996.

CHAPTER 12

NAZI POLITICS: THE ROAD TO WAR AND THE HOLOCAUST

In *Mein Kampf* Hitler defined politics as manipulation. "The people in their overwhelming majority are so feminine by nature and attitude that sober reasoning determines their thoughts and actions far less than emotion and feeling . . . The masses are slow-moving, even to notice a thing, and only after the simplest ideas are repeated thousands of times will the masses finally remember them." Incapable of rational thought, the masses must be manipulated, through simple repeated slogans, and through careful staging of political rallies. Propaganda is essential for a movement and for a government, but it must be "limited to a few points, devised exclusively for the masses, carried on with indefatigable persistence." The leader must be active, heroic. "Anyone who wants to win the broad masses must know the key that opens the door to their heart. Its name is not objectivity (read weakness), but will and power."[1]

However, in *Triumph of the Will*, as Hitler speaks and the crowd erupts with applause, Riefenstahl's camera catches Hitler pausing, reading in the audience's response something he has not expected. He glances at his notes in surprise with raised eyebrows, and then accepts their response and feeds it into his next point. That is, rather than cynical manipulation from the top down, the regime also reacted to the needs and desires pressing from the bottom upward. Hitler repeatedly insisted, "That I found you, and that you found me. That is the miracle!" and this may have been more than mere rhetoric. For Riefenstahl, and possibly for both Hitler and many ordinary German women and men, the will that triumphed was not simply Hitler's will, but Germany's.

The contradictory perspectives of Nazi politics as top-down manipulation, or as something more complex, have led to competing interpretations of Nazi society, the war, and the Holocaust. From the outside the Nazi regime appeared monolithic, a totalitarian dictatorship ruled by a man who played the role of charismatic leader. In theory, nothing could happen without Hitler's approval. However, the regime was divided against itself, and each decision came only after intense debate. Senior leaders struggled for power and for additions to their bureaucratic empires. Competition severely reduced efficiency, even in those areas the Nazis considered most important. In the view of Karl Dietrich Bracher, Hitler pursued a set of consistent goals, but deliberately divided power among his subordinates, in order to prevent any of them from becoming powerful enough to challenge his leadership.[2] Martin Broszat in contrast argued that Hitler lacked any systematic policy, but that his inconsistent interventions created competing agencies that struggled to anticipate the will of the Führer, and that it was out of this administrative chaos that the greatest Nazi crimes emerged.[3]

The war has been described simply as "Hitler's war," but it has also been seen as the outcome of deeper processes operating on German society. Germany remained as it had been before the First World War, a powerful state situated uncomfortably in the middle of Europe. Russia, transformed into the Soviet Union and revivified by a state-sponsored Communist ideology, threatened to the east. Vengeful France and suspicious Britain hampered Germany's freedom from the west. On the other hand, all of the internal tensions that had tempted Germany's leaders to break out of their dilemma by seeking external triumph remained, magnified by the frustrations of defeat and depression. Klaus Hildebrand emphasizes the consistency of Hitler's desire to conquer living space in Eastern Europe, establish a racially based empire, and make Germany a dominant world power, but also his gift for improvisation and tactical flexibility.[4] Others see Hitler's alleged flexibility merely as inconsistency and the absence of clear goals, and Marxist historians see Hitler not as autonomous but as the agent of an expansionist German capitalism.

Similarly, historians have viewed the Holocaust as Hitler's personal project, as the outcome of the broad sweep of German history, or as something in between. Leah Greenfeld believes that the Holocaust was a possibility from the moment the German national character took form in the Napoleonic wars.[5] Daniel Goldhagen believes Germans shared an "eliminationist anti-Semitism" that predisposed them to become Hitler's "willing executioners."[6] Others disagree and follow Hannah Arendt's lead, struck by the ordinariness of those responsible, by "the banality of evil."[7] For some, Nazi crimes may simply exemplify the potentially brutal impulses lurking in all human beings.[8] Still other approaches trace the Holocaust and other cases of genocide to the deep flaws common to all societies in the twentieth century, either a fanatic but rational modernity, determined to perfect human beings no matter what the cost,[9] or the system of national states, within which difference cannot be tolerated.[10]

There are also those who regard the Holocaust as an event so far beyond the pale of normal experience as to be quite literally incomprehensible and therefore inexpressible in any meaningful way.[11] Theodor Adorno wrote in 1949, "After Auschwitz to write a poem is barbaric." Even a work of art that successfully confronts horror, by doing so gives horror form, legitimizes it esthetically, sets limits to it, and transforms it into "cultural property" for appropriation.[12] Poems were written after Auschwitz, and paintings painted, but there seems some residue, something that cannot be and possibly should not be said. As seen in the chapters that follow, German art, like Germany itself, has remained in the problematic shadow of Nazism, of the Holocaust, of Auschwitz.

The political context

Hitler

Hitler's personality lies at the center of the Nazi enigma. Karl Dietrich Bracher and others have argued that Nazism is "Hitlerism" and that Hitler's intentions mapped out the broad outlines, if not the details of Nazi policy, from economic recovery to rearmament, to war, and to the Holocaust. Frequently, however, these studies have simply taken Hitler's program as given and not probed the psychological dimension for an explanation of his policies.[13] This may in part be because, like Immanuel Kant, we sense a moral imperative that "great events have great causes." We are uncomfortable with the idea that fortune and history might be simply irrational, for, if they were, the human condition would reduce, in Kant's phrase, to a "farcical comedy" and our essential human dignity would be violated.[14] More specifically, in the 1960s a number of West German historians worried that, if Hitler were made solely responsible for Nazism and the Holocaust, then Germans as a whole would be less likely to come to terms successfully with their past, and those who had participated in Nazi crimes could evade personal responsibility for their complicity.

In fact we know a great deal about Hitler.[15] And much of what we know bears directly on possible psychological origins of his program. The evidence is subject to different interpretations, and his anti-Semitism, desire for conquest, and rigid gender attitudes all are overdetermined. Alice Miller emphasizes the abuse he suffered at the hands of his father Alois. Born in 1837, a minor official in the Austrian government, Alois was a rigid, authoritarian man who beat Adolf regularly from the age of 3 or 4 and called him with the same whistle he used for the dog. Alois' mother had been a 42-year-old unmarried peasant's daughter, and she had been working in the household of a Jewish merchant at the time of Alois' birth. Rumors circulated that this Jewish merchant had been Alois' father, and through his childhood Alois lived not with his mother but with the brother of her later husband. Alois was punishing his son for his own insecurities, and Adolf's failures in school, his fantasies of a glorious future destiny, and his desperate need to possess absolute power can be traced to this history of abuse.[16] However, during the war these and other pieces of evidence also suggested to a team of American psychiatrists that he might be monorchid, that is, suffering from a missing or undescended testicle. The autopsy performed by Soviet authorities after Hitler's suicide in 1945 reported that one testicle was missing. Robert Waite, using analogies drawn from clinical studies of monorchid boys, traces the possible consequences of this deformity through Hitler's childhood and later career.[17]

Rudolf Binion concentrates on the relationship between Adolf and his mother Klara. Having lost two previous children, she was lavishly overprotective of him as a child. She breastfed him well beyond the teething stage, extremely unusual in the border districts of Austria and Bavaria in the 1880s. In January 1907, when Adolf was 17, she consulted Eduard Bloch, a Jewish physician with a reputation as a "poor folks' doctor," about a pain in her chest, was diagnosed as having breast cancer, operated on, and released. Adolf left for Vienna to take the entrance exam for the painting school of the Academy of Fine Arts. He failed. Klara's condition suddenly worsened, and he returned home and nursed her through her final months as she died of the spreading cancer. Bloch applied a caustic packing of crystallized iodine, an expensive and ultimately poisonous treatment that he must have known was useless in Klara's advanced case. Indirect evidence suggests that Adolf insisted on the treatment. Klara died on December 21 and Adolf paid Bloch his final bill of 300 crowns, about 10 per cent of his inheritance, on December 24, Christmas Eve.

Hitler remained in contact with Bloch. He sent a postcard from Vienna in 1909 signed "Your ever grateful AH." Bloch sent Hitler a framed photo of himself in his office. Twenty years later, when Austria was absorbed into Germany, Hitler as Chancellor issued a special decree granting Bloch "all possible alleviations" from the Reich's anti-Jewish legislation. But, after returning to Vienna the young Hitler had ample opportunity to absorb the arguments of the anti-Semitic party of long-serving mayor Karl Lueger.[18] Fantasies of the malevolent power of the Jew fused with doubts about his own identity and self-worth, and with the trauma of his mother's death, and resurfaced in his anti-Semitic rhetoric. *Mein Kampf*, written during Hitler's imprisonment following the failed 1923 putsch, is saturated with medical imagery, of the Jew as a cancer and a poison, "brushing up and down the body politic, or eating like poisonous abscesses into the nation." Germans, said Hitler, "saw at most the form of our general disease and tried to combat them, but blindly ignored the virus." The source of Germany's problems was the Jew, and the humiliation of defeat and the pernicious consequences of the revolution would only be made good when the Jew was eliminated. This would require desperate measures, and Hitler repeatedly warned that the treatment might be fatal to the patient, to Germany, as well as to the disease, the Jew.[19]

Hitler became a charismatic political leader and one of the great orators of modern history. But during the First World War his superiors believed him lacking in leadership potential. Further, his fellow soldiers listened to him as he insisted that Germany would still win, long after most had come to believe victory impossible, and those tirades had no effect. How did a young man of limited academic achievement, no leadership capacity, and no speaking ability, transform himself so completely? Blinded in a poison gas attack, he was still hospitalized in November 1918 when the revolution broke out, and the shock of the news may have caused a relapse. "Again everything went black before my eyes," he later recalled.[20] In the early 1920s, the Nazi Party circulated a story of a miracle cure that had restored Hitler's sight and given him his mission to save Germany. In the 1930s, the Gestapo seized the records of Hitler's treatment, and the doctor who treated him was hounded from his position. Binion sifts the remaining evidence and argues the doctor may have used hypnosis and post-hypnotic suggestion to give Hitler the "will" to become a leader.[21]

As Jews were eliminated, at the same time German men would be restored to their rightful place as rulers of their own homes. Women would be banished from public life. Hitler's childhood was a caricature of the fantasy of male domination. Klara had been born in 1860, the daughter of the brother of Alois' stepfather. She lived in Alois' household from 1876 onward and referred to him as "uncle." Alois had separated from his first wife, and when she died in 1883, he immediately married another young woman living in the household who already had borne him one child and was pregnant with another. This second wife died on August 10, 1884, and Klara gave birth to her first child by Alois on May 17, 1885, meaning the baby was conceived within days of the wife's death. Klara was completely subject to Alois, and unable to protect Adolf from his father's beatings, which continued until Alois died. After Alois' death, Klara emphasized particularly grave or important points by gesturing toward his pipes, kept on the same shelf in the kitchen as when he was alive. Hitler said in the 1920s, "My only bride is my motherland," and slept with his mother's picture over his bed. In 1928, however, he took his half-niece Geli Raubal to live in his apartment in Munich where he kept her a virtual prisoner. She called him "uncle" and was younger than him by exactly the same amount as Klara had been to Alois. The attempt to become his father failed. Geli died in 1931, a reported suicide, but there is enough evidence to lead some to suspect that Hitler may have killed her because she tried to leave him.[22]

The Nazi leadership

How Hitler came to power and how the regime secured its position have been outlined in Chapters 10 and 11. In power, Hitler's position depended in the first instance on the support of a relatively small number of men, a group that fluctuated somewhat but remained largely constant from the 1920s to the collapse in 1945. These were the architects of the New Order, the "true believers" who established and operated the Nazi organizations that came to penetrate virtually all aspects of the lives of ordinary Germans. Martin Bormann, director of the Nazi Party Chancellery and Hitler's personal secretary, Joseph Goebbels, head of the Ministry for Popular Enlightenment and Propaganda, Hermann Goering, head of the air force and of the Four-Year Plan office, Heinrich Himmler, head of the SS and of the security services and responsible for "racial questions" on the Eastern Front, Robert Ley, head of the Labor Front and the Strength Through Joy organization, Fritz Todt, head of the autobahn project and Minister for Armaments until his death in an airplane crash in 1942—these and a few others had joined the party early in the 1920s and remained throughout.

As seen at several points in Chapter 11, these men were not united. The entire period was marked by conflicts over the meaning of national renewal and over the content of the Nazi revolution. Just below the surface of the ideological conflicts, and never concealed, was a continual struggle for power. In these battles some dropped by the wayside. Ernst Röhm, head of the SA, wanted the SA to replace the army and in this also competed with Himmler and the SS. He died in the purge of June 30, 1934. Rudolf Hess, deputy Führer and Hitler's secretary, failed to establish an administrative apparatus to exercise his theoretical power over regional Nazi leaders and lost influence to his subordinate Bormann. Hess flew to Scotland in 1941 to make peace overtures to the British government. A few others rose into the inner circle, most notably Albert Speer, Hitler's architect and then Todt's successor as Minister for Armaments.

The personality profiles of Nazi leaders reveal very little in common. Some had suffered failure and humiliation in Germany's inherited social structures, but not all. They displayed a range of psychopathologies, but did not share a single set of symptoms. The Allies administered Rorschach inkblot projective tests to major Nazi war criminals at Nuremberg in 1945 and 1946. The supervisors of the original studies disagreed over the results. One believed that the defendants were essentially normal, while the other was convinced that they represented a distinctly aberrant personality type. Their conflict ended in an impasse, and neither published a study of the tests. More recently, using the refined Rorschach Comprehensive System, with computerized interpretations, control groups, and a combination of blind and non-blind evaluation, a team of specialists concluded that the tests "failed to identify a homogeneous Nazi personality," and that the Nazi leaders "shared few common traits or characteristics with the exception of above average intellectual functioning."[23]

One trait they did share was an unswerving commitment to Nazism and to Hitler personally. This shows as well in others such as Admiral Karl Dönitz, whose tests indicate that he was a convinced Nazi, not an "unpolitical" soldier as sometimes claimed. Another common element is a conversion experience during their initial meeting with Hitler. Goering, whose father was a minor official in the consular service and who grew up in a small house on the estate of the man who kept his mother as a mistress, a war hero but at loose ends after the war, heard Hitler speak in 1922, requested an interview, swore allegiance on the spot, and never deviated in his devotion. "I have no conscience. Adolf Hitler is my conscience," he said.[24] Speer, from a solid upper-middle class family, a young architect teaching at the University of Berlin, was persuaded by his students to hear Hitler in 1931, fell under his spell, and joined the Nazi Party several weeks later. In early 1933, Hitler noticed the work he had done designing decorations for rallies and renovating offices for the new Nazi government, and invited him to dinner. Thereafter, like Goering, he never considered anything other than the Führer's will. "Completely under the sway of Hitler, I was henceforth possessed by my work. Nothing else mattered."[25]

Hitler on his part rewarded loyalty rather than competence. As it happened, Speer proved an organizational genius, but Goering was spectacularly corrupt, unable to master the intricacies of economic planning, and optimistic to the point of dishonesty about the capabilities of his air force. Rather than dismiss Goering, Hitler created new agencies or allowed others to encroach on his areas. The Four-Year Plan office, the armaments ministry, and the SS vied for control over the economy, for instance. The resulting administrative confusion led to inefficiency and waste. From one perspective, the competition among agencies left Hitler as the supreme arbiter and reinforced his power. From another point of view, this left Hitler a "weak dictator" who lost control of agencies, and the competition among the agencies then led to a radicalization of policies, in particular toward the Jews. Throughout, however, "Hitler was hypersensitive toward any attempts to impose the slightest institutional or legal restriction upon his authority, which had to be completely untrammeled, theoretically absolute, and contained within his own person."[26]

Just below this group were the *Gauleiter*, the leaders of the Nazi Party's regional administrative units. Like the senior leaders, most were long-time Nazi Party members, and like them they were intensely loyal to Hitler personally. Again, Hitler reciprocated, and in case after case intervened on the side of "his" *Gauleiter* in any dispute with central authority or with specific government ministries. Although most did not achieve quite the lavish lifestyle of Hans Frank in the General Government in Poland, a substantial fraction was corrupt, many were incompetent administrators, and all resented any intrusion into their district, for whatever purpose. Neither Hess nor Bormann as Nazi Party secretary, nor interior minister Frick, was able to establish effective control over the *Gauleiter*. Himmler also failed to bring the *Gauleiter* under his power when he became interior minister in 1943. From another direction and in competition with Himmler, Speer struggled constantly with individual *Gauleiter* in his attempts to gain control over resources for armaments production. He also failed, although he could force their compliance on single issues by obtaining specific orders from Hitler demanding resources for the production of given numbers of individual weapons.

One step further down from the senior Nazi leaders and *Gauleiter* we find a substantial number of people who made careers in Nazi organizations. Leaders of women's associations, artistic and cultural chambers, agencies of the Labor Front, and others all grasped the opportunities. Elite organizations appeared to provide the best opportunities, and they attracted large numbers of aspiring young men from affluent and educated backgrounds. The Security Police and Security Service recruited over half their personnel from professional, bureaucratic, and independent business families. Nearly two-thirds had received the *Abitur*, and over half had proceeded on to university. Of the young men who volunteered and were accepted into the various SS units, from a third to a half possessed the *Abitur* and from 12 to 23 per cent had completed a university degree. Their personal psychologies are largely inaccessible, and they undoubtedly spread across an even broader spectrum than the top leaders, but they suffered from a collective psychosis. They believed in the regime. As an elite, even as a "new aristocracy," as Herbert Ziegler calls them, they were eager to prove themselves through their diligence, not only to follow orders to seek out and destroy the regime's enemies, but also to anticipate orders that had not yet been given.[27]

The Nazis and the old elites

Many intellectuals were disappointed with the Nazis. Carl Schmitt had provided significant theoretical legitimacy to the regime, but in 1936 his jealous opponents within the Nazi movement used his contacts with the Catholic Church to undermine his influence. Martin Heidegger celebrated the "inner greatness and grandeur" of the Nazi movement, but resigned his rectorship following disputes over appointments, and became disillusioned with the Nazi leadership when it became apparent that he would not gain real influence. Ernst Jünger was highly regarded for his call for military leadership and mobilization for war, but he was an elitist who disdained most ordinary Nazi Party members. He refused the offer of membership in the academy of poetry and traveled extensively in the 1930s. His novel, *On the Marble Cliffs* (*Auf den Marmorklippen*, 1939), tells of the destruction of an idyllic, cultured community by a vicious Head Forester. The narrator, whose contemplative devotion to botany symbolizes the life of the superior intellect, discovers a hut where the Head Forester has been torturing his victims. Government censors banned the book and Goebbels wanted Jünger arrested, but was prevented by Hitler. Critics have noted that the narrator of the novel does not disapprove of the Head Forester's actions, but rather seems to enjoy the prospect for new growth that the destruction will bring. Jünger returned to the army in the Second World War, and was stationed in Paris at the time of the 1944 coup against Hitler. He avoided committing himself because he did not believe the generals were good enough politicians to be successful.[28]

Neither the aristocracy nor business leaders played the role that they and their predecessors had in Weimar or before 1914. Local Nazi groups had frequently depended on influential landowners or industrialists for contributions and organizational support before 1933. Farmers were generally celebrated in Nazi mythology, and after the war began, estate owners in the east profited directly from foreign workers, brought to Germany and forced to labor under brutal conditions. But farmers, whether large or small, had no say in the formulation or implementation of agricultural policy. Well-connected businesses such as Krupp, the Deutsche Bank, IG Farben, and Allianz Insurance all benefited, from the expansion of the economy, from the opportunity to take over Jewish-owned firms and other property in occupied territories, and from the employment of conscripted foreign workers. Nevertheless, the businessmen who had supported the Nazis discovered that they had no more influence over the Nazi regime than the politicians and generals who actually placed Hitler in power. Fritz Thyssen, son of steel magnate August Thyssen and chairman of the United Steelworks, had been a major donor to Nazi Party. After the seizure of power, his proposals for a corporatist restructuring of German industry were ignored. Alienated from the Nazi government, he opposed the war and fled Germany in 1939. He was captured in Vichy France, shut in a mental hospital from 1941 to 1943, and then confined in a concentration camp until the end of the war. Imprisoned by the victorious Allies for four further years, he was finally released, emigrated to Latin America, and died deeply embittered in 1951.

Army officers had been attracted in increasing numbers to National Socialism, for many of the same reasons as other Germans. The promise of strong leadership had an additional appeal to the army, since it promised increased military budgets and the possibility of action and promotion. Large numbers of junior officers were involved with the Nazis, and among senior officers Werner Blomberg was well known for his sympathetic attitude toward Nazism and Hitler personally. Blomberg became defense minister and defended the 1934 purge. As seen above, the Nazi government began to increase military spending almost immediately. From 1936 onward, the regime directed the economy toward a war footing and pursued an active and expansionist foreign policy. Within the army, Georg Thomas, in charge of the mobilization section from 1928, pressed for expanded production of synthetic materials and for agencies to control supplies of raw materials as in the First World War. In 1936, Blomberg and the army seemed poised to work closely with Goering's new Four-Year Plan office.

But Goering, after defeating Schacht and the representatives of heavy industry, attacked the war ministry and attempted to deprive it of any influence over economic policy. Then, in 1937, planners in the army, including the Commander-in-Chief Werner von Fritsch and the Chief of Staff Ludwig Beck, became alarmed at Hitler's grandiose military plans, believing that reserves of manpower and raw materials were already drying up and fearing Germany's continued dependence on imports. In January 1938, Blomberg remarried. Hitler and Goering served as principal witnesses, but several days later Goering produced evidence that Blomberg's new wife had a police record for theft and indecent behavior. Hitler dismissed Blomberg. Then Himmler accused Fritsch of being a homosexual, and Hitler dismissed him as well. Hitler abolished the post of war minister and assumed personal command of the armed forces. A new high command was created as his personal military staff, and the new Commander-in-Chief, Walter von Brauchitsch, was a devoted follower. Another sixteen generals were relieved of their commands and 44 transferred.

The army had been brought to heel, but Hitler hedged his bets. Brauchitsch may have received money to help with his own divorce, and from 1938 onward he received a monthly check as "compensation for expenses." In the summer of 1940, other senior officers began to receive large, tax-free payments from a discretionary account in the Reich Chancellery, 4000 marks a month for twelve newly promoted field marshals and 2000 a month for each remaining *Generaloberst*. These payments can be compared to annual salary levels of 26,500 and 24,000 marks for field marshals and senior generals respectively. Recipients were informed by a letter from Hans-Heinrich Lammers, chief of the Reich Chancellery, that "Whether and in what amount one can expect further compensation for expenses . . . remains reserved for my decision in [each] individual case, based on the authorization given to me by the *Führer*." Hitler also made "bequests" of 250,000 marks to senior officers on significant birthdays (fiftieth, sixtieth, sixty-fifth), and a number also received large landed estates, in the case of famous tank commander Heinz Guderian a property worth 1.24 million marks. The timing and manipulation of the gifts show that Hitler intended them not as rewards but as bribes to ensure obedience.[29]

Politics and everyday life

A social consensus supported the Nazi regime. Hitler had provided jobs, and he was building the highways. In his study of Bavaria published in the 1980s, Ian Kershaw documented the widespread and active enthusiasm of ordinary Germans for their new rulers, their delight that the economy had finally recovered, and their pride in Germany's return to international power. Kershaw's biography of Hitler continues in this vein, framed as a general history of Nazism and its appeal rather than as a study of an individual. Germans, concludes Kershaw, willingly wagered their futures on Hitler and Nazism. They did not expect to be repaid with the Holocaust and they certainly did not expect to lose the war, but they did accept the Nazi government even when its policies appeared arbitrary, unclear, contradictory, or inconsistent.[30] Those people recognized as "German" in the annexed territories proved even more enthusiastic. Although there were some reservations in conservative Catholic areas, Austrians of all social classes accepted unification with Germany and eagerly embraced Nazism. Anti-Semitism was especially widespread and virulent in Austria. Some 8 per cent of the total population of Greater Germany, Austria contributed 14 per cent of SS personnel and 40 per cent of the "special" units assigned to killing operations.[31]

The extent and quality of popular support for the regime remains in dispute, as does the question of what the support was for. Some historians believe the atomization of society and especially the destruction of the power of organized labor gave the Nazi regime total power. In the small industrial city of Osterode, for instance, the lack of any independent basis of organization meant that after 1934 resistance was impossible.[32] Others are less certain. Detlev Peukert pointed to the variety of individual and group experiences of the Nazi generation, but also to the underlying commonalities of belief, commitment, and material interest. Competition and violence were celebrated as normal, but, at the same time, often reluctant boys and girls were drilled to obey orders in the name of the Führer and the Fatherland.[33] Michael Geyer has extended this line of argument and noted the degree to which the Nazi regime depended on self-mobilization. *Triumph of the Will* portrayed a people on the rebound from depression and humiliation. Not only could ordinary Germans demonstrate their superiority in public spectacle, but they could also impose their will on the other peoples of Europe. The "honor" that had been the exclusive prerogative of the upper classes could now be shared by all. "For if the First World War was fought for a way of life which a good part of German society had come to reject, the Second World War was fought for the construction of a better life which a good part of German society strove very hard to achieve. This is the space where identity and terror could merge."[34]

Hitler declared that Germany was surrounded by enemies, and that there were enemies within as well. The authorities encouraged patriotic Germans to report any person who opposed the regime or any action that violated any of the new laws, and to observe and report on any suspicious individuals. Enemies of the regime were the enemies of all, and this applied most particularly to "race enemies."[35] As seen in Chapter 11, Gentile Germans knew their Jewish neighbors were being rounded up, and many of them benefited. In Osterode, for example, by late 1938 most Jewish stores had passed to new owners. The government intended the ultimate fate of the Jews to remain secret. Himmler told senior SS officers that the murder of the Jews would be discussed openly "among ourselves" but never mentioned to outsiders. Nevertheless, police reports monitored and reported on widespread awareness of the Final Solution as it was being implemented. Participants told their families and friends what they had seen, and it became known that the public statements by Hitler himself and other senior Nazi leaders that the Jews would be exterminated were not merely rhetoric or figures of speech.[36]

In 1942, an article in the local newspaper in Osterode mentioned the extermination of Jews.[37]

Among industrial workers, fathers who refused to allow their sons to join the Hitler Youth [*Hitler Jugend* or HJ] could find themselves in serious trouble with the police. In the early 1980s, elderly workers remembered conflicts with their fathers, and how for a rebellious son the new Nazi organizations could provide a source of support they could never have expected from the schools or churches.

> "Papa, I'm joining the HJ." "Join the HJ, and you don't have to stick your feet under my table any more." And these words put many in the KZ [*Konzentrazionslager*, concentration camp], many fathers of families. Without evil intention, not meaning to denounce the father, just because it was asked, "Why don't you join the HJ?" "Papa forbids me!"[38]

The fathers often lived under suspicion as either known or suspected former Socialists or Communists. "Do you know what anxiety [*Angst*] is?" one interviewee asked his much younger interviewer. During the war, the aspects of Nazi labor relations that had tilted toward workers lessened. The Labor Front became less of an advocate for workers and more of a command mechanism to extract maximum effort and enforce discipline. Police, party, and Labor Front might compete, but all worked to repress any signs of discontent.

The Nazi regime did not countenance any behavior by young people that might be construed as opposition, however. Informal groups of urban youths, gangs with names such as the Edelweisspiraten and Navajos, mostly but not exclusively male and usually between the ages of 15 and 20, continued to form themselves as they had before. Their appeal may have increased as the degree of regimentation rose, but they exhibited no political tendency and were united only by a shared lifestyle and general hostility toward authority. Nevertheless, police and party agencies treated them as if they were genuine illegal opposition organizations. Some were arrested and some of their members were publicly hanged to serve as examples.[39]

Among the jealous middle class, a young woman living alone with no visible job could be repeatedly denounced. In the case of Ilse Totzke, detailed by Robert Gellately, her neighbors suspected her of being a spy because she stayed out late, always seemed to have money, appeared to "know a lot" about the army, and associated with another women who "looked" Jewish. She, in fact, had been forced out of a musical career in the early 1930s because of a motorcycle accident, and lived on an inheritance. However, she had become friendly with a Jewish woman, and when after four years of denunciations from 1936 to 1940 she was finally called in for questioning, she refused to give up the friendship. In November 1941, it became a crime to show such friendship by appearing with a Jew in public. In 1942, Totzke was denounced again, and fled, first to Berlin and then to Switzerland. She and her Jewish friend were arrested by Swiss police and turned over to German border guards. Both disappeared into the concentration camps, Totzke because she was "beyond redemption."[40]

The trauma of defeat led many to forget their support of the regime, or to remember themselves as having "resisted" to some degree. In West Germany, the Protestant and Catholic Churches supported research that detailed cases of resistance, and in East Germany Communist resistors were similarly celebrated. In fact, active resistance involved only individuals or very small groups; Communist and Socialist leaders were in prison or in exile, and neither Catholic nor Protestant Church leaders ever challenged the regime.[41] Some religious leaders opposed the Nazis' anti-Christian propaganda, and a few spoke out openly against the murders. In sermons delivered in 1943 and 1944, Catholic Archbishop Josef Frings condemned killing innocent people merely because they belonged to another race.[42] The Catholic Church opposed forced sterilization, but conceded the principle, and asked merely that Catholic doctors, who were mostly male, be exempted from performing the actual operations. The Church propounded a vague distinction between "formal" and "active" participation for Catholic social workers and nurses, who were mostly female, and some lost their jobs as a result. Protestant clergy supported the regime's eugenics measures enthusiastically.[43] Neither Catholic nor Protestant Church leaders opposed the lengthening list of anti-Jewish laws.

Those who did resist the regime, even in a minor way such as Ilse Totzke or members of youthful gangs, could be denounced, hunted down, silenced, imprisoned, and tortured and killed. The forms of legality might be observed, but in fact the security services were not bound by the laws. Those who had done nothing might still be harassed, visited in their homes, commanded to appear for interrogation, threatened, and then either released or not. This was known, even if not discussed openly.[44] It was also known that Nazi agencies disagreed with one another, and that the system was frequently corrupt. Therefore those with doubts or reservations about specific policies might, for instance, prevent the sterilization of a particular individual or have another included in one of the categories of privileged Jews. Respectable and not-so-respectable people who ran foul of one agency might be able to appeal to friends in other agencies for help. A worker whose employer ordered the army to mobilize him could use his influence with the local Nazi Party cell to have the order reversed. In the town of Trossingen in Württemberg, prominent businessman Fritz Kiehn gained control over a number of Jewish firms between 1938 and 1945, sometimes with the help of his connections in the SS. He alienated the regional *Gau* leaders of the Nazi Party, but with the help of those SS connections he survived several investigations into his business affairs by the regional Party Court.[45]

Those subjected to the brutal underside of the regime—the slave laborers brought into Germany and set to work in fields, mines, and factories—were among those most likely to resist, through attempted escape, malingering, or sabotage.[46] The conditions under which Jews were rounded up, sent to camps, and then systematically murdered did not often allow for resistance, but a few did escape, there were riots in the camps, and among Polish Jews calls for violent resistance culminated in the uprising in the Warsaw ghetto in April and May 1943. Some opposition to the regime arose from dissatisfaction with the way in which the benefits of the new national community were being distributed. Evan Bukey documents the unhappiness of Austrians, not with the Nazi ideology which most accepted, but with the takeovers of Austrian firms by Germans, favoritism shown Germans in jobs and pay scales, and the relegation of Vienna to the status of a second-class provincial capital.[47] Finally, it was only in the occupied territories that nationalism provided the motive and the breadth of organization to oppose the German invaders, in the French resistance or as partisan guerrillas in the east.

Some in the army eventually came to believe that Hitler would lose the war and destroy Germany. However, most of Germany's soldiers unhesitatingly condemned the attempted assassination of Hitler in July 1944 when the news was broadcast.[48] With very few exceptions, ordinary German soldiers, like most other ordinary Germans, believed in Hitler and in the Nazi ideal of a harmonious community marching forward toward a new and better world. Further, many ordinary German soldiers also inflicted atrocities on those they regarded as their inferiors, both

Jews and others. Most believed in the "Jewish–Bolshevik conspiracy" and believed themselves to be protecting German civilization against the inhuman hordes of the east. Not all were Nazis, but most were thoroughly imbued with Nazi ideology. On the home front, there were no spontaneous parades when the war broke out as in 1914, but rather a cautious sense that in this new war the hardships and privations of the First World War must be avoided, and that if there must be sacrifices then they must be shared equally by all classes.[49]

The Second World War

Hitler's foreign policy

The foreign policy of Nazi Germany is another area of contention among specialists. Opinions differ over Hitler's goals. In *Mein Kampf* he announces his intention to reunite Germany and Austria on the first page. In later chapters, he concludes regretfully that war with England is likely. War with France he regards as inevitable because France has been completely taken over by Jews. However, to restore the necessary balance between population and land for the German people, conquest of large amounts of territory is necessary, and this can only take place in the east. Germany, says Hitler, must "take up where we broke off six hundred years ago [and] shift to the soil policy of the future." But "if we speak of soil in Europe today, we can primarily have in mind only Russia and her vassal border states."[50]

However, in power Hitler and other Nazi leaders articulated aims ranging from moderate demands for the restoration of Germany's status in Europe, to a war of conquest against the Soviet Union, to further ambitions to replace Britain and France as the preeminent powers in the Near East, to a future confrontation with the United States and literal world power, but how much weight to give each statement remains open to debate. In addition, all of the questions of Hitler's personal role present themselves, and again interpretation depends on the view of Hitler. If he was essentially rational, a calculating opportunist who then lost the war because he committed crucial errors of diplomacy and military leadership, then possibly some alternate policy by other nations might have prevented the war, or some other policy by Hitler might even have led Germany to victory. If he was essentially irrational, driven either by some inner personal compulsion or by the internal conflicts among Nazi agencies, then the war was inevitable, and could only end with the destruction of the Nazi regime.[51]

In addition, there are several possible systemic explanations of the war, and, viewed from these perspectives, Hitler's desires may have been less important than the logic of Germany's situation. Joshua Goldstein places the Second World War in the context of long swings in world economic development and cycles of major power conflict. In this view war, though not necessarily the war that actually took place, was the final round in a cycle of "hegemonic" conflict resulting from the emergence of new major powers, similar to the Thirty Years War of 1618 to 1648 and the French Revolutionary and Napoleonic Wars from 1789 to 1815—in effect, a continuation of the First World War, and ultimately attributable to the instability caused by Germany's emergence as a major industrial power.[52] For East German Marxist historians, the Nazi regime was the political expression of a late stage in capitalist development, a "state monopoly capitalism" in a last desperate attempt to maintain the rate of profit by oppressing the German working class and expanding outward. From an internal perspective, Tim Mason saw the war as the outcome of the contradictions of Nazi policies that required successful foreign expansion to satisfy the material wants of the mass of the population, but at the same time could not impose significant sacrifices on the population in order to achieve those goals. The increasing labor shortage led to upward pressure on wages even in the absence of labor unions, and the economic crisis therefore developed into a political crisis for the regime and forced it into war.[53]

The disorganization and hesitancy of the other major powers allowed Hitler to achieve a very impressive alteration of Germany's position with remarkable ease. All countries suffering from the depression concentrated on their internal problems. France was seriously divided internally between right and left. British leaders were also divided, not only over the best means of restraining Germany, but also over the balance between European concerns and Britain's overseas interests. In the United States, a strong isolationist movement opposed any involvement in European affairs. Further, until the crisis was nearly upon them, none of the leaders of these three capitalist countries would contemplate alliance with the Socialist Soviet Union.

Until 1939, Hitler argued with some plausibility that Germany's gains represented reasonable demands, either revisions of unjust treaties or responses to the desires of ethnic Germans. In 1936, the German army marched into the demilitarized Rhineland. This unilateral move violated both the Versailles Treaty and the Locarno agreements. However, Hitler insisted that he had merely acted to restore German sovereignty over its own territory, and no power was prepared to undertake the invasion that would have been required to force the German troops back out of the region. Austria, paralyzed by internal conflict, was occupied and annexed in March 1938. British leaders, for instance, regarded the unification or *Anschluss* as inevitable, and they justified their acceptance of this new expansion of German power on the grounds that it reflected the desires of the majority of Austrians.

In September 1938, British, French, Italian, and German representatives met in Munich and agreed to detach the Sudetenland, the western segment of Czechoslovakia, and add it to Germany. The Western powers then pressured Czechoslovakia to give in to the German demands. British Prime Minister Neville Chamberlain returned from the Munich meeting and claimed to have secured "peace in our time." His policy of "appeasement" has ever since been regarded as a failure. However, at the time the decision could be seen as both inevitable and justifiable on national grounds. The inhabitants of the Sudetenland were predominantly German speaking, and many supported the demonstrators who demanded freedom from Czechoslovakia and unification with Germany. Hitler announced that this was his final demand, and the remainder of Czechoslovakia was guaranteed against unprovoked aggression.

Blitzkrieg

In early 1939, Germany absorbed most of the remainder of Czechoslovakia. Now, however, Hitler's claim that the new "protectorates" of Bohemia and Moravia had been German provinces for a thousand years was clearly false. British and French policy began to harden. Later in 1939, Hitler suddenly allied himself with the Soviet Union. Britain and France, who had been courting Stalin as well, now concluded that Hitler's ambitions went well beyond the unification of ethnic Germans, and they pledged support to Poland. Hitler, apparently convinced they would back down once again, invaded western Poland on September 1. To his surprise, Britain and France declared war on September 3. German forces destroyed the Polish army, Soviet forces occupied eastern Poland, and Russians and Germans met at Brest-Litovsk.

Map 5 The Nazi empire in 1942, showing the borders of Germany 1919–37, the Greater German Reich, and the furthest extent of the German advance

The British and French could have attacked in the west, where they outnumbered the remaining German divisions, but they did not. In April 1940, Hitler outmaneuvered them again and occupied Denmark and Norway. Then, in May, German armored columns struck the Netherlands and Belgium, while another pressed through the Ardennes and reached the Somme, splitting and cutting off the Allied armies. A delay gave the British an opportunity to evacuate over 300,000 men from Dunkirk. The disorganized French fell back. The German army occupied Paris on June 14. A week later, a new French government under 84-year-old Marshall Henri Pétain, commander at Verdun during the First World War, signed an armistice in the same railroad dining car and in the same place where the armistice had been signed in 1918. Hitler then ordered the car destroyed.

This was *Blitzkrieg*, Hitler's preference, a "lightning war" of tanks, accompanied by motorized infantry and supported by fighter bombers, intended to break through and behind the front line, cut communications between the enemy's headquarters and the troops at the front, and force the disorganized foe to surrender. Blitzkrieg was a strategic as well as a tactical conception. Each campaign could be separate, directed against a single foe; each campaign could be organized by a single commander appointed by the Führer. Stockpiles of raw materials won from previous campaigns and synthetic (*Ersatz*) replacements could compensate for the loss of resources imposed by the Treaty of Versailles. Even more important, the blitzkrieg strategy would not require a higher proportion of national income to be devoted to the military than had already been achieved. Civilian consumption must be maintained. The German people must not suffer. Hitler consistently said the hardships imposed on ordinary people during the First World War had fatally undermined Germany's morale, and he did not intend to repeat that mistake.

However, Britain did not give up the fight, and Hitler faced the problem of defeating a "world empire" that could draw resources from a range of colonial possessions across the globe. Not everyone agreed how this should be achieved. Blitzkrieg was "armament in width" and was opposed by military experts who favored "armament in depth," a program of large-scale investment in military industries to support a long war against major opponents. Hitler was not entirely consistent, and some specialists argue that the blitzkrieg represented not a strategic concept, but the lack of planning and the organizational chaos of Nazi Germany.[54] Hitler had approved plans for a fleet of heavy bombers and for a large fleet of battleships, neither of which could be ready before the mid-1940s. Bottlenecks and shortages resulted, but Hitler was not particularly interested in questions of economic management and had no sense for balancing resources against his goals. He preferred as always to let overlapping and competitive agencies fight with each other, believing that the struggle for survival would ensure that the strongest would win. As a result, German military planning suffered from the competition among the war ministry, which argued for armament in depth, the Four-Year Plan office under Goering which preferred *Ersatz* materials for use in the blitzkrieg strategy, the economics ministry which believed itself responsible for overall control of the economy, and the armaments ministry under Fritz Todt and then Albert Speer.

Some specialist military historians believe Hitler and Germany could have won the war. He appears brilliant as politician and military leader to 1940, but was then "diverted" from completing the defeat of Britain. The diversions were the attack on the Soviet Union and the extermination of the Jews, which together "consumed most of Hitler's attention and the vast bulk of the resources and manpower of the German Reich."[55] Hitler himself identified the need to fight on two fronts at once as the crucial strategic error made by Germany's leaders in the First World War. But, allied with the Soviet Union and at war with Britain and France, he then turned on the Soviet Union and invaded the vast expanses of the east before Britain had been defeated. At war with both Britain and the Soviet Union, he then declared war on the United States as well following the Japanese attack on Pearl Harbor in the Pacific.

Errors of strategy in the major theaters compounded these fundamental errors. Old soldiers say that success has many fathers, but failure is an orphan. Hitler claimed to have been the one who saw the opportunity to thrust through the Ardennes into France in 1940. After the war, others claimed credit both for the original insight and for the necessary staff work, and, after the war, these surviving generals also argued that the early victories convinced Hitler of his own genius and that his overconfidence then led to the attack on Russia and to defeat. However, following the fall of France they all hailed Hitler's genius, and none opposed any of his subsequent decisions. A fleet was assembled to invade Britain, but air attacks on London left the British air bases intact, and when the "Eagle attack" (or the Blitz, as the British called it) failed, the fleet was dispersed. The failure of the Blitz is usually attributed to Goering's incompetence, but Hitler had diverted the attacks to London and did nothing to enforce cooperation between Goering's air force and the other services. In the meantime, Hitler added new fronts in support of Italy in North Africa, and in Bulgaria, Yugoslavia, and Greece. Successful again, he also insisted that "If Russia is destroyed, Britain's last hope will be shattered," and he ordered preparations for an attack on the Soviet Union.

Army leaders accepted all these decisions. On June 22, 1941, Operation Barbarossa launched 187 German divisions into the Baltic republics, through Belarus, into central Russia, and across the Ukraine. The initial victories had virtually destroyed the Red Army's ability to resist in the central area of the advance by July 1941, and the Germans should have been able to press on to Moscow. But instead, Hitler first ordered a halt, and then diverted some of his spearhead motorized divisions south to secure the oil fields of the Caucasus and another force northward toward Leningrad. As a result, the Soviet capital was not taken and the Soviet leaders were given two crucial months to recruit, equip, and train new units.[56] When the German advance resumed, it was already late in the year, and as fall and then winter approached, the failure to plan for a cold-weather campaign began to take its toll. Tanks and transport vehicles, not prepared for the sub-freezing temperatures, stalled. Troops without winter clothing suffered. Dangerously long supply lines were vulnerable to disruption.

Stalled in the Russian winter, the Germans now needed the support of the local population. In many districts the advancing German armies had been greeted warmly by people who had suffered the effects of Stalin's dictatorship, the collectivization of agriculture, and the purges. But behind the German armies came the *Einsatzgruppen*, special units of the Security Police and Security Service. Under the direction of Reinhard Heydrich and under the authority of Heydrich's superior Heinrich Himmler, their assignment was to eliminate potential sources of future resistance by killing all those belonging to groups the Nazis identified as enemies, including Jews, Gypsies, government officials, and military prisoners of war. Mass executions began almost immediately. At the edges of ravines or trenches, successive lines of victims were methodically shot and fell, each row on top of the other. In late 1941, some of the units began to operate mobile gas vans that pumped carbon monoxide into their sealed rear sections to kill the victims. The reports submitted by the *Einsatzgruppen* themselves indicate that these 3000 men killed at least 700,000 persons in the Soviet Union between June 1941 and December 1942.[57]

After the war, army veterans such as Erich von Manstein distanced themselves from these atrocities and portrayed themselves as purely professional soldiers whose victories had been thrown away by Hitler and fanatical Nazis such as Himmler. During the invasion of Poland, army commanders had objected to the intrusion of Himmler's units into their sphere of operations, and a few local commanders protested against the murders of noncombatants and prisoners. Himmler appealed to Hitler and received authority to act directly behind the army's front lines. In addition, however, army Commander-in-Chief Brauchitsch had explicitly instructed the officer corps to master National Socialist principles and to act according to those principles in every situation. Hitler described the impending attack on the Soviet Union to army leaders as a "race war" and as "a war of extermination." They in turn passed those descriptions on to their subordinates. Army leaders accepted and implemented the "Barbarossa order" to collaborate with the

Einsatzgruppen. While the SS was to eliminate the "Jewish–Bolshevik intelligentsia" among the civilian population, army personnel were to execute any person suspected of connections with the Communist Party apparatus among captured Soviet soldiers. Army units cooperated with the mass executions of the *Einsatzgruppen*, regularly used additional mass executions as reprisals for suspected acts of sabotage, and murdered additional thousands of people as "suspected criminal elements" among the civilian population.[58]

In addition to the systematic murder of suspects and potential enemies, and mass reprisals, individual soldiers committed further brutalities against both enemy soldiers and the civilian population. Official reports detail indiscriminate shootings, rapes, robberies, and destruction of property and livestock. Survivors recounted the raping of women accompanied by the murder of their children. Hitler had pardoned individual soldiers who had committed "excesses" against the Polish population, and he issued a blanket pardon in advance for such excesses committed against Russians. Field officers, although they complained that their troops were "running wild," and warned repeatedly against unauthorized and undisciplined crimes, did not usually punish them. They believed they were fighting a war for survival against a culturally and racially inferior enemy, and their concern was not excessive severity but a possible decline in discipline. Their response was drastic. Over the course of the eastern campaign some 15,000 soldiers were executed, but these soldiers were punished not for crimes against civilians or prisoners, but for desertion, cowardice, or self-inflicted wounds.[59]

The war economy

In contrast to military historians, economists see little or no chance of Germany winning a long war against Britain, the Soviet Union, and the United States together. When Germany launched the Second World War in 1939 there was very little slack left in the economy. Germany's allies, Italy and Japan, were also close to their maximum output in 1939. In contrast, the burst of expansion in Britain and the United States in 1940 reflected British mobilization and American "armed neutrality" and preparation for impending war. Labor shortages restricted British output from 1943, but the United States continued to expand. The depressed American economy was still over three and one-half times the size of Germany in 1939; by 1944 it was nearly seven times as large.

The Soviet Union survived the horrors of the German invasion. A decade of experience in central economic planning came into play. Factories were dismantled, the machinery shipped eastward, and the workers put them back into operation in makeshift buildings. Men and women were mobilized into new factories and new farms, as well as into new army units. By the end of the war, estimates show the Soviet Union producing three-quarters of prewar output despite losing control of all the major industrial and food-producing areas of the west, and despite over 20 million deaths.[60]

Concern for civilian morale and the belief that Germany had been "stabbed in the back" during the First World War led Hitler and senior leaders to worry about the food supply. The army encouraged planning for wartime rationing in 1936–37, and rationing cards were already printed and distributed at that time. From 1938 onward, the army pressed for an expanded form of "economic management" including control over food supplies. Goering's Four-Year Plan office and Walter Darré's deputy Herbert Backe argued for expansion of easily produced basic foodstuffs such as potatoes, rye, and sugar beet. The desires of consumers for more variety and of farmers for greater autonomy were rejected. Germans were eating less than either Americans or the British in 1939, and the brutal exploitation and destruction in the occupied territories reduced potential supplies, but, for the non-Jewish population in Germany itself, levels of consumption were maintained until late in the war, and the class divisions that had embittered social relations during the First World War were avoided.[61]

Only when the German armies stalled in Russia in the winter of 1941–42 did Hitler become convinced of the need to increase the share of the military in the economy. He had ordered cuts in military production in 1940 after the fall of France and cuts in the size of the army in July 1941 after the initial successes in Russia. Then, beginning in September, came much larger losses of tanks, a result of both weather conditions and improved Russian tanks. From December, Germany was at war with the United States as well, and something had to be done to prevent American aid from reaching Britain. As always, Hitler did not consider the problem from an aggregate economic perspective, but simply ordered the production of increased numbers of tanks for use in Russia and submarines for deployment in the Atlantic.

Fritz Todt, who as armaments minister had been given the assignment of increasing tank production, died in a plane crash in February 1942.

Albert Speer happened to be at Hitler's East Prussian headquarters on the day Todt died. Hitler called him in and appointed him Todt's successor. As Speer said in his memoirs he protested, "But I don't know anything about . . . " To which Hitler replied, "I have confidence in you. I know you will manage it. Besides, I have no one else. Get in touch with the Ministry at once and take over!"[62] Speer faced formidable competition from other leaders, but by combining a system of alliances with potential enemies (he held a high rank in the Four-Year Plan office, for instance) with the full weight of Hitler's approval for allocations of raw materials and labor to produce specific numbers of weapons, he succeeded in creating an organization that expanded to control much of the economy. From an average of 400 per month in late 1941 and early 1942, tank production rose steadily to its peak of 1854 in December 1944. Speer's ministry took over submarine production in July 1943 and increased new launchings from 23 a month to a peak of 38 full-sized and another 20 midget submarines in December 1944. In June 1944, Hitler gave Speer authority over fighter aircraft production, and output rose from 2449 to a peak of 3375 in September.

In part, these increases in output reflected Speer's ability to redirect raw material supplies into the priority areas. There were some productivity gains through standardization and concentration. Most important, Speer could draw on supplies of labor from the occupied territories. In March 1942, Hitler appointed Fritz Sauckel, long-time Nazi Party member and *Gauleiter* of Thuringia, as head of a new office for the mobilization of labor. Over the next three years, Sauckel's agency brought 5.3 million foreign workers into Germany, housed in 22,000 camps. As noted above, thousands were used on agricultural estates in the east. Also as noted above, many were treated harshly, and conditions worsened as the situation became more desperate. One of the largest employers of forced labor was Speer's sprawling industrial empire, and he therefore both cooperated and fought with Sauckel over the supply of workers. Speer preferred to keep French workers in "protected factories" in France, where they could be more easily fed, for instance. After the war, Speer managed to persuade Allied prosecutors that he had opposed Sauckel's increasingly brutal methods. Speer served his twenty-year sentence and lived to write his memoirs; Sauckel was hanged.[63]

Goebbels gave a carefully staged speech at the Berlin Sportpalast in February 1943 in which he announced mobilization of the economy for "total war," a phrase going back to Ludendorff's demands in 1917 and

THE ROAD TO WAR

Ernst Jünger's book *Total Mobilization* (*Die Totale Mobilmachung*) published in 1931. Once again, ideology and practice conflicted. Nazi ideology hampered effective economic organization in many ways. As seen in Chapter 11, German women were not mobilized to the same degree as in other countries. As part of his campaign, Goebbels attempted to push through an order to conscript women for work and close all non-essential shops and businesses, including luxury restaurants. This would have included Goering's favorite restaurant, and he told the owner to keep operating as before. Goebbels organized a demonstration and the restaurant's windows were broken. As *Gauleiter* of Berlin, he told Goering he had authority to close the restaurant, and Goering replied that he, as head of the air force, could turn it into an officers' club and keep it open, and he did. The campaign for total war faded. Speer never gained complete control over the economy. Himmler's SS kept its own industrial base, and even after Speer was given authority over fighter plane production, Sauckel managed to get Hitler's approval to construct a huge underground plant in his own *Gau* district to produce the Me-262. Hitler remained committed to maintaining civilian consumption. Most consumers did not experience significant shortages until 1943, and, as noted above, many Germans only really sensed the war when the Allied bombing raids began.

The Axis could not outproduce the Allies. German submarines initially sank huge amounts of American shipping, a peak of 722,000 tons in November 1942. Increased production made good the losses, and by mid-1943 improved countermeasures allowed the Allies to sink submarines faster than German shipyards could build them. German fuel production peaked in 1943 and then declined, and, by late 1944, Speer's factories were producing more tanks, submarines, and aircraft than could be operated. The fuel shortages had cut pilot training to the point that Speer estimated as many as a quarter of the fighter planes crashed while being flown from the factories to operational bases. The mobilization of labor resulted in large but temporary increases in production, but this worked to conceal from the leadership, including Speer, the seriousness of the larger underlying crisis.[64]

Collapse

The Axis also could not outfight the Allies. At the Battle of Stalingrad during the winter of 1942–43, the German army lost 240,000 dead and another 90,000 taken prisoner. Through 1943 and 1944 the Soviet army advanced, despite desperate German resistance, American and British forces landed in Normandy, and further American forces advanced north through Italy. The weaknesses of Goering's air force were laid bare, and Germany lost control of the air. Allied leaders believed that strategic bombing could destroy Germany's industrial capacity and by "de-housing" the population could destroy Germany's will to resist. The range of bombing raids spread from 1942 onward, and from February 1944 all of Germany lay open to daylight raids. The western industrial cities all became prime targets. Central Hamburg disappeared in a fire-storm, and the raid on Dresden killed more people than the atomic bomb dropped on Hiroshima.

The final attempts at resistance became increasingly suicidal and bizarre. On the home front, Goebbels' propaganda machine spread stories and newsreels of Russian atrocities, broadcast the plan of American Treasury Secretary Henry Morganthau to reduce Germany to a "primarily agricultural country," and produced its last major feature film, *Kolberg*, with its mythic victory over the French in the Napoleonic wars. Pre-adolescent boys were mobilized to make a last stand against the invading Allies. The apparatus of surveillance and terror expanded, although it also fractured along regional lines as each *Gauleiter* demanded control in his district. In March 1945, the Me-262 program was placed under the SS, and SS personnel appeared in the aircraft factories to terrorize the workers into higher productivity. The "night and fog" decree provided for anyone resisting the regime to disappear, and thousands did disappear.

As the battle front collapsed, in February 1945 soldiers were told that if they surrendered, their families would be exterminated. Special courts martial were established to judge "readiness to fight and devotion unto death"—the only possible sentences were exoneration, or death. The massive bribes Hitler paid to the generals may have purchased loyalty. A number, such as Erich von Manstein, whose influential postwar memoirs portrayed the army leaders as purely professional soldiers, shrewdly shifted their accounts from banks in the path of the advancing enemy to other banks in safer locations. The final payment made in May 1945 was twice the usual monthly rate.[65] In the ranks, Omer Bartov has argued that the draconic disciplinary measures taken against deserters held units together even in the face of obvious defeat.[66] Guilt and fear of the vengeance that the Russians would exact for Nazi crimes may have kept many fighting as well. The Russians, to their own surprise and dismay, were forced to fight for Berlin street by street against a beaten foe who would not surrender, and Soviet casualties in this action alone exceeded 300,000.

At the end, Hitler's position remained ambiguous. Isolated in the complex of bunkers below the Reich Chancellery, he at times issued orders to non-existent armies and insisted that new miracle weapons would turn the tide. There were no miracles. The Me-262, the first jet-propelled fighter, had successfully flown in July 1942, but conflicts among agencies, and Hitler's insistence that it be designed as a bomber, slowed development. Nearly 1500 were available by the end of the war, but they were not deployed to challenge the Allies' control of the air. The attacks by V-1 and V-2 rockets did not significantly damage Britain's industrial capacity. The V-1 was essentially a pilotless plane and could be intercepted. The V-2, a genuine ballistic missile, could not be intercepted, but it was still only a single large conventional bomb. As noted above, Germany had been slow to begin work on nuclear weapons, partly because the underlying theory was "Jewish" science and partly because there seemed no urgency early in the war. The delivery system was in place, but nuclear warheads remained several years' of development in the future.

But Hitler also had his moments of lucidity, and in these he perceived clearly that the war he had launched and led could not be won. Examples of his assessments of the military situation are if anything more pessimistic than those offered by the army leadership. Yet he made no effort, for instance, to split the Allies through diplomatic overtures, and he continued to press further offensives and to forbid retreat. Why? Had he persuaded himself that his vengeful enemies, the Jews, had come to control all the Allied countries, and therefore that negotiation was impossible? Or was the war intended only to destroy the Jews, or if that failed, to be destroyed in the attempt? The so-called "Nero Order" directed that all productive plant and equipment be destroyed, and the entire population was to be evacuated from threatened areas and moved to the south for a last stand. Speer protested, and Hitler replied,

> If the war is lost, the people will also be lost also. It is not necessary to worry about what the German people will need for elemental survival. On the contrary, it is best for us to destroy even these things. For the nation has proved to be the weaker, and the future belongs solely to the stronger eastern

nation. In any case only those who are inferior will remain after this struggle, for the good have already been killed.[67]

Hitler devoted a considerable effort to "staging defeat." If the war could not be won militarily, then it must be lost in a way that would leave future generations awestruck. Or, as Goebbels put it, when one leaves the stage of world history, one can at least "slam the door so that the world hears it."[68] Binion is persuaded that the shockingly poor planning for the invasion of Russia can only be explained by an unconscious intention to fail. Even before the war, Hitler insisted that Speer's buildings in Berlin all be designed so that they would provide impressive ruins for future generations, and he commissioned massive sculptures by Arno Breker and others so that "If time were to blot out our soldiers' deeds, the monuments I shall have set up in Berlin will continue to proclaim their glory a thousand years from today."[69] With Soviet soldiers only streets away from the Chancellery building, Hitler exited history by suicide followed by an unsuccessful attempt to burn his body.

Others preferred to survive rather than merely be remembered. Although they did not oppose the Führer openly, Speer and other Nazi leaders did not always implement Hitler's orders to destroy everything, and some of them began to think of escape. Outside the immediate inner circle such thoughts were already spreading. In early 1944, Hermann Abs, head of the Deutsche Bank, met with a number of leading industrialists, officials, and economist Ludwig Erhard, director of the Nuremberg Institute for Industrial Research. Erhard and others had been considering ways in which the problems of Nazi economic planning could be overcome. The meeting looked beyond the Nazi regime and impending defeat toward the future, to plan for the best possible economic terms that might be obtained from the Allies, and to organize reconstruction. Jews were not discussed.

The Holocaust

As the Nazi empire expanded, and then as it collapsed, six million Jews perished. As we have seen, explaining this monstrous fact has stimulated much of the research in German history since 1945. Historians have mapped the stages in the process of extermination and sought explanations. Did Hitler and his followers intend from the outset literally to exterminate millions of children, women, and men, old and young,

simply because they were Jews? Or did the contradictory internal structures of the Nazi system lead to ever more radical policies, taking on a
kind of momentum that drove even senior Nazi leaders further than they
may have originally intended? And, awful as it is to contemplate, is the
genocidal destruction of the Jews unique, or is it only one example
among others of the seemingly limitless capacity of human beings to
inflict pain and suffering on each other?[70]

Jews were not the only victims of the Nazi regime. Some 90,000
homosexuals were arrested and 10,000 sent to concentration camps.[71]
Beginning in late 1942, over 20,000 criminal offenders who had been
identified as "asocial"—that is, according to Security Police head Reinhard Heydrich, anyone who "demonstrates through conduct opposed to
the community . . . that he does not want to adapt to the community"—
were removed from detention and transferred to the police for "annihilation through labor." The majority were guilty only of repeated minor
property offenses, but had been condemned to "security confinement"
under the Nazi law directed against "dangerous habitual criminals."
Hitler believed the habitual criminals to be "vermin" who could not be
allowed to live while "the bravest" died at the front. "If I decimate the
good, while conserving the bad, then what happened in 1918, when five
or six hundred ruffians raped the nation, will happen again."[72] Gypsies
(the Sinti and Roma) were also classified as "asocial" and in addition as
an undesirable racial group. Those already in prison were condemned
along with other "habitual" criminals. In addition, a Central Office to
Combat the Gypsy Menace registered, classified, and organized camps
to hold Gypsies. Across Europe over 500,000 were detained and at least
250,000 perished. Further millions of "Slavs" perished in the east.

As seen above, the Nazis intended to improve the Aryan race itself by
eliminating the physically and mentally unfit. The first gas chamber
designed for killing people was constructed in an unused prison in
Brandenburg during the winter of 1939–40. Its victims were psychiatric
patients. Nazi leaders had singled out this group as the first targets of
the "euthanasia operation," codenamed T-4. Patients were at first told
they were entering an "inhalarium," to be followed by a shower. Actual
showerheads were a later addition. Those in charge debated killing by
lethal injection, a suggestion to release the gas in hospital dormitories
while patients slept, and finally decided in favor of gas chambers after
the success of the Brandenburg experiment. Pomeranian and Polish
handicapped persons, and foreign forced workers with tuberculosis,

were condemned and killed in the same manner. In addition, the victims were not only to be selected, lured into the chambers, and killed, but their bodies were then to be processed to extract whatever might be of value, such as their hair or gold dental fillings.

Those in charge of the euthanasia programs developed the entire range of techniques used a short time later in the extermination of the Jews, including the procedures of selection, the technologies used in killing, and the methods of processing the bodies. Many concentration camp administrators and technicians began their careers in the euthanasia program, and former T-4 participants eventually composed "almost the entire personnel" of the extermination camps of "Operation Reinhard" at Belzec, Sobibor, and Treblinka, where nearly 2 million people perished. The perpetrators were doctors, nurses, support and security personnel, and photographers. Some were "ideologically motivated" but many were not, and Henry Friedlander finds them generally "dull and uninteresting men and women."[73]

In addition to the actions of the *Einsatzgruppen*, early local instances of killing of Jews and other targeted groups often arose out of the actions of local commanders keen to make their mark. Nazi officials regarded Jews as a drain on the local economy, as "extraordinarily destructive eaters," in Hans Frank's phrase. They portrayed themselves as responding to emergency situations, but the emergencies were of their own making, and their decision was always to murder. First in Poland and then in the Soviet Union, immediate shortages of food and housing, slowness in deciding what should be done with Jews already concentrated into temporary holding camps, the need to eliminate Eastern European Jews to make room for new arrivals of German Jews, the problems of Jews too young or too old to work, the need to reduce food consumption in order to provide supplies for the German army, or a conviction that, for example the population of northern Russia was superfluous, all became excuses simply to murder thousands of the people in question.[74]

In Serbia during the fall of 1941, the majority of Jewish men were murdered. In the annexed province of the Wartheland, mass murders of Jews began in late September or early October 1941. French Jews began to be shipped to the east in September. In the second week of September 1941, Hitler approved a program to deport German Jews to the eastern territories. Himmler, Heydrich, and some of the regional *Gauleiter* had been pressing him to do so for some time. Transportation of German

Jews to Lodz, Minsk, Kaunas, and Riga began in mid-October 1941. However, these were still interim measures, and organizational problems limited the deportations to a small fraction of Jews living in Germany. Those close to the center of power insisted on control over policy and its implementation. Himmler appears to have wished to prevent the shooting of some one thousand Berlin Jews killed near Riga on November 30, 1941. On the next day, he sent a radio transmission that "unauthorized actions" with respect to treatment of the Jews would be "punished."[75]

The final question of when and how the decision to exterminate, to murder every single Jewish man, woman, and child, was made relates to the manner in which Nazi Germany functioned. How broadly is responsibility for the Holocaust spread? Did Hitler alone decide and then dictate to others? Did a few others share in decisions? Or did major decisions emerge from the collective desires and actions of a large number of Nazi Party members and state officials? On January 30, 1939, Hitler said in a speech to the Reichstag, "If the world of international financial Jewry, both in and outside of Europe, should succeed in plunging the nations into another world war, the result will not be the Bolshevization of the world and thus a victory for Judaism. The result will be the extermination of the Jewish race in Europe." He repeated this threat on a number of subsequent occasions. Richard Breitman argues that although "surviving documents may not reflect the full reality," they "suggest that Hitler had made a fundamental decision to exterminate the Jews" in early 1941, that by March 1941 planning had begun, and from then onward "the Final Solution was just a matter of time." Once Hitler had reached his decision, Himmler led the gigantic process of planning the organization necessary to implement the extermination policy. For Himmler and the SS this meant beating off challenges from rival agencies, preparing procedures, and mobilizing subordinate units. All these institutional developments evolved gradually during the latter part of 1941.[76]

Other specialists believe Breitman has placed the date too early, and possibly misread the lines of responsibility. On July 31, 1941, Goering sent an order to Heydrich to produce a plan for all "organizational and financial matters for bringing about the complete solution of the Jewish question in the German sphere of influence in Europe." Such an order could only have emanated from Hitler, and many historians have picked this as the crucial date. On December 7, 1941, Japan attacked the United States and invaded Southeast Asia. On December 11, Hitler announced his declaration of war on the United States in the Reichstag. So the war was now a world war, and, as he had threatened, Hitler then announced his decision to exterminate all Jews in Europe. On the afternoon of December 12, Hitler addressed a meeting of senior Nazi Party officials, national section leaders (*Reichsleiter*), and regional leaders (*Gauleiter*). Goebbels' notes on the meeting record Hitler's speech.

> Regarding the Jewish question, the *Führer* is determined to clear the table. He warned the Jews that if they were to cause another world war, it would lead to their own destruction. Those were not empty words. Now the world war has come. The destruction of the Jews must be its necessary consequence. We cannot be sentimental about it. It is not for us to feel sympathy for the Jews. We should have sympathy rather with our own German people. If the German people have to sacrifice 160,000 victims in yet another campaign in the east, then those responsible for this bloody conflict will have to pay for it with their lives.

This speech was public in the sense of moving beyond the inner circle of Hitler's confidents, to a group of over fifty persons including all party leaders with administrative responsibility for the regions affected by the decision and all those whose agencies would be involved in implementing the decision. It was not rhetorical, nor was it ambiguous. It was an announcement that previous threats "were not empty words," and that they would now be acted upon.

Programs of mass murder presented both external and internal problems for the regime. There had been strong objections by religious leaders to the euthanasia program. The police reported in February 1942 that "anonymous letters are constantly arriving, from practically all areas of the Reich" concerning executions of Jews. In official circles, military authorities in the east objected to the excessively large numbers of deportees. Civilian authorities worried that the mistaken deportation of non-Jews or of privileged Jews who had not been targeted might jeopardize political support for anti-Jewish measures as a whole. They worried about "part-Jews" who were not Jews under the Nuremberg Laws, Jews married to Aryans, relatives of army servicemen, veterans of the First World War, and categories of workers such as Jews working in the armaments industry. But others pressed for broader definitions and for even more rapid executions. None opposed the idea of killing very large numbers of human beings, but they required a set of clear guidelines as to who should be included and how to proceed.

The conference of January 20, 1942, held at Heydrich's office in the Berlin suburb of Wannsee, was intended to resolve these problems.[77] The meeting opened with Heydrich reviewing Goering's commission. He claimed overall responsibility and authority, and then outlined his plan for the murder of all Jews in the German sphere of Europe, without exception. Some would be employed as forced labor first. He foresaw no serious diplomatic problems, though the plan depended on military developments in the east. He then presented ideas for expanding the definition of "Jewish." Heydrich wanted all half-Jews, some quarter-Jews, and Jews with non-Jewish spouses to be included. There were objections and no agreement was reached. There was further disagreement over which areas of Europe should be affected first, and over who should be responsible. But Heydrich's authority was unchallenged, and no one opposed the murder of the Jews, including those in Western Europe and the German Reich.

Heydrich did not present a "complete proposal" as Goering had instructed. The Wannsee minutes are vague about the means of extermination, though they are very clear about the end planned for the Jews.

> In the course of the final solution, the Jews should be brought in an appropriate manner and under appropriate direction to work in the east. In large detachments, with the sexes separated, the Jews who are able to work will construct roads in these regions. It is to be expected that a sizeable number will disappear due to natural causes. The Jews who survive, however many there may be, will no doubt be the hardiest. They will have to be treated accordingly. Otherwise these select few, should they escape, could form the basis for a new Jewish line of descent. (See the experience of history.)

Heydrich died on June 4, 1942, victim of an assassination, and his outline was not followed. Deportation orders continued to follow the Nuremberg Laws. Jews with non-Jewish spouses, Jewish foreigners, Jewish workers in armaments plants and in agriculture, and elderly Jews continued to be exempted. There was no agreement reached on the status of part-Jews, and most continued to be exempted. Proposed attempts at geneological tracing were abandoned because they were too difficult. Heydrich had wanted to begin in the west and work eastward. Hitler also said in May 1942 that the process should begin in the west. In fact, the extermination campaign had already begun in the occupied territories of the Soviet Union and the General Government of Poland.

The expansion of the killing was made possible by a large build-up of SS personnel ordered by Himmler during the second half of 1941. The forced labor projects were never implemented.

Construction of extermination camps in Chelmno, near Lodz, had already begun and *Einsatzgruppen* units had used gas vans to kill Jews from neighboring districts. On January 16, 1942, the execution of Polish Jews from Lodz itself began. German Jews in Riga and Minsk now began to be selected openly for deportation. Deportations began in the German Reich, but Speer said on January 26 that further deportations would have to be postponed until April because of the shortage in rail transport. In April, the railroad office said it had trains available, and from May 1943 a coordinated program of deportations from the Reich began. The trains, with their slatted railroad cars that have become the image of the Holocaust, ran to tight schedules, day after day. Raul Hilberg's classic study detailed the institutional and organizational structures that moved Jews from their homes into collection centers, onto the railroad cars, and toward the death camps. There, as fore-shadowed in the T-4 program, they were separated into those who could be forced to work for a while before execution and those who were to be killed immediately. All possessions and clothes were collected. Gassed, the dead victims were then processed, and the bodies finally burned, either in the industrial ovens or in open pits when the numbers became too large.[78]

The slaughter continued to the end. As the Soviet armies advanced, SS headquarters in Berlin issued orders that killing centers should be destroyed and their inmates killed before they could be liberated. Treblinka, Sobibor, and Belzec were evacuated in the fall of 1943. Auschwitz continued to operate until January 1944, when the remaining inmates were either shot or marched westward through the snow. Soviet soldiers found hundreds of thousands of items of clothing, and seven tons of women's hair, that had been collected but not yet shipped. Across Germany, a further 250,000 Jews and other prisoners died in the forced marches, and further tens of thousands were shot and carefully reported to headquarters.

Who was responsible? Hitler did at several points merely approve plans or actions taken by others. He himself never produced a plan for extermination. However, he did not have to produce a plan, for although they might take the initiative, no one in the party hierarchy would act in a manner that Hitler might disapprove. Other possibilities were advanced, including deportation to the east or to Madagascar. Finally, though, once Hitler had announced his decision in principle, "for the National Socialists, the various decisions to proceed with the exterminations were political and not moral decisions. They could thus be made and applied in limited fashion to specific territories or to particular groups of people—those 'incapable of work,' for example."[79]

A few did survive. Victor Klemperer lived in Dresden. A sympathetic official had warned him that at some point he would have to escape and go into hiding to avoid being killed. He did nothing, but the Allied air attack on February 13, 1945, and the resulting firestorm not only gave him his opportunity but also miraculously spared both him and his wife. Reunited, they fled west and later returned to their previous home. Klemperer lived in East Germany for another fifteen years, and remarried after his first wife's death. His second wife transcribed his diaries, and the collapse of the East German regime in 1989 finally created conditions in which they could be published.

Notes

1. *Mein Kampf*, Vol. I, Chs. 3, 6, 12.
2. Bracher 1973.
3. Broszat 1969.
4. Hildebrand 1995, p. 572.
5. Greenfeld 1992.
6. Goldhagen 1996.
7. Arendt 1965.
8. Clendinnen 1999.
9. Bauman 1989.
10. Levene 2000.
11. Braun 1994; LaCapra 1994.
12. Adorno 1949, p. 34.
13. Kershaw 2000b, pp. 70–9.
14. Moses 1998, p. 200.
15. Kershaw 1998; 2000a.
16. Miller 1980.
17. Waite 1977.
18. Pulzer 1988.
19. *Mein Kampf*, Vol. I, Chs. 4, 11.
20. *Mein Kampf*, Vol. I, Ch. 7.
21. Binion 1976.
22. Rosenbaum 1992.
23. Zillmer *et al.* 1995, pp. 99, 192.

24. Overy 1984.
25. Speer 1970, pp. 45–8, 66.
26. Kershaw 2000b, Ch. 4 and p. 82.
27. Ziegler 1989; Wegner 1990; Banach 1998.
28. Nevin 1997.
29. Goda 2000.
30. Kershaw 1998; 2000a.
31. Bukey 2000.
32. Struve 1992, p. 530.
33. Peukert 1987.
34. Geyer 1996, p. 159.
35. Gellately 2001.
36. Bankier 1996.
37. Struve 1992.
38. Zimmermann 1986, p. 99.
39. Klenkmann 1996.
40. Gellately 1993, pp. 53–5.
41. Hoffmann 1988.
42. Bankier 1996, pp. 217–18.
43. Koonz 1993.
44. See Mallmann and Paul 1994.
45. Berghoff and Rauh-Kühne 2000.
46. Herbert 1997.
47. Bukey 2000.
48. Geyer 1996, p. 155.
49. Geyer 1996, pp. 155–7.
50. *Mein Kampf*, Vol. I, Ch. 1 and Vol. II, Ch. 14.
51. See Kershaw 2000b, Ch. 6.
52. Goldstein 1988.
53. Mason 1993.
54. Overy 1988; Gregor 1997.
55. Alexander 2000, p. x.
56. Stolfi 1991.
57. Headland 1992.
58. Förster 1996.
59. Bartov 1991; 1996.
60. See the output figures in Maddison 1995, Table C.
61. Corni and Gies 1997.
62. Speer 1970, p. 276.
63. Zilbert 1981; Herbert 1997.
64. Naasner 1994, p. 473.
65. Goda 2000.
66. Bartov 1991.
67. Speer 1970, Ch. 29.
68. Wegner 2000, p. 509.
69. Trevor-Roper 1988, p. 72; Richie 1998, pp. 450–1.

70. Brecher 1999.
71. Rector 1981.
72. Wachsman 1999.
73. Friedlander 1995, pp. 187, 297.
74. Black 2000.
75. Gerlach 1998, p. 766.
76. Breitman 1991, pp. 153, 247.
77. Gerlach 1998.
78. Hilberg 1961.
79. Gerlach 1998, p. 810.

CHAPTER 13

ABSTRACT EXPRESSIONISM AND SOCIALIST REALISM: DIVIDED GERMANY IN AN AGE OF ECONOMIC MIRACLES

The first postwar generation's experience reflected three fundamental facts. For Germans, the essential fact about their nation was that it was now divided. Large territories east of the Oder and Neisse rivers were lost to Poland and the Soviet Union. The Soviet Union, the United States, Britain, and France all occupied separate zones in what remained of Germany. Out of these zones emerged West Germany, the Federal Republic of Germany, and East Germany, the German Democratic Republic. Austria, also occupied, again emerged as a separate country as well. In addition, a second fact about Germany was that neither West Germany nor East Germany was an independent actor. Both became embedded in separate and hostile networks under the domination of the United States and the Soviet Union. For two generations these two morose and humorless superpowers regarded each other with gloomy foreboding. On one side, the United States feared the expansion of Soviet power and of Communism. On the other side, the Soviet Union feared encirclement by a ring of hostile countries allied with and armed by the United States. Both East and West feared both external threats and internal enemies and possible corruption from foreign influences.

The third fact about the first postwar generation was the extraordinarily rapid growth of the economy, an "economic miracle" and a new golden age. As the economies of East and West Germany recovered and grew, culture also took on the forms of the Cold War, and solidified into the representative shapes of public and residential architecture. Official culture in West Germany adopted a bland modernism exemplified in the clean, square forms of Abstract Expressionism. The American military government invited expatriate Mies van der Rohe to return to Germany to lecture on modern architecture. The new building style, the

496

Americans believed, would help teach Germans the meaning of freedom and democracy. His New National Gallery in West Berlin (1965–68) was intended to display works of German art that had not fallen to East Germany. Its flat roof, column-free interior space, and glass wall linking the interior with the exterior terrace epitomized his minimalist principle "less is more" enunciated in the 1920s.[1] The Hansaviertel residential development included buildings by other leading modern architects including Walter Gropius and Le Corbusier. American High Commissioner James B. Conant said it would help the city to become the cultural capital and "showcase" for West Germany.[2]

West German popular culture in contrast adopted the fluid, unsquare forms of rock and roll. Both official "high" culture and popular "mass" culture depended on American models, and the "Americanization" of the German economy and German society became one of the most debated topics among contemporary observers.[3] West Germany's leaders cited the economic miracle within the framework of a managed "social market economy" to prove the superiority of Western capitalism. More recently, however, critical historians have questioned both the successes of economic management and the gendered processes of cultural reproduction in West Germany.[4] Glass walls are not in fact a very good exterior for a museum. As West Germany's public architecture repeated tedious glass and concrete rectangles, the Hansaviertel's monotonous apartments and barren open spaces led even Gropius to say it was "more a chart of modern architecture than an organic setup from a community point of view."[5] The same boring square boxes, however, spread along the rail lines on the outskirts of all West German cities.

"Over there," the "other Germany" developed very different patterns of economic, social, and political relations. The Soviet model of official Socialist Realism dominated cultural life, and the Soviet models of economic planning and single-party government dominated social relations and political structures. The Soviet War Memorial in East Berlin's Treptow Park (1946), constructed largely from stones taken from the ruined Reich Chancellery building, features two huge stylized flags made from red marble and three enormous muscular figures towering over the graves of Soviet soldiers. The massive housing project along the Stalinallee with its decorated marble façades and commemorative statues was, according to East Germany's President Wilhelm Pieck, "the greatest, widely visible symbol of our policy of peace and the improvement in conditions for all our population."[6]

Plate 13.1   Ludwig Mies van der Rohe, New National Gallery, Berlin, 1962–68. A glass, steel, and concrete manifestation of Abstract Expressionism, explicitly intended to epitomize the integration of West Berlin and West Germany into the democratic capitalist system of the West. The interior curtains necessary to protect the art works from the sunlight shining through the glass walls are visible to the left and right. Photo: Gerhard Murza, 1993, Bildarchiv Preussischer Kulturbesitz.

Economic growth seemed very rapid as well, and "concretely existing Socialism" offered opportunities to women and young people from working-class families. East German leaders argued that rapid growth and more equal opportunities proved the superiority of the Socialist system. Here, too, more recently historians have questioned both the simple pictures from the Cold War and later more positive accounts, and have begun to look at the tensions and ambiguities of East German developments within the framework of the debates over reunification and the "German question."[7] The Stalinallee's decorations sent costs well over its budget, and following Stalin's death it was announced that it was "not necessary to make a modern apartment building into a church or museum." The new principles that all ground and floor plans be identical and that there be no more than nine square meters per

Plate 13.2 Soviet War Memorial, Treptow, Berlin, 1946. Socialist Realism in action. Anonymous but presumably happy citizens of the emerging German Democratic Republic on an edifying Sunday stroll through the memorial to the Soviet soldiers killed in the Battle of Berlin. The ruins of Speer's Reich Chancellery building provided the materials. Photo: Bildarchiv Preussischer Kulturbesitz.

person in each apartment "resulted in the construction of the ugliest buildings in Berlin's history."[8] As in West Germany, the same square style spread to the suburbs of other cities.

In both East and West, squareness and economic growth displaced discussion of the past. Many of the members of the generations of Abstract Expressionism and Socialist Realism had belonged to the Nazi generation. The rupture of defeat and division led them to reinterpret and repress that earlier history, but the mournful footsteps of the past continued to echo in the present.

Zero hour and occupation

Plans for Germany

The Allies, remembering the aftermath of the First World War, forced Germany to surrender unconditionally on all fronts. Admiral Doenitz was kept as a figurehead successor to Hitler just long enough to ensure that it was explicitly the Nazi regime that surrendered and therefore bore blame for the defeat. The Allies announced their intention to occupy Germany. They also announced plans to destroy German "militarism" and restructure both German government and German society, the "four Ds" of demilitarization, denazification, decartalization, and decentralization. Outraged German leaders protested that such plans went far beyond the rights of military occupation authorities under the Hague Convention of 1907.[9] More significantly, because the Allies disagreed over both the specific policies to be implemented and the manner of their implementation, the results fell far short of the original intent.

The Allies explicitly rejected the idea of a dismemberment of Germany. They did, however, agree to give German territory to Poland to make up for Poland's losses to the Soviet Union. In addition, in Quebec in 1944, British Prime Minister Winston Churchill and United States President Franklin Roosevelt had adopted the plan of United States Treasury Secretary Henry Morganthau for a "pastoralization" of Germany intended to prevent German rearmament by severely limiting industrial production. The mines of the Ruhr would be sealed, for instance. At Yalta and Potsdam in February and July 1945, the Allies agreed to separate zones of occupation. Soviet leader Josef Stalin insisted on retaining possession of the Polish territories that the Soviet Union had conquered in 1940. At Potsdam, the new United States President Harry Truman and the new British Prime Minister Clement Atlee agreed. East Prussia was divided between the Soviet Union and Poland, and Poland was given German territory extending to the Oder and Neisse rivers.

All Nazi organizations were abolished, and some such as the SA, SS, and Gestapo were declared "criminal organizations." "War criminals" were to be tried and punished. All individuals who had been "more than nominal" participants were to be excluded from public office. The judicial and educational systems were to be restructured. The most spectacular demonstration of the Allies' commitment to punishing the guilty

Map 6 The Allied zones of occupation in Germany, 1945

was the trial of 22 prominent officials and supporters of the Nazi regime by the International Military Tribunal at Nuremberg. Three, including Franz von Papen and Hjalmar Schacht, were acquitted. Of the remainder, twelve were sentenced to death and the others to prison terms ranging from ten years to life. Hans Frank was among those executed, Hermann Goering escaped his death sentence by committing suicide, and Albert Speer served a twenty-year prison term and later published his best-selling memoirs.[10]

The broader attempt at denazification proved difficult. On the one hand, speed seemed necessary to ensure a clean break with the past, but, on the other hand, a slower process might be more thorough. There was also the question of whether the process should be carried through by the Germans themselves, to drive the lesson home, or rather by the Allies, to ensure that all the guilty were judged properly. While such questions were debated, large numbers of soldiers and suspected Nazis were rounded up and kept in camps, in some cases the same concentration camps that had housed political prisoners under the Nazi regime. Some died, of disease or malnutrition. Eventually, some 11.5 million individuals completed questionnaires intended to provide preliminary evidence for potential prosecutions. In 1949, the Allies' authorities placed denazification in the hands of Germans to administer. As seen below, by that time this meant that the process would be carried out by the separate West and East German governments.

Economic policy also caused problems. The Morganthau Plan was unworkable. As millions of Germans fled or were forced westward, the population of the remaining German territories increased. The areas ceded to Poland included mostly agricultural lands, and therefore Germany could not feed itself. In addition, the recovery of the rest of Europe depended on German industrial resources, such as the coal from the mines of the Ruhr, as did any future plans for European integration. Therefore Germany could not simply be de-industrialized. As a result, the proposed limits on industrial production were never enforced. In addition, United States policy changed rapidly from a desire to reduce German industrial capacity to a determination to push industrial development throughout Western Europe as a counterweight to the Eastern European bloc emerging under Soviet sponsorship.

One area in which cooperation proved impossible was reparations. Soviet leaders wanted large amounts of goods and dismantled industrial plants to be reassembled in the Soviet Union. The United States and Britain agreed only to a small amount, and they refused to agree to requisitions and removals from their zones of occupation. The American Secretary of State suggested that the Russians would have to be satisfied with whatever they could extract from their zone. Eventually, the United States made any reparations settlement dependent on prior German economic recovery and on the cooperation of a new united German government. Soviet leaders saw this as evidence of Western hostility and duplicity.[11]

The question of the political structures of the new Germany bore directly on the conflict of interest and ideology between the Western Allies and the Soviet Union. The Western powers distrusted any political activity by Germans, and they were slow to grant any political parties the right of organization. They were not united, however, and the French argued that Germany should become a loose confederation of states. Konrad Adenauer, jailed after the 1944 assassination attempt, was released by the Americans and returned to his position as Mayor of Cologne in March 1945. In October, the British authorities dismissed him for "unauthorized political activity." He had returned to his old idea of an independent Rhineland, and had been negotiating with the French for the creation of a state that would include the Ruhr, the Palatinate, and parts of Hesse.

In the East, Soviet authorities believed that the future Germany would be more easily contained if it were a centralized unitary state, and they began to implement their preferred model in their zone. In contrast to the Western powers, they had reliable German allies in the exiled leaders of the Communist Party as well as support from former Socialist and Communist Party members. The Russian zone therefore quickly acquired a set of highly centralized institutions, both the administrative apparatus and other organizations.

The zones and the establishment of two Germanies

The tension and suspicion between the Soviet Union and the Western powers led to the division of the world in the Cold War and to Germany's division. This was not the result intended by Stalin, Roosevelt, and Churchill, or by Harry Truman and Clement Atlee when they came to power. Although their private agendas called for a Germany that tilted their way, all senior leaders of the Big Three believed that a united and neutral Germany was the best guarantee of postwar stability. However, the divergence of the interests of the United States and the Soviet Union affected the implementation of even agreed policies from the outset. In addition, influential members of the Soviet and American occupation administrations in Germany moved well ahead of their superiors in Moscow and Washington. Russian Colonel Sergei Tiul'panov and American General Lucius Clay both anticipated and worked for the division of Germany, either because they desired it, or because they saw it as inevitable and sought to gain the greatest advantage for their own country.[12]

The differences among the Allies led quite rapidly to differences among their zones. In all of the zones, however, we can trace a shift from hostility to the Germans as the authors of the war and as criminals, to an emphasis on creating the conditions for recovery and stability. Blanket amnesties were granted to specific categories of persons to overcome the difficulties of administration and economic reconstruction. At the local level, government workers had to remain in their jobs if life was to continue. These frequently included police officials who had cooperated with the Nazi security services. The Allies protected individuals they considered useful. The British, for instance, prevented Hermann Abs, head of the Deutsche Bank, from being prosecuted by the Americans.[13] The Americans allowed rocket scientist Werner von Braun and a number of his co-workers to move to the United States in violation of American law.[14] They also employed Klaus Barbie, a senior SS official responsible for suppressing resistance in occupied France, to use his expertise on Eastern Europe, and then helped him escape to South America.[15]

As a result, neither West nor East Germany began from "zero hour." In the West, business and financial institutions remained essentially unchanged. Political leaders, though they could not have been too prominent under the Nazi regime, were men who had been active before the war. The profile of the East German leadership differed in that the path to high office was a long pedigree of Communist Party activism, but these too were men who had been active in Weimar politics. Owners of business firms were expropriated, but many managers and most workers remained in their existing jobs. In both East and West, at the lower levels the government bureaucracy remained largely the same.

Hoping to speed the creation of a new unified German government, the United States proposed to unify its zone with that of any other power. The Soviet Union refused, as this would have made it impossible to extract further reparations. The French also refused, unless the Ruhr, the Rhineland, and the Saar districts were all separated from Germany. The British, however, accepted. The creation of the combined zone or "Bizonia" ensured the eventual division of Germany. As United States and British policy moved to sponsoring German recovery, this came in fact to mean West German recovery. In contrast, the Soviet authorities only called a final halt to the dismantling of factories in early 1948.

In their desire to begin planning for German economic recovery, the Western powers began to act without waiting for approval of the Soviet authorities. After a series of protests and confrontations, on March 20, 1948, the Soviet representatives walked out of the four-power central council in Berlin. In the aftermath, the French, yielding to American and British pressure, agreed to merge their zone with Bizonia, creating a

Trizone. Soviet authorities had printed large amounts of money, legal tender in all zones under the occupation agreements, which they used to purchase items they could not seize as part of the reparations. In addition to angering the Western Allies, this contributed to the suppressed inflation discussed below. On June 20, the Western powers announced a deflationary currency reform that would apply to their zones only. In response the Soviet Union began the blockade of Berlin.

The Berlin Blockade is important as a stage in the division of Germany, as a marker of the division of the world by the Cold War, and also as an example of the sort of legalistic distinctions made by both the Soviet Union and the United States to try to gain an advantage over the other but not to push the other to the point of confrontation and war. The Soviet Union never admitted officially that the blockade existed. Rather, authorities announced that the roads and canals leading through the Soviet zone to Berlin would be closed because of "technical difficulties." The Soviet commander, Colonel General V. D. Sokolowski, unofficially but openly let it be known that the blockade would remain in force until the Western allies gave up their plans for an independent West German state.

Clay, the American commander, proposed to force his way to Berlin with an armed convoy. United States leaders rejected this as too risky. However, the designated air corridors from Hanover, Hamburg, and Frankfurt remained open, and the United States and Britain assembled transport aircraft to fly supplies to their zones in Berlin. Capacity increased from 1000 tons a day in July 1948 to 13,000 tons a day by April 1949. This operation also posed risks. Industrial production in Berlin dropped by half and unemployment rose sharply. Coal was in very short supply, and only a mild winter prevented a disaster. Within Berlin itself, riots organized by the Soviet authorities disrupted the meetings of the city legislature in the Soviet sector, and it was transferred to the Western sector. Elections held in the Western sector in December 1948 resulted in an overwhelming 65 per cent vote for the Socialist Party (SPD) and divided the city's government.

On the other side, the Soviet Union did not challenge the passage of the aircraft that were feeding the population of the Western sector of Berlin. They also did not challenge the move of the city legislature to the Western sector, or the elections in that sector. Like their counterparts in the United States, the leaders of the Soviet Union saw direct confrontation as too risky. When it became obvious that the blockade was not preventing the creation of a West German state, and in fact was accelerating it by making firmer allies of the Western powers, the West Germans, and the West Berliners, Soviet leaders dropped it. On May 4, 1949, the blockade ended.[16]

During early 1949, work on a new "Basic Law" for West Germany was slowed by disagreements among the Western powers, but also by German fears that adoption of an independent constitutional structure in West Germany would lead to division. Among the Western Allies the United States in particular forced the pace, for instance by promising to reduce or eliminate restrictions on West German industrial output. Among the Germans, Konrad Adenauer in particular was willing to dispense with the Soviet zone if necessary to achieve an independent German government as quickly as possible. After his dismissal as Mayor of Cologne, he had joined the recently formed Christian Democratic Union (CDU) and become leader of the party in the British zone. The creation of Bizonia allowed him to forge alliances with other regional leaders of the CDU and a coalition with the Free Democratic Party (FDP). As head of this grouping he chaired the Parliamentary Council that drafted the Basic Law. The need for haste also reflected the general increase in international tension resulting from the Berlin Blockade, the Communist takeover in Czechoslovakia, and in Asia the defeat of the Nationalists by the Communists in China.

The Basic Law (*Grundgesetz*) was announced as a provisional arrangement, not a constitution. Although it applied only to the three Western zones of occupation, it provided that the Soviet zone could join at any time, and foresaw the regaining of the lost territories in the east, designated as "presently under Polish/Russian administration." Legislative and administrative powers were carefully divided between the federal and state governments, as were the contentious sources of tax revenue, but the draft followed the Weimar constitution in tipping the balance toward the federal government. The draft did not please all Germans, and it was rejected by Bavaria because it did not guarantee sufficient powers for the states.[17] Allied authorities overruled this regional declaration of independence, and the Basic Law was promulgated on May 23, 1949. The Basic Law addressed the "German question" by asserting that there was only one Germany, and that the West German government was the only legitimate German government. It was, after all, the Federal Republic *of Germany*.

The establishment of the new government of East Germany followed almost immediately after the promulgation of West Germany's Basic Law. The Soviet authorities passed over government of their zone to a German administration two weeks after the Western powers recognized West Germany. The constitution adopted shortly afterward also included features from Weimar. There was to be a president and two legislative chambers. Individual rights were guaranteed. In addition, as a Socialist state the new government would control productive resources directly. There would be an economic plan and private property would disappear. Provisions for reunification were included, but not surprisingly the new state rejected West Germany's interpretation of the "German question" and declared through its name, the *German* Democratic Republic, that there might be more than one German state, and that they might have very different forms.

The economic context

Expellees, refugees, and migrants

As the Nazi empire collapsed, millions of Germans fled westward. In the Soviet Union and Poland the retreating German armies destroyed everything they could; pressed back into Germany they demolished productive plants and transportation. Then, as they advanced into Germany, Soviet soldiers looted, raped, and sometimes killed German civilians. Soviet propaganda explicitly encouraged them to take revenge on all Germans. Stories of their behavior preceded them, stimulated and exaggerated by Germany's own propaganda. Women later reported feeling they were living through newsreels already experienced. The number of women raped, many repeatedly, lies at a minimum in the tens of thousands, most probably in the hundreds of thousands, and some insist that it reached into the millions. Many of the rapes occurred from April 24 to May 5, 1945, following the Soviet army's final victory in Berlin.

There were many gruesome murders along with or following rapes, but there were no mass killings such as the Germans had inflicted in the Soviet Union. Notorious for their capacity for rape, Russian soldiers also became famous for their tenderness toward children, and for sharing their food. The threat of rape, particularly by drunken soldiers, continued well after the establishment of Soviet rule, only abating when the Soviet army began to enforce a policy of separation from the German population. Moroccan troops in the French zone also committed many rapes, but non-fraternization rules in the American and British zones reduced contact with civilians and therefore reduced the occasions for violence.[18] Even so, as a bitter joke had it, the difference between East and West might have been that, whereas an American or British soldier would take you to dinner before forcing you to bed, with Russians it was the opposite.[19]

Czechs and Poles also attacked Germans, exacting vengeance for the years of oppression and brutality under the Nazi regime. The victims included all ethnic Germans, not only government officials and the several hundred thousand new settlers, but also those whose families had lived in these regions for generations. At the Potsdam Conference, the Allies had ordered that Germans who had been "left behind" were to be removed and transferred to Germany, and this appeared to license wholesale expulsion. In East and West Prussia, Posen, Silesia, and the Sudetenland the new Polish and Czech authorities pursued a ruthless policy of pushing all Germans out, regardless of length of residence, political affiliation, class, or religion.

In June 1946 alone, over half a million people arrived in the Soviet occupation zone, mostly from Czechoslovakia, and mostly shipped in boxcars. The conditions under which Germans were transported improved, but the numbers continued to grow. By the middle of 1949, there were some 4.3 million expellees and refugees in the Soviet zone, close to a quarter of the population. West Germany absorbed an influx of over 10 million persons. One-third of the population of Schleswig-Holstein were expellees and refugees in 1951. There was of course no housing, nor were there social services to accommodate this mass of people. The Allies rejected German claims that they should be considered an international problem.

The East German government described the new arrivals as "settlers" and sought to integrate them into the emerging Socialist system. The West German government also granted expellees and refugees citizenship, and guaranteed them pension rights based on their previous social and occupational status. A certain number were also granted compensation for their lost property. Beyond that, little was done for them as a group. The East German government encouraged them to blame Hitler rather than the Russians for the loss of their previous homes, and cautioned them not to fantasize about returning. In West Germany, organizations of expellees, particularly those from Silesia, achieved a certain political importance, but never influenced policy decisively. The West

German government blamed the Russians for the expulsions, spoke of reunification, and refused to accept the new eastern boundaries, but could do nothing in the context of the Cold War deadlock. Both governments therefore avoided the need to develop an independent policy, and thereby evaded the responsibilities of power that had troubled Weimar leaders such as Stresemann. Neither was moved to act on the refugees' behalf so long as they did not pose a serious political threat.

Initially, the sudden increase in population simply added to the burdens of reconstruction, particularly in the Soviet zone because of the continued extraction of reparations. Expellees and refugees who had been farmers or small-scale artisans were difficult to employ. West Germany settled some 40,000 expellees and refugees in the countryside with a range of programs and benefits, relocated around a half a million others directly into housing in the west and southwest, and provided preferred access to the new housing being constructed. These programs benefited only a small fraction of the expellees and refugees, and they aroused deep hostility among West Germans. State governments resented being forced to accept responsibility for them, families resented being forced to share their homes with them, and individuals resented being forced to compete with them for jobs.

As recovery and expansion began, the expellees and refugees proved more of a benefit than a burden. They tended to be relatively young, and many, especially from the Sudetenland, were experienced industrial workers. As such they made a valuable addition to the labor force. They took the low-paying jobs, and their numbers held wages down. Particularly in the West, their desire to regain their lost status made them extremely mobile and competitive. They put in long hours and extra shifts. Later, many of them recalled these years as the hardest working but also the most exciting and enjoyable of their lives. Over the next two decades their demand for housing and for furnishings and appliances provided the basis for further growth.

The flow of people into West Germany continued. As seen below, the restructuring of the East German economy caused hardship and unhappiness, and many wished to escape. Between 1949 and 1961 over 2.5 million persons moved from East to West Germany. The West German government attempted to distinguish carefully among the migrants, because "accepted refugees" were granted benefits under the welfare system and given privileged access to housing. West German leaders wanted to encourage migration to reinforce their claim to represent the

German nation, but they wanted to limit the flow, because a flood of migrants could overwhelm West Germany's capacity to absorb them. The attempt failed, and West Berlin was very nearly overwhelmed, forcing the government to distribute large numbers of migrants among the other West German states. Eventually nearly all refugees were "accepted" because it proved impossible to make distinctions on the basis of motivation.[20]

Because the situation had changed, the East German migrants did not cause the resentment that the expellees and refugees had. Previously, West Germans had been desperately short of food, housing, and most essential goods. In contrast, when the migrants arrived the economic miracle had begun, and the sacrifices were much less painful. By 1958, the federal states no longer resisted the allocation of refugees. Instead both state governments and employers had become eager to acquire more workers to prevent labor shortages.

At first East German officials did not worry about the exodus, but this changed. Through the mid-1950s, because so many of the migrants claimed to be suffering from political persecution, it appeared that they were potentially troublesome dissidents, who by leaving were improving the chances of establishing a stable Socialist system. However, as the numbers of migrants did not decline, the regime began to become concerned. A worryingly high proportion of the migrants were young adults, and many of them were skilled workers and professionals. Their loss threatened to restrict economic growth. Leaving East Germany without permission was made a crime. This did not stop the flow, and may have accelerated it.

Finally the East German government acted, cutting off the flow of people and creating the Wall, the definitive symbol of the Cold War and of Germany's division. On the night of August 12–13, 1961, construction crews moved in to seal off the border between East and West Berlin. To the first layers of bricks and mortar were added barbed wire, watchtowers, floodlights, cleared fields of fire, and the system of checkpoints, especially Checkpoint Charlie, the most common point of entry to and exit from East Berlin. Eventually the entire border between East and West Germany was sealed off, continually patrolled along a dead zone where anyone seen would be shot. The suddenness of the move divided families, friends, and lovers. Over the next 28 years, hundreds of East Germans were killed attempting to escape over the border, and thousands arrested and imprisoned.[21]

In 1986, East Germany issued a set of postage stamps celebrating the twenty-fifth anniversary of the "Anti-Fascist Protective Wall." From without, the Wall symbolized the repression of the East German system. From within, it provided a dike against the outward flow of people and the inward flow of potentially subversive influences. The Wall stabilized both the East German economy and the East German social system. Germany was divided, it seemed, forever.

Reconstruction

The 1948 currency reform has been seen as the crucial policy decision in the reconstruction of the West German economy. The large increases in government debt and the money supply under the Nazis had not led to price increases, because prices and wages were both set by the government. Instead, individuals and firms accumulated bonds and money in bank accounts. This "suppressed inflation" continued following the war, and Soviet attempts to purchase scarce goods aggravated the problem. Black markets and complex barter arrangements had become widespread. On the black market prices were rising rapidly, and those with goods to sell refused to offer them at the low official prices. Rather, owners of firms attempted to accumulate stocks, exchanged their goods for other goods when necessary, and paid their workers in kind. Workers in turn traded their goods for other goods. Wendy Carlin and others have estimated that well over half of all transactions were taking place outside official channels.

On June 21, 1948, the Western Allies withdrew the old currency and replaced it with a new "Deutsche Mark" at the rate of one DM for every ten of the old reichsmarks. In addition, government and private debts were wiped away, as were private savings. This eliminated the "monetary overhang." It also discriminated in favor of those holding real assets, that is, owners and employers, and against those holding monetary assets, particularly workers but also firms with large credit balances and bank deposits. At the same time, most prices were also decontrolled, and they jumped upward despite the reduction in the money supply. Labor leaders agreed to accept a 15 per cent increase in wages despite a 25 per cent rise in prices. This kept export prices low and allowed firms to make higher profits. Domestic profits and foreign exchange earnings in turn were fed back into the economy as increased investment.

In addition, the United States had offered direct aid to stimulate economic recovery. Secretary of State George Marshall made the initial offer in 1947, and the institutional machinery for administering the European Recovery Program was finalized at the same time as the currency reform in June 1948. Funds were to be made available for medium-term investment to restore specific industries to operation, and, possibly even more importantly, participating countries would receive grants to overcome their shortage of foreign exchange. The United States set up an Economic Cooperation Administration (ECA) in Paris to evaluate and coordinate requests for aid, and the Organization for European Economic Cooperation (OEEC, the forerunner of the Organization for Economic Cooperation and Development, the OECD) was established to oversee a multilateral payments network and to reduce barriers to trade among Western European countries.

The economic impact of the Marshall Plan varied from country to country, but it was important in West Germany. Bottlenecks had emerged in the supply of coal, and in the steel, power, and transport sectors as well. In these industries prices were still controlled. Profits were low and investment therefore was also low, and might have remained so. The funds provided by the Marshall Plan helped to overcome the bottlenecks. An aid package organized by the ECA and OEEC in 1949–50 helped overcome a sudden balance of payment crisis caused by imports of raw materials as West German industry began to recover. The Marshall Plan also demonstrated the commitment of the United States both to economic recovery and to maintaining the positions of existing West German owners and managers. The plan therefore helped to reestablish confidence and stimulate further investment.[22]

The sudden reappearance of goods in the stores after the currency reform appeared miraculous, and the belief that the miracle had resulted purely from the creation of a new currency and the reestablishment of a free market economy became one of West Germany's founding myths. Forty years later, as we will see in Chapter 15, excessive faith in the mark and in the market contributed to the severe problems of reunification. It is therefore important to note that the success of the reform depended on very favorable circumstances. The design of the reform left employers with physical assets and their accumulated stocks of goods, but very little money. Because they now needed to sell, they released their stocks. One crucial fact was that those stocks already existed. Even more important, despite the visible destruction, West Germany actually possessed larger and more modern industrial plants than before the war. In addition, as seen above, migrants greatly increased the supply of labor. The restoration of the railroad service immediately made raw material and energy supplies more reliable, and of course allowed delivery of goods to domestic and foreign customers. By 1951, West Germany had regained prewar levels of output.[23]

The Soviet Union rejected Marshall Plan aid, saying it interfered in the sovereign rights of other countries. Soviet policy also changed, from an apparent willingness to tolerate national variations among Socialist countries, to an insistence that the Soviet model be accepted regardless of local conditions. Fear of the widespread popular dissatisfaction with the slowness of recovery in Eastern Europe compared to Western Europe, and the split with Yugoslavia that placed an alternative Socialist model in view, both seem to have influenced Stalin's thinking.[24] In 1949, the Soviet Union founded the Council for Mutual Economic Assistance (CMEA, also known as Comecon), which included all the Socialist countries except Yugoslavia, as a counterweight to the Western European OEEC. The CMEA organized trade bilaterally, that is, between pairs of countries, and by manipulating the prices of goods exchanged in these agreements the Soviet Union extracted roughly the same amount from Eastern Europe as the United States granted to Western Europe through the Marshall Plan.

Soviet policy in Germany was inconsistent and opportunistic,[25] based on the desire to reconstruct the Soviet economy and to exploit German resources for this purpose. Soviet authorities dismantled something over 20 per cent of the capital stock, and later transfers and trade took place at prices set to benefit the Soviet Union. However, like West Germany, East Germany inherited a modern industrial base from the Nazi war economy. Saxon machine tools, Berlin electronics, the aircraft complexes in Dessau and Rostock, and the organic chemical industry centered around Leuna and Bitterfeld, all were substantial industrial assets. As in West Germany, wartime destruction was less severe than the initial impression of rubble-filled streets suggested, and the expellees provided labor.

Even more than direct exploitation, however, the shift to Stalinist planning appears to have hampered East German recovery. Although official statistics showed productivity increases that almost exactly matched those enjoyed by West Germany, more recent estimates indicate that productivity in many industries in 1950 was still around 20 per cent below prewar levels. Internal reports of the Soviet economic administration identified imperfections in planning, incorrect prices leading to poor allocation of resources, and, most importantly, a pervasive "lack of work discipline" as the sources of low productivity.[26]

Workers were systematically squeezed. After dismissing or demoting specialists, engineers, and managers in the immediate aftermath of the war, the emerging planning regime reinstated most of them. Pay levels for managers rose quickly and they gained control over the distribution of bonuses, whose division quickly became corrupt. In the general scarcity this meant that pay for ordinary workers remained very low and working conditions worsened. It also meant that workers who had belonged to the Socialist or Communist Parties before 1933, and who had suffered under the Nazi regime, now saw their bosses who had collaborated with the Nazis enjoying relatively high standards of living while they were exhorted to sacrifice and threatened with punishment if they did not conform. "Technical work norms" imposed blanket targets, while privileged, highly paid "shock workers" who exceeded the norms were used to push the expected norms for all workers upward. Continual driving of workers and machines often proved counter-productive, leading to more frequent breakdowns, increased accidents, and higher sick rates. The regime blamed enemy agents and saboteurs for the resulting shortfalls in output, and redoubled the pressure on the workers.[27]

The unhappiness of the workers was one of the reasons for the 1953 uprising. Another was the possibly even greater unhappiness of East German farmers. The regime had expropriated some 7000 Junker landlords and distributed the land to over 500,000 small farmers, landless laborers, and expellees. Important elements within the regime and the party regarded this as a step backward, granting private property to an inefficient and potentially reactionary class of peasants. Many urban consumers, who still had to travel in the countryside to obtain food, resented the high prices charged by farmers. In 1952, the announced "transition to Socialism" meant the beginning of collectivization, with over 100,000 farmers forced into collectives almost immediately and all farmers confronted with new and oppressive demands from the regime.

The age of economic miracles

West Germany went from recovery to the Korean War boom; East Germany stumbled in 1953, but the regime survived with Soviet support and moved economically toward prewar levels. The German economies did more than merely recover, however; both East and West Germany grew very rapidly during the 1950s and 1960s. West German output rose more than 6 per cent per year in real terms from 1950 to 1970. East Germany's growth is more contentious. The East German government's own statistics showed output rising even more rapidly, at more than 7 per cent per year. Western estimates were more modest, but were still over 4 per cent per year. Substantial increases in total and per capital output appeared to have been achieved despite the heavy loss of population before the closure of the border in 1961 and despite the burden of reparations and occupation costs imposed by the Soviet Union.

Charles Maier argued in an influential article that the main difference between the two postwar eras in twentieth-century Europe, and the reason for the social and political stability of the generation following the Second World War, was the ability of governments to deliver the economic goods, "both figuratively and literally."[28] In contrast to Weimar, both West and East Germany delivered the literal goods through the 1950s and 1960s, although they delivered them in different ways and displayed them in quite different figurative wrapping. In West Germany, Ludwig Erhard, the economist who had attended the 1944 meeting of industrial and financial leaders, had received his doctorate in economics in 1924 and became director of the Nuremberg Institute for Industrial Research in 1942. He worked for the American occupation authorities as minister for commerce and trade in Bavaria and then as chairman of the Bizonal Commission for Money and Credit in Frankfurt, which laid the foundations for the 1948 currency reform. Following the 1949 elections, he became minister of economics in the new government of Konrad Adenauer. In 1963, he replaced Adenauer as Chancellor, but he lost office in 1966 when the economy stumbled into recession.

Erhard, "Mr. Economic Miracle" (*Herr Wirtschaftswunder*), believed in "prosperity through competition"[29] and opposed central planning, but this did not mean that government would be inactive. In Alfred Müller-Armack's phrase, the "social market economy" would both guarantee individual freedom and protect those most in need. Private property was the basis of the family and of individual freedom. The market would allow individuals and families to accumulate property, and active social engineering would insure against the negative consequences of economic change.[30] The notion of the social market economy rested on the ideas of a group of economists known as the Freiburg School, neo-liberals, or "Ordoliberals," including Müller-Armack,

Wilhelm Röpke, and Walter Eucken. They echoed Hegel's faith in the superior abilities of public servants responsible for the general interest, and his link between private capital and the family in the limited private sphere. Eucken meant by "Ordo" the medieval concept of the natural and harmonious order, an ideal that could be identified and then approached in reality by proper policy. The state was not to be simply a "night watchman" but rather a strong force that would act as a counter-weight and arbiter, responsible for the inherently complex tasks of central administration. Private interests were best left to operate freely within this framework.[31] Competition was good, but private interests would need to be restrained and guided. Röpke favored free markets, but he also advocated government intervention to prevent excessive urbanization and to protect the lifestyles of small farmers and of artisans in small towns.[32]

In East Germany, Günter Mittag, son of a laborer, worked as a railroad inspector, completing a home study course and finally a doctorate, also in economics. He moved up through the Socialist Unity Party. Through the 1960s and again from the late 1970s onward he dominated the economic planning apparatus in East Germany, but his preferred policies always had to fit the official Marxist ideology. He later portrayed himself as working in the "field of tension between two systems." As a Marxist–Leninist system, the regime believed in the role of a small vanguard party and in the direct role of the state. Ruling in the name of the working class, the party would institute Socialist modes of production, using the state apparatus to overcome opposition and redirect resources. Over time, repression would become unnecessary, the social product could be distributed according to need rather than work, and the state would "wither away." Sadly, in a world where Socialist states were threatened by Western capitalist imperialist forces, the state and the party had to be retained to protect against foreign aggression.[33]

Initially the regime directed high levels of investment through centralized ministries for each industry. The resulting rigidities and inefficiencies were recognized, and in line with reforms in the Soviet Union following Stalin's death, in the early 1960s Mittag introduced the changes labeled the New Economic System and targeted "structure determining industries" that received favored treatment as the leading edge of economic development. The reforms did not lead to increases in the rate of growth, and when Erich Honecker replaced Walter Ulbricht as leader of the Socialist Unity Party, Mittag was dismissed.[34]

In West Germany, industrial structures proved difficult to change. Decartelization had ranked as one of the four Ds on the Allied agenda for Germany, and the picture of competition among many small firms accorded with the dreams of the Ordoliberals as well. The project failed, and large West German firms remained large. In part, the ideal simply did not fit the technological realities of modern industry. IG Farben was divided, but the successor companies were the same huge firms that had dominated the international market for chemicals before 1914, and which continue to do so today, notably BASF, Hoechst, and Bayer. In addition, the politics of the new West German state and the Cold War played a role. As noted above, Hermann Abs remained as head of the Deutsche Bank, which retained its interests in other large firms such as Daimler–Benz. Although losing from the division of Germany and moving its headquarters to Munich, the Allianz insurance group kept most of its gains made during the Nazi era. Alfred Krupp, tried and convicted as a war criminal and sentenced to twelve years' imprisonment, was freed by American High Commissioner John McCloy in 1951, and his industrial empire was restored to him. Overextended and in debt, Krupp was rescued by the government and the firm reorganized as a joint stock company in 1967.

Erhard drafted a law that would have banned the formation of cartels and forbidden other forms of anticompetitive behavior. Industrial groups opposed the law and favored a return to the legal situation of the 1920s, when cartels had been explicitly legal and could only be dissolved if they were proven to have abused their market power. The debate extended over seven years, and the final Antimonopoly Law passed in 1957 provided for cartels to be formed in exceptional circumstances, to avoid excessive competition that would damage the public interest, to alleviate emergencies, or to foster restructuring of an industry. Cynical observers and foreigners dealing with West German firms continued to perceive cooperation and collusion as typical behavior, but more sympathetic students argued that they came increasingly to resemble United States firms.[35]

Encouraged by favorable government policies, West German savings and investment rose to historically high levels. Most saving was done by businesses. Interest rates were low and businesses were allowed to value assets at high initial levels and then to take very generous tax deductions for depreciation. As Henry Wallich concluded in an early study, "German business pulled itself up by its tax-exempt bootstraps."[36] Banks continued to dominate the economy through direct holdings and proxies, and persevered in their preference for large firms and mergers that provided them with business, but, as in the 1895–1913 upswing, this conservative bias did not hamper growth. Technical advances that had lain fallow during the interwar years now blossomed. A revolution in consumer spending patterns marked the upswing. West Germans spent a rapidly increasing percentage of their rising incomes on durable goods, especially the automobile. The share of food and drink in total consumption had declined only slightly from 60 per cent in 1850 to 52 per cent in 1910; now it dropped from 46 per cent in 1950 to 29 per cent in 1967. The number of automobiles in West Germany increased by 18 per cent per year from 1950 to 1970.

In East Germany, with wages and prices set and labor and raw materials allocated by central agencies, the problem of matching savings and investment faced by western governments did not arise. Under the New Economic System, industry ministries were abolished and planning placed under looser cartel-like organizations guided by indirect "economic levers" of credit, taxes, new sets of prices, and new accounting procedures. Already in 1965, however, a new layer of central planning was added over this decentralized system, with recreated industry ministries and five-year planning targets. Opposition to the reforms had come not only from Stalinist conservatives but also from individual enterprise managers, who preferred central directives that created a predictable and comfortable framework of routine decisions.[37] Policy continued to favor heavy industry, but consumer durables fed the upswing as well. Though their incomes were only half those of their West German cousins, East Germans came to enjoy substantially higher living standards than other Eastern Europeans. By 1970, 92 per cent of East German families owned a radio and 69 per cent owned a television.

Rapid growth required increased numbers of workers. In both West and East Germany a shift out of agriculture moved workers from low to high productivity employment. The share of agriculture in employment had dropped to 6 per cent in West Germany and 10 per cent in East Germany by the 1970s. Industry rose to just under half of the total. West German industry employed workers drawn from agriculture and also from foreign countries. Between 1960 and 1973, some 8 million "guest workers" came to West Germany from Mediterranean countries, first Italy, then Yugoslavia, and then Turkey. Their numbers fluctuated with the economic cycle. Around 5 million returned to their home countries, but 3 million remained as long-term residents, creating a new group of minorities. East Germany also redeployed agricultural workers, and also employed migrants from other Socialist countries, but in much smaller numbers. East German growth depended more on the mobilization of women. Eventually, official figures reported that 91 per cent of women were employed, the highest female participation rate in the world.

The golden age

The Germanies were not alone. The international upswing of the 1950s and 1960s embraced both Western and Eastern Europe, the United States, and Japan. In the 1960s, policy-makers seemed to have discovered the secrets of unending wealth at last. They and their economic advisors basked in international acclaim, and their ability to deliver the literal economic goods became the primary evidence of their success. Conversely, failure to deliver was punished. The difficult period of slow growth after 1970 lay in the future, but, even during the golden age, leaders who did not deliver could lose their jobs, as both Erhard and Mittag discovered.

International cooperation accompanied and supported the boom. A general lowering of trade barriers recalled the liberalization of the 1860s. A European Coal and Steel Community established in 1952 managed change in those industries in Western Europe.[38] Success here contributed to the foundation of the European Economic Community in 1958—comparisons were made with the Zollverein, because many believed the EEC to be the first step toward political unification of the member countries. On a worldwide basis, the International Monetary Fund provided resources to support countries with temporary deficits in their balance of payments, the World Bank assisted with loans for major infrastructure projects, and the General Agreement on Tariffs and Trade (GATT) extended a web of bilateral reductions in tariff through most-favored nation agreements.

Once again, foreign trade was one of the key forces driving economic growth. The golden age resembled the previous long booms from 1850 to 1873 and from 1896 to 1914 in that all countries enjoyed very rapidly rising exports. The role of the United States was crucial. As the world's largest economy, it was also the world's largest market. In 1970, the United States produced roughly twice the output of the Soviet Union, three times that of Japan, four times that of West Germany, and five times that of Britain. From 1950 to 1970, imports into the United States increased on average by 5.1 per cent per year. In 1970, the United States ranked among the top five trading partners of all sixteen Western European countries, and was among the top three partners of ten of them, including West Germany.

West Germany occupied a central position in the Western trade system. West German exports rose 12.9 per cent per year during the 1950s and 1960s. West Germany was the first or second most important trading partner of all of the countries of continental Western Europe and the third most important for Britain. Except for Italy, France, and Britain, West Germany exported two or three times as much as it imported from all European countries. These surpluses offset the large deficits that West Germany ran in its trade with the United States until the late 1960s. The overall surplus in the United States balance of payments in turn was important because it made possible large capital outflows, investments by United States firms in Western Europe that contributed to the modernization and technological transformation of a number of key industries.

Eastern Europe also enjoyed the long upswing, and, as in the West, trade played an important role. Also, as in the West, the role of the hegemonic power was crucial. Recent estimates indicate that the Soviet Union grew at nearly 5 per cent per year, faster than the United States.[39] The Soviet Union's own official figures were even higher, and the numbers caused anxiety and occasional panic among American and other Western leaders. For Eastern Europe, the important point was that Soviet supplies of energy and raw materials and the huge Soviet market now benefited their economies. In part because of changes in relative prices and in part because of a more liberal Soviet policy, the Soviet Union came to exchange these goods at quite favorable rates, in effect granting substantial subsidies to the other Socialist countries.

East Germany benefited particularly as a major supplier of industrial products to eastern Europe. Most trade remained bilateral and the Soviet Union remained the major trading partner for each of the other Socialist countries. The CMEA under Soviet leadership made periodic attempts to allocate production among the members, to create a "Socialist division of labor" that would lead to greater efficiency. These projects were not entirely successful, but the sensitive role of divided Germany meant that East Germany had a privileged position among Eastern European countries. East Germany was the most important trading partner of the Soviet Union, and overall East Germany's official statistics show foreign trade rising 6.6 per cent per year in 1985 prices. In addition, East Germany enjoyed a "back door" for exports into the European Economic Community. West Germany's "one Germany" policy in this case meant that the EEC's common external tariff did not apply to goods from East Germany. West Germany was East Germany's second or third most important partner after the Soviet Union and Czechoslovakia. Trade between the two Germanies was approximately balanced and trebled from 1960 to 1974.

The social and cultural context

Can there be art after Auschwitz?

Many regard the Holocaust as inexpressible. Adorno later regretted his blunt assertion that poetry after Auschwitz is barbaric, and, as Lisa Saltzman argues, his statement may indicate his commitment to an ethical involvement of the viewer or reader confronting an artistic work, rather than a blanket prohibition on representation.[40] To express the Holocaust artistically one would not necessarily need to have suffered and survived oneself. One would, however, need to have absorbed the experience, have the ability to translate experience into artistic form, and also have one's work published, exhibited, reviewed, and, importantly for a professional artist or writer, purchased. This was difficult. There were few survivors, and fewer still with both the talent and the desire to reveal their experiences artistically. It was forty years before Auschwitz survivor Paul Steinberg wrote his disturbing memoir, and he said, "the one thing I am sure of is that writing this will knock me off balance, deprive me of a fragile equilibrium achieved with the utmost care."[41] In both West and East Germany, most practicing artists and writers had other concerns, and the agendas of official bodies did not support works that broke from the established consensus. Also, as seen below, there was very little inclination among ordinary Gentile Germans to reflect on or ponder the meaning of the Holocaust.

Paul Celan's poem "Death Fugue" ("Todesfuge," 1945) is not the only work to attempt to come to grips with the horror of the Holocaust, but it became one of the best known. Celan, born in Romania to German-speaking Jewish parents, composed the poem in Czernowitz in late 1944 shortly after the Soviet armies drove the Germans out of Bukovina. It is written in the present tense, with the plural pronoun "we" placing the speaker and the reader in an extermination camp as witnesses. The repetitions of the musical form lend rhythm and power to successive images of black milk, ashes, and human hair. Death, "a master from Germany," orders his victims to "play death more sweetly" while he drives them to prepare "a grave in the clouds" where they will "rise as smoke to the sky." The German, the figure of Death, has a beloved in Germany to whom he writes, Margarete, golden-haired, "straw blond," an evocation of German womanhood. She is paired and contrasted with Shulamith, a Jewish woman with "ashen" hair, ashen because it is black, and ashen because she will die and be burned as well. The "black milk of daybreak" is drunk at night, midday, evening, and morning, as the victims die and the smoke from burning bodies in the industrial ovens darkens the sky. The poem ends with the workers in the camp being set on by the German's dogs and then shot, and concludes with an image evoking the two women through their hair, golden for Margarete and ashen for Shulamith.

It was not Celan's delicate but frightening metaphors, however, but Abstract Expressionism that became West Germany's recognized style. For architects this meant simplification of forms as in Mies van der Rohe's New National Gallery. For authors it meant a "clear felling" (*Kahlschlag*) to cut down the forest of corrupt ideas and language in favor of an "unmediated realism." This was, however, a realism without politics, concentrating on the struggle for survival in postwar Germany, or the personal traumas of individual soldiers returning home from the war, the abbreviated descriptions abstracted from their wider contexts and broader meanings. As economic growth gathered momentum, novels appeared that considered the danger of lost values amid affluence, often with alienated outsiders as narrators, but these too often focused on the family, cut off from the public sphere.

There were critical voices. In 1947, the American occupation banned the journal *Der Ruf* because of its open advocacy of Socialism. This led to the formation of Gruppe 47, which included a number of influential writers. In Heinrich Böll's *Billiards at Half Past Nine* (*Billiard um halb zehn*, 1959), the eightieth birthday of a Rhenish architect allows monologs and flashbacks to review German history from the Bismarckian era through the 1950s. Günter Grass' first novel, *The Tin Drum* (*Die Blechtrommel*, 1959), features a narrator, Oskar Matzerath, who consciously decides not to grow up, remaining a child and therefore able to observe the absurdities of the adult world of Danzig in the Weimar period, the rise of Nazism, and the war. The novel mocks at once the canonical German literary tradition of the *Bildungsroman*, the values of the German middle classes, and Germany itself as a recalcitrant child. Critical voices enjoyed international acclaim. Böll received the Nobel Prize in 1972. *The Tin Drum* became the first West German novel to achieve international recognition, and Grass received the Nobel Prize in 1999. Criticism was not valued so highly at home. West Germans said they could not understand Grass' popularity with foreigners, and when Böll's *The Clown* (*Ansichten eines Clowns*, 1963) raised the embarrassing issue of the relations of the Catholic Church both to the Nazi state and to the contemporary CDU, he was bitterly attacked.[42]

Among painters, many artists in West Germany, hoping to reenter the international art community, repudiated the immediate past. Wilhelm Nay following the surrender in 1945 said, "what more will happen? . . . Hopefully art will now regain its freedom after these 13 evil years." The search for a metaphysically centered artistic style continued. Yule Heibel notes the "rapid return of idealisms of various kinds . . . manifesting themselves most often in fantasies of synthesis." Initially, a wide range of styles competed. Nay's works were Expressionistic and abstract but contained colorful recognizable images and mythical themes. He straddled the divide between abstraction, represented by Willi Baumeister in Stuttgart, and figurative realism as practiced by Karl Hofer in Berlin.[43]

Art did not completely regain its freedom, for at the same time both the federal and state governments directed official support toward high culture as a way of reestablishing their, and Germany's, credentials as members of the Western cultural community. Works could be monumental but they had to be respectable. In addition, in art too the Cold War cast its long shadow. The shift in the economic center toward the United States meant that New York, where a number of important European dealers had fled from Nazism, emerged as the preeminent artistic market place. The powerful Museum of Modern Art actively promoted Abstract Expressionism, "free enterprise painting" in the words of its co-founder Nelson Rockefeller. In Europe, American interests funded exhibitions of abstract art because it was seen as an "anti-Communist ideology, the ideology of freedom, of free enterprise. Non-figurative and politically silent, it was the very antithesis of socialist realism."[44]

Like many writers, painters avoided politically divisive, confrontational art. They had worked under a system established and controlled by the Nazis. They worked under very difficult conditions in the immediate postwar years. Some had suffered—Nay, Baumeister, and Hofer all had their works exhibited in the Degenerate Art exhibition in 1937. Artists remembered the dangers of experimentation, and at the same time they wanted to portray themselves as different from and opposed to the tendencies fostered by the Nazis. Abstract art, which the Nazis had disliked and which was also disliked by official Soviet circles, at the same time was also static, conservative, and not realistic. It was individualistic but not socially critical, and hence not revolutionary or Communist. It also enjoyed the support of official bodies, crucial when private collectors were still few. In 1959, the *documenta II* exhibition in Kassel celebrated abstract painting as an exemplification of the personal freedom available within a capitalistic, democratic society.

In East Germany, writers and artists were caught up in the attempts to create the "Socialist citizen" and an "East German" identity. At first, as in West Germany, a range of styles opposed to official Nazi art were supported. The first major postwar art exhibition in Dresden in 1946 displayed a wide array of modernist approaches. Bertolt Brecht, persecuted in the United States for his Marxism, accepted an offer to settle in East Berlin as artistic director of the Berliner Ensemble in 1948 and remained until his death in 1956. Quite quickly, however, the new regime imposed severe restrictions on permissible modes of expression. Soviet-style Socialist Realism meant that artists needed first to consider their responsibilities to society. "Formalism" and bourgeois individualism became things to be avoided. Art was not simply to reflect individual experience, and it was not to look critically at the new political and social system. It was to be accessible to ordinary working people, not only to sophisticated critics and patrons. Its role was to support the regime and to encourage ordinary working people to greater efforts in building a Socialist society. Artists would have to conform, though in return they could expect the security of regular state patronage.

By 1953, the Third German Art Exhibition featured "agitation art" and naturalist illustrations, interspersed with symbolic peace doves, clasped hands, and massed flags. Johannes Becher, who had returned from exile in 1945 and played a prominent role in organizing the cultural life of the Soviet zone, became East Germany's first minister of culture in 1954 and served until his death in 1958. He wrote the East German national anthem, but the line "Germany, united fatherland" was later deleted as it conflicted with the regime's policy on unification. Anna Seghers, building on a reputation earned with publications in English while in exile, served as president of the writers' union for twenty-five years. She and Becher both mediated between individual writers and the regime, and Seghers was an important influence on the large number of women writers in East Germany, but the pressure on writers to produce "positive" heroes and heroines and to write stories with "non-antagonistic" conflicts remained. Specialists judge the work of both Becher and Seghers personally to have suffered from the tension between their creativity and the need to conform, and their combination of official success and unrealized artistic potential typified the East German experience.

Women, families, and social control

In gender relations and family structures the heritage of the Nazi regime proved as difficult as in any other area. Defeat and occupation added a further element of instability in marriage relationships. In addition, in the immediate aftermath something had to be done about the consequences of mass rape and pregnancy. Occupation authorities quickly settled on abortion as the solution, and this medicalization of the problem allowed a quick organizational resolution through the existing public health authorities. Plans devised by the Nazis to eliminate unwanted racially inferior children were in fact implemented after the defeat of the Nazi regime. The law forbidding abortions was ignored, and, despite shortages of medical supplies, abortions were "performed on a fast assembly line." As many as 90 per cent of the pregnancies in Berlin may have been terminated. However, a sort of half-silence then descended. Rape was clear evidence of victimization, but in the East the rapes had been committed by Russians, who were now the friends and protectors of the emerging East Germany. In the West, those same Russians were coded as enemies, and the French troops as black and therefore alien, but the "remasculinization" of West Germany meant that discussion of the topic quickly became too humiliating for men and too risky for women.[45]

Reconstruction meant "rubble-women" clearing the debris of bombed-out buildings from the streets, and then clearing the building sites themselves, by hand. The question was what they would do after the rubble was cleared. As always, the role of women was tied to the structure of the family, and to the definition and delimitation of sexual expression. On the one hand, the attempts of the Nazi regime to intervene directly in marriage and procreation to pursue its dream of racial purification were rejected. On the other hand, many of the same doctors and other public officials remained in office. Therefore, with regard to the ideal images of the family, a woman's role, and sex, there were important continuities from Weimar, through the Nazi period, and into the postwar era. Both East and West Germany built policy on "the Weimar 'motherhood–eugenics consensus,' which stressed the importance of fertility regulation and heterosexual intimacy leading to healthy offspring and stable marriages." They ignored the conviction of Weimar reformers, eradicated after 1933, that "heterosexual satisfaction, family stability, and eugenic health were also tied to abortion and homosexual rights or sex counselling for adolescents."[46]

In both East and West, marriage became the expectation for women. And the norm was fulfilled, even among the war generation. Despite concerns over a "lost generation" of husbands and a surplus of women left behind by the war, and despite the image of the war widows as victims standing alone, the marriage rate actually increased. By the 1960s, women of the war generation were as likely to be married as women of their age before the war.[47] In East Germany, as noted above, the regime actively encouraged women to take waged work. Further, despite prejudice and legal disabilities, the number of women in paid employment in West Germany continued to increase in line with trends extending back into the nineteenth century. Therefore, in both East and West, working women married and had children, but married women with children worked.

In East Germany, women's wage labor was a social goal as well as an economic necessity. Explicit planning of the economy meant control over the workplace, but also linked workplace to home and family through the provision of housing, childcare, and medical services. The equality that Marxist theory assumed meant that women ought to have the right to work on the same terms as men. The pressure on the economy led the government to transform this right into an obligation. The norm for women became a combination of work and motherhood. Women were expected to be housewives as well, but this double burden disappeared from view. In theory, there could be no double burden, because the provision of facilities for children by neighborhood and enterprise as well as by the state educational system removed the burden of childcare from working women. In fact, development was gendered along traditional lines. In the previously non-industrial Prignitz district of Brandenburg, the government first erected a textile factory that hired women, and then opened a metalworking factory that hired men, with the explicit purpose of providing husbands for the women textile workers and thereby creating families to provide a permanent recruiting pool for the future.[48]

In West Germany, women in theory moved from the streets into homes as housewives. Women's wage labor might be necessary, but it was regarded as regrettable, an aberration of the war and postwar period, and something to be overcome as quickly as possible. The marriage law was reformed in 1957, but still stipulated that women's waged work outside the home must not interfere with "marital and family obligations." This provision remained in force until 1977. The assumption that a family was headed by an employed male who functioned as the breadwinner became the basis of the welfare system, first in theory and then increasingly in practice. Frankly discriminatory legislation prevented women from entering a range of occupations. Legislation also reinforced an officially sanctioned prejudice against single women. To be unmarried and female was to be marginalized.

Neo-liberalism and the social market economy rested on the family. Sociologist Helmut Schelsky began his academic career during the Nazi period and became one of the government's key advisors on social issues, parallel to the economic Ordoliberals. "A sociologist for all seasons," in Robert Moeller's phrase, Schelsky argued that the natural division of labor in the family had the male as breadwinner in the public realm and the female as homemaker in the private realm.[49] Again, with phrasing lifted from Hegel and subsequent commentators, Schelsky insisted that waged work for women outside the home threatened to subject them to the same conflicts between "primary and abstract relationships" that dominated men's lives in the public arena. Women would obviously resign their jobs if they could, for they would prefer to be spared subjection to "bureaucratic power and abstract authority"—the deplorable situation in East Germany—if the position of their families could be made secure. As the declining birth rate showed, however, the family, despite being a natural and unchanging structure, was under threat and required protection. Demographers, also with academic careers extending back through the Nazi period, worried that West

Germany was becoming a land of two-child families, and they pressed urgently for policies to increase the amount of "human capital" by raising the birth rate.[50]

What should be done? Erhard resisted increases in welfare spending and argued that government should not grant favors to any specific groups. Instead, the partial privatization of state-owned firms such as Volkswagen would create a "people's capitalism" in which many individuals could become responsible shareholders. In addition, the government could commit itself to certain clearly recognized "common tasks" such as infrastructure, education, and culture. Erhard's phrase for this was the *"formierte Gesellschaft"* or "formed" society, which retained the central role of government policy.[51] Schelsky argued that the new West German society had already in fact largely eliminated the problem of class conflict, and had become a *"nivellierte kleinbürgerlich-mittelständische Gesellschaft,"* that is, a "leveled" society of the small *Bürgertum* and middle class, a reassuring phrase that recalled the peaceful small town environments that the Ordoliberals saw as the basis of their social market economy.[52]

Within this leveled society men and women were equal under the Basic Law, but it was "equality in difference." The 1957 legislation stipulated that, though husbands and wives bore mutual responsibility for decisions affecting their life together, "The wife carries sole responsibility for the running of the household." Within the private realm, housewives were supposed to replicate the planning of the social market economy. The economy promised, and indeed required, increasing levels of consumption, but the economic miracle also required savings, and to consume and save at once required careful planning.[53] In addition, as a consumer in her own right, woman was both object and subject, since even when she purchased goods for the entire family, much of what she consumed was also for her personal use. Female fashion played a particularly ambivalent role in this respect, being at once a highly profitable segment of the "culture industry" and at the same time a quintessentially unproductive kind of expenditure. Popular images, in film especially, focused on the subversive potential of unrestrained female consumer desire, and linked fashion, espionage, and criminal deviance.[54]

Sociological analyses, market research, and books of practical advice appeared to analyze and guide "irrational" female impulses, to create a female "consumer-citizen" who would stabilize the social and economic orders. Erica Carter identifies a conservative "rational order of domestic femininity" based on planned, enlightened spending and on deferred gratification. Economics matched morality; the Conservative Catholic Franz-Josef Wuermeling, head of the new ministry for family questions, cited scriptural texts to prove the natural subordination of wife to husband. The domestic ideology figured the housewife both as manager of the household and as servant to her husband and children, creating the "warmth of the nest" as an antidote to the "furnace" of the workplace.[55]

Housing and social control

In the 1960s, a wit in the Rhineland explained the difference between a Communist and a Socialist. A Socialist, he said, is a Communist with a wife, two children, and a mortgage. The provision of housing was one of the most contentious issues in postwar Germany. Success in providing housing became one of the standards by which both the West and East German governments measured themselves. But as they placed their citizens in housing, both governments attempted to fit them to a particular mold. Possession of an apartment or a house improved the quality of life and lowered potential levels of discontent. In addition, the fear of losing one's residence in the East, and the long-term commitment of a mortgage debt in the West, bound individuals and families within the system.

Millions of women and men in West and East Germany had either been driven from their homes or bombed out in the final phases of the war. The provision of housing therefore became one of the main problems confronting governments in the postwar era. Providing housing was not easy. The expense was enormous. Almost as difficult, however, were the divisions and disagreements among levels of government and between competing visions of what postwar German society should look like. Housing became one of the aspects of the creation of the West German social market economy and a key element in the self-image of the new West German polity. In West Germany, 3 million housing units were constructed between 1949 and 1953, and by 1964, a total of 8 million units had been constructed. They were boring, but they were solid, with insulated internal doors that allowed thrifty families to heat only one room at a time. In the East, as well, the creation of the East German Socialist system rested on the claim that it too could provide adequate housing for all. Many new units were constructed, though for many the claim was deferred into the future, in view of the pressing needs of the present. Following the collapse and reunification, it became obvious that large numbers of the families in East Germany had remained in prewar buildings.

In West Germany, the federal government in Bonn provided most of the money, but always with conditions imposed on its use, and therefore disputes over policy and jurisdictional conflicts were inevitable. The debate continued themes from the Weimar years, and the men involved drew on their experiences of town planning under the Law for the Redesign of the German Cities of 1937 decreed by Hitler, and Albert Speer's Working Staff for the Reconstruction and Planning of Destroyed Cities established in 1943.[56] The question of what sort of housing to provide raised both social and political issues. To subsidize apartment dwellings would provide low-cost housing for poor workers convenient to their places of employment, but also implied a paternalistic concern with their welfare. To subsidize home ownership would reinforce private property and might help ensure social stability, but it was more expensive and implied that the benefits would go to those who were already affluent enough to contribute to the cost of the new houses.

The shortage was so desperate that the initial consensus that the government must be involved in the housing market was easily achieved. Federal laws passed in 1950 and 1956 provided that the federal government would finance housing. However, the obvious need and the rapidity of the passage of the laws paradoxically cut off systematic discussion of exactly what sort of housing was to be provided. Programs were driven by changing balances of political forces and the pressure of special interest groups. Paul Lücke, federal housing minister and Christian Democrat, strongly supported home ownership. He believed that owning a home would provide a new bulwark for private property, for the family, and for social stability in the face of the threat from Communism. On the other hand, authorities in densely settled states such as North Rhine-Westphalia preferred apartment developments, which consumed less land, provided more housing for less money, and promoted economic development by placing residences close to jobs.

The situation in 1950 was exceptional, not only because so many people needed housing but also because so many of them were not poor. It therefore proved easy to agree to offer subsidized housing to these people because they had the resources to contribute to construction costs. From the government's perspective this meant that more units could be constructed for the same amount of money. The Socialist Party attempted to introduce programs to support housing for the poorest families, but these efforts were opposed by some of the party's own supporters, including the labor unions, the non-profit housing societies, and the state and local governments controlled by the SPD. In 1960, with the crisis apparently past, a law passed by the Bundestag abolished government intervention in the housing market. Without representation the poor suffered, and their needs were only met later, after the more affluent had been housed. Those at the very bottom of the pyramid suffered the most, or had to wait the longest, with housing for them drawn from the funds of state and local governments.[57]

Labor relations and social control

In West Germany, the Basic Law guaranteed workers the right of association, although it also forbade compulsory union membership and outlawed "political" strikes. The collective bargaining law of 1949 was based on the 1918 law that had governed labor relations under Weimar. In addition, in 1951 a "co-determination" (*Mitbestimmung*) act was passed that applied in the coal, iron, and steel industries. The supervisory boards of these firms were to include equal numbers of representatives of workers and of shareholders, and the workers' representatives were given the right to veto the appointment of the personnel manager. A "worker director" with full equal rights was also to be added to the management board. In 1952, a somewhat weaker act was applied to firms in other industries with over 500 employees. In smaller firms, works councils were established that had powers similar to those under Weimar. Management was required to consult the works council on a range of issues. In 1976, a general co-determination law standardized representation, with a majority of members on the supervisory board going to shareholders' representatives and management.

Employers resisted these changes. They were forced to accept the initial introduction of co-determination because British authorities favored it and simply imposed the new system on the coal and iron firms in their zone. Employers attempted to reverse this defeat in 1951; the division between the coal, iron, and steel industries with "parity co-determination" and other industries, and the limitation to large firms, were compromises reached after intense dispute, including a mass strike in May 1952. The struggle of labor leaders for parity in other industries during the 1960s led eventually to the further compromise in 1976. On balance, the system served employers well, and West Germany enjoyed relatively peaceful labor relations. The major confrontations made a relatively short list—in addition to the co-determination strikes of 1952, there were disputes over sick days in 1958, a series of wildcat strikes in 1971, strikes following the oil crisis in 1976, a major steel strike in 1978, and a strike for shorter hours in 1984.

The German Confederation of Labor Unions (*Deutsche Gewerkschaftsbund* or DGB) reestablished itself in 1949. Even more centralized than before, it consisted of sixteen national unions. Hans Böckler, first chairman of the DGB, believed the ideological and confessional divisions within the labor movement had weakened workers in the confrontation with Nazism. He worked to spread the new organization across all trades and industries, and was supported by local officials who favored a non-partisan but politically active movement. Forbidden from enforcing compulsory membership, the unions enrolled only 30 to 40 per cent of workers but negotiated agreements that covered 90 per cent of workers. This reduced their potential income from dues and increased the risk that a strike might not be supported by non-members, who, however, would share in any benefits. Consistently, the unions restrained wage demands in return for employment guarantees. They preferred stability over radical experiment. Strikes became a last resort, requiring approval by a 75 per cent majority in most unions, but ended at the leaders' discretion if only 25 per cent of the members approved. Instead of strikes, unions protected terms of employment with a thicket of legal provisions and procedures. Although this reduced arbitrary actions by employers, legalism further reduced the range of tactics available to the unions.[58]

The emerging legal and institutional framework might be designed for stability, but it could not completely insulate firms and workers from change. In the Ruhr, for instance, once the mines returned to production the crucial question became how to get and keep sufficient numbers of workers in the area. Incentive programs were used first, and then after the currency reform, the lure of subsidized housing. Managers and local officials hoped their new hostels, apprenticeship programs, and housing estates would not only attract new workers to the mines, but also reshape the culture of the workers. They wanted to avoid the labor disputes of the Weimar era by creating a "new" miner with more cooperative values. They failed. Their authoritarian and paternalistic approach took little or no account of what the miners and their families actually wanted. When jobs opened in other areas in the mid-1950s, workers left the mines for more pleasant and less restrictive environments.[59]

In East Germany, the labor unions became explicit instruments of political control. The Free German Confederation of Trade Unions was formed in 1948. Like the DGB it had sixteen member unions, but unlike the West, union membership in the East was compulsory, and also unlike the West, the movement included all members of the intelligentsia as well as manual workers. Every enterprise and every institution contained a branch representing the relevant union. The unions' functions included the implementation of government policy and particularly the execution of production plans. Although they were responsible for ensuring that managers abided by health and safety regulations, for instance, they played no role in setting wages, which were determined by the central Council of Ministers as part of the planning process. The right to strike, included in the 1949 constitution, disappeared from the new constitution of 1968, because, the regime said, a strike in a workers' state could only represent the nonsensical act of workers striking against themselves.

The unions did not, and probably in general could not, protect East German workers against adverse conditions such as increasing pollution to the extent that West German unions did. However, they did enforce a range of legal measures that governed the pace of work and protected workers against unfair dismissal. Under the New Economic Policy, and after the party congress of 1971, the unions gained increased rights of consultation in the overall planning process, and in administration at the enterprise level. By the 1980s, the union movement, the largest mass organization in the country, was seen as at least a junior partner with the ruling party in the state apparatus.

Photographs from the late 1960s onward show that the leaders of the labor unions in East Germany dressed in the same suits as the leaders of the ruling party. Closer inspection reveals that these suits were almost certainly purchased in the West. And in the West, the "labor directors" of large firms, and the leaders of the union movement, also came to wear suits indistinguishable from those worn by senior executives, senior bureaucrats, and senior politicians. In the early 1960s, in one large firm, the head of the works council and the plant manager joked about how the former had organized a protest during the war. The plant manager had contacted the army to call him up, but he in turn had contacted a friend in the Nazi Party apparatus to have the mobilization order canceled. "Ah, but those were different times," they laughed.

The members of the new elite of labor leaders were men. The wife of the head of that same works council had great difficulty fitting in with the wives of the senior executives that her husband now associated with. She and those other affluent wives probably did not work. In East Germany, the wives of senior labor leaders probably did work, but even as privileged members of the elite they found that their chances of rising to positions of real power were restricted.

Rock'n'roll: youth, education, and social control

As with other aspects of German society, the Allies originally intended that the German educational system would be restructured in ways that would produce more democratically inclined citizens. United States officials pushed for a comprehensive system and advocated the abolition of the *Gymnasium*. German officials, all of them products of the *Gymnasium* system and holders of the *Abitur*, opposed what they saw as a threat to the quality of education itself. The British, who after decades of debate were themselves implementing a dual track system that separated a talented elite from the masses of ordinary students, agreed with the Germans. So did the French, who also possessed a system geared to the training of a small elite. In the Soviet zone, two-thirds of existing teachers were dismissed, and a six-month training course for new teachers launched. The Russians insisted that returning teachers, even those declared to have been only "nominal" participants in the Nazi regime, were not to replace or to supervise these new teachers. All teachers in the Soviet zone were told that the schools were engaged in a life-and-death struggle between reactionary and democratic forces. More than loyalty was expected. Teachers must develop a "firm belief in the strength of scientific socialism, in the teachings of Marx–Engels–Lenin–Stalin, in the power and greatness of the Soviet Union."[60]

The desperate economic situation of the immediate postwar years meant the reconstruction of school buildings and any restructuring of the system itself had to be postponed, and this in turn meant that control over the systems was returned to the new German governments. In East Germany, the attempt to force teachers to become committed Marxists failed through the 1950s. Until 1961, unhappy teachers could leave for the West. Others stayed, but left teaching for better-paying jobs in industry or government. Beginning in the late 1950s and continuing through the 1960s, the East German government constructed a highly centralized system, in which virtually all students moved from primary schools into comprehensive polytechnical upper schools. These originally introduced students to specific trades, but became more generalist over time. By 1974, 90 per cent of children were staying in school until the age of 16. Of these, about 13 per cent proceeded on to extended upper schools and took their *Abitur* at the age of 18. The rest moved to two or three-year courses leading to practical qualifications, and in the case of the three-year courses, to the *Abitur* as well.

East Germany introduced a comprehensive system of preschools, a correlate of the rising proportion of women in full-time employment. By the 1980s, 80 per cent of children attended day care centers for ages 1 to 3, and 90 per cent attended preschools for ages 3 to 6. At the other end of the educational spectrum, the government committed itself to increasing the proportion of students from working-class and peasant families who attended university. In the 1950s, bridging courses such as that completed by Günter Mittag, provided a path to university for workers and peasants, a total of some 34,000 students by 1963 when they were phased out. In 1960, the proportion of university students from working-class families had risen to 50 per cent, compared to 5 per cent in 1949. In the 1960s, the proportion dropped again, as the children of the "Socialist service class" of party officials and white-collar workers increased in numbers.

Throughout, ideological indoctrination and training supported the system's primary aims. A series of myths, reinterpretations of Germany's past and representations of the present, were developed and deployed through school lessons, explicit political indoctrination, field trips, festivals, organized rituals, and mass meetings. Textbooks, supported by children's literature, poster art, and the media, were all structured around the canonical themes. German culture, anti-Fascism, the "great Socialist Soviet Union," and the "Socialist fatherland" became symbols reinforcing an East German identity. East Germany embodied the best aspects of German culture, including literature (Goethe) and music (Beethoven). Later, the figure of Martin Luther appeared as a symbol of an independent Germany whose heritage East Germany maintained, as did Frederick the Great, and the Wars of Liberation against Napoleon. During the dark days of the Nazi era, the German Communist Party had led the fight against Fascism, and the anti-Fascist resistance had ultimately triumphed and resulted in the foundation of the German Democratic Republic. Patriotic German Communists had been assisted by the Soviet Union, and the image of the great Socialist Soviet Union reinforced the inculcation of Socialist values. This included veneration of Stalin until the de-Stalinization of 1956. The Soviet victory in 1945 was therefore a victory for East Germany. The creation of the Socialist fatherland was portrayed as the culmination of all of Germany's previous history.[61]

Indoctrination alone might be insufficient to produce Socialist citizens. Youth needed to be protected from comic books, escapist literature, and the dangers of West German commercial television. Students were observed, particularly in the early years if they came from suspect family backgrounds. In the 1960s, authorities began to place less emphasis on social background in selecting students, but political reliability remained crucial. Courses in Marxism–Leninism were compulsory. Although there were no fees, students worked in industry and agriculture during vacations, experience intended to reinforce their commitment to the worker–peasant orientation of the regime. At all levels students were pointed toward the careers that planning officials regarded as the most necessary.[62]

The East German system included a large number of research institutes, but their agendas were set by the government and directed toward practical applications, especially after a major reorganization in the late 1960s. Academic careers were redesigned into a secure sequence of steps, and the lower classes received much greater access to academic careers than before. Explicit ideological control bore far more heavily on teachers and researchers in the humanities and social sciences than on their colleagues in the natural sciences, but, on balance, university instructors became an "unremarkable" part of the elite "service class" of the East German regime.[63]

In West Germany, in 1955, the state ministers of culture decided to maintain the traditional separate tracks throughout the system. The *Gymnasium* remained, a secondary school offering nine years of schooling to follow the initial four years of primary schooling, intended to prepare students for the *Abitur* and for university study. English replaced Latin as the first foreign language in most schools. Otherwise little changed in the structure of the curriculum for the elite. A second track, the ten-year middle school, prepared students to enter technical schools for career training. The third track, the general school (*Hauptschule*) of nine years, was intended to be followed by at least three years of vocational training. Throughout the system most teachers returned to their jobs providing they could prove they had not been excessively active in Nazi organizations.

The system did provide for more flexibility than before. Students could shift from one stream to another, and over time the proportion of students aiming for the *Abitur* rose. In addition, a number of states introduced new comprehensive schools in the early 1970s and these enrolled 166,000 students in 1975. In 1960, only 24 per cent of secondary school students attended a *Gymnasium* and fewer than half of those earned the *Abitur*. By 1975, the proportion of students attending a *Gymnasium* had risen, but still only to 30 per cent. The proportion of students entering the middle schools, 12 per cent in 1960, increased to 19 per cent in 1980, and the proportion entering the general schools dropped from 60 to 41 per cent.

The system remained rigid in other important ways. The proportion of girls who received the *Abitur* increased only slowly, from 30 per cent in 1950, to 36 per cent in 1960, and 39 per cent in 1975. The large majority of girls continued to receive only a primary education. Those who, if they had been boys, would have moved to the general or middle schools and then on to technical training were discouraged or explicitly prohibited from doing so. For the boys and the small numbers of girls the training was thorough, but unimaginative. Diligent and precise, but slow and unwilling to change, the graduates of West Germany's technical training programs had been well trained in the technologies of the late nineteenth and early twentieth centuries. During the golden age this was an advantage, but it was not the best preparation for the next generation.

The number of university students rose in line with the increase in absolute numbers of *Gymnasium* students, from 239,000 in 1960 (16 per cent female) to 412,000 (about 25 per cent female) in 1970. New universities were opened and other institutions upgraded, raising the total to around eighty. Enrollments would nearly double again in the next decade, but it was this initial generation of "mass" educated university students who confronted the problems of outdated teaching styles, inadequate accommodation, and unsympathetic administrations. These new students were not the sons and daughters of the lower classes. In stark contrast to East Germany, in West German universities the students continued to come from the middle and upper classes. The share of farmers' children remained small, 4 per cent in the early 1950s and 2 per cent in the late 1960s, and the proportion of children of workers increased only slightly, from just under 4 per cent to 5.5 per cent.

As in previous generations, what youth did in their spare time worried adults. Youth were also consumers, and as affluence increased the dangers of temptation grew. When they were not in school, they continued to form informal groups that concerned West German authorities as they had concerned their Weimar and Nazi predecessors.[64] Young people also went to movies such as Willi Forst's *Die Sünderin* (*The Sinner,* 1951), in which a woman named Marina resorts to prostitution as her middle-class family disintegrates during the war. Her labor as a prostitute brings her wealth and luxury, as well as sexual satisfaction and power over men, first Nazis and then Americans. She finds emotional redemption through her love for Alexander, a reformed alcoholic artist, but then kills him to spare him death from a brain tumor and herself commits suicide and dies in his arms. Supported with newly introduced government subsidies and promoted partly by Forst's deliberate provocation of the censorship board, *Die Sünderin* became the most popular film of the year. It also became a scandal, with public protests by Catholic youth groups. The controversy led to increased "public" representation on the national censorship board, which meant Christian Democrat appointees who were representatives of conservative Catholic opinion, the creation of another film board by state cultural ministers that could grant or withhold tax incentives to producers, and the establishment of Catholic film leagues that issued ratings and monitored attendance.

Film-makers in general avoided controversy when they could. Twenty per cent of all German films during the 1950s, including Forst's next film in 1952, were *Hematfilm* ("homeland film"), a genre that embodied the static nostalgic vision of the Ordoliberals, family sociologists, and Catholic conservatives. In the typical plot outline, a city girl returns to the country, discovers the charm of the close-knit community with its folk dancing and festivals, falls in love with a local woodsman or squire, and gives up the city, her effete urban boyfriend, and her job.[65]

Popular culture also took on the forms of American rock and roll. Like jazz in the 1920s and 1930s, American popular music of the 1950s was equated by both West and East German authorities with blackness, a stereotyped racialized other that threatened the social and sexual order. The "orgiastic hysteria" that *Der Spiegel* attributed to Elvis Presley's young female fans concerned authorities in both West and East

Germany, and so did their tendency to adopt American clothing and hairstyles. The press detailed the unhealthy and disorderly appearance of girls who danced "boogie" in ponytails, jeans or pedal-pusher pants, and short jackets. In the West, Christian civilization seemed under attack; in the East, American popular culture was another aspect of capitalist imperialism.[66]

It was extremely important to West Germany's leaders that whatever it was that youthful West Germans were doing, it should not be political. Erhard argued that, as wealth increased and class differences declined, social policy could and should be placed beyond any political ideology.[67] Helmut Schelsky again produced the necessary research. *The Skeptical Generation* (*Die skeptische Generation*, 1957) congratulated West Germany's youth on their "skepticism," by which he meant that they had moved beyond belief in any particular ideology. Any rebellion they might show, Schelsky assured his readers, was a purely "private" matter. In addition to rejecting the "politicized" stance of the Weimar and Nazi generations, West German youth had also rejected the search for Utopian ideals such as "community" or "wholeness" that had led previous generations from the pre-1914 youth movement onward to reject modern industrial civilization. Indeed, West German youth not only accepted industrial society, but they were also instinctively anti-Communist. They were, Schelsky concluded, "nonpolitically democratic" and, indeed, possibly more thoroughly non-political and more democratic than other contemporary youthful Western Europeans or Americans.[68]

In East Germany, the regime maintained its blanket ban on rock and roll. West Germany in contrast discovered ways to accommodate the new style. Home-grown dance and singing stars modeled the new fashions for German "teenagers"—the term that replaced *Halbstarken* ("semi-strong," or half-grown, potentially rowdy young men) and *Backfisch* ("fried fish," previously a common term for a girl in her teen years, which disappeared between 1956 and 1958). Magazines such as *Bravo* reported on the stars and advertised the products. "We teenagers have our own style. And that's what makes many people see red," an advertisement for Triumph underwear proudly asserted in 1958.[69] Indeed, the point was precisely that many people had feared a red menace. Uta Poiger argues that the depoliticizing and domestication of rock and roll opened the possibility of consolidating youth into a consumer culture while at the same time contrasting the freedom of choice of "style" in the West with the lack of choice in the East.[70]

The political context

The war altered the social basis of politics in several significant ways. The old military elite disappeared. Of some 9000 members of the nobility, nearly 5000 had been killed in the fighting and another 1500 had perished in air raids, died in detention camps, or been murdered by the foreign workers on their estates or by Soviet soldiers. In Poland and the Soviet zone, large agricultural estates were expropriated. As seen above, farmers were a rapidly declining percentage of the population. The decline of agriculture remained a problem, but farmers could never provide sufficient votes to elect important numbers of representatives. In East Germany their votes would not have mattered in any case. Here a new party elite arose, though the leaders were often older men from the Weimar Communist Party. In West Germany, the business elites and bureaucracy remained essentially unchanged, and many party leaders had also begun their careers in Weimar, but the power of elected political leaders was unchallenged. In West Germany, observers also noted the continued importance of religion and of class. However, both the Catholic and working-class milieus seemed to dissolve over time, though when this occurred and exactly why is still disputed.

West Germany: consensus politics

The new political parties reflected the emerging identity of West Germany. The Socialist Party (SPD) descended from the old Socialist Party outlawed in 1933. Kurt Schumacher, an editor and Socialist representative in the Reichstag, and an outspoken critic of both Communists and Nazis, had been arrested in 1933 and spent ten years in concentration camps. He had begun to reform the SPD even before the final collapse in 1945. He opposed the new Socialist central committee under Otto Grotewohl in Berlin because of its willingness to cooperate with the Communists and therefore with the Russians. He became the leader of a separate Western SPD in May 1946. His experiences gave him an unquestionable moral authority. He personified the "other" or "good" non-Nazi Germany, and he opposed the notion of "collective guilt," the idea that all Germans were implicated in the crimes of the Nazi regime. He was also strongly nationalist. He regarded the occupation as illegitimate and pressed the Allies to lift the restrictions on German industrial expansion, demanded reunification, and opposed policies such as the Schumann Plan that led to the European Coal and Steel Community, membership in the Council of Europe, and especially rearmament.

Under Schumacher, the party had reaffirmed the Marxist principles of the Erfurt Program. This appeared anachronistic to some, but to others the immediate postwar period appeared to offer an opportunity for fundamental social reform. In addition, however, in the context of the Cold War, left-wing parties across Western Europe needed to distinguish their position from Communism in order to appeal to voters. In 1959, the SPD adopted the Godesberg Program, which abandoned the demand for nationalization and state ownership of industry and defined Socialism as the outgrowth of a broad Western ethical tradition. At the state level, the SPD led reformist coalition governments. In successive federal elections, the SPD attempted to break out of its previous limits in the working-class milieu by appealing directly to the interests of farmers and to the white-collar middle classes.

The Christian Democratic Union (CDU) and their Bavarian allies, the Christian Socialist Union (CSU), were the successors of the prewar Catholic Center and the Bavarian People's Party, which had dissolved themselves in 1933. Building on debates within the Catholic Center Party extending back before the First World War, the Christian Democrats also attempted to break out of their confinement to a restricted milieu. The CDU presented itself as a popularly based party that aimed to unite disparate groups and interests into a non-denominational movement committed to Christian ethics and democratic institutions.

In the old Reich, Catholics had been a minority of just above a third of the population. In West Germany, the balance between Catholics and Protestants was very nearly equal. It has been argued that the CDU integrated "those who needed to be integrated—the cultural and political conservatives—into a durable liberal order."[71] However, the old divisions could still be seen. Among Catholics not all believed that the new party served their interests. The Catholic influence remained in some areas, particularly in social questions, and in an intransigent opposition to Communism, but integration meant less emphasis on the agenda of the Catholic Church hierarchy and the desires of devout lay Catholics. The gap between Catholics and Protestants remained as well. The CDU/CSU won a majority of the Catholic vote in every election, and usually won over 60 per cent, but they never won more than 40 per cent of the Protestant vote.

The role of Konrad Adenauer remains contentious. His negotiations with the French for an independent Rhineland after both the First and Second World Wars caused a scandal when they were publicized in the 1960s, as they appeared to Conservatives to throw a shadow across his record as a national statesman. Viewed from the left, under Adenauer the CDU/CSU coalition became increasingly conservative. Adenauer was consistently and strongly anti-Communist. He saw the SPD as only slightly less evil, an "enemy within" that could not be trusted with power. Riding the wave of economic growth, Adenauer and his supporters succeeded in demonizing radicals and choked off the potential for significant social reform. In the context of the Cold War, Adenauer's principled anti-Communism meant automatic support for United States policies. Autocratic and authoritarian, his insistence on integrating West Germany into a Western alliance directed against the Soviet Union was broadly unpopular until at least 1952, and many blamed him for contributing to Germany's division.[72]

From 1961 to 1983 there were only three parties represented in the federal parliament, the Bundestag. The third after the CDU/CSU and the SPD was the Liberals or Free Democratic Party (FDP), which gained from 7 to 13 per cent of the vote and between 34 and 67 of just under 500 voting representatives in the Bundestag. Despite its small size, the FDP played a crucial role, since the close balance between the two large parties frequently made it a necessary coalition partner. The party claimed descent from the Liberal parties of the imperial and Weimar systems. Its leaders had all made careers in Weimar politics. Founded in December 1948, it was a loose and sometimes undisciplined coalition of regional parties, some more democratic and progressive and some more nationalistic and business-oriented. The first leader was Theodor Heuss, allied with Adenauer on the Parliamentary Council in the drafting of the Basic Law, and then supported by Adenauer to become West Germany's first President. A high point for the party came in the early 1960s, when its largest Bundestag vote was matched by participation in nine of the eleven state governments.

The first elections under the Basic Law were very close. The CDU/CSU coalition gained 139 seats, the SPD 131, and the FDP 52. The remainder of 402 seats was scattered among a number of other parties ranging from the Communists to the Conservative right wing. Adenauer stitched together an alliance with the FDP and other Conservative parties and became West Germany's first Chancellor by a single vote.

The new electoral law came into force in 1953. Half of the members were to be elected from party lists as in Weimar. In contrast to Weimar but resembling the pre-1914 imperial constitution, half would be directly elected to represent local constituencies. In addition, no party that did not gain 5 per cent of the national vote would receive any representation in the Bundestag. The 5-per-cent rule wiped out the small parties, but it became the basis of the FDP's continued influence. The party was unlikely ever to elect representatives directly, but as long as it won 5 per cent of the national vote it gained proportional representation in the Bundestag.

Rapid economic recovery translated into electoral success for Adenauer. Cold War crises helped as well. From 243 seats in 1953 following the uprising in East Germany, the CDU/CSU moved to 270 and an absolute majority in 1957 following the Hungarian revolt in 1956. In 1959, "*der Alte*" (the Old Man; he had been born in 1876) first decided to run for the office of Federal President and then withdrew. He wanted to retain control of foreign policy, and when this was rejected he argued that his likely successor as Chancellor, Ludwig Erhard, was unsuitable. In 1961, Willy Brandt, the Socialist Mayor of West Berlin, captured the mood of anger and defiance during the Berlin crisis and the construction of the Wall; Adenauer seemed lethargic by comparison. In the national elections, the CDU/CSU lost votes, and the Liberals agreed to continue the coalition only on condition that Adenauer retire by 1965. Then in 1962 came the "*Spiegel* affair," when the defense minister ordered raids on the magazine's offices and arrests of journalists following articles in *Der Spiegel* critical of the combat-readiness of the army. Franz Josef Strauss, head of the CSU and the minister responsible, was forced to resign, and the FDP now insisted that Adenauer must go in 1963.

Erhard did finally replace Adenauer in 1963, and despite gloomy predictions led the CDU/CSU to an increased representation in the 1965 elections. Unfortunately, Erhard's government then bore the blame for one of the golden age's few recessions. His electoral gains had come at the expense of the FDP, and the government was weakened by disputes between the coalition partners. Erhard was forced to resign and was replaced by Kurt Kiesinger, who advocated cooperation with the Socialists.

Aside from the economic recession, the major parties also feared a sudden rise of radical right-wing agitation. Formed in 1964, the National Democratic Party (NPD) rode dissatisfaction with the economy to a peak that almost gave it representation in the Bundestag. Anti-capitalist and anti-democratic, it carefully claimed publicly to support the existing political system, and was studiously vague about its program. In 1965, it gained 664,000 votes, 2 per cent of the total. In the economic downturn in 1966, it passed the 5-per-cent barrier in state elections in Hesse and Bavaria. In 1969, despite the recovery of the economy, the NPD still won 1.4 million votes, 4.2 per cent. The emergence of a serious right-wing party widely regarded as favoring a restoration of the Nazi regime and committed to regaining the lost territories alarmed foreign observers and seemed to call into question the depth of West Germany's commitment to democracy.

Kiesinger formed a "grand coalition" with the Socialists, with Brandt, now the leader of the SPD, serving as foreign minister. Balancing the desires of left and right was difficult, but Kiesinger managed the process successfully for three years. Compromises were hammered out at weekly meetings of senior ministers known as the Kressbronn Circle. The process of elite negotiation on behalf of a range of potentially conflicting interests resembled techniques coming into fashion elsewhere in Europe, notably in Sweden. "Democratic corporatism" embodied in a coalition commanding 90 per cent of the seats in the Bundestag might promise stability, but it also removed political decisions from the voters and placed them in the hands of politicians, bureaucrats, and representatives of organized interest groups. It could be argued that this ensured better decisions, since the process of negotiation was in the hands of experts.[73] More cynically, some saw the grand coalition as a panicked response by elite politicians to the challenge from the right, a tacit admission that they had not yet learned how to overcome the weaknesses of Weimar, and an admission as well that they did not trust German voters.

Brandt gained stature for his dramatic overtures to Eastern Europe, the beginnings of West Germany's new *Ostpolitik* or Eastern Policy. In addition, Socialist Karl Schiller served as economics minister while Strauss returned as finance minister, and the SPD gained credibility as a party capable of governing because of the rapid recovery of the economy. In 1969, the Socialists won over 40 per cent of the vote, widely regarded as the symbolic boundary of their traditional working-class support base. The FDP continued its decline, and within the party the left wing gained power. Seeing an opportunity, Brandt broke from the grand coalition and allied with the FDP. In addition to the Eastern Policy, the Socialist–Liberal government introduced a series of social reforms, including changes to the marriage and family law and an attempt to legalize abortion that was rejected by the Federal Court. Social welfare measures were extended with family allowances, rent subsidies, and improvements in sickness benefits. Expansion and restructuring of both schools and universities was begun. The government also favored an extension of co-determination, with a compromise passed finally in 1976.[74]

Conservatives opposed both the Eastern Policy and the social reform program. In 1972, CDU leader Rainer Barzel launched an attempt to unseat Brandt. One of the provisions in West German parliamentary procedures intended to help ensure stability is the "constructive vote of no confidence." Simply losing a majority is not enough to end a government. There must be a new leader already available, someone able to command a working majority. Brandt survived the vote, but he then stage-managed a no-confidence vote in himself and ordered his own supporters to abstain. He perceived, correctly, that many voters disliked the opposition's tactics. In the elections forced by the no-confidence vote, the Socialists and Liberals both gained, the CDU/CSU lost, and Barzel was replaced by Helmut Kohl. Brandt's position seemed secure.

East Germany: the structure and functioning of a one-party state

As in West Germany, the new political parties demonstrated the new identity most clearly. The Soviet authorities forced the merger of the old Socialist and Communist parties into a new Socialist Unity Party (SED). The leader of the SED was Walther Ulbricht. Born in 1893, he had been one of the founders of the Communist Party in 1918, had fled the Nazis, and had been in Moscow during the war. As was the case in the other countries of East Europe, as a long-time Communist and as a supporter of the Soviet Union, he was promoted by the occupying authorities to leadership. The SED was structured on the model of the Communist Party in the Soviet Union, highly centralized, with a restricted membership, but with a network of cells reaching down to the local level parallel to all other governance structures. To deflect the criticism that this was a one-party state, several minor parties continued to function, but without real power. The two political systems became completely separate when the West German courts declared the Communist Party to be "opposed to the constitution" in 1956 and directed that it be banned.

In the 1950s, adopting Soviet forms also meant adopting the final extreme form of the personal cult surrounding Stalin.[75] Ulbricht's rule was not popular. Expropriation of property and anti-religious policies of course had alienated many. Even among initially enthusiastic supporters, the purges of former Socialist Party members from the SED, the hardships imposed on workers, the unhappiness of farmers, and the frustrations of artists and writers meant that when Stalin died in March 1953 the regime had disappointed and angered very broad segments of society. Ulbricht and Grotewohl had been ordered by the new leaders of the Soviet Union to moderate their policies, but had only partially complied. Prices on sugar and meat had been increased, and food supplies had deteriorated to near-crisis conditions. On June 16, 1953, Berlin building workers struck and demonstrated to protest a blanket increase in work norms, and the strike movement spread to nearly every city and town. The SED and the government were paralyzed, and were only saved when the Soviet commander in Berlin proclaimed a state of siege, moved in tanks and troops, and imposed a curfew, forcing the demonstrators off the streets.

Ulbricht might have been removed by the new Soviet leadership, but was in effect saved by the uprising. Surviving, he systematically eliminated his opponents within the SED. Government institutions came under closer party control. Although the increase in work norms was rescinded and the existing plan was revised to allow for increases in consumer goods, there was no suggestion of a loosening of the reins of power. The overwhelming demonstration of the regime's unpopularity worked the other way. As Jeffrey Kopstein emphasizes, the uprising reduced the range of policy options available to the government, giving labor a "paradoxical sort of veto power,"[76] but it also had the effect of cutting off voices within the party that might have argued for more popular participation in decision-making, more freedom of expression, and for more openness to the possibility of reunification with West Germany. Similar to Adenauer in the West, Ulbricht led East Germany to closer integration with the Soviet Union and the Socialist bloc.

The Wall stabilized the regime by cutting off the opportunity to flee. Ulbricht consolidated both his own role and the position of the SED with the new constitution adopted in 1968. The new document defined the German Democratic Republic as "a Socialist state of the German nation" and also specifically celebrated the "fraternal ties" with the Soviet Union. The Leninist principle of democratic centralism meant that the state would be led by "the working class and its Marxist–Leninist party." Ulbricht, rigidly dogmatic, remained committed to dictatorship and to repression of opposition. Although he sponsored the New Economic System to improve economic efficiency, his willingness to impose reduced living standards to pay for investment in the targeted industries and his open advocacy of his own "German" path to Socialism created both opposition at home and enemies in the Soviet Union. As in 1953, further changes in the Soviet Union left him vulnerable in the late 1960s. Erich Honecker, former leader of the youth league and the security apparatus and Ulbricht's designated successor, conspired with Soviet leaders and replaced him as first secretary of the SED in 1971. Ulbricht retained honorific posts as party chairman and chair of the state council, and died in 1973.[77]

The "German question" and the past that would not go away

Germans in the postwar era were more than happy to talk about the Nazi period. Claudia Koonz recalls how easy it was in the late 1950s and early 1960s, as a hitch-hiking student, to stimulate reminiscences about the 1930s and the war years:

> I stumbled onto my own interview format with my standard opener, "What wonderful highways you have here."
> "You like our autobahn?"
> "Oh, yes, it seems very fast, and scenic, too."
> "You would never guess who built it."

And the unwitting interviewee would continue with an earnest explanation of how it had really been, what Germany was really like, to share

> their memories of a Nazism without genocide, racism, or war . . . a social world of close families, sports activities and vacations, a strong community spirit, high moral standards, and economic security . . . sad only about the war—that is, the defeat, not the brilliant military victories before the Battle of Stalingrad.[78]

The conversations with foreigners tended to have an odd tone about them, didactic, sometimes almost hectoring, and a bit defensive. Germans knew that foreign observers monitored Germany's pulse, questioned how completely West Germany had become integrated into Western Europe, and continued to fear the rise of a new right-wing movement. Germans felt misunderstood. They wanted to explain, they wanted understanding, but for the foreign observer the odd thing remained that Germans did not seem to know about the crimes of the Nazi regime that stood so clearly in the historical record.

As seen in Chapters 11 and 12, a great deal of the scholarship of the past forty years has been devoted to determining just how many Germans participated in Nazi crimes, and how many more knew. The answer in short is that many participated, and most knew. Although there was much to talk about and much to remember, there were many things it was best not to talk about and not to remember. When those things were talked about, when they had to be remembered, the process was difficult.

Victimhood

As we have seen, most ordinary Gentile Germans did not experience substantial hardship until late in the war, and for many the war in effect only began when bombs began to fall, or Soviet troops fought their way into the neighborhood. At the end of the First World War, although final defeat in 1918 came as a shock, both soldiers and civilians had been coping for a long time with increasing privation caused by the inequity of Germany's institutions and the incompetence of its leaders. In 1945, the "collapse" (*Zusammenbruch*) that most experienced was much more sudden, and therefore traumatic in a different way. In 1918, Germans felt betrayed, and began to argue over who was responsible for the betrayal. In 1945, many felt that the war had descended on them from the heavens, totally unexpected and totally undeserved. They were victims.

German leaders reversed the poles of responsibility. Germans were not guilty. They were victims of Hitler, indeed they were Hitler's first victims, and Hitler's rise to power was ultimately the fault of the Western countries whose leaders shared responsibility for the depression. Now those same powers insisted on occupying Germany, and Germans were victims again. Both CDU leader Adenauer and SPD leader Schumacher refused to accept German responsibility for the war or for its outcome, and each tried to outdo the other in denouncing the occupation as immoral and illegal, and the occupation authorities as incompetent and irrational. Catholic Archbishop Josef Springs, who had preached openly against the murder of Jews during the war, now described the occupation as "scarcely different from a totalitarian state."[79]

Those who served in the occupation at the local level were continually surprised at the absence of Nazis. No one, it seemed, had supported the regime. No one, it seemed, had the least knowledge of Nazi crimes, even when they lived in the immediate vicinity of one of the concentration camps. No one, it seemed, had known any Jews. However, everyone remembered bombs destroying their homes or workplaces, often the exact dates, and everyone remembered incidents of harassment or oppression inflicted by the Allied soldiers. In 1965, the housewife from the southwest quoted at the beginning of Chapter 11 still remembered vividly how "the evil (böse) Americans invaded Swabia, and shot our pelicans that roosted in the chimney of the old factory." Her husband, a prisoner in France after the war, remained outraged that the French had stationed "black soldiers, Africans" in their zone. "Intentional—they knew what would happen—just like the French," he said. Interviewers of Rhenish workers noted that those who lived through the "good times" of the Nazi period described their experiences only in general terms of employment, marriage, homes, and children. In contrast, they had very detailed recollections of the crisis periods of the 1918 revolution, Weimar, and the depression, and their precise chronology began again with the bombing, defeat ("Hitler's only mistake"), and the immediate aftermath of the war.[80]

East Germans also saw themselves as victims, but in a slightly different way. In the West, war widows became a representation of the victimized *Volk*, part of the general sense that Germans were the ones who had suffered. In the East this was not possible, because the government insisted that the East German state rested on a history of heroic resistance to Fascism. The Western image of the brave woman "standing alone" (*alleinstehend*) was not repeated, because it was too obvious that her dead husband was a Nazi soldier. Rather, two parallel myths emerged, of the heroic resistance of Communist leaders, and of the innocence of the masses, workers and peasants. The term "Fascist" applied not only to the Nazis but also to contemporary Britain and the United States. The British and Americans were villains, because they had not come to the aid of the Soviet Union, because they had delayed opening a "second front" until 1944, and particularly because they had bombed German cities. The bombing, East Germans said, on the one hand was inadequate and ineffectual in a military sense, and on the other hand was intended to destroy German productive capacity. This was part of the official historiography of the East German regime, but many individuals were determined to take foreign visitors to bombsites in order to impress them with the fundamental injustice of the Western attacks on Germany.[81]

There were real victims. The large numbers of those who had fled the Nazi regime, the large numbers of Socialist and Communist workers who suffered suspicion and harassment if nothing worse under the Nazis, the large numbers of women who were raped, the large numbers of families who lost their homes, the large numbers of soldiers who had suffered in varying degrees, all tended to escape the notice of foreign observers. Although, as seen above, rape victims faded into a semi-silence and left-wing workers found life difficult in East Germany, the East German regime and West German churches celebrated Communists and Christians who had resisted the Nazis. In the West, as well, organizations representing the expellees from the lost eastern territories continued to agitate, veterans' organizations represented another important interest group, and all parties campaigned with demands for the return of German prisoners of war from the Soviet Union.

But victimhood was problematic in a number of ways. While "victims" in the abstract received sympathy, real individual victims often suffered alone. Émigrés such as Thomas Mann were criticized for having watched from the "box seats" while others suffered. The abstract raped "German woman" might in reality be ostracized and denied welfare payments. In the East, her neighbors knew who the "Russian baby" was, and, similarly in the West, liaisons with occupation soldiers (common after the troops who had fought in the war were replaced and the non-fraternization rules were relaxed) were remembered twenty years later. The abstract widow "standing alone" might in reality lose her job to a returning male soldier and be forced into the streets as a rubble-woman. Later she was subjected to the same restrictions imposed on other women. The male soldier, whose deeds had appeared heroic during Nazi Germany's expansion, now needed to conceal what he had done. Defeat was shameful. He might be conceived abstractly as a suffering victim, but if he was disfigured or too badly damaged psychologically to function effectively, he might find himself pushed aside and hidden from view. Similarly, the victims of the Nazi security services could be portrayed as heroic resistors in abstract terms, but as individuals they might in reality be forced to live with the same neighbors who had denounced them.

Allied soldiers and the first occupation officials regarded all Germans as equally guilty, and they were angered to find that most Germans regarded them as the invaders and themselves as innocent victims. Of course, all Germans were not equally guilty, but, in addition, those with something to hide proclaimed their innocence. Army generals blamed Hitler for losing the war, the SS for committing the atrocities in Russia, and in Heinz Guderian's case the Communists for the division of Germany and the loss of his country estate.[82] Veterans, notably those who had served in the Waffen-SS, presented themselves as "ordinary soldiers" in the "struggle against Communism." Popular novelists such as Heinz Konsalik portrayed ordinary soldiers coping as best they could with the hardships of war. Stalingrad, the massive defeat that marked the war's military turning point, became the backdrop for stories of individual heroism against insurmountable odds.[83] Others insisted and have continued to insist not only on their innocence, but also that they resisted the regime. In interviews, the wives of Protestant pastors remember visits from the Gestapo and mention jail terms and death, although in fact there were very few members of the clergy who opposed the regime at any time.[84] For these women, and for many other Germans in both East and West, the continued blame of outsiders was unjustified, and Germany remained a victim, the unwilling recipient of advice and pressure from Russia in the East and the United States in the West.

Denazification

Coming to terms with the past meant coming to terms with the Nazi pasts of many, many individuals. In 1949, the Allies passed responsibility to German authorities for the prosecution of Nazi war criminals. The International Military Tribunal had laid down definitions, guidelines, and principles, and the ground had been prepared through the widespread responses to questionnaires detailing activities during the Nazi period. Nothing happened in West Germany until 1958, when an office in Ludwigsburg began to assemble evidence and prepared to begin criminal proceedings. Through the early 1990s, a total of over 100,000 preliminary proceedings were begun. These had resulted in about 6500 convictions. In East Germany, the regime proclaimed that it had convicted nearly 13,000 Nazi war criminals, but these figures included a substantial number of persons who appear to have been victims of political purges.[85]

The conflict between denazification and reconstruction, and the Cold War conflict between the United States and the Soviet Union, meant that denazification in both the East and the West became not an end in itself but a piece to be played in other more pressing games. In West Germany, the "131 Law" based on Article 131 of the Basic Law ensured reinstatement or retirement on full pension to the overwhelming majority of public officials and military personnel who were deemed to have been mere "accessories" to Nazi crimes or indeed to have done nothing blameworthy at all. Institutional continuities included academic professions such as musicology and folklore studies, where periodic disputes over specific individuals' involvement reflected what Jeffrey Herf calls Germany's "divided memory" and the reinterpretation of the Nazi past to suit the needs of the two regimes.[86] Over the years, East German "Brown Books" denounced former Nazis who achieved high office in West Germany, and West German observers periodically announced the continued presence of former Nazis in East Germany.

We might say the Nazi past was often forgiven, but not exactly forgotten. Rather, it was repressed. It was not mentioned, but at the same time contacts from the Nazi period could be useful. At the national level, for instance, Hans Globke, an official in the interior ministry until 1945, had drafted the official commentary on the Nuremberg Laws, held special responsibility for nationality affairs, and had been directly involved in providing legal justifications for actions against Jews and foreigners. He not only escaped prosecution, but in 1949 he became Adenauer's advisor on senior bureaucratic appointments, and from 1953 he served as state secretary in the Chancellery, an office that Adenauer used to bolster his personal control over policy. Adenauer believed Germany desperately needed the services of capable and experienced civil servants, and relied on Globke for recommendations. Many of those who benefited, not surprisingly, were Globke's former colleagues in the Nazi interior ministry, but critical observers believed Globke and his protégés to have been far more than mere public servants during the Nazi period. Globke's fate was tied up with Adenauer's political fortunes. In 1960, *Der Spiegel* published details of his involvement in Jewish deportations, and in 1962, the East German Supreme Court convicted him *in absentia* of war crimes. In the resulting scandal and amidst the crisis over Adenauer's leadership, he was forced to resign in 1963.[87]

At the local level, as well, there were significant continuities in the structure of business firms, their leadership, and consequently in the leadership of local and regional communities. Fritz Kiehn, who had led the Nazi Party to victory in Trossingen, Württemberg, benefited from questionable business deals including the acquisition of Jewish properties through his contacts in the SS. He was arrested in 1945 and interned. For a time he became the scapegoat for Nazism in Trossingen, and his archrival Ernst Hohner returned to the position of leadership of the local community from which Kiehn had ousted him. However, Kiehn was released in 1949 and returned to control of Efka, his paper-manufacturing firm. He became a respected figure once again, primarily because of his success in providing jobs and taxes for the community. He received a substantial government loan to take over the rescue of another company.

Like Globke, Kiehn's past was forgiven but not exactly forgotten. He gave up active politics, but he employed numbers of former Nazis and maintained the social connections he had made during the Nazi period, continuing on friendly terms with the family of Baldur von Schirach. Most important to him was that he recovered his local social prominence. But he did not change, and he did not admit his guilt. Specifically, he never admitted his role in the "Aryanization" of Jewish properties, and in general he never confronted the essential criminality of the Nazi regime. He was less successful in the 1960s, although Efka remained profitable, and a bank bailout removed him from management in 1972. When he died in 1980, his obituary in the local paper celebrated his achievements and ignored his Nazi connections.[88]

Atonement

The preeminent victims, the central focus of Nazi hostility and the primary object of Nazi policy, were absent. The Jews were not there. Celan's "Death Fugue" is well known because it became the single Holocaust piece in many school anthologies, a tokenism that eventually led Celan to cease reading it in public. Celan himself left Germany in 1948 and committed suicide in 1970, and "the virtual absence of German-Jewish voices from post-war literature compounded the effects of genocide itself."[89] There were only 15,000 Jews residing in West Germany in 1950, and three-quarters were refugees from Eastern Europe. Their numbers increased to 25–28,000 in the 1960s. There were only a few thousand Jews in East Germany in 1945. The regime at first had celebrated them as victims of Fascism, but when Stalin launched his anti-Semitic purges in 1952, Jews in East Germany were denounced as

Zionists and their communal organizations dissolved. Only a few hundred remained by the 1960s. The "Oath of Buchenwald," presented to the schoolchildren and foreigners who visited the site and viewed Fritz Cremer's memorial sculpture portraying resistance to Fascism, listed sixteen national groups among the "inmates" but did not mention Jews.[90]

Adenauer's willingness to employ former Nazis in his government represented one aspect of the desire to put the Nazi past behind. Compensation to the victims was another, and also reinforced West Germany's claim to represent all Germans. In 1949, Adenauer indicated that he was willing to discuss compensation with the new state of Israel. David Ben-Gurion withstood strong opposition within Israel to negotiations for "blood money," and under the Luxemburg Agreement of 1952 West Germany agreed to deliver US$ 1 billion to Israel, mostly in industrial goods, and another US$ 500 million to a Claims Conference, over a ten-year period. West Germany and Israel established full formal diplomatic relations in 1965.[91] East Germany, consistent with its self-image as a blameless heir to the resistance to Hitler, refused to negotiate with either Israel or other representatives of Jewish victims regarding compensation. In addition to anti-Zionist propaganda, East Germany offered support and material aid to Arab and Palestinian groups in the hope of achieving diplomatic recognition, and the visit of Ulbricht to Egypt in 1965 contributed to the final opening of full relations between West Germany and Israel.

There were other victims besides the Jews. In Europe, East Germany of course accepted the boundaries laid down at the end of the war, but refused to accept responsibility for Nazi crimes. West Germany did not accept the eastern boundaries, and continued to insist that the loss of German territory was illegitimate, as was the existence of East Germany. Walter Hallstein, selected by Adenauer to serve first in the Chancellor's office and then in the foreign ministry, gave his name to the Hallstein Doctrine, which mandated that West Germany would break diplomatic relations with any country that recognized East Germany. It was central to the German sense of victimhood that not only German women, but Germany itself had been raped by the invading Russians. Soviet demands for reparations, and the dismantling of German factories, were unjustified, and Germany owed nothing as compensation for the invasion of the Soviet Union or other Eastern European countries. One of Adenauer's greatest apparent successes, the freeing of remaining

German prisoners of war, was extorted by the Soviet Union in 1955 in return for diplomatic recognition in violation of the Hallstein Doctrine.

Brandt's *Ostpolitik* cut across two decades of West German foreign policy. Rejecting the Hallstein Doctrine, he opened formal relations with Romania and Yugoslavia. As Chancellor he continued the Eastern Policy, negotiating treaties with the Soviet Union, Poland, and Czechoslovakia that recognized the existing borders and surrendered German claims to the old borders of 1937. A new four-power agreement on the status of Berlin in 1971 and a treaty with East Germany in 1972 provided for the continuation of West Germany's relations with West Berlin and for the recognition of East Germany within a framework of "two German states, but one German nation."

The Eastern Policy aroused bitter opposition. Brandt insisted at the time, and continued to insist over the next two decades, that normalization of West Germany's relations with the East was a necessary precondition for reunification.[92] But as his opponents protested, *Ostpolitik* meant admitting the loss of the eastern territories to Poland, it meant accepting the permanent division of Germany, and it meant accepting the Socialist regime of East Germany as legitimate. Franz Josef Strauss and the Bavarian government mounted a legal challenge to the treaty with East Germany. *Ostpolitik* also meant coming to terms with and atoning for the crimes of the Nazi era. Internationally, one of Brandt's most applauded gestures was to fall to his knees at the memorial for the victims of Nazism in the Warsaw ghetto. In West Germany many saw it as humiliating, and those who had lost homes in the East were offended. Ironically, Brandt was forced to resign, not because of *Ostpolitik*, and not because of the costs of his social policies, but when one of his aides was unmasked as an East German spy. He was succeeded by Helmut Schmidt in 1974.

Notes

1. Belting 1998, pp. 104–5.
2. Richie 1998, pp. 704–5.
3. Pommerin 1995.
4. Fulbrook 1992; Moeller 1997.
5. Richie 1998, pp. 704–5.
6. Richie 1998, pp. 711–12.
7. Fulbrook 1992; 1995; Jarausch 1999.
8. Richie 1998, pp. 711–12.

9. Foschepoth 1997.
10. Marrus 1997.
11. Naimark 1995, pp. 167–8.
12. Naimark 1995; Eisenberg 1996.
13. Czichon 1970.
14. DeVorkin 1992.
15. Paris 1986.
16. Tusa 1989.
17. Dorondo 1992.
18. Naimark 1995, Ch. 2, pp. 106–7.
19. Grossmann 1997.
20. Heidemeyer 1994, p. 191.
21. Wyden 1989.
22. Milward 1984; Hogan 1987; Maier 1991.
23. Carlin 1996.
24. Pritchard 2000, pp. 161–2.
25. Naimark 1995, p. 9.
26. Ritschl 1996, p. 511.
27. Kopstein 1997; Pritchard 2000, Ch. 8.
28. Maier 1981, p. 334.
29. Erhard 1957.
30. Müller-Armack 1946.
31. Eucken 1952.
32. Röpke 1944. See Peacock and Willgerodt 1989; Giersch *et al.* 1994, pp. 26–32.
33. McCauley 1979.
34. Mittag 1991.
35. Berghahn 1986, Ch. 1; Reich 1990.
36. Wallich 1955, p. 166.
37. Hübner 1998, p. 76.
38. Gillingham 1991.
39. Maddison 1995.
40. Saltzman 1999, pp. 17–23.
41. Steinberg 2001.
42. Conrad 1992.
43. Heibel 1995, p. 102.
44. Guilbaut 1983; Saunders 1999, p. 254.
45. Grossmann, 1997.
46. Grossmann 1995, pp. 136, 209.
47. Heineman 1999, p. 242.
48. Ansorg and Hürtgen 1999.
49. Moeller 1993, p. 191.
50. Moeller 1993, pp. 117–19.
51. Giersch *et al.* 1994, pp. 161–2.
52. Moeller 1993, pp. 119–20.
53. Wildt 1995.
54. Carter 1997, pp. 206, 230.

55. Moeller 1993, pp. 121, 122; Carter 1997, pp. 206, 230.
56. Diefendorf 1993.
57. Wagner 1995.
58. Fichter 1995.
59. Roseman 1992.
60. Naimark 1995, p. 457.
61. Nothnagle 1999.
62. Bernhardt and Kuhn 1998.
63. Jessen 1999a, p. 439.
64. Klenkmann 1996.
65. Fehrenbach 1995; 1997.
66. Poiger 1997.
67. Erhard 1957.
68. Poiger 1997; Moses 1999.
69. *Bravo*, no. 42, 1958, cited in Carter 1997.
70. Poiger 1997, pp. 398–400, 403 note 99, 408.
71. Cary 1996, p. viii.
72. Köhler 1994.
73. Hancock 1989.
74. Braunthal 1994.
75. Lemke 1999.
76. Kopstein 1997, p. 18.
77. Grieder 1998.
78. Koonz 1986, pp. xviii–xix.
79. Foschepoth 1997.
80. Herbert 1986.
81. Richie 1998, p. 738; Fulbrook 1999, pp. 55–9.
82. See Goda 2000.
83. Heinz Konsalik, *The Heart of the 6th Army* (trans. Oliver Cobern; Henley-on-Thames, 1977); Theodor Pluvier, *Stalingrad: Roman* (Munich: Bertelsmann Lesering, 1959).
84. Thomas 1995. See Hoffmann 1988.
85. Grabitz 1988.
86. Lixfeld 1994; Herf 1997; Potter 1998.
87. Garner 1997, pp. 148–7; Fulbrook 1999, pp. 60–4.
88. Berghoff and Rauh-Kühne 2000.
89. McGowan 1997, p. 449.
90. Fulbrook 1999, pp. 30–1.
91. Zweig 2001.
92. Cary 2000.

CHAPTER 14

A POSTMODERN GENERATION:
WEST AND EAST GERMANY
AFTER THE MIRACLE,
1973–89

In 1983, Hanne Darboven completed a work entitled *Cultural History 1880–1983*.[1] It consists of 1590 "sheets" contained in identical wooden frames, and nineteen "elements/sculptures." When installed, the sheets cover the entire wall space of a very large room. The elements/sculptures standing in the open space of the room include an antique rocking horse and two mannequins in jogging suits.

The sheets on the walls are predominantly brown and red in tone, and the framed materials include covers and articles from German magazines, postcards, posters, and photographs. They divide roughly into nine areas: the two world wars, an extensive collection of knitting and weaving patterns, articles from the magazines *Stern* and *Der Spiegel* that relate to the debate over the fraudulent Hitler diaries, posters and postcards about the Russian Revolution, a "cultural timetable" (*Kulturfahrplan*) of Germany listing events in art, politics, and science, articles and examples from the history of popular printing and postcards, pictures and posters of movie and rock stars, and a collection of photographs of doorways in New York City.

Despite its title, the work does not tell a "story" and does not offer an analysis of German cultural history over the century from the Bismarckian empire to the 1980s. The date 1880 is arbitrary. Darboven has produced other works structured around the idea of a century. *One Century* (*Ein Jahrhundert*, 1975) includes 365 binders with one page for each day, with, for instance, all the January 1s in one binder. *One Century: Dedicated to Johann Wolfgang von Goethe* (1988) consists of pages of typed numbers, extending by one each day, with each sheet of paper framed individually. Here the beginning point reflects no more than the fact that Darboven began the work in 1980. Similarly, the end date is simply the year in which Darboven completed the work. The areas covered reflect Darboven's personal history, including a number of years in New York, and her hobbies. The "cultural timetable" consists of parallel lists with no grouping, hierarchy, or connections among the events.

The work attempts to place itself beyond criticism precisely because it offers no analytical framework. It invites the viewer to consider the idea that the world wars and the Russian Revolution are of no more importance than the artist's photos of New York doorways. As history, this is worse than amateurish; as politics, many would see it as worse than irresponsible. But that is not the point. Darboven and other postmodernist thinkers and artists are not claiming to be professional historians, and they are not interested in politics as normally conceived. Rather, Darboven's work has been praised for her "obsessive" accumulation images, which some critics believe offers a "deconstructive challenge" to the "totalizing, mythologizing art of mainstream modernism." In the 1980s, some saw her work as "deeply political," not for its possible political references, but because it raised the problem of representation itself. "Darboven's 'presence' wordlessly traces the passage of its own absence, its own death and unaccountability in languages."[2]

The essence of postmodern art is self-reflexivity. The world, and any work representing the world, is to be experienced or "read" by each individual rather than interpreted, and each reading by each individual is unprivileged, undetermined, and unrelated to other readings. Anything can be a text, and there is simply nothing beyond the text itself. Darboven frequently copies passages because she "cannot improve on them," and she fills pages with cursive "ls" because "the writing fills the space as a drawing would." She in fact prefers numbers. "I choose numbers because they are so steady, limited, artificial. The only thing that has ever been created is the number. A number of something (two chairs or whatever) is something else. It is not pure number, and has other meanings."[3]

In the modern world numbers are important. In West Germany, the numbers did not look as good as for the previous generation. The divergent trends in cultural life, and perhaps the postmodernist perspective itself, can be traced to the new social fault-lines that opened as the economy slowed and failed to deliver the goods. Not only how to manage the economy, but the question of whether the economy could or should be managed at all divided economists. The demands of marginalized groups also called the principles of social management into

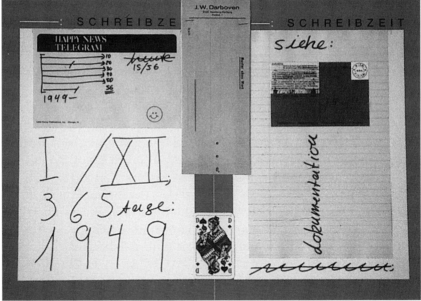

Plate 14.1   Hanne Darboven, *Kulturgeschichte 1880–1983* (*Cultural History 1880–1983*), 1980–83, installation at Dia Center for the Arts, New York, March 28, 1996–June 29, 1997. One of a number of massive projects Darboven has structured with reference to a century, this work consists of 1590 framed "sheets" and 19 "elements/sculptures." *Top:* This overview of the installation shows the sheets on the walls and some of the elements/sculptures in the middle of the room. *Bottom:* Detail: one of the 1590 "sheets" that make up the bulk of the work. Photo: Cathy Carver. Courtesy Dia Art Foundation.

question. And in the cultural realm, the claims of postmodernists undermined the foundations of any single perception of "reality." New social movements linked to new cultural forms, a new feminism, and new attempts to master the past. Historians, now in close competition with social scientists and cultural theorists, entered the debates over economic development, social change, and cultural transformations. In addition, their own professional debates over the course and meaning of German history themselves became public events.

In East Germany, the rate of growth also slowed, but East Germany's official numbers appeared to show that growth remained more rapid than in West Germany. Socially, the regime appeared to have achieved at least acceptance if not enthusiastic support, and it easily contained and controlled overt opposition. Some limited space opened for hopeful reformers, but the extremes of Western popular culture, postmodernist high culture, and protest movements had no place. Then suddenly the economy appeared to lurch into crisis. Equally suddenly, fringe groups such as disaffected urban youths took on much greater significance as evidence that the level of support for the regime was not nearly so high as the leadership had hoped.

The economic context: the era of slow growth

The lost golden age

The long upswing ended in the late 1960s. The slowdown affected the United States and Japan as well as both Western and Eastern Europe. (See Table 14.1.) Growth in West Germany averaged under 2 per cent per year in 1971 to 1986, and total output declined in 1975, 1981, and 1982.[4] East Germany's official measure of net material product also showed a decline in the rate of growth, from over 7 to 4.6 per cent.[5] The less favorable Western estimates of East German growth still showed a similar decline, from over 4 to 2.3 per cent per year.[6]

In the West, from the mid-1970s onward, levels of unemployment not seen since the 1930s created unhappiness and discontent. As economic growth stagnated, prices rose, a perverse and unexpected development that seemed to require a new name—"stagflation." West Germany had the reputation for being the country whose monetary authorities exercised the most restraint. As seen in Table 14.2, this reputation may have been justified. However, the figures also show first that inflation was a

Table 14.1 International comparison of growth rates, 1950–70 and 1970–90 (per cent per year)

	West Germany	East Germany	France	Britain	Italy	USSR	USA	Japan	Indonesia	Argentina
1950–70	6.28	4.15	5.08	2.76	5.93	4.99	3.75	9.62	3.75	3.68
1970–90	2.48	2.30	2.74	2.29	2.99	1.95	2.97	4.31	5.90	0.99

Source: Calculated from data in Angus Maddison, *Monitoring the World Economy 1820–1992* (Paris: Development Centre of the Organization for Economic Cooperation and Development, 1995), Table B-7 and Table C. For East Germany the final year is 1989.

world phenomenon, and second that West Germany did not escape. The indices for both wholesale prices and the cost of living in West Germany doubled from 1970 to 1985. As elsewhere in Europe, in the United States, and in Japan, the rise in prices began in the late 1960s before the "oil shock" of 1973, accelerated through the mid-1980s, and only abated in the recession that followed the collapse in world stock markets in late 1987.

Table 14.2 International comparison of price changes, 1950–88

	West Germany (1953 = 100)	France (1953 = 100)	Italy (1953 = 100)	Britain (1953 = 100)	USA (1938 = 100 to 1975; then 1980 = 100)	Japan (1970 = 100; then 1985 = 100)
1950	85	78	93	93	202	62
1955	101	98	100	105	217	86
1960	104	130	99	104	234	88
1965	109	145	113	111	239	90
1967	109	148	114	113	247	94
1970	112	177	128	135	273	100/49
1975	153	278	246	335	432/65	76
1980	189	435	530	673	100	101
1985	222	681	908	926	115	100
1987	198	614	936	883	114	88
1988	200	700	970	911	119	87

Source: Calculated from data in B. R. Mitchell, *International Historical Statistics*, 3 vols. (Basingstoke: Macmillan and New York: Stockton, 1992–95). Indices of wholesale prices.

In the East, ordinary people might be employed, but the lack of goods also created unhappiness and discontent. The East German government reported no increase in the cost of living from 1965 to 1988, but this was fraudulent. Official prices for a range of commodities were fixed. Food, clothing, housing, medical care, childcare, and education were all subsidized or provided free, and so too were a range of domestic appliances. But demand was pressing on supplies. The Soviet Union began charging higher prices for oil and other raw materials provided to East Germany and other Socialist countries. In turn, the East German regime had to exchange greater quantities of goods to obtain the necessary energy and raw material imports, and therefore less was available for investment and consumption. Travel was a privilege reserved for the elite and the politically reliable, and higher quality goods were often unobtainable. Consumer durables, such as refrigerators, washing machines, and automobiles, might be available but were restricted in supply and rationed by waiting lists. The result was suppressed inflation. Excess purchasing power, the savings that ordinary East Germans could not spend, accumulated.

What had happened, and who was to blame? International factors played a role. World trade slowed and markets became more competitive. Table 14.3 shows the export performance of West Germany, other countries in Western Europe, the United States, and Japan. The contrast between the high rates of growth of exports in the 1950s and 1960s and the slow rates of the 1970s and 1980s is striking. The growth of West German exports dropped to from 12.9 to 5.3 per cent per year. East Germany's official statistics showed a decline in the growth of foreign trade from 6.6 per cent to 2.4 per cent per year. East German producers

Table 14.3 International comparison of rates of growth of exports, 1950–70 and 1970–88 (per cent per year)

	West Germany	France	Italy	Britain	USA	Japan
1950–70	12.9	7.3	11.0	4.5	5.7	14.3
1970–88	5.3	5.1	5.6	2.2	3.8	5.8

Value of exports in current prices, deflated using indices of wholesale prices.

Source: Calculated from data in B. R. Mitchell, *International Historical Statistics*, 3 vols. (Basingstoke: Macmillan and New York: Stockton, 1992–95).

found that their markets in Eastern Europe grew more slowly, and so too did the markets of Western Europe that they had reached via West Germany. West Germany in turn suffered from slower growth in the European Communities and the United States, and from the rise of new competitors, especially Japan.[7]

Across the industrialized world, the distinctive forces that had fashioned the golden age weakened. In Chapter 13, we saw that all countries in both Eastern and Western Europe shared in the long boom, as did the United States and Japan, and that they did so for broadly similar reasons. Now, as shown in Table 14.4, if we decompose the overall rates of growth into their components, we see that in all of the wealthy Western countries and Japan, the factors that had contributed most strongly to growth slackened. This reflected both social and economic changes.

The rates of increase of both labor and capital slowed. Decline or slow growth in total hours worked resulted from declining birth rates and the slower growth of the labor force, but also the general reduction in hours worked per week. The capital stock grew at a lower rate, because changes in government policy, alterations in lifestyle, and the beginnings of the aging of the populations lowered the proportion of national product that was saved each year. In both Germanies investment slackened relative to the upswing. In West Germany, government reports, similar to those that appeared during the interwar downswing, criticized the large West German banks' influence over industry and accused them of increasing financial instability.[8] The East German regime attempted to meet the demands of its subjects, but found it could not both maintain the previous high rate of investment and increase the supply of consumer goods.

The ways in which resources were used also changed. During the golden age, each additional hour of labor and each added unit of capital brought large increases in output. This was less true in the era of slow growth, and overall the continued increases in capital did not in themselves raise output. Labor and capital of course need to be considered together, and total factory productivity is an estimate of the ratio of output to all of the inputs. The measure here includes an upward adjustment to the input of labor to account for increasing educational levels. This must decline as the proportion of the population with first primary, then secondary, and finally tertiary education rises. The rising levels of education, although they contributed to the increase in total

Table 14.4 The sources of growth, 1950–73 and 1973–92 (average annual percentage change)

	West Germany	France	Netherlands	Britain	United States	Japan
Gross domestic product (GDP)						
1950–73	5.99	5.02	4.74	2.96	3.92	9.25
1973–92	2.30	2.26	2.14	1.59	2.39	3.76
Total hours worked						
1950–73	0.00	0.01	− 0.04	− 0.15	1.15	1.44
1973–92	− 0.38	− 0.46	− 0.07	− 0.57	1.27	0.61
Labor productivity (GDP per hour worked)						
1950–73	5.99	5.11	4.78	3.12	2.74	1.44
1973–92	2.69	2.73	2.21	2.18	1.11	0.61
Total non-residential capital stock						
1950–73	5.93	4.80	4.55	5.17	3.27	9.18
1973–92	3.37	4.30	3.07	3.32	3.13	6.81
Capital productivity (GDP per unit of non-residential capital)						
1950–73	0.05	0.22	0.18	− 2.10	0.63	0.06
1973–92	− 1.04	− 1.96	− 0.90	− 1.67	− 0.72	− 2.85
Total factor productivity						
1950–73	4.05	3.22	2.71	1.48	1.72	5.08
1973–92	1.54	0.73	0.77	0.69	0.18	1.04
Foreign trade effect						
1950–73	0.48	0.37	1.32	0.32	0.11	0.53
1973–92	0.15	0.12	0.32	0.15	0.05	0.09
Structural change in labor force distribution						
1950–73	0.68	0.36	− 0.07	0.10	0.10	2.10
1973–92	0.17	0.15	− 0.12	− 0.09	− 0.17	0.09
Scale effect						
1950–73	0.18	0.15	0.14	0.09	0.12	0.28
1973–92	0.07	0.07	0.06	0.05	0.07	0.11
Unexplained residual						
1950–73	2.71	2.34	1.32	0.97	1.39	2.17
1973–92	1.15	0.39	0.51	0.58	0.23	0.75

Gross domestic product refers to the total value of goods and services produced within the country, before taking account of the depreciation and replacement of worn-out capital equipment.
Source: Angus Maddison, *Monitoring the World Economy 1820–1992* (Paris: Development Centre of the Organization for Economic Cooperation and Development, 1995), Table 2.6.

output, therefore account for some of the observed decline in the *rate* of growth of productivity.

In the era of low growth, improvements in productivity were far lower than in the golden age. The relatively easy gains from exploiting the backlog of technical innovations from the interwar era had now been exhausted. The discovery of genuinely new technologies is a costly and risky business that requires heavy investments over long periods of time. In the Germanies, the aftereffects of the Nazi era and the occupation continued, despite the restoration and expansion of the university systems and the creation of new research institutes. Some of the scientists and technicians taken to the Soviet Union returned to East Germany during the 1950s, but most of those who had emigrated during the Nazi period or moved to the United States after the war did not return.[9] The worldwide percentage of scientific articles published in German declined from 44 in 1920 to 21 in 1950 and 10 in 1970, and the proportion of German-speaking Nobel Prize winners dropped from 33 per cent or more in all the decades before 1940, to less than 10 per cent in the 1970s.[10]

Markets grew less rapidly, and this may have slowed the introduction of new technologies. In West Germany the initial boom in consumer durables had passed. The number of automobiles rose 5.5 per cent per year during the 1970s, less than a third of the rate during the upswing. As rapid growth reinforced itself during the boom by leading to rapid construction and replacement of plants and equipment, so now slow growth meant that almost by definition new techniques would spread relatively slowly. The large numbers of medium-sized firms in West Germany, without the resources of the giants such as Bayer or Siemens, often found the new conditions of slow growth extremely difficult.

The effects of more open markets—lower tariffs, dropping of quotas on manufactured goods, and removal of foreign exchange controls—can be seen in the large positive impact of foreign trade on growth in the golden age. Increased international integration also increased competition, but during the golden age rapid growth made participants more willing to absorb the costs. In West Germany, for instance, the expansion of employment and output in the Ruhr coal industry with reconstruction and the beginnings of the boom had been followed in the late 1950s by forced lay-offs as increasing costs, cheaper imports from the United States, and the reopening of the Suez Canal put the Ruhr mines under pressure. The European Coal and Steel Community had coordinated these and other changes, and the West German government absorbed much of the expense through welfare payments and retraining initiatives. This sort of cooperation was less easy to achieve in the era of slow growth. Protective cartels, disputes over access to markets, and non-tariff barriers marked trade relations. In contrast to the golden age, the negotiations of the General Agreement on Tariffs and Trade (GATT) became exercises in frustration. A chart of "GATT-speak" circulated, with parallel columns of subjects, verbs, adverbs, and objects, that would allow the user to speak for a claimed three hours without repetition and without making a single substantive statement.

Structural changes accounted for much of the success of the golden age, and for much of the difference between the golden age and the era of slow growth. The changes in labor force distribution—the final large declines in agricultural employment and in self-employed and employment of family members—had been greatest in West Germany and in Japan, and once again they were unique to the golden age. Once the shifting of workers from agriculture to industry had been completed, these gains were exhausted. The remaining small numbers of farmers became a highly protected minority that planners in both Japan and Europe hoped would disappear as they grew old and retired. Small shopkeepers, and in West Germany large numbers of artisan handicraft workers, also demanded and received protection through licensing requirements, restricted trading hours, and fixed retail prices.

The scale effect shows the impact of the trend toward larger units of production, more rapid in the golden age than ever before or since. Mass production reached limits in each successive new product market, and, as overall growth slowed, again the opportunities for introduction of new technologies and for further expansion declined. This links back to labor productivity and to the final unexplained residual. Large firms are generally more efficient than small firms. However, large firms require large amounts of information, and the number of workers devoted to collecting, distributing, and preserving information increased dramatically. From the 1960s through the 1980s, expanding offices housed multiplying batteries of typists and file clerks. The demand for their services was one of the great forces driving the rising number of women in the labor force. In West Germany, as elsewhere, at some point in each firm and in each industry, the gains in efficiency realized by the bureaucratization of management information systems began to decline.

Economists like to think of themselves as objective social scientists, but it was typical of the postmodern generation that the previous consensus on the process of economic growth dissolved. Each of the factors touched on above seemed to some to be "the" cause of the slowdown. In addition, Marxist economists argued that the deeper causes of these changes lay in a crisis of accumulation. The emphasis of capitalists on accumulating masses of physical capital had led to declining productivity and therefore to declining profits. Capitalists, caught in competition with one another, attempted to reduce costs to restore their profits. In earlier periods of freer competition this had caused instability, but had also forced the adoption of new technologies, raising productivity. Now, in a world of multinational enterprises and stagnant technologies, employers fell back on their one remaining tactic, direct reductions in the cost of labor. Lay-offs and attempts to cut wages led to unrest, and employers therefore called on government authorities for assistance in repressing the working class. Marxist analysts saw Margaret Thatcher in Britain and Ronald Reagan in the United States as the representatives of this conservative response to the crisis.[11]

Competing visions: West Germany's social market economy under challenge

In West Germany as well, through the 1970s and 1980s, slow growth called the previous consensus on the "social market economy" and economic management into question. Policy choices and structures that had seemed so successful now suffered criticism. Conservatives and monetarist economists blamed excessive spending on social welfare and overly generous wages and unemployment benefits. To them, West Germany appeared an example of "Eurosclerosis," the reduced inefficiency that resulted from the power of entrenched interests, especially labor unions, to protect their members. The Bundesbank became notorious for its insistence that wages must be held in check in order that profits could be increased to the levels of the 1950s and 1960s. Bank officials believed higher profits would lead to increased investment and to rapid growth as in the golden age. Those on the left and Keynesian economists blamed large firms and their monopoly power, but also the political influence of particular groups, although for them the guilty parties were farmers and industrialists. Farmers received massive subsidies. Declining "sunset" industries, such as coal mining, iron and steel, textiles, and clothing, were protected by tariffs and non-tariff barriers. The resulting high prices reduced the purchasing power of all consumers, and these observers argued that it was this lowering of aggregate demand, rather than the low rate of profits, that was inhibiting investment and slowing growth.[12]

West Germany was not an autonomous actor, however. Policies were negotiated within the framework of the European Community. The commitment to protecting existing interests and shielding producers from the effects of competition resulted in programs of subsidies and subventions. German steel-makers, for instance, were irritated that their share of production was limited in order to preserve less efficient firms elsewhere in the EC. Under the Common Agricultural Policy, EC authorities accumulated infamous "lakes" of wine and "mountains" of butter in attempts to hold prices at remunerative levels. Within the EC itself, a large fraction of the budget went to translating all documentation into every member country language. For ordinary citizens, and for many ordinary government officials, the Eurocrats in Brussels seemed very distant, out of touch with economic and social realities, and above all privileged.

In addition, there were international pressures. In 1975, the OECD had suggested "the locomotive concept" as a solution to world economic problems. The so-called "strong" countries with relatively low inflation and positive trade balances were called upon to increase government spending. This would reduce their levels of unemployment, and also increase demand for imports, and this in turn would benefit the economies of the "weak" countries. United States and West European leaders condemned West German and Japanese policy-makers for their caution, for failing to turn West Germany and Japan into locomotives of growth in their respective regions. In 1978, at a summit meeting held in Bonn, West Germany and Japan agreed to stimulate their economies, the United States agreed to reduce its demand for oil by decontrolling prices, and all participants committed themselves to a quick conclusion of the "Tokyo round" of GATT negotiations. Unfortunately for West Germany, the additional government spending and reduced interest rates came as the economy approached the peak of an upward cycle. Then came the second "oil shock" in 1979–80. The resulting high inflation and trade deficits left West Germany "uniquely ill equipped for the severe slump that was to come in the early 1980s."[13]

Unions on balance became less able to protect their members' interests. The compromise law of 1976 changed the co-determination system for large firms of over 2000 employees, but, although supervisory board members were now split equally between representatives of shareholders and of workers, the chair, representing the shareholders, was given an additional casting vote in case of ties. In addition, seats on the board were reserved specifically for representatives of middle management, technically employees but generally disposed toward shareholders. In 1986, new legislation altered the conditions under which strikes and lockouts could be conducted. Workers who were laid off as the result of a strike elsewhere in their industry were denied government unemployment benefits if they were likely to benefit indirectly from the strike. This threw the burden of supporting all laid-off workers onto the unions and made it far more difficult for them to call strikes. Employers in turn were allowed to use lockouts as a tactic in wage disputes, although they were limited in applying defensive lockouts to about a ratio of one locked-out worker to each three strikers.[14]

Compared to Italy, Britain, or France, West Germany did not experience a great number of strikes. As we have seen, the unions preferred to cement employment conditions into legally binding agreements. In 1978, however, the DGB pulled out of the "concerted action" sessions in which possible wage increases were discussed with employers and government officials. They complained in particular of rising unemployment. Subsequent strikes in the printing, machinery, and steel industries were defeated by lockouts. Employers gained the power to cut jobs, subject only to the requirement to offer retraining to displaced workers.[15]

Crumbling concrete: East Germany in crisis

Contemporaries noted that East Germany and the other Socialist economies of Eastern Europe appeared to be managing better than Western Europe or the United States. For a time it seemed that more direct government control over the economy might be better than the indirect Keynesian techniques of adjustments to monetary and fiscal policy, and this became part of a generally more positive evaluation of Socialist systems. With hindsight we now can see that East Germany and Eastern Europe did escape the slowdown for a time, but then fell suddenly into a period of stagnation and decline. After the dissolution of the Soviet Union and reunification, Charles Maier and others argued that the larger problems of Communist regimes created a systemic economic crisis, leading to a terminal structural crisis and collapse.[16] Economic "failure" clearly undermined the credibility of the regime, but politics still took command. East Germany survived as long as the Soviet Union provided support.

Governments in Eastern Europe all recognized the continuing problem of productivity. Central planning made it difficult to provide incentives for the managers of individual enterprises to introduce new technologies. Various mechanisms were introduced to address the issue. East Germany had returned to the older style of planning by national ministries after the experiments of the 1960s. In 1976, Günter Mittag returned to his old position as head of the Central Committee's economic committee. Government planners attempted to improve their control over the economy by grouping enterprises into some 250 new "combines" (*Kombinate*). These were supposed to be both vertically and horizontally integrated, pulling together suppliers and producers across an entire industry. Each was in effect a national monopoly production and distribution unit. The director general of each *Kombinat* was supposed to work in tandem with the relevant minister. In theory, the director generals, in addition to their overall responsibilities, would directly manage the largest single enterprise in the industry. This was to give them hands-on access to production costs and prices and direct contact with other managers in the industry.

From the outside the system appeared to be functioning reasonably well. Then, at some point in the mid-1980s, the difficulties of providing both increased consumer goods and adequate levels of investment began to strain available resources. The problem was still productivity. Honecker and Mittag now designated certain industries and "key technologies" for encouragement and channeled funds in their direction. As experience in Western Europe and in Asia has shown, it is much easier to "pick winners" during a general upswing than in a period of generally slow growth. In retrospect, it appears Honecker and Mittag did not select the best targets, and the system of prices did not provide accurate evaluation of the program. More resources were provided to the favored industries than they could use effectively, while at the same time others were starved of the resources they needed to remain viable. However, at the time East Germany remained well in advance of the Soviet Union and most other Eastern European countries. In the late 1980s, hopeful observers noted that this meant that East Germany would benefit from any flow of Western capital eastward.[17]

External factors also played a role. The embargoes on exports of advanced technologies imposed by the United States remained a hindrance.[18] The embargoes led to expensive alternative solutions—an East German 256 Kb computer chip reportedly cost 534 marks to produce when a similar one cost only 17 marks abroad. The CMEA failed to break out of its original pattern of bilateral relationships, and individual countries remained too committed to the Leninist vision of autarchy, each country with a complete set of industries and relatively independent of foreign sources of supply. East European leaders failed to find a "Socialist division of labor" that would satisfy the national aspirations of all. They thus lost the potential benefits of specialization, and remained too dependent on the Soviet Union for raw materials and energy. In East Germany's case, the Soviet Union cut oil shipments from 19 to 17.1 million tons in 1981, reducing both energy supplies and the raw material for petroleum-based export products.

The distortions and the general decline in efficiency remained largely hidden until the collapse. Mittag used censorship to prevent bad news leaking to the public, and threats of dismissal to silence subordinates who might criticize his policies. The increase in oil prices made international borrowing more difficult. Foreign debt had jumped from 2 to 11 billion marks from 1970 to 1975, a reflection of the first oil crisis, but it more than trebled to nearly 35 billion in 1987. Despite his public commitment to reunification and hostility to East Germany, Franz Josef Strauss, in his capacity as Bavarian Minister-President, arranged a credit line of DM 1 billion in 1983.[19] Exports had to be increased to service the debt, leaving less for investment. Investment as a proportion of national product declined from 20 per cent in 1970 to 11 per cent in 1987. The military and police budgets absorbed over 16 billion marks annually in the late 1980s, equal to a third of the estimates of total productive investment. Alexander Schalk-Golodkowski, the State Secretary for Commercial Coordination, organized sales of items that might earn Western currency, and after the collapse became notorious as details of his deals became known. He sometimes sold paintings of dissident artists, and sometimes the dissidents themselves. The proceeds went to cover deficits in the military budget and to make up embarrassing civilian shortages, for instance, of bananas.[20]

One possible explanation of the "crisis" of the 1980s is that previously recorded rates of growth were exaggerated. The measurement of economic performance is always politically sensitive, and during the Cold War era this was especially true, for the figures became propaganda weapons in the struggle between the Socialist and capitalist systems. The

East German government's estimate of "net material product" included elements of double counting and made insufficient provision for changes in the price level, and this had the effect of making growth appear more rapid than it was. On the other hand, the value of services was substantially underestimated, and this lowered the overall levels of measured national product and possibly reduced the measured rate of increase.

As seen in Chapter 13, Western estimates of East German growth lay substantially below the official figures, but they did place per capita income in East Germany at about three-quarters of West Germany and about two-thirds of the United States. East Germany appeared to have performed best among the Eastern European economies by a substantial margin. However, the estimates relied on partial data and a large number of assumptions. Following the collapse of East Germany and reunification, the first measures of per capita income in the "new states" showed income levels less than half of those estimated only a year before. Some of this resulted from the widespread closures of plants and rising unemployment. Measurement remained politically sensitive, because the West German government did not want to accept responsibility for destroying the East German economy.

Taking an estimate of the income of the regions that became East Germany in 1936 and the figures for 1990 as benchmarks would imply that per capita income had risen at only 0.33 per cent per year, rather than the 2.64 per cent shown in previous Western estimates. In the absence of complete recalculations, Angus Maddison concludes the most plausible approach is to compare East Germany with Czechoslovakia, a country broadly similar in structure. "If East German per capita growth performance in 1950–89 had in fact been like that of Czechoslovakia, its 1989 level would have been less than two-thirds of what it was imagined to be." But, this would still mean that income levels dropped by over 25 per cent from 1989 to 1990.[21] The consequences will be examined in Chapter 15.

The cultural context: postmodernism as leitmotiv

West Germany: America's most boring colony

"We are America's most boring colony," burst out a university student in Heidelberg in 1985. "I am emigrating as soon as I get my degree." Asked where he might choose to emigrate, he replied equally emphatically

"It doesn't matter. There is no center anymore." His not terribly consistent argument could be dismissed as an adolescent complaint. But he
typified many West Germans in the vague resentment against an over-
bearing American cultural imperialism. And he was typical as well in
asserting at the same time that there is no center, for the notion that
there is no privileged place, no perspective that can be identified as
objectively valid, defined the postmodern position. On the one hand,
"Coca-Colonization" and Americanization seemed to threaten German
values, but on the other hand challenges to existing structures placed the
very notion of a single German culture in question.

In fact, West German culture in the postmodern generation was anything but boring. At the 1966 Princeton meeting of the Gruppe 47, Peter
Handke achieved instant notoriety when he accused the German literary
establishment of "impotence of description." He denounced descriptive
realism and political literature as empty rhetoric. From the other side,
Gruppe 47 was also attacked by those who demanded that writers play
an active political role, and that literature as such should either be abolished entirely, or functionalized, subordinated to higher social purposes.
Left-wing radical students disrupted the 1967 meeting, and in 1977 the
organization was dissolved in the aftermath of the rise and repression of
terrorist movements.

Handke's experimental plays of the later 1960s and early 1970s, for
instance, *Self-Accusation* (*Selbstbezichtigung*, 1966) and *The Ride across
Lake Constance* (*Der Ritt über den Bodensee*, 1971), were deliberately
structured to "expose" conventional language and theatrical practices.
He criticized stereotyped, predictable language, but also attempted to
show the role of language in maintaining an authoritarian system and
specifically the power of language over the individual. In novels
beginning in the early 1970s and continuing through the 1990s, however, Handke moved away from his critical stance and began to assert
that literature could become a counter-reality with the potential to
preserve individuality. In *Der Chinese des Schmerzes* (1983) the
protagonist, Loser, is an "observer" who exists in isolation until he
murders a man who has defaced nature with a swastika, but his emergence from the static state of isolation is not a triumph, but a violation of his conditions of existence. Handke's style also became more
consciously poetic, using archaic forms to evoke a past or trans-
historical Utopia. His intent was to restore a sense of wonder at the
world, but critics who celebrated his earlier criticism of existing social

structures began to accuse him of an irresponsible narcissistic self-absorption.[22]

Not all postmodernist or conceptual artists avoided the political implications of their art. One of the most influential figures in postwar German art was Joseph Beuys. Appointed professor at the Düsseldorf Art Academy in 1961, he was dismissed in 1972, an action held to have been illegal following a court challenge. Beuys' works seem opaque and non-referential like Darboven's *Cultural History*, but on second glance they have an ironic quality and an anti-elitist message. One is *Felt Suit* (1970), a brown suit on a hanger, tailored to his own measurements. Another is a lamp consisting of a yellow light bulb, plugged into a lemon and powered by the acid in the lemon. Both of these are or could become "multiples," and both are criticisms of the materialism of West German society. "The idea of multiples is the distribution of ideas," said Beuys. His major installations included honey and wax, connected with bees, communities of individuals that accommodate themselves to the needs of the whole, and mythical emblems of healing such as stags and horses. He insisted that "everybody is an artist" and attempted to admit anyone to the Düsseldorf academy who wanted to attend. *7000 Oaks* (1982–87) encouraged plantings throughout the greater Kassel metropolitan area. Each tree was planted together with a dark stone column. The work was to be continued and effect environmental change, or as Beuys put it, "an idea takes root." Creative activity, he said, was "social sculpture," and he led several organizations dedicated to direct democracy and in 1979 ran for the European Parliament as a candidate of the Greens.

Better known internationally were the directors of the "new German cinema," such as Werner Herzog, Rainer Werner Fassbender, Wim Winders, and Margarethe von Trotta. Concentrating on outsiders or those trapped by social convention, their films characteristically criticized the platitudes of the economic miracle and the social market economy. However, American films, with German voices dubbed in, were far more popular in West Germany. Both the famous and the large numbers of less famous West German film-makers depended on government funding. The fearful censorship of the 1950s gave way to a much more innovative approach, particularly by public television authorities in the 1970s. Support for film and the arts generally became one of the sources of regional pride, and state and municipal governments competed to demonstrate their commitment even, and in some cases especially, when the artist in question adopted an idiosyncratic or critical stance.[23]

Along with American films, translations of popular novels that had become best-sellers in the United States dominated the West German market. British author Frederick Forsythe, whose works featured British intelligence agents but with much of their action set in Germany, was better known to German readers than most German writers. Johannes Mario Simmel, Heinz Konsalik, and Uta Daniel enjoyed huge sales, but best-sellers were not "literature" and none of the three appears in the index of the *Cambridge History of German Literature*. At the other end of the scale, the works of Günter Grass, Heinrich Böll, and Peter Handke definitely qualified as literature, but their commercial success in Germany rested in part on their international reputations as critics of the existing West German order. Films and books, like other cultural products, required advertising to succeed, part of the feedback loop connecting producer, consumer, and media, and the resulting rapid turnover in fashions, styles, and subjects linked with the proliferation of viewpoints characteristic of postmodernism.

East Germany: Socialist realism in a postmodern age

It seems unlikely that any East German students would have referred to their country as "Russia's most boring colony." Some certainly did refer to East Germany as a Soviet colony, if they were in private, among trusted friends. But the level of living in East Germany was so obviously in advance of the rest of Eastern Europe that the admission of dependent status was always tinged with pride. Nevertheless, East Germany's heavy-handed attempts to create Socialist women and men began to backfire at some point in the late 1970s or early 1980s. At lower levels, the conflicts between official culture and the demands of a popular youth culture led to resentment. Students dropped out and either became openly rebellious or drifted along in a sullen compliance.[24] At higher levels, lip service to Marxism—Leninism accompanied a manipulative careerism. Across a range of academic disciplines, works appeared with an obligatory first page or first chapter citing works from the Marxist classics, but with the body of the work more or less divorced from the supposed theoretical introduction. Many East Germans retreated into a private realm of family and friends.

The difficulties of creating Socialism were largely of the regime's own making. The government supported the entire range of artistic activity. The state-owned Deutsche Film-Aktiengesellschaft (DEFA) was already producing "anti-Fascist" films in 1946, and became the largest studio facility in Europe. Of very high technical quality, DEFA's films were attacked by the party leadership in 1965 and thereafter consistently lacked the critical stance that would have made them interesting, or the entertainment value that would have allowed them to compete in international markets. A number featured the transformation of a rowdy delinquent worker, who, however, has a heart of gold, into a committed political activist. Rejected by his previous circle of friends, he succeeds in rebuilding his life because of his qualities of true leadership.[25]

Under Johannes Becher, the Academy of the Arts had begun its sponsorship of a broad range of publications, including editions of exile literature. East Germany became the third largest producer of books per capita in the world, after the Soviet Union and Japan. But the official cultural standards remained so constricting, and the repression of unapproved cultural expression so pervasive, that talented writers and artists were virtually forced into opposition. Stefan Heym, who like Brecht left the United States because of the violent anti-Communist climate in the early 1950s, found himself periodically at odds with the authorities. His work on the 1953 uprising, *Five Days in June*, was only published in West Germany in 1974, and other works were refused publication as well. He instead satirized the East German system obliquely in works set in historical or mythical surroundings. This kind of indirect criticism in literary works became the main vehicle for oppositional expression, and resulted both in some very subtle writing and in the growth of a very sophisticated readership.

A significant aspect of official culture was the relatively stable career paths available to members of the Writers Union. Many journalists, editors, and dramaturges were publishing writers. Many of them were also women, who struggled with the inconsistencies of theoretical equality and actual double and triple burdens. Christa Wolf worked as a reviewer for large publishing houses, and became the best-known woman writer in East Germany, especially with her *The Quest for Christa T.* (*Nachdenken über Christa T.*, 1968), in which the narrator attempts to assemble the literary fragments left behind by her nonconformist friend after her premature death, exploring as well the meanings of their two lives. Wolf also defined the Utopian role of prose writing:

> Prose can expand the limits of what we know about ourselves. It keeps alive in us the memory of a future which we cannot disown, on pain of destruction. It supports the process by which man becomes a free individual. It is

revolutionary and realistic: it seduces and encourages us to do the impossible.[26]

Wolf became a candidate member of the SED central committee in the early 1960s, but her party career suffered after she defended the rights of young writers in 1965. *The Quest for Christa T.* was only released for general readers in 1971 as part of Honecker's liberalization of the censorship. She continued to fill official positions and to receive honors, but also came into periodic conflict with the authorities. She and Heym were among many who signed a letter of protest when dissident poet and musician Wolf Biermann was first allowed to leave the country and then stripped of his citizenship and forbidden to return in 1976. In the aftermath of the Biermann "affair," censorship tightened again and a large number of younger writers left for the West.

The social context: postmodernism as lived experience

Not only did serious writers and artists question received styles, but also the arts as such splintered and overflowed into channels previously regarded as beyond the bounds of serious discussion. Once again Germany participated in international trends. As we have seen, since the late nineteenth century the media had provided the avenue for expressions of mass culture. Newspapers, magazines, and popular novels all required sensation to boost sales. Their search for sensation led them to highlight the shocking, the exotic, and above all the new. The media also depended on advertising. Advertisers hoped to reach consumers who might purchase their products or potential customers seeking entertainment—reading, film, music, clothing, food, drink. The content of stories in the media and the products and services offered for sale through advertisements existed in a symbiosis. Anything reported as new and currently fashionable could be packaged and sold, and then reported on again. The many industries that arose from popular culture were dedicated to fostering consumption. Popular culture was therefore diametrically opposed to the moral restraint and self-sacrifice demanded by official culture and generations of commentators.

The 1920s had added radio to the print media, and the 1950s added television. As we have seen in the case of radio, the government regulated the electronic media even more strictly than the print media. The same was true of television. However, in the postwar world usage escaped control. In all countries licensing requirements broke down or were abandoned.[27] Commercial radio and television broadcasters emerged to compete with state broadcasters where they did not exist from the beginning. Further, as in the case of print media, content also escaped control, partly because of the sheer volume of material required and partly because of the need to appeal to the audience. Television is notorious among practitioners as a "carnivorous" medium with a voracious appetite for new material. Listeners and viewers were already experienced readers, and if the material presented did not appeal to their tastes, they would not listen or watch. What they did listen to or watch could not be effectively controlled because electronic signals passed across national boundaries.

As Table 14.5 shows, the audience for the new mass media was far better educated than previous generations, and the levels of education continued to increase. The figures, produced by economists, are also interesting in giving greater weight to secondary and tertiary education, based on evidence that increased education leads to substantially higher income. The audience was not only more highly educated, it was also far more affluent, and as hours worked per week declined, leisure time increased.

The result, from an individual perspective, was a fragmented identity. The expanded public realm of popular culture, and the expanded number of voices competing for attention, almost guaranteed of themselves that this should be so. West and East Germans, but also the postwar members of many other national communities, held multiple identities. With regard to the previous history of German nationalism, we can note

Table 14.5 Weighted average of years of education per person aged 15–64 in major countries, 1820–1992

	USA	Germany	France	Britain	Japan
1820	1.75	na	na	2.00	1.50
1870	3.92	na	na	4.44	1.50
1913	7.86	8.37	6.99	8.82	5.36
1950	11.27	10.40	9.58	10.60	9.11
1992	18.04	12.17	15.96	14.09	14.87

Primary education is given a weight of 1, secondary 1.4, and higher 2, based on evidence of relative earnings associated with different levels of education.

Source: Angus Maddison, Monitoring the World Economy 1820–1992 (Paris: OECD, 1995), p. 37.

that membership in the national community was certainly one such identity, but it was not the only one, and it might not be the most important one for any given individual. As with popular culture generally, this was not a completely new phenomenon, but it was more common in an increasingly well-educated and affluent world.

The effects of mass media and popular culture caused concern in West Germany, but in East Germany they posed serious problems, because they forced East Germany's leaders to confront the lack of real enthusiasm among the population. The media in the East were highly centralized and Western newspapers and magazines virtually unobtainable. However, Western radio and television could be received. The televised version of West Germany and the consumer goods on display could raise expectations, and images of the United States could lead to a sort of second-hand Americanization. Jokes circulated about certain times of the evening when all curtains would be closed because everyone was watching forbidden Western programs—no one noticed because the security services were watching as well. Under Honecker, the regime in effect abandoned previous attempts to prohibit listening and watching Western programs. Attempts were made to compete by improving the entertainment value of East German programs. News broadcasts remained a black spot, however, leaden and largely ignored.

Churches and workers: the end of separate milieus?

The separate milieus that had defined social and political life for previous generations appeared to dissolve. In West Germany, the fundamental principle of the CDU/CSU coalition's electoral policy was that it represented all Germans, not only Catholics. As the ruling party under Adenauer, Catholics were not oppressed and therefore one of the key forces maintaining their previous sense of unity had disappeared. Conservative Protestant milieus had re-formed themselves after the war, but the explicit nationalism that had been their integrating force disappeared. The repression of memories of the Nazi past in some cases, the sense that extreme nationalism was embarrassing internationally in others, and in some cases a genuine sense that previous faith in the German nation had been misplaced, all contributed. The common enemies they recognized were Communism, the Soviet Union, and the East German regime, but they shared these enemies with Catholics and Adenauer's coalition.[28]

It was fashionable among sociologists such as Helmut Schelsky to declare the end of the working class. The SPD was as determined as the CDU/CSU to portray itself as a party of the whole people. Participation in the grand coalition and Willy Brandt's final victory appeared to confirm the Socialists' success. The shift in employment toward the service sector and toward part-time work undermined one of the presumed principles of working-class consciousness, proletarian labor in an industrial firm, with the worker figured implicitly or explicitly as a married man supporting his family. As housing improved, the new physical structures such as interior toilets tended to decrease personal communication among residents in the streets and public parts of buildings. When workers moved to better housing in better parts of town, made use of modern mass transportation, took advantage of new forms of recreation, and spent more time in their homes, the cultural and political content of more traditional working-class housing was undermined. Some older districts had fallen victim to wartime bombing or now fell victim to urban renewal, and other areas saw greater differentiation within the working class, and greater contact between classes, which further undermined workers' sense of separateness and solidarity.

In East Germany, since the regime defined itself as an alliance of the workers and peasants, in theory there could be no separate workers' milieu. The clumsiness of the ruling oligarchy was possibly never so evident as when dealing with the question of workers' culture. In the early 1980s, leading economic and social historian Jürgen Kuczynski insisted in the fourth volume of his history of the working class that the creators of German workers' culture before the First World War were the leaders of the Socialist Party and its leading intellectual figures. "Now for the period under consideration the great ones are well known— Marx and Engels, Wilhelm Liebknecht and Bebel, Karl Kautsky, Rosa Luxemburg and Franz Mehring, as well as many others."[29] Culture for the regime remained classic German high culture, although it also included a number of modernist figures, such as Bertolt Brecht, honored for their Marxism and their support of the regime. Culture also remained something to be instilled in schoolchildren and in adult workers. Cultural activities were accordingly subsidized by the state, but they acted as additional arms of the state-sponsored media, working, as Lenin had put it, as "collective propagandist, collective agitator, and collective organizer."

Officially the Socialist regime was opposed to religion. Separate religious milieus would not have been tolerated. Catholics remained a small minority in what had been central Germany, and the Catholic Church traded the right to continued religious observance for political passivity. The national organization of Protestant churches was illegal under the 1968 constitution. East German Protestant leaders decided in 1969 to form a separate organization and to work not "against" or even "alongside" the regime, but rather to work "within" Socialism, as Bishop Schönherr put it in 1971. The regime in turn found the social welfare institutions of the churches, their homes for the elderly, hospitals, and childcare centers, extremely useful. In 1978, Honecker explicitly recognized the Church as an autonomous social institution. A protected sphere emerged, and within this sphere a substantial amount of discussion of the shortcomings of the regime and of potential changes took place. The churches were used in this way by a range of oppositional groups, not always Christian, and as a result were often split between more radical members who wanted reforms and senior members of the hierarchy who appreciated the delicate and potentially dangerous position they occupied.[30]

Minorities

As the old milieus appeared to decline, somewhat paradoxically minorities and marginal groups appeared, demanding recognition. This posed problems. Not only how to alleviate want and suffering, but the question of whether marginals could, should, or even would want their "problems" addressed divided sociologists and political scientists. More groups appeared to need help, but the assumption on which social security had been traditionally based, the presumption that all members of the community were fundamentally the same, was challenged. Groups who demanded aid also demanded the right to be and remain different. But partial, fragmentary, or serial identifications intersected with and cut across these definitions. Those who spoke for each group were themselves divided, and, within groups, members might or might not identify continuously with the group. Again, this was an international phenomenon, but Germany's history ensured that such problems would be taken especially seriously within Germany, and that German responses would be particularly closely monitored by outsiders.

The Jewish community remained small. In West Germany, the 25,000 to 28,000 Jews were divided between the few German survivors of the Holocaust and a larger number of Eastern European migrants. Adults existed in an uncomfortable relationship with Gentile Germans. Despite the reparations made available, some had disappointing experiences with the officials who considered claims for compensation. For children, a forced philo-Semitism sometimes saw the single Jewish student in a school asked repeatedly to talk about the Holocaust for the benefit of his or her fellow pupils, or given preferential treatment in order to avoid any hint of anti-Semitism.[31] In contrast, the single focus on the Jews as the victims of the Nazi regime meant that other survivor groups, particularly the Sinti and Roma (Gypsies), continued to suffer from stereotyping and prejudice.

Citizenship remained based on the law of 1913, meaning that only those with German blood could claim membership in the national community. Persons of German descent, wherever they had been born and however long ago their ancestors had left Germany, were German by right. Immigrants who were not of German descent were excluded, and naturalization was made extremely difficult. The exception rather than the presumed rule, naturalization required marriage to a German citizen, or ten years of continuous residence and a "clear identification" with German culture. However, the "guest workers" of the 1950s and 1960s had frequently remained, married among themselves, and had children. Recruitment ceased in 1973, and the number of guest workers declined to 1.8 million (still over 8 per cent of the labor force), but their families and dependants continued to increase. In the late 1980s, some 5 million persons or 7 per cent of West Germany's population were technically foreigners, with the 1.7 million Turks the largest single group. Children of foreign families suffered prejudice at school, hostility from their fellow students, and lack of sympathy from their teachers.

Social marginals also included the handicapped. Building on Weimar legislation, the West German government extended medical, vocational, and social rehabilitation benefits from invalids of war or work accidents to include broader groups. In 1974, existing programs were extended to all disabled persons, some 600,000 in 1990. The broadening of scholarly perspectives on the Nazi period also revealed the impact of Nazi eugenics policies on groups with disabilities. Discrimination continued, however. A stubborn insistence on attributing disabilities to some flaw in character or moral shortcoming marked relations of the majority to the handicapped minority. Well-meaning friends would explain earnestly to others that the handicapped individual was "really a good person" despite the disability.

Sexual minorities also emerged into the public sphere. In East Germany, the old law against homosexuality was reformed in 1968 and repealed in 1988. However, the regime banned homosexual organizations and publications, and in effect pretended that homosexuals did not exist and therefore could not suffer discrimination—the fate of the many lesbian women sent to the Ravensbrück camp by the Nazi regime received no mention in the official guides to the memorial site.[32] Some groups began to meet under the protection of the Protestant Churches in the 1980s. In West Germany, hostility toward homosexuals was reinforced in the 1950s by the panicky fear that they were contributing to the declining birth rate. The old law remained in force, though the Nazi additions were repealed in 1969. In addition to ongoing campaigns for repeal of the anti-homosexual law by gay groups, the Green Party succeeded in securing access to compensation for homosexual victims of Nazism in 1988.

Women and feminism

What women did was gradually transformed. The decline and virtual disappearance of domestic service eliminated the largest category of non-agricultural employment for women. In West German industry, the share of women rose until 1962 and then stabilized, but women came to occupy over half of the positions remaining in agriculture and nearly half of those in the rapidly expanding service sector. In the early 1980s, the proportion of working women who were married had risen to 42 per cent. Significantly, of women married to industrial workers, fully 90 per cent were in gainful employment outside the home—economic structures had changed, but the necessity for women in poorer families to work remained. The gap between female and male earnings also remained, and additional lines of cleavage opened between those with high levels of education and those with lower qualifications. The growing service occupations were sales and clerical work, primarily low income and female, and professional services, typically more highly paid and predominantly male. Private sector management remained overwhelmingly male, as did the upper levels of academic disciplines. The share of government employees who were women rose from 20 to 30 per cent from the early 1960s to the mid-1970s, but most were secretaries. Women in the middle levels generally worked as teachers and health workers, and only 9 per cent of upper level officials were women.[33]

In East Germany, as we have seen, the chronic shortage of labor accelerated the increase in the number of female workers, and, in the 1980s, 91 per cent of East German women of working age were either employed or in training, the highest female participation rate in the world. But state-regulated gender quotas meant there remained fields from which women were effectively excluded, and in positions of real power women were progressively less visible the higher the level. In the late 1980s, one-third of all managerial positions were held by women, but only 8 per cent of deputy directors or division heads were women, and women headed only 3 per cent of all *Kombinate*, typically the smallest. In the party and bureaucracy, 34 per cent of those in leadership positions were female, with the fewest in ministries such as industry and construction and the most in "non-productive" ministries such as education, trade and food supply, and especially health. Beginning at the level of section head and moving up to ministers, the share of women declined progressively from 17 to 1.5 per cent. A third of mayors were women, but only one head of a district (*Bezirk*) council. Twenty per cent of the members of the state council were women, but only one woman belonged to the Council of Ministers—Margot Honecker, wife of Erich Honecker since 1953 and education minister since 1963.[34]

Working women continued to pose problems for both systems. "Work" in both West and East Germany meant full-time, paid employment, outside the home. In West Germany, "work" was further conceived as male. As before, women in West Germany were not supposed to work, and a host of legal regulations continued to exclude them from many training programs and from a broad range of jobs. In East Germany, women were supposed to work, but what they did was not "women's work" but simply work itself, and, therefore, although a broader range of jobs was open to women than in West Germany, and although there was support for children, no additional concessions were made to the women who might hold those jobs.

Part-time work cut across these definitions. In West Germany, "part-time workers" had always been assumed to be women. This rested on the further assumption that married women could not hold full-time jobs because of their obligation to maintain the household. But part-time work could also act as the first step toward more extended employment outside the home. West Germans gradually reconceived women's roles, and part-time work was both a sign of this underlying social change and a contribution to it. Public discourse, the legal system, large firms, and male-dominated labor unions had all opposed the idea of married women working in the 1950s. But the "household model" was challenged continuously, by women's groups, by female trade unionists, by some of the press (particularly popular magazines that depended on women for their readership), and by citizens' complaints to government officials and legal challenges to discrimination mounted in the courts.

Employers began to tolerate, and then to recruit, women, married or not, because of the increasing shortage of labor. Christine von Oertzen presents the case of a cookie factory in Hanover that eventually employed part-time married women as a large part of its labor force. The firm's success apparently depended in part on the female and motherly image of making and packaging cookies, despite the fact that the work itself was on a mechanized production line. For the women this image allowed them to regard themselves as having a higher status than full-time "factory workers" or those engaged in the excessively masculine "machine work" in the other factories in the city. Politicians followed behind, and by the 1960s even quite conservative CDU leaders became more tolerant of wives and mothers working. In 1969, the SPD government introduced part-time work in the government service, and by the mid-1970s over 80 per cent of women employed by government agencies worked part-time.[35] Part-time workers who worked more than 24 hours per week won the right to unemployment and insurance benefits. A new discourse emerged that credited women with creating a "new blueprint for life" that included the desire for higher income for the family but also for an independent existence outside the home.

In East Germany, the regime encouraged female work, but here too the presumption that this would be full-time paid employment broke down. Large numbers of women began to work only part-time, and the regime decided that female part-time work was also acceptable. Industrial concerns offered little resistance once the decision had been made; labor unions simply implemented the new policy. It appears that there was a continuing difference in the way in which women conceived of their part-time jobs. In the West, part-time work was seen as a path toward full-time employment, a way to escape the defining constrictions of the housewife ideology. In the East, part-time employment was a way of escaping the obligation of a full-time job and being able to devote more energy to the "second job" of maintaining the family home.[36]

In 1968, groups of women in Frankfurt and Berlin split from the radical student movement. Like women members of student movements elsewhere in Europe and the United States, they rebelled against the leaders' sexism and lack of concern for women's issues. The new women's movement divided between Marxists who believed that women's oppression grew out of capitalist relations of production, and those who saw patriarchy, the structuring of power and privilege on gender lines, as the more fundamental problem. However, women's organizations found broad support, and a focus on the issue of abortion. A campaign begun in 1971 with dramatic public confessions of abortions culminated in 1975 when the Bundestag passed legislation that substantially liberalized access to abortions.

The new feminism rested on women's more active involvement in the paid labor force. Being employed meant having control over money, and being employed part-time could offer the opportunity to care for children and also contribute to initiatives in cooperation with other women. Women supported a broad range of new institutions—ranging from coffee shops, women's centers, theater groups, and lesbian support organizations, to refuges and homes for battered women and children. Women also patronized specialist bookstores catering to their needs. New publishing houses were founded, and journals appeared such as Alice Schwarzer's mass circulation *Emma, Courage*, published by a West Berlin collective, and film-maker Helke Sander's *Frauen und Film*. A generation of feminist scholars, many born during the 1940s and 1950s, analyzed the forms of male domination.

In 1975 appeared the first *Women's Yearbook (Frauenjahrbuch '75)* published by a Frankfurt collective, landmark books by Schwarzer, *The Small Difference and Its Big Consequences (Der kleine Unterschied und seine grossen Folgen)*, Margot Schröder, *I Can Take It Like a Woman (Ich stehe meine Frau)*, and Verena Stefan, *Shedding (Häutungen)*, and also Sander's film *REDUPERS—The All-Around Reduced Personality*. Sander's work is identified as the first feminist film. Schwarzer, Schröder, and others recounted autobiographical narratives of female experience that allowed other women to recognize themselves, in Schröder's case from a working-class perspective. Stefan's *Shedding* is important for both its structure and its theme. Stefan worked through her writing to find a mode of expression that would break the constraints on women's expression imposed by inherited patriarchal forms of language. Stefan's narrator, disillusioned by her loss of self in heterosexual structures, returns from the "Other" to the "One" and rediscovers the harmony and wholeness of her childhood in lesbian relationships. Theater and dance were particularly important in the 1980s, with Pina Bausch's dance pieces and the essays and plays of Gisela von Wysocki. Wysocki's *Actor, Dancer, Chanteuse* (*Schauspieler, Tänzer, Sängerin*, 1988) dramatized the fact that woman's role in cultural history has been precisely to "play" the socially scripted role of woman.

Parallel to the movements of minority groups, the contribution of feminism to the postmodernist generation was to announce and support new alternative modes of social interaction. Open advocacy of single-parent families, lesbian families, and communal arrangements challenged the model of the family that we have traced from the early nineteenth century, and as such may constitute one of the key dividing points in women's history.[37] However, the movement also typified the postmodernist generation in its divisions. Not only the split between Marxists and theorists of patriarchy, but also deep divisions over specific programs marked the movement through the 1970s and 1980s. Some feminists opposed the campaign to secure wages for housework because it might restrict women to their traditional roles. Some opposed the campaign against pornography, on the grounds that women were entitled to read or see whatever they themselves wished; this dispute led to a debate over the precise boundaries between pornography and erotica. Some women made careers as feminists or as feminist scholars, and concerns emerged that in doing so they lost touch with the concerns of ordinary women. In the early 1980s, a series of international conferences on women's history highlighted the contributions of West German feminist academics, but in the aftermath of the 1985 meeting in Bonn there were worries about the tensions between professionalization and personal growth, accusations of a new "feminist historicism," and fears of a conservative "turn" (*Wende*) in women's studies parallel to the conservative shift in politics.[38] In addition, as elsewhere, postmodernist assertions had provoked counterattacks. The new liberal abortion law was struck down by the Constitutional Court in 1976, a severe and disheartening setback.

The political context: the expansion of the public sphere

The effects of the continued growth of mass media and rising education on politics were mediated through the public sphere. In addition to the expression of a non-political mass culture, the new media also provided the avenue for new political voices. Again this was not completely new.

The search for sensation that led the media to highlight the shocking, the exotic, and the new in popular culture also led them to report on political movements outside the mainstream. National elites found this deeply troubling. "The journalist belongs to a sort of pariah caste," said Weber in his 1918 piece on politics as a profession. The Nazi regime had suppressed the public sphere, and the East German regime attempted to do so as well. During the 1950s, political leaders in West Germany would also have preferred to restrict access. From the 1960s onward, however, the number of voices proliferated. Minority groups, women, youth, some in the labor movement, and left-wing intellectuals gained access to the public realm in new ways. Affluence and leisure provided the market, and the public sphere became saturated with messages emanating from the popular culture industries. Even when non-political, popular culture exercises a political effect in displaying alternative lifestyles and raising expectations, something that concerned the East German leadership in particular. In addition, the line between frivolous popular culture and serious discussion of public issues blurred. Political parties learned that they must advertise. Media figures leveraged their recognition factor into public careers. All movements across the spectrum, from radical feminists to the racist new right, exploited popular culture modes of expression, especially graphic art and music, to sell their message.

In addition to the dissatisfaction of the left in the labor movement and the rising number of women's groups, the initial expansion of university enrollments had laid the basis for youth cultures and a self-conscious counterculture. Since the 1940s, the Socialist German Student League (*Sozialistischer Deutscher Studentenbund*, or SDS) had agitated for increased representation of ordinary people. The SDS represented a radical Marxist, but anti-Soviet, alternative to the Socialist Party leadership. SDS activists were egalitarian and redistributive, deeply anti-authoritarian, and profoundly critical of both the Soviet Union and the anti-Communist hysteria that eventually included the SPD leadership. Following the adoption of the reformist Godesberg Program, in 1960 the SDS was expelled from the party. The SDS advocated opening universities to the children of poorer parents, and they agitated against the student fraternities (some of which still fought duels into the 1960s), which the SDS regarded as glorifiers and defenders of the worst aspects of Germany's past. The generational gap opened in their opposition to the accommodations made with the heritage of Nazism, whose remnants they detected in virtually every institution in West Germany. The

SDS also demanded that the West German government make restitution to the victims of Nazism, especially Jews and Poles. In this they anticipated the later special relations of West Germany with Israel and the adoption of *Ostpolitik*, two of the keys to West German political identity and long-term legitimacy.[39]

In 1972, two of the intellectual leaders of the radical student movement, Oskar Negt and Alexander Kluge, published *Public Sphere and Experience*.[40] The book was an engagement with Jürgen Habermas' *The Structural Transformation of the Public Sphere: An Enquiry into a Category of Bourgeois Society*, published ten years earlier. Habermas had attacked the student movement for their dogmatic intransigence and accused them of "left Fascism." Negt had edited the immediate response *The Left Answers Habermas* (*Die Linke antwortet Habermas*) in 1968. Negt and Kluge offered both a prediction and a theoretical analysis of the continuing proliferation of public voices in the context of the 1960s and 1970s. As indicated in their title, they argued that the public sphere not only demarcates "specific institutions, agencies, practices," but was "also a general social horizon of experience in which everything that is actually or ostensibly relevant for all members of society is integrated." It therefore constituted a "dimension of consciousness" for the participants. The crucial second point was contained in their subtitle, "toward an analysis of the bourgeois and proletarian public sphere." They contended that the bourgeois and proletarian public spheres organize experience in radically different ways. As Marxists, they highlighted the class interests at stake. In the bourgeois public sphere, they said, the proletarian life-situation can only be incorporated insofar as it can be "domesticated" in the interests of profit-making. In the twentieth century, the bourgeois public sphere had changed, from the classic form analyzed by Habermas (clubs, parties, newspapers, parliaments) to "public spheres of production" linked to the "consciousness industry" and mediated through advertising, the mass consumption it engenders, and the new applications of public relations techniques in politics. Television in particular they identified as the "concrete technique" that breaks down the previous barriers between the processes of production and the private sphere of individuals.

In contrast to Habermas, Negt and Kluge insisted on a plurality of public spheres. As argued above, this is one of the defining characteristics of the postmodern generation, but at the time Negt and Kluge privileged the proletarian public sphere. The proletarian public sphere,

they said, is the form that sets in motion repressed emancipatory potential, embodied in both experience and fantasies. They believed that,
within a "counterpublic sphere" defended against the existing bourgeois
sphere, a "sociological imagination" could create new active relations
between producers and audiences. The "horizon of social change" would
move closer, offering new ways of organizing experience. Negt and Kluge
anchored their argument in what they regarded as the essential qualities
of capital and labor, but they also severely criticized what they called the
"ideology of the camp," the tendency of leftist organizations to isolate
themselves, for instance, in the separate working-class milieu of the
imperial and Weimar periods. The way therefore seemed open to groups
not necessarily defined as working class to appropriate and re-form the
public sphere, to emancipate themselves and realize their fantasies.

From different directions activist intellectuals such as Rudi Dutschke
and Petra Kelly developed these themes of active involvement of new
groups organized in new ways. Dutschke argued against the Soviet
model of Marxism, not because he rejected the principles but because of
his opposition to rigid bureaucratic power structures, and his conviction
that the experience of the Russian Revolution was historically specific
and therefore not a guide to action elsewhere.[41] Kelly based her approach
on non-violent grassroots organization. She supported certain positions
consistently, notably feminism and opposition to nuclear power and
military armaments, but also opposed dogmatic rigid orthodoxies.[42]
Neither would have accepted Darboven's refusal to engage with the
political, but their support of a plurality of self-reflexive positions suggests her eclectic mixing of themes and the indeterminacy of what
exactly politics is or where its limits might lie.

Habermas of course did not agree. In addition in the 1980s, he
extended his critique to include postmodernist philosophers as well.
More voices might be heard, he insisted, but this neither broadened nor
improved the public sphere. His point against cultural conservatives was
that they had confused and conflated the processes of economic modernization and cultural modernization. As the subsystems of the market
economy and the administrative state had expanded, they had "colon-
ized" and "impoverished" the "lifeworld." At the same time, cultural
modernization resulted in an increasing differentiation, because of the
professionalization of previously unified areas such as science, law, ethics,
and esthetic criticism. The right demanded repression of expression,
when the pathologies they decried (hedonism, narcissism, lack of social

identity, withdrawal from achievement competition) in fact resulted from the very process of modernization that the right wanted to defend. The left in turn was simply the obverse of the right, hence his epithet "left Fascism" for the Marxist student radicals.

Postmodernist thinkers in Habermas' view had simply despaired of addressing the pathologies of modernity and had abandoned the faith in rational communication. The dispute here traces back to opposed notions of the structure and use of language. For Habermas, language was a tool of potentially rational communication. For postmodernist philosophers language itself structured social reality. For postmodern artists such as Darboven language in fact could and should be dispensed with altogether. Habermas believed the radical relativism and the antimodernity of the line of philosophers from Nietzsche to Heidegger and Bataille, Foucault, and Derrida, linked to the politics of neo-Conservatism as a parallel and reinforcing trend. Habermas defined the age as postmodern, and argued it was no coincidence that neo-Conservatism and postmodernism emerged and spread at the same time. Nevertheless, he insisted that the reasoned discourse of the public sphere was the only basis on which "the lifeworld can develop institutions of its own in a way currently inhibited by the autonomous system dynamics of the economic and administrative system."[43]

East Germany

There were very few fantasies realized in East Germany under Erich Honecker, and the autonomous system dynamics of the Socialist administrative regime appeared insurmountable. There were, however, many areas of repressed potential, and the failure to realize the fantasies and the final failure of repression eventually marked the end of the regime. As the new leader in the early 1970s, Honecker also attempted to create a new relationship between the state and the workers. His phrase for this was the "unity of social and economic policy," and the new approach included more substantial rewards for improvements in productivity. Higher pay, if it were to mean anything, would require larger amounts of consumer goods. This in turn implied that the rates of investment in heavy industry would have to decline. As seen above, this imposed severe strains on the economy and posed very difficult problems for planners. But, while the West faltered, East Germany and Eastern Europe generally reported continued substantial economic growth.

Despite the constant sense of living behind the Wall, East Germans responded positively to Honecker's new approach. As seen above, the pressure on writers was relaxed for a time. The government moved to improve housing. Consumer goods and especially consumer durables became more easily available. The regime discovered and addressed a "youth market," and jeans, cosmetics, and other items targeted at young consumers appeared in department stores. In the workplace, "brigades for Socialist work" exercised considerable independent power in relations with managers, who could find themselves caught between directives from above and the need to negotiate with workers over whom they had no real power. Women's issues were addressed. In 1972, abortion during the first trimester of pregnancy was made legal, the result of a campaign waged within the regime and the influence of the rising number of women doctors (18 per cent of physicians in 1946, but 36 per cent of physicians and just over half of medical students in the early 1960s), who pointed to the physical, social, and economic costs of the large numbers of illegal abortions.[44]

In the 1980s, problems emerged in all these areas. The economic situation deteriorated, although the seriousness of the difficulties was concealed. Honecker himself appears never to have recognized the threatening crisis. In the workplace, the balance tipped back toward managers, now increasingly perceived as more distant and less interested in the welfare of their workers, who were "hardly ever to be seen in the production halls."[45] In consumption, the "youths" of the late 1960s and early 1970s discovered that, as married workers with children, despite subsidies, there was very little left after rent, utilities, and food expenses. For this crucial generation, born after the war and subjected to intense programmatic indoctrination in the school system, the gap between the goods that appeared to have been promised and the goods that had been delivered was substantial. It was also widening in comparison with the West, and as Socialist societies moved away from satisfying needs to fulfilling wants, this was the comparison that mattered. One of the crucial markers of status became access to Western currency and therefore to the goods at the Intershops.[46]

The privileged, those who could travel, those with access to Western goods, belonged to the "Socialist service class" of party officials, managers, and professionals such as teachers, doctors, and engineers. In the 1950s, this was the most open group in East German society, but by the 1980s it had become the most closed. In the 1950s, the son of a working-class family had an equal chance of gaining entry to the service class, but, during the 1960s and 1970s, the chances of sons of service-class families tripled, and by the 1980s the son of a service-class family was seven to eight times as likely to secure a position in the service class as a young man from a working-class background. Further, at the top, those who enjoyed privilege stayed in their positions, blocking the access of those below. Male leaders over age 55 rose to 25 per cent of the total, and the share of those under 25 dropped sharply. Honecker retained power despite declining health, and his wife Margot remained education minister from her appointment in 1963 to the collapse.[47]

West Germany

In West German politics, the 1970s began in 1968. During the year of protests and violent confrontations on university campuses and in the streets of major cities, the carefully nurtured consensus on the economy, society, and politics came undone. Once again, Germany was not alone, and 1968 saw similar protests across the United States, in France, where the "days of May" caused a change in government, and in Japan, where ongoing confrontations peaked in 1970. One of the points of similarity was opposition to the war being waged by the United States in Vietnam. Another was Marxism, not the Soviet or East German variety, but a broad range of theories derived from Socialist thinkers and deployed to analyze, unmask, and denounce existing institutions. SDS leader Rudi Dutschke, for instance, synthesized ideas drawn from George Lukács, Herbert Marcuse, and Ernst Bloch.[48]

The grand coalition, the alliance with the Conservative parties, made the Socialist Party more acceptable to a broad spectrum of moderate voters, but it also caused protests on the left and especially in the universities. For the protesters, the SPD was merely another branch of the establishment. The activism of the SDS linked with the Campaign for Democracy and Disarmament, and also with some of the labor unions. This broad "extra-parliamentary opposition" (*Ausserparlamentarische Opposition* or APO) focused on the National Emergency Act, first proposed by the CDU/CSU in 1960. Leftists viewed the provisions for restricting civil liberties during a "state of defense," "state of tension," or "state of internal emergency" as serious threats to democratic rights, and compared them to the emergency decrees that had undermined the Weimar Republic. The accusation implied here was clear: the generation of 1968 was accusing their fathers and mothers of "being the Nazis that the Hitler Youth had trained them to be."[49] Another target was West German rearmament and the continued alliance with the United States, and hence complicity in capitalist imperialism.

The high point of the protest movement came in the spring and early summer of 1968. However, the grand coalition government commanded the two-thirds majority necessary for constitutional changes, and the laws were passed. Nor could the APO halt West Germany's rearmament. The end of the grand coalition, Brandt's alliance with the FDP, and the combination of *Ostpolitik* and social reform addressed some of the reformers' concerns. Nevertheless, Brandt's policies as Chancellor were not radical, and they certainly were not revolutionary. They aroused opposition on the right, but they disappointed many in the APO.

In the frustrating aftermath of these defeats, the APO split, those favoring more moderate tactics separating from the more radical confrontationalist groupings.[50] "Postmaterialist" groups, including environmentalists, opponents of nuclear power and weapons, and feminists, organized to campaign at the local level, and by the mid-1970s had moved to state politics. These made up the basis of the Greens. Leftist intellectuals such as Rudi Dutschke played a role in negotiating alliances among the groups, though Dutschke himself died in 1979 of complications from wounds suffered in an assassination attempt in 1968. Petra Kelly returned to Germany from ten years in the United States in 1970, moving from her American experiences in civil rights, women's, and anti-Vietnam War movements, to anti-nuclear and alternative health issues, and a founding role in the Greens. In 1979, a coalition campaigned in the first European Parliament elections, and gained enough votes to qualify for substantial federal funding, which was used to create the organizational basis for a national Green party. Success in local and state elections was followed in 1983 by winning 5.6 per cent of the national vote and gaining representation in the Bundestag. In 1987, the Greens increased their vote to 8.3 per cent, less than 1 per cent behind the Liberals.[51]

A minority on the extreme left concluded that only violence could change the system, and they turned to terrorism in an attempt to provoke a confrontation and crisis. Ulrike Meinhof and Andreas Baader formed the Baader–Meinhof Group in the late 1960s. With Gudrun Ensslin, Jan-Carl Raspe, and a few others they launched a countrywide bombing campaign. In June 1972, police arrested leading members of the group. They were held, tried, and then sentenced to detention in a specially built prison in Stammheim in 1974. Remaining members of the Group formed the Red Army Faction in 1972, proclaimed they would organize a military assault on the state, and began to attack United States army units stationed in West Germany. Authorities attributed 28 deaths, another 93 injured, and fifteen kidnappings to the Group and the RAF over the ten years to 1978.[52]

As the party in power, the SPD had to cope with the violence of the extreme left wing. Their credentials as pragmatic managers at stake, and in a quasi-crisis atmosphere created by media reports of terrorist actions (the conservative Springer publishing group and its lead paper *Die Welt* were particular targets of the SDS and other radical groups), SPD leaders responded by deploying the state apparatus to repress dissent and spy on suspected radicals. Hans-Dietrich Genscher of the FDP, interior minister since 1969, introduced a series of broad laws intended to make surveillance and control more effective. Some, such as the provision allowing searches of all apartments in a building in which a terrorist might be hiding, and the broad censorship provisions of 1976 (repealed in the 1980s), reduced the civil liberties of the entire population. In addition, the government promulgated the "Radical Decree" that made appointment to government positions dependent on an evaluation of the potential future behavior of the candidate, and denied employment to anyone connected with any organization or guilty of any activity held to be "opposed to the constitution." The SPD, facing an election, hoped to prevent the demands of the CDU/CSU for exclusion of "radicals" from becoming an issue. Through 1980, nearly 1.5 million people were investigated and over 1000 were denied government employment because of their left-wing politics or association with "extremist" organizations or individuals. Opposition to the law itself was construed as "opposed to the constitution." In one case reminiscent of the pre-1914 situation, an applicant was denied employment for allegedly being a "renter in a house, in which Communists also live."[53]

Helmut Schmidt replaced Brandt as Chancellor in 1974 and led the SPD to further victories in the elections of 1976 and 1980. He had served first as Brandt's minister of defense, but was better known for his period as finance minister. Twenty years before, he had been among those who advocated reform within the SPD, "reform" meaning abandoning the party's Marxist ideology in order to attract voters from the middle class. For Schmidt this meant stepping out of the old working-class milieu, jettisoning "illusionary doctrinaire-ism" and presenting an image of a true "people's party" that would appeal to as many groups as possible. This is what SPD strategists believed the CDU/CSU to have done in the 1950s, by moving beyond the confines of the Catholic milieu.

During the golden age, the assertion that growth and welfare could be achieved at the same time had become accepted as conventional wisdom, and the only remaining question appeared to be which of two groups of political leaders could "manage" economic and social change more successfully. In the new era of slow growth, things were not so simple. Schmidt confronted the rising public debt and budgetary problems that followed from the social security and tax reforms of the early 1970s. His policies were restrictive. He enjoyed international praise for his "pragmatism," for combating inflation, and for maintaining the strength of the West German mark, but he was less popular with those who suffered. Unemployment rose from 300,000 in 1973 to 600,000 in 1974 and 1.1 million in 1975. Schmidt insisted this was the necessary price to pay for curbing inflation, which rose to nearly 8 per cent in 1973 but then declined.

Ulrike Meinhof died in May 1976, an alleged suicide but without a really satisfactory explanation. To force the release of the other prisoners the Red Army Faction and other sympathizers launched a series of actions. The president of the employers' association, Hanns Martin Schleyer, was kidnapped on September 5, 1977. On October 13, Palestinians hijacked a Lufthansa jet en route from Majorca to Frankfurt. The hijackers also demanded the release of the prisoners. On October 18, the plane was stormed by German troops as it stood on the runway in Mogadishu. Hours after the storming of the plane, Baader, Raspe, and Ensslin died in the prison at Stammheim. They committed suicide with the assistance of their lawyers, but in a way intended to make it appear they had been murdered. Schleyer's body was found shortly afterward. Despite Schleyer's death and the doubts over the prisoners' deaths, the success at Mogadishu was widely credited with saving Chancellor Helmut Schmidt's government. The decisive use of force was indeed portrayed as a sign of the Federal Republic having finally come of age.[54] In the aftermath, some left-wing extremists attempted to continue the campaign of terrorism. Some established connections with the East German security police and others with left-wing nationalists in the Middle East and elsewhere, while still others merged into loose groups of anarchist *Autonomen* ("autonomists") in the cities who pursued violence as a means to realize a revolutionary self-identity.

There also existed a right-wing world including extreme Conservatives, former Nazis, and younger enthusiasts. Supported by wealthy patrons such as Maximiami Portas (Savitre Devi) they maintained links with British and American neo-Nazis.[55] Five small terrorist groups appeared on the right in the late 1970s and early 1980s. Their agendas varied, but all rejected the ideal of rule by constitutional law and planned to seize power to impose an authoritarian, nationalistic order. The Otte Group of the late 1970s was explicitly neo-Nazi. As with the left-wing groups, they faded after arrests of key members, but before being broken up they planned and sometimes carried out attacks on public buildings, West German and American military bases, asylum seekers, Jews (including several murders), and memorials to the Holocaust. A bomb planted by the Hoffmann Group in September 1980 killed thirteen and wounded 219 others at the Munich Oktoberfest.[56]

Parallel to the *Autonomen*, groups of violent neo-Nazi youths appeared in the cities, living in abandoned buildings and like the *Autonomen*, they were sometimes supported by government welfare agencies. Street battles between neo-Nazis and *Autonomen* could see both masked in Palestinian scarves, the former supporting Palestinian independence because they were explicitly anti-Semitic, and the latter because they opposed Zionist imperialism.[57] In 1985, the Bundestag passed a law prohibiting the wearing of masks and the carrying of "protective" weapons, and reinforcing the powers of the police to disperse threatening demonstrations.

In foreign policy Schmidt again played the pragmatic manager. Under continual pressure to prove that West Germany was no longer an "economic giant but political dwarf," he insisted that Germany's economic and diplomatic policies overlapped and should be pursued in common. In addition, they needed to be pursued cooperatively with other countries. Not only was there no place for abstract political ideologies in the modern interdependent world; there also was no place for nationalism or isolated national policies.[58] The need for European unity was another article of faith among pragmatic political leaders. Schmidt and French President Valery Giscard d'Estaing pressed for the creation of the European Monetary System in 1979. Although incomplete and ambiguous in its effects, the EMS was valued by Schmidt and others for its symbolic value, and was intended as much as a further step toward European integration as for its specific economic impact.

Schmidt endorsed the idea of reinforcing a strong defense, but at the same time exploring the possibility of "détente" with the eastern bloc. Under Genscher, now head of the FDP and foreign minister since 1974, this came to mean a much more cautious pursuit of Brandt's Eastern Policy, combined with the traditional Atlantic alliance with the United States and commitment to NATO. This "dual-track" policy had been recommended by the 1967 Harmel Report, and it implied strengthening the military as well. In 1977, Schmidt and Genscher recommended the deployment of intermediate-range missiles armed with nuclear warheads on West German territory. Seen by Conservatives and pragmatists as a response to Soviet deployment of their SS-20 intermediate range missiles, the Pershing II and cruise missiles became symbols of the dependent relationship between West Germany and the United States, and of a dangerous resurgent German militarism. They were opposed by the Greens, and opposition also mounted within the left wing of the SPD.

As the recession of the early 1970s gradually extended to a new period of slow growth, the distribution of the economic surplus also became more of an issue. This led to tensions over economic policy between the Socialists and the Liberals, whose support they still required to remain in power. In the 1980 elections, the SPD vote held steady but the FDP rose to over 10 per cent, its highest level since 1961. Predictably, this increased the pressure for the Liberals to exercise more of a voice in the government. Some observers believed the voters were expressing their satisfaction with the existing coalition, but the conservative business-oriented wing of the FDP led by Otto Lambsdorff, serving as finance minister, disagreed. A member of the German Baltic aristocracy, seriously wounded toward the end of the war, and a successful commercial banker and business leader before his entry into the Bundestag in 1972, Lambsdorff was congenitally uncomfortable working with the Socialists. He supported the market-oriented Kiel Theses adopted by the FDP in 1977. He produced a report critical of the Keynesian emphasis on demand and advocating reductions in social welfare spending and policies intended to stimulate production. Lambsdorff argued that the resulting growth would in itself solve the social problem and preserve financial stability in the difficult recession environment. The "Lambsdorff Paper" has been called the German version of supply-side economics.[59]

A constructive vote of no confidence forced Schmidt from office in 1982. Brandt opposed the deployment of the intermediate-range missiles and Schmidt's support within the SPD eroded. Genscher concluded that "NATO's two-track resolution could no longer be realized with the SPD."[60] The dispute over economic policy and specifically over the Lambsdorff Paper, and finally the failure to agree on a budget, triggered a crisis in the coalition. The beneficiary of the break-up of the Socialist–Liberal coalition was Helmut Kohl. He had led the CDU/CSU in 1976, but, although winning the highest share of the vote (48.8 per cent) since 1957, he did not gain a majority, and he lost the leadership in the 1980 elections to CSU head Franz Josef Strauss. He remained as CDU head and chair of the parliamentary caucus, however, and as such was well placed to take advantage of the instability in the Socialist–Liberal coalition.

Chancellor Kohl announced a "change of course" (*Tendenzwende*), and in the 1983 elections the CDU/CSU increased its vote by two million. The FDP lost nearly two million votes, but together they still commanded a majority. The SPD also lost nearly two million, and the new Greens won just over two million. The SPD lost some middle-class and white-collar votes to the CDU/CSU, and larger numbers of younger left-leaning voters to the Greens. The Conservative *Wende* meant that the emergency laws, the new police powers (and their new computer systems for collating data on all citizens), and the Radical Decree all remained in place. In 1983, Kohl and Genscher implemented the deployment of the intermediate-range missiles, over further protests and a 386–14 vote against deployment at the SPD party congress (the missiles were eventually removed as a result of the 1987 Intermediate Nuclear Forces Treaty). The new climate also allowed Franz Josef Strauss to complain openly about Germany being "swamped" by foreigners and to insist on the need to maintain a "healthy" demographic balance.

Could Germany become normal? Postmodern identity and coming to terms with the past

Remembering and forgetting

Old habits of concealment and denial continued. Unable to secure funding for her film projects after the war, Leni Riefenstahl turned to Africa and ethnographic photography. Her portfolios of photographs published in the 1970s earned further praise for her technical achievement and blame for her political and social insensitivity. She published her memoirs in 1987 and once again failed to admit to any sort of culpability or complicity in Nazi crimes, portraying the entire twentieth century as not much more than a sort of backdrop to her artistic accomplishments.[61] Composer Carl Orff, who wrote some of the music for the opening ceremony of the 1936 Olympics, remains known as a musical educator who believed in the innate musical potential of children and in folk music as a medium for learning. He was also an egocentric careerist, and in 1945 his long-standing active commitment to Nazism was concealed with the help of a former student who happened to be on the staff of the American military government. Michael Kater's frank discussion of Orff's unattractive character and the way in which he reestablished his reputation "has rendered Kater unwelcome in American Orff circles to this day."[62] Michael Verhoeven's 1989 film *The Nasty Girl* recounted the scandal caused when a young woman historian from the Bavarian town of Passau began to dig into the archival material detailing the complicity of local political, religious, and business leaders in Nazi crimes.

On the other hand, some former Nazi leaders sought exposure and recognition. Gertrud Scholz-Klink resented the attention gained by Albert Speer with his memoirs. In her interview with historian Claudia Koonz in 1981 she expressed no remorse, but rather continued to take pride in her accomplishments. She wanted the recognition given to other prominent Nazis.

> You know, if our politicians learned from the past, they would not have to complain about the unruly youth of today. Why don't they ask us for advice on social problems? We senior citizens could tell them a thing or two. In the Depression, we sponsored a national labor service that took teenagers off the streets and taught them patriotism.[63]

Scholz-Klink was riding the *Hitlerwelle*, the "Hitler wave." Joachim Fest's biography of Hitler published in 1976 became a perennial best-seller. The film based on the book, *Hitler: A Career* (1977), has been described as "hagiographic" and slightly more sympathetically as showing the Nazi period "as a form of collective madness, a murderous opéra bouffe, a demented aberration in the history of a great nation."[64] Photo albums and other popularized histories of the Nazi period proliferated to fill this new market, accompanied by a boom in collectable relics such as *Wehrmacht* and Nazi Party insignia, SS daggers, and original editions of *Mein Kampf*. Novels and popular films such as Wolfgang Petersen's gripping drama *Das Boot* (*The Boat*, 1982) continued the established themes of stoical heroism by German soldiers. "You have to have good men," says the commander of the submarine in *The Boat*, but the sacrifices are in vain, for after surviving its epic voyage to port, the vessel is then abruptly and ignominiously destroyed by an Allied bombing attack.

Writers who addressed the Nazi past critically were harshly criticized. In 1963, Rolf Hochhuth's first play *The Deputy* (*Der Stellvertreter*) had condemned Pope Pius XII for failing to oppose Nazi crimes and for possible complicity in the deportation of Jews from Rome. The play was not based on documentary evidence, though its central insight regarding Pius' anti-Semitism has in fact been confirmed by subsequent historians, but at the time it created an international sensation. Chancellor Erhard publicly attacked Hochhuth, and German critics denounced the play, one exception being Marcel Reich-Ranicki, who wrote that the embarrassed silence of other writers arose from their failure to confront the theme of the Holocaust at all. In 1979, Hochhuth's *Lawyers* (*Juristen*) considered the postwar careers of men who had served as judges in the Nazi courts. Critics again accused Hochhuth of both artistic failings and falsifying the facts, but the ensuing controversy resulted in the resignation of the Minister-President of Baden-Württemberg, Hans Filbinger.[65]

Painters who examined the Nazi past were equally rare, and equally contentious. Georg Baselitz, who left East Germany to complete his education in West Berlin, refused to adopt the fashion of Abstract Expressionism and created a scandal in the mid-1960s with his figurative works ironically labeled "heroes" that portray hulking male figures in devastated landscapes, men shattered by their war experiences, their impotence figured by flaccid genitals exposed by the open flies of their baggy fatigues. Anselm Kiefer, a student of Josef Beuys, caused an uproar with a series of photographs and paintings produced in 1969 and 1970 with the title *Heroic Symbols*, which show Kiefer dressed in riding breeches or a long coat, his arm raised in the Nazi salute, in a number of locations in France, Italy, and Switzerland. Part of the point for both was Germany's division and refusal to look at its past. Baselitz's *Divided Hero* (1966) has his head, not cut off and not separated from his body, but simply displaced to one side by a straight line drawn across the canvas. Kiefer's photographed gestures, and by implication the recognition of the past, could only take place outside of West Germany, where it was illegal to raise one's arm as Hitler and his millions of followers had done.[66]

In 1980, Baselitz and Kiefer were selected to represent West Germany at the Venice Biennale. In addition to several paintings, Baselitz contributed *Model for a Sculpture*, a deliberately incomplete sculpture, a rather cheerful and chubby male figure emerging from a wooden block, partly painted in red and black, with its right arm outstretched in the Nazi salute and a hint of a Hitler-style mustache. In two adjacent rooms, Kiefer's works were displayed, including massive mixed-media paintings dealing with the myths of the Nibelungen, Wagnerian scenarios, German intellectual history, and German militarism. German critics violently denounced the two artists and the organizers of the exhibition. Baselitz's sculpture, said one, greeted the visitor with a gesture that "was equated immediately with a German [*sic*] salute," and its brown, red, and black coloring "further suggests the idea of German imperialism." Kiefer's paintings, said another, were "technically lamentable, coloristically hopeless and compositionally pathetic" and "in dangerous proximity to glorifying German megalomania."

The point of the controversy, as Lisa Saltzman argues, was not what Baselitz and Kiefer showed, but how their works might affect West Germany's image. Critics worried explicitly how "a stream of visitors (primarily non-German)" might react. The hysterical reaction resulted from the fear that foreigners might question the genuineness of West Germany's commitment to constitutional democracy. So dangerous did it seem, and so unsure of their own identity were the critics, that it was unacceptable that any one or two artists should refer to the past at all.

As it happened, thanks partly to the controversy, partly to some clever marketing, and partly to his own talent, over the next decade Kiefer became popular and successful internationally and especially in the United States, precisely because he did confront German history, Nazism, and the Holocaust.[67] *Athanor* (1991), named after the furnace used by alchemists to transmute lead into gold, shows a charred picture of the Reichstag, possibly after it burned down in 1933. It was auctioned for US$ 1,116,750 in New York in November 2001.[68] The massive *Germany's Spiritual Heroes* (1973) shows a huge timbered hall receding into the distance, torches burning in niches along the sides, with the names of cultural figures ranging across the nineteenth and twentieth centuries, including both Wagner and Beuys, scribbled beneath them. Superficially similar to Darboven's "cultural timetable," this and other similar works require the viewer to confront the simultaneously crowded and empty, multi-layered and dangerous German cultural inheritance.[69] A series of works, particularly *Margarete* (1981) and *Sulamit* (1983), refer to Celan's "Death Fugue." As in the poem, the women are absent, figured in *Margarete* by her name floating in the center of the canvas and by literal straw growing in clumps from the soil, and in *Sulamit* only by her name scratched on a brick archway at the extreme upper left-hand corner of the canvas. The tufts of blond straw in *Margarete* end in flames. The massive vaulted interior space in *Sulamit* is an exact portrayal of the Nazi Mausoleum for German War Heroes designed by Wilhelm Kreis. Here, the torches that celebrate the German dead are extinguished and black, but in the distance at the end of the hall burns a fire whose shape resembles a menorah, the Jewish candelabrum.[70]

At a more popular level, the need to be seen to have rejected the past could also be observed in the reaction to the American television series *Holocaust*, broadcast in West Germany in January 1979. Estimates placed the audience at 20 million, half the adult population. Despite prohibitions, many East Germans watched as well, and in the aftermath teachers and students had to refrain from mentioning the series for fear of admitting to having seen it. In West Germany, 58 per cent of those asked wanted it repeated. Of the 5200 phone calls after the first episode, 72.5 per cent were positive and only 7.3 per cent negative. The stations received 12,000 letters, telegrams, and postcards. A large number expressed shock and surprise on learning about the Holocaust. One woman wrote,

> After *Holocaust* I feel deep contempt for those beasts of the Third Reich. I am twenty-nine years old and the mother of three children. When I think of the many mothers and children sent to the gas chambers, I have to cry. (Even today the Jews are not left in peace. We Germans have the duty to work every day for peace in Israel.) I bow to the victims of the Nazis, and I am ashamed to be a German.

The producers made it easy to identify with the central characters. The Weiss ("White") family portrayed in *Holocaust* are educated and impeccably middle class, designed to appeal to an American audience, but for Germans also instantly recognizable as members of the solid, respectable *Bürgertum*.[71] Of course one worries about one's own children, and it is easy to shed tears for victims of tragedy. Twelve years later, during the Gulf War, the Israeli embassy in Bonn was inundated with panicky phone calls from Germans wanting to know if they could help Israeli children if something terrible happened. Most also wanted to know whether they could return the children after the war.[72] But this particular woman had distanced herself from both "those beasts of the Third Reich" and from the Jews. Born in 1950, she had grandparents who were adults when the Nazis came to power, and parents who were still in school in 1933 and who were young adults during the war. Many of her own schoolteachers began their careers under the Nazis. Yet, despite being "ashamed to be a German," she did not refer to her own family's activities during the Nazi period, and she forgot that "the Jews" portrayed in *Holocaust* were German.

Neo-Conservatism and the inability to mourn

Franz Josef Strauss belonged to a minority who openly disliked the *Holocaust* series. He agreed with left-wing intellectuals who dismissed it because it was so "American" and so obviously commercial in its motives. However, the more important reason he and other Conservatives objected to it was because it cast Germans in a hopelessly negative light. It was time, Strauss argued repeatedly, for Germany finally to put the past behind: "It is now high time for us to step out of the shadow of the Third Reich and the aura of Hitler and become a normal nation once again." Joachim Fest, as editor of the influential *Frankfurter Allgemeine Zeitung*, also called repeatedly for Germany to become a normal, responsible power once again, in particular by using force to achieve its ends in foreign policy.

One thing normal nations do not do is surrender territory willingly. The CDU/CSU Conservatives had opposed Brandt's Eastern Policy at every step. Strauss and the Bavarian government took the treaty with East Germany to the Constitutional Court, on the grounds that it was incompatible with the Basic Law. In June 1985, Chancellor Kohl, on the advice of Conservative historians, addressed the annual meeting of the Association of Silesian Refugees. Strauss also contributed by sending a telegram in which he insisted that, in his view, the German Reich as a legal entity continued to exist in its 1937 boundaries. The treaties of the early 1970s, said Strauss, could not alter this fact. However, Strauss, as noted above, had also arranged for large credits to East Germany in

1983. Strauss later claimed he had negotiated specific concessions in return, such as increased travel permits for East Germans. How should we interpret these moves? In 1985, there was simply no chance of overcoming the division of Germany or of regaining the lost territories in the east, and the East German regime used West German financial aid and other concessions as a means of avoiding substantial internal reform.[73] Writing in 1987, historian Volker Berghahn suggested that, rather than a genuine attempt to reopen the "German question,"

> Kohl's advisors who, as Bismarck experts, have studied the Iron Chancellor's manipulative approach to politics closely, are more concerned to mobilise the presumed emotional potential of a German nationalism not because they consider reunification a realistic option, but because it appears to be an integrating device in domestic politics.[74]

One thing normal nations do is to remember those who have died in their defense. Kohl's address to the Silesian expellees came only a month after the embarrassing culmination of his attempts to stage a visit by United States President Ronald Reagan to the military cemetery in Bitburg. Intended to commemorate the fortieth anniversary of the end of the Second World War, the visit's more important purpose was to put the past behind. The two countries could "achieve peace and reconciliation . . . across the graves" and mourn the sacrifices that both had made in the war, now to be seen as their shared tragedy. Reagan himself initially refused a proposal that he also visit a concentration camp, because he believed that among Germans "very few . . . even remember the war . . . They have a guilt feeling that's been imposed on them, and I just think it's unnecessary." Kohl attempted to claim the high moral ground, and despite having repeatedly referred to the "blessing of late birth" (he was born in 1930, and therefore was still a child during the war) now insisted on Germany's responsibility "for the crimes of Nazi tyranny . . . a responsibility reflected not least in never-ending shame." The news that 49 of the dead buried at Bitburg had served in the Waffen-SS led to extensive protests in both countries. Kohl and a still reluctant Reagan visited the memorial at Bergen-Belsen in the morning and then stopped briefly at the Bitburg cemetery in the afternoon.

Normal nations also have normal histories. In 1984, five years after the *Holocaust* series, at least 25 million West Germans watched one or more of the eleven episodes of *Heimat*. The family saga produced by Edgar Reitz began with the return of a young man from French captivity in 1919 and followed successive generations through to the early 1980s. Languidly paced, the series portrayed a Germany of small towns, close-knit communities, and above all families. The depression, the rise of Nazism, and the war impinged on their lives from outside. The characters have no control over their destiny. They are innocent victims who focus on their daily concerns, have no knowledge of or complicity in Nazi crimes, work to overcome the tragedy of the war and occupation, and then cope with the problems of affluence. Again, the characters were easy to identify with, but in this case the other groups who suffered and who did not survive the war are effaced by the images of "normal" Germans and their lives.[75]

Among professional historians, Ernst Nolte, author of one of the best-known books on Fascism, insisted in essays published in 1985 and 1986 that it was time to cease regarding German history as exceptional. There were, he said, many cases of genocide in world history. In addition, he argued that Hitler and the Nazi regime might have acted as they did because "Hitler had good reasons to be convinced of his enemies' determination to annihilate him" and because the Nazis "regarded themselves as the potential or real victims of an 'Asiatic' deed." He cited a claim by Chaim Weizmann in September 1939 that "Jews in the whole world would fight on the side of England," and the Soviet threat to "exterminate the bourgeoisie" as evidence that Germany might have simply acted to defend itself, brutally to be sure, but not more brutally than other states in the twentieth century.

Jürgen Habermas attacked Nolte. Habermas insisted that "after Auschwitz our national self-consciousness can be derived only from the better traditions of our history, a history that is not unexamined but appropriated critically." The great achievement of West Germany had been that it had "opened itself without reservation to the political culture of the West" and abandoned the old exclusionary nationalism and replaced it with a "constitutional patriotism." But Habermas believed that this consensus, on which the official understanding of the Federal Republic was based, had been terminated by right-wing politicians such as Strauss.[76] In addition to faulting Nolte's use of evidence and the logic of his argument, Habermas accused him and other Conservative historians of attempting to create a mythical nationalistic vision of Germany's past that Conservatives could use to bolster their position internally and to make Germany a stronger power externally.

Nolte and his supporters counterattacked, and the resulting conflict divided the historical profession. Those who supported Nolte in the "historians' dispute" (*Historikerstreit*) demanded that German history be normal, that, for instance, the Nazi regime be regarded as a case study of Fascism, and the Holocaust as a case study of genocide, different certainly from other cases but also alike in many ways. Those on the other side insisted that German history was not normal, and the Nazi regime and the Holocaust were the unique outcome of that history. No other regime in history, they pointed out, had ever decided to exterminate a group of its own citizens without exception, and for no material, economic, or territorial advantage.[77]

Women's history, when the women in question were Nazi women, could not be normal either. The issues again were victimization, responsibility, and the previous course of German history. Helma Sanders-Brahms' 1980 film *Germany, Pale Mother* (*Deutschland, bleiche Mutter*) celebrated the strength and resourcefulness of a German mother and daughter in the aftermath of the war. Again, as in the 1950s, the war only begins for them in 1945 with rape by Allied soldiers and the return of brutalized German veterans. The rapist, however, is American not Russian, a shift in perspective to seeing West Germany as subjugated and victimized by the United States. The film encapsulated much of the West German historical work of the 1970s on women in the postwar era, which, although revealing their suffering and their contribution to reconstruction and the boom, nevertheless repeated the claims of blameless victimhood.[78]

As to what women had experienced before 1945, some West German feminists insisted that women had been victims of the Nazi regime, not perpetrators, agents, collaborators, or beneficiaries. Claudia Koonz's 1986 book *Mothers in the Fatherland* was attacked by Gisela Bock. Koonz, as we have seen, detailed the enthusiastic support many women gave the Nazi Party before 1933, their collaboration with the new Nazi government, their disappointment when they failed to gain effective power over their own separate sphere, and their accommodation within the regime. Bock faulted Koonz for minimizing the victimization of non-Jewish German women by the Nazis (particularly those forced to undergo sterilization, Bock's special subject), for not highlighting the resistance of Christian women to the Nazis, and, most importantly, for criticizing the ideology of the separate female sphere and the notion of women as the mothers of society. According to Bock, Koonz's argument that the inherited ideas and structures of the German feminist movement had made German women susceptible to Nazism was not only incorrect, but was also undermining the contemporary project of those "who see in the emancipation of women (also) their right, to be 'different' and to live 'differently' from men, without suffering discrimination."[79] Koonz defended her approach. The following debate divided historians and feminists, again between those who saw German history as normal, a case study this time of patriarchy and gender discrimination, and those who viewed it as unique—a battle not only "to reinterpret a national history" but also a battle "for the identity of West German women and feminists."[80]

What was wrong? Why was the German past unmasterable? Why did the past refuse to become history? One answer is the conflict between generations. The "forty-fivers" stood condemned by their children, the "sixty-eighters," of silence regarding the Nazi crimes, for not having confronted *their* parents, the previous generation of perpetrators. An entire genre of "father-literature" focused on the failings of the wartime generation.[81] The sixty-eighters in turn were accused of simply repeating the sins of their fathers, but with the sign reversed, and, among other things, of not having rid themselves of anti-Semitism.[82] Many on the West German left adopted the East German regime's anti-Israeli stance. "They believed that being on the left was a vaccination against being anti-Semitic," said a West German Jew, who had migrated from Russia as a child.[83]

A much-discussed attempt to explain the problematic relationship of Germans to their past had been published the year before the 1968 demonstrations. Alexander and Margarethe Mitscherlich's *The Inability to Mourn* (*Die Unfähigkeit zu trauern*, 1967) became one of the sticks the sixty-eighters used to beat their parents. Harshly critical of West German society, the Mitscherlichs accused West Germans of a "psychic immobilism" and a "political apathy" that hindered the adoption of important reforms. They believed "the political and social sterility of present-day Germany" had been brought about by "a denial of the past." They applied ideas developed by Freud in his 1921 work *Group Psychology and the Analysis of the Ego*. Freud asked what it was that held large bodies of people together in, for instance, churches or armies, and found the answer in the identification of the individual with an external object, an ego ideal. Members of a church or soldiers in an army could all focus their psychic energies on the leader, and, confident that the leader regarded all his followers as equal, they could then attach themselves to other members of the group, individuals with whom they might objectively have nothing in common.

The Mitscherlichs argued that in Nazi Germany Hitler had functioned as the ego ideal. For all Germans, "identifications that had filled a central function in the lives of his followers were attached to his person." The loss of the war, and the loss of Hitler, broke this psychic structure. Worse, "the country was reduced to rubble" and "the Führer himself was exposed by the victors as a criminal of truly monstrous proportions." As a result, "the ego of every single German individual suffered a central devaluation and impoverishment." Germans should have come to terms with their identification with Hitler and therefore with their complicity in the crimes of the Nazi regime. They did not, because the loss was too great. Instead of mourning the loss, accepting their complicity, and moving on, they denied their participation in the Nazi regime and their celebration of Hitler. They would not, or could not, confess their crimes. Refusal to admit guilt enabled them to shield themselves not only from guilt and punishment, but also from the sense of impotence that followed defeat. Instead, they concentrated on the economy. The failure to confront the past was made possible by building for the future, a massive self-investment in the "expansion and modernization of our industrial potential right down to the kitchen utensils."

As critics at the time and since have pointed out, the argument reflects the Mitscherlichs' frustration with German politics in the late 1960s. Further, some have argued, the sixty-eighters took the assertion of their parents' guilt as a means of avoiding empathetic engagement with their parents, which would have entailed assuming the burden of a tainted family and national legacy. This was a sort of escapism itself. In Freud's terms, an unresolved complex in the parent becomes a primary cause of disturbance in the child. Those who are critical of the sixty-eighters argue that their failure of empathy put off the necessary work of national mourning for at least another decade.[84]

We can also consider the divisions among the reformers and protesters of the sixties, and the subsequent disputes over the economy, social structures, and cultural forms. Identity was a problem for the postmodern generation. Artists experienced "the loss of ego ideals, those tainted and disavowed paternal signifiers, and with that, the loss of an ability to unselfconsciously articulate and embody a German identity."[85] They were not alone. All Germans were not the same, any more than in any previous generation. There could be no single identity of the simple and undifferentiated sort the Mitscherlichs and other critics envisaged. However, something was lacking. The identities offered as substitutes for a German identity by the elites of both East and West Germany were deeply unsatisfactory to many. The sudden opportunity to bring them together brought with it the need to confront the problem of forging a single identity once again.

Notes

1. Hanne Darboven, *Cultural History 1880–1983 (Kulturgeschichte 1880–1983)*, 1980–83. Dia Center for the Arts, New York, ⟨diacenter.org/exhibs/darboven/darboven.html⟩.
2. J. Fisher, "Hanne Darboven, Costelli," *Artforum* 23/4 (1984): 88.
3. Hanne Darboven, interview. The Dia Center website includes a systematic introduction to Darboven's treatment of numbers, based on calendar dates, some of which have been used as the base for musical compositions. See Dia Center for the Arts, New York, ⟨diacenter.org/exhibs/darboven/darboven.html⟩.
4. Organization for Economic Cooperation and Development, *OECD Economic Surveys—Germany 1975* (Paris: OECD), pp. 5–18; *Germany 1982–83*, pp. 7–23; *Germany 1987–1988*, pp. 33–4.
5. East Germany, *Jahrbuch 1988*, pp. 13, 15, 105, 356.
6. Maddison 1995, Table B-7 and Table C.
7. United Nations, *Statistical Yearbook 1981*; West Germany, *Jahrbuch 1988*, p. 88; East Germany, *Jahrbuch 1988*, pp. 239, 291; Vienna Institute for Comparative Economic Studies, *Comecon Data 1985* (London: Macmillan, 1986), p. 236.
8. Smith 1983, pp. 230–4, 267–9.
9. Gimbel 1990.
10. Ammon 1990.
11. Mandel 1978; Armstrong *et al.* 1984, Chs. 13–15.
12. Carlin 1996, pp. 474–9.
13. Giersch *et al.* 1994, p. 243.
14. Silvia 1988.
15. Armstrong *et al.* 1984, pp. 379–80.
16. Maier 1997, Ch. 2.
17. Bentley 1984; OECD, *Germany 1987–1988*.
18. Spaulding 1997, pp. 349–59.
19. Jarausch 1994, p. 100.
20. Bryson and Melzer 1991; Jarausch 1994, pp. 99–100.
21. Maddison 1995, pp. 131–3.
22. DeMeritt 1987; Firda 1993.
23. Silberman 1995.
24. Hasselbach 1996.
25. Merkel 1999, pp. 102–3.

26. Christa Wolf, *Dimension des Autors* (1986), p. 332, cited in Fehervary 1997, p. 422.
27. See the source notes to the tables in Mitchell 1992–95.
28. See Lösche and Walter 2000.
29. Lidtke 1996, p. 290, quoting Kuczinski 1961ff, Vol. 4, pp. 255–6.
30. Goeckel 1990.
31. Rabinbach and Zipes 1986.
32. Fulbrook 1999, p. 31.
33. Wunder 1986, p. 172.
34. Langenhan and Ross 1999, pp. 182–3.
35. Wunder 1986, p. 172.
36. Oertzen 1999.
37. Abrams and Harvey 1996; Janssens 1997.
38. Annette Kuhn, "Einleitung: Frauengeschichte zwischen Professionalisierung und Selbsterfahrung," in Dalhoff *et al.* 1985.
39. Albrecht 1994.
40. Negt and Kluge 1972.
41. Dutschke 1974.
42. Kelly 1983.
43. Habermas 1981, pp. 52–3; 1985. See D'Entrèves 1996.
44. Harsh 1997.
45. Wierling 1996; Hübner 1999.
46. Merkel 1999.
47. Jessen 1999b.
48. Dutschke 1974.
49. Moses 1999, p. 105.
50. Burns and van der Will 1988.
51. Eley 1988.
52. Aust 1987; Markovits and Gorski 1993.
53. Wunder 1986, pp. 176–83.
54. Aust 1987.
55. Goodrick-Clarke 1998.
56. Hoffman 1986.
57. Hasselbach 1996.
58. Schmidt 1985.
59. Lambsdorff 1980.
60. Cary 2000, p. 372.
61. Riefenstahl 1987.
62. Celia Applegate, review of Kater 2000, in *Central European History* 34 (2001): 140.
63. Koonz 1986, pp. xxi–xxiv.
64. Saltzman 1999, p. 145 note 11; Buruma 1994, p. 19.
65. Buruma 1994, p. 83; McGowan 1997, pp. 461–2, 466–7.
66. Belting 1998, p. 95; Biro 1998, pp. 24–31; Saltzman 1999, Ch. 2.
67. Archer 1997, Ch. 4.
68. Anselm Kiefer, *Athanor*, 1991. Oil, sand, ash, gold leaf, and lead foil on canvas, 281.9 × 381.6 cm. Auction details recorded by Sotheby's, ⟨www.sothebys.com⟩.

69. Anselm Kiefer, *Deutschlands Geisteshelden*, 1973. Oil and charcoal on burlap, mounted on canvas, 307 × 682 cm. Collection of Barbara and Eugene Schwartz, New York. Reproduced in Biro 1998, pp. 32–5.

70. Anselm Kiefer, *Margarete*, 1981. Oil and straw on canvas, 280 × 380 cm. Private collection. Reproduced in Saltzman 1999, pp. 29–30, and in Archer 1997, p. 152. Anselm Kiefer, *Sulamit*, 1983. Oil, acrylic, emulsion, shellac, and straw on canvas, with woodcut, 290 × 370 cm. Private collection. Reproduced in Saltzman 1999, pp. 29–30. See Biro 1998; Arasse 2001.

71. Buruma 1994, pp. 88–91. See Herf 1980.

72. Buruma 1994, p. 18.

73. Cary 2000, pp. 253, 261.

74. Berghahn 1987, p. 251.

75. See Kaes 1989; Moeller 1996, pp. 1038–40; Confino 1998.

76. Habermas 1990b, pp. 227, 234, 246–7.

77. Maier 1988, Ch. 3; Evans 1989.

78. Heineman 1996, pp. 388–92; Moeller 1996, pp. 1037–8; 2001.

79. Bock 1989, p. 565; 1992; Koonz 1992; see Grossmann 1991; Saldern 1994.

80. Heineman 1996, p. 392.

81. McGowan 1997, pp. 463–4.

82. Moses 1999.

83. Buruma 1994, pp. 17–19.

84. Moses 1999.

85. Saltzmann 1999, p. 94.

CHAPTER 15

NEO-REALISM: REUNIFICATION AND REUNITED GERMANY

Run Lola Run (*Lola Rennt*) appeared in 1999.[1] The film opens with a desperate phone call. Manni, a minor criminal, has lost a bag containing 100,000 marks belonging to his boss. His girlfriend Lola failed to meet him as planned, and he took the subway instead, but panicked when he saw two security guards and left the bag, which was then picked up by a bearded derelict. He must deliver the money in half an hour or he will be killed. He is considering robbing the store across the street. He calls Lola, who explains she could not meet him because her motor scooter had been stolen. She then tells him to wait for her.

Lola quickly reviews all her acquaintances in her mind, looking for one who can provide a large amount of money at short notice. She settles on her father, a senior official at a bank. She runs through the streets to the bank, where she interrupts a confrontation between her father and his mistress, who is telling him she is pregnant. He refuses to give Lola the money. She runs out of the bank and races to meet Manni, but she is late and he has begun to rob the store. She helps him with the robbery, but the police corner them as they run away from the store, and a young policeman accidentally shoots Lola in the chest.

But Lola refuses to die. In fact, she refuses to accept this version of the story, and resolves to return to the place where it went wrong. Back in her apartment after the phone call, she again decides to confront her father. This time she is tripped by a small boy as she runs out of the building, and is slightly delayed. Coming in at a later point in the conversation between her father and his mistress, who has just told her father that the baby is not his, she trades insults with both. Her father orders her to leave, but she takes a gun from the bank guard, takes her father hostage, robs the bank, and escapes. The police have surrounded the bank, but when she emerges they rush her off to the side—"Do you want to get killed?" one says. However, Lola's delay has also caused an ambulance to run through a sheet of plate glass being carried across the street by some workmen. This confuses the driver, and as Lola runs up to Manni, the ambulance smashes into him.

Lola, of course, refuses to accept Manni's death either. Back to her apartment, this time leaping over the boy's outstretched leg. Slightly ahead this time, she is almost run over by a business associate of her father's. This delays him, and prevents him from having the minor accident he has had in the previous two versions. However, this also means that he is on time for his appointment to pick up Lola's father, and she arrives at the bank to see the two men driving away. She runs into a casino instead, talks the cashier into giving her a 100-mark chip for the 99.50 she has, and wins the 100,000 marks she needs. While she is running to meet Manni, her father and his associate have a serious accident, and both are killed. In addition, this time Manni spots the derelict and retrieves the original bag. Lola arrives with her 100,000 marks to see Manni being congratulated by his boss. Manni then demands to know why she is late, and they walk away, holding hands.

The film is darkly humorous, and there are even darker undercurrents. The plot's structure reflects the course of German history with its tragic path and its multiple turning points. We each have our preferred point from which we would like to rerun the past, but everything is contingent, and all stories depend on the complex intersection of multiple events. A woman pushing a baby carriage, whom Lola first bumps into, then narrowly misses, and then simply runs past, shouts a different insult after her each time, but subsequently experiences three completely different futures. The film also satirizes Germany's authority structures. We see the bank's rigid hierarchy in the obsequiousness of the lower-level employees toward Lola's father. The guard outside the armored door protecting the bank's interior apes generations of petty officials. Deferential at first, he becomes both officious and lecherous when he sees that Lola's father has rejected her. The police are tremendously efficient in tactical deployment, but incompetent in the actual performance of their real duties. The emptiness of authoritarian family relations is clear in the generational conflict between daughter and father.

In the most recent generation, neo-realism appears as a dominant motif. Neo-realism as a style does not mean photographic re-creation. There are animated sequences in *Run Lola Run*, in addition to the physical impossibility of the plot. Neo-realism may be non-representational, but it represents reality without comment. It minimizes feeling, emotion, and connectedness. In domestic politics, this means accepting severe limits on the reach of the public realm and the role of the state. In economics, it means economic rationalism, accepting the decisions of the market. The key to this neo-realist text is the matter-of-fact selfishness of the characters. They are completely self-absorbed, and they all believe the world revolves around their problems. We learn in intermezzo scenes that Manni and Lola both think that, if they died, the other would quickly attach themselves to someone else. Manni blames Lola for his predicament, she blames her father for not providing the money she needs, and he in turn blames her and her mother for his involvement with the mistress. He asks why she needs the money, she replies, "for Manni"; he asks, "Who is Manni?" and she wails, "My boyfriend, for a year now," but she has obviously made no attempt to introduce them. Money is the link between individuals, and its loss is the only real tragedy, but one to be made good as quickly and easily as possible, by asking a rich relative, winning in a casino, or by robbing a convenient store or bank.

As with previous generations, the historical field is contested. Critics of neo-realism in politics and economics have pointed to the impoverished view of social life that it presents. The film appears to make no moral judgments, but in doing so it comments on the characters. Although the story revolves around choices and turning points, a large number of choices are not examined. Manni has chosen to work for a drug dealer. He chooses to rob the store, instead of, for instance, going to the police and informing on his criminal boss. Lola has chosen him as her boyfriend. She has also chosen to turn her back on her affluent family background, but only until she needs a large amount of money. Her father is systematically betraying his wife, but treats the crisis with his mistress as a minor irritant in his working day.

Reunification

For Germany, reunification was the rupture between the postmodern and the neo-realist generations. Reunification, the turning point or *Wende* that overshadowed and replaced Kohl's *Tendenzwende* of 1982, which has been described as a process, a movement, or an event,[2] was read as it occurred, not as a postmodern but as a neo-realist text. The availability of electronic as well as print media meant that a bewildering variety of forms of information became available. However, each story, each report, each image, was presented as a simple fact, added to the accumulating pile. Repeatedly it was announced that "events" were moving too rapidly for their "meaning" to be determined. Like Lola, characters simply responded as best they could. Significantly, the reports included a continual stream of opinion surveys that purported to identify what "Berliners," or "West Germans," or "East Germans," or some other group "thought" about some development. Again, the meaning of these opinions remained obscure. That is, the indeterminate and unprivileged individual readings of postmodernism were tabulated, averaged, and presented as the uncontested but also unanalyzed facts of neo-realism. The surveys also assumed their respondents to be selfish, that their main concern would be the cost, first of the grants to émigrés, then of possible increases in welfare expenditures, then of potential increases in taxes.[3] Although grouped and averaged, the respondents like Lola were isolated individuals whose main concern was money and the inconvenience of its loss.

Like other ruptures in German history, no one expected reunification. In 1985, Dietrich Staritz and Hermann Weber, leading West German experts on East Germany, both published general histories of the German Democratic Republic. Though they disagreed, neither predicted collapse. Staritz judged East Germany's problems to be serious but not insuperable: higher living standards combined with incentives to improve productivity, and the difficulties of motivation in the face of widespread cynicism regarding Socialism. Staritz thought the regime flexible and capable of adjusting. Weber, in contrast, believed East Germany faced an unresolvable contradiction, a foreign form of government imposed by the "backward" Soviet Union, confronting the demands of an advanced society. Weber concluded that the regime would not adjust, but periodically would crush demands for change arising both inside and outside the party.

As we have seen, East Germany, like the other economies of Eastern Europe, grew through the 1970s and early 1980s, but then lurched into crisis. In the 1950s or 1960s this would not have mattered; the police, the East German army, and the Russian army together would have suppressed any open demonstrations of discontent, as they did in 1953. Nor was there any particular reason why it should have mattered in the 1980s. As we have also seen, there was no organized opposition to the regime. If there was any movement in culture and politics it was rather toward a greater acceptance of the regime and a sense that ultimately changes would come from within. Overt repression was less common and more diversity was tolerated. The leadership, the party, and the people existed in a stable if not always comfortable relationship. The regime was known to be divided. If the current balance appeared to be in favor of the older generations of conservatives, the logic of the situation appeared to favor younger pragmatic reformers in the longer term.

A shifting balance could be seen in the Soviet Union, with new leader Mikhail Gorbachev returning to the reform initiatives of the 1960s. Gorbachev's policies of "openness" and "restructuring" encountered opposition within the Soviet regime, and senior East German leaders also regarded Gorbachev with suspicion. However, if there were to be reforms in the Soviet Union, and if the Soviet Union tolerated reform movements elsewhere in Eastern Europe, then the balance would tip toward reform in East Germany as well. The essential facts were the continued reality of Soviet power and the half-century tradition of Soviet domination across Eastern Europe.

West Germany appeared stagnant, recession and decline in 1981 and 1982 followed by a slow growth of less than 2 per cent average from 1983 to 1987. There were embarrassing political scandals, and a general dissatisfaction with the major parties. In 1984, reports of questionable campaign contributions by the Flick family's holding company led to the resignation of Rainer Barzel, the former CDU leader, who had served in Kohl's cabinet as minister for inter-German relations and then as parliamentary president. The "Flick Affair" also nearly ended the career of Otto Lambsdorff, who was forced to resign from his position as economics minister. He was indicted for having abetted tax evasion by collecting unreported business contributions to the FDP. The case concluded in 1987 with a guilty verdict, but resulted only in a fine, and, in 1988, Lambsdorff was elected to leadership of the FDP. Kohl was reelected in the 1987 elections, but with a lower voter turnout and a declining share of the vote. The CDU/CSU lost the two million votes they had gained in 1983. Kohl was saved by the failure of the SPD to win back the Green voters. The Socialists lost another 800,000 votes, and the Greens gained nearly 1 million and increased their share of the vote to 8.3 per cent. The CDU suffered a series of defeats in state elections, and Kohl's popularity was clearly in decline.

Ironically, relations between the two Germanies had reached new levels of amicability in the mid-1980s. Over one hundred agreements had been signed since the Basic Treaty of 1972. A news photo of Helmut Kohl and Erich Honecker in 1984 showed them smiling, in the identical suits worn by members of the elite, representative of increasingly frequent contacts between leaders. Honecker made a highly successful trip to West Germany in 1987, followed by further agreements. In 1988, negotiations were begun for construction of a high-speed rail link from Berlin to Hanover. For ordinary East Germans, travel was eased somewhat.

There is also a nice irony in the fact that it was people on their annual summer vacations who began the East German revolution. There were protests in early 1989. In May, opposition groups had organized to monitor the local elections, and they accused the regime of falsifying the results. Additionally, the partial liberalization of travel created a sort of "exit opposition." By 1989, the backlog of requests had reached 1.5 million. Nevertheless, as pessimists such as Hermann Weber might have predicted, 120 election protesters were arrested, and in June the People's Chamber passed a resolution supporting the suppression of Chinese dissidents in Tiananmen Square in Beijing.

In early May 1989, Hungarian soldiers began to allow East Germans to cross the border into Austria. Some were turned back, but they and then others began flocking to West German embassies in Budapest, Warsaw, Prague, and Berlin. They could claim "German" citizenship under existing West German law, and if they could pass over into West Germany they were assured of the traditional friendly welcome. Their numbers swelled to thousands. In Budapest, the Red Cross set up tent camps to accommodate them. Kohl urged the Hungarian government to open its borders. East German foreign minister Oskar Fischer threatened "dire consequences" if they did so. West Germany also promised Hungary economic support. The Hungarian government, already committed to internal reform, decided to gamble that the Soviet Union would not intervene. At midnight on September 10–11 Hungary opened its border with Austria. The waiting cars and buses flowed across, 8000 people in the first twenty-four hours. Others drove north from vacations in Bulgaria and Romania, and more simply got on the train. Through Austria and into West Germany in a few hours, they were greeted with beer and balloons in the Bavarian town of Passau, and the televised images passed instantly around the world, including back to East Germany.

By the end of September, 30,000 had fled through Hungary and Austria. The East German government restricted travel to Hungary, and when the flow shifted to Czechoslovakia, travel to Prague without a permit was also forbidden. Attempts to enforce the new restrictions in

October led to violent confrontations between police and people desperate to seize the opportunity to leave. A series of negotiations with West Germany, and compromises followed by new restrictions, only worsened the situation. Soviet leaders refused to intervene. Gorbachev, visiting East Berlin for the celebrations of the fortieth anniversary of East Germany's foundation on October 6 and 7, warned the East German regime to implement reforms parallel to those already announced elsewhere in Eastern Europe. Honecker, recovering from surgery, still fixated on the celebrations, possibly not aware how serious the economic crisis was, and also unaware of the deep dissatisfaction with the government and with him personally, refused. Mass protests began in Magdeburg and Dresden, and reached what appeared to be a climax on October 16 when 120,000 demonstrated in Leipzig. Although there was considerable tension and apprehension, the local authorities decided not to use force. The next day Honecker resigned after a majority of the Central Committee turned against him, and was replaced by Egon Krenz.

On November 6, the government announced a new travel law, but it remained hedged with restrictions. Outrage brought huge crowds into the streets again. Krenz and the other leaders revised the draft, hoping to gain popularity. On November 9, an evening press conference announced that "applications for private trips abroad may be submitted without further preconditions . . . Permission will be granted immediately." The result was the "Opening of the Wall," a flood that overwhelmed the officials at the Berlin checkpoints, who stopped even attempting to stamp passports around midnight. The government, again, decided not to use force to disperse the masses of people.

The flood continued. During 1989, a total of 343,854 people, more than 2 per cent of the population, left East Germany. They tended to come from East Berlin, the industrial cities of Dresden, Chemnitz, and Leipzig in Saxony, and from smaller cities in the south. They were young (56 per cent between the ages of 18 and 45, compared to the national average of 34 per cent), and tended to be single. There were more men than women. They were also predominantly working class, with steady jobs in industry, construction, and transportation. Two-thirds of them were skilled workers with advanced qualifications. In addition, around one in six had completed a tertiary degree, usually medicine or teaching. Typically somewhat better off than average, they reported that they wanted to improve their positions and seized what they feared might be their only chance to do so.[4]

The emigrants differed from the protesters, at least initially. Workers, though officially a privileged class in the "worker—peasant" state, in fact were excluded from political life except for ritual observances. Students, the sons and daughters of the elite of party members, officials, and managers, could look forward to careers that would bring them influence, but they chafed under the restrictions on expression and the slowness of promotion they foresaw as the existing leaders refused to retire. Workers therefore had little sense of commitment to the system. Students did not object to the system as such, but wanted changes to give their generation more opportunity. The initial thousands who left the country through Hungary in the summer of 1989 were primarily young male workers. The demonstrations from September onward were predominantly by those committed to remaining but demanding reform. Workers joined the demonstrations generally only after the opening of the Wall. In a November 1989 survey, 54 per cent of foremen and 39 per cent of skilled workers supported immediate reunification with West Germany, but only 4 per cent of students. Students overwhelmingly favored a reformed East Germany in preference to reunification.[5]

The calls for reform and for democratic rights, however, were as deadly a threat to the existing leadership as the flow of migrants. The pattern repeated: demonstrations and pressure on the government, concessions, always seen as grudging and insufficient, further demands and further demonstrations, followed by further concessions. The people in the streets were not a leaderless crowd. The demonstrations centered around the tolerated social movements that had grown up in spaces separate from the ruling apparatus, particularly the churches. East Germany in this resembled similar developments elsewhere in Eastern Europe, especially Poland, Hungary, and Czechoslovakia, but differed from them in that the current leaders were more intransigent and in that there was another Germany to which dissidents could look for inspiration, or asylum.[6]

The East German regime suffered a double weakness. First, the Soviet Union refused to guarantee the existence of East Germany. Soviet motives are disputed. Philip Zelikow and Condolezza Rice argue that Gorbachev had so many problems at home that he was forced to yield on the German question. If he had seized the initiative he might possibly have achieved the neutralized state advocated by many. Other specialists believe Soviet leaders no longer felt their Eastern European empire was worth the cost.[7] Second, the East German administration began to disintegrate. Nothing could be hidden. The accumulated weaknesses, inefficiencies, and corruption became common and embarrassing knowledge. Crowds broke into offices of the security police (Stasi), beginning the revelation of the shocking extent of surveillance. The economy began to stall because of the loss of skilled workers, and health services deteriorated because of the loss of medical personnel. Output declined and unemployment rose. The demands of the demonstrators shifted away from reform and toward a demand for unification with West Germany. "We are the people"—that is, the regime was not the people and could not speak in the people's name—became, more threateningly, "we are one people." Johannes Becher's line from the East German national anthem, "Germany, united fatherland," that had been deleted as it implied the desirability of unification, was also taken up as one of the chanted phrases.

Kohl spoke to the Bundestag on November 28. He proposed a Ten Point Plan for German Unity. Informed that the Soviet leadership were thinking about "the quasi-unthinkable" and already certain of United States support, and under intense pressure to demonstrate his own leadership, he decided to seize what had come to look like a historic opportunity. He offered humanitarian aid and continued practical cooperation for instance in postal services. Further aid would be forthcoming as long as the East German reforms became "irreversible." The SED Party monopoly must be ended and free elections held. The economy must be converted to a market economy. In addition, Kohl agreed to the idea of a "treaty community" based on existing bilateral relations, as suggested by the East German leaders. Most daring was his proposal for "confederative structures," including a shared parliamentary body, although "nobody knows today how a reunited Germany will look in the end." With a nod toward the Soviet Union, Kohl also committed himself to Gorbachev's "common European house" and increased European integration and disarmament.[8]

Krenz was replaced by Hans Modrow, a known reformer and untainted by corruption, on December 3. He began negotiations with opposition groups represented at the Round Table forum. The announcement of free elections opened opportunities for West German parties to agitate. The CDU promised that living standards in the East would be brought rapidly up to the levels of the West, which convinced more people that reunification was preferable to reform. In addition, Kohl promised that if the coalition Conservative Alliance for Germany won the election, then East Germany could simply join West Germany under the existing constitution rather than following drawn-out negotiations as both the reformers in East Germany and his opponents in West Germany preferred, and also that the East German and West German currencies would be equal. The elections in March 1990 brought victory to counterparts of the West German parties and formation of a grand coalition of CDU, SPD, and FDP with Lothar de Maizière of the CDU as Minister-President.

In East Germany, the leaders of the citizens rights movement represented in the discussions of the Round Table still hoped for reform and a new but separate constitution. They had been left behind by the solid majority of working-class voters who had decided they wanted reunification. In West Germany as well growing majorities favored reunification. Those who were opposed or hesitant, the Greens, the left wing of the SPD, and intellectuals such as Jürgen Habermas, found themselves isolated. In the negotiations with West German representatives, the East Germans were at a constant disadvantage, as their economy continued to decline, as their government budget deficit rose, as the flow of people continued (74,000 in January and 64,000 in February), and without external support.

In February, Kohl pushed for a rapid monetary union as a step toward reunification. The number of migrants and demands by East Germany that the West German government provide welfare relief in the East meant increasing costs. But polls showed that 75 per cent of West Germans opposed increased taxes to pay for reunification. Kohl, now facing an election, argued that unification of the currency systems would stimulate the economy, and the resulting growth he vowed would make new taxes unnecessary. Polls showed 91 per cent in the East in favor of currency union, and 76 per cent in favor in the West, in both countries because the respondents believed it would bring reunification without cost.[9] The treaty that emerged in May was dictated to the East German negotiators, but provided for fairly generous exchange rates, and in fact was opposed initially by the Bundesbank. The West German mark was introduced as the currency of East Germany on July 1, 1990. The political effect was to erode the authority of the East German government even further.

Negotiations for a Treaty of German Unity began in early July. Again the terms were dictated by West German negotiators. "This is the accession of the German Democratic Republic to the Federal Republic of

Germany and not the reverse," said West German interior minister Wolfgang Schäuble. "We want to do everything for you. You are cordially welcome. We do not want to trample coldly on your wishes and interests. But this is not the unification of two equal states." Divisions between the SPD and the CDU/CSU over the imposition of West Germany's anti-abortion legislation on East Germany threatened ratification by the West German Bundestag, but the parties agreed on a transitional period and committed themselves to pass a new law in 1992. The treaty was signed on August 31, 1990.

The Allied powers, caught by surprise at the rapidity of the East German collapse and the West German moves for rapid unification, insisted on their rights under the agreements that had ended the Second World War. The United States had decided in early 1989 to move toward Germany as its main security partner in Europe. President George Bush had met with Gorbachev in early December 1989, and had communicated Soviet willingness to agree to unification to Kohl. His support for Kohl's plan for quick unification was also important because both French President François Mitterand and British Prime Minister Margaret Thatcher opposed immediate unification.[10] The ensuing "Two-plus-Four" negotiations, among the four Allied powers and the two Germanies, concluded on September 12, 1990. An additional treaty recognized the Oder-Neisse border with Poland on September 13. Soviet leaders offered substantial concessions—as a result of their own mounting crisis—including accepting unification itself and the membership of united Germany in NATO. In return, West Germany offered compensation by paying the costs of the withdrawal of Soviet troops. An offer to limit the size of the German army was backed by a guarantee of the United States not to make unification of Germany an opportunity to strengthen NATO further.

The unification treaty went into effect, and the two Germanies became one, on October 3, 1990. In the aftermath, opinions diverged over who merited the most credit for the achievement. Kohl, of course, claimed credit and compared himself to Bismarck seizing the hem of God's cloak. Others saw "a Kohl-shaped hole" in the version of events presented by the official documentary collection, particularly regarding the point at which Kohl decided reunification was both desirable and possible.[11] American scholars Zelikow and Rice argued that George Bush grasped the opportunity to support Kohl and accomplish an objective set by the West early on in the Cold War era, the reunification

Map 7 Germany in 1990

Plate 15.1   Anselm Kiefer, *Twilight of the West*, 1989. Lead sheet, synthetic polymer paint, ash, plaster, cement, earth, varnish on canvas, wood, 400 × 380 × 12 cm. National Gallery of Australia, Canberra. The German title is simply *Abendland*, a reference to Spengler's *Decline of the West* (*Untergang des Abendlandes*). No one today can view a portrayal of railroad tracks by a German artist and not be reminded of the railroad lines leading to the death camps. The materials of this work, particularly ash, remind the viewer of the fate of those who were shipped to the camps in the trains. However, the stylized mechanical sun is in fact an impression of a manhole cover on the lead sheet that forms the sky and that also cuts off the receding perspective of the foreground. Lead was the material that alchemists hoped to transform into gold; in the year of reunification and the West's triumph over the East, this might suggest a possible escape from the branchings of Germany's past history. © National Gallery of Australia, Canberra.

of Germany under a Western-style liberal democratic regime, within the NATO alliance (Rice later became a senior advisor to Bush's son George W. Bush when he became President).[12] Former leaders such as Willy Brandt took a longer view and argued that the previous twenty years of *Ostpolitik* had laid the foundation for unity, but they disagreed over which of them and which specific acts had contributed the most.[13] Konrad Jarausch, reconstructing events day by day, emphasized the role of the people. Leaders did not lead, but were forced to recognize the new situation created by popular protest. They did, however, seize the agenda. The people were not consulted about the form of the new state.[14] Initially, this did not seem to matter.

The economic context: reunified Germany in the global economy

The economics of German unification

Ordinary East Germans expected reunification would bring them Western standards of living; ordinary West Germans did not expect to have to pay; political leaders expected to reap the credit for the simple and smooth imposition of the West German system in the "new federal states" in the East. All were disappointed. The euphoria of reunification rapidly gave way to disillusionment. One cartoon showed a couple, the man labeled West and the woman labeled East, awakening on a disheveled bed labeled Germany, empty champagne bottles on the floor and the sun of reunification coming up through the window, regarding each other dubiously and asking, "What now?" Another showed two men on either side of a broken fence. One, thin, haggard, and shabbily dressed, is proclaiming, "We are one people!" The other, fat and well dressed, is replying with a scowl, "So are we!"

The Western economic agenda, as Kohl had emphasized in his original Ten Point Plan speech, was first and foremost the dismantling of the Socialist system and its replacement by a market economy. Faith in the market solidified into dogma. Former Chancellor Ludwig Erhard, "Mr. Economic Miracle," insisted that reunification "must take place by means of the market economy." Believing that the new currency and market forces alone had caused the recovery in 1948–51 and laid the basis for the long boom of the 1950s and 1960s, he was certain that introduction of the West German currency and reliance on private initiative would work a similar miracle in East Germany. He believed "widespread fears about tragic material effects on individual lives" to be "unfounded." There might be some need for government assistance, but he predicted "German reunification will unleash forces" that government planners could not imagine.[15]

In addition, the collapse of the other Eastern European economies and the dissolution of the Soviet Union were not only taken as proof of the failure of Socialism, but were also seen as an opportunity for an immediate transition to a market economy, a "big bang" that influential economists said would lead to prosperity.[16] The International Monetary Fund published a study in 1990 that outlined two possible scenarios for the East German economy following reunification. The "optimistic" scenario showed output rising 7.5 per cent in 1991, then 17.5 per cent in 1992, and substantial growth at well over 6 per cent per year over the next decade. The "pessimistic" scenario suggested that output might decline by 2.5 per cent in 1991, but then would rise nearly 10 per cent in 1992, and again would grow at over 6 per cent until 2001. The IMF team believed that, despite possible difficulties, high levels of investment and the inherited traditions from before the Second World War would bring levels of productivity in the East rapidly up to those in the West, laying the basis for a "new Wirtschaftswunder."[17]

As seen in Chapter 13, in 1948 the success of the currency reform depended on a very favorable set of circumstances. East German firms did not possess large stocks of goods that could be sold immediately, and East Germany's capital stock was severely outmoded. But West German authorities believed in the myth, and they accepted the idea that the new currency and the market together would ensure success. They therefore did not attempt to steer the transition, for instance by establishing a sequence of areas to be opened to market forces, controlling the flow of credit, and subsidizing potentially competitive firms while modernizing their technologies.

The monetary union replaced the East German mark with the West German mark. Wages, salaries, and pensions were converted at 1:1, debts at 2:1, and foreign accounts at 3:1. Savings were treated on a graduated scale, from 2000 marks at parity for children, to 6000 for retired persons, with the remainder usually exchanged at 2:1. Further clauses introduced "the free, democratic, federal, legal, and social order" of West Germany's Basic Law, and specifically the provisions of West German labor law, welfare funding, private health care, and various types of insurance. The deficit of the East German government was to be covered by privatizing state enterprises, cutting subsidies, and reducing personnel expenses. Funding was provided to begin all these undertakings, but the amounts were strictly limited, and new customs duties and taxes were to be levied to cover the expenses of the transition.

The first sense of wonder as the stores filled with Western goods quickly evaporated. When the subsidies ended, prices of basic commodities doubled and tripled in price. Eastern goods became unsaleable, not always because of their poor quality. East Germany's most important markets in Eastern Europe disappeared as the Socialist regimes collapsed. Western retail chains moved into the East, but they sourced their products in the West, so that even potentially competitive Eastern goods were shut out of the market. The loss of half their savings above the minimum amounts substantially reduced the wealth of ordinary East Germans. After the new taxes, retirement, and insurance contributions were deducted, those who had jobs found their net income was 15 per cent lower than before. Jobs themselves became a problem as many firms, struggling with old debts, abandoned by previous joint venture partners, shut out of previous markets, and refused support by Western banks, continued to lay off workers.

To move toward a market economy, but also to help pay the government's expenses and cover the accumulated deficit, in March 1990 the East German government accepted a suggestion of the Round Table to establish a "trustee corporation" (*Treuhandsanstalt*, or simply *Treuhand*) to oversee the transformation of state enterprises into joint stock corporations while preserving the genuinely public portion of the "people's wealth." The process moved too slowly to satisfy West German authorities, and in June de Mazière restructured the *Treuhand*. Its new mission was to reduce the size of the state sector and introduce "privatization as quickly and thoroughly as possible." Legally the *Treuhand* became a private corporation free from government control, and not for instance a public limited company, which would have been subject to the provisions of the Co-Determination Law, including the right of employees to be consulted about a decision to sell or close down the company. Profits from the break-up and sale of state enterprises were to be used first to meet government expenses; anything left over would be distributed as public shares. The process was to be completed by 1994.

Detlev Rohwedder, a Western economist who had guided the Hoesch steel firm through a drastic restructuring in the early 1980s, from the SPD but with cross-party experience as a state secretary, became the first president of the *Treuhand*. His attempt to operate as a small holding company failed, and the *Treuhand* rapidly became a large bureaucracy of over 3000 with branch offices throughout the East in addition to the headquarters in Berlin. Enterprises were graded on a scale of six to determine their saleability. Those in the bottom category were condemned to a "gentle closure" (*behutsame Stillegung*), a phrase later changed to *Abwicklung* or winding down. In early 1991, the *Treuhand* board was enlarged to include representatives of the Eastern state governments as well as the labor unions. Review commissions and temporary employment programs were also established. The *Treuhand* began to consider ways of salvaging firms rather than simply either selling or closing them. The presumption remained that privatization was the desirable norm, however, and so did the pressure to work quickly.

Treuhand managers were generally recruited from large West German firms. They were paid high salaries, and, following Rohwedder's murder (the Red Army Faction claimed responsibility), his successor Birgit Breuel introduced additional bonuses depending on the number of firms they sold. As one said, "We had to privatize, privatize, and privatize again. It was expected that we should dispose of the firms in our portfolio as quickly as possible." Managers also received a government guarantee of freedom from liability for negligence or maladministration. They were uniformly disliked by Easterners for their arrogance, and of course were not popular with workers in firms condemned to *Abwicklung* or dismissed after a sale. "How's it going?" was the morning greeting; "Feeling a bit wound down" was the reply.

Scandals accompanied the transition. In addition to possible cases of actual corruption and insider deals, there were systematic flaws in the process. The *Treuhand* made its decisions on the basis of immediate profitability, in secrecy and without accountability, and in the rush was almost certain to make some bad decisions. Although there were exceptions, most of the viable firms were sold at absurdly low prices. The values used by the *Treuhand* to set selling prices were excessively depressed by the inclusion of previous debts on the firms' books from before the unification of the currencies. West German finance minister Theodor Waigel rejected the idea of canceling these debts. He believed to do so would cost the government more in continued subsidies, but given the massive de-industrialization and eventual need for government intervention and support, this proved to be wrong. In addition, cases were revealed in which the *Treuhand* itself had assumed the debts in order to secure the sale.[18]

As the East German economy collapsed, Western leaders repeated that recovery and a new economic miracle would begin at any moment. Short-term pain, they said, would be worth the long-term gain. A propaganda campaign was launched to stimulate small business. But the miracle was not repeated. The East German economy did not take off. Measuring the pain depends on estimates of total output before reunification. These, as we have seen, are disputed, and not surprisingly debate continued.[19] Total product may have declined more than 14 per cent in 1990, and another 30 per cent in 1991. More reliable is the index of industrial output, which fell by two-thirds from 1989 to 1991. Though mixed, on average prices rose 12 per cent in 1991. Unemployment had already risen to 1 million before reunification and estimates indicated that another 1.6 million were working on reduced hours. Then, over the next eighteen months, another 1.8 million jobs were lost. Altogether half of the jobs in East Germany may have disappeared. In late 1993, unemployment in the East was over 15 per cent, and 65 per cent of the unemployed were women.

Something had to be done. The Eastern Recovery Program began in March 1991 and transferred 135 billion marks to the eastern states by the end of the year. In 1992, the total of direct transfers, loans, investment, and interest on debt was 218 billion marks, roughly equal to the total of goods and services actually produced in the eastern states. The flow continued at over 100 billion marks a year for most of the rest of the decade, though estimates of the total depend on what is included. In addition the government subsidized investment in the East. Officials argued that the backward state of the capital stock and, equally important, the poor reputation of the East meant that without subsidies no investment would take place—though the financial weakness of eastern firms resulted from the burdens imposed by the monetary union, and the uncertainty about property ownership in the East from a commitment to "restore" property to those who had lost it forty years before. Taxes had to rise to cover these costs, and they did, to a total of 45 per cent of gross domestic product in 1995, the highest ratio among the major industrialized countries. The "Solidarity Surcharge" of 7.5 per cent on personal and corporate income taxes (introduced for two years in 1991 and 1992, then extended in 1993), and increases in the value added tax and other indirect taxes, painfully reduced disposable incomes.[20]

West Germany had grown by over 5 per cent in 1990 and still over 4 per cent in 1991, but the costs of reunification depressed growth in united Germany to 2 per cent in 1992, and the economy contracted in 1993. Over the next four years, growth averaged less than 2 per cent annually. Higher growth in 1998 and 1999 was then followed by sluggish growth if not contraction in 2000 and 2001. Nationally, unemployment averaged 9 per cent from 1991 to 1997, but remained higher in the eastern states, where on average one in seven workers was still unemployed in 1995 and some districts still suffered unemployment rates of 20 per cent in 2000–01. Within this framework the painful economic restructuring of East Germany continued. At first, the transfer payments to maintain incomes in the East were spent largely on goods produced by West German manufacturers, increasing the pressure on firms in the East. There was some recovery of industrial output in the East in 1992 and 1993 following the collapse, and growth of 9 per cent in 1994 and 10 per cent in 1995. Gradually, surviving firms updated their technology, branches of West German firms expanded, and new firms emerged, but in the eastern states' total output in the late 1990s still lay well below the levels of the late 1980s.

Germany in the European and world economies

Internationally, the 1990s were marked by the very rapid growth of Asian economies. Astute observers had already taken notice of the "four tigers," South Korea, Taiwan, Hong Kong, and Singapore. Now Thailand, Indonesia, and Vietnam accelerated as well. Looming in the background was China, with growth of 8 to 10 per cent per year from the "opening" of 1978 onward.[21] The "Asian crisis" of 1997 slowed growth, but China was unaffected, and although Indonesia stumbled into political turmoil the other Asian economies recovered rapidly.

At the same time, the international economy as a whole continued to grow relatively slowly, because of the continued trend of slow growth in Europe, the United States, and especially Japan, still the three dominant economic areas. For Japan this was the "lost decade" of stagnation. For the United States the record was mixed. Moderate growth overall concealed serious problems in older industrial and service sectors. The exceptionally rapid expansion of the computer industry led to a speculative stock market boom and sudden collapse, the "tech wreck" of 2000, and stagnation in 2000 and 2001. Although revived by the move to unify the European market in 1992, the admission of new members, and the long-awaited currency union in 2000, the European Union also did not rediscover the secrets of rapid growth.

Slow overall growth combined with the entry of new competitors made life difficult for older firms and older regions. Despite the slower growth of their labor forces, none of the industrialized countries managed to expand rapidly enough during periods of expansion to absorb workers thrown off during periods of stagnation or recession. Among economists, the Keynesian conception of unemployment, that workers could be put back to work by an expansionary government policy, was replaced by the harsher neo-realist notion of a "natural" rate of unemployment that could not be permanently reduced by macro-economic policy. Increases in government spending, or lower interest rates, might reduce unemployment for a short time, but it would rise again, and in the meantime the rate of inflation would have risen as well. European states were accused of maintaining "rigidities" in their labor markets, and it was broadly accepted that only microeconomic reforms leading to lower labor costs would reduce the natural rate of unemployment.[22]

Conservative politicians seized on the shift in economic opinion. Economic growth had been the policy of the left: Democrats in the United States, Labour in Britain, and the SPD in West Germany. Growth, achieved by stimulating demand, seemed to offer the key to balancing social equity against economic incentives. In the 1980s and 1990s, however, growth became the watchword of Conservative parties, Republicans, Tories, and the CDU/CSU. Growth now was to be achieved through supply-side reforms, and became a doctrine deployed to revitalize and implement a Conservative and anti-statist vision of government. Economist Milton Friedman and social theorist Friedrich von Hayek were often cited, though perhaps not as often read.[23] Looking back from the mid-1990s, Charles Maier said, "no one in the late 1970s would have envisaged the triumph of market forces during the Reagan–Thatcher era."[24] Democrats under Bill Clinton, "New Labour" under Tony Blair, and the SPD of the "middle way" under Gerhard Schröder, all found they needed to speak the language of fiscal responsibility and microeconomic reform.

The European Union's new European Central Bank inherited this Conservative mindset, and was widely regarded as having inherited the biases of the West German Bundesbank as well. German leaders, including the SPD, were among the strongest advocates of a central financial institution completely independent of elected politicians. The ECB's position was buttressed by the Maastricht Treaty and the Stability and Growth Pact, which obligated member governments to observe limits on their annual borrowing and total debt and to achieve balanced budgets over the medium term. Officially, the ECB regarded the rate of inflation as its core concern.[25] Unofficially, a "strong" currency was also one of its priorities. When the new Euro declined against the United States dollar the bank increased interest rates. Employment was not a priority. Prices rose only 2 per cent in 1999–2000 and not at all in 2000–01, but recorded unemployment in the Euro zone was 9.4 per cent in 2000 and 8.8 per cent in 2001. Germany, the EU's largest economy and more committed to monetary union than any other member, was now constrained in any policy it adopted by the limits set by the central bank.

The large positive trade balances traditionally enjoyed by West Germany (an average of 4 per cent of gross domestic product in 1988–90) became negative trade balances from 1991 through 1997. Through the mid-1990s, the German government announced a series of reforms intended to improve the efficiency and competitiveness of Germany in the globalized market place. Licensing procedures were to be simplified, corporate taxes lowered, government enterprises privatized, restrictions on working hours reduced, welfare provisions restricted, and the financial, transportation, and communications sectors liberalized. Competitiveness had two sides. One was to make Germany a desirable location for investors, both to encourage foreign firms to locate in Germany and to encourage German firms to keep their capital at home. The other was to reduce the cost of German exports and restore the positive trade balance. International agencies applauded, but complained that a business license could still take two years, that German banks were too conservative, that the service sectors were still protected, that the federal and especially the state governments owned too many businesses, that retail opening hours were still restricted, and above all that German workers were too expensive—that minimum wages, job security, unemployment benefits, and welfare entitlements were too high.[26]

The 1990s saw a very large number of mergers. The Cartel Office, notorious over the years as a "toothless tiger," scrutinized applications for cartel agreements carefully, but approved virtually all mergers proposed to it. From 600 per year in the early 1980s, mergers rose to 900 a year in the late 1980s, peaked at 2007 in 1991 in the aftermath of reunification, but then averaged 1500 each year through the remainder of the 1990s. Further, the proportion of "horizontal" mergers between potentially competitive firms in a single industry rose dramatically, and the average size of the merged firms also increased substantially. In the late 1990s, any hesitancy the Cartel Office might have had regarding particularly large mergers became effectively irrelevant, because responsibility for approval of mergers of companies with more than 5 billion ECU turnover was taken over by the European Commission. The Commission was widely perceived as favoring cross-border mergers of EU firms as a defensive strategy to protect European interests against the United States and Japan.[27]

What might this mean? For example, the employees of Lufthansa had enjoyed the same status as public servants, with virtually guaranteed lifetime employment after fifteen years' service and high wages and retirement benefits. Eight complete crews served each aircraft, and a senior pilot earned roughly the same salary as an under-secretary in a federal government department. Limited in its markets but with its revenues protected by international agreements and domestic monopoly, the airline concentrated on its image as a provider of superb service in the latest models of aircraft. From the 1980s onward, however, deregulation in the United States reduced profits for United States airlines, and they began to discount fares on their flights to Europe. The European Commission also moved to break down national monopolies within the European Union. A thin profit in 1990 was followed by large losses in 1991 and 1992. New managing director Jürgen Weber froze wages for twelve months, spun off segments of the company in order to avoid long-term wage agreements, and transferred pensions from federal and state funds to a pension insurance association. He also reduced the remaining work force from 50,000 to fewer than 47,000. Productivity rose 31 per cent, the company's publicly listed shares rose, and in 1994 the government took advantage of the high price and sold much of its holding.[28]

The market could give, but it could also take away. Weber's decision to retain and expand Lufthansa's freight services earned increasing profits over the next four years, as did the subsidiary Sky Chef catering and Technik maintenance units, which sold their services to other airlines. But then the overseas demand for German machine tools shrank, as did German demand for computer components, cut flowers, and other expensive or perishable goods typically shipped by air. Revenues from freight declined drastically in 2001. Pilots, now poorly paid by industry standards, struck in April, leading to lost earnings and a large settlement for back wages. Weber announced his intention of cutting costs further, but his profit forecasts failed to convince analysts, and Lufthansa's shares dropped 36 per cent. Worldwide the deregulated airline industry faced severe overcapacity in major markets and was predicted to be entering a phase of bankruptcies, consolidations, and mergers. Employees faced a difficult future, and passengers and freight customers could expect higher prices and reduced services as existing airlines disappeared or merged, even before the terrorist attacks in the United States in September further damaged prospects.[29]

Was Germany competitive? A journalistic account might carry the title "Germany, Inc." in reference to the many descriptions of Japanese business–government cooperation, but in fact the conclusion was that German managers were "defensive" and needed to escape the "self-contained, even incestuous" economic culture dominated by the Deutsche Bank and Allianz Insurance. The most successful had moved significant portions of their operations to the United States or allied themselves with American firms.[30] German exporters enjoyed great success in the newly developing post-Socialist economies of Eastern Europe, but Germany's overall share of the world market for manufacturing exports was declining, and the proportion of goods sourced externally by German firms had risen dramatically since the 1980s.

Some of the problem resulted from exchange rate changes. The strong mark made German goods more expensive in foreign markets, and foreign goods cheaper in Germany; after 2000 a strong Euro would have the same effect. In addition, structurally Germany remained specialized in what were now regarded as medium-level technologies, particularly non-electronic machinery, transportation equipment, and chemicals. Studies showed that, even in traditional core areas of manufacturing such as automobiles and machine tools, Germany had become less competitive. Overall, Germany lagged in cutting-edge technologies. The share of high technology industries (drugs and medicines, electronic goods, office and computing machinery, professional equipment, and aircraft) in both output and exports was lower than in either Japan or the United States.[31]

Small and medium-sized firms remained in general not competitive in the global market place. In 1996, there were 33,000 bankruptcies, and the chair of the Federation of Small Business claimed that two-thirds of small firms were "fighting for their lives" and demanded government aid to alleviate the looming "crisis in the Mittelstand."[32] Training programs for young workers, one of the proud traditions of Germany's employment system, continued to provide excellent instruction in skilled positions in industrial firms, but were criticized for concentrating on too narrow a range of skills and for inflexibility and inability to adapt to changes in technology.[33] The inherited system drilled young German workers in careful, attentive approaches to the details of their craft, but did not reward originality. It also remained gender-biased, built on the assumption that a worker would be male, and locally or regionally oriented.[34] In the context of the more open European Union and the world economies, these were disadvantages.

A longer-term problem shared with other Western European countries and Japan was the aging of the population. There were fewer children. Despite child support programs, the birth rate had declined below replacement levels. At the other end of the age distribution, the legal retirement age was 65, but, in the 1990s, half of workers retired earlier. Older workers thrown out of their jobs by restructuring and closure of firms in the East had often retired. A person who had been "wound down" at the age of 55 in 1990 could expect to live in retirement until 2020 or beyond. This exceptional bulge in numbers added to the underlying trend. The "elderly dependency ratio" relates the number of persons of 65 and over to the number of persons between the ages of 15 and 65. From just over 22 per cent in the late 1990s it was projected to rise to 55 per cent in 2035, meaning roughly that, instead of four persons of working age per retired person, there would be fewer than one. The unfunded obligations to provide for these large numbers of elderly people placed increasing pressure on government budgets.

One solution was higher rates of growth, achieved through increases in efficiency. Combined with this were calls to reduce social security benefits and wages. International agencies criticized Germany for its high levels of taxation and excessively generous welfare system. While 5 per cent of taxpayers paid 37 per cent of the revenue received from income tax, unemployment benefits could extend indefinitely. This lowered savings and therefore reduced investment, and also discouraged employers from taking on new workers. From the perspective of low-wage workers, the withdrawal of benefits as income increased in effect imposed marginal tax rates of 90 to 100 per cent, discouraging them from seeking jobs and trapping them in unemployment.[35] As seen below, the CDU/CSU–FDP coalition reduced taxes, and so too did the

SPD–Green coalition when they came to power. In addition, following international fashion, in 2001 Chancellor Schröder announced initiatives to apply information technology to the delivery of government services. By 2005, about 1200 government services would be available over the Internet. Echoing officials in many other countries, he said that this would unlock enormous potential gains in efficiency.

Another solution was to break the dependence on growth. In West Germany, campaigns by the APO and then the Greens had halted earlier ambitious plans to construct nuclear reactors to provide electricity. A government projection in 1979 had foreseen two new reactor plants opening each year until 2000. Direct protest action, combined with arguments about both the environmental dangers and the long-term economic viability of nuclear energy, altered policy, and in fact the last orders for new plants were placed in 1982. Following reunification, the low safety standards of East Germany's four nuclear power plants also caused a scandal. This meant that in Germany as elsewhere energy became more expensive. Restructuring the East German economy also meant coping with the environmental damage, again raising costs but also presenting an opportunity to evaluate alternative solutions.

The costs of growth could be seen in the significantly higher levels of allergic disease and obesity in West Germany than in East Germany at the time of reunification, attributed by allergy specialists to the higher levels of automobile exhaust fumes and greater reliance on processed food. East Germany's notorious haze resulted from coal not automobile exhaust, which had been less bad, and East Germans ate much higher proportions of fresh, unprocessed foods, which had been unambiguously good. Following reunification, the differences narrowed as Ossis (Easterners) began to eat the same processed foods as Wessis (Westerners). Children in the East became more likely to suffer allergic conditions, and the number suffering from obesity doubled.[36] Studies also showed a higher proportion of income in the eastern states went to purchase automobiles. The Trabant, the automobile that East Germans had waited for before reunification, but which became the despised symbol of a defunct system, continued to pose environmental problems because the chemical composition of its body made it difficult to dispose of safely. The new cars in the East were most often produced by West German subsidiaries of United States, Japanese, or Korean firms.

The social and cultural context: neo-realism as leitmotiv

Integration

The imposition of West German institutions on the East, as seen above in the economic sphere, was neither simple nor costless. It appeared that, rather than answering the German question, reunification had instead posed it again. Legal scholars earnestly debated whether or not the German Reich remained in legal existence, or not. The point was that the answer would determine the validity of specific laws dating from the imperial, Weimar, and Nazi periods. In fact, the specific answers reflected Germany's external position and an internal Conservative agenda. Constitutionally, for example, the Basic Law contained provisions for the reincorporation of the lost territories in the East (Article 23) and for a fundamental reconsideration of the form of government after reunification (Article 146). Ways were found to finesse these issues, disappointing both Conservative expellees and their descendants on the one hand, and leftists who wanted to reform the inherited West German system on the other. In the economic sphere, compensation for victims of the East German regime was limited to expropriated property owners. In social relations, the West German law prohibiting abortion was imposed on the East. Throughout, the emphasis on what lawyers call "black letter law" and what German lawyers refer to as the traditions of the *Rechtsstaat* allowed changes that affected many individuals to be presented in a manner that made them appear not only legal, but inevitable.[37]

Reunification had severe consequences for universities and for research in the physical and social sciences in East Germany. East German institutions had been quite severely out of touch in both teaching and research. However, the blanket adoption of West German research and teaching systems had the effect of reducing the number of academic positions, particularly in pure research. Industrial research carried out in the large state enterprises fell victim to their break-up and privatization. The Academy of Sciences was closed under the provisions of the reunification treaty, and many of the large university research institutes were closed. Some physical and biological scientists were absorbed by West German institutions or found places in new institutions, but those in less desirable areas generally lost their jobs. Scientists who had held upper-level party positions, who had cooperated with the security police, or who were otherwise ideologically "tainted" lost their jobs.[38] In the social sciences, entire fields of study that had received support, including any associated with Marxist philosophy or economics, were closed down. The results could be ugly indeed, with the publications of East German academics carefully picked over in order to justify their dismissal. Horst Groschopp, who had taught at Humboldt University since the early 1970s and published a series of books on labor history, including one translated into English, was dismissed in 1993. He was told he did not satisfy the "professional prerequisites" of his position because his work was "limited" in considering "exclusively working-class culture" without sufficient comparisons to other classes, and was "oriented around a not very subtly developed Marxist paradigm."[39]

In addition, following the reorganizations came a series of budget cuts to universities across reunified Germany. Overall, the system in the late 1990s, like many elsewhere in Europe, was diverse, rather amorphous, overcrowded, and underfunded. The abstract commitment to pure research remained, but the ideal of disinterested scholarship contrasted uneasily with the more concrete promise to provide tertiary education to all who desired it. The system was responsible for training very large numbers of students for white-collar careers, but in a rapidly changing environment. The rigidity of disciplinary boundaries worked against the flexibility in education that all recognized as necessary to cope with the very uncertain future.

Taxes, wealth, and class

Since the *Wende* of 1982, the CDU/CSU government had pressed reform of the tax system as one of its central policies. Mindful of the connections between growth, competitiveness, corporate restructurings and mergers, and jobs, Kohl and other leaders had emphasized the need to make West and then reunited Germany a more favorable location for investors. Kohl said in 1993,

> It is completely undeniable that there is a close connection between investments, growth and jobs on the one hand and the level of taxes and social insurance contributions on the other . . . with the "Location Protection Law" we have decided to lower taxes on commercial income noticeably . . . We wish thereby to encourage investments and to facilitate the creation of jobs.

Taxes on wages and personal consumption increased, while taxes on corporate incomes declined. The total share of tax revenue raised by taxes on profits declined from 35 per cent in the early 1960s, and 27 per cent in the late 1970s, to 12 per cent in the mid-1990s, while the share raised by the wages tax rose from 15 to over 35 per cent. The taxes paid by Siemens on its profits declined from 48 per cent in 1990–91 to 20 per cent in 1994–95.

The emphasis on the market and on exports posed problems for ordinary Germans. The government's concern to make Germany a more desirable investment location arose from the heavy flow of German capital outward, particularly to Eastern Europe and overseas to the United States. As with Siemens, large firms derived rising shares of their sales outside of Germany, in the case of chemical giants BASF, Bayer, and Heochst from 70 to 80 per cent of their turnover, and in the case of automobile manufacturer Daimler–Benz over 60 per cent in 1995. This was also true of their labor forces. The share of the foreign-based work force among BASF employees was 40 per cent, for Bayer 52 per cent, and for Hoechst 62 per cent. The Deutsche Bank cut its German work force by 15 per cent from 1992 to 1995, but increased its foreign-based work force, to 30 per cent of the total.

The effect of tax reform was a very large redistribution of wealth from individuals to corporations and from the less affluent to the wealthy. Jeremy Leaman has estimated that the net transfer of income away from wage-earning families to corporations amounted to nearly 800 billion marks from 1983 to 1996, and that the shift had accelerated from the early 1990s. This suggested that the economy had lost mass demand equivalent to over 540 billion marks. From a Keynesian economic perspective, the reduction in demand accounted for the sluggish rate of growth and persistent high unemployment.[40] Information on the distribution of wealth is scarce. Such as they are, the figures show that already in the early 1980s the top 10 per cent of households in West Germany possessed at least 48.8 per cent of all private assets, and the bottom 10 per cent only 2.4 per cent. Estimates in the early 1990s indicated that some 1.8 million households enjoyed incomes over 10,000 marks per month, the level at which a luxurious lifestyle could be combined with savings of 30 per cent of income or more. In 1996, the households headed by self-employed persons reported an average of over 20,000 marks per year in unearned income from their accumulated wealth. At the lower end of the spectrum, the number of welfare recipients had tripled since 1980.[41]

The 1.8 million households with enough income to consider the acquisition of significant new assets each year included many self-employed, either affluent professionals or owners of firms, senior executives in larger corporations, upper-level politicians and government officials, and smaller numbers of media and sports personalities. Some of them had inherited wealth from parents, grandparents, and great-grandparents. Clearly, being the child of one of these households guaranteed access to education, contacts to help in one's career, or entry into the family firm. Nevertheless, it was far more difficult than in previous generations to identify a cohesive ruling class. The visible marks of class had become far less visible, an effect of the pervasive forms of mass culture. Wealth and political power were no longer intertwined as they had been in the past. Competition for positions in large organizations was more open and transparent. The interlocking relationships that had allowed wealth to be transmitted across generations had become weaker, and the position of high-income earners less secure. The 33,000 bankrupts of 1996 had been high-income earners in 1995, and the entire small and medium business sector was under intense pressure. Life was not easier for those at the top in large corporations, entertainment, politics, or even in the bureaucracy, when the judgment of impersonal markets could change abruptly and blight or end a career.

Women

In the heady days of late 1989, a widely based women's movement emerged in East Germany. Local groups from throughout the country, academic feminists in Berlin, and reformist women within the SED Party apparatus and government agencies came together in the Independent Women's Association (*Unabhängiger Frauenverband* or UFV). For a few months, as they looked toward a reformed East German government, the leaders of the UFV also looked forward to playing an important role in that new structure. However, the organization was divided, especially between those who had belonged to oppositional movements and those who had belonged to the party. And when the elections were opened to West German parties, UFV leaders suddenly found themselves sidelined by parties that had always refused to give women real power.[42]

In the realm of gender relations, as elsewhere, reunification meant the imposition of West German structures. Economically women suffered disproportionately from the dislocation and then the privatization and winding down of state enterprises. Textiles, the industrial sector in which women were most heavily represented, contracted drastically. In other industries, West German norms of sex segregation and access to training sharply reduced opportunities for women. Legal changes impinged on women particularly severely. The issue of abortion had almost derailed the unification treaty. Legalized in East Germany in 1972, abortion was again criminalized after a two-year transition period. In this case, however, the final result was a compromise that eased access to reform for West German women. From 1995, a new national law allowed abortion on medical grounds. It prohibited all other abortions, but also provided that abortions in the first twelve weeks of pregnancy, though illegal, should not be punished.

With reunification, in East Germany the childcare previously available through neighborhood, university, and workplace centers disappeared. Hanna-Beate Schopp-Schilling, General Director of Women's Affairs in the Federal Ministry of Women and Youth, justified the loss of these and other rights on neo-realist grounds:

> I consider it politically naïve to expect that those specific rights which GDR women enjoyed within the context of an undemocratically governed society and a centrally planned socialist economy—and which were given to them less for reasons of equal rights and equal opportunities but for general economic and demographic reasons—should be adopted by the West German government and a West German society as a whole, which for the past 15 years did not find a political consensus to legislate these very rights for its women.[43]

This ignored the fact that the CDU/CSU had not only never attempted to create such a consensus, but had since its foundation campaigned and legislated to confine women to the roles of wives and mothers, and on two occasions taken the abortion issue to the Constitutional Court to have reform legislation overturned.

In the aftermath of reunification, the absence of feminist influence was striking. In *Run Lola Run*, almost as remarkable as the stereotyped gender structures is the fact that they are simply accepted without comment by the characters. Lola's mother does not appear, rejected by her husband, attacked by the mistress, and ignored by her daughter. The mistress's ambition is to force Lola's father to leave his wife and to marry her. In the final sequence the father walks out on her to meet his associate. The male, public realm takes precedence over the private, female realm. Manni assumes, and Lola accepts, that it is somehow Lola's responsibility to do something to free him from his predicament, without question and without recognition. Lola, as we see, is a strong runner and a resourceful friend, but at the end of the film she accepts Manni's failure even to ask what she has been doing.

An important reason for the marginalization of women's issues during and after reunification was the lack of coordination between the UFV and West German feminists. Frustrated by the defeat of the abortion reform bill in 1975, many West German feminists rejected mainstream politics and concentrated on local issues and grassroots projects. Explorations of patriarchy often portrayed women as victims of an ahistorical male violence, immutable and incapable of change. For instance, feminist film-maker Helke Sander's book and film *Liberator and Liberated* (*BeFreiter und Befreite*, 1992) emphasizes the large number of German women raped by Soviet soldiers at the end of the war. The film offers "projections" of 1.9 million raped women. The film, however, does not blame the Russians as such, but rather all men. The opening shots of Soviet soldiers posing with loot are accompanied by a voice that insists "just like in Kuwait, just like in Yugoslavia," and images of raped and murdered women by one that repeats "German women, Russian women, German women, Russian women." But, the images in fact come from the German films produced by Goebbels' propaganda ministry near the end of the war to portray the Russians as beasts that must be resisted at all costs. Sander is also the author of a short story that refers to the "exterminatory will" of the five books of Moses and the "literally murderous patriarchy" of the Old Testament, and is contemptuous of those who emphasize Jewish victims of the Holocaust. The purpose of the very high estimates of raped women is to bring the number of female victims of patriarchal violence toward parity with Jews murdered in the Holocaust, a "competitiveness about the status of victim" and "a lust for generally portraying women as victims that seems central to her particular historical and feminist agenda."[44]

As a result, although feminist initiatives played important roles in the lives of individual women, at the national level women's issues were left to sympathetic but not necessarily feminist parties, the SPD and the Greens. Writing in 1993, Dorothy Rosenberg was blunt: "In fact, aside from the unsuccessful abortion campaign, the West German feminist movement has agitated politically for none of the improvements in social welfare policy which have been implemented in the past 15 years."[45]

Their anti-state stance made West German feminists instinctively suspicious of the UFV's ambitions for a national role in a reformed East German state, but their isolation from national politics in West Germany also meant that they offered no alternative that might have ameliorated some of the negative effects of reunification on East German women.[46]

Whether they desired it or not, in the 1990s part-time work was the norm for many women. In 1988, 44 per cent of housewives in West Germany reported they would like to take paid employment, but 90 per cent said they could work only part-time because of their family responsibilities. The expense of childcare, the failure to provide lunches and the irregular hours at schools, and the necessity to supervise hours of homework in addition to time in school, all continued to exclude women from advanced training and from full-time jobs. In the late 1990s, over 30 per cent of women worked part-time, and four out of five women working part-time were married. In poor households wives had to work, in low-skill service industries such as retail, cleaning, and catering that provided no opportunity for further training or advancement. Full-time jobs declined as employers replaced their full-time workers with part-time employees who did not enjoy social insurance and fringe benefits. For women in particular, the clerical positions that expanded through the 1960s and 1970s now contracted as record keeping was increasingly computerized. For the one in five women working part-time who were single, in the 1990s as in the 1890s the pay they received was insufficient to support themselves. For women with full-time jobs, the gendered segmentation of the labor market and the glass ceiling that limited promotion opportunities meant that women earned less than 70 per cent of average male earnings.

Wayward youth

The peak and then decline in population was reflected in school enrollments. Primary students in West Germany rose to nearly 4 million in 1970, but had dropped to 2.4 million in 1985. Secondary enrollments peaked in 1978, and then they too declined. The percentage of students enrolled in a *Gymnasium* leading potentially to the *Abitur* and university continued to rise, though with declining numbers. As in other areas, following reunification East Germany adopted the West German system. This meant that the new state governments controlled education, but most adopted the West German structure, abandoning their comprehensive schools in favor of class-based separate tracks. Each of the new eastern states was adopted by a partner state in the West, and the advisors seconded to the East often stayed as permanent senior officials in the reorganized state education ministries.[47]

In 2001, Chancellor Schröder said that 95 per cent of German schools were already equipped with multimedia capable computers, and that by 2002 every school in the country would have Internet access. On the other hand, nearly one-third of primary school teachers were over fifty years old, and all teachers had been vetted by state authorities under the Radical Decree to ensure they had never had contacts with potentially subversive organizations. University and other tertiary sector enrollments continued to rise, but reorganization and cuts in budgets placed severe constraints on the quality of teaching.

The quality of education posed serious problems for the future, but, as with previous generations, it was what young people did outside of school that most concerned adults. Late entry into the labor market combined with high levels of affluence made youthful consumers a crucial market segment for the culture industries. Supported by their parents but continually interacting with peers of both sexes, young Germans, girls and boys on their way to becoming women and men, read magazines, listened to music, and above all purchased products designed to reflect their emerging personal identities. These identities were gendered and class specific. However, the traditional imposition of role definitions from the top down through the schools and legal system was less effective, as girls and boys studied together and increasingly studied similar subjects, and as girls and boys from all classes enjoyed more equal opportunities to move through secondary and on to tertiary education. Identities developed in dialog with the media and with products. Marketing research showed repeatedly that young people preferred to socialize with their peers, and that they responded to images more readily than to text. In 1999, the publishers of *BRAVO* collaborated with an opinion research institute to produce a full-scale report on the opinions and preferences of their target cohort of 14- to 18-year-olds, *Generation BRAVO*. Conscious that their readers resented authority, the editors minimized the number of overt advertisements and opted instead for repeated portrayals of branded items embedded in illustrations of stories and advice columns.

American models continued to dominate. Well over 80 per cent of the films shown in Germany were American. Germany was the third largest market for CDs in the world, behind the United States and Japan, but whereas in Japan native pop groups dominated hit lists, in Germany American or other English-speaking groups were the top sellers. The influence of American models could be seen even in the fad in the eastern states for rock bands from the former East Germany—"the more 'eastward leaning' (ostiger) the better"—including an underground boom in Sandow's "Born in the GDR."[48] It was also true of the enthusiasm for rap, popular among Turkish-German groups who ostentatiously emphasized the analogies between their position in Germany and Blacks in America.[49]

Mainstream youth publications avoided politics. A partial exception was portrayal of female empowerment, but this was shown as gaining freedom and sexual success through purchase of products designed to enhance physical attractiveness. Nevertheless, the old boundary between the public and private spheres had shifted. By implication, freedom and success were not only sexual but also financial, and success stories for both boys and girls involved jobs in media and information technologies as well as the fantasy world of models, actors, and musicians. Pop and rock music could be self-consciously feminist, left wing, and anti-racist, but it was more often simply romantic portrayals of heterosexual love. It could also be aggressively anti-feminine and could also deploy right-wing, racist, and even neo-Nazi tropes. In all cases the producers attempted desperately to stay the essential half-step ahead of the market, looking both for the profitable niche among definable subcultures and for the subcultural style with "crossover" appeal that could be sold to the mainstream.

Young German women and men typically reported themselves as uninterested in or "bored" by politics. However, the violence against foreigners that followed reunification was committed overwhelmingly by young people, mostly but not exclusively male. Through 1991 and peaking in 1992, a series of individual assaults, violent demonstrations, riots, and firebombings of immigrant hostels shocked the country. Seventy per cent of those arrested for acts of racist violence in 1992 were between sixteen and twenty-one years old. Surveys showed 28 per cent of all German youth were hostile to foreigners, especially asylum seekers. In the East the figure was 54 per cent, and was accompanied by disturbing levels of anti-Semitism, despite relatively low proportions of foreigners and the virtual absence of Jews in the East. Anti-foreign violence was not the same thing as neo-Nazism. Police reports indicated that only a small fraction of the perpetrators of the violence were linked to established right-wing organizations. More of them came from the small groups in the right-wing youth subculture. Most were non-political in any organized sense, but responded to a vague sense of "Germany for Germans."[50]

Citizenship and identity

But what was Germany and who were the Germans? In 1990, a loosening of restrictions on the naturalization of second and third-generation foreigners, and more frequent granting of dual citizenship, meant that among the communities of "foreigners" there were more with German citizenship. The severe restrictions on asylum seekers passed in 1993 worked in the other direction, but the greater freedom of movement within the EU and potentially more liberal immigration policies adopted by the EU as a whole would open Germany further.[51] There are no migrants in *Run Lola Run*. All of the characters are "German," and again the film does not comment but simply represents this as a fact by excluding non-"German" faces. There is also no working class, and the only hint that all Germans are not all alike is a procession of Catholic nuns that impedes Lola as she runs up a street. There is no reason for this scene, and it can only be read as a distant echo of the old suspicion that Catholics were a hindrance to Germany's progress.

The debate over German identity was not merely academic; it impinged on the lives of ordinary people every day. In mid-1997, on a flight from Sydney to Amsterdam were seated a family group, father, mother, and three children aged between roughly six and eleven. Black-haired, very dark-skinned, with aquiline features, they were conversing in fluent colloquial German with a strong Swabian accent. They were Turkish. Both the father and the mother were children of "guest workers" who had migrated to West Germany in the 1950s. The father had completed his *Abitur* before joining his father in business. The mother had completed secondary school and had an additional teaching certificate. The children will almost certainly all go on to university. They were returning home after a holiday in Australia.

The conversation turned to the role of religion in politics. The family are Muslim. They consider themselves "devout," although the mother and daughter do not cover their heads. They felt emphatically that religion is a personal matter and should be kept separate from public life. The father in particular emphasized that it is "highly dangerous" to mix religion and politics. However, the cautionary example he had in mind was not contemporary Islamic fundamentalism, but "Luther's Reformation" and the religious wars of the sixteenth century. He was not making invidious comparisons; this was simply the example from the German history learned in school that would come to mind for a member of the educated middle classes.

The members of this family are not German citizens. They are excluded from full participation in German society by the immigration law that restricts automatic German citizenship to those with "German blood." The detailed application of the law has so far excluded their children from citizenship as well. They personally have suffered only minor and irritating instances of discrimination, some of them amusing, for instance the repeated question, "Where are you from?" "Stuttgart." "Yes, but where are you *really* from?" They have friends who were injured in 1992, and they worry about their children's safety in the streets at night. The father and mother are resigned to the situation, but they are hopeful that the law will someday be changed so their children "may be allowed to become what they are—German."

Culture

One of the requirements for naturalization remained a clear identification with German culture. But was there a "German" culture? Official ideologies in the arts remained suspect and subject to continued questioning. This could come from the left, from the right, or from supposedly apolitical artists and writers, who moved away from the self-referential works that typified postmodernism, but who adopted painting practices and writing forms that often leave meanings deliberately obscure. The popularity of conservative authors could be read as a symptom of neo-realism, but also as nostalgia for the days when German was unambiguously a world language across the arts, sciences, and social sciences. Ernst Jünger continued writing through a long postwar career to his death in 1999, including a description of his drug experiences published in 1970 and *A Dangerous Meeting* (*Eine gefährliche Begegnung*, 1985), a novel centered on the clash of aristocratic characters with the machine age. Carl Schmitt lost his teaching position at the Friedrich-Wilhelm University (Humboldt University) in 1945, but he lived until 1985 and continued to publish on constitutional law, including a study of the distinction between "enemy" and "criminal" in 1950. Martin Heidegger remained a professor at Freiburg until his death in 1976. His later work identified technology as the culmination of Western metaphysics, and he argued that technology's attempt to understand reality as purely objective must fail, because "being" is not an object and therefore requires a different means of expression.

All three benefited from their alienation from the Nazi regime, as their supporters could minimize the support they had given the Nazis and emphasize the positive aspects of their thought. Heidegger's conception of man's position in the universe and his doubts about technology continue to interest philosophers. His concern with the impact of technology has influenced the more recent work of Anselm Kiefer.[52] Schmitt's studies of modern society, the role of the state, and his critique of liberal democracy were all translated in new English editions in the late 1970s and 1980s and enjoyed renewed popularity with political scientists. Jünger's consistent anti-democratic elitism, his estheticism, and his celebrations of sacrificial death continued to be controversial, but his distinctive style and his emphasis on the need somehow to preserve individuality in the homogenized mass society of the modern world also continued to attract readers.

If there was a German culture, what should it be? Botho Strauss argued in 1989, in a special issue of *Der Spiegel* marking Adolf Hitler's one hundredth birthday, that all German writing was haunted by "the ugliest German." In another *Spiegel* essay in 1993 he denounced the "disastrous" state of German culture and German politics, both before and after reunification. He sharply criticized the left and accused them of abandoning any project that might even hint at nation-building. Born in 1944, Strauss had been a prominent playwright since the 1970s. Often identified as a postmodern author because of his subjectivity and refusal of authorial statement, he nonetheless repeatedly asserted the need for myth, for some form of transcendental belief to ground human existence. His novel *The Young Man* (*Der Junge Mann*, 1984), with its multiple layers, interweaving of novellas, satirical set pieces, and other structures recalls Goethe's *Wilhelm Meister*. It has been seen as an attempt to come to terms with the evolving relationship between German culture and historical consciousness, and also more ambitiously as an attempt to define a notion of "right" living free of the taint of politics and grounded in an abstract philosophical vision.

Like those of many on the right, Strauss' arguments were elliptical, implicit, and often difficult to extract. His prose, even in the eyes of sympathetic readers, became nearly impenetrable, in *Congress: The Chain of Humiliations* (*Kongress: Die Kette der Demütigungen*, 1989), *Fragments of Ambiguity* (*Fragmente der Undeutlichkeit*, 1989), and *Without Beginning* (*Beginnlosigkeit*, 1992). Strauss believed in the notion of a German nation and a German culture, and asserted the position of the poet/author as a privileged visionary, but he was suspicious of linear argument and dubious of the possibility of achieving a simple correspondence between meaning and its representation. A sympathetic argument would say he left readers themselves to extract meaning from his texts, or indeed from Germany's history; critics suspect his motives and believe his underlying message to be reactionary, and some have accused him of "Fascist" tendencies.[53]

Many prominent East German authors and artists had opposed reunification. Christa Wolf urged East Germans not to leave but to stay and help reform their country. This was not a popular position, and, as seen above, those working for a reformed East Germany were swept aside. In 1990, Wolf published an account of a day spent under police surveillance, *What Remains* (*Was bleibt*), which she had written in 1979. The publication and the timing suggested self-pity and opportunism at the same time. She was accused of enjoying a privileged position as a "state author" and of supporting a regime despite knowing its repressive nature. She was then caught up in the stream of revelations concerning those who had reported on their associates, friends, and families to the Stasi. The debate broadened into an attack on East German writers and their work in general, for not having opposed the regime forthrightly. Conservative West German commentators insisted that the East German government was totalitarian, essentially the same as the Nazi regime, and therefore denounced anyone who had collaborated.[54]

A number of writers on the left in West Germany portrayed reunification as a brutal takeover of East Germany by West Germany. Rolf Hochhuth's play *Westerners in Weimar—Scenes from an Occupied Country* (*Wessis in Weimar—Szenen aus einem besetzten Land*, 1993) met with outrage even before its premiere. Chancellor Kohl denounced Hochhuth and the play, as Chancellor Erhard had attacked *The Deputy*. In the opening scene, the president of the *Treuhand* is murdered, which was in fact what happened to Detlev Rohwedder, the trust's first president. Subsequent scenes portray the actions of the *Treuhand* as an occupation, an occasion for civil war. Hochhuth disowned the production, but the director accused Hochhuth of revising the published version to make it less inflammatory.[55]

Günter Grass was particularly scathing, and in his fictionalized account of reunification and winding down he added the additional element of "the—alas—weather-resistant anti-Semitism in this country." In *Too Far Afield* (*Ein breites Feld*, 1995), an East German legal scholar, who is Jewish, commits suicide after being dismissed from his university post following a drawn-out inquisitorial "evaluation" process. The main character, Theo Wuttke, finally leaves Germany: "I must get out, get far, far away! . . . Everything tells me: Get out of this country, where, for all eternity, Buchenwald lies down the road from Weimar." Wuttke is an elderly semi-retired filing clerk working in Goering's air ministry building, formerly used by the East German government, and now the home of the *Truehand*. He had a career as a lecturer for the East German culture ministry. A specialist in the life and works of novelist Theodor Fontane, he has adopted Fontane's personal habits and dress and believes himself possibly to be Fontane's reincarnation. The neo-realism of the text emerges in the way in which Grass portrays these mannerisms as the affectation of a slightly dotty but likeable old man, rather than in the way that for instance Oskar in *The Tin Drum* remembers his own birth and literally decides to remain physically a child.

Grass pairs Wuttke with another character named Hoftaler, an official in the state security bureaucracy, Wuttke's "day and night shadow," who has had him under surveillance for so many years that they have become firm friends. In fact, Hoftaler worked for the Nazi regime and followed Wuttke's youthful involvement with the French underground during the war, and after the winding down of the Stasi, he moves smoothly to a new assignment under the unified German government. Further, as Wuttke may be the reincarnation of Theodor Fontane, so Hoftaler may be the reincarnation of the police official who dogged Fontane through the middle decades of the nineteenth century. Fontane is never mentioned by name, but Grass adopts Fontane's flowing, oblique style and uses continual quotations and references from Fontane's works to drive home his message that nothing has changed, that all the negative aspects of the German character and all the repressive aspects of German institutions remain.

The political context: the search for a new national identity

The global public sphere

The rhetoric of globalization and competitiveness deployed by political leaders and international agencies was questioned. The assumption that market solutions would be the right ones did not satisfy workers who lost their jobs or small businesses facing ruin. It also did not satisfy large firms when their own interests were at stake. And, despite their rhetoric, it also did not satisfy political leaders when national interests were threatened, or when too many of their constituents protested and threatened to vote for their opponents. Inchoate protests led to a series of violent confrontations at international meetings.

Jürgen Habermas offered a different critique of globalization, one based on his previous description of the public sphere and his analysis of the pathologies of modernity. If the public sphere is the arena where free and equal persons can come together and discuss issues of common concern rationally, then the agreements reached in the public sphere can be implemented by a properly constructed state. Habermas was far from believing that the German state was perfect, or indeed that the national state as such was perfect, caught as it was between the opposed principles of inclusion of all members of the national community and exclusion of outsiders. Nevertheless, the public realm, if it could be made to operate in a number of national states, did open the possibility that the citizens of those states might decide to cooperate. If members of one national community could recognize others as both different and equal, the resulting "public, discursively structured formation of opinion" would also "make a rational political understanding possible among foreigners." The integration of the European Union might foreshadow what appeared on the face of it to be a Utopian project, the creation of a genuinely cosmopolitan world order.

However, said Habermas, economic globalization and a corresponding reduction of the capacity for action of Western liberal states had undermined this project. The subsystems of the market economy and the administrative state had continued their colonization and impoverishment of the lifeworld. More concretely and more immediately, they had also removed the causes of economic and social problems beyond the confines of single states. Thus national governments found themselves unable to cope with mass unemployment, poverty, migration, and environmental damage. Further, because the causes lay beyond their borders, so did the solutions. Habermas suggested that regional solutions, for instance by the European Union, were likely only to reproduce destructive competition among individual nations at a higher level, among the EU, the United States, and Asian blocs (it has to be added that he was less well informed about Asia than about Europe and the United States). The logic of the global situation, said Habermas, called for global solutions, and his analysis attempted not only to present an inclusive sense of global citizenship and action as a norm, but also to explain why in the current situation the norm was unlikely to be realized. Most importantly, perhaps, at present "the governing elites have to concern themselves with consensus and re-election within their own national arenas," and this lessened the likelihood that they would do what they ought to do, that is, to attempt "to initiate a debate on the future of Europe, and in the process articulate interests that cross national boundaries."[56]

Parties and elections

The major parties in reunified Germany were indeed far more interested in reelection than in articulating interests across national boundaries. Predictably, in 1990 the CDU/CSU rode to victory in the aftermath of reunification. Under Oskar Lafontaine the SPD was punished both for its hesitancy and vacillation during the negotiation and ratification of the unity treaties, and for its perceived inability to manage the economy successfully. Then, again predictably, Kohl and the CDU/CSU lost popularity when they failed to master the economic problems of reunification. More difficult to predict was the series of tactical errors that new SPD leader Rudolf Scharping committed during the 1994 campaign. The CDU/CSU and the FDP lost votes, but managed nevertheless to win an election many observers believed they must lose. In 1998, in turn, despite economic recovery nationally and substantial expansion in the East, the CDU/CSU suffered large losses, the SPD increased its vote beyond the symbolic 40 per cent, and new Chancellor Gerhard Schröder entered office at the head of a coalition of the SPD and Greens.

Both of the major parties confronted challenges. The SPD now had two rivals on the left, the Greens and the Party of Democratic Socialism (PDS), the revived East German SED, now committed to democratic competition and portraying itself as a defender of social justice. The

CDU/CSU also faced a new rival on the right in addition to the FDP, the Republicans (*Die Republikaner* or REP). In addition, specialists noted that both the SPD and the CDU were in fact coalitions of groups with opposed interests. The SPD contained a "materialist" wing devoted to economic growth and the more direct interests of the party's traditional working-class constituency, and a "post-materialist" wing closer to the Greens that was more concerned with the environment and with social reform. The CDU encompassed groups committed to social reform and groups opposed, and also included broadly secular as well as traditionalist conservative Catholic groupings. Scanning the opinion polls, many observers also detected a widespread disillusionment (*Verdrossenheit*) with elections and with parties. As in the case of young people, this could lead to reduced participation in elections, and this would hurt the major parties the most, since the small parties' more focused commitment to specific issues meant their core constituencies were relatively more reliable.

Among the small parties, the Greens adhered to what at first glance appears a relatively simple and appealing set of principles: concern for the environment, nonviolence, participatory grassroots democracy, and a broad "social responsibility." However, they had great difficulty defining consistent policies to deal with specific issues. In part this reflected their internal divisions. A mix of a very broad spectrum of opinion, they included the genuinely "green" environmentalists, a "brown" element opposed to capitalism and industrialism with roots in the pre-First World War and Nazi youth movements, and "red" groups ranging from Communists to anarchists and syndicalists. Decision-making was slowed by the principle of consensus, which often meant that extreme minority positions exercised an effective veto over the majority. To prevent the growth of an entrenched party apparatus, the Greens adopted a principle of rotating representation. All Green representatives were replaced half-way through each parliamentary session. The only exception was Petra Kelly, who served from 1983 to 1990, stepping down when her Bavarian district voted to limit candidates to serving a maximum of two legislative periods. She had been named as a Green candidate for the 1994 European Parliament elections, but died in 1992.

The Greens split between two broad factional groupings divided over tactics. The "Realists" (*Realos*) were more willing to work within the existing system to achieve specific if limited goals, whereas "Fundamentalists" (*Fundamentalos* or *Fundis*) believed that only a continued position of radical opposition could prevent their principles from being compromised. The specific issue was whether to cooperate with other parties. In the early 1980s, they joined in a coalition with the SPD in Hesse, but their state environment minister Joschka Fischer was caught between uncompromising grassroots Green activists on the one hand and obstructionist industry groups and bureaucratic officials on the other. The divisions between the two factions effectively paralyzed the national party in the mid-1980s.

The Greens initially opposed reunification. They favored reform in East Germany that would reflect the desires of people in the East and opposed the proposed "takeover" of the East by the West. Faced with overwhelming public support for reunification, they then accepted unity, but only grudgingly. In the 1990 elections, in the West they refused to ally with other parties, and dropped below the 5-per-cent line. In the East, they allied with civil rights groups (*Bündnis 90*), and because of the transitional provision for separate voting lists they gained seats. The Fundamentalists left to form their own party in 1991. In addition, dissatisfaction with the process of reunification made the Greens' initial opposition seem less obtuse than before. In 1994 with 7.8 per cent and again in 1998 with 7.3 per cent they won more votes than the FDP, and in 1998 entered government with the SPD.

The FDP had already begun to shift its platform toward the right from the late 1970s. The Freiburg Theses of 1971 had expressed a social reformist outlook corresponding to the coalition with the Socialists in 1969. However, the Kiel Theses of 1977 and the Liberal Manifesto of 1985 emphasized reliance on individual initiative and especially on the market to solve social problems, early expressions of the neo-realist style in economic management. Leader Otto Lambsdorff argued in favor of market solutions to environmental protection, such as payments by firms for permission to pollute. The FDP continued to present itself as a balancing force in politics, but now glossed with an additional responsibility to preserve the free market in ideas and political options by avoiding the "sole rule" (*Alleinherrschaft*) of either of the two large parties. Both the Socialists and the Christian Democrats, argued the FDP, were statist, whether they advocated "Socialism" in the guise of social reform, or "clericalism" in the guise of social order.[57]

In the 1990 elections the FDP achieved its best result ever, 11 per cent of the national vote and over 13 per cent in the East. During the debate over reunification, Lambsdorff opposed any new taxes to finance reunification. He later recanted and admitted he had underestimated the economic and financial difficulties of reconstructing the East German economy. In the meantime, as forthright exponents of the market, the FDP benefited from the revulsion against Socialism. In addition, Hans-Dietrich Genscher, long-serving foreign minister, had been born in Halle in 1927. After serving briefly in the war he had studied law in East Germany, before fleeing to the West in 1952. He was among many West German leaders who had cultivated contacts in the East, and as a native Easterner enjoyed great popularity there.

FDP success in the 1990 elections enabled Lambsdorff to survive a challenge to his leadership. He resigned as planned in 1993, following Genscher who had retired in 1992. However, the intended generational shift preceding the next election failed to throw up either convincing leaders or credible policies.[58] In 1994, tactical voting by CDU/CSU supporters, according to some estimates more than 1.5 million, saved the FDP from dropping below the 5-per-cent line and out of the Bundestag. In 1998 they survived again, but with a further reduced share of 6.2 per cent of the national vote.

On the far right, the National Democratic Party and the German People's Union remained confined to the older right-wing subculture. The Republicans (REP) aimed for a broader constituency. The party was formed in Bavaria in 1985. Founding leader Franz Schönhuber had belonged to the circle of Conservative Catholic politicians around Franz Josef Strauss. He was also a media personality, deputy editor of the Bavarian television network, newspaper editor, columnist, and talk show host. He published an autobiography, in which he was frank about his service in the Waffen-SS, he did not conceal his early admiration for Hitler, and he was scornful of other ex-Nazis in public life who had hidden their involvement. The book caused a scandal, and he was dismissed. He portrayed his sacking as an example of the very hypocrisy he had denounced, and when he sued the courts found his dismissal unlawful and the book not to be an (illegal) glorification of the Nazi regime.

The Republicans were not successful in state elections until January 1989 in Berlin. The issue they discovered was the growing numbers of foreign migrants. Instead of the circumlocutions of the major parties, the REP campaigned on the blunt assertion that Germany was not and should not become an "immigrant state," swamped by "alien" cultures. The anti-immigrant campaign of the REP intersected with the attacks on foreigners in 1992.[59] Internal factionalism then led to a split, though not to dissolution. The REP won 8.3 per cent of the vote in Hesse in 1993, but in the Bundestag elections they failed in both 1994 and 1998 even to approach the 5-per-cent level. An important part of their program had been hijacked by the major parties. The CDU/CSU, with the support of their FDP partners and also with the support of the SPD, passed a revision to the Basic Law that severely restricted the rights of foreigners to seek political asylum in Germany. From another direction, the REP also suffered from a popular backlash from grassroots citizens' movements opposed to anti-foreignism and racism. Mass demonstrations against racism brought tens of thousands into the streets, more people in fact than the REP or any other right-wing party could ever mobilize.

In the aftermath of the 1998 election, the CDU was thrown into a crisis when a scandal involving illegal campaign contributions led to the resignation of the defeated Helmut Kohl, who refused to name the contributors involved, and left the party struggling with a large debt. Under Schröder, the "Red—Green" coalition introduced a tax reform to reduce taxes on wage earners. However, the loss of revenue had to be funded by cuts in welfare expenditures, and the government, with a view to the impending rise in the number of retired persons, also announced plans for reductions in pension entitlements. Lafontaine, originally finance minister and broadly Keynesian in approach, resigned and was replaced by Hans Eichel, a pragmatic neo-realist. These changes created severe tensions with the Greens, and did nothing to alleviate the continued suffering in the East, where the SPD and Greens did badly in a series of state elections.

For the future, the government hoped its information technology program would boost the economy. In addition, Schröder, speaking to a conference of senior federal government officials, insisted that e-government would streamline government services, making the bureaucracy more efficient, transparent, and user-friendly. He said, "I am convinced such modernisation will change our understanding of administration, the tasks of the state and citizens' self-determination." The first positive steps were confined to applications for identity cards, drivers' licenses, and passports. In addition, interior minister Otto Schilly announced that elections would also soon be conducted over the Internet. Online voting in local and state elections could be possible as early as 2006, and in federal elections by 2010.[60]

Germany, the European Union, and a world with one superpower

Two incidents may be cited to indicate the sometimes painful relations between Germany and the world's hegemonic power. In March 1999, Chancellor Schröder visited Washington. High on his agenda was the hope that the United States would agree to return the files of the East German Stasi, spirited away by the United States Central Intelligence Agency following the fall of the Berlin Wall. The so-called "crown jewels" of the East German security apparatus are said to contain the identities, code names, and other vital data of thousands of Stasi foreign agents, the vast majority of whom of course worked in West Germany. Total numbers of West Germans working for East Germany are believed to range from 20,000 to 30,000. The CIA, however, insisted that the files could not be handed over to Germany, because doing so would jeopardize American agents still at large. The American government accepted that view, and President Clinton refused even to discuss the issue with Schröder. Schröder publicly announced there had not been enough time to discuss the files, but let it be known that he was outraged at the insult to German sovereignty. A senior official remarked that it was ironic that the United States, a champion of free speech and openness, should ally itself with former Communists and their sympathizers, who might still be at large and holding influential positions in Germany.[61]

Schröder had also promised during the election campaign that under him Germany would abandon its postwar policy of non-assertiveness in international affairs. He demonstrated this new assertiveness by insisting that Germany had the right to nominate a German to become the new head of the International Monetary Fund. The headquarters of the IMF are located in Washington, but the United States generally accepts that the head will be a European. United States officials indicated they were happy to accept a German, provided the nomination was backed by the rest of the EU. Schröder nominated the German deputy finance minister, Caio Koch-Weser, and began organizing support for him among EU members. However, Larry Summers, United States Secretary of the Treasury, told US President Clinton that Koch-Weser was unacceptable, and persuaded Clinton to veto the nomination. For Schröder the Clinton veto was a serious embarrassment.

Furious, Schröder dropped Koch-Weser and nominated a second candidate, Horst Koehler, a banker who had served as chief economic advisor to former Chancellor Helmut Kohl. Europeans agreed Koehler was a very good choice, but in Washington Summers was still unhappy, and was only persuaded to accept Koehler reluctantly after high-level contacts and lobbying efforts. Michael Steiner, senior economic advisor to Schröder, said, "we have discovered that the superpower sees its global role not only in the military area but also in setting the rules of globalization through the IMF. But Europeans are also gaining consciousness of themselves and cannot share the view that the role of the IMF is to simply transmit the philosophy of the superpower."[62]

Schröder also favored a federal European government. This intersected with the government's budget problems, as a stronger European executive might be able to deal more effectively with the social problems of slow growth, and if necessary confront the European Central Bank. He proposed to transform the current unelected European Commission into a governmental body headed by a president, probably to be elected by the European Parliament. Schröder's plan resembled the German federal system in some respects. However, Britain, France, and Spain all seemed opposed to any substantial increase in the powers of a central EU government. It was also not clear how the United States would react to a genuinely united Europe able to act as a great power in its own right.

The past that has still not gone away

The search for a German history

Two competing interpretations of reunification emerged almost immediately, supported by two definitions of the German national identity and two views of German history.[63] The official West German version became a heroic tale of liberation and unification, of narrow windows of opportunity seen and of fleeting chances seized. This version also celebrated the victory of capitalism over Socialism, and of democracy over Communism. Helmut Kohl, the "unification Chancellor," became a hero to be compared to Bismarck. The problems of adjustment had been ameliorated by generous support, a successful implementation of the principles of West Germany's traditional social market economy in a new situation. The official version of reunification extended backward in time. Not only was Kohl compared to Bismarck, but also Bismarck's empire was given a positive evaluation by a broad range of historians.[64] The underlying assumption was that there was nothing questionable or problematic in the statement that "the Germans should be and want to be one nation," the title of a newspaper piece by Thomas Nipperdey.[65]

The alternative version lamented the missed opportunity of the popular revolution. Rather than resourceful, Kohl was portrayed as either clueless or duplicitous. The imposition of West German capitalism on East Germany was not a triumph but a disaster leading to mass unemployment and ruined lives. Socially, the imposition of the West German legal system disadvantaged groups in East Germany, particularly women, who had enjoyed substantial benefits under the Socialist regime.[66] The alternative version also implied a selective reading of history. Hans Magnus Enzensberger, writer and essayist since the 1940s, asked in "The Great Migration" (1992), "What, then, is so special about the Germans?" Xenophobia is a universal phenomenon, but the extreme form, and the extreme polarization of Germans, has not caused the "historical guilt" felt by Germans. Rather, "the causes go further back. They lie in the precarious self-consciousness of the nation. It is a fact that Germans like neither each other nor themselves [and] someone who dislikes himself is going to find it difficult to love those who are not even his neighbours."[67] Günter Grass believed the very existence of a single German state posed a risk:

> A complex-riddled megalomania induced the Germans to forfeit their opportunity to establish themselves as a nation based on a common culture in a federal state and instead with ruthless single-mindedness to force through the foundation of a unitary state in the form of an empire. It was the initial precondition for Auschwitz . . . Whoever reflects about Germany and seeks answers to the German question must automatically think about Auschwitz.[68]

Divided memory

The past therefore continues to divide Germans. In this, Germany does not differ from other countries. Anti-Semitism remains widespread around the world, and there are professional Holocaust deniers in a number of countries.[69] There are uncomfortable events in the past histories of all countries. Where current agendas overlap with historical memory, history is mobilized and reinterpreted in the service of those agendas.[70] But in Germany, overt anti-Semitism and attempts to relativize or minimize the ugly past appear exceptionally problematic. Where Germany does differ from other countries may be in the exceptional sensitivity of public opinion to these attempts. Germany's past history itself ensures that history is never "merely" history.

At the level of popular culture, Joseph Vilsmeier's *Stalingrad* (1992), from the same production team as *The Boat*, continued to portray German soldiers as ordinary men simply caught up in the extraordinary situation of the battle, although there are now "bad" as well as "good" Germans. The film shows its central characters struggling stoically against both the Russian foe on the one hand, and the brutality of the rigid German military hierarchy on the other. They are condemned to dangerous mine clearing when they force a doctor to treat one of their comrades, and thwart a sudden Russian tank attack. They have a chance to flee on the final flight out of the encircled city, but decide to stay. They attempt to avoid shooting civilian prisoners when ordered to do so, and they refuse to participate in the rape of a Russian woman soldier. All eventually die, including the Russian woman, who is shot by unseen Russian soldiers in the film's final scene.

When portrayals of the Nazi period strayed outside of the conventional bounds, they became controversial. We can contrast the reception of the *Holocaust* television miniseries with that of the film *Hitlerjunge Salomon* (1992), released internationally with the title *Europa, Europa*. The title recalls *Hitlerjunge Quex*. In this case, the story is based on the account of a Holocaust survivor, Salomon Perel, who escaped death first by fleeing to Poland and then by pretending to be an ethnic German (*Volksdeutsche*). The production of *Holocaust* was shallow and sentimental, but, as noted in Chapter 14, the characters were solid members of the educated middle classes, and German viewers found them easy to identify with. Salomon is a far more interesting and much less instantly likeable character. His main problem is his circumcized penis, which if revealed would give him away instantly. His story, very funny at times, reveals the corruption, banality, and stupidity of the Germans as he manipulates situations in order to escape discovery. Equally significantly, the *Holocaust* series was American, but *Hitlerjunge Salomon* was German. *Hitlerjunge Salomon* was very successful internationally and particularly in the United States, but it was not popular in Germany. It was harshly criticized, precisely because it was a German production, for being cheap sentimental melodrama, unworthy of its theme. And it was then rejected as a possible German entry for the Academy Awards, apparently on the dubious grounds that the director, Agnieszka Holland, was Polish.[71]

Public history also remained contentious. The basements of the Gestapo headquarters in Berlin, accidentally uncovered in 1987, became a permanent "site of memory" but probably would not have survived the sudden jump in real estate values following reunification. In 1993, a life-size cloth replica of the façade of the eighteenth-century royal palace was erected in Berlin, and set off a debate over whether the original building—or even perhaps only its façade—should be reconstructed.[72] In 1995 and 1996, a traveling exhibition mounted by the Hamburg Institute for Social Research on the atrocities committed by the regular army in the East during the war attracted large audiences but caused an uproar, particularly in Munich. There, 90,000 viewers endured waiting times of up to three hours, but the official CSU newspaper accused the exhibitors of faking the photographs, and described the exhibition as an attempt "to sharpen the punitive measures of Nürnberg against Germany and carry on a campaign of extermination against the German people." When 5000 right-wing extremists attempted to demonstrate, they were blocked by a counter-demonstration of some 10,000 people assembled by labor unions, Young Socialists, Antifascist Action, and the Greens.[73]

As had happened before in the disputes over Fritz Fischer and Ernst Nolte's works, Daniel Goldhagen's 1996 book, *Hitler's Willing Executioners*, created a controversy among professional historians that spilled over into the public realm. Goldhagen, as noted in Chapter 12, accused all Germans of sharing an "eliminationist anti-Semitism" and therefore made all Germans equally guilty of perpetrating the Holocaust.[74] Condemned by many professional historians for its methodological weaknesses and overinterpretation of a narrow range of evidence, the book nevertheless became a best-seller in German translation. Goldhagen was warmly received and supported by appreciative audiences at lectures across Germany. This may result from one of the book's major inconsistencies, the assertion that in 1945 Germans suddenly abandoned their alleged centuries old anti-Semitism, thereby laying the foundation for postwar democracy and successful integration into the Western community of nations. This comforting interpretation meant that, while reading his graphic portrayals of the violence against Jews, none of Goldhagen's readers or listeners would see themselves among his perpetrators. More optimistically, it may reflect a general increase in the willingness of ordinary Germans to read and reflect on all aspects of their history.[75]

Professional historians also came to an accounting with the involvement of their own profession in the Nazi period. A session at the 1998 meeting of the German Historians' Association featured papers detailing the careers of several prominent historians under the Third Reich, and their subsequent concealment of their activities. As with other professions, historians not only accepted the Nazi regime, but also offered interpretations of history that supported Hitler's expansionist and racist agendas. Several, especially Werner Conze and Theodor Schieder, became prominent leaders of the profession in the postwar era, and as such were the teachers and mentors of the subsequent generation of historians. The accusations at the 1998 meeting were leveled not only at those who had served the Nazis directly, but also at their students, now themselves the senior leaders of the profession, who sometimes knew but said nothing of their teachers' involvement. The subsequent controversy involved not only reputations, but also disputes over the relative merits of different methods of historical research.[76] As with the Goldhagen debate, this could reflect simply point-scoring by younger scholars, or those whose methodologies had been denigrated by the accused or their students, or, more optimistically, it could indicate a broader readiness to confront the past.

A concluding symbol

Christo's wrapping the Reichstag in 1995 stands as a symbol of the ambiguous nature of that German past—hidden, closed, ominous, concealing some portentous and possibly dangerous secret. This was not Christo's intent. He said, "fabric, like clothing or skin, is fragile," and "will create a sumptuous flow of vertical folds . . . revealing the essence of the building's architecture." This was slightly disingenuous, for the fabric and its steel framework in fact were very high-strength and fireproof. It was also not the intent of the politicians who favored the project. Aware that Germany must continually prove its commitment to democracy, they intended that the "seeming iconoclasm" of the wrapping would be a totally unambiguous symbol of Germany's new tolerant disposition, "visual proof" of its definitive acceptance of Western values. "It is good for the building, for the German parliament and German democracy, at home and abroad," said the spokesperson in the Bundestag debate. Best of all, it could be done "without spending one penny of the taxpayers' money," because Christo Business Limited would underwrite all costs, recouping expenses through the sale of pre and after-project memorabilia, and promised a profitable surge in tourism during the two weeks of the proposed wrapping.[77] It would make the world forget the anti-foreign violence, the economic collapse in the East, the silencing of dissent, and all the other mournful footsteps echoing through Germany's two hundred years of modern history. Like so many texts, it deconstructed itself, and like so many events over that history, its meaning remained for each generation to discover for itself.

Notes

1. *Run Lola Run (Lola Rennt)*, 1999, written and directed by Tom Tykwer, starring Franka Potente and Moritz Bleibtreu; *Run Lola Run: The Soundtrack*, X-Filme Creative Pool GmbH/Warner Music, 1999.
2. Jarausch 1994; Maier 1997, Ch. 5.
3. Jarausch 1994.
4. Jarausch 1994, p. 24.
5. Wierling 1996, p. 59 note 59.
6. See Joppke 1995; Maier 1997, Chs. 1 and 3.
7. Zelikow and Rice 1995; Cary 2000.
8. Jarausch 1994, pp. 67–9.
9. Jarausch 1994, pp. 142–4.
10. See Hutchings 1998.
11. McElvoy 1998, reviewing Küsters and Hofmann 1998.
12. Zelikow and Rice 1995.
13. See Cary 2000.
14. Jarausch 1994.
15. Jarausch 1994, pp. 154–5.
16. See Lange and Pugh 1998.
17. McDonald and Thumann 1990.
18. Halsall 1995.
19. Hickel 1993; Jarausch 1994, Ch. 7; Koch 1995; Maier 1997, Ch. 6; Lange and Pugh 1998.
20. OECD, *Germany 1992*; *Germany 1994*; Leaman 1995.
21. Tipton 1998b.
22. Bean 1994.
23. Hayek 1944; 1960; Friedman 1962; 1968.
24. Maier 1996, p. 155; see Collins 2000.
25. European Central Bank, *Monthly Bulletin*, January 1999.
26. OECD, *Germany 1994*; *Germany 1996*.
27. Leaman 1997b.
28. Meyer-Larsen 2000, Ch. 10.
29. *Financial Review*, September 13, 2001, from *Business Week*.

30. Meyer-Larsen 2000, pp. 30–2.
31. Leaman 1996; 2001; Lindlar and Holtfrerich 1997; Naschold 1997.
32. Leaman 1997b, p. 248.
33. OECD, *Germany 1994*.
34. Herrigal 2000.
35. OECD, *Germany 1996*.
36. *Sydney Morning Herald*, October 4, 1997, from *The Guardian*; *Sydney Morning Herald*, September 27, 2001.
37. Quint 1997.
38. Bentley 1992.
39. Groschopp 1994, p. 244.
40. Leaman 1997b; 2001.
41. Huster 1995; Eissel 1999.
42. Young 1999.
43. Rosenberg 1993, p. 119.
44. Grossmann 1997, pp. 34–6. See Sander 1987; Sander and Johr 1992.
45. Rosenberg 1993, p. 125.
46. Einhorn 1995; Young 1999.
47. Neather 1995.
48. Wicke 1998.
49. Cheesman 1998.
50. See Hasselbach 1996.
51. See Fijalkowski 1993; El-Tayeb 1999.
52. Biro 1998.
53. See Adelson 1984; Rohlfs 1995; McGowan 1997.
54. Melis 1995.
55. Rohlfs 1995, pp. 255–6.
56. Habermas 2001.
57. Søe 1989.
58. Søe 1993.
59. Roberts 1992; Anti-Defamation League 1993.
60. *The Australian*, May 22, 2001, AFP report of conference "BundOnline 2005, e-Government for a Modern Administration."
61. *Sydney Morning Herald*, March 6, 1999, from *Washington Post*.
62. *Sydney Morning Herald*, March 18, 2000.
63. See Betts 2000.
64. Tipton 1998a.
65. *Frankfurter Allgemeine Zeitung*, July 13, 1990. Jarausch 1994, p. 5.
66. Grass 1990; Habermas 1990a.
67. Enzensberger 1994, p. 130.
68. Quoted in Burns and van der Will 1993, p. 137.
69. Lipstadt 1993.
70. See Bartov 1998.
71. Buruma 1994, p. 84–5.
72. Ladd 1997.
73. Hamburg Institute for Social Research, *Viernichtungskrieg: Verbrechen der*

Wehrmacht 1941 bis 1944 (War of Extermination: Crimes of the German Army 1941–1944), traveling exhibition 1995; see Rosenhaft 1997.

74. Goldhagen 1996.
75. Rosenhaft 1997; Moses 1998.
76. Schulze and Oexle 1999.
77. Leslie 1996.

BIBLIOGRAPHY

Material on German art and German artists, including images of many of the works mentioned, can be located through web search engines such as Alta Vista. Mark Harden's texas.net Museum of Art, ⟨lonestar.texas.net/ ~mharden/artchive⟩, includes the German painters commonly included in the canonical history of modern art, especially of course the Expressionists. The site ⟨www.kunst-und-kultur.de/Kuenstler/bin/index⟩ covers a broader range of German artists, although the links to museums are less useful, as many of the museums' sites are limited to brochure ware and do not display images of their holdings.

An excellent selection of historical maps of Germany can be accessed at ⟨www.hoeckmann.de/index.html⟩.

Abrams, Lynn (1990) 'From control to commercialization: the triumph of mass entertainment in Germany, 1900-1925," *German History* 8: 278-93.

Abrams, Lynn, and Elizabeth Harvey (1996) 'Introduction: gender and gender relations in German history," in Lynn Abrams and Elizabeth Harvey, eds., *Gender Relations in German History*. Durham: Duke University Press.

Adams, Carole E. (1988) *Women Clerks in Wilhelmine Germany*. Cambridge: Cambridge University Press.

Adelson, Leslie A. (1984) *Crisis of Subjectivity: Botho Strauss's Challenge to West German Prose of the 1970s*. Amsterdam: Rodopi.

Adorno, Theodor (1949) 'Cultural criticism and society," in *Prisms*, trans. Samuel and Sherry Weber. London: Neville Spearman, 1967.

Albisetti, James (1988) *Schooling German Girls and Women: Secondary and Higher Education in the Nineteenth Century*. Princeton: Princeton University Press.

Albrecht, Willy (1994) *Der Sozialistische Deutsche Studentenbund (SDS): Vom parteikonfomen Studentenverband zum Repräsentanten der Neuen Linken*. Politik- und Gesellschaftsgeschichte, 35. Bonn: J. H. W. Dietz.

Aldenhoff, Rita (1996) 'Agriculture," in Chickering, ed., *Imperial Germany*, pp. 33-61.

Alexander, Bevin (2000) *How Hitler Could Have Won World War II: The Fatal Errors That Led to Defeat*. New York: Crown Publishers.

Alings, Reinhard (1996) *Monument und Nation: Das Bild vom Nationalstaat im Medium Denkmal; zum Verhältnis von Nation und Staat im deutschen Kaiserreich 1871–1918*. Beiträge zur Kommunikationsgeschichte, 4. Berlin and New York: Walter de Gruyter.

Allen, Ann Taylor (1991) *Feminism and Motherhood in Germany, 1800–1914*. New Brunswick, NJ: Rutgers University Press.

Ammon, Ulrich (1990) "German as an international language," *International Journal of the Sociology of Language* 83: 135–70.

Anderson, Margaret L. (1991) "Piety and politics: recent work on German Catholicism," *Journal of Modern History* 63: 681–716.

Anderson, Margaret L. (2000) *Practicing Democracy: Elections and Political Culture in Imperial Germany*. Princeton: Princeton University Press.

Anderson, Margaret L., and Kenneth D. Barkin (1982) "The myth of the Puttkamer purge and the reality of the Kulturkampf: some reflections on the historiography of imperial Germany," *Journal of Modern History* 53: 647–86.

Andrzejewski, Marek (1994) *Opposition und Widerstand in Danzig: 1933 bis 1939*. Politik- und Gesellschaftsgeschichte, 36. Bonn: J. H. W. Dietz.

Ansorg, Leonore, and Renate Hürtgen (1999) "The myth of female emancipation: contradictions in women's lives," in Jarausch, ed., *Dictatorship*, pp. 163–76.

Anti-Defamation League (1993) "The German neo-nazis: ADL investigative report," ADL Special Report. New York: ADL.

Applegate, Celia (1990) *A Nation of Provincials: The German Idea of Heimat*. Berkeley: University of California Press.

Arasse, Daniel (2001) *Anselm Kiefer*. London: Thames and Hudson.

Archer, Michael (1997) *Art since 1960*. London: Thames and Hudson.

Arendt, Hannah (1965) *Eichmann in Jerusalem: A Report on the Banality of Evil*, 2nd edn. New York: Viking Press.

Armstrong, Philip, Andrew Glyn, and John Harrison (1984) *Capitalism since 1945: The Making and Breakup of the Great Boom*. London: Fontana.

Aschheim, Steven E. (1992) *The Nietzsche Legacy in Germany, 1890–1990*. Berkeley: University of California Press.

Ash, Mitchell G. (1995) *Gestalt Psychology in German Culture: Holism and the Quest for Objectivity*. Cambridge: Cambridge University Press.

Aust, Stefan (1987) *The Baader–Meinhof Group: The Inside Story of a Phenomenon*. London: Bodley Head.

Bajohr, Stefan (1982) "Illegitimacy and the working class: illegitimate mothers in Brunswick, 1900–1933," in Richard J. Evans, ed., *The German Working Class, 1888–1933*. London: Croom Helm, pp. 142–73.

Balfour, Michael (1972) *The Kaiser and His Times*, 2nd edn. New York: Norton.

Banach, Jens (1998) *Heydrichs Elite: Die Führerkorps der Sicherheitspolizei und des SD 1936–1945*. Paderborn: Ferdinand Schöningh.

Bankier, David (1996) "German public awareness of the Final Solution," in Cesarani, ed., *The Final Solution*, pp. 215–27.

Baranowski, Shelley (1995) *The Sanctity of Rural Life: Nobility, Protestantism, and Nazism in Weimar Prussia*. New York: Oxford University Press.

Barclay, David E. (1995) *Frederick William IV and the Prussian Monarchy, 1840–1861*. Oxford: Clarendon Press.

Barkai, Avraham, Paul Mendes-Flohr, and Steven M. Lowenstein, eds. (1998) *German Jewish History in Modern Times*, Vol. 4: *Renewal and Destruction, 1918–1945*. New York: Columbia University Press.

Barkin, Kenneth D. (1970) *The Controversy over German Industrialization, 1890–1902*. Chicago: Chicago University Press.

Barkin, Kenneth D. (1987) "1878–1879: the second founding of the Reich, a perspective," *German Studies Review* 10: 220–35.

Barnett, Victoria J. (1999) *Bystanders: Conscience and Complicity during the Holocaust*. Christianity and the Holocaust—Core Issues. Westport, CT: Greenwood.

Barron, Stephanie (1991) *Degenerate Art: The Fate of the Avant-Garde in Nazi Germany*. Los Angeles: Los Angeles County Museum of Art.

Bartov, Omer (1991) *Hitler's Army: Soldiers, Nazis, and War in the Third Reich*. New York: Oxford University Press.

Bartov, Omer (1996) "Operation Barbarossa and the origins of the Final Solution," in Cesarani, ed., *Final Solution*, pp. 119–36.

Bartov, Omer (1998) "Defining enemies, making victims: Germans, Jews, and the Holocaust," *American Historical Review* 103: 771–816.

Bauer, Yehuda (1994) *Jews for Sale? Nazi–Jewish Negotiations, 1933–1945*. New Haven: Yale University Press.

Bauman, Zygmont (1989) *Modernity and the Holocaust*. Oxford: Oxford University Press.

Baumgarten, Hermann (1866) *Der deutsche Liberalismus: Eine Selbstkritik*. Frankfurt: Wissenschaftliche Buchgesellschaft, 1974.

Baumgarten, Marita (1997) *Professoren und Universitäten im 19. Jahrhundert: Zur Sozialgeschichte deutscher Geistes- und Naturwissenschaftler*. Kritische Studien zur Geschichtswissenschaft, 121. Göttingen: Vandenhoeck Ruprecht.

Bean, Charles R. (1994) "European unemployment: a survey," *Journal of Economic Literature* 32: 573–619.

Beck, Hermann (1995) *The Origins of the Authoritarian Welfare State in Prussia: Conservatives, Bureaucracy, and the Social Question, 1815–70*. Social History, Popular Culture, and Politics in Germany. Ann Arbor: University of Michigan Press.

Belting, Hans (1998) *The Germans and Their Art: A Troublesome Relationship*. New Haven: Yale University Press.

Bentley, Raymond (1984) *Technological Change in the German Democratic Republic*. Boulder, CO: Westview Press.

Bentley, Raymond (1992) *Research and Technology in the Former G.D.R.* Boulder, CO: Westview Press.

Berend, Ivan T., and Gyorgy Ranki (1974) *Economic Development in East Central Europe in the 19th and 20th Centuries.* New York: Columbia University Press.

Bergengrün, Alexander (1908) *Staatsminister August Freiherr von der Heydt.* Berlin.

Berghahn, Volker R. (1986) *The Americanisation of West German Industry, 1945–1973.* Leamington Spa: Berg.

Berghahn, Volker R. (1987) *Modern Germany: Economy, Society and Politics in the Twentieth Century.* New York: Cambridge University Press.

Berghahn, Volker R. (1993) *Germany and the Approach of War in 1914*, rev. edn. London: Macmillan.

Berghoff, Hartmut, and Cornelia Rauh-Kühne (2000) *Fritz K.: Ein deutsches Leben im zwanzigsten Jahrhundert.* Stuttgart: Deutsche Verlags-Anstalt.

Berkner, Lutz (1972) "The Stem family and the developmental cycle of the peasant household: an eighteenth-century Austrian example," *American Historical Review* 77: 398–418.

Berman, Russell A. (1997) "How to think about Germany: nationality, gender, and obsession in Heine's 'Night thoughts,'" in Herminghouse and Miller, eds., *Gender and Germanness*, pp. 66–81.

Bernhardt, Christoph, and Gerd Kuhn (1998) *Keiner darf zurückgelassen werden! Aspekte der Jugendhilfepraxis in der DDR 1959–1989.* Münster: Votum.

Bernstein, Eduard (1909) *Evolutionary Socialism.* New York: Schocken, 1970.

Betts, Paul (2000) "The twilight of the idols: East German memory and material culture," *Journal of Modern History* 72: 731–65.

Beyerchen, Alan D. (1977) *Scientists under Hitler.* New Haven: Yale University Press.

Biefang, Andreas (1994) *Politisches Bürgertum in Deutschland 1857–1868: Nationale Organisationen und Eliten.* Beiträge zur Geschichte des Parlamentarismus und der politische Parteien, 102. Düsseldorf: Droste.

Binion, Rudolph (1976) *Hitler among the Germans.* New York: Elsevier.

Biro, Matthew (1998) *Anselm Kiefer and the Philosophy of Martin Heidegger.* Cambridge: Cambridge University Press.

Black, Peter (2000) "Central intent or regional inspiration? Recent German approaches to the Holocaust," *Central European History* 33: 533–50.

Blackbourn, David (1987) "Between resignation and volatility: the German petty bourgeoisie in the nineteenth century," in David Blackbourn, ed., *Populists and Patricians.* London and Boston: Allen & Unwin, pp. 84–113.

Blackbourn, David (1997) *The Long Nineteenth Century.* The Fontana History of Germany, 1780–1918. London: Fontana Press.

Blackbourn, David, and Geoff Eley (1984) *The Peculiarities of German History: Bourgeois Society and Politics in Nineteenth-Century Germany.* Oxford: Oxford University Press.

Blackbourn, David, and Richard J. Evans, eds. (1991) *The German Bourgeoisie.* New York: Routledge.

Blaich, Fritz (1973) *Kartell- und Monopolpolitik im kaiserlichen Deutschland.* Beiträge zur Geschichte des Parlamentarismus und der politischen Parteien, 50. Düsseldorf: Droste.

Blaschke, Olaf (1997) *Katholizismus und Antisemitismus im Deutschen Kaiserreich.* Kritische Studien zur Geschichtswissenschaft, 122. Göttingen: Vandenhoeck & Ruprecht.

Blasius, Dirk (1976) *Bürgerliche Gesellschaft und Kriminalität.* Göttingen: Vandenhoeck & Ruprecht.

Blasius, Dirk (1994) *"Einfache Seelenstörung": Geschichte der deutschen Psychiatrie 1800–1945.* Frankfurt: Fischer Taschenbuch.

Blaug, Ricardo (1999) *Democracy, Real and Ideal: Discourse Ethics and Radical Politics.* Albany: State University of New York Press.

Blue, Gregory (1999) "Gobineau on China: race theory, the 'yellow peril,' and the critique of modernity," *Journal of World History* 10 (1): 93–142.

Bock, Gisela (1986) *Zwangssterilsation im Nationalsozialismus: Studien zur Rassenpolitik und Frauenpolitik.* Opladen: Westdeutscher Verlag.

Bock, Gisela (1989) "Die Frauen und der Nationalsozialismus," *Geschichte und Gesellschaft* 15: 563–79.

Bock, Gisela (1992) Reply to Koonz, *Geschichte und Gesellschaft* 18: 400–4.

Bock, Gisela (1994) "Antinatalism, maternity and paternity in National Socialism," in Crew, ed., *Nazism and German Society.*

Bopp, Karl R. (1954) "Die Tätigkeit der Reichsbank von 1876 bis 1914," *Weltwirtschaftliches Archiv* 72: 179–224.

Borchardt, Knut (1961) "Zur Frage des Kapitalmangels in der ersten Hälfte des 19. Jahrhunders in Deutschland," *Jahrbücher für Nationalökonomie und Statistik* 173. Translation in Borchardt, *Perspectives.*

Borchardt, Knut (1973) "The Industrial Revolution in Germany," in Carlo Cipolla, ed., *The Fontana Economic History of Europe,* Vol. 4, part 1. Glasgow: Fontana, pp. 76–160.

Borchardt, Knut (1991) *Perspectives on Modern German Economic History and Policy.* Cambridge: Cambridge University Press.

Bordo, Michael D., and Finn E. Kydland (1995) "The gold standard as a rule: an essay in exploration," *Explorations in Economic History* 32: 423–64.

Bowie, Andrew (1998) "Critiques of culture," in Kolinsky and van der Will, eds., *The Cambridge Companion to German Culture,* pp. 132–52.

Boyle, Nicholas (1991, 2000) *Goethe: The Poet and the Age,* 2 vols. Oxford: Clarendon Press.

Bracher, Karl Dietrich (1973) *The German Dictatorship*, trans. Jean Steinberg. Harmondsworth: Penguin, 1978.

Braun, Robert (1994) "The Holocaust and the problems of historical representation," *History and Theory* 33 (1994): 172–90.

Braunthal, Gerard (1994) *The German Social Democrats since 1969: A Party in Power and Opposition*. Boulder, CO: Westview Press.

Brecher, Bob (1999) "Understanding the Holocaust: the uniqueness debate," *Radical Philosophy* 96 (July/August): 17–28.

Breckman, Warren G. (1991) "Disciplining consumption: the debate about luxury in Wilhelmine Germany, 1890–1914," *Journal of Social History* 24: 485–505.

Breitman, Richard (1991) *The Architect of Genocide: Himmler and the Final Solution*. New York: Alfred A. Knopf.

Brenner, Michael (1996) *The Renaissance of Jewish Culture in Weimar Germany*. New Haven: Yale University Press.

Brettell, Richard R. (1999) *Modern Art 1851–1929*. Oxford and New York: Oxford University Press.

Breuilly, John (1996) *The Formation of the First German Nation-state 1800–1871*. London: Macmillan.

Breuilly, John, ed. (2001) *Nineteenth-Century Germany: Politics, Culture, and Society, 1800–1918*. London: Arnold.

Brophy, James M. (1998) *Capitalism, Politics, and Railroads in Prussia, 1830–1870*. Columbus: Ohio State University Press.

Brose, Eric D. (1993) *The Politics of Technological Change: Out of the Shadow of Antiquity, 1809–1848*. Princeton: Princeton University Press.

Broszat, Martin (1969) *The Hitler State: The Foundation and Development of the Internal Structure of the Third Reich*. London and New York: Longman, 1981.

Brubaker, R. (1992) *Citizenship and Nationhood in France and Germany*. Cambridge, MA: Harvard University Press.

Brustein, William (1996) *The Logic of Evil: The Social Origins of the Nazi Party, 1925–1933*. New Haven: Yale University Press.

Bryson, Phillip J., and Manfred Melzer (1991) *The End of the East German Economy: From Honecker to Reunification*. New York: St. Martin's Press.

Bucholz, Arden (1991) *Moltke, Schlieffen, and Prussian War Planning*. New York: Berg Press.

Bukey, Evan Burr (2000) *Hitler's Austria: Popular Sentiment in the Nazi Era, 1938–1945*. Chapel Hill: University of North Carolina Press.

Bungert, Heike (1997) *Das Nationalkomitee und der Westen: Die Reaktion der Westalliierten auf das NKFD und die Freien Deutschen Bewegung 1943–1948*. Transatlantische Historische Studien: Veröffentlichungen des Deutschen Historischen Instituts Washington, D.C., 8. Stuttgart: Franz Steiner.

694

BIBLIOGRAPHY

Burleigh, Michael (2000) *The Third Reich: A New History*. London: Macmillan.

Burns, Rob, and Wilfried van der Will (1988) *Protest and Democracy in West Germany: Extra-Parliamentary Opposition and the Democratic Agenda*. New York: St. Martin's Press.

Burns, Rob, and Wilfried van der Will (1993) "Angst vor Deutschland? A review of recent literature on the German question," *Debatte* 1: 135–53.

Buruma, Ian (1994) *The Wages of Guilt: Memories of War in Germany and Japan*. New York: Penguin/Meridian.

Buse, Dieter K., and Juergen C. Doerr, eds. (1998) *Modern Germany: An Encyclopedia of History, People, and Culture, 1871–1990*. New York and London: Garland Publishing Inc.

Bussmann, Klaus, and Florian Matzner, eds. (1993) *Hans Haacke. Bodenlos: Biennale Venedig 1993, Deutscher Pavilion*. Stuttgart: Edition Cantz.

Caldwell, Peter C. (1997) *Popular Sovereignty and the Crisis of German Constitutional Law: The Theory and Practice of Weimar Constitutionalism*. Durham: Duke University Press.

Calomiris, Charles W. (1995) "The costs of rejecting universal banking: American finance in the German mirror, 1870–1914," in Naomi R. Lamoreaux and Daniel M. G. Raff, eds., *Coordination and Information: Historical Perspectives on the Organization of Enterprise*. Chicago and London: University of Chicago Press, pp. 257–321.

Campbell, Joan (1989) *Joy in Work, German Work: The National Debate, 1800–1945*. Princeton: Princeton University Press.

Canis, Konrad (1997) *Von Bismarck zur Weltpolitik: Deutsche Aussenpolitik 1890 bis 1902*. Studien zur Internationalen Geschichte, 3. Berlin: Akademie.

Canning, Kathleen (1992) "Gender and the politics of class formation: rethinking German labor history," *American Historical Review* 97: 736–68.

Canning, Kathleen (1996) *Languages of Labor and Gender: Female Factory Work in Germany, 1850–1914*. Ithaca, NY: Cornell University Press.

Carlin, Wendy (1996) "West German growth and institutions, 1945–90," in Nicholas Crafts and Gianni Toniolo, eds., *Economic Growth in Europe since 1945*. Cambridge: Cambridge University Press, pp. 455–97.

Carter, Erica (1997) *How German Is She? West German Reconstruction and the Consuming Woman*. Ann Arbor: University of Michigan Press.

Cary, Noel D. (1996) *The Path to Christian Democracy: German Catholics and the Party System from Windhorst to Adenauer*. Cambridge, MA: Harvard University Press.

Cary, Noel D. (2000) "Reassessing Germany's *Ostpolitik*," (2 parts) *Central European History* 33: 235–62, 369–90.

Cecil, Lamar (1989, 1996) *Wilhelm II*, 2 vols. Chapel Hill: University of North Carolina Press.

Cesarani, David, ed. (1996) *The Final Solution: Origins and Implementation.* London and New York: Routledge.

Chambers, Simone (1996) *Reasonable Democracy: Jürgen Habermas and the Politics of Discourse.* Ithaca, NY: Cornell University Press.

Chandler, Alfred D. (1990) *Scale and Scope: The Dynamics of Industrial Capitalism.* Cambridge, MA: Harvard University Press.

Chatterjee, Partha (1986) *Nationalist Thought and the Colonial World: A Derivative Discourse.* London: Zed Books.

Cheesman, Tom (1998) "Polyglot politics: hip hop in Germany," *Debatte* 6: 191–214.

Chickering, Roger (1984) *We Men Who Feel Most German: A Cultural Study of the Pan-German League, 1886–1914.* Boston: Allen & Unwin.

Chickering, Roger (1993) *Karl Lamprecht: A German Academic Life (1856–1915).* Atlantic Highlands, NJ: Humanities Press.

Chickering, Roger, ed. (1996) *Imperial Germany: A Historiographical Companion.* Westport, CT, and London: Greenwood Press.

Chickering, Roger (1998) *Imperial Germany and the Great War, 1914–1918.* Cambridge: Cambridge University Press.

Childers, Thomas (1983) *The Nazi Voter: The Social Foundations of Fascism in Germany, 1919–1933.* Chapel Hill: University of North Carolina Press.

Childers, Thomas, and Jane Caplan, eds. (1993) *Reevaluating the Third Reich.* Europe Past and Present Series. New York and London: Holmes and Meier.

Clendinnen, Inga (1999) *Reading the Holocaust.* Cambridge: Cambridge University Press.

Collins, M. (1991) *Banks and Industrial Finance in Britain 1800–1939.* London: Macmillan.

Collins, Robert M. (2000) *More: The Politics of Economic Growth in Postwar America.* Oxford: Oxford University Press.

Confino, Alan (1998) "Edgar Reitz's Heimat and german nationhood: film, memory, and understanding the past," *German History* 16 (2): 185–208.

Confino, Alan, and Rudy Koshar (2001) "Regimes of consumer culture: new narratives in twentieth-century German history," *German History* 19 (2): 135–61.

Conrad, Christoph (1994) *Vom Greis zum Rentner: Der Strukturwandel des Alters in Deustschland zwischen 1830 und 1930.* Kritische Studien zur Geschichtswissenschaft, 104. Göttingen: Vandenhoeck & Ruprecht.

Conrad, Robert C. (1992) *Understanding Heinrich Böll.* Durham: South Carolina University Press.

Corni, Gustavo, and Horst Gies (1997) *Brot, Butter, Kanonen: Die*

Ernährungswirtschaft in Deutschland unter der Diktatur Hitlers. Berlin: Akademie Verlag.

Cornwall, Mark (1995) "Serbia," in Wilson, ed., *Decisions for War*, pp. 55–96.

Craig, Gordon A. (1955) *The Politics of the Prussian Army, 1640–1945.* Oxford: Oxford University Press.

Craig, Gordon A. (1964) *The Battle of Königgrätz.* Oxford: Oxford University Press.

Craig, Gordon A. (1978) *Germany, 1866–1945.* Oxford: Clarendon Press.

Crew, David (1979) *Town in the Ruhr: A Social History of Bochum, 1860–1914.* New York: Columbia University Press.

Crew, David, ed. (1994) *Nazism and German Society.* London and New York: Routledge.

Crew, David (1998) *Germans on Welfare: From Weimar to Hitler.* Oxford: Oxford University Press.

Czichon, Eberhard (1970) *Der Bankier und die Macht: Hermann Josef Abs in der deutschen Politik.* Cologne: Pahl-Rugenstein.

Dahrendorf, Ralf (1967) *Society and Democracy in Germany.* London: Weidenfeld and Nicolson.

Dalhoff, Jutta, Uschi Frey, and Ingrid Schöll, eds. (1985) *Frauenmacht in der Geschichte: Beiträge des Historikerinnentreffens 1985 zur Frauengeschichtsforschung.* Düsseldorf: Schwann.

Daniel, Ute (1989) *The War from Within: German Working-class Women in the First World War*, trans. Margaret Rees. Oxford: Berg, 1997.

Davis, Belinda (1996) "Food scarcity and the empowerment of the female consumer in World War I Berlin," in Victoria deGrazia and Ellen Furlought, eds., *The Sex of Things: Gender and Consumption in Historical Perspective.* Berkeley: University of California Press, pp. 287–310.

Deist, Wilhelm (1992) "Verdeckter Militärstveik im Kriegsjahr 1918?" in Wolfrom Wette, ed., *Der Kriege des Kleiner Mannes.* Munich: C. H. Beck, pp. 146–57.

DeMeritt, Linda C. (1987) *New Subjectivity and Prose Forms of Alienation: Peter Handke and Botho Strauss.* New York: Lang.

Denham, Scott (1992) *Visions of War: Ideologies and Images of War in German Literature before and after the Great War.* Berne and New York: P. Lang.

D'Entrèves, Maurizio P. (1996) "Introduction," in D'Entrèves and Benhabib, eds., *Habermas and the Unfinished Project of Modernity*, pp. 1–36.

D'Entrèves, Maurizio P. and Seyla Benhabib, eds. (1996) *Habermas and the Unfinished Project of Modernity.* Cambridge: Polity Press.

Derks, Hans (1999) "Social sciences in Germany, 1933–1945," *German History* 17 (2): 177–90.

DeVorkin, David H. (1992) *Science with a Vengeance.* New York: Springer.

Dickinson, Edward R. (1996) *The Politics of German Child Welfare from the Empire to the Federal Republic*. Harvard Historical Studies, 121. Cambridge, MA: Harvard University Press.

Diefendorf, Jeffrey M. (1980) *Businessmen and Politics in the Rhineland 1789–1830*. Princeton: Princeton University Press.

Diefendorf, Jeffrey M. (1993) *In the Wake of War: The Reconstruction of German Cities after World War II*. New York and Oxford: Oxford University Press.

Dorondo, David R. (1992) *Bavaria and German Federalism: Reich to Republic, 1918–33, 1945–49*. New York: St. Martin's Press.

Dorpalen, Andreas (1957) *Heinrich von Treitschke*. New Haven: Yale University Press.

Dorwart, Reinhold A. (1971) *The Prussian Welfare State before 1740*. Cambridge, MA: Harvard University Press.

Dube, Wolf-Dieter (1972) *The Expressionists*. London: Thames and Hudson.

Dutschke, Rudi (1974) *Versuch, Lenin auf die Füsse zu stellen: Über den halbasiatischen und den westeuropäischen Weg zum Sozialismus*. Berlin: E. Wagenbach.

Dyzenhaus, David (1997) *Legality and Legitimacy: Carl Schmitt, Hans Kelson and Herman Heller in Weimar*. Oxford: Clarendon Press.

Eichengreen, Barry (1992) *Golden Fetters: The Gold Standard and the Great Depression, 1919–1939*. Oxford: Oxford University Press.

Eichengreen, Barry, and Peter Temin (2000) "The gold standard and the Great Depression," *Contemporary European History* 9 (2): 183–207.

Einhorn, Barbara (1995) "Feminism in crisis: the East German Women's Movement and the 'New Europe,'" *Australian Journal of Politics and History* 41: 14–28.

Eisenberg, Carolyn W. (1996) *Drawing the Line: The American Decision to Divide Germany, 1944–1949*. Cambridge: Cambridge University Press.

Eissel, Dieter (1999) "Distribution policy in the Kohl era: the impact of neo-liberalism on wealth and poverty in Germany," *Debatte* 7: 39–55.

Eksteins, Modris (2000) *Rites of Spring: The Great War and the Birth of the Modern Age*. Basingstoke: Macmillan.

Eley, Geoff (1986) *From Unification to Nazism: Reinterpreting the German Past*. Boston: Allen & Unwin.

Eley, Geoff (1988) "Germany since '68: from the APO to the Greens," *Socialist Review* 18: 130–42.

Eley, Geoff (1991) *Reshaping the German Right: Radical Nationalism and Political Change after Bismarck*, 2nd edn. Ann Arbor: University of Michigan Press.

Eley, Geoff (1996) *Society, Culture, and the State in Germany, 1870–1930*. Ann Arbor: University of Michigan Press.

Eley, Geoff (1998) "Problems with culture: German history after the linguistic turn," *Central European History* 31: 197–227.

El-Tayeb, Fatima (1999) "'Blood is a very special juice': racialized bodies and citizenship in twentieth-century Germany," *International Review of Social History* 44, supplement, pp. 149–69.

Emmrich, Irma (1989) *Carl Blechen*. Munich: C. H. Beck.

Engelberg, Ernst (1990) *Bismarck*, 2 vols. Berlin: Akademie Verlag.

Engels, Frederick (1851–52) *Germany: Revolution and Counter-Revolution*, ed. Eleanor Marx. New York: International Publishers, 1969.

Enzensberger, Hans Magnus (1994) *Civil War*, trans. Piers Spence and Martin Chalmers. London: Granta.

Erhard, Ludwig (1957) *Prosperity through Competition*. English translation, London: Thames and Hudson, 1958.

Eucken, Walter (1952) *Grundsätze der Wirtschaftspolitik*. Bern.

Evans, Richard (1989) *In Hitler's Shadow: West German Historians and the Attempt to Escape from the Nazi Past*. New York: Pantheon.

Eyck, Erich (1956–57) *A History of the Weimar Republic*, 2 vols. Cambridge, MA: Harvard University Press, 1962.

Faber, Karl Georg (1966) "Realpolitik als Ideologie: Die Bedeutung des Jahres 1866 für das politische Denken in Deutschland," *Historische Zeitschrift* 203 (1): 1–45.

Fairbairn, Brett (1996) "Political Mobilization," in Chickering, *Imperial Germany*, pp. 303–42.

Fairbairn, Brett (1997) *Democracy in the Undemocratic State: The German Reichstag Elections of 1899 and 1903*. Buffalo, NY: University of Toronto Press.

Falter, Jürgen (1991) *Hitlers Wähler*. Munich: C. H. Beck.

Falter, Jürgen (1998) "Die 'Märzgefallenen' von 1933," *Geschichte und Gesellschaft* 24: 595–616.

Fehervary, Helen (1997) "The literature of the German Democratic Republic (1945–1990)," in Watanabe-O'Kelly, ed., *Cambridge History of German Literature*, pp. 393–439.

Fehrenbach, Heide (1995) *Cinema in Democratizing Germany: Reconstructing National Identity after Hitler*. Chapel Hill: University of North Carolina Press.

Fehrenbach, Heide (1997) "The fight for the 'Christian West': German film control, the churches, and the reconstruction of civil society in the early Bonn republic," in Moeller, ed., *West Germany*, pp. 321–45.

Feldenkirchen, Wilfried (1994) *Werner von Siemens: Inventor and International Entrepreneur*. Historical Perspectives on Business Enterprise Series. Columbus: Ohio State University Press.

Feldman, Gerald D. (1966) *Army, Industry and Labor in Germany 1914–1918*. Princeton: Princeton University Press.

Feldman, Gerald D. (1977) *Iron and Steel in the German Inflation, 1916–1923*. Princeton: Princeton University Press.

Feldman, Gerald D. (1993) *The Great Disorder: Politics, Economics, and Society in the German Inflation, 1914–1924*. Oxford: Oxford University Press.

Felix, David (1971) "Reparations reconsidered with a vengeance," *Central European History* 4 (2).

Fellner, Fritz (1995) "Austria-Hungary," in Wilson, ed., *Decisions for War*, pp. 9–26.

Ferguson, Niall (1995) *Paper and Iron: Hamburg Business and German Politics in the Era of Inflation, 1897–1927*. Cambridge: Cambridge University Press.

Fichter, Michael (1995) *Labor in Germany, 1945–1990*. New York: Berg.

Fijalkowski, Jürgen (1993) "Aggressive nationalism, immigration pressure, and asylum policy disputes in contemporary Germany," German Historical Institute, Occasional Papers, 9. Washington, D.C.

Finney, Gail (1997) "Revolution, resignation, realism," in Watanabe-O'Kelly, *Cambridge History of German Literature*, pp. 272–326.

Firda, Richard A. (1993) *Peter Handke*. New York: Twayne.

Fischer, Conan (1991) *The German Communists and the Rise of Nazism*. New York: St. Martin's Press.

Fischer, Conan, ed. (1996) *The Rise of National Socialism and the Working Classes in Weimar Germany*. Providence and Oxford: Berghahn Books.

Fischer, Fritz (1961) *Germany's Aims in the First World War*. New York: Norton, 1967.

Fischer, Klaus P. (1996) *Nazi Germany: A New History*. New York: Continuum.

Fohlin, Caroline (1999) "Universal banking in pre-World War I Germany: model or myth?" *Explorations in Economic History* 36: 305–43.

Förster, Jürgen (1996) "The relation between Operation Barbarossa as an ideological war of extermination and the Final Solution," in Cesarani, ed., *The Final Solution*, pp. 85–102.

Förster, Stig (1996) "The armed forces and military planning," in Chickering, ed., *Imperial Germany*, pp. 454–88.

Foschepoth, Josef (1997) "German reaction to defeat and occupation," in Moeller, ed., *West Germany*, pp. 73–89.

Frampton, Kenneth (1980) *Modern Architecture: A Critical History*. London: Thames and Hudson.

Freeman, Christopher, ed. (1996) *Long Wave Theory*. International Library of Critical Writings in Economics. Cheltenham and Brookfield: Edward Elgar.

Fremdling, Rainer (1975) *Eisenbahnen und deutscher Wirtschaftswachstum 1840–1879*. Dortmund.

Fremdling, Rainer (1977) "Railroads and German economic growth: a leading sector analysis with a comparison to the United States and Great Britain," *Journal of Economic History* 37: 583–604.

Frese, Matthias (1991) *Betriebspolitik im "Dritten Reich": Deutsche Arbeitsfront, Unternehmer und Staatsbürokratie in der westdeutschen Grossindustrie 1933–1939.* Forschungen zur Regionalgeschichte, 2. Paderborn: Ferdinand Schöningh.

Friedburg, Robert von (1997) *Ländliche gesellschaft und Obrigkeit: Gemeindeprotest und politische Mobilisierung im 18. und 19. Jahrhundert.* Kritische Studien zur Geschichtswissenschaft, 117. Göttingen: Vandenhoeck & Ruprecht.

Friedlander, Henry (1995) *The Origins of Nazi Genocide: From Euthanasia to the Final Solution.* Chapel Hill: University of North Carolina Press.

Friedlander, Saul (1997) *Nazi Germany and the Jews*, Vol. 1: *The Era of Persecution, 1933–1939.* New York: HarperCollins.

Friedman, Jonathan (1998) *The Lion and the Star: Gentile–Jewish Relations in Three Hessian Communities, 1919–1945.* Lexington: University Press of Kentucky.

Friedman, Milton (1962) *Capitalism and Freedom.* Chicago: University of Chicago Press.

Friedman, Milton (1968) "The role of monetary policy," in *The Optimum Quantity of Money.* London: Macmillan, 1969, pp. 95–110.

Friedrichsmeyer, Sara, Sara Lennox, and Susanne Zantop, eds. (1998) *The Imperialist Imagination: German Colonialism and Its Legacy.* Ann Arbor: University of Michigan Press.

Fritz, Stephen G. (1995) *Frontsoldaten: The German Soldier in World War II.* Lexington: University Press of Kentucky.

Fritzsche, Peter (1990) *Rehearsals for Fascism: Populism and Political Mobilization in the Weimar Republic.* Oxford: Oxford University Press.

Fritzsche, Peter (1996) "Did Weimar fail?" *Journal of Modern History* 68: 629–56.

Fritzsche, Peter (1998) *Germans into Nazis.* Cambridge, MA: Harvard University Press.

Führer, Karl Christian (1995) *Mieter, Hausbesitzer, Staat und Wohnungsmarkt: Wohnungsmangel und Wohnungswirtschaft in Deutschland 1914–1960.* Vierteljahrschrift für Sozial- und Wirtschaftsgeschichte, Beiheft 119. Stuttgart: Fritz Steiner.

Führer, Karl Christian (1997) "A medium for modernity? Broadcasting in Weimar Germany, 1923–1932," *Journal of Modern History* 69: 722–53.

Fulbrook, Mary (1992) *The Two Germanies, 1945–1990: Problems of Interpretation.* Basingstoke: Macmillan.

Fulbrook, Mary (1995) *Anatomy of a Dictatorship: Inside the GDR, 1949–1989*. New York and Oxford: Oxford University Press.

Fulbrook, Mary (1999) *German National Identity after the Holocaust*. Cambridge: Polity Press.

Fulbrook, Mary (2000) *Historical Theory: Or, Talking Sense about History*. London.

Fussell, Paul (1975) *The Great War and Modern Memory*. New York: Oxford University Press.

Gall, Lothar (1993) *Germania: Eine deutsche Marianne? Une Marianne allemande?* Bonn: Bouvier.

Garner, Curt (1997) "Public service personnel in West Germany in the 1950s: controversial policy decisions and their effects on social composition, gender structure, and role of former Nazis," in Moeller, ed., *West Germany*, pp. 135–95.

Gay, Peter (1952) *The Dilemma of Democratic Socialism: Eduard Bernstein's Challenge to Marx*. New York: Collier.

Gay, Peter (1968) *Weimar Culture: The Outsider as Insider*. New York: Harper & Row.

Gay, Peter (1978) *Freud, Jews and Other Germans: Masters and Victims in Modernist Culture*. Oxford: Oxford University Press.

Gellately, Robert (1974) *The Politics of Economic Despair: Shopkeepers and German Politics 1890–1914*. London and Beverly Hills: Sage Publications.

Gellately, Robert (1993) "Enforcing racial policy in Nazi Germany," in Childers and Caplan, *Reevaluating the Third Reich*, pp. 42–65.

Gellately, Robert (2001) *Backing Hitler: Consent and Coercion in Nazi Germany*. Oxford: Oxford University Press.

Gerlach, Christian (1998) "The Wannsee Conference, the fate of German Jews, and Hitler's decision in principle to exterminate all European Jews," *Journal of Modern History* 70 (4): 759–812, trans. Stephen Duffy. Earlier version in *Werkstatt Geschichte* 18 (October 1997).

Geyer, Michael (1996) "Restorative elites, German society and the Nazi pursuit of war," in Richard Bessel, ed., *Fascist Italy and Nazi Germany: Comparisons and Contrasts*. Cambridge: Cambridge University Press, pp. 134–64.

Geyer, Michael, and Konrad H. Jarausch, eds. (1989) *German Histories: Challenges in Theory, Practice, Technique*, special issue of *Central European History* 22 (3/4).

Giersch, Herbert, Karl-Heinz Paqué, and Holger Schmieding (1994) *The Fading Miracle: Four Decades of Market Economy in Germany*, rev. edn. Cambridge: Cambridge University Press.

Gillingham, John (1991) *Coal, Steel and the Rebirth of Europe 1945–51*. Cambridge: Cambridge University Press.

Gillis, John R. (1971) *The Prussian Bureaucracy in Crisis, 1840–1860: Origins of an Administrative Elite*. Stanford: Stanford University Press.

Gimbel, John (1990) *Science, Technology and Reparations: Exploitation and Plunder in Postwar Germany*. Stanford: Stanford University Press.

Goda, Norman J. W. (2000) "Black marks: Hitler's bribery of his senior officers during World War II," *Journal of Modern History* 72: 413–52.

Goeckel, Robert F. (1990) *The Lutheran Church and the East German State: Political Conflict and Change under Ulbricht and Honecker*. Ithaca, NY: Cornell University Press.

Goldhagen, Daniel J. (1996) *Hitler's Willing Executioners: Ordinary Germans and the Holocaust*. New York: Alfred A. Knopf.

Goldstein, Joshua S. (1988) *Long Cycles: Prosperity and War in the Modern Age*. New Haven: Yale University Press.

Gollwitzer, Heinz (1957) *Die Standesherren: Die politische und gesellschaftliche Stellung der Mediatisierten, 1815–1918*. Stuttgart.

Goodrick-Clarke (1998) *Hitler's Priestess: Savitre Devi, the Hindu-Aryan Myth, and Neo-Nazism*. New York: New York University Press.

Grabitz, H. (1988) "Problems of Nazi trials in the Federal Republic of Germany," *Holocaust and Genocide Studies* 3: 209–23.

Grass, Günter (1990) *Deutscher Lastenausgleich. Wider das dumpfe Einheitsgebot*. Berlin.

Green, Abigail (2001) *Fatherlands: State-Building and Nationhood in Nineteenth-Century Germany*. Cambridge: Cambridge University Press.

Greenfeld, Leah (1992) *Nationalism: Five Roads to Modernity*. Cambridge, MA: Harvard University Press.

Gregor, Neil (1997) "Big business and the 'Blitzkriegwirtschaft': Daimler–Benz AG and the mobilisation of the German war economy 1939–42," *Contemporary European History* 6: 193–208.

Grieder, Peter (1998) "The overthrow of Ulbricht in East Germany," *Debatte* 6: 8–45.

Grill, Johnpeter Horst (1983) *The Nazi Movement in Baden, 1920–1945*. Chapel Hill: University of North Carolina Press.

Grisebach, Lucius (1999) *Ernst Ludwig Kirchner, 1880–1938*. Cologne: Taschen.

Groschopp, Horst (1994) "Dokumentation einer Kündigung," *Geschichte und Gesellschaft* 20: 242–50.

Gross, Michael B. (1997) "Kulturkampf and unification: German liberalism and the war against the Jesuits," *Central European History* 30 (4): 545–66.

Grossmann, Atina (1991) "Feminist debates about women and National Socialism," *Gender and History* 3: 350–8.

Grossmann, Atina (1995) *Reforming Sex: The German Movement for Birth Control and Abortion Reform, 1920–1950*. New York: Oxford University Press.

Grossmann, Atina (1997) "A question of silence: the rape of German women by occupation soldiers," in Moeller, ed., *West Germany*, pp. 33–52.

Guilbaut, Serge (1983) *How New York Stole Modern Art: Abstract Expressionism, Freedom, and the Cold War*. Chicago: University of Chicago Press.

Gutman, Yisrael (1996) "The response of Polish Jewry to the Final Solution," in Cesarani, ed., *Final Solution*, pp. 151–8.

Habermas, Jürgen (1962) *The Structural Transformation of the Public Sphere: An Enquiry into a Category of Bourgeois Society*. Cambridge, MA: Harvard University Press, 1992.

Habermas, Jürgen (1981) "Modernity: an unfinished project," in D'Entrèves and Benhabib, eds., *Habermas and the Unfinished Project of Modernity*, pp. 38–55.

Habermas, Jürgen (1985) *The Philosophical Discourse of Modernity*, trans. Frederick Lawrence. Cambridge: Polity, 1990.

Habermas, Jürgen (1990a) *Die nachholende Revolution*. Frankfurt: Suhrkamp.

Habermas, Jürgen (1990b) *The New Conservatism: Cultural Criticism and the Historians' Debate*, trans. Sherry Weber Nicholson. Cambridge: Polity.

Habermas, Jürgen (2001) *Post-National Constellations*, trans. Max Pensky. Cambridge: Polity.

Hagemann, Karen (1996) "Of 'old' and 'new' housewives: everyday housework and the limits of household rationalization in the urban working-class milieu of the Weimar Republic," *International Review of Social History* 41: 305–30.

Hahn, Hans-Werner (1982) *Wirtschaftliche Integration im 19. Jahrhundert: Die hessischen Staaten und der Deutsche Zollverein*. Kritische Studien zur Geschichtswissenschaft, 52. Göttingen: Vandenhoeck & Ruprecht.

Halsall, Robert (1995) "The Treuhand: a look back in anger," *Debatte* 3: 85–104.

Hamerow, Theodore S. (1958) *Restoration, Revolution, Reaction*. Princeton: Princeton University Press.

Hamerow, Theodore S. (1983) "Guilt, redemption, and writing German history," *American Historical Review* 88: 53–72.

Hamilton, Richard (1982) *Who Voted for Hitler?* Princeton: Princeton University Press.

Hancock, Donald (1989) *West Germany: The Politics of Democratic Corporatism*. Chatham: Chatham House.

Hardach, Gerd (1987) *The First World War 1914–1918*. Harmondsworth: Penguin.

Harrington, Anne (1996) *Reenchanted Science: Holism in German Culture from Wilhelm II to Hitler*. Princeton: Princeton University Press.

Harris, James F. (1994) *The People Speak! Anti-Semitism and Emancipation in Nineteenth-Century Bavaria.* Social History, Popular Culture, and Politics in Germany. Ann Arbor: University of Michigan Press.

Harsh, Donna (1993) *German Social Democracy and the Rise of National Socialism.* Chapel Hill: University of North Carolina Press.

Harsh, Donna (1997) "Society, the state, and abortion in East Germany, 1950–1972," *American Historical Review* 102: 53–84.

Hasselbach, Ingo (1996) *Führer-Ex: Memoirs of A Former Neo-Nazi,* with Tom Reiss. London: Chatto and Windus/Random House.

Hausen, Karin (1981) "Family and role-division: the polarisation of sexual stereotypes in the nineteenth century—an aspect of the dissociation of work and family life," in Richard J. Evans and W. R. Lee, eds., *The German Family: Essays on the Social History of the Family in Nineteenth- and Twentieth-Century Germany.* London: Croom Helm, and Totowa, NJ: Barnes and Noble, pp. 51–83.

Hawkins, Mike (1997) *Social Darwinism in European and American Thought 1860–1945: Nature as Model and Nature as Threat.* Cambridge: Cambridge University Press.

Hayek, Friedrich A. von (1944) *The Road to Serfdom.* London: Routledge.

Hayek, Friedrich A. von (1960) *The Constitution of Liberty.* London: Routledge.

Headland, Ronald (1992) *Messages of Murder: A Study of the Reports of the Einsatzgruppen of the Security Police and the Security Service, 1941–1943.* Rutherford, NJ: Fairleigh Dickinson University Press.

Heberle, Rudolf (1963) *Landbevölkerung und Nationalsozialismus: Eine soziologische Untersuchung zur politischen Willensbildung in Schleswig-Holstein 1918–1932.* Stuttgart.

Hefeker, Carsten (2001) "The agony of central power: fiscal federalism in the German Reich," *European Review of Economic History* 5: 119–42.

Heibel, Yule F. (1995) *Reconstructing the Subject: Modernist Painting in Western Germany, 1945–1950.* Princeton: Princeton University Press.

Heidemeyer, Helge (1994) *Flucht und Zuwanderung aus der SBZ/DDR 1945/ 1949–1961: Die Flüchtlingspolitik der Bundesrepublik Deutschland bis zum Bau der Berliner Mauer.* Beiträge zur Geschichte des Parlamentarismus und der politischen Parteien, 100. Düsseldorf: Droste.

Heilbronner, Oded (1998) *Catholicism, Political Culture, and the Countryside: A Social History of the Nazi Party in South Germany.* Ann Arbor: University of Michigan Press.

Heilbronner, Oded (2000) "From ghetto to ghetto: the place of German Catholic society in recent historiography," *Journal of Modern History* 72: 453–595.

Heineman, Elizabeth (1996) "The hour of the woman: memories of

Germany's 'crisis years' and West German national identity," *American Historical Review* 101: 354–95.

Heineman, Elizabeth D. (1999) *What Difference Does a Husband Make? Women and Marital Status in Nazi and Postwar Germany.* Studies on the History of Society and Culture, 33. Berkeley and Los Angeles: University of California Press.

Heither, Dietrich, *et al.*, eds. (1997) *Blut und Paukboden: Eine Geschichte der Burschenschaften.* Frankfurt: Fischer Taschenbuch.

Held, D. (1980) *Introduction to Critical Theory: Horkheimer to Habermas.* Berkeley: University of California Press.

Helling, Gertrud (1965) "Zur Entwicklung der Produktivität in der deutschen Landwirtschaft im 19. Jahrhundert," *Jahrbuch für Wirtschaftsgeschichte* (1): 129–91.

Henderson, W. O. (1959) *The Zollverein,* 2nd edn. London: Frank Cass.

Henderson, W. O. (1963) *Studies in the Economic Policy of Frederick the Great.* London: Frank Cass.

Henderson, W. O. (1968) *The State and the Industrial Revolution in Prussia.* Liverpool: Liverpool University Press.

Henderson, W. O. (1975) *The Rise of German Industrial Power, 1834–1914.* London: Temple Smith.

Herbert, Ulrich (1986) "'Die guten und die schlechten Zeiten.' Überlegungen zur diachronen Aanalyse lebensgeschichtlicher Interviews," in Lutz Niethammer, ed., *"Die Jahre weiß man nicht, wo man sie hinsetzen soll." Faschismus Erfahrungen im Ruhrgebiet.* Lebensgeschichte und Sozialkultur im Ruhrgebiet 1930 bis 1960, Vol. 1. Berlin and Bonn: J. H. W. Dietz Nachf, pp. 67–96. Partial translation in Richard Bessel, ed., *Life in the Third Reich.* Oxford: Oxford University Press, 1987.

Herbert, Ulrich (1997) *Hitler's Foreign Workers.* Cambridge: Cambridge University Press.

Herbert, Ulrich, ed. (1998) *Nationalsozialistische Vernichtungspolitik, 1939–1945: Neue Forschungen und Kontroversen.* Frankfurt: Fischer.

Herf, Jeffrey (1980) "The *Holocaust* reception in West Germany: Right, Center, and Left," *New German Critique* 19: 30–52.

Herf, Jeffrey (1984) *Reactionary Modernism: Technology, Culture and Politics in Weimar and the Third Reich.* Cambridge and New York: Cambridge University Press.

Herf, Jeffrey (1997) *Divided Memory: The Nazi Past in the Two Germanies.* Cambridge, MA: Harvard University Press.

Herminghouse, Patricia (1997) "The Ladies' Auxiliary of German Literature: nineteenth-century women writers and the quest for a national literary history," in Herminghouse and Miller, eds., *Gender and Germanness,* pp. 145–58.

Herminghouse, Patricia, and Magda Miller, eds. (1997a) *Gender and Germanness: Cultural Productions of Nation*. Providence, RI, and Oxford: Berghahn Books.

Herminghouse, Patricia, and Magda Miller (1997b) "Introduction: looking for Germania," in Herminghouse and Miller, eds., *Gender and Germanness*, pp. 1–18.

Herrigal, Gary (2000) *Industrial Constructions: The Sources of German Industrial Power*. Cambridge: Cambridge University Press.

Hickel, Rudolf (1993) "Transforming the East German Economy," *Debatte* 1: 65–84.

Hiery, Hermann Joseph (1995) *The Neglected War: The German South Pacific and the Influence of World War I*. Honolulu: University of Hawaii Press.

Hilberg, Raul (1961) *The Destruction of the European Jews*, rev. edn. 3 vols. New York: Holmes & Meier, 1985.

Hildebrand, Klaus (1995) *Das vergangene Reich: Deutsche Aussenpolitik von Bismarck bis Hitler 1871–1945*. Stuttgart: Deutsche Verlags-Anstalt.

Hitler, Adolf (1925) *Mein Kampf*, trans. Ralph Manheim. Boston: Houghton Mifflin, 1971.

Hobson, John M. (1997) *The Wealth of States: A Comparative Sociology of International Economic and Political Change*. Cambridge: Cambridge University Press.

Hochstadt, Steve (1999) *Mobility and Modernity: Migration in Germany 1820–1989*. Ann Arbor: University of Michigan Press.

Hodenberg, Christina von (1996) *Die Partei der Unparteiischen: Der Liberalismus der preussischen Richterschaft 1815–1848/49*. Kritische Studien zur Geschichtswissenschaft, 113. Göttingen: Vandenhoeck & Ruprecht.

Hoffman, Bruce (1986) *Right-wing Terrorism in Germany*. Santa Monica: Rand Corporation.

Hoffmann, Peter (1988) *German Resistance to Hitler*. Cambridge, MA: Harvard University Press.

Hoffmann, Walther G. (1965) *Das Wachstum der Deutschen Wirtschaft seit der Mitte des 19. Jahrhunderts*. Berlin: Springer.

Hogan, Michael J. (1987) *The Marshall Plan: America, Britain and the Reconstruction of Western Europe, 1947–1952*. Cambridge and New York: Cambridge University Press.

Hohendahl, Peter Uwe (1989) *Building a National Literature: The Case of Germany, 1830–1870*. Ithaca, NY: Cornell University Press.

Holtfrerich, Carl-Ludwig (1986) *The German Inflation (1914–1923)*. Berlin: Walter de Gruyter.

Holtfrerich, Carl-Ludwig (1988) "Relations between monetary authorities and governmental institutions: the case of Germany from the 19th century to the present," in Gianni Toniolo, ed., *Central Banks' Independence in Historical Perspective*. Berlin: Walter de Gruyter.

Homburg, Heidrun (1991) *Rationalisierung und Industriearbeit: Arbeitsmarkt—Management—Arbeiterschaft im Siemens-Konzern Berlin 1900–1939*. Schriften der Historischen Kommission zu Berlin. Beiträge zur Inflation und Wiederaufbau in Deutschland und Europa 1914–24, 1. Berlin: Haude und Spener.

Hong, Young-sun (1997) "Gender, citizenship, and the welfare state: social work and the politics of femininity in the Weimar Republic," *Central European History* 30: 1–24.

Hong, Young-sun (1998) *Welfare, Modernity, and the Weimar State, 1919–1933*. Princeton: Princeton University Press.

Howell, Martha (1988) *Women, Production, and Patriarchy in Late Medieval Cities*. Chicago and London: University of Chicago Press.

Hubert, Peter (1992) *Uniformierter Reichstag: Die Geschichte der Pseudo-Volksvertretung 1933–1945*. Beiträge zur Geschichte des Parlamentarismus und der politischen Parteien, 97. Düsseldorf: Droste.

Hübinger, Gangolf (1996) "Confessionalism," in Chickering, ed., *Imperial Germany*, pp. 156–85.

Hübner, Peter (1998) "Industrielle Manger in der SBZ/DDR: Sozial- und mentalitätsgeschichtliche Aspekte," *Geschichte und Gesellschaft* 24: 54–80.

Hübner, Peter (1999) "Stagnation of change? Transformations of the workplace in the GDR," in Jarausch, ed., *Dictatorship*, pp. 285–306.

Hull, Isabel V. (1996) *Sexuality, State, and Civil Society in Germany, 1700–1815*. Ithaca, NY: and London: Cornell University Press.

Hundt, Michael (1996) *Die mindermächtigen deutschen Staaten auf dem Wiener Kongress*. Veröffentlichungen des Instituts für Europäische Geschichte Mainz, Abteilung Universalgeschichte, 164. Mainz: Philipp von Zabern.

Huster, Ernst-Ulrich (1995) "Wealth in Germany: the difficulty of talking about a taboo," *Debatte* 3: 46–64.

Hutchings, Robert (1998) *American Diplomacy and the End of the Cold War*. Baltimore: Johns Hopkins University Press.

Iggers, Georg G., and James M. Powell (1990) *Leopold von Ranke and the Shaping of the Historical Discipline*. Syracuse, NY: Syracuse University Press.

Imhof, Arthur E. (1981) "Women, family and death: excess mortality of women in childbearing age in four communities in nineteenth-century Germany," in Richard J. Evans and W. R. Lee, eds., *The German Family*. London: Croom Helm, pp. 148–74.

Imle, Fanny (1905) *Gewerbliche Friedensdokumente*. Jena.

Jackson, James H. (1981) "Overcrowding and family life: working-class families and the housing crisis in late nineteenth-century Duisburg," in Richard J. Evans and W. R. Lee, eds., *The German Family*. London: Croom Helm, pp. 194–220.

James, Harold (1992) "Introduction: Central Bank cooperation in the interwar period," *Contemporary European History* 1 (3): 227–31.

James, Harold (1993) "Innovation and conservatism in economic recovery: the alleged 'Nazi recovery' of the 1930s," in Childers and Caplan, eds., *Reevaluating the Third Reich*, pp. 114–38.

Janssens, Angélique (1997) "The rise and decline of the male breadwinner family? An overview of the debate," *International Review of Social History* 42: supplement, pp. 1–23.

Janz, Oliver (1994) *Bürger besonderer Art: Evangelische Pfarrer in Preussen 1850–1914*. Veröffentlichungen der Historischen Kommission zu Berlin, 87. New York: Walter de Gruyter.

Jarausch, Konrad (1973) *The Enigmatic Chancellor: Bethmann-Hollweg and the Hubris of Imperial Germany*. New Haven: Yale University Press.

Jarausch, Konrad H. (1990) *The Unfree Professions: German Lawyers, Teachers, and Engineers, 1900–1950*. New York: Oxford University Press.

Jarausch, Konrad H. (1994) *The Rush to German Unity*. New York: Oxford University Press.

Jarausch, Konrad H., ed. (1999) *Dictatorship as Experience: Towards a Socio-Cultural History of the GDR*. New York and Oxford: Berghahn Books.

Jay, Martin (1973) *The Dialectical Imagination: A History of the Frankfurt School and the Institute for Social Research, 1923–1950*. Boston: Little, Brown & Co.

Jessen, Ralph (1999a) *Akademische Elite und kommunistische Diktatur: Die ostdeutsche Hochschullehrerschaft in der Ulbricht-Ära*. Kritische Studien zur Geschichtswissenschaft, 135. Göttingen: Vandenheock & Ruprecht.

Jessen, Ralph (1999b) "Mobility and blockage during the 1970s," in Jarausch, ed., *Dictatorship*, pp. 341–60.

Johnson, Eric A. (1995) *Urbanization and Crime: Germany, 1871–1914*. Cambridge: Cambridge University Press.

Jones, Larry E. (1988) *German Liberalism and the Dissolution of the Weimar Party System, 1918–1933*. Chapel Hill: University of North Carolina Press.

Joppke, Christian (1995) *East German Dissidents and the Revolution of 1989: Social Movement in a Leninist Regime*. New York: New York University Press.

Jünger, Ernst (1920) *The Storm of Steel: From the Diary of a German Storm Troop Officer on the Western Front*. New York: Howard Fertig, 1999.

Kaelble, Hartmut (1983) "Der Mythos von der rapiden Industrialisierung in Deutschland," *Geschichte und Gesellschaft* 9 (1): 108–18.

Kaes, Anton (1989) *From Hitler to Heimat: The Return of History as Film.* Cambridge, MA: Harvard University Press.

Kaplan, Marion A. (1991) *The Making of the Jewish Middle Class: Women, Family, and Identity in Imperial Germany.* Oxford: Oxford University Press.

Kaplan, Marion A. (1998) *Between Dignity and Despair: Jewish Life in Nazi Germany.* New York: Oxford University Press.

Kater, Michael (1983) *The Nazi Party: A Social Profile of Members and Leaders 1919–1945.* Oxford: Oxford University Press.

Kater, Michael H. (1992) *Different Drummers: Jazz in the Culture of Nazi Germany.* New York: Oxford University Press.

Kater, Michael H. (1997) *The Twisted Muse: Musicians and Their Music in the Third Reich.* New York: Oxford University Press.

Kater, Michael H. (2000) *Composers of the Nazi Era: Eight Portraits.* New York: Oxford University Press.

Kehr, Eckart (1970) *Der Primat der Innenpolitik,* ed. Hans-Ulrich Wehler, 2nd edn. Berlin: Walter de Gruyter. Selections published as *Economic Interest, Militarism, and Foreign Policy: Essays on Germany History,* ed. Gordon Craig, trans. Greete Heinz. Berkeley: University of California Press, 1977.

Keiger, John F. V. (1995) "France," in Wilson, ed., *Decisions for War,* pp. 121–50.

Keisch, Claude, and Marie Ursula Riemann-Reyher, eds. (1996) *Adolf Menzel: Between Romanticism and Impressionism.* New Haven and London: Yale University Press.

Kele, Max H. (1972) *Nazis and Workers. National Socialist Appeals to German Labor, 1919–1933.* Chapel Hill: University of North Carolina Press.

Kelly, Petra (1983) *Fighting for Hope,* trans. Marianne Howarth. London: Hogarth Press, 1984.

Kennedy, Paul (1984) *Strategy and Diplomacy 1870–1945.* Aylesbury: Fontana.

Kershaw, Ian, ed. (1990) *Weimar: Why Did German Democracy Fail?* London: Weidenfeld and Nicolson.

Kershaw, Ian (1998) *Hitler, 1889–1936: Hubris.* London: Allen Lane.

Kershaw, Ian (2000a) *Hitler, 1936–1945: Nemesis.* London: Allen Lane.

Kershaw, Ian (2000b) *The Nazi Dictatorship: Problems and Perspectives of Interpretation,* 4th edn. London: Arnold.

Kershaw, Ian, and Moshe Lewin, eds. (1997) *Stalinism and Nazism: Dictatorships in Comparison.* Cambridge: Cambridge University Press.

Kiesewetter, Hubert (1988) *Industrialisierung und Landwirtschaft: Sachsens Stellung im regionalen Industrialisierungsprozeß Deutschlands im 19. Jahrhundert.* Cologne: Böhlau.

Kitchen, Martin (1976) *The Silent Dictatorship: The Politics of the German*

High Command under Hindenburg and Ludendorff, 1916–1918. London: Croom Helm.

Klein, Gotthard (1996) *Der Volksverein für das Katholische Deutschland, 1890–1933: Geschichte, Bedeutung, Untergang.* Paderborn: Ferdinand Schöningh.

Klemperer, Victor (1999) *I Shall Bear Witness: The Diaries of Victor Klemperer, 1933–41,* ed. and trans. Martin Chalmers. London: Phoenix.

Klemperer, Victor (2000) *To the Bitter End: The Diaries of Victor Klemperer, 1942–45,* ed. and trans. Martin Chalmers. London: Phoenix.

Klenkmann, Afons (1996) *Wilde Jugend: Lebenswelt grossstäsdtischer Jugdendlicher zwischen Weltwirtschaftskrise, Nationalsozialismus und Währungsreform.* Essen: Klartext.

Koch, Karl (1995) "The German economy: decline or stability?" in Lewis and McKenzie, eds., *The New Germany,* pp. 127–47.

Kocka, Jürgen, (1969) *Unternehmensverwaltung und Angestelltenschaft am Beispiel Siemens, 1844–1914.* Stuttgart: Klett-Cotta.

Kocka, Jürgen (1973) *Facing Total War: German Society, 1914–1918.* Cambridge, MA: Harvard University Press, 1985.

Kocka, Jürgen (1978) "Entrepreneurs and managers in German industrialization," in Peter Mathias and M. M. Postan, eds., *The Cambridge Economic History of Europe,* Vol. 7. Cambridge: Cambridge University Press.

Kocka, Jürgen (1981) *Die Angestelleten in der deutschen Geschichte.* Göttingen: Vandenheock & Ruprecht.

Köhler, Henning (1994) *Konrad Adenauer.* Berlin: Propyläen.

Kohn, Hans (1960) *The Mind of Germany: The Education of a Nation.* New York: Harper.

Kohut, Thomas A. (1991) *Wilhelm II and the Germans: A Study in Leadership.* Oxford and New York: Oxford University Press.

Kolb, Eberhard (1988) *The Weimar Republic,* trans. P. S. Falla. London and New York: Routledge.

Kolinsky, Eva, and Wilfried van der Will, eds. (1998) *The Cambridge Companion to German Culture.* Cambridge: Cambridge University Press.

Kollander, Patricia (1995) *Frederick III: Germany's Liberal Emperor.* Contributions to the Study of World History, 50. Westport, CT: Greenwood.

Kondratiev, Nikolai D. (1928) "Long cycles of economic conjuncture," in *The Works of Nikolai D. Kondratiev,* 1: 25–63. London: Pickering & Chatto, 1998.

Koonz, Claudia (1986) *Mothers in the Fatherland: Women, the Family and Nazi Politics.* London: Methuen, 1988 (paperback edn.).

Koonz, Claudia (1992) Reply to Bock, *Geschichte und Gesellschaft* 18: 394–9.

Koonz, Claudia (1993) "Eugenics, gender, and ethics in Nazi Germany: the debate about involuntary sterilization 1933–1936," in Childers and Caplan, eds., *Reevaluating the Third Reich,* pp. 66–85.

Kopstein, Jeffrey (1997) *The Politics of Economic Decline in East Germany, 1945–1989*. Chapel Hill: University of North Carolina Press.

Kracauer, Siegfried (1947) *From Caligari to Hitler: A Psychological History of the German Film*. Princeton: Princeton University Press.

Krahe, Enno (1963, 1983) *Metternich's German Policy*. Vol. 1: *The Struggle with Napoleon*; Vol. 2: *The Congress of Vienna, 1814–1815*. Princeton: Princeton University Press.

Kraus, Hans-Christof (1994) *Ernst Ludwig von Gerlach: Politisches Denken und Handeln eines preussischen Altkonservativen*. Schriftenreihe des Historischen Kommission bei der Bayerischen Akademie der Wissenschaften, 53, 2 vols. Göttingen: Vandenhoeck & Ruprecht.

Kreimeier, Klaus (1996) *The Ufa Story: A History of Germany's Greatest Film Corporation 1918–1945*, trans. Robert Kimber and Rita Kimber. New York: Hill and Wang.

Kriedte, Peter, Hans Medick, and Jürgen Schlumbohm (1977) *Industrialization before Industrialization*, trans. Beate Schempp. Cambridge: Cambridge University Press, 1981.

Krieger, Leonard (1957) *The German Idea of Freedom: History of a Political Tradition*. Chicago: University of Chicago Press.

Kruedener, J., ed. (1990) *Economic Crisis and Political Collapse: The Weimar Republic, 1924–1933*. New York: Berg.

Kuczinski, Jürgen (1961–) *Geschichte der Lage der Arbeiter under dem Kapitalismus*, 17 vols. East Berlin: Akademie Verlag.

Kühne, Thomas (1994) *Dreiklassenwahlrecht und Wahlkultur in Preussen 1867–1914: Landtagswahlen zwischen korporativer Tradition und politischem Massenmarkt*. Beiträge zur Geschichte des Parlamentarismus und der politische Parteien, 99. Düsseldorf: Droste.

Kunz, Andreas (1994) "The economic performance of inland navigation in Germany, 1835–1935," in Andreas Kunz and John Armstrong, eds., *Inland Navigation in 19th Century Europe*. Mainz: Verlag Philipp von Zabern, and Manchester: Manchester University Press, pp. 47–78.

Küsters, Hanns Jürgen, and Daniel Hofmann, eds. (1998) *Deutsche Einheit. Sonderedition aus den Akten des Bundeskanzleramtes, 1989–1990*. Munich: Oldenbourg.

LaCapra, Dominick (1998) *Representing the Holocaust: History, Theory, Trauma*. Ithaca, NY: Cornell University Press.

Ladd, Brian (1990) *Urban Planning and Civic Order in Germany, 1860–1914*. Cambridge, MA: Harvard University Press.

Ladd, Brian (1997) *The Ghosts of Berlin: Confronting German History in the Urban Landscape*. Chicago: University of Chicago Press.

Lamberti, Marjorie (2001) "German schoolteachers, National Socialism, and the politics of culture at the end of the Weimar Republic," *Central European History* 34: 53–82.

Lambsdorff, Otto Count (1980) *Bewährung: Wirtschaftspolitik in Krisenzeiten*. Düsseldorf: Econ-Verlag.

Lange, Thomas, and Geoffrey Pugh, eds. (1998) *The Economics of German Unification*. Cheltenham: Edward Elgar.

Langenhan, Dagmar, and Sabine Ross (1999) "The Socialist glass ceiling: limits to female careers," in Jarausch, ed., *Dictatorship*, pp. 177–91.

Lapp, Benjamin (1997) *Revolution from the Right: Politics, Class and the Rise of Nazism in Saxony, 1919–1933*. Boston: Humanities Press.

Laqueur, Walter (1962) *Young Germany: A History of the Youth Movement*. London: Routledge & Kegan Paul.

Lässig, Simone (1995) "Wahlrechtsreform in den deutschen Einzelstaaten: Indikatoren für Modernisierungstendenzen und Reformfähigkeit im Kaiserreich?," in Simone Lässig, *et al.*, eds., *Modernisierung und Region im wilhelminischen Deutschland*. Bielefeld: Verlag für Regionalgeschichte, pp. 127–69.

Leaman, Jeremy (1995) "Taxation and taxation policy since the Wende," *Debatte* 3: 143–53.

Leaman, Jeremy (1996) "Renewed growth weakness of the German economy," *Debatte* 1: 124–44.

Leaman, Jeremy (1997a) "Germany's economy in the context of 'globalization,'" *Debatte* 5: 91–104.

Leaman, Jeremy (1997b) "Mergers in the unsocial market economy," *Debatte* 5: 234–48.

Leaman, Jeremy (2001) "Spring 2001 growth trends," *Debatte* 9: 88–95.

Lees, Andrew (1975) "Debates about the big city in Germany, 1890–1914," *Societas* 5: 31–48.

Leitz, Christian (1996) "Hermann Goering and Nazi Germany's economic exploitation of nationalist Spain, 1936–1939," *German History* 14 (1): 21–37.

Lemke, Michael (1999) "Foreign influences on the dictatorial development of the GDR, 1949–1955," in Jarausch, ed., *Dictatorship*, pp. 19–107.

Lemmons, Russel (1994) *Goebbels and Der Angriff*. Lexington: University Press of Kentucky.

Lepsius, Rainer (1993) "Parteiensystem und Sozialstruktur: Zum Problem der Demokratisierung der deutschen Gesellschaft," in Rainer Lepsius, *Demokratie in Deutschland*. Göttingen: Vandenhoeck & Ruprecht, pp. 25–50.

Lerman, Katherine A. (1990) *The Chancellor as Courtier: Bernard von Bülow and the Governance of Germany, 1900–1909*. Cambridge: Cambridge University Press.

Leslie, Esther (1996) "Wrapping the Reichstag: re-visioning German history," *Radical Philosophy* 77: 6–16.

Levene, Mark (2000) "Why is the twentieth century the century of genocide?" *Journal of World History* 11: 305–36.

Levy, Richard S. (1975) *The Downfall of the Anti-Semitic Political Parties in Imperial Germany*. New Haven: Yale University Press.

Lewis, Derek, and John R. P. McKenzie, eds. (1995) *The New Germany: Social, Political and Cultural Challenges of Unification*. Exeter: University of Exeter Press.

Lidtke, Vernon (1985) *The Alternative Culture: Socialist Labor in Imperial Germany*. New York: Oxford University Press.

Lidtke, Vernon (1996) "The Socialist labor movement," in Chickering, ed., *Imperial Germany*, pp. 272–302.

Liedtke, Christian, ed. (2000) *Heinrich Heine: Neue Wege der Forschung*. Darmstadt: Wissenschaftliche Buchgesellschaft.

Liefmann, Robert (1910) *Kartelle und Trusts und die Weiterbildung der volkswirtschaftlichen Organisation*, 5th edn. Stuttgart, 1922.

Lindenberger, Thomas (1995) *Strassenpolitik: Zur Sozialgeschichte der öffentlichen Ordnung in Berlin 1900 bis 1914*. Politik- und Gesellschaftsgeschichte, 39. Bonn: J. H. W. Dietz.

Lindenfeld, David F. (1997) *The Practical Imagination: The German Sciences of State in the Nineteenth Century*. Chicago: University of Chicago Press.

Lindlar, Ludger, and Carl-Ludwig Holtfrerich (1997) "Geography, exchange rates and trade structures: Germany's export performance since the 1950s," *European Review of Economic History* 1: 217–46.

Linton, Derek S. (1991) *"Who Has the Youth, Has the Future": The Campaign to Save Young Workers in Imperial Germany*. New York: Cambridge University Press.

Lipstadt, Deborah E. (1993) *Denying the Holocaust: The Growing Assault on Truth and Memory*. New York: The Free Press.

Lixfeld, Hannjost (1994) *Folklore and Fascism: The Reich Institute for German Volkskunde*, ed. and trans. James R. Dow. Folklore Studies in Translation. Bloomington: Indiana University Press.

Loetz, Francisca (1993) *Vom Kranken zum Patienten: "Medikalisierung" und medizinische Vergesellschaftung am Beispiel Badens 1750–1850*. Medizin, Gesellschaft und Geschichte, Beiheft 2. Stuttgart: Franz Steiner.

Loewenberg, Peter (1971) "Origins of the Nazi Youth Cohort," *American Historical Review* 76: 1457–502.

Lönne, Karl-Egon (2000) "Katholizismus-Forschung," *Geschichte und Gesellschaft* 26: 128–70.

Lösche, Peter, and Franz Walter (2000) "Katholiken, Konservative und

Liberale: Milieus und Lebenswelten bürgerliche Parteien in Deutschland während des 20. Jahrhunderts," *Geschichte und Gesellschaft* 26: 471–92.

Lowenstein, Steven M. (1980) "The rural community and the urbanization of German Jewry," *Central European History* 13: 218–36.

Lowenstein, Steven M. (1994) *The Berlin Jewish Community: Enlightenment, Family, and Crisis, 1770–1830.* Studies in Jewish History. New York: Oxford University Press.

Lukas, Richard C. (1994) *Did the Children Cry? Hitler's War against Jewish and Polish Children, 1939–1945.* New York: Hippocrene.

McAleer, Kevin (1994) *Dueling: The Cult of Honor in Fin-de-Siècle Germany.* Princeton: Princeton University Press.

McCauley, Martin (1979) *Marxism–Leninism in the German Democratic Republic.* London: Macmillan.

McClelland, Charles (1980) *State, Society, and University in Germany, 1700–1914.* Cambridge: Cambridge University Press.

McCloskey, Barbara (1997) *George Grosz and the Communist Party: Art and Radicalism in Crisis, 1918 to 1936.* Princeton: Princeton University Press.

McCormick, John P. (1997) *Carl Schmitt's Critique of Liberalism: Against Politics as Technology.* Cambridge: Cambridge University Press.

McDonald, Donogh, and Günther Thumann (1990) "East Germany: the new Wirtschaftswunder?" in Leslie Lipschitz and Donogh McDonald, eds., *German Unification: Economic Issues.* Washington, D.C.: International Monetary Fund.

McEligott, Anthony (1998) *Contested City: Municipal Politics and the Rise of Nazism in Altona, 1917–1937.* Ann Arbor: University of Michigan Press.

McElvoy, Anne (1998) "The forgotten mystery: how Helmut Kohl secretly plotted to reunite Germany," *The Times Literary Supplement*, December 11.

McGowan, Morray (1997) "German writing in the West (1945–1990)," in Watanabe-O'Kelly, ed., *Cambridge History of German Literature*, pp. 440–506.

Maddison, Angus (1982) *Phases of Capitalist Development.* Oxford: Oxford University Press.

Maddison, Angus (1987) "Growth and slowdown in advanced capitalist economies," *Journal of Economic Literature* 25: 649–98.

Maddison, Angus (1989) *The World Economy in the Twentieth Century.* Paris: Organization for Economic Cooperation and Development.

Maddison, Angus (1995) *Monitoring the World Economy 1820–1992.* Development Centre Studies. Paris: Organization for Economic Cooperation and Development.

Magnus, Shulamit (1997) *Jewish Emancipation in a German City: Cologne, 1798–1871.* Stanford Studies in Jewish History and Culture. Stanford: Stanford University Press.

Mah, Harold (2000) "Phantasies of the public sphere: rethinking the Habermas of historians," *Journal of Modern History* 72: 153–82.

Maier, Charles S. (1975) *Recasting Bourgeois Europe: Stabilization in France, Germany, and Italy in the Decade after World War I*. Princeton: Princeton University Press.

Maier, Charles S. (1981) "The two postwar eras and the conditions for stability in twentieth-century Western Europe," *American Historical Review* 86: 327–67.

Maier, Charles S. (1988) *The Unmasterable Past: History, Holocaust and the German National Identity*. Cambridge, MA: Harvard University Press.

Maier, Charles S., ed. (1991) *The Marshall Plan and Germany: West German Development within the Framework of the European Recovery Plan*. New York: Berg.

Maier, Charles S. (1996) "The postwar social contract: comment," *International Labor and Working Class History* 50: 148–56.

Maier, Charles S. (1997) *Dissolution: The Crisis of Communism and the End of East Germany*. Princeton: Princeton University Press.

Mallmann, Klaus-Michael (1996) *Kommunisten in der Weimarer Republik: Sozialgeschichte einer revolutionären Bewegung*. Darmstadt: Wissenschaftliche Buchgesellschaft.

Mallmann, Klaus-Michael, and Gerhard Paul (1994) "Omniscient, omnipotent, omnipresent? Gestapo, security, and resistance," in Crew, ed., *Nazism and German Society*.

Mandel, Ernest (1978) *The Second Slump*. London: New Left Books.

Mannheim, Karl (1928) "The problem of generations," in Karl Mannheim, *Essays on the Sociology of Knowledge*, ed. Paul Kecskemeti. London: Routledge & Kegan Paul, 1952. pp. 276–320.

Markovits, Andrei, and Philip S. Gorski (1993) *The German Left: Red, Green and Beyond*. New York: Oxford University Press.

Marks, Sally (1969) "Reparations reconsidered: a reminder," *Central European History* 2 (4).

Marrus, Michael (1997) *The Nuremberg War Trials*. Boston: Bedford.

Mason, Timothy W. (1972) "The primacy of politics: politics and economics in National Socialist Germany," in Henry A. Turner, ed., *Nazism and the Third Reich*. New York: Quadrangle, pp. 175–200. Also in Mason, *Nazism, Fascism and the Working Class*.

Mason, Timothy W. (1977) *Sozialpolitik im Dritten Reich: Arbeiterklasse und Volksgemeinschft*. Opladen: Westdeutscher Verlag.

Mason, Timothy (1993) "The domestic dynamics of Nazi conquests: a response to critics," in Childers and Caplan, eds., *Reevaluating the Third Reich*, pp. 161–89. Also in Mason, *Nazism, Fascism and the Working Class*.

Mason, Timothy W. (1995) *Nazism, Fascism and the Working Class*, ed. Jane Caplan. Cambridge: Cambridge University Press.

Mau, Rudolf (1994) *Eingebunden in den Realsozialismus? Die Evangelische Kirche als Problem der SED*. Sammlung Vandenhoeck. Göttingen: Vandenhoeck & Ruprecht.

Mayer, Arno J. (1967) *The Politics of Peacemaking: Containment and Counterrevolution at Versailles*. New York: Alfred A. Knopf.

Mayer, Arno J. (1981) *The Persistence of the Old Regime: Europe to the Great War*. New York: Pantheon Books.

Mazon, Patricia (2000) "Germania triumphant: the Niederwald national monument and the liberal moment in imperial Germany," *German History* 18 (2): 162–92.

Meinecke, Friedrich (1907) *Weltbürgertum und Nationalstaat*, 7th edn. 1927, ed. Hans Herzfeld. Darmstadt: Wissenschaftliche Buchgesellschaft, 1969.

Meinecke, Friedrich (1946) *The German Catastrophe: Reflections and Recollections*, trans. Sydney B. Fay. Boston: Beacon Press, 1960.

Melis, James (1995) "Writers in transition: the end of East German literature?," in Lewis and McKenzie, eds., *The New Germany*, pp. 220–42.

Mendels, Franklin (1972) "Proto-industrialization: the first phase of the industrialization process," *Journal of Economic History* 32: 241–61.

Mergel, Thomas (1994) *Zwischen Klasse und Konfession: Katholisches Bürgertum im Rheinland 1794–1914*. Bürgertum 9. Göttingen: Vandenhoeck & Ruprecht.

Merkel, Ina (1999) "Working people and consumption under really-existing Socialism: perspectives from the German Democratic Republic," *International Labor and Working-Class History* 55: 92–111.

Merkenich, Stephanie (1998) *Grüne Front gegen Weimar: Reichs-Landbund und agrarischer Lobbyismus 1918–1933*. Beiträge zur Geschichte des Parlamentarismus und der politischen Parteien, 113. Düsseldorf: Droste.

Meyer-Larsen, Werner (2000) *Germany, Inc.: The New German Juggernaut and Its Challenge to World Business*, trans. Thomas Thornton. New York: John Wiley & Sons, Inc.

Michels, Robert (1915) *Political Parties: A Sociological Study of the Oligarchical Tendencies of Modern Democracy*, trans. Eden and Cedar Paul. New York: Collier, 1962.

Miller, Alice (1980) *For Your Own Good: The Roots of Violence in Childrearing*, trans. Hildegarde and Hunter Hannum. London: Virago, 1983.

Milward, Alan S. (1984) *The Reconstruction of Western Europe 1945–51*. Berkeley and Los Angeles: University of California Press.

Mitchell, Allan (1965) *Revolution in Bavaria 1918–1919: The Eisner Regime and the Soviet Republic*. Princeton: Princeton University Press.

Mitchell, B. R. (1992) *International Historical Statistics: Europe 1750–1988*, 3rd edn. Houndmills: Macmillan, and New York: Stockton Press.

Mitchell, B. R. (1993) *International Historical Statistics: The Americas 1750–1988*, 2nd edn. Houndmills: Macmillan, and New York: Stockton Press.

Mitchell, B. R. (1995) *International Historical Statistics: Africa, Asia & Oceania 1750–1988*. 2nd rev. edn. Houndmills: Macmillan, and New York: Stockton Press.

Michell, Sonya, and Seth Koven (1990) "Womanly duties: maternalist politics and the origins of the welfare state in France, Germany, Great Britain, and the United States, 1880–1920," *American Historical Review* 95: 1076–108.

Mittag, Günter (1991) *Um jeden Preis: Im Spannungsfeld zweier Systeme.* Berlin.

Mitterauer, Michael (1986) *Sozialgeschichte der Jugend.* Frankfurt: Suhrkamp.

Moeller, Robert G. (1993) *Protecting Motherhood: Women and the Family in the Politics of Postwar West Germany.* Berkeley: University of California Press.

Moeller, Robert G. (1996) "War stories: the search for a useable past in the Federal Republic of Germany," *American Historical Review* 101: 1008–48.

Moeller, Robert G., ed. (1997) *West Germany under Construction: Politics, Society, and Culture in the Adenauer Era.* Ann Arbor: University of Michigan Press.

Moeller, Robert G. (2001) *War Stories: The Search for a Useable Past in the Federal Republic of Germany.* Berkeley: University of California Press.

Mommsen, Hans (1964) "The political effects of the Reichstag fire," in Hajo Holborn, ed., *Republic to Reich: The Making of the Nazi Revolution.* New York: Vintage, 1972, pp. 129–222. Also in Henry A. Turner, ed., *Nazism and the Third Reich.* New York: Quadrangle, 1972, pp. 109–50. Originally published in *Vierteljahrschrift für Zeitgeschichte* 12: 351–413.

Mommsen, Hans (1989) *The Rise and Fall of Weimar Democracy*, trans. Elborg Forster and Larry Eugene Jones. Chapel Hill: University of North Carolina Press, 1996.

Mommsen, Wolfgang J. (1974) *The Age of Bureaucracy: Perspectives on the Political Sociology of Max Weber.* Oxford: Basil Blackwell.

Moses, A. Dirk (1998) "Structure and agency in the Holocaust: Daniel J. Goldhagen and his critics," *History and Theory* 37: 194–219.

Moses, A. Dirk (1999) "The forty-fivers: a generation between Fascism and democracy," *German Politics and Society* 17: 94–126.

Moses, John A. (1975) *The Politics of Illusion: The Fischer Controversy in German Historiography.* London: George Prior Publishers.

Mosse, George (1964) *The Crisis of German Ideology: Intellectual Origins of the Third Reich.* New York: H. Fertig, 1981.

Mühlberger, Detlef (1991) *Hitler's Followers: Studies in the Sociology of the Nazi Movement.* New York: Routledge.

Müller, Dirk (1996) *Arbeiter, Katholizismus, Staat: Der Volksverein für das katholische Deutschland und did katholischen Arbeiterorganisationen in der Weimarer Republik.* Bonn.

Müller-Armack, Alfred (1946) *Wirtschaftslenkung und Marktwirtschaft.* Hamburg.

Naasner, Walter (1994) *Neue Machtzentren in der deutschen Kriegswirtschaft, 1942–1945.* Boppard: Harald Boldt.

Naimark, Norman M. (1995) *The Russians in Germany: A History of the Soviet Zone of Occupation, 1945–1949.* Cambridge, MA: Harvard University Press.

Namier, L. B. (1946) *1848: Revolution of the Intellectuals.* London: Oxford University Press, 1971.

Naschold, Frieder (1997) "Industrial policy in Germany: old issues and new challenges," in Michio Muramatsu and Frieder Naschold, eds., *State and Administration in Japan and Germany: A Comparative Perspective on Continuity and Change.* Berlin: Walter de Gruyter, pp. 184–219.

Neather, Edward (1995) "Education in the new Germany," in Lewis and McKenzie, eds., *The New Germany,* pp. 148–72.

Negt, Oskar, and Alexander Kluge (1972) *Public Sphere and Experience: Toward an Analysis of the Bourgeois and Proletarian Public Sphere,* trans. Peter Lubanyi *et al.* Minneapolis and London: University of Minnesota Press, 1993.

Nelson, Keith (1995) "Russia," in Wilson, ed., *Decisions for War,* pp. 97–120.

Neuberger, Hugh and Houston H. Stokes (1974) "German banks and German growth, 1883–1913: an empirical view," *Journal of Economic History* 34: 710–31. See Rainer Fremdling and Richard H. Tilly, "German Banks, German growth, and econometric history," *ibid.* 36 (1976): 416–24, and reply by Neuberger and Stokes, *ibid.,* pp. 425–7.

Neumann, Eckard (1993) *Bauhaus and Bauhaus People,* 2nd edn. New York: Van Nostrand.

Nevin, Thomas (1997) *Ernst Jünger and Germany: Into the Abyss, 1914–45.* London: Constable.

Nichols, J. Alden (1958) *Germany after Bismarck: The Caprivi Era, 1890–1894.* Cambridge, MA: Harvard University Press.

Nipperdey, Thomas (1993a) *Deutsche Geschichte 1806–66: Bürgerwelt und starker Staat,* 6th edn. Munich: C. H. Beck. Translated as *Germany from Napoleon to Bismarck.* trans. Daniel Nolan. Dublin: Gill & Macmillan, 1996.

Nipperdey, Thomas (1993b) *Deutsche Geschichte 1866–1918, Erster Band: Arbeitswelt und Bürgergeist*, 3rd edn. Munich: C. H. Beck.

Nipperdey, Thomas (1993c) *Deutsche Geschichte 1866–1918, Zweiter Band: Machtstaat vor der Demokratie*, 2nd edn. Munich: C. H. Beck.

Nolan, Mary (1994) *Visions of Modernity: American Business and the Modernization of Germany*. New York: Oxford University Press.

Nolte, Paul (1994) *Gemeindebürgertum und Liberalismus in Baden 1800–1850: Tradition, Radikalismus, Republik*. Kritische Studien zur Geschichtswissenschaft, 102. Göttingen: Vandenhoeck & Ruprecht.

Nonn, Christoph (1996) *Verbraucherprotest und Parteiensystem im wilhelminischen Deutschland*. Beiträge zur Geschichte des Parlamentarismus und der politischen Parteien, 107. Düsseldorf: Droste.

Nothnagle, Alan L. (1999) *Building the East German Myth: Historical Mythology and Youth Propaganda in the German Democratic Republic, 1945–1989*. Social History, Popular Culture, and Politics in Germany. Ann Arbor: University of Michigan Press.

Oertzen, Christine von (1999) *Teilzeitarbeit und die Lust am Zuverdienen*. Kritische Studien zur Geschichtswissenschaft, 132. Göttingen: Vandenhoeck & Ruprecht.

Ogilvie, Sheilagh C. (1996) "The beginnings of industrialization," in Sheilagh C. Ogilvie, ed., *Germany: A New Social and Economic History, II: 1630–1800*. London: Edward Arnold.

Opelland, Torsten (1995) *Reichstag und Aussenpolitik im Ersten Weltkrieg: Die deutschen Parteien und die Politik der USA 1914–1918*. Beiträge zur Geschichte des Parlamentarismus und der politischen Parteien 103. Düsseldorf: Droste.

Overy, R. J. (1984) *Goering: The "Iron Man."* London: Routledge & Kegan Paul.

Overy, R. J. (1988) "Mobilisation for Total War in Germany 1939–1941," *English Historical Review* 103: 613–39.

Palatschek, Sylvia (1990) *Frauen und Dissens: Frauen im Deutschkatholizismus und in den freien Gemeinden, 1841–1852*. Göttingen: Vandenhoeck & Ruprecht.

Palmowski, Jan (1999) *Urban Liberalism in Imperial Germany: Frankfurt am Main, 1866–1914*. Oxford Historical Monographs. New York: Oxford University Press.

Paret, Peter (1980) *The Berlin Succession: Modernism and Its Enemies in Imperial Germany*. Princeton: Princeton University Press.

Paris, Erna (1986) *Unhealed Wounds: France and the Klaus Barbie Affair*. New York: Grove Press.

Parsons, Talcott (1951) *The Social System*. Glencoe: The Free Press.

Parsons, Talcott, and Neil Smelser (1956) *Economy and Society*. London: Routledge & Kegan Paul.

Patch, William L. (1998) *Heinrich Brüning and the Dissolution of the Weimar Republic*. Cambridge and New York: Cambridge University Press.

Patton, Craig D. (1998) *Flammable Material: German Chemical Workers in War, Revolution, and Inflation, 1914–1924*. Berlin: Haude and Spener.

Peacock, Alan, and Hans Willgerodt, eds. (1989) *German Neo-Liberals and the Social Market Economy*. London: Macmillan.

Pesch, Volker (1997) "Die künstliche Wilden. Zu Daniel Goldhagens Methode und theoretischem Rahmen," *Geschichte und Gesellschaft* 23: 152–62.

Petersen, Klaus (1992) "The Harmful Publications (Young Persons) Act 1926: literacy, censorship, and the politics of morality in the Weimar Republic," *German Studies Review* 15: 505–25.

Peterson, Brent O. (1997) "The Fatherland's kiss of death: gender and Germany in nineteenth-century historical fiction," in Herminghouse and Miller, eds., *Gender and Germanness*, pp. 82–97.

Peukert, Detlev J. K. (1986) *Die Grenzen der Sozialdisziplinierung: Aufstieg und Krise der deutschen Jugendfürsorge 1878–1932*. Cologne: Kiepenheuer and Witsch.

Peukert, Detlev J. K. (1987) *Inside Nazi Germany: Conformity, Opposition and Racism in Everyday Life*. New Haven: Yale University Press.

Pflanze, Otto (1963, 1990) *Bismarck and the Development of Germany*, 3 vols. Princeton: Princeton University Press.

Pinson, Koppel (1954) *Modern Germany*. New York: Macmillan.

Poiger, Uta (1997) "Rock'n'Roll, female sexuality, and the Cold War battle over German Identities," in Moeller, ed., *West Germany*, pp. 373–410.

Polenz, Peter von (1978) *Geschichte der deutschen Sprache*, 9th edn. Berlin and New York: Walter de Gruyter.

Pommerin, Reiner, ed. (1995) *The American Impact on Postwar Germany*. Providence, RI, and Oxford: Berghahn Books.

Potter, Pamela M. (1998) *Most German of the Arts: Musicology and Society from the Weimar Republic to the End of Hitler's Reich*. New Haven and London: Yale University Press.

Prelinger, Catherine (1987) *Charity, Challenge and Change: Religious Dimensions of the Mid-Nineteenth-Century Women's Movement in Germany*. New York: Greenwood.

Pridham, Geoffrey (1973) *Hitler's Rise to Power: The Nazi Movement in Bavaria, 1973–1933*. New York: Harper & Row.

Pritchard, Gareth (2000) *The Making of the GDR 1945–53: From Antifascism to Stalinism*. Manchester: Manchester University Press.

Pulzer, Peter G. J. (1988) *The Rise of Political Anti-Semitism in Germany and Austria*, rev. edn. New York: Wiley.

Pyta, Wolfram (1996) *Dorfgemeinschaft und Parteipolitik 1918–1933: Die Verschränkung von Milieu und Parteien in den protestantischen Landgebieten Deutschlands in der Weimarer Republik*. Beiträge zur Geschichte des Parlamentarismus und der politischen Parteien, 106. Düsseldorf: Droste.

Quataert, Jean H. (1995) "Survival strategies in a Saxon textile district during the early phases of industrialization, 1780–1860," in Daryl M. Hafter, ed., *European Women and Preindustrial Craft*. Bloomington: Indiana University Press, pp. 153–78.

Quint, Peter E. (1997) *The Imperfect Union: Constitutional Structures of German Unification*. Princeton: Princeton University Press.

Rabinbach, A., and J. Zipes, eds. (1986) *Germans and Jews since the Holocaust*. New York: Holmes and Meier.

Raeff, Marc (1983) *The Well-Ordered Police State: Social and Institutional Change through Law in the Germanies and Russia, 1600–1800*. New Haven: Yale University Press.

Rauh, Manfred (1977). *Die Parlamentarisierung des Deutschen Reiches*. Düsseldorf: Droste.

Reagin, Nancy R. (1995) *A German Women's Movement: Class and Gender in Hanover, 1880–1933*. Chapel Hill: University of North Carolina Press.

Reagin, Nancy R. (2001a) "The imagined *Hausfrau*: national identity, domesticity, and colonialism in imperial Germany," *Journal of Modern History* 73: 54–86.

Reagin, Nancy R. (2001b) "*Marktordung* and autarkic housekeeping: housewives and private consumption under the Four-Year Plan, 1936–1939," *German History* 19 (2): 162–84.

Rector, Frank (1981) *The Nazi Extermination of Homosexuals*. New York: Stein and Day.

Reich, Simon (1990) *Fruits of Fascism: Postwar Prosperity in Historical Perspective*. Ithaca, NY: Cornell University Press.

Reif, Heinz (1993) *Die verspätete Stadt: Industrialisierung, städtischer Raum und Politik in Oberhausen 1846–1929*. Landschaftsverband Rheinland, Rheinisches Industrie Museum, Schriften, 7. Cologne: Rheinland.

Reinharz, Yehuda (1975) *Fatherland or Promised Land: The Dilemma of the German Jew, 1893–1914*. Ann Arbor: University of Michigan Press.

Remak, Joachim (1964) *The Gentle Critic. Theodor Fontane and German Politics, 1848–1898*. Syracuse, NY: Syracuse University Press.

Rentschler, Eric (1996) *The Ministry of Illusion: Nazi Cinema and Its Afterlife*. Cambridge, MA: Harvard University Press.

Retallack, James (1995) *Germany in the Age of Kaiser Wilhelm II*. London: Macmillan.

Retallack, James (1998) "Society and politics in saxony in the nineteenth and twentieth centuries," *Archiv für Sozialgeschichte* 38: 396–457.

Retallack, James (1999) "Conservatives and antisemites in Baden and Saxony," *German History* 17 (4): 489–506.

Richie, Alexandra (1998) *Faust's Metropolis: A History of Berlin*. London: HarperCollins.

Richie, J. M. (1983) *German Literature under National Socialism*. London: Croom Helm.

Rickman, H.-P. (1988) *Dilthey Today: A Critical Appraisal of the Contemporary Relevance of His Work*. New York: Greenwood.

Riefenstahl, Leni (1987) *Leni Riefenstahl: A Memoir*. New York: St. Martin's Press, 1992 (English translation).

Riehl, Wilhelm Heinrich (1854) *Die Naturgeschichte des Volkes als Grundlage einer Deutschen Sozial-Politik*. Stuttgart.

Riley, James C. (1986) "Insects and the European mortality decline," *American Historical Review* 91: 833–58.

Ringer, Fritz (1979) *Education and Society in Modern Europe*. Bloomington: Indiana University Press.

Ritschl, Albrecht (1996) "An exercise in futility: East German economic growth and decline, 1945–89," in Nicholas Crafts and Gianni Toniolo, eds., *Economic Growth in Europe since 1945*. Cambridge: Cambridge University Press, pp. 498–540.

Ritschl, Albrecht (1998) "Reparation transfers, the Borchardt hypothesis and the Great Depression in Germany, 1929–32: a guided tour for hard-headed Keynesians," *European Review of Economic History* 2: 49–72.

Ritschl, Albrecht (2001) "Deficit spending in the Nazi recovery, 1933–1938: a critical reassessment," abstract at ⟨www.eh.net/AEH⟩; text at ⟨papers.ssrn.com/sol3/papers⟩.

Ritter, G. A. (1983) *Regierung, Bürokratie und Parlament in Preussen und Deutschland von 1848 bis zur Gegenwart*. Düsseldorf: Droste.

Roberts, Geoffrey K. (1992) "Right-wing radicalism in the new Germany," *Parliamentary Affairs* 45 (3).

Robertson, Richie (1988) *Heine*. London: Hallan.

Rochau, Ludwig August von (1853) *Grundsätze der Realpolitik*, ed. Hans-Ulrich Wehler. Frankfurt: Wissenschaftliche Buchgesellschaft, 1972.

Rohe, Karl, ed. (1990) *Elections, Parties and Political Traditions: Social Foundations of German Party Systems 1867–1987*. New York.

Rohe, Karl (1992) *Wahlen und Wählertradition in Deutschland: Kulturelle Grundlagen deutscher Parteien und Parteisysteme im 19. und 20. Jahrhundert*. Frankfurt: Suhrkamp.

Röhl, John C. G. (1967) *Germany without Bismarck: The Crisis of Government in the Second Reich 1890–1900*. Berkeley and Los Angeles: University of California Press.

Röhl, John C. G. (1977) "Beamtenpolitik im wilhelminischen Deutschland," in Michael Stürmer, ed., *Das kaiserliche Deutschland: Politik und Gesellschaft 1870–1918*. Düsseldorf: Droste, pp. 287–311.

Röhl, John C. G. (1987) *The Kaiser and His Court: Wilhelm II and the Government of Germany*, trans. Terence F. Cole. New York: Cambridge University Press, 1994.

Röhl, John C. G. (1995) "Germany," in Wilson, ed., *Decisions for War*, pp. 27–54.

Rohlfs, Jochen (1995) "German literature after unification," in Lewis and McKenzie, eds., *The New Germany*, pp. 243–58.

Rollins, Wilhelm H. (1997) *A Greener Vision of Home: Cultural Politics and Environmental Reform in the German* Heimatschutz *Movement, 1904–1918*. Social History, Popular Culture, and Politics in Germany. Ann Arbor: University of Michigan Press.

Rooth, Tim (1993) *British Protectionism and the International Economy: Overseas Commercial Policy in the 1930s*. Cambridge: Cambridge University Press.

Roper, Katherine (1991) *German Encounters with Modernity: Novels of Imperial Berlin*. Boston: Humanities Press.

Röpke, Wilhelm (1944) *Civitas Humana: Grundfragen der Gesellschafts- und Wirtschaftsreform*. Zurich.

Rose, Sonya O. (1992) *Limited Livelihoods: Gender and Class in Nineteenth-Century England*. Berkeley: University of California Press.

Roseman, Mark (1992) *Recasting the Ruhr, 1945–1958: Manpower, Economic Recovery and Labor Relations*. New York: Berg and St. Martin's Press.

Roseman, Mark (1995) "Gender in German history," *German History* 13 (1): 83–90.

Rosenbaum, Ron (1992) "Hitler's angel," *Vanity Fair* (April): 83–90, 130–9.

Rosenberg, Dorothy (1993) "The new home economics: women in the united Germany," *Debatte* 1: 111–34.

Rosenberg, Hans (1943) "Political and social consequences of the depression of 1873–1896 in Central Europe," *Economic History Review* 13. Reprinted in Sheehan, ed., *Imperial Germany*, pp. 39–60.

Rosenberg, Hans (1958) *Bureaucracy, Aristocracy and Autocracy: The Prussian Experience 1660–1815*. Boston: Beacon Press.

Rosenberg, Hans (1967) *Grosse Depression und Bismarckzeit*. Berlin: Walter de Gruyter.

Rosenhaft, Eve (1983) *Beating the Fascists? The German Communists and Political Violence, 1929–1933*. Cambridge: Cambridge University Press.

Rosenhaft, Eve (1997) "Facing up to the past—again? 'Crimes of the Wehrmacht,'" *Debatte* 5: 105–18.

Roth, Ralf (1996) *Stadt und Bürgertum in Frankfurt am Main: Ein besonderer*

Weg von der ständischen zur modernen Bürgergesellschaft 1760–1914. Stadt und Bürgertum, 7. Munich: R. Oldenbourg.

Rouette, Susanne (1997) "Mothers and citizens: gender and social policy in Germany after the First World War," *Central European History* 30: 48–66.

Rudloff, Wilfried (1998) *Die Wohlfahrtsstadt: Kommunale Ernährungs-, Fürsorge-, und Wohnungspolitik am Beispiel Münchens 1910–1933*, 2 vols. Schriftenreihe der Historischen Kommission bei der Bayerischen Akademie der Wissenschaften, 63. Göttingen: Vandenhoeck & Ruprecht.

Rupp, Leila J. (1978) *Mobilizing Women for War: German and American Propaganda 1939–1945.* Princeton: Princeton University Press.

Sabean, D. W. (1990) *Property, Production and Family in Neckarhausen, 1700–1870.* Cambridge: Cambridge University Press.

Sachs, Jeffrey (1988) "International economics: unlocking the mysteries of globalization," *Foreign Policy* 110: 97–111.

Sackett, Robert E. (1982) *Popular Entertainment, Class and Politics in Munich, 1900–1923.* Cambridge, MA: Harvard University Press.

Saldern, Adelheid von (1990) "The hidden history of mass culture," *International Labor and Working Class History* 37: 32–40.

Saldern, Adelheid von (1994) "Victims or perpetrators? Controversies about the role of women in the Nazi state," in Crew, ed., *Nazism and German Society.*

Saldern, Adelheid von (1995) *Häuserleben: Zur Geschichte städtischen Arbeiterwohnens vom Kaiserreich bis heute.* Politik- und Gesellschaftsgeschichte, 38. Bonn: J. H. W. Dietz.

Saltzman, Lisa (1999) *Anselm Kiefer and Art after Auschwitz.* Cambridge: Cambridge University Press.

Sander, Helke (1987) "A telephone conversation with a friend," in *The Three Women K*, trans. Helen Petzhold. London: Serpent's Tail, 1991, pp. 118–130.

Sander, Helke, and Barbara Johr, eds. (1992) *BeFreier und Befreite: Krieg, Vergewaltigungen, Kinder.* Munich: Verlag Antje Kunstmann.

Saul, Nicholas (1997) "Aesthetic humanism (1790–1830)," in Watanabe-O'Kelly, ed., *Cambridge History of German Literature*, pp. 202–71.

Saunders, Frances S. (1999) *Who Paid the Piper: The CIA and the Cultural Cold War.* London: Granta Books.

Saunders, Thomas J. (1994) *Hollywood in Berlin: American Cinema and Weimar Germany.* Berkeley: University of California Press.

Schambach, Karin (1996) *Stadtbürgertum und industrieller Umbruch: Dortmund, 1780–1870.* Stadt und Bürgertum, 5. Munich: R. Oldenbourg.

Scheck, Raffael (1998) *Alfred von Tirpitz and German Right-wing Politics, 1914–1930.* Boston: Humanities Press.

Schlumbohm, Jürgen (1994) *Lebensläufe, Familien, Höfe: Die Bauern und*

Heuerleute des Osnabrückischen Kirchspiels Belm in proto-industrieller Zeit, 1660–1860. Veröffentlichen des Max-Planck-Instituts für Geschichte, 110. Göttingen: Vandenhoeck & Ruprecht.

Schmidt, Helmut (1985) *A Grand Strategy for the West: The Anachronism of National Strategies in an Interdependent World.* New Haven: Yale University Press.

Schmitt, Carl (1927) *The Concept of the Political.* New Brunswick: Rutgers University Press, 1976 (English translation).

Schmitt, Carl (1985) *The Crisis of Parliamentary Democracy.* Cambridge, MA: MIT Press.

Schorsch, Ismar (1972) *Jewish Reactions to German Anti-Semitism, 1870–1914.* New York: Columbia University Press.

Schorske, Carl E. (1955) *German Social Democracy 1905–1917.* Cambridge, MA: Harvard University Press.

Schröder, Wilhelm H. and Reinhard Spree, eds. (1980) *Historische Konjunkturforschung.* Stuttgart: Klett-Cotta.

Schüler-Springorum, Stefanie (1996) *Die jüdische Minderheit in Königsberg/Preussen, 1871–1945.* Schriftenreihe der Historischen Kommission bei der Bayerischen Akademie der Wissenschaften, 56. Göttingen: Vandenhoeck & Ruprecht.

Schulze, Winfried, and Otto Gerhard Oexle, eds. (1999) *Deutsche Historiker im Nationalsozialismus.* Frankfurt: Fischer Verlag.

Schwartz, Michael (1995) *Sozialistische Eugenik: Eugenische Sozialtechnologien in Debatten und Politik der deutschen Sozialdemokratie 1890–1933.* Forschungsinstitut der Friedrich-Ebert-Stiftung, Reihe Politik- und Gesellschaftsgeschichte, 42. Bonn: J. H. W. Dietz.

Scott, Joan W. (1988) "Gender: a useful category of historical analysis," in Joan Scott, *Gender and the Politics of History.* New York: Columbia University Press.

Secombe, Wally (1986) "Patriarchy stabilized: the construction of the male breadwinner wage norm in nineteenth-century Britain," *Social History* 11: 53–76.

Sheehan, James J., ed. (1976) *Imperial Germany.* New York: New Viewpoints.

Sheehan, James J. (1989) *German History 1770–1866.* Oxford: Clarendon Press, 1993 (paperback edn.).

Siegel, Tilla (1985) "Wage policy in Nazi Germany," *Politics and Society* 14: 31–60.

Siegel, Tilla (1989) *Leistung und Lohn in der nationalsozialistischen "Ordnung der Arbeit."* Opladen: Westdeutscher Verlag.

Sieglerschmidt, Jörn (1996) "Social and economic landscapes," in Sheilagh C. Ogilvie, ed., *Germany: A New Social and Economic History, II: 1630–1800.* London: Edward Arnold.

Silberman, Marc (1995) *German Cinema: Texts in Context*. Detroit: Wayne State University Press.

Silverman, Dan P. (1998) *Hitler's Economy: Nazi Work Creation Programs, 1933–1936*. Cambridge, MA: Harvard University Press.

Silvia, Stephen J. (1988) "The West German labor controversy: a struggle for the factory of the future," *Comparative Politics* 22: 155–74.

Simms, Brendan (1997) *The Impact of Napoleon: Prussian High Politics, Foreign Policy and the Crisis of the Executive, 1797–1806*. New York: Cambridge University Press.

Simon, Wilhelm M., ed. (1968) *Germany in the Age of Bismarck*. London: Harper Torchbooks, pp. 111–12.

Smith, Helmut W. (1995) *German Nationalism and Religious Conflict: Ideology, Politics, 1870–1914*. Princeton: Princeton University Press.

Smith, Owen E. (1983) *The West German Economy*. London: Croom Helm.

Søe, Christian (1989) "'Not without us!' The FDP's survival, position, and influence," in Peter H. Merkl, ed., *The Federal Republic of Germany at Forty*. New York: New York University Press.

Søe, Christian (1993) "Unity and victory for the German Liberals: little party, what now?" in R. Dalton, ed., *The New Germany Votes*. Oxford: Berg, pp. 99–134.

Solomou, Solomos (1987) *Phases of Economic Growth, 1850–1973: Kondratieff Waves and Kuznets Swings*. Cambridge: Cambridge University Press.

Solomou, Solomos (1998) *Economic Cycles: Long Cycles and Business Cycles Since 1870*. Manchester: Manchester University Press.

Sondhaus, Lawrence (1997) *Preparing for Weltpolitik: German Sea Power before the Tirpitz Era*. Annapolis, MD: Naval Institute Press.

Sorkin, David (1987) *The Transformation of German Jewry, 1780–1840*. New York: Oxford University Press.

Spaulding, Robert M. (1997) *Osthandel and Ostpolitik: German Foreign Trade Policies in Eastern Europe from Bismarck to Adenauer*. Providence, RI, and Oxford: Berghahn.

Speer, Albert (1970) *Inside the Third Reich*, trans. Richard and Clara Winston. London: Sphere Books Limited, 1978.

Spencer, Elaine G. (1992) *Police and Social Order in German Cities: The Düsseldorf District, 1848–1914*. DeKalb: Northern Illinois University Press.

Sperber, Jonathan (1984) *Popular Catholicism in Nineteenth-Century Germany*. Princeton: Princeton University Press.

Sperber, Jonathan (1991) *Rhineland Radicals: The Democratic Movement and the Revolution of 1848–1849*. Princeton: Princeton University Press.

Sperber, Jonathan (1997a) "*Bürger, Bürgertum, Bürgerlichkeit, Bürgerliche Gesellschaft*: studies of the German (upper) middle class and its socio-cultural world," *Journal of Modern History* 69 (2): 271–97.

Sperber, Jonathan (1997b) *The Kaiser's Voters: Electors and Elections in Imperial Germany*. Cambridge: Cambridge University Press.

Spoerer, Mark (1997) "Weimar's investment and growth record in intertemporal and international perspective," *European Review of Economic History* 1: 271–97.

Spree, Reinhard (1978) *Wachstumstrends und Konjunkturzyklen in der deutschen Wirtschaft von 1820 bis 1913: Quantitativer Rahmen für eine Konjunkturgeschichte des 19. Jahrhunderts*. Göttingen: Vandenhoeck & Ruprecht.

Spree, Reinhard (1980) "Was kommt nach der 'langen Wellen' der Konjunktur?" in Schröder and Spree, eds., *Historiche Konjuncturforschung*, pp. 304–15.

Stackelberg, Roderick (1999) *Hitler's Germany: Origins, Interpretations, Legacies*. London and New York: Routledge.

Staritz, Dietrich (1985) *Geschichte der DDR 1949–1985*. Frankfurt: Suhrkamp.

Steger, Manfred B. (1997) *The Quest for Evolutionary Socialism: Eduard Bernstein and Social Democracy*. New York: Cambridge University Press.

Steinberg, Jonathan (1965) *Yesterday's Deterrent: Tirpitz and the Birth of the German Battle Fleet*. New York: Macmillan.

Steinberg, Paul (2001) *Speak You Also: A Survivor's Reckoning*, trans. Linda Coverdale and Bill Ford. London: Allen Lane.

Steinmetz, George (1993) *Regulating the Social: The Welfare State and Local Politics in Imperial Germany*. Princeton: Princeton University Press.

Steinweis, Alan E. (1993) *Art, Ideology, and Economics in Nazi Germany: The Reich Chambers of Music, Theater, and the Visual Arts*. Chapel Hill and London: University of North Carolina Press.

Stephenson, Jill (1975) *Women in Nazi Society*. New York: Barnes and Noble.

Stephenson, Jill (1981) *The Nazi Organization of Women*. London: Croom Helm.

Stern, Fritz R. (1961) *The Politics of Cultural Despair: A Study of the Rise of the Germanic Ideology*. Berkeley: University of California Press, 1974.

Stern, Fritz R.(1977) *Gold and Iron: Bismarck, Bleichröder and the Building of the German Empire*. New York: Knopf.

Stieg, Margaret (1990) "The 1926 law to protect youth against trash and dirt," *Central European History* 23: 22–56.

Stoehr, Irene (1985) "Neue Frau und Alte Bewegung? Zur Generationskonflikt in der Frauenbewegung der Weimarer Republik," in Jutta Dalhoff, Uschi Frey, and Ingrid Schöll, eds., *Frauenmacht in der Geschichte*, pp. 390–402.

Stolfi, R. H. S. (1991) *Hitler's Panzers East: World War II Reinterpreted*. Norman: University of Oklahoma Press.

Struve, Walter (1992) *Aufstieg und Herrschaft des Nationalsozialismus in einer industriellen Kleinstadt: Osterode am Harz 1918–1945*. Essen: Klartext.

Sugiyama, Chuhei (1994) *Origins of Economic Thought in Modern Japan*. London: Routledge.

Sun, Raymond C. (1999) *"Before the Enemy Is Within Our Walls." Catholic Workers in Cologne, 1885–1912*. Boston: Humanities Press.

Tarrant, V. E. (1995) *Jutland: The German Perspective*. London.

Tatar, Maria (1995) *Lustmord: Sexual Murder in Weimar Germany*. Princeton: Princeton University Press.

Taylor, A. J. P. (1946) *The Course of German History*. London: Hamish Hamilton.

Taylor, Peter K. (1994) *Indentured to Liberty: Peasant Life and the Hessian Military State, 1688–1815*. Ithaca, NY: Cornell University Press.

Temin, Peter (1971) "The beginning of the depression in Germany," *Economic History Review* 24: 240–8.

Temin, Peter (1989) *Lessons from the Great Depression*. Cambridge, MA, and London: MIT Press.

Theweleit, Klaus (1977–78) *Male Fantasies*, trans. Stephen Conway. Minneapolis: University of Minnesota Press, 1987–89.

Thomas, Theodore N. (1995) *Women against Hitler: Christian Resistance in the Third Reich*. Westport, CT: Praeger.

Thompson, Alastair P. (2000) *Left Liberals, the State, and Popular Politics in Wilhelmine Germany*. Oxford and New York: Oxford University Press.

Thorpe, Wayne (2000) "Keeping the faith: the German syndicalists in the First World War," *Central European History* 33 (2): 195–216.

Tilly, Richard H. (1966a) *Financial Institutions and Industrialization in the Rhineland, 1815–1870*. Madison: University of Wisconsin Press.

Tilly, Richard H. (1966b) "The political economy of public finance and the industrialization of Prussia, 1815–1866," *Journal of Economic History* 26: 484–97.

Tilly, Richard H. (1975) "Germany," in Charles Tilly, Louise Tilly, and Richard Tilly, *The Rebellious Century, 1830–1930*. Cambridge, MA: Harvard University Press, pp. 191–238.

Tilly, Richard H. (1986) "German banking, 1850–1914: development assistance for the strong," *Journal of European Economic History* 15: 113–52.

Tilly, Richard H. (1989) "German industrialization and Gerschenkronian backwardness," *Revista di storia economica* 6: 139–64.

Tilly, Richard H. (1990) *Vom Zollverein zum Industriestaat: Die wirtschaftlich-soziale Entwicklung Deutschlands 1834 bis 1914*. Munich: Deutscher Taschenbuchverlag.

Tilly, Richard H. (1991) "An overview of the role of the large German banks up to 1914," in Youssef Cassis, ed., *Finance and Financiers in European History, 1880–1960*. Cambridge: Cambridge University Press, pp. 94–112.

Tipton, Frank B. (1974) "The national consensus in German economic history," *Central European History* 7: 195–224.

Tipton, Frank B. (1976) *Regional Variations in the Economic Development of Germany during the Nineteenth Century*. Middletown, CT: Wesleyan University Press.

Tipton, Frank B. (1994) "The regional dimension in the historical analysis of transport flows," in Andreas Kunz and John Armstrong, eds., *Inland Navigation in 19th Century Europe*. Mainz: Verlag Philipp von Zabern, and Manchester: Manchester University Press, pp. 167–80.

Tipton, Frank B. (1998a) "A new German identity? Or the ghost of German idealism?," in Peter Monteath and Frederic S. Zuckerman, eds., *Modern Europe: Histories and Identities*. Adelaide: Australian Humanities Press, pp. 61–72.

Tipton, Frank B. (1998b) *The Rise of Asia: Economics, Society, and Politics in Contemporary Asia*. Houndmills: Macmillan.

Tipton, Frank B. (2002) "Japanese nationalism in comparative perspective," in Sandra Wilson, ed., *Nation and Nationalism in Japan*. London: Curzon, pp. 146–62.

Tobias, Fritz (1962) *The Reichstag Fire*. New York, 1964 (English translation).

Tönnies, Ferdinand 1887. *Community and Civil Society*, ed. and trans. José Harris. Cambridge: Cambridge University Press, 2001.

Tooley, J. Hunt (1997) *National Identity and Weimar Germany: Upper Silesia and the Eastern Border, 1918–1922*. Lincoln: University of Nebraska Press.

Trevor-Roper, Hugh, ed. (1988) *Hitler's Table Talk 1941–1944*. New York: Oxford University Press.

Trippe, Christian (1995) *Konservative Verfassungspolitik 1918–1923: Die DNVP als Opposition in Reich und Ländern*. Beiträge zur Geschichte des Parlamentarismus und der politischen Parteien, 105. Düsseldorf: Droste.

Turnbull, John (2000) "How Conventional Was Nazi Economic Policy?" Thesis, University of Sydney.

Turner, Henry A. (1985) *German Big Business and the Rise of Hitler*. New York and Oxford: Oxford University Press.

Turner, Henry A. (1996) *Hitler's Thirty Days to Power: January 1933*. Reading, MA: Addison-Wesley.

Tusa, Ann (1989) *The Berlin Blockade*. Sevenoaks: Coronet.

Tylecote, Andrew (1993) *The Long Wave and the World Economy: The Current Crisis in Historical Perspective*. London: Routledge.

Usborne, Cornelie (1992) *The Politics of the Body in Weimar Germany: Women's Reproductive Rights and Duties*. Social History, Popular Culture, and Politics in Germany. Ann Arbor: University of Michigan Press.

Verhey, Jeffrey (2000) *The Spirit of 1914: Militarism, Myth and Mobilization in Germany*. Cambridge: Cambridge University Press.

Volkov, Shulamit (1978) *The Rise of Popular Antimodernism in Germany: The Urban Master Artisans, 1873–1896*. Princeton: Princeton University Press.

Wachsman, Nikolaus (1999) "'Annihilation through labor': the killing of state prisoners in the Third Reich," *Journal of Modern History* 17: 624–59.

Wagner, Georg (1995) *Sozialstaat gegen Wohnungsnot*. Forschungen zur Regionalgeschichte, 11. Paderborn: Ferdinand Schöningh.

Waite, Robert (1977) *Adolf Hitler: The Psychopathic God*. New York: Da Capo Press, 1993.

Walker, Mack (1971) *German Home Towns: Community, State, and General Estate 1648–1871*. Ithaca, NY: Cornell University Press.

Walker, Mark (1989) *German National Socialism and the Quest for Nuclear Power, 1939–1949*. Cambridge: Cambridge University Press.

Wallerstein, Immanuel (1974) *The Modern World System I: Capitalist Agriculture and the Origins of the European World Economy in the Sixteenth Century*. New York: Academic Press.

Wallich, Henry C. (1955) *Mainsprings of the German Revival*. New Haven: Yale University Press.

Watanabe-O'Kelly, Helen, ed. (1997) *The Cambridge History of German Literature*. Cambridge: Cambridge University Press.

Wawro, Geoffrey (1996) *The Austro-Prussian War: Austria's War with Prussia and Italy in 1866*. New York: Cambridge University Press.

Weber, Hermann (1983) *Kommunismus in Deutschland 1918–1945*. Darmstadt: Westdeutscher Verlag.

Weber, Hermann (1985) *Geschichte der DDR*. Munich: Deutscher Taschenbuch.

Weber, Max (1893) "Capitalism and rural society in Germany," in *From Max Weber: Essays in Sociology*, ed., trans., and with an introduction by H. H. Gerth and C. Wright Mills. New York: Oxford University Press, 1958, pp. 363–85.

Weber, Max (1904–05) *The Protestant Ethic and the Spirit of Capitalism*, trans. Talcott Parsons. New York: Charles Scribner's Sons, 1958.

Weber, Max (1918) "Politics as a vocation," in *From Max Weber: Essays in Sociology*, ed., trans., and with an introduction by H. H. Gerth and C. Wright Mills. New York: Oxford University Press, 1958, pp. 77–128.

Wegner, Bernd (1990) *Hitlers politische Soldaten: Die Waffen SS, 1933–1945: Leitbild, Struktur und Funktion einer nationalsozialistischen Elite*, 4th edn. Paderborn: Ferdinand Schöningh.

Wegner, Bernd (2000) "Hitler, der Zweite Weltkrieg und die Choreographie des Untergangs," *Geschichte und Gesellschaft* 26 (3): 493–518.

Wehler, Hans-Ulrich (1973) *The German Empire 1871–1918*, trans. Kim Traynor. Leamington Spa: Berg, 1985.

Wehler, Hans-Ulrich (1995) *Deutsche Gesellschaftsgeschichte*, Vol. 3: *Von der "Deutschen Doppelrevolution" biz zum Beginn des Ersten Weltkrieges, 1849–1914*. Munich: C. H. Beck.

Wehler, Hans-Ulrich (1996) "A guide to future research on the Kaiserreich? Society, culture, and the state in Germany, 1870–1930, edited by Geoff Eley," *Central European History* 29: 541–72.

Weichlein, Siegfried (1996) *Sozialmilieus und politische Kultur in der Weimarer Republik: Lebenswelt, Vereinskultur, Politik in Hessen*. Kritische Studien zur Geschichtswissenschaft, 115. Göttingen: Vandenhoeck & Ruprecht.

Weindling, Paul (1989) *Health, Race and German Politics between National Unification and Nazism 1870–1947*. Cambridge: Cambridge University Press.

Weinhauer, Klaus (1994) *Alltag und Arbeitskampf im Hamburger Hafen: Sozialigeschichte der Hamburger Hafenarbeiter 1914–1933*. Sammlung Schöningh zur Geschichte und Gegenwart. Paderborn: Ferdinand Schöningh.

Welch, David (1983) *Propaganda and the German Cinema, 1933–1945*. Oxford: Clarendon.

White, Dan S. (1992) *Lost Comrades: Socialists of the Front Generation, 1918–1945*. Cambridge, MA: Harvard University Press.

Whitford, Frank (1984) *Bauhaus*. London: Thames and Hudson.

Wicke, Peter (1998) "'Born in the GDR': ostrock between ostalgia and cultural self-assertion," *Debatte* 6: 148–55.

Wierling, Dorothee (1996) "Work, workers, and politics in the German Democratic Republic," *International Labor and Working-Class History*, 50: 44–63.

Wildt, Jürgen (1995) "Plurality of taste: food and consumption in West Germany during the 1950s," *History Workshop Journal* 39: 23–41.

Willett, John (1978) *Art and Politics in the Weimar Period: The New Sobriety, 1917–1933*. New York: Da Capo Press, 1996.

Williamson, John G. (1971) *Karl Helfferich, 1872–1926: Economist, Financier Politician*. Princeton: Princeton University Press.

Williamson, Samuel R. Jr. (1991) *Austria-Hungary and the Origins of the First World War*. Houndmills: Macmillan.

Wilson, Keith (1995a) "Britain," in Wilson, ed., *Decisions for War*, pp. 175–208.

Wilson, Keith, ed. (1995b) *Decisions for War, 1914*. London: University College of London Press.

Winkler, Heinrich A., ed. (1974) *Organisieter Kapitalismus: Voraussetzungen und Anfänge.* Göttingen: Vandenhoeck & Ruprecht.

Winkler, Heinrich A. (1993) *Weimar, 1918–1933: Die Geschichte der ersten deutschen Demokratie.* Munich: C. H. Beck.

Witt, Peter-Christian (1970) *Die Finanzpolitik des Deutschen Reiches von 1903 bis 1913.* Lübeck and Hamburg: Mathiesen.

Wolin, Richard, ed. (1993) *The Heidegger Controversy: A Critical Reader.* Cambridge, MA: MIT Press.

Woods, Roger (1996) *The Conservative Revolution in the Weimar Republic.* New York: St. Martin's Press.

Wunder, Bernd (1986) *Geschichte der Bürokratie in Deutschland.* Frankfurt: Suhrkamp.

Wunder, Bernd (1993) "Das Prüfungsprinzip und die Entstehung der Beamtenschaft in Deutschland," *Jahrbuch für Wirtschaftsgeschichte,* Jg. 1993 (1–2): 11–26.

Würgler, Andreas (1995) *Unruhen und Öffentlichkeit: Städtische und ländliche Protestbewegungen im 18. Jahrhundert.* Frühneuzeit-Forschungen, 1. Tübingen: Bibliotheca Academica.

Wyden, Peter (1989) *Wall: The Inside Story of a Divided Berlin.* New York: Simon and Schuster.

Yaney, George (1994) *The World of the Manager: Food Administration in Berlin during World War I.* Studies in Modern European History, 11. New York: Peter Lang.

Young, Brigitte (1999) *The Triumph of the Fatherland: German Unification and the Marginalization of Women.* Ann Arbor: University of Michigan Press.

Zelikow, Philip, and Condolezza Rice (1995) *Germany Unified and Europe Transformed: A Study in Statecraft.* Cambridge, MA: Harvard University Press.

Zerback, Ralf (1997) *München und sein Bürgertum: Eine Residenzstadt als Bürgergemeinde, 1780–1870.* Stadt und Bürgertum, 8. Munich: R. Oldenbourg.

Ziegler, Herbert (1989) *Nazi Germany's New Aristocracy: The SS Leadership, 1925–1939.* Princeton: Princeton University Press.

Zilbert, Edward R. (1981) *Albert Speer and the Nazi Ministry of Arms: Economic Institutions and Industrial Production in the German War Economy.* Rutherford, NJ: Fairleigh Dickenson University Press.

Zillmer, Eric A. *et al.* (1995) *The Quest for the Nazi Personality: A Psychological Investigation of Nazi War Criminals.* The LEA Series in Personality and Clinical Psychology. Hillsdale, NJ: Lawrence Erlbaum.

Zimmermann, Clemens (1991) *Von der Wohnungsfrage zur Wohnungspolitik:*

Die Reformbewegung in Deutschland 1845–1914. Kritische Studien zur Geschichtswissenschaft, 90. Göttingen: Vandenheock & Ruprecht.

Zimmermann, Michael (1986) "Aufbruchshoffnung: Junge Bergleute in den Dreißiger Jahren," in Lutz Niethammer, ed., *"Die Jahre weiß man nicht, wo man sie hinsetzen soll": Faschismus Erfahrungen im Ruhrgebiet*, 2nd edn. Berlin and Bonn: Dietz, pp. 97–132.

Zweig, Ronald W. (2001) *German Reparations and the Jewish World: A History of the Claims Conference*, rev. edn. London: Frank Cass Publishers.

INDEX

An 'f' after a page number indicates the inclusion of a figure; an 'm' indicates the inclusion of a map; a 'p' indicates the inclusion of a plate, and a 't' indicates the inclusion of a table.

714